When chemicals come to school.

The Student Assistance Program Model

Gary L. Anderson

CRP

Published by **Community Recovery Press**

P.O. BOX 20979
GREENFIELD, WISCONSIN 53220

Published by Community Recovery Press,
3767 South 81st Street, Milwaukee, WI 53220.

Printed in the United States of America.

ISBN: 0-9618023-0-8

Cover illustration: Thomas Schroeder

First Printing . . . . April 1987
Second Printing . . . . . January, 1988

DEDICATION

To my parents, Gordon and Eva.

* * * * * * * *

If it were not for the miracle of Alcoholics Anonymous and the fact that recovery is real and possible, this book and the approaches it describes would not have been possible.

It is inspired by all of the young people who have recovered from alcoholism and other chemical dependencies.

It is for all those who have not.

TABLE OF CONTENTS

APPENDICES

LIST OF TABLES

LIST OF FIGURES

ACKNOWLEDGEMENTS

NOTES ON THE TEXT

It appears that no satisfactory scheme has as of yet gained currency for replacing the generic pronoun he/his/him. Ubiquitous locutions such as he/she, his/her, etc., seem only slightly less clumsy than the use of s/he. I have chosen, instead to alternate the use of "his" and "her" and the other members of their paradigm within and between paragraphs.

"Student Assistance Program" is capitalized in the text when it refers to a specific school's program; it is set in lower case when it refers to the concept in general. I have also chosen to use "SAP" as the abbreviation rather than "SA Program" as can be found in some other discussions.

Many readers may not be familiar with "AODA" as the abbreviation for "alcohol and other drug abuse." Abbreviations are explained at their first occurrence in the text.

References are made periodically to a hypothetical school district, "Midville Public Schools," in order to illustrate concepts presented in the text. Such references are not intended to portray any actual community or school district.

The "Wisconsin Experience"

In the eight years since 1978, when consultation and training at the State level were first available for Student Assistance Programming, 180 of Wisconsin's 434 public school districts (or 41%) either have Student Assistance Programs or are in various stages of implementing them. For a complex and comprehensive joint school-community effort to achieve this level of popularity, on a voluntary basis, is partial testimony to the effectiveness of this approach in helping students cope with AODA-related problems.

In retrospect, three factors have been most responsible for the origins of Student Assistance Programming in Wisconsin in 1974. First and foremost was *need*. National and regional surveys of adolescent alcohol and other drug use were showing alarming increases during the early 1970's; people working in schools, law enforcement, and local alcohol/drug agencies were experiencing these changes in an immediate way, as were parents and kids themselves.

The second factor contributing to the emergence of the Student Assistance Program model was what was almost an obsession for and repeated disillusionment with "prevention." Each year saw the publication of a new solution to the "drug problem": scare tactics, get-tough policies, accurate information, values clarification, decision-making skills, and so on. Each existed in the absence of evaluation data to prove its effectiveness, or was followed shortly by data demonstrating either no effect on student drug use or actual *increases*.

The third and most important factor was the increasing momentum of Employee Assistance Programs [EAP's], the obvious namesake of the Student Assistance Program model. Here was a program which proved to be the most successful means of reaching adults with alcohol and other drug problems. It addressed the needs of both employees *and* their families; it benefited employer as well as employee; it saved jobs, families, and money. EAP's were received enthusiastically by labor and management alike.

The success of the EAP model was due in large part to the structure of the model itself, to the fact that it addressed the problem by examining the *functional* necessities for helping rather than arguing over the merits of "prevention" or "intervention," and by the fact that it addressed the *context*, or work environment, more than it focussed on employees themselves.

Employee Assistance Programs are highly structured, which is to say, formalized. Most standard descriptions would include components such as policy review and revision, role clarification, a focus on job performance as the identification criterion, and the training of all key staff as crucial elements in both the design and implementation of an EAP.

A first step in coping with troubled employees was to *have* a formal policy on "behavioral/medical" problems, especially those such as alcoholism and drug abuse, which are characterized by formidable social stigma and hence denial. The major advancement in such policies was their public recognition of the existence of AODA problems, their recognition of chemical dependency as an illness, and the explicit declaration that no one would be punished for having such problems. Thus, policies were written which addressed both the belief system and the procedures by which employee problems would be addressed. Policies were, more than anything else, an offer of help.

EAP's also succeeded by addressing organizational issues. They recognized that support always had to come from the top management and from all other levels as well. Also significant was the insistence that two formal roles be recognized and clarified; the role of the supervisor was to develop clear standards of performance, enforce them, and offer employees help (via referral to the EAP) if they needed help to maintain satisfactory job performance; "counseling" was recognized to be incompatible with the competence as well as the role of most supervisors. Thus, the second role of "referral resource person," which could be fulfilled by virtually anyone, was formally distinguished from that of "supervisor."

Another of the major contributions of EAP's was their insistence that the criteria for supervisory identification and referral was to be *job performance only*. Supervisors were not to look for or diagnose "alcoholism" or any other behavioral/medical problem. By looking for patterns of unsatisfactory performance they were, in fact, intervening much earlier, since these signs become apparent much sooner to the untrained eye than would the symptoms of alcoholism. Moreover, various program elements were designed to encourage self-referral—the earliest identification possible.

In order to accomplish these procedural ends training was crucial in three areas. First, all supervisory and management staff required orientation to the principles of early identification by job performance, and training in the procedures of making referrals to EAP resource staff. Secondly, those designated as resource persons received training in interviewing skills, EAP procedures, the nature of various behavioral/medical problems, and in the availability local community resources. Finally, employees and their families were oriented to the new program via staff meetings and mailed announcements.

In sum, Employee Assistance Programs did not have a narrow, pinpoint, "local" focus on the individual employee who had an AODA-related problem or any other. Instead, EAP's represented a *global* response to the mutual tragedies which employee AODA problems caused for employers, employees, and their families.

The Employee Assistance Program model was also not "invented" as a result of ideology. It was not deduced from abstract notions concerning "prevention" or "intervention" but discovered and refined over 40 years through a commitment to common sense and practicality. Everyone got what they needed and people got well. One of the contributing factors to this process was the design of a program model based not on conformity to such definitions but on its ability to carry out the necessary conditions for providing help: identification, assessment, motivation, and referral.

Lastly, one aspect of the success of EAP's is often overlooked. Programs sought, though often not explicitly, a change in the environment or context, not in the individual employee. The former was a necessary precondition for the latter. They did not clarify employees' values, arm them with "accurate information," enhance their decision-making skills, or raise the drinking age to 65 to prevent employee alcohol abuse. Obtaining changes in employees required making changes in the working environment in the areas of attitudes, knowledge, and behavior. In the broadest sense, EAP's actually worked because they examined those factors which unwittingly contributed to employee problems going ignored, unidentified, and untreated. Today we recognize these factors as components of the "enabling system."

All of the factors above, in a fairly direct way, contributed to the development and initial form of the Student Assistance Program model. We essentially asked: what features of EAP's—which make them such a successful means of helping adults with AODA-related problems in the work setting—can we apply to students with AODA-related problems in the school setting? And, what adjustments need to be made, taking into account the uniqueness of youth and of the school setting? Much of the result is contained in the model described in this book.

The need, the disaffection with prevention, and the availability of a viable model simply created the appropriate conditions for conception all around the country. Two other developments were more directly responsible for the "birth" of the 180 SAP's in Wisconsin mentioned initially. In 1978, what was then the Bureau of Alcohol and Other Drug Abuse of the State of Wisconsin's Department of Health and Social Services created the position of "Student Assistance Program Consultant." The position was created to design a Student Assistance Program Model and to promote its implementation on a statewide basis by providing consultation and training to interested districts.

The final piece to be put in place was the enactment by the Wisconsin legislature, in 1979, of what is now popularly called "Chapter 331." Chapter 331 of the Laws of 1979 contained several provisions designed to address the growing problems associated with youthful alcohol and other drug abuse. Among its major provisions were the following:

1. The creation of a grant program, administered by the Wisconsin Department of Public Instruction, whereby school districts could apply for up to $25,000 a year to develop and implement "joint school/community alcohol and drug abuse prevention, intervention, treatment, and rehabilitation" programs: in other words, SAP's;

2. A section making it illegal for anyone to consume alcoholic beverages on school grounds or at school sponsored activities;

3. A section liberalizing provisions for minor's consent for treatment.

4. A section declaring that alcohol/drug information disclosed to school staff by students is to be regarded as *privileged communication* protected by confidentiality;

5. A section mandating the establishment of working referral relationships, between school superintendents and local AODA agencies, on behalf of students with AODA-related problems;

6. A section protecting school officials from legal liability solely for referring a student to an alcohol/drug agency.

The major psychosocial impact of the legislation was to give public permission to school districts and their communities to admit "having a drug problem," which is the first step in working toward its resolution.

A final factor in the development of so many Student Assistance Programs in Wisconsin has been their very success. Each year school districts begin implementing SAP's because of the experience their neighbors have had with them. This factor, in concert with those mentioned above, have contributed to the development of student Assistance Programs in over a third of Wisconsin's public schools in just under eight years.

| Part One | # "What Can I Do To Help?" |

It is fair to assume, at the very least, that most readers bring to this book some curiosity regarding the alcohol and other drug problems of youth, and perhaps even the assumption that school systems are appropriate contexts within which to work to ameliorate them. Others may be interested in how to bring about specific school/community changes in order to cope more effectively, successfully, and healthfully with the alcohol and other drug problems of young people.

Characterization of the abuse of alcohol and other drugs by young people as "epidemic" by the press, professionals, and the public alike is no longer shocking or unexpected. The numbers of kids in trouble with drugs and the numbers of drugs they are regularly using have been steadily increasing for the past two decades. And, they are discovering mood-altering chemicals at younger and younger ages. We also know that the problem is sufficiently complex that it will be many more years before a complete, considered, and cogent explanation of its causes is within our reach. It is clear, however, that the problem has continued to grow despite major investments of time, money, and expertise in attempts to resolve it.

Background

Whether looked at within the narrow confines of the school building, or in the light of the global trends noted above, the history of the past two decades' attempts at "prevention" is in many ways a catalogue of the things that we have learned do not work. Experience has shown many strategies to have been ineffective in forestalling drug abuse either because they were flawed in principle, or because any one of them alone was insufficient.

Denial. Deciding not to recognize the problem as a problem has always been the first and most frequent strategy. Youthful drug abuse is often perceived as either an individual or a social phase which, like other

"fads," will pass. Many adults will also observe that "we drank when we were kids and it didn't hurt us." That this strategy has not worked is obvious to the casual observer; it is understandable to anyone familiar with the dynamics of denial.

Scare Tactics. As one of the first active strategies to be employed, it was the utter failure of scare tactics that taught us our first lessons about coping with youthful drug abuse. The logic and psychology behind the scare tactics approach is unimpeachable: educators and other adults projected their own irrational or exaggerated fears of drugs upon young people. Educators reasoned that if they could effectively communicate the horrors of drugs to youth, the latter would be prevented from using them. What was often taught was that trying one marijuana cigarette would inexorably lead to death in a slum from a heroin overdose.

While accurately representing the clear and present dangers of a situation does have some preventive value, this approach to drug abuse failed, and continues to fail, for two basic reasons. First, the early scare tactics approach was based on the irrational projection of narrow social statistics onto individuals. What may have been true for a small percentage of the population was not applicable to the majority of teenagers on Mainstreet, USA. Moreover, scare tactics were based on the logical fallacy of *post hoc propter hoc* ("after the fact, therefore because of the fact"). It was illogical to argue that because some heroin addicts admitted to earlier use of marijuana then anyone who uses marijuana will become a heroin addict.

Secondly, this approach failed simply because of the day-to-day experiences of youth. Kids did not see that these arguments were illogical: they saw, day by day, that they were not true. Increasingly, most young people knew of others who used drugs, or used them themselves. Their daily experience demonstrated to them overwhelmingly that the mere use of drugs did not lead to the problems their elders predicted. Consequently, scare tactics produced two casualties: kids kept on using, and educators employing such strategies lost credibility.

Objective Information. Educators and prevention specialists learned from experience, too, and concluded that what was needed was objective information about drugs in place of value-laden preachments. Millions of dollars were spent by the federal government in support of prevention programs designed to teach kids objectively about drugs: what drugs there are, what they look like, their street names, how they affect the body and mind, etc. Subsequent evaluation revealed that as a direct result of such approaches student drug use actually *increased*—so much so that the federal government declared a funding moratorium on drug education as a prevention strategy.

The objective approach failed for a practical reason that was unforeseen. Many students were afraid to try drugs. Providing objective, cognitive information merely reduced the anxieties they had and made them better consumers. Now they knew what to ask for. The approach also failed because it, too, was based on false assumptions: that drug use is primarily a cognitively-based phenomenon, that kids use drugs because they don't know something, and that cognitive knowledge alone is preventive.

"Responsible Drinking." "Responsible drinking" appeared to address these shortcomings by targeting behavior change as the goal of prevention and by addressing the value systems and decision-making skills which students bring to their decisions about whether or not to use drugs. While it appeared to be a major step in the right direction, the "responsible use" approach was also fraught with complexities. In the first place, in many instances this approach had the effect of condoning drug use if it was done responsibly. Young people don't need to be taught how to use drugs responsibly: they *do* need to be taught how to make healthy, responsible decisions about drug use.

Secondly, although the responsible drug use approach supplied students with competencies in discovering their values and making decisions, it frequently left them to apply these skills to drug use "on their own," and often without communicating to them the set of values by which adults in the school setting judged drug use as harmful. Most were left, under this generic approach, to "make up their own minds."

This isn't the way families work. Even those families which consider themselves to be the most liberal in allowing their children to make up their own minds will subtly reinforce attitudes and behaviors which parents themselves endorse. Socializing children in the closely knit, interpersonally intense environment of the family is difficult enough. To expect children to "make up their own minds" on alcohol and drug matters in the comparatively impersonal environment of the classroom or school building is unrealistic. In other words, what the "responsible drinking/drug use" strategies have often lacked is the support of a well-thought out and effectively communicated belief system that tells students in what ways drug use and underage drinking are unacceptable and dangerous.

Getting Tough. To some schools it became apparent that something more concrete had to change: student drug use and its disruptive consequences were becoming unavoidable in the hallways, classrooms, and offices. Often a large drug bust, an overdose, a traffic fatality, or a community alarmed by survey results prodded a school into an apparently proactive stance: the birth of the "get tough" policy designed to get the problems out of the school. Such policies suspended or expelled any student who became involved with drugs in any way in school. This approach enjoyed some apparent short-term success but failed as any long-term response by driving problems underground, by reinforcing the fears of students, parents, and staff regarding getting help, by failing to get troubled students the help they needed, and by creating an environment that precludes students from accepting help if it was offered. Such a punishment-only policy is like the proverbial raindance: it doesn't make it rain, but allows everyone to feel better about the drought.

Dogs and Stars. Many schools tried other "quick fixes": drug-sniffing dogs, massive locker searches, or the celebrity expert. In the latter case, a single charismatic speaker came into the school and aroused in students an intense but momentary conviction against drug use. By all reports student drug use always returned to its former level within days when such approaches were utilized in isolation or lacked long-term, school-wide follow-up.

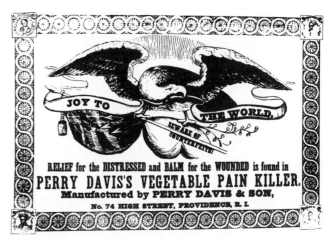

Hiring an Expert. Often the solution seemed to be to employ a full-time alcohol/drug counselor or specialist in the high school who can deal with such problems expertly. Or, the school formed a working relationship with a community alcohol/drug counselor who visited the school for a few hours each day or week. However, at best, the counselor could see only a fraction of the students who have AODA-related problems. Often too, counselor turnover either in the school or in the agency meant spending months re-establishing contacts, working relationships, and credibility among all concerned. More serious was the implication that others in the school, or the system itself, did not have to examine or change the factors that were allowing drug problems to persist or to worsen. For a school to expect an outside expert to solve its alcohol/drug problems made about as much sense as for a family to expect that hiring a drug counselor would solve the problems of alcoholism in its household.

Community Solutions. Finally, in many places it was recognized that such problems were, after all, community problems that required community-wide solutions. Task forces, advisory panels, or Chemical People groups were organized. Often, however, such community-wide efforts suffered because they lacked or failed to develop an action agenda. Membership and involvement declined as the group was exposed to an endless round of speakers, panels, and films but took no action: as people were given nothing to do, attendance declined. Other times, the agenda they did develop was inappropriate. Youth centers, alternatives programs, recreational opportunities, and other projects were implemented but could not be sustained or did little to impact on youthful drug abuse.

Many times the energy of community members was also allowed to dissipate itself in piecemeal projects. This was often due to the absence of AODA specialists as consultants to community groups or to the former's failure to provide appropriate technical assistance and guidance. Frequently the prevention specialists expected the lay people to be experts. Having discovered the "nominal group process," they allowed communities to identify their own problems and solutions without providing them with information about more workable, appropriate strategies.

Rather than documenting our failures, the foregoing should be testimony to the great investment of effort in trying to combat such problems and to the things that have been learned in the process. One lesson is that effective strategies of dealing with youthful drug-related problems must appreciate their complexity and scope as well as their context. Problems that took decades to develop will not be resolved by a single policy or person, nor will they go away overnight. Moreover, it is necessary to recognize that everyone has been affected by alcohol and other drug abuse, if not through intimate personal experience then by growing up in a society whose fears and judgemental attitudes about such problems severely erode our abilities to be helpful.

In addition, the systems within which individuals live and work have also been affected in the sense that they, too, in varying degrees have become dysfunctional in successfully handling young people with alcohol and other drug-related problems. The result is that we have learned that it is impossible to affect the AODA-related problems of youth if systems and individuals within them remain dysfunctional.

That systems can change in the direction of health, and that individuals within them can change are among the beliefs behind this book. Moreover, that systems and the individuals within them must change as a prerequisite to "helping" is perhaps its chief assumption.

What Can I Do to Help?

Another assumption behind this book is that the reader will bring to this material some curiosity as to what he or she can do to help. However, the leap from "What can I do to help?" to "How do I change the system?" is often made too easily and automatically. It is easy to miss altogether the individual nature of "helping." It is simply true that after all the books have been read, after all the talks are presented and meetings are over, after all the decisions have been made and the policies enacted, after all the structures are in place—"helping" finally occurs within the more limited boundaries of one person dealing intimately with another.

The arena of change is ultimately the individual.

Therefore, in order to answer the question "What can I do to help?" it is necessary to ask "How do I help just one student?" To do this, answering three additional, more basic questions is a prerequisite:

(1) What problem does this student have?
(2) What does this student need?
(3) What must *I* do to get them what they need?

Furthermore, it is only after we have answers to these questions that it makes sense to focus attention on changing the various systems with which young people interact, and then to ask:

(4) What aspects of the *system* need changing—
    (a) in order to get them what they need,
    (b) in order to help as many as possible,
    (c) and to remove obstacles to (a) and (b)?

The five chapters in PART ONE deal with each of these questions in greater detail, as prerequisites to designing and implementing a given version of the Student Assistance Program model.

Chapter 1 introduces student assistance programming through an essay that equates the process of program implementation with the process of recovery: one of the central themes of the book.

Assuming that one of the answers to the question "Why Do We Need a Student Assistance Program?" can be found in looking at their prevalence, Chapter 2 examines the nature and scope of alcohol and other drug abuse problems that can affect young people.

Chapter 3 examines who such programs are for. While they are obviously for young people with alcohol and other drug-related problems, it is not as obvious just what such problems are. To a large degree, conventional wisdom sees the "drug problem" as a large and amorphous one that is nevertheless a singular phenomenon that can be resolved with a singular response: funding, a curriculum, or a law. Chapter 3, however, describes the different ways in which youth can be affected by mood-altering chemicals and points out that these different experiences imply different needs. Thus, an assistance program will recognize these discrete target groups, and will design procedures and structures unique to each. Finally, it is not often appreciated that a student assistance program is also "for" others: that it has concrete and primary benefits for staff, parents, and the community as a whole as well.

Chapter 4 then turns to ways of defining the concept "Student Assistance Program" in logical and operational terms, outlining additional philosophical tenets that underlie the concept as presented here, and suggesting some reasonable goals for those engaged in Student Assistance Programming. It also explores the role of the school system, and its limitations, in coping with AODA-related problems.

Finally, Chapter 5 returns to the concept that in varying degrees the school setting is dysfunctional with respect to coping with the alcohol and other drug abuse problems of its students. This is not to say that schools cause or are in any sense responsible or to blame for drug problems. It is merely to confront the global issue of "enabling" as defined by those working in the field of drug abuse and dependency. Our individual failures to help or to be helpful can often be traced to our own patterns of "enabling": the patterns of what we think, feel, and do (or fail to know, feel, and do) that contribute to the continuation of alcohol and other drug-related problems.

Ultimately, Student Assistance Programming is equivalent to the process of recovering from the ways in which enabling has been institutionalized in the school setting as well as in others. Consultants, trainers, and other change agents may find it useful to see their role as helping school systems (or any system) to recover from the effects of drug problems in a way which parallels the recovery process for chemically dependent persons and their families.

Chapter 1 | "Student Assistance" Means "Community Recovery": A Personal View

In a small Wisconsin school system a caring, well-intentioned teacher confronted an intoxicated student and referred him to the principal, who suspended him in accordance with a long-standing school policy. The parents, outraged at what they saw as the school's accusation that their son had a 'drinking problem,' appeared at the next school board meeting with an attorney, demanding that their son be reinstated, compensated, and that references to the incident be expunged from his school records. The Board acquiesced.

We would do well to ask ourselves what each of the participants in this drama—parent, teacher, administrator, or community members—has learned, and if these are the things we want to teach.

Although nearly everything in this manual is directed at defining "student assistance program" [SAP], or describing a given realization of the model, I wish to take some time at the beginning to focus a stronger light on the concept. Over the years, three broad ways of answering the question "What is a student assistance program" have suggested themselves. Each illuminates this notion from a different perspective.

Consider, first, the following:

> [I] *A student assistance program consists of a team of staff who draft policy language, design procedures, train others, and promote program awareness in order to identify, assess, refer, and support students with alcohol and other drug-related problems in proportion to their numbers.*

Many would consider Definition [I] to be a good, logical example of what we mean by "student assistance program." It contains four significant elements.

First, such programs, to succeed, are never the

result of an individual, solitary effort. Rather, a program consists of a team of individuals—a group united by a common goal and responsibility. Secondly, the definition identifies the tasks ("draft policy language...promote program awareness") which involve the team in the design and implementation process. Third, the program must perform certain functions ("identify, assess, refer, and support") to be an effective student assistance program. And finally, a program functions on behalf of certain target groups: "students with alcohol and other drug-related problems."

However, as anyone who has been connected with student assistance programs will attest, if this is all such programs are then they are unexciting objects indeed. In fact, some of the challenge of being involved in student assistance programming can be captured by defining such programs from an additional perspective, and by bearing two things in mind. I suggest that we must continually ask who such programs are for, and we must continually remember that *recovery* — not "prevention" or "intervention" — is our ultimate as well as our primary concern.

As to the first, while it is clear that student assistance programs are for students, it is not as apparent that good programs are much more than that. If a student assistance program is not for ourselves, no matter who we are in a school system — teacher, administrator, counselor, etc. — then it is misguided and deficient. For in the context of an effective program, I feel better about myself, my work with kids, and my ability to help. More generally, a good program is also for the community at large, from families and neighborhoods to community organizations, agencies, and institutions. On the one hand, we have an investment in becoming more effective at minimizing the alcohol and other drug-related problems of the kids we care about; on the other, we have an investment in becoming healthier individuals in healthier environments.

Secondly, it is easy to see that formal treatment is what we would want an adequate student assistance program to offer its chemically dependent youth, for example. Similarly, we also want to offer "treatment" for the other ways in which youth are affected by their own or others' use of mood-altering chemicals. However, a fundamental assumption behind this manual is that everyone has been affected by alcohol and other drug abuse, if not through personal experience with drugs or those with drug-related problems, then through growing up and living in a cultural context characterized by inaccurate knowledge, harmful attitudes, negative feelings, and inaction: in other words, denial. A change in these personal and social conditions is only one result of implementing a student assistance program. Hence, we might advance the following definition to complement the first:

[II] *A student assistance program is the system of all of the things it is necessary to know, think, feel and do in order to help students deal with all of the ways in which they are affected by their own use of mood-altering chemicals or someone else's.*

Those aspects of knowledge, feeling, and action that characterize our individual stance with respect to alcohol and other drug abuse problems and which have become institutionalized in our social systems constitute those areas within which our own "recovery" must take place. In this sense, recovery is as much a cause, or precondition for a good program as it is an effect of one.

I would like to devote the rest of my comments to just this issue: that 'Student Assistance' means 'community recovery.' It is my belief that the process of implementing an effective student assistance program is fundamentally similar to the process which caring individuals go through in recovering from the ways in which they have been affected by their own chemical use or that of those close to them. The steps in this recovery process supplement the "cookbook" implementation tasks of Definition [I] above. Moreover, this recovery is not limited to individuals within a school system alone, but extends to those other segments of the community with which the school system is necessarily involved.

In this connection, the experience of recent years confirms my belief that it is useful to see school systems (as only one segment of the community) as dysfunctional families, at least with respect to the ways in which they have been affected by the drug problems in their midst, and that in becoming more effective at helping youth with such problems they go through a recovery process similar to that of other "families." Hence, Definition [III]:

[III] *A student assistance program is the result of the process of recovering as individuals, systems, and as a community from the effects of alcohol and other drug abuse.*

The Family Illness Analogy

It is challenging to attempt in a few paragraphs a characterization of chemical dependency—a topic about which many substantial books have been written (Johnson (1980), Milam (1981), McAuliffe (1975a, 1975b)). However, even a partial list of the broad characteristics of chemical dependency would include the following: (a) loss of control, over both chemical use and its consequences (b) increasing frequency of harmful consequences as a result of chemical use, (c) much emotional pain, and (d) the presence of an elaborate denial system.

If one is chemically dependent, increasing loss of control will result in his/her inability to predict the outcome, or consequences, of chemical use once the drug is ingested. What typically begins to happen is that the chemical user experiences harmful consequences- accidents, family arguments, violence, and other irresponsible conduct—directly related to alcohol /drug use. It is important to understand that the harmful consequences consist of behavior that is atypical in the sense that it violates the individual's system of values.

These increasingly frequent, unpredictable violations of one's values are the source of the growing emotional distress—pain, guilt, shame, anger, fear, loneliness, etc. Episode by episode, defense mechanisms prevent the dependent person from experiencing these emotions and from seeing their connection to chemical use. Instead, the events and their painful emotional consequences are rationalized, excused, suppressed, minimized, and blamed away. Thus, the pain goes unrecognized by the individual as well as by family and friends.

Defense mechanisms and impairments to perception, judgement, and memory prevent the dependent person from gaining insight into his condition. Aside from failing to realize that he is dependent, the individual has even more fundamentally lost the ability to see the clear and definite connection between chemical use and the nature and scope of the harmful consequences that follow. Also a crucial part of this denial system is the "enabling" of those around him: the responses to the dependent's behavior by family members which ironically have the effect of preventing him from fully experiencing the consequences of his chemical use— covering up, hiding feelings, accepting excuses, blaming self and others, etc.

The denial system that supports the delusion of the dependent person and family alike is perfectly understandable when seen as a general human trait. As Gorski (1976a, p.3) has pointed out so simply, our denial systems accomplish four things for us:

(1) They maintain a sense of self-esteem and self respect;
(2) They make reality seem manageable;
(3) They provide a "myth" of control over situations;
(4 They provide a mythical solution.

Faced with the shaming attitudes of a culture that stigmatizes alcoholism, the dependent and family member alike have a great deal invested in protecting their self-image and self-esteem. No one is eager to admit having it if the price to be paid is public shame. The denial of chemical dependency is fully understandable on these grounds alone. In addition, the denial that drug use is a problem, or is the problem, allows one to feel that life still makes sense, that one can still control daily actions as well as destinies, and that solutions to the problem lie elsewhere—usually in more "acceptable" areas: family counseling, or simply "trying harder."

In addition to denial, there is also a logical and psychological process that helps to explain the degree to which family members, and the public at large, become increasingly entangled in their own dysfunction. To the extent that they are unaware of the dynamics of chemical dependency, family members are likely to subscribe to the following five fallacies concerning the drug user's behavior:

1. The individual can control his drug use (i.e., there is no distinction between drug use, drug abuse, and drug dependency);

2. I can help the individual to control her chemical use and its consequences (i.e., the drug user is inadequate to do what the rest of us have the personal strength to do);

3. Thus, I am now responsible for the individual's drug use and its consequences.

As a family member, I am now "hooked" too. And, as the chemical use and its harmful consequences continue, I am forced to conclude at some conscious or unconscious level:

4. I am to blame for the continuing chemical use;

5. I have failed to control the behavior because I am inadequate (i.e., I'm no good).

Just as dependency follows a predictable progression, the disease process in the family typically evolves in predictable stages as its members attempt to cope with the problem. (For some descriptions of family dynamics, see Wegscheider (1981), McCabe (1978), and Jackson (1954)). The family initially becomes aware of changes in the dependent's personality and behavior, but is unaware that the changes are related to chemical use. Protected by their own defense mechanisms from the painful feelings associated with the harmful consequences, the family members hope that their experience is temporary, that it is "only a phase" that will pass.

In the next phase, the family becomes aware that chemical use has become a problem, but is unaware that the problem is dependency. Likewise, family members continue in their belief that the dependent person can control his behavior, but needs a little help from them. They become increasingly manipulative in their attempts to control. As these attempts fail, the family members conclude they are at fault, that they are responsible for the chemical use and the results, and that the unhappy situation is due ultimately to their own personal inadequacies. Embarrassment or shame leads the family and those within it to isolate themselves from society and from each other.

The final phase is dominated by resentment, anger, and despair, Family members will often resent each other for failing to solve the problem or "fix" the person. Family members at this point may choose to do one of four things: (1) keep on keeping on, (2) escape the family, (3) expel the dependent person—or (4) seek appropriate treatment for themselves and the persons they care about.

Thus, the affected family member largely mirrors the same feelings and dynamics as the drug abuser. We become as preoccupied with the user's behavior as she is with her chemical use. Feelings of fear, shame, guilt, anger, and hurt arise from many sources—chiefly from the user's behavior and prevailing social stigma—but go unrecognized due to similar defensive patterns.

Family secrets and "no talk rules" predominate around the subject of alcohol/drug abuse and the increasing family pain. The self-esteem of family members and of the family as a unit is vigorously protected.

The denial and defensiveness of the family serves to protect the family's image to the outside world, since no one wants to admit publicly what the public regards as a shameful problem.

All of these traits comprise an elaborate "enabling system," which prevents the abuser and family system alike from experiencing the consequences of chemical abuse, and unwittingly allows the disease to progress to more severe stages.

In all of the above, one is justified in regarding chemical dependency as a "family illness"—the caring person's disease—in whose context neither the individual family member nor the dependent person can achieve health and growth.

The Dysfunctional School System

While our school systems are very efficient at handling most other problems, to the extent that they lack SAP-like approaches they become increasingly unable to provide help to youth who are affected by their own use of chemicals or someone else's. The brief outline above illustrates a situation in

which the family is unable to meet its own emotional needs or those of the drug using persons within it. Many school systems and their communities also become dysfunctional with regard to managing chemical abuse. Schools become dysfunctional in ways which are strikingly similar to the ways in which family systems do. While individual students in such a setting will certainly suffer, the school itself often suffers through the inability of staff to refer successfully, low staff and student morale, high dropout rates, vandalism, declining test scores, and so on.

"To the extent that a school system resembles an alcoholic family, in order to have a student assistance program it needs to recover from the ways it has been affected by alcohol and other drug-related problems."

Thus, there are many areas of similarity between the affected families discussed earlier and school systems which have "the caring person's disease." Before continuing, two points are worth emphasizing. First, even though we may have difficulties in coping with the problem—as schools, families, or individuals—we are nevertheless doing the best we can with what we know and with the resources we have. And secondly, we experience difficulties in managing students' alcohol/drug problems precisely because we care: we have some personal investment in the well-being of kids.

As systems made up of individuals, school systems suffer from the same inadequacies that families do regarding the dynamics of chemical dependency. Probably nothing contributes more to our ineffectiveness than our lack of accurate information about such problems and our tendency to subscribe to the fallacies and prevailing public attitudes about them.

One of the most noteworthy similarities between affected families and school settings can be seen in the feelings that are shared. Feelings of fear, shame, guilt, anger, powerlessness, and inadequacy are not hard to identify in many school buildings. Fear may be expressed as "apprehension" about the growing drug problem, or it may be seen in a staff member's reluctance to confront an intoxicated student, or in a teacher's fear of being in certain areas of the high school building. I have also visited school systems where individual staff members have expressed their frustration at being unable to cope with the growing numbers of drug-affected youth as well as feelings of inadequacy in dealing with the problems of individual students. In terms of such feelings, is there any difference between "If I were a better wife my husband wouldn't drink" and "If I were a better teacher, counselor, or principal we wouldn't have these problems?"

Perhaps there is no more consistent similarity between school settings and the dysfunctional alcoholic family than the persistence of each system's denial and its sources. The denial extends far beyond the overt "We don't have a problem here" so often voiced by administrators, school boards, or parent groups. As with families, the need to protect the image of the system is typically very strong: it is directly proportional to the degree of student alcohol/drug involvement, and accounts for most of the overt denial or minimization of the alcohol/drug problems of students.

Another area of similarity between the school setting and dysfunctional families lies in our understandable tendency to do the best we know how based on inadequate information. Families typically lack the crucial awareness that chemical dependency differs from other varieties of chemical use due to the phenomenon of "loss of control." Thus, we see a given individual's chemical use as just like everyone else's, but differing in degree and consequences. We therefore conclude that we can help the individual (i.e., we can control their using behavior), and when the outcome doesn't change we attribute it to the student's moral or psychological weakness, to "bad parents," to our own inadequacy as people or as helpers, or to all of the above. At some point our own defensive postures come to our aid, and we rationalize, blame, avoid or withdraw from the situation. It is thus that we also fail to recognize our own role in the problem as participants in the "enabling" system.

There are three final areas in which we can see a school system's dysfunctions regarding helping those students who suffer from their own or others' chemical problems: policy, procedure, and structure.

Policy. In school settings where there is no SAP-like program we often find two kinds of policy statements regarding student alcohol/drug use. The "written" policies, at least until a few years ago, usually read something like this:

The manufacture, use, possession, delivery or sale of controlled substances by students is a violation of state and federal laws. The school system will turn over students, and evidence of their use of controlled substances, to law enforcement officials immediately.

The "unwritten" policy would go something like this:

We will suspend or expel students for conduct which violates school rules without seeking to see if it is alcohol or drug-related. We will avoid confronting the issue of chemical behavior in hopes that students will outgrow it, graduate, or drop out, where social service agencies can deal with the problem.

While few would consciously "own" such a policy, it is nonetheless an accurate description of much of our behavior. Such "policies" are also descriptions of how many families respond to their chemically dependent members.

In examining these written policy stances three deficiencies often stand out. First, they are much too brief. Chemical abuse by young people is probably one of the most complex human problems we are currently attempting to cope with and understand, and no simple response is going to be adequate. Simply put, different youngsters have different varieties of chemical experience, and have different needs. These differing needs should dictate appropriately different responses which are reflected in policy, procedure, and structure.

"I submit that it feels better to confront a student with what I have observed and how I feel about it than to retreat into my classroom and nurse the conviction that junkies are just bad people."

Secondly, the brief "written" policies are admittedly punitive, at least in tone. In examining school policy language regarding drug use I suggest that school officials ask themselves one basic question: "If I were a student, teacher, or parent, how likely am I to believe that the school system is offering "help," and how likely am I to accept it if it is offered?" I submit that it is unlikely that a teacher will refer a student— especially one he/she cares about—for suspected or observed drug involvement if the official policy requires automatic legal action and nothing else. For the same reasons, such policy language makes it equally unlikely that students or their parents will contact the school for assistance once they begin to experience real problems around chemical use.

And finally, in addition to being simplistic and punitive in tone, most policy stances of whatever sort go largely unenforced. Inadequately trained staff members, given the choice between punitive action and no action at all, too often find the latter course the most attractive. Where policies are not enforced students learn there are no consequences for their actions. If there are no consequences, why should they change?

Procedures. The procedures which grow out of such written or unwritten policies are equally narrow and disjointed at times. While a procedure for dealing with students who are intoxicated in school is usually a part of most school systems, what about procedures for those who abuse chemicals outside of school but whose in-school conduct suffers as a result—grades, attendance, behavior, and so on? Or what about those students whose poor school performance is related not to their own abuse of chemicals, but to the alcohol/drug problems of parents? Again, our procedures may often be inappropriate to a given student, or may attempt to correct a problem over which the student has no control. Surely, there must be additional procedural choices we can give ourselves and our students.

Structure. A major symptom of the dysfunctional school "family" is the absence of a structure, or the presence of a dysfunctional structure, for dealing with kids who have AODA-related problems. While our system may indeed have administrative, pupil services, and academic structures in place, a major symptom of the dysfunctional system is the degree to which "It's the other guy's job" is an unspoken belief by staff. Very often the administrator (who can implement policy), the counselor (who can assess and recommend action) and the classroom teacher (who can best monitor school performance and identify problem students) are unable to function together, at least with respect to meeting the needs of chemically-affected youth. One of the things I learn in a dysfunctional family is mistrust: I can't depend on others to be there when I need them. In a dysfunctional school setting, I learn that if I play my part I can't depend on others to play theirs. And nothing undermines my participation in a process faster or more thoroughly than failing to see changes occur after I attempt to utilize it. At best we become "loners" and attempt to work with a given student alone. At worst we decide that nothing can, after all, be done.

In sum, we are faced with a "school/family system" in which we are unable or unwilling to admit the existence of a drug problem as well as its nature and scope. We are underinformed or misinformed, and we suspect that somehow the drug problem is our fault. We remain unaware of how our attitudes and behavior have given us an unwitting role in allowing the problem to continue. We react with rigidity to crises or we fail to confront issues at all. And still we often feel that it is solely our responsibility to change things.

There must be a better way.

Recovery

As I mentioned at the beginning, student assistance programs are certainly for students—for those 25 percent to 40 percent of all of our kids who suffer with their own chemical problems or those of their families. However, programs must also be for ourselves. Our school systems need recovery from the attitudes, feelings, and behaviors which render us incapable of meeting the needs of these students and which in fact perpetuate these problems.

Thus, I would like to look at the implementation process from an additional perspective. While it is true that there are definite stages of program implementation [see Part Four], this process can also be seen as identical to the process which family members go through in recovering from the dysfunctions brought on or aggravated by chemical abuse and dependency. Stated in its strongest form, the major thesis of this book is that *to the extent that a school system resembles an alcoholic family, in order to have a student assistance program it needs to recover from the ways it has been affected by alcohol and other drug-related problems.* I would like to spend the rest of our time looking briefly at seven distinct stages in this recovery process.

1. THE DECISION TO RECOGNIZE. Effective changes can begin within this dysfunctional system to the extent that key persons within the family or school system recognize that there is indeed a problem. For a hypothetical school system this simple step entails quite a bit: recognizing the scope of the problem (it's not just a few "visible" kids), recognizing that our past attempts to deal with it are not adequate (whether it's "coming down hard" or just believing drug abuse is a passing social phase), and becoming aware that there are successful alternatives. It means struggling with the conscious choice between taking action or continuing as we have. It also means admitting to ourselves and to others that "We need help." Deciding to recognize that there was a problem leads us to ask questions.

2. ACQUIRING ACCURATE KNOWLEDGE. Having decided to do something, acquiring accurate knowledge is a crucial step, since most of what we absorb from our culture regarding chemical problems is wrong, inadequate, and negative. Moreover, probably no other human problem is as complex or as pervasive. So much of what we constructively do about alcohol/drug problems relies on what we know about them.

Among the first things to learn are the distinctions between use, abuse, and dependency, the family dynamics involved, and the enabling process. We have encountered the denial of others: now we discover our own. We also learn that the problem is not our fault: we did not, individually or as a system, cause the problem.

3. _REGAINING SELF ESTEEM_. With accurate information, we realized we were not at fault. Armed with appropriate information, we need not be preoccupied with an irrational fear of the judgment of our communities that the school system is to be blamed for the "drug problem." In addition, we stopped scape-goating others (the police, parents, pushers). At the very least our system can regain its self-esteem, and be strengthened enough to risk the remaining steps. Perhaps more importantly, the fact that a student uses, or continues to use chemicals does not mean we are inadequate as people, or as principals, teachers, counselors, or coaches. Having discovered our worth, we also discovered the courage to take risks.

4. _SELF-KNOWLEDGE_. New knowledge and a sense of our potential makes the next difficult step easier: having the courage to look at what our role in the problem has been. We begin to examine our own enabling behavior. How have we failed to confront students? How have we failed to invoke consequences for behavior which we have told students is unacceptable? How have our own feelings and attitudes prevented us from talking to kids in a way that they can hear? How have we provoked their defenses? How have we hidden behind our own?

What have we been explicitly teaching through our own behavior with alcohol and other drugs: the staff parties and athletic banquets, not to mention our failure to confront and help the 10 percent of our own staff that is chemically dependent?

How have the working relationships between administration, pupil services, and teachers allowed students' alcohol/drug problems to worsen? In whom does my mistrust reside? With a healthier concept of our possibilities, we examined what our role in the problem has been, which pointed the way toward change.

5. _CHANGING OUR BEHAVIOR_. After such an examination, which can be painful, the crucial step is to begin to change those behaviors, feelings, and attitudes which have enmeshed us in the problem, whether as individuals or as a system. These changes take two complementary forms. The first involves avoiding these dysfunctional styles: beginning to talk openly about alcohol/drug problems; violating the "no talk" rules; writing firm, flexible, appropriate, positive policy language; enforcing policies; developing appropriate procedures; giving up the safety of our own defensive attitudes and postures.

On the other hand, we also change our behavior because it is healthy for us. We acquire conduct, and the attitudes behind it, of which we can be publicly and openly proud. In other words, we learn to do what is good for ourselves apart from the fact that it is good for kids. I submit that it feels better to confront a student with what I have observed and how I feel about it than to retreat into my classroom and nurse the conviction that junkies are just bad people.

6. _LEARNING TO CONFRONT_. We learned to confront, which gave us strength. As individuals and as a system we begin to feel comfortable in taking the risk to say what we see and how we feel about it. We confront the problem by deciding to take action: as a classroom teacher I involve the alcohol/drug specialists in my building when I see or suspect problems with my students. I confront my students with my concerns, the facts I have seen, and refer them to the building specialists.

We also confront our own negative attitudes and behaviors and those we see in each other. Just as there is behavior we will no longer tolerate in the classroom, there is behavior that is no longer acceptable in the staff lounge. We challenge the system, the Board of Education, and the community. When we encounter obstacles in the course of a program's development we say what we see, and force those involved to consciously choose to impede progress. And, we do so because it feels better to talk about the elephant in the living room instead of blaming others for not seeing it too.

7. _SURRENDER_. Finally, we let go. Surrender is a phenomenon that probably no one masters completely or all of the time. By surrendering, or "letting go," the recovering family member realizes that just as he/she was not responsible for an individual's chemical use, neither is he/she responsible for their recovery. Similarly, as a staff and as a system we understand that we do not trade being to blame for the problem for being entirely responsible for its solution. This means simply getting in touch with our limitations as persons and as a school system. This is not a negative step, and it does not mean quiet desperation. It means we will not be overwhelmed by having to change everyone, or even one student. It means we will set reasonable goals and help those we can because it feels good to do so.

This recovery process is clearly one which runs parallel to the "cookbook" implementation strategies. The two are, in fact, different ways of looking at the same thing: becoming more adequate to meet the needs of students with AODA-related problems and to meet our own.

By going through a process similar to this, school systems "recover" from the negative impact which alcoholism, chemical dependency, and drug abuse have had upon them. The same process extends outward to the community at large. While at first only a handful of individuals within the school system may be bringing about changes in themselves and the system, they gradually attract others and expand their numbers. Just as one family member making such changes can alter the constellation of the family system, so the school district can become a powerful force for change-gradual though it may be—in its community.

Conclusion

Though I have directed my observations toward only one system—the school setting—clearly the deficits and failures of coping with the drug-related problems of youth exist in other systems, too. Individuals who are experiencing drug-related problems themselves or in their loved ones exist in every social setting (churches, civic organizations, softball teams) and in every community institution (the criminal justice system, the human services system, employment settings, etc.). I will risk noting that in many communities, at least with respect to managing alcohol and other drug-related problems, each of these is as dysfunctional as the school setting in the ways I have suggested.

This has two large and immediate implications. Each of these "systems," too, needs to recover from the ways in which it is dysfunctional if it is to help its clients or its members. And, closer to our topic, each must do so in cooperation with local school districts as part of a community recovery process. There is victory in the recovery of one family member if only because they have saved themselves. How much better when the whole family smiles.

I wish to conclude this essay by relating a recent experience which helps to clarify for me why I feel student assistance programs are vital and why the recovery perspective is a fruitful one. I had returned to a school district with which I had worked about a year earlier. The school system had implemented "affected others groups" for those youngsters who were reacting to alcoholism in their families. The staff had been unsuccessful in getting a particular third grade boy to join this group and we brainstormed a list of possible strategies. All of these strategies had been tried and had failed.

We were all feeling somewhat despondent when I was suddenly struck by the fact that the community—quite literally, the world in which this boy was growing up—had changed profoundly in a year. We did not have just one chance with him. Because the school district has implemented a program, and because many

of the staff were intimately involved with it, and because the structure of the district had changed, the staff had nine more years to help the boy. And for the next nine years he would be living in a system and a community which was recovering from chemical dependency, too.

Student assistance programs, like recovery, are not something to have but something to do, something to become a part of, something which helps to form what a district is. We implement programs for the same reason that families and their chemically dependent members recover: it simply feels better this way.

Chapter 1 | Supplements

Supplement 1.1 is a list of statements which allow individuals or groups within a school district to evaluate its current climate with respect to dealing with alcohol and other drug-related problems.

Supplement 1.2 is a restatement of the three definitions of the term "Student Assistance Program" presented in Chapter 1. A fourth definition has been added which defines such a program using language drawn from Wisconsin statutes (Chapter 331, Laws of 1979).

Supplement 1.1

The "WHERE DOES OUR DISTRICT STAND" worksheet is a list of 21 statements which draw upon the concepts presented in Chapter 1. Responding within a "Strongly Disagree" to "Strongly Agree" range, individuals may assess the location of their school system along the dysfunctional/recovery continuum. Individual worksheets can be scored simply by adding the number of responses in each column and multiplying by the number of the column. Adding the five column scores gives an overall rating. Ratings will range between 105 (all "Strongly Agree) and 21 (all "Strongly Disagree"). High scores would be consistent with the existence of a Student Assistance Program.

If responses are entered on the worksheet provided, a graph such as the one below may result. Graphed responses above the "3" level indicate perceptions of the school district in the "recovery" range. Groups of individuals (teachers, board members, etc.) can be given the worksheet and their collective responses graphed to illustrate consensus within groups or comparisons between groups.

The checklist can also be utilized to demonstrate changes in perception of the district before and after a program has been implemented. Figure 1.1 also illustrates scores received prior to implementing a program plotted against those received after its implementation.

Figure 1.1

"WHERE DOES OUR SCHOOL DISTRICT STAND?"

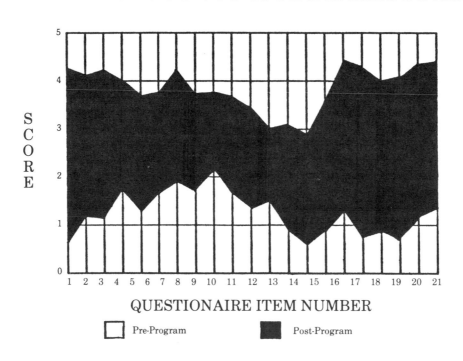

Supplement 1.1

Where Does Our District Stand?

Evaluate your school system in the light of each of the following statements. Indicate your assessment on the "agree/disagree" continuum. Transfer your responses to the grid provided (Figure 1.2).

STRONGLY DISAGREE		NEUTRAL		STRONGLY AGREE		
1	2	3	4	5		1. There is widespread, open acknowledgement by the board of education, administrators, staff, students, and parents of the scope of AODA-related problems affecting students in the community.
1	2	3	4	5		2. There is agreement that our current strategies for helping students who have AODA-related problems are successful.
1	2	3	4	5		3. There is cooperation and teamwork among school staff, and between the school system and other segments of the community in resolving AODA-related issues.
1	2	3	4	5		4. All levels of the school system are aware of fundamental AODA concepts, such as the distinctions between drug abuse and dependency, family dynamics involved, denial and enabling, effective intervention, etc.
1	2	3	4	5		5. All levels are aware of the different needs of students who are abusing drugs, who are affected family members, and who are recovering from chemical dependency.
1	2	3	4	5		6. The school has been involved in significant AODA inservice education for students, staff, and parents.
1	2	3	4	5		7. The school system does not feel responsible for causing the drug problem, and does not place blame for it on other segments of the community (e.g., parents, the police, etc.).

STRONGLY DISAGREE		NEUTRAL		STRONGLY AGREE	
1	2	3	4	5	8. The staff feels adequate and competent to deal with AODA issues in general, and with respect to individual students in particular.
1	2	3	4	5	9. The system is not fearful of being judged at fault for drug problems by other segments of the community, parents, or neighboring school districts.
1	2	3	4	5	10. Administrators, pupil services staff, and teachers have examined and corrected their enabling behavior.
1	2	3	4	5	11. Procedural aspects of enabling have been examined and corrected.
1	2	3	4	5	12. Most in the district have a good sense of how their individual, personal attitudes and behavior can foster either chemical problems or chemical health.
1	2	3	4	5	13. Changes have been made in policies, procedures, and services offered to students, which allow AODA problems to be managed effectively.
1	2	3	4	5	14. Student alcohol and other drug abuse is discussed openly and publicly within the district. Respect for privacy is not confused with secrecy.
1	2	3	4	5	15. Students and staff openly discuss feelings and attitudes about alcohol and other drug abuse in a constructive manner.
1	2	3	4	5	16. Staff members frequently confront students with their concerns in a caring but firm manner.
1	2	3	4	5	17. Counselors are knowledgeable regarding alcohol and other drug abuse and routinely confront such issues in their students.

STRONGLY DISAGREE		NEUTRAL		STRONGLY AGREE
1	2	3	4	5

18. There is an effort by staff to confront negative and harmful attitudes and behavior in each other.

1	2	3	4	5

19. The school has develped close ties with AODA services as well as with the community at large—police, parents, service organizations, clergy, etc.—to help resolve alcohol/drug problems.

1	2	3	4	5

20. There is a healthy, positive grasp of the school's possibilities as well as limitations in coping with alcohol and other drug abuse.

1	2	3	4	5

21. School staff frequently reassess goals and redefine limitations with respect to AODA programming.

Total "1" responses _____ x 1 = _____

Total "2" responses _____ x 2 = _____

Total "3" responses _____ x 3 = _____

Total "4" responses _____ x 4 = _____

Total "5" responses _____ x 5 = _____

TOTAL = _____

Figure 1.2

"WHERE DOES OUR DISTRICT STAND?"

Response Sheet

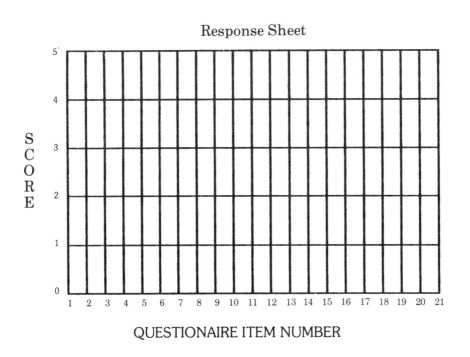

QUESTIONAIRE ITEM NUMBER

Enter the number of your response (score) to each of the checklist items in the appropriate column.

SUPPLEMENT 1.2
PROGRAM DEFINITIONS

[I]   A Student Assistance Program consists of a *team* of staff who draft policy language, design procedures, train others, and promote program awareness in order to identify, assess, refer, and support students with alcohol and other drug-related problems in proportion to their numbers.

[II]   A Student Assistance Program is the system of all of the things it is necessary to know, think, feel and do in order to help students deal with all of the ways in which they are affected by their own use of mood-altering chemicals or someone else's.

[III]   A Student Assistance Program is the result of the process of recovering—as individuals, systems, and as a community—from the effects of alcohol and other drug abuse.

[IV]   A Student Assistance Program is a comprehensive and integrated, joint school-community program for providing to students prevention, intervention, support, and instructional services for the amelioration of alcohol and other drug-related problems.

Why Implement Student Assistance Programs: The Scope of Student Drug Use

Abuse of substances, licit and illicit, is so widespread in our present societal context that we might well ask why some adolescents abstain, rather than why most do not. (Baumrind and Moselle, p. 44)

Introduction

The major motivation for implementing student assistance programs must reside in the nature and scope of the AODA-related problems of young people. The past two decades have witnessed the progression from a time when a handful of young people became involved with drugs to a period when approximately one third of all school-aged youth are harmed either by their own use of mood-altering chemicals, or by that of family members.

Thus, we have found that the use of alcohol and other drugs is now commonplace among teenagers and preadolescents; that for many, drug use begins prior to secondary school; that while there is some evidence that the precipitous increase in alcohol/drug use is moderating, it is stabilizing at perilously high levels; that there are only slight variations between national regions and rural, urban, suburban locales; and that particularly dangerous patterns of multiple drug use are common among a significant percentage of young people. Finally, at least 25% of all school children are seriously affected by the alcohol/drug abuse of parents.

Additional reasons for implementing SAP's have to do with the role of school systems first as educational institutions, and secondly as forces for change in their respective communities and in society as a whole. Common sense is supported by statistics on the degree to which students' drug use hampers attendance, academic achievement, and school conduct. Drug abuse compromises any school system's primary function: to teach. More generally, school systems are also in the best position to help individual students and to create climates that militate against drug abuse.

In describing the nature and scope of alcohol and other drug abuse, we will examine three areas: (1) data concerning overall prevalence, or how many students are using what drugs and how often; (2) data concerning "problem use," (3) and data relating to the number of children affected by parental alcoholism.

Prevalence of Alcohol and Other Drug Use

We suffer, to an extent, from an abundance of statistics gathered since the early 70's. Several studies, national in scope, have been conducted under the auspices of the National Institute on Alcohol Abuse and Alcoholism (NIAAA) and the National Institute on Drug Abuse (NIDA). Numerous other studies of alcohol/drug prevalence have also been conducted by individual researchers, and many more by communities and school districts. The great majority of such work supports the generalizations made earlier.

Table 2.1 summarizes the prevalence data that NIDA has collected since 1972 on drug abuse by 12 to 17 year-olds, or those in the 7th to 12th grades, in a national household survey. (Tables 2.1 through 2.10 are appended as Supplement 2.1). The table illustrates that 26.7% of secondary aged youth have had some lifetime experience with marijuana, 1 out of 5 (20.6%) have used marijuana during the past year, with 11.5% using within the past month.

For alcohol, 65.2% of those in grades 7 through 12 have used alcohol at some point in their lives; 47.3% report drinking during the past year, and 26.9% during the past month. The slight reduction in all three frequencies of marijuana and alcohol use since 1979 is born out by other studies, which nevertheless show that the use of these two drugs is moderating at high levels.

For the other three categories of drugs listed in Table 2.1 the situation is different. Cocaine use has escalated from 1.5% of this age group having some lifetime experience with it in 1972 to 6.5% in 1982. Stimulants and tranquilizers show a similar pattern of increase. As of 1982, Table 2.1 indicates that somewhere between 1% and 3% of 7th through 12th graders have had some experience with drugs other than marijuana and alcohol within the past month.

Table 2.2 summarizes the results of the Monitoring the Future Surveys, which have been conducted annually since 1975. These surveys are conducted among high school seniors only in a national sample of public and private schools, using urban and rural samples in all four demographic regions of the country. The table depicts the patterns of drug use for the same categories of drugs as Table 2.1, and includes rates of daily use.

The Monitoring the Future survey for the class of 1984 indicates that, overall, 61.6% of the senior class reports some illicit drug use; 21.3% report using marijuana only; and 40.3% have used some illicit drug other than marijuana.

Note that by the 12th grade, nearly 55% of high school students have had some experience with marijuana, and 92.6% have used alcohol. One out of six (16.1%) have some experience with cocaine, and more than one out of four (27.9%) report having used stimulants, including over-the-counter and look-alike drugs. Of more importance, 5% report using marijuana daily, and 4.8% report daily drinking.

"Problem Use"

According to some points of view, any use of drugs by young people is problematic: i.e., represents real or potential harm, and is not to be condoned. For the purposes of this book, we will distinguish three major "varieties" of chemical experience: drug use, drug abuse, and drug dependency, which will be dealt with in greater detail in Chapter 3. For now, it is necessary to observe that, on clinical grounds, not all students who use drugs have "a drug problem." While many might agree with the philosophical standpoint described above, it is nonetheless true that a student who drinks every day and uses four other types of drugs has a different type of "drug problem" than one who has smoked marijuana twice in the past year. In other words, at what point does an individual's drug "use" become "problematic?" When does it cease to be "experimental," "social," recreational," etc., and become pathological, harmful or dangerous? The numbers of young people involved in these patterns of chemical experience will define the extent of "the drug problem" in an additional way.

The major difficulty in defining "problem use" involves the absence of objective, widely accepted criteria (clinical or statistical) that universally separate "normal" from "pathological" chemical use. In other words, it is not possible to invoke standards such as "use of 2 or more drugs," "use of marijuana twice a week," or "drinking everyday," to separate those with drug problems from those without them. On the other hand, there are a number of criteria which clearly are correlated with the development of a drug problem.

For example, higher frequency of drug use can indicate a greater potential for drug problems in several ways. Frequent use argues for a greater emotional commitment to drugs as well as for a more harmful impact on psychosocial development. Moreover, for drugs with long half-lives (the period of time it takes the body to metabolize one-half the given dose), even consumption on a weekly basis can cause physiological damage. Secondly, simultaneous use of two or three types of drugs clearly multiplies the potential for physical and psychosocial harm, and indicates the degree of emotional commitment to drug use as well. Finally, the incidence of problems in living caused by one's drug use is a self-evident indication of a "drug problem."

The statistics cited above merely indicate the prevalence of students' experience with mood-altering chemicals. An increasing body of data also allows us to estimate the number of students experiencing real or potential harm from their chemical use.

Problem Drinking. The most rigorous study of adolescent problem drinking was conducted in 1974, and is reported in Donovan and Jessor (1978). Adolescents in grades 7-12 in the 48 contiguous states were sampled (N = 13,122). The survey collected data concerning frequency of drinking, amounts consumed per occasion, and problems subsequently encountered. Of the total sample of 13,222 students, 57% (7,481) were categorized as "moderate drinkers."

Table 2.3 shows the results of applying three different definitions of "problem drinking" to the sample of students drinking at or above the "moderate" level. Definition I is based on the conception of "problem drinking" as the combination of frequency of drunkenness and pattern of negative consequences caused by drinking. Almost 30% of the moderate-or-above sample fit this definition, or 18.8% of the total sample of 7th through 12th graders. Definitions II and III involve frequency of drunkenness and frequency of consequences alone, respectively, as definitions of problem drinking. These definitions reveal 9.4% and 8.9% of the total sample, respectively, as "problem drinkers."

The Adolescent Alcohol Involvement Scale (Mayer and Filstead, 1980) has been used in two studies that employ somewhat different criteria to establish "problem drinking" but whose results support the ranges indicated above. Mayer and Filstead's survey of Chicago-area high school students found that 19.1% scored in the "problem use" range; Moberg's application of the scales to adolescents in Dane County, Wisconsin found that 19.8% scored in the same range (Moberg: 1983, p. 705).

All of these studies support a conclusion that at least 20%, or 1 out of 5 secondary school students, drink in a manner that causes a pattern of harmful personal and social consequences.

Polydrug Use. One of the changes that has slowly occurred since we have been measuring such things is the movement toward greater polydrug use. It is now rare to encounter a student who has only had experience with one drug. (Tables 2.4-2.7, below, summarize some relevant statistics). Polydrug use clearly multiplies the potential for harm. On physiological grounds alone, for example, the concurrent ingestion of different types of drugs, with different manners of action, different metabolic pathways, different behavioral effects, etc., makes this an extremely dangerous pattern of drug behavior.

However, on psychological grounds also, one should be concerned about multiple drug use. Regular use of two, three, four, or more different types of drugs illustrates the degree of commitment on the part of an individual toward drug use ("preoccupation" or "obsession," in clinical terms). Commitment to drug-taking or to drug-highs is directly related to the risk of both "problem use" and alcoholism or other chemical dependencies. It is also true that psychosocial development is impaired to the degree that a young person has adopted multiple drug use as a part of his/her life-style.

Tables 2.4 and 2.5 depict the results of two different studies of multiple drug use by adolescents. Table 2.4 is based on a survey of 1,970 students in the 9th-12th grades in New Jersey (Pandina, et al., 1981). Only 22% of the students report no current or former drug use; and only 44% report use of alcohol only. More than a third (36%) report using two or more drugs; 19% use three or more; and 14% use four or more. This particular study also exemplifies the degree to which concurrent alcohol and marijuana use form the predominant "core" of drug use.

Table 2.5 is based on the Monitoring the Future Surveys of high school seniors only. It, too, illustrates the alcohol-marijuana use core, and indicates that 23.4% of students surveyed reported using three or more drugs. In addition, it shows the high correlation between daily use of marijuana ("commitment" measured in terms of frequency) and simultaneous use of other drugs.

The data in Table 2.6 demonstrate in another way the positive correlation between increased severity of alcohol use and polydrug use. The percentages of those involved with other drugs climbs steadily with increased alcohol involvement. Table 2.7 illustrates the same linear relationship in terms of numbers of drugs used. This study also indicates that 10.9% of all students surveyed (10th through 12th grades) report using 3 or more drugs; 7.4% use four or more drugs; and 4.4% use five or more drugs.

This comparatively brief survey of a portion of the statistical record illustrates its abundance and in some respects its diversity. However, in view of the data on problem drinking alone, and in view of these statistics on polydrug abuse, the conclusion that at least 20% of secondary students are harmfully involved with alcohol or other drugs is conservative.

Alcoholism and Other Drug Dependencies. Chemical dependency, of which alcoholism is but one variety, is the most severely harmful relationship one can have with mood-altering chemicals. Most definitions of this illness stress its progressive (always worsening), chronic (incurable), and ultimately fatal nature. While 10 percent reliably represents the prevalence of chemical dependency among the adult population, somewhat less certainty exists with respect to adolescents. For example, in Donovan and Jessor's study (1978), the 18.8% rate of "problem drinking" is also to be interpreted as including an indeterminate percentage of "alcoholics."

In estimating the rate of chemical dependency among adolescents one must rely on some assumptions applied to the data cited above, and upon only a few studies. For the purposes of this book, we will assume that the rate of chemical dependency among adolescents is at least 5%. This assumption is based on the following considerations:

1. In applying their Adolescent Alcohol Involvement Scale (AAIS) to a population of Chicago adolescents, Mayer and Filstead (1979, 1980) discovered that 4% of the adolescents sampled scored in the "alcoholic" range. This is the only survey instrument, whose reliability and validity have been established, which measures "alcoholism" as opposed to "alcohol misuse." Since the AAIS measures alcohol use only, other drug use would add to the 4% figure.

2. Table 2.2 indicates that nearly 5% of high school seniors use marijuana daily. Since tolerance and dependence to marijuana develop within 14-21 days of daily use (Maykut: 1984, p. 105), it can safely be assumed that most of this 5% are dependent.

3. On the grounds of polydrug use, Table 2.5 indicates that 5.4% of the Class of 1980 consisted of daily marijuana smokers who also used four other drugs, including alcohol. Table 2.4 reports that 11.0% of the 9-12th graders surveyed were using four or more drugs simultaneously.

4. According to Farley et al (1979; pp. 153), adolescents in treatment for chemical dependency have, on the average, used 5.1 substances in their lifetime, and regularly use 3.8 substances. Applying these criteria to the data in Table 2.7, between 4.4% and 7.4% of students in grades 10-12 have patterns of drug use typical of chemically dependent adolescents.

The Children of Alcoholics

To have a drug problem has most often meant to have a problem with one's own chemical use. Thankfully, there is an increasing awareness of the problems faced by the "other victims" of drug abuse: the children and adult children of chemically dependent parents. While few studies of scientific rigor have been done on the number of children who have alcoholic parents, those that have been conducted support the conclusion that one out of four students, or 25% of students in all grades have at least one biological parent who is an active alcoholic, and with whom they may or may not now be living.

Table 2.8 displays the frequency of secondary school students' "yes" and "no" responses to a survey question concerning whether they had ever wished one of their parents would stop drinking. ("CAF" = "Children of Alcoholic Families"). The responses ranged between 27% and 30% across a span of six survey years. School districts in Wisconsin, which have asked similar questions on student self-report surveys have received almost identical results, regardless of the size of the school system, its urban/suburban/rural setting, or the age of the students surveyed.

The specific needs of these children will be reviewed in detail in the next chapter. For now it is only necessary to note that they represent the single largest AODA-related target group, and that they are at the greatest risk for developing alcohol and other drug problems, either in adolescence or by young adulthood.

Finally, if one adds to these children those students concerned about a friend's chemical use, or those concerned about the drug problems of siblings, 25% becomes a very conservative figure as an estimate of "concerned" or "affected others."

Conclusion

The discussion above does not reflect an increase in the consumption of over-the-counter drugs (sleeping aids, antihistamines, cough syrups, "alertness" drugs, etc.), of the "look alikes," which are sold most often as amphetamines but which consist mainly of caffeine, and of the mail-order inhalants ("Locker Room," "Rush," etc.), consisting of butyl nitrite. The most disturbing recent trend is toward "designer drugs": drugs similar in effect to narcotics, for example, but whose chemistry is altered slightly enough to make them "legal" (i.e., ineligible for inclusion on the controlled substances schedules). The creation and manufacture of such drugs by amateur chemists is difficult to control, and the drugs are literally tested on the street. Incidents of death or irreversible central nervous system damage as a result of using "designer drugs" are reported daily.

The data in Tables 2.1 and 2.9 illustrate that experience ("lifetime" prevalence) with alcohol and illicit drugs by adolescents has been steadily increasing since 1972, although rates of monthly, weekly, and daily use have been slightly decreasing for most drugs. The rates of cocaine and stimulant use are the exceptions, showing slow but steady increases.

The research also demonstrates that significant numbers of teenagers—as many as one in five—are using drugs frequently, in combination, and with demonstrable personal and social harm. Furthermore, the studies reviewed above support an estimate of 5% as the rate of chemical dependency among adolescents. Looking at all school-aged children, at least 25% are classified as "children of alcoholics," and suffer the increased risk for later dependency and the developmental deficits that this problem creates.

No other problem threatens the health, safety, welfare, and development of children to as great an extent as do the problems suffered by young people because of alcohol and other drug abuse.

Chapter 2 | Supplements

Table 2.1

DRUG USE BY 12 TO 17 YEAR OLDS: 1972-1982
National Survey on Drug Abuse

DRUG CLASS	1972	1974	1976	1977	1979	1982
MARIJUANA						
Lifetime	14.0	23.0	22.4	28.0	30.9	26.7
Past Year	——	18.5	18.4	22.3	24.1	20.6
Past Month	7.0	12.0	12.3	16.6	16.7	11.5
ALCOHOL						
Lifetime	——	54.0	53.6	52.6	70.3	65.2
Past Year	——	51.0	49.3	47.5	53.6	47.3
Past Month	——	34.0	32.4	31.2	37.2	26.9
COCAINE						
Lifetime	1.5	3.6	3.4	4.0	5.4	6.5
Past Year	1.5	2.7	2.3	2.6	4.2	4.1
Past Month	.6	1.0	1.0	.8	1.4	1.6
STIMULANTS						
Lifetime	4.0	5.0	4.4	5.2	3.4	6.7
Past Year	——	3.0	2.2	3.7	2.9	5.6
Past Month	——	1.0	1.2	1.3	1.2	2.6
TRANQUILIZERS						
Lifetime	3.0	3.0	3.3	3.8	4.1	4.9
Past Year	——	2.0	1.8	2.9	2.7	3.3
Past Month	——	1.0	1.1	.7	.6	.9

Source: Adapted from Clayton and Ritter (1985), p. 78.

Interpretation: 54.0% of 12-17 year olds in 1974 reported some use of alcohol during their lifetime; 32.4% reported some alcohol use during the past month.

The 1982 survey is the seventh in a series conducted since 1971-72. Designed to represent rates of drug use among households, the survey has been sponsored by the National Institute on Drug Abuse (NIDA) since 1974. Sample size has varied between N = 880 (1972) to N = 2,165 (1979).

Marijuana and alcohol use at all frequencies appear to have peaked in 1979, and decreased slightly since. Use of cocaine, stimulants, and tranquilizers have steadily increased since 1972.

Table 2.2

PREVALENCE RATES FOR FOURTEEN TYPES OF DRUGS
Class of 1984

SUBSTANCE	LIFETIME	ANNUAL	MONTHLY	DAILY
Alcohol	92.6	86.0	67.2	4.8
Marijuana	54.9	40.0	25.2	5.0
Inhalants	19.0	7.9	2.7	0.2
Amyl/Butyl Nitrite	8.1	4.0	1.4	0.1
Hallucinogens	13.3	7.9	2.6	0.2
LSD	8.0	4.7	1.5	0.1
PCP	5.0	2.3	1.0	0.1
Cocaine	16.1	11.6	5.8	0.2
Heroin	1.3	0.5	0.3	0.2
Other Opiates	9.7	5.2	1.8	0.1
Stimulants	27.9	17.7	8.3	0.6
Sedatives	13.3	6.6	2.3	0.1
Methaqualone	8.3	3.8	1.1	0.0
Tranquilizers	12.4	6.1	2.1	0.1

Source: Johnston, Lloyd D., et. al. *Use of Licit and Illicit Drugs by America's High School Students 1975-1984*. Rockville, MD.: National Institute on Drug Abuse, 1985. Pp. 34-37.

Interpretation: 92.6% of the graduating class of 1984 had used alcohol by 12th grade; 4.8% were drinking daily.

Alcohol and marijuana use continue to form the "core" of most students' drug experience, and each is used on a daily basis by approximately 5% of the seniors surveyed.

Table 2.3

INCIDENCE OF PROBLEM DRINKING: GRADES 7-12

DEFINITION OF PROBLEM DRINKING	PERCENT OF MODERATE DRINKERS	PERCENT OF N = 11,663
(I) Drunkenness 6 or more times and/or negative consequences 2 or more times in past year in at least 3 of 5 areas:	29.3*	18.8
(II) Drunkenness once a month or more times in past year:	14.7	9.4
(III) Drinking-related negative consequences at least 2 times in a single area and once in another area in the past year:	13.9	8.9

* PROBLEM AREAS:
- trouble with a teacher or principal
- trouble with friends over drinking
- driving when drunk
- being criticized for drinking by a person one is dating
- trouble with police

Source: Donovan and Jessor (1978), pp. 1511-1512.

The survey was conducted in 1974 among 13,222 students in grades 7-12 in all 48 contiguous states. Of the total sample, 57% were categorized as "moderate drinkers."

Interpretation: 29.3% of "moderate drinkers," or 18.8% of the total sample, are problem drinkers according to Definition (I).

Table 2.4

MULTIPLE DRUG USE OF SEVEN CLASSES OF DRUGS
Grades 9-12

SUBSTANCE USE CLASS	PERCENT
1. Abstainers: no use of any drug at any time	6.0
2. "Stoppers": some past use, none at time of survey	16.0
3. Alcohol use only	41.0
4. Alcohol and marijuana use only	17.0
5. Alcohol and marijuana use, plus use of one other drug	5.0
6. Alcohol and marijuana use, plus use of two or more others	11.0
7. Use of one or more drugs in other combinations	3.0

(N = 1,970)

Source: Pandina, et al. (1981), p. 21.

Results are based on a survey of 1,970 students in grades 9-12.

Table 2.5

MULTIPLE DRUG USE PATTERNS
AMONG DAILY MARIJUANA USERS

TYPOLOGY OF DRUG USERS	PERCENT USING MARIJUANA DAILY	NUMBER	% of N
1. No use of any drug, or use of cigarettes and/or alcohol only:	0.0	6,839	41.4
2. Cigarettes and/or alcohol and marijuana:	5.6	3,426	20.7
3. Cigarettes, alcohol, and marijuana, and one or two of the following: tranquilizers, cocaine, amphetamines:	24.5	2,972	18.0
4. Cigarettes, alcohol, marijuana, tranquilizers, amphetamines, and cocaine:	54.1	889	5.4

Source: Clayton and Ritter (1985), p. 88.

Interpretation: 54.1% of those students reporting daily use of marijuana also used cigarettes, alcohol, tranquilizers, amphetamines, and cocaine. This pattern is true of 5.4% of the total sample.

Figures are based on those high school seniors using marijuana daily (>20 times in past month) who also report any other drug use within the past year. Thus, 5.4% of the sample report using six drugs more than 20 times in the past month; this accounts for 54.1% of the daily marijuana users.

The sample consists of 16,524 seniors from the Monitoring the Future surveys, Class of 1980.

Table 2.6

ALCOHOL AND POLYDRUG USE: Grades 10-12

DRUG TYPE	Ab-stainers	Infre-quent	Light	DRINKING LEVEL: Moder-ate	Mod. to Heavy	Heavy	All Students
Barbiturates	0.3	1.0	1.0	1.2	3.2	5.6	1.9
Cocaine	0.0	0.3	0.7	2.6	6.6	10.2	3.1
Hallucinogens	0.5	0.8	1.3	1.2	4.7	1.2	2.9
Heroin	0.1	0.0	0.2	0.3	0.4	1.6	0.5
Inhalants	0.7	1.3	0.9	3.5	4.2	6.5	2.7
Marijuana	3.6	8.5	20.8	35.9	52.5	62.7	29.6
Stimulants	0.3	0.7	2.3	4.5	9.4	16.1	5.1
Tranquilizers	0.3	0.5	0.7	3.2	6.0	8.4	3.0

Source: Lowman (1982), p. 42. N = 4,918.

Interpretation: 0.3% of alcohol abstainers use barbiturates; 35.9% of moderate drinkers use marijuana.

The table also illustrates that the likelihood of use of a given drug increases with frequency of alcohol use.

Table 2.7

NUMBER OF DRUGS USED BY DRINKING LEVEL:
Grades 10-12

NUMBER OF DRUGS USED DRUG TYPE	Ab-stainers	Infre-quent	Light	Moder-ate	Mod. to Heavy	Heavy	All Students
None	89.7	78.5	60.1	43.0	31.4	22.5	55.5
1 Drug	8.5	19.2	31.3	37.6	38.4	35.8	27.6
2 Drugs	0.7	1.0	4.2	9.4	10.4	10.8	6.0
3 Drugs	0.5	0.5	2.1	3.9	5.2	9.1	3.5
4 Drugs	0.1	0.6	1.0	2.0	4.9	10.5	3.0
5 Drugs	0.2	0.2	0.6	2.2	4.4	4.1	1.9
6 Drugs	0.1	0.0	0.3	1.0	2.9	4.1	1.4
7 Drugs	0.2	0.0	0.4	0.8	1.9	2.3	0.9
8 Drugs	0.0	0.0	0.0	0.1	0.5	0.8	0.2
TOTAL:	100.0	100.0	100.0	100.0	100.0	100.0	100.0

Source: Lowman (1982), p. 45.

Interpretation: 89.7% of alcohol abstainers also used no other drugs; 10.5% of "heavy" drinkers used 4 drugs; 4.4% of all students use 5 or more drugs.

The table also indicates the linear relationship between severity of alcohol use and likelihood of multiple drug use.

Table 2.8

CHILDREN OF ALCOHOLIC PARENTS

SURVEY YEAR	PARENTS ABSTAIN	"YES" TO CAF ITEM	"NO" TO CAF ITEM
1976	9.5	27.4	63.0
1978	13.8	30.1	56.1
1981	16.9	29.5	53.5

Source: DiCicco, et al (1984), p. 5.

Interpretation: 9.5% of students indicated in 1976 that their parents abstain from alcohol; 27.4% answered "Yes" to the "children of alcoholics" survey item: "Have you ever wished one of your parents would stop drinking?"

Table 2.9

DRUG USE AMONG HIGH SCHOOL SENIORS: 1975-1984
Monitoring the Future Surveys

DRUG CLASS	1975	1976	1977	1978	1979	1980	1981	1982	1983	1984
MARIJUANA										
Lifetime	47.3	52.8	56.4	59.2	60.4	60.3	59.5	59.0	57.0	54.9
Past Year	40.0	44.5	47.6	50.2	50.8	48.8	46.1	44.3	42.3	40.0
Past Month	27.1	32.2	35.4	37.1	36.5	33.7	31.6	28.5	27.0	25.2
Daily	6.0	8.2	9.1	10.7	10.7	10.3	9.1	6.3	5.5	5.0
ALCOHOL										
Lifetime	90.4	91.9	92.5	93.1	93.0	93.2	92.6	92.8	92.6	92.6
Past Year	84.8	85.7	87.0	97.7	88.1	87.9	87.0	86.8	87.3	86.0
Past Month	68.2	68.3	71.2	72.1	71.8	72.0	70.7	69.7	69.4	67.2
Daily	5.7	5.6	6.1	5.7	6.9	6.0	6.0	5.7	5.5	4.8
COCAINE										
Lifetime	9.0	9.7	10.8	12.9	15.4	15.7	16.5	16.0	16.2	16.1
Past Year	5.6	6.0	7.2	9.0	12.0	12.3	12.4	11.5	11.4	11.6
Past Month	1.09	2.0	2.9	3.9	5.7	5.2	5.8	5.0	4.9	5.8
Daily	.1	.1	.1	.1	.2	.2	.3	.2	.2	.2
STIMULANTS										
Lifetime	22.3	22.6	23.0	22.9	24.2	26.4	32.2	35.6	35.4	27.9
Past Year	16.2	15.8	16.3	17.1	18.3	20.8	26.0	26.1	24.6	NA
Past Month	8.5	7.7	8.8	8.7	9.9	12.1	15.8	13.7	12.4	8.3
Daily	.5	.4	.5	.5	.6	.7	1.2	1.1	1.1	NA
TRANQUILIZERS										
Lifetime	17.0	16.8	18.0	17.0	16.3	15.2	14.7	14.0	13.3	12.4
Past Year	10.6	10.3	10.8	9.9	9.6	8.7	8.0	7.0	6.9	6.1
Past Month	4.1	4.0	4.6	3.4	3.7	3.1	2.7	2.4	2.5	2.1
Daily	.1	.2	.3	.1	.1	.1	.1	.1	.1	.1

Source: Johnson et al., (1985), 34-37.

Interpretation: 10.7% of high school seniors reported daily marijuana use in 1979.

The Monitoring the Future Survey is sponsored by the National Institute on Drug Abuse (NIDA) and is conducted annually among high school seniors only. Those absent on the survey day, and the approximately 20% of high school-age youth who drop out, are not represented. Since is is widely acknowledged that these adolescents have high rates of alcohol/drug use, the results above somewhat conservative when applied to all 17-year olds.

Table 2.10

GRADE OF FIRST USE OF FOURTEEN TYPES OF DRUGS
Class of 1984

SUBSTANCE	GRADE IN WHICH DRUG WAS FIRST USED						
	6th	7th-8th	9th	10th	11th	12th	NEVER
Alcohol	10.4	22.4	23.6	18.4	12.0	5.9	7.4
Marijuana	4.3	14.1	13.6	11.2	7.3	4.4	45.1
Inhalants	1.3	3.1	2.7	2.9	2.0	2.4	85.6
Amyl/Butyl Nitrite	.6	1.5	1.7	1.7	1.3	1.3	91.9
Hallucinogens	.1	1.2	2.5	3.0	2.6	1.2	89.3
LSD	.1	.7	2.0	2.1	2.1	1.0	92.0
PCP	.5	.5	1.3	1.2	1.0	.5	95.0
Cocaine	.1	.7	2.3	3.4	5.0	4.6	83.9
Heroin	—	.2	.4	.3	.2	.2	98.7
Other Opiates	.2	.8	2.3	2.5	2.3	1.6	90.3
Stimulants	.5	3.1	8.9	7.9	4.9	2.6	72.1
Sedatives	.4	1.8	4.2	3.8	2.1	1.0	86.7
Methaqualone	.1	1.0	2.6	2.5	1.6	.5	91.7
Tranquilizers	.2	1.4	3.5	2.5	3.1	1.7	87.6

Source: Johnston et al. (1985), p. 66.

Interpretation: 4.3% of the high school seniors who reported using marijuana in 1984 indicate first using it by 6th grade.

Table 2.11

DEMOGRAPHICS OF ADOLESCENT DRINKING PRACTICES: 1980

DEMOGRAPHIC VARIABLE	Non-Drinkers	Infre-quent	Light	Moderate	Heavier	Heaviest
OCCUPATIONAL STATUS OF FAMILY:						
Professional	39	14	19	12	10	7
Manager, executive, proprietor	30	14	22	15	12	6
Clerical, sales, office worker	42	10	21	6	14	6
Skilled worker	42	16	19	8	10	4
Farmer	46	23	8	15	8	0
Semiskilled or unskilled	45	11	15	10	13	6
PARENTS' EDUCATIONAL LEVEL:						
College graduate or more	44	14	19	11	10	1
Some college	36	19	17	12	12	4
Completed H. S. or tech school	41	10	21	9	11	8
Some high school	50	8	12	12	9	9
8th grade or less	50	3	19	16	9	3
GEOGRAPHICAL AREA OF RESIDENCE:						
Northeast	47	13	18	9	10	3
South	44	12	19	11	10	4
North Central	42	12	17	9	13	7
West	42	15	16	12	8	6

Source: Zucker and Harford (1983), pp. 979-80. Figures are reported in percentages and indicate the number of students in each drinking category who fit the demographic variable. Row totals do not add up to 100% due to rounding.

With the exception of the lowest occupational level, heavy alcohol use is associated with increasing occupational status of the family. Highest levels of heavy alcohol use were reported by students in the North Central region.

Supplement 2.2

STADUS: STUDENT ALCOHOL/DRUG USE SURVEY

STADUS is a simple, three-page survey instrument which can be utilized by any group wishing to gather information regarding the patterns of alcohol/drug experience of youth. It can be administered to large groups (i.e, a high school population), to classrooms (i.e., as part of an alcohol/drug instructional unit), to small groups (i.e., as a "drug history questionnaire" for support groups), or to individuals as an assessment tool.

The investigator is invited to use Supplement 2.2: STADUS, which follows, as a master from which sufficient copies of the survey and/or answer sheet may be reproduced. Appropriate attribution is requested.

THE GOAL OF STUDENT AODA SURVEYS

One could probably fill a good-sized library with the results of all of the student alcohol/drug surveys that have been done since the 1960's. They are hardly new, and frequently unnecessary. As a rule, utilizing a student survey to "prove" the existence of a "drug problem" in the school setting is not among the best reasons for conducting one. In the first place, only slight variations have been demonstrated between geographic regions, and between urban/suburban/rural localities. In other words, the data available from reliable national surveys are widely applicable to most community settings. Secondly, if staff, parents, or the decision makers in a school system are not convinced by *applied* statistics, the reasons usually have to do with the emotional dynamics of denial, which do not usually respond to statistical arguments.

Therefore, it is wise for the individual school system or educator to be clear as to the specific purpose(s) that a large-scale student survey will serve. Aside from the specific applications mentioned above, the decision to conduct a large-scale survey of a student population can serve some limited ends.

New Information. Gathering information for which there are no national correlates is one viable goal for a student alcohol/drug use survey. For example, data demonstrating correlations between drug use and academic performance, or between drug use and extracurricular activities are difficult to find. A survey can also help to combat stereotypes concerning the "typical drug abuser" by demonstrating the degree to which students who get high grades or who are involved in extracurricular activities (e.g., athletics) are also involved in alcohol/drug use.

PART THREE of the STADUS survey also allows the school to estimate the number of students concerned and/or affected by others' chemical use, and to identify the person of concern (e.g., family members, friends, etc.).

In addition, since there is no definition of the term "drug abuse" which is widely accepted by or applicable to all communities, a survey allows a given community to develop its own definitions, to apply these standards to survey results, and thus to estimate the number of students whose patterns of drug use fit these criteria.

Evaluation. Surveys can also provide reliable, individualized base-line data to a school system as it begins to implement a student assistance program. It can assist in estimating the size of various target groups (see Chapter 3), and thus in the formulation of concrete goals and objectives for the program. If a survey is conducted periodically (e.g., annually, or every other year) it can contribute to measures of a program's overall effectiveness.

ADMINISTRATION

The large-scale use of a survey requires attention to uniformity, credibility, and confidentiality, if the results are to be reliable and valid. The survey should be uniformly administered. Ideally, the same individuals (or class of individuals, such as members of the student council, or of an external agency), will be administering the survey. Giving a survey simultaneously to all students eliminates the possibility of student's minimizing or exaggerating their responses as survey "rumors" propagate throughout the day. Administering the survey with uniform explanations as to its purpose, and as to directions, also help to assure validity. Uniformity is also important in eliminating the bias of those giving the survey. If done by classroom teachers, for example, it is vital that everyone regard the survey with the same degree of seriousness.

Credibility has to do with explaining to students the purpose for the survey. The major issue is to assure them that the purpose is not to justify a "witch-hunt", but to help the school plan ways of helping those students who are in trouble. Care should thus be taken in the selection and preparation of those who will be administering the survey.

Confidentiality is most important. Pains must be taken to assure students that the survey is confidential: that there is no way for them to identify themselves, or for someone to identify them from their survey responses.

TABULATION

STADUS has been constructed to permit ease of tabulation as well as ease of administration. Responses of all students can be tabulated, or they can be grouped by age and grade, by sex, by drug used, etc. Regardless of the complexity of the investigator's design, at least three areas of analysis will probably be most rewarding.

Simple Tabulations. Results can be reported as raw tabulations of students' responses to each of the items in the survey, by grade level, by school (e.g., middle school versus high school) or as totals. Figures 2.1 and 2.2 represent blanks that can be used to tabulate and display the responses to PART ONE and PART TWO, respectively. The Anwser Sheet itself can be easily adapted as a tabulating and reporting format for all responses.

Simple tabulations alone will provide a wealth of data concerning the kinds, amounts, and frequencies of alcohol and other drug use, the degree of problems encountered in drug use, and the number of students who are concerned about their own and/or others' drug use.

Polydrug Use and Problem Use. One of the advantages of the STADUS format is that it permits easy cross-tabulations that revel the number of students involved in polydrug use, and thus the number of students at greatest risk. Such an analysis can be carried out in three steps. First, decide on the criteria concerning frequency of use. For example, in correlating "numbers of drugs used" and "number of problems encountered", one might be concerned with "current use" responses only, and perhaps only those at the "D" level and above ("1 to 4 times per month" or more). Establishing this criterion is more likely to rule out "experimental" use, and to include students with greater "committment" to drug use.

Second, construct a grid with "Number of drugs used" as the "Y" axis, and "Number of problems" as the "X" axis. Third, tabulate the results by recording which box each answer sheet fits in. Figure 2.3 provides an example of results reported as percentages of the total sample in an actual school district in rural Wisconsin.

Correlates of Drug Use. The most complex analysis consists of correlating various responses in BACKGROUND INFORMATION and in PART THREE with other responses.

The following exemplify the types of correlations that may be most revealing:

1. GRADE-POINT-AVERAGE correlated with:

   -Number of Drugs Used
   -Frequency of Drug Use
   -Frequency of "Quitting"
   -Number of Problems Reported

2. EXTRACURRICULAR ACTIVITY correlated with:

   -Number of Drugs Used
   -Frequency of Drug Use
   -Number of Problems Reported
   -Number of Affected Family Members (i.e., Item 1 in
     PART THREE)

STADUS: Student Alcohol/Drug Use Survey

Part One

Which of the following best describes your current experience with alcohol or other drugs, as of today?

Place the letter of your response in the appropriate blank on the answer sheet.

SUBSTANCE CATEGORY:	COMMON NAMES:	NO CURRENT USE			CURRENT USE			
		NEVER USED	DID USE BUT QUIT	less than Once per Month	1 to 4 Times per MONTH	1 to 4 Times per WEEK	1 or More Times per DAY
1. TOBACCO	Cigarettes, Cigars, Snuff, Chewing Tobacco	A	B	C	D	E	F
2. ALCOHOL	Beer, Wine, Hard Liquor	A	B	C	D	E	F
3. MARIJUANA	Marijuana, Hashish, Hash Oil, "grass," "Pot"	A	B	C	D	E	F
4. COCAINE	Snow, "Nose Candy," "coke"	A	B	C	D	E	F
5. OTHER STIMULANTS	Amphetamines, Dexedrine, Diet Pills, "speed," "Uppers"	A	B	C	D	E	F
6. DEPRESSANTS	Barbiturates, Tranquilizers, PCP, Reds, "Downers," Sleeping Pills	A	B	C	D	E	F
7. INHALANTS	Glue, Gasoline, Aerosols, Amyl Nitrite, "poppers," "RUSH"	A	B	C	D	E	F
8. NARCOTICS	Heroin, Morphine, Codeine	A	B	C	D	E	F
9. HALLUCINOGENS	LSD, Mescaline, Peyote, "acid"	A	B	C	D	E	F
10. OVER-THE-COUNTER DRUGS	cold pills, diet pills, cough syrups, "No Doz," "Compose"	A	B	C	D	E	F

STADUS: Student Alcohol/Drug Use Survey

Part Two

Some people occasionally have problems because of their use of alcohol or other drugs.

Indicate on your answer sheet whether your use of any of the substances listed has ever caused you problems. You may select more than one response.

SUBSTANCE CATEGORY:	DOES NOT APPLY	Problems With My PARENTS	Problems With OTHER FAMILY	Problems With the POLICE	Problems With MONEY OR JOB	Problems With My FEELINGS	Problems in SCHOOL	Problems With My HEALTH	Problems With My FRIENDS
1. TOBACCO	A	B	C	D	E	F	G	H	I
2. ALCOHOL	A	B	C	D	E	F	G	H	I
3. MARIJUANA	A	B	C	D	E	F	G	H	I
4. COCANE	A	B	C	D	E	F	G	H	I
5. OTHER STIMULANTS	A	B	C	D	E	F	G	H	I
6. DEPRESSANTS	A	B	C	D	E	F	G	H	I
7. INHALANTS	A	B	C	D	E	F	G	H	I
8. NARCOTICS	A	B	C	D	E	F	G	H	I
9. HALLUCINOGENS	A	B	C	D	E	F	G	H	I
10. OVER-THE-COUNTER DRUGS	A	B	C	D	E	F	G	H	I

STADUS ANSWER SHEET

*Your answers on this survey are **completely confidential**. Please do not write your name anywhere on this answer sheet.*

BACKGROUND INFORMATION

Today's Date: _____

Sex: Male _____
          Female _____

Grade in School: _____

Grade-point average: _____

What school activities do you Participate in?
_____ *Athletics*
_____ *Cheerleading*
_____ *Student Government*
_____ *Clubs*
_____ *Music or Drama*
_____ *Others?* _____ *None*

PART ONE	PART TWO: Shade in the letter of your response.
1. _____	1. [A] [B] [C] [D] [E] [F] [G] [H] [I]
2. _____	2. [A] [B] [C] [D] [E] [F] [G] [H] [I]
3. _____	3. [A] [B] [C] [D] [E] [F] [G] [H] [I]
4. _____	4. [A] [B] [C] [D] [E] [F] [G] [H] [I]
5. _____	5. [A] [B] [C] [D] [E] [F] [G] [H] [I]
6. _____	6. [A] [B] [C] [D] [E] [F] [G] [H] [I]
7. _____	7. [A] [B] [C] [D] [E] [F] [G] [H] [I]
8. _____	8. [A] [B] [C] [D] [E] [F] [G] [H] [I]
9. _____	9. [A] [B] [C] [D] [E] [F] [G] [H] [I]
10. _____	10. [A] [B] [C] [D] [E] [F] [G] [H] [I]

PART THREE

1. Have you ever wished that one of the following would stop drinking or using other drugs? *You may check more than one.*

_____ *Mother*   _____ *Brother*   _____ *Other?* _____
_____ *Father*   _____ *Sister*
_____ *Guardian*   _____ *Friend*

2. Which of the following best applies to you?

_____ *I think I may have an alcohol/drug problem and **would like** to talk to someone about it.*
_____ *I think I may have an alcohol/drug problem but would **not** like to talke to someone about it right now.*
_____ *I don't think I have an alcohol/drug problem.*

Figure 2.1
FREQUENCY TABULATION

SUBSTANCE CATEGORY:	NO CURRENT USE		CURRENT USE			
	NEVER USED	DID USE BUT QUIT	Less than Once per MONTH	1 to 4 Times per MONTH	1 to 4 Times per WEEK	1 or More Times per DAY
1. TOBACCO						
2. ALCOHOL						
3. MARIJUANA						
4. COCAINE						
5. OTHER STIMULANTS						
6. DEPRESSANTS						
7. INHALANTS						
8. NARCOTICS						
9. HALLUCINOGENS						
10. OVER-THE-COUNTER DRUGS						

Figure 2.2

PROBLEM ALCOHOL/DRUG USE

SUBSTANCE CATEGORY:	NONE	1 - 2	3 - 4	5 - 6	7 - 8	9 -10	NUMBER OF REPORTED PROBLEMS: 11 - 12	13 - 14	15+
1. TOBACCO									
2. ALCOHOL									
3. MARIJUANA									
4. COCAINE									
5. OTHER STIMULANTS									
6. DEPRESSANTS									
7. INHALANTS									
8. NARCOTICS									
9. HALLUCINOGENS									
10. OVER-THE-COUNTER DRUGS									

Figure 2.3

SIGNIFICANT POLYDRUG USE
AND NUMBER OF PROBLEMS

NUMBER OF DRUGS USED	NUMBER OF PROBLEMS:						TOTAL
	0	1-2	3-4	5-6	7-8	9-15	
NONE	62.2	---	---	---	---	---	62.2
1 DRUG	9.0	8.0	3.0	1.1	.2	.9	22.2
2 DRUGS	2.0	3.0	1.7	.6	.6	.5	8.4
3 DRUGS	1.0	1.0	.8	.5	.3	.7	4.3
4 DRUGS	.3	.3	.3	.6	.2	.1	1.8
5 DRUGS	.1	.1	.2	.3	.1	.1	.9
6 DRUGS	---	---	---	---	---	.1	.1
7 DRUGS	---	---	---	---	---	.1	.1
TOTALS:	74.6	12.4	6.0	3.1	1.4	2.5	100.0

Figure 2.3 is an example of a tabulation which can be performed on STADUS results, based on an actual school survey done in 1980. "Significant Use" was defined here, for example, as "current use of a drug from 1 to 4 times per month or more" for all substances, excluding tobacco products and over-the-counter drugs.

Row totals indicate the percentage of students with "significant use" patterns who report using various numbers of drugs regularly. Column totals indicate the percentage of students reporting various numbers of problems occurring as a direct result of their drug use in PART TWO of the survey.

Chapter 3

Who Are Student Assistance Programs For? AODA Target Groups

The story is told of how, during the World Series, a reporter asked three umpires to explain how they made their decisions. The young rookie, thinking he already had the last word, said, "I call 'em the way I see 'em."

His more experienced colleague thought to do him one better, adding "I call 'em the way they are."

To which the third, a seasoned veteran, merely responded, "They ain't nothin' until I call 'em."

In the past, once they have begun to recognize the scope of young peoples' alcohol/drug involvement, school systems and/or their communities have often been tempted by magical thinking: there must be something simple, quick, and effective that can be done. The fact of the matter is that many preventive or interventive strategies have often been inappropriate, narrowly focussed, or short-lived. One of the reasons for their ineffectiveness is their failure to appreciate the complex manner in which problems related to alcohol and other drug abuse are manifested in individuals, families, systems, or in society as a whole.

In other words, there are different varieties of chemical experience. Most authorities recognize that experience with alcohol and other drugs can progress through a number of predictable stages. A brief period of experimentation may be followed by a period of more regular use. The data indicate that some 20 percent of adolescents progress to a period of harmful involvement; a few succumb to one of the various forms of addiction covered by the term "chemical dependency." The progression from initial experimentation to chemical dependency is not inevitable. Steps can be taken at each stage to interrupt the progression and bring about a return to healthier, safer conduct.

For our purposes, an awareness of the scope of student drug-related problems must be accompanied by an appreciation of these different ways in which students can be affected by drugs, of the different needs which they therefore possess, and of the different structures and strategies that consequently must be enlisted in the resolution of such problems. Just as there is no one thing called "The Drug Problem," there is no single, quick "fix."

Target Groups

In the Student Assistance Program model a target group is defined on the basis of a group of students' uniform experience with alcohol and other drug use and the unique needs dictated by such unique experiences. The criteria which define a single target group also distinguish one such group from another. Each of the target groups must be addressed by any program that claims to be a comprehensive effort to address the AODA-related problems of youth in the school/community setting. Thus, the recognition of at least six different target groups has acquired the force of orthodoxy in student assistance programming:

1. Students who are chemically dependent: the 5% of adolescents who are the most seriously affected by their alcohol/drug use;

2. Students who abuse alcohol or other drugs: the 15% or more of adolescents whose alcohol/drug use is causing them problems in their daily lives;

3. Students who are affected by others: the 25% of all school-aged youth who are concerned about or affected by someone else's alcohol/drug abuse;

4. Recovering students: those who are returning to the school setting from an alcohol/drug treatment program, or who are attending school and primary treatment concurrently;

5. Non-using and non-abusing students: the majority of students who need help in avoiding alcohol/drug abuse or who need support for their decision to remain chemically free;

6. Students with other, non-AODA-related problems: separation and divorce, death and loss, suicide, sexuality issues, child abuse and neglect, etc.

Chemical Dependency.

Chemical dependency represents the most severe way in which young people can be damaged through their own chemical use. Approximately 5 percent of those in the 12 to 17 age group are believed to be chemically dependent (compared to a rate of 10 percent among adults). The classical view of chemical dependency describes it as a disease, characterized by the development of tolerance, a tendency to increase the dosage, preoccupation with the drug and its use, loss of control over the outcomes of chemical use, and harmful consequences in personal and social functioning.

Chemical dependency is usually described as a pattern of drug involvement which has evolved beyond drug abuse and has reached the proportions of an autonomous disease—one which is "primary, progressive, chronic, and fatal" (Johnson, 1980). "Primaryness" refers to the autonomous character of the illness. In other words, although chemical dependency—like any other condition—has antecedent causes, the disease has reached a point where it progresses in a manner independent of the presence or absence of these predisposing factors. The disease is also progressive but in a dual sense. Without intervention, the condition always worsens over time; it is not a phase which the individual will grow out of with maturity or the passage of time. The disease is also progressive in the sense that it affects the whole person: emotionally, intellectually, socially, spiritually, and physically.

"This book is based on a rather conservative view of adolescent alcohol/drug use: any use of mood-altering chemicals by adolescents constitutes abuse, on the grounds that it is not personally and socially constructive."

Chronicity refers to the fact that the condition is incurable. The course of the disease can be interrupted through intervention and treatment, and recovery is possible, but is based on abstinence from further use of mood-altering chemicals. Finally, unless interrupted and treated, the disease always causes premature death, either from the immediate physical damage of drug abuse or from its complications or secondary effects: suicide, homicide, drownings, automobile accidents, etc.

In addition to these immediate threats to health, most experts agree that chemical dependency seriously interrupts normal adolescent development. The most frequently heard rule is that "once dependency develops, development stops." For those in treatment, drug use has typically begun by age 11-12, and dependency can develop rapidly—by age 12 to 14 on the average (Farley et al: 1979, pp. 152ff). Thus, the development of dependency for most adolescents coincides with the need to accomplish the significant developmental tasks that make up the transition from childhood to adulthood. Unless the chemical dependency is addressed these students will suffer from serious, lifelong developmental deficits.

The serious impairments caused by chemical dependency inevitably affect school performance at some point. The National Youth Polydrug Study revealed a clear pattern of problems in school performance among students in treatment for alcoholism, drug addiction, and other varieties of chemical dependency (Santo: 1979, pp 137-138; Cohan and Santo: 1979, pp. 242ff). Among the most significant findings:

- patients had a mean age of 16.4 years

- the mean grade completed was 9.1

- 54% of the patients were retarded by one grade level

- 25.9% had dropped out of school at least once

- 40.5% reported patterns of suspension and expulsion

- 55.5% reported serious problems in school, including expulsion, suspension, and fighting with teachers

Santo observes that "there is a clear association between applying for treatment for drug abuse and being retarded in school attainment" (p. 138).

Friedman et al (1985) p. 25) have shown that "earlier substance use predicted to a statistically significant degree later failure to graduate from high school." Similarly, Barnes and Welte (1985, p.53) discovered that heavy drinking correlated with frequent school misconduct, early onset of drinking, and low grades.

Many other studies have demonstrated the significant correlation between the use of alcohol and other drugs and poor scholastic achievement. Kirk (1979: p. 390) notes the following correlations between use of beer or marijuana and grade-point average among rural students he studied:

Among A students, 14.3% used beer > 50 times
Among B students, 27.5% used beer > 50 times
Among C students, 38.9% used beer > 50 times
Among D students, 52.9% used beer > 50 times

Moreover,

Among A students, 57.1% are marijuana abstainers
Among B students, 39.9% are marijuana abstainers
Among C students, 35.6% are marijuana abstainers
Among D students, 17.7% are marijuana abstainers

Hubbard et al. have studied the living problems which adolescents in residential drug treatment programs have in addition to their drug abuse. Over one-fourth (26.8%), for example, were referred to drug treatment programs by the criminal justice system (p. 52). Table 3.1 summarizes other drug-related problems which adolescents in treatment report occurring during the year prior to their treatment.

These examples represent fairly mild instances of the damage to physical health, human growth and development, and school performance caused by chemical dependency. Without early identification and proper treatment, the chemically dependent adolescent will suffer lifelong damage.

The needs of the chemically dependent student with respect to treatment and recovery from this complex illness are enormous. Many will require intensive residential treatment followed by long-term aftercare. Effective treatment and recovery from this "whole person" illness will require repairing the damage done to all aspects of the adolescent's life. However, with respect to the school system the needs of chemically dependent students are simpler. These students will not outgrow their chemical use; it will not pass with time or maturity; it will not respond to "alternatives" or involvement in extracurricular activities; films, discussions, pamphlets, and talks with the guidance counselor will not arrest the chemical use.

These students have an immediate need to be

Table 3.1

DRUG-RELATED PROBLEMS OF ADOLESCENTS IN TREATMENT

DRUG-RELATED PROBLEM	MALES	FEMALES	BOTH
Medical problems	35.5	59.0	47.3
Psychological problems	42.3	73.8	58.1
Family problems	71.5	82.0	76.8
Legal problems	44.5	37.7	41.1
Work or school problems	50.4	62.3	56.4
Financial problems	39.4	37.7	38.6
Suicidal thoughts	21.0	23.0	22.0
Suicide attempts	17.4	49.2	33.3
Predatory illegal acts	68.4	52.9	60.7
Not in school when admitted	89.9	83.6	86.7

Source: Hubbard, et al., pp. 55ff.

N = 250 adolescents 17 years of age or under, in federally funded residential drug treatment programs, from 1979-1981. Figures represent the percentage of patients reporting the problems indicated occurring during the year prior to their admission to the treatment programs.

identified and referred successfully to treatment programs outside of the school. Thus, in terms of in-school structures the needs of these students are simple. However, it requires careful and enlightened action on the part of the school system to intervene effectively, to gather the relevant data, to work with the fear and denial of both the student and his/her family, and so on. Policies, procedures, and educational strategies which assume that everyone has control over their own chemical behavior will be ineffective with these students.

Alcohol/drug Abuse.

"Drug Abuse" is a term which will mean different things to different people because individual values lie at the heart of any application of it to an individual's behavior. On religious grounds, for example, one person might regard any use of alcohol as unacceptable (i.e., as "alcohol abuse") whereas someone with different beliefs can accept "drinking in moderation." What each has done, however, is to apply a similar standard to individual behavior. For our purposes, an instance or episode of "drug abuse" will be distinguished from an episode of "drug use" based on whether the individual's behavior with respect to the chemical is "personally and socially constructive." In applying this standard, any two individuals will come to different conclusions depending on the values they bring to the criterion of "personally and socially constructive."

This book is based on a rather conservative view of adolescent alcohol/drug use: any use of mood-altering chemicals by adolescents constitutes abuse, on the grounds that it is not personally and socially constructive. The basis for this view is independent of legal or moral issues that can change from person to person, community to community, or decade to decade. Whether they are legal or not, drugs will always be potentially detrimental to human health, and especially to that of adolescents. It would be difficult for anyone to claim that mood-altering chemicals, used for the purpose of recreationally altering moods, promote or enhance adolescent growth and development.

Exceptions, as they say, prove the rule. Use of alcohol with meals, especially when a part of a family tradition or ritual, is clearly an exception. Note that in these instances alcohol is used as a beverage, not as a drug. Similarly, medication taken in the manner and degree prescribed represents an exception on similar grounds.

It is necessary, however, to recognize that there are degrees of severity of chemical experience. As noted above, if one applies certain statistical criteria to student alcohol/drug behavior, there is reason to believe that 20 percent of those in grades 7 through 12

are having serious problems as a result of their chemical use. Included in this 20 percent are the 5 percent who are chemically dependent. This leaves at least 15 percent who are involved in other harmful patterns of alcohol/drug use and who can modify their alcohol/drug behavior with the help of services other than treatment.

These students are not chemically dependent, and consequently are not traditionally thought of as candidates for treatment. Many of their needs are similar in terms of damage to physical health, psychosocial development, school performance, and so on. These students, however, can benefit from education, personal and social skill development, and individual and group counseling within the school setting. They will also benefit from experiencing clear, reasonable consequences for violating school policies regarding chemical use.

"It would be difficult for anyone to claim that mood-altering chemicals, used for the purpose of recreationally altering moods, promote or enhance adolescent growth and development."

While a definitive explanation of the causes of drug abuse among young people remains elusive, the major correlates of drug abuse are well-known. (For a complete discussion see NIDA (1976) and NIDA (1979). The consequences of adolescent drug abuse are also well-known. By definition, drug abuse involves drug use which causes problems, aggravates existing ones, or prevents their normal resolution. The most global consequence of drug abuse lies in its potential for preventing adolescents from successfully accomplishing the developmental tasks associated with adolescence.

'Affected Others.'

Until recently, most prevention, intervention, and treatment programs have ignored this target group. Approaches aimed at reaching either of the two groups above have usually failed to meet the needs of the third and largest risk group: students who are negatively affected by others' drug abuse or chemical dependency. If "child of an alcoholic parent" alone is the criterion, this group includes upwards of 25% of the entire student body in grades K through 12. If we add students who are affected by chemical dependency or drug abuse in siblings, or those simply worried or concerned about the drug problems of peers, the percentage of "concerned persons" is considerably higher.

Those living with an actively chemically dependent

parent figure are the most severely affected. Sexual abuse and violence are more often present in alcoholic families than in others, and contribute most to an environment that is both emotionally and physically unsafe. Schoolwork frequently suffers due to children's mental and emotional preoccupation with tensions at home. Others act out their anger in school. Most suffer from chronic feelings of guilt, shame, loneliness, fear, anger and hurt. Perhaps the greatest impact of family alcoholism is on childhood development. There is widespread agreement that alcoholism results in one or both parents becoming physically or emotionally unavailable to children, disrupting the parenting that promotes healthy development. Claudia Black has summarized the effects on children (and adult children) of alcoholics by noting the three "rules" learned in the alcoholic family: "Don't Talk," "Don't Trust," and "Don't Feel." To these we could add a fourth: "Don't Know," or find out anything about alcoholism and chemical dependency.

Finally, these children also are the group at greatest risk for developing problems related to drug abuse themselves by adolescence, or risk developing chemical dependency by the time they reach young adulthood. Statistically, approximately 50 percent of the children of alcoholics become alcoholic or chemically dependent themselves.

While the "no talk rule" is first learned at home, it is reinforced by children's experience of the shaming and judgemental attitudes of society. These they will frequently find reinforced in school, by peers, classmates, and teachers. The major task in identifying such children in the school setting involves creating an emotionally safe and knowledgeable environment in which they can admit their concern and accept the help that is offered.

In addition to needs for physical and emotional safety, the following is a partial list of needs which the school system can meet in these children:

1. Affected family member children need to know that they are not alone, and that there are many others with the same experiences who know how they feel;

2. Children of alcoholics desperately need accurate information concerning the difference between drug abuse and drug dependency. This helps them realize that the alcoholism is not their fault;

3. They need help in understanding that they are not "crazy": that their parent's unpredictable behavior is understandable in terms of the disease;

4. The need help in sorting out their confusion about their ambivalent feelings toward their parents: "I love my dad but I hate him";

5. They also need help in separating the person from the disease—sorting out their parent's ambivalent behavior toward them;

6. These children also need to know that they are not helpless victims, but can do things for themselves which will help them to be safe, healthy, and happy;

7. They need to be made aware of their risk of becoming chemically dependent themselves if they use chemicals;

Education and support groups have proven to be the most effective means of meeting some of these basic needs. (For a complete discussion of the influence of parental chemical dependency on children see Ackerman (1978), Wegscheider (1981), Woititz (1983), Deutsch (1982) and McCabe (1978).

Recovering Students.

Students who do complete drug treatment programs and return to the school setting have needs which set them apart from each of the other target groups. Their ultimate need is to stay chemically free; a "relapse," or return to drug use, reactivates the disease whose devastation precipitated their treatment in the first place. For the chemically dependent youth, staying drug-free is a life-and-death issue. Most of their unique needs revolve around this central task. They have poor academic histories and must face, upon returning to school, a host of unrealistic expectations on the part of the staff. They have poorly developed personal and social skills, retarded by the onset of dependency early in adolescent development. Their family environments are typically disrupted and are often hostile to recovery. Moreover, they must cope with stresses caused by these deficits without utilizing the coping strategy previously available to them: mood-altering chemicals.

Thus, among the factors that commonly contribute to relapse are the absence of an environment (among staff as well as students) that positively supports sobriety, the presence of strong "peer pressure" to get high again, and the developmental deficits of recovering students themselves. These students respond well to support groups, to the availability of counselors knowledgeable about chemical dependency, and to the development of a process that eases their re-entry into the school setting (see Chapter 15).

These four target groups are composed of those students who are most severely affected by their own chemical use or that of a family member or friend. Two additional groups must be acknowledged by a comprehensive student assistance program.

Non-users and Non-abusers.

Students who have not become problem users constitute what has been traditionally regarded as the target group for "primary prevention": strategies designed for those without problems, and which are intended to keep them from developing them. Those students who have not begun experimentation or regular drug use are those who benefit most from prevention-oriented curricula begun in the primary grades. These strategies also benefit students who have begun chemical use, but who may also require drug education and counseling strategies that provide an opportunity to examine their individual drug behavior and to acquire skills in responsible decision-making, coping positively with peer pressure, and so on.

Other Students With Other Problems.

A comprehensive student assistance program will not focus solely on alcohol and other drug abuse. A school with a comprehensive program will also make the means of assistance available, within the limitations of its resources, to students with other problems as well: coping with separation and divorce, grief and loss resolution, teenage sexuality, generic problem-solving and growth groups, etc.

Strategies that are successful in managing students in the first four target groups will also be effective in working with students in the remaining two. Most past strategies have been developed for students without serious problems, and have thus been ineffective in reaching those most seriously affected.

Application:
Midville Public Schools

Let us look at the implications of this for a hypothetical school system, Midville Public Schools in Midville, USA—a community of 40,000 people. Midville Public Schools has a total enrollment of 10,000 students. The school system is organized as follows:

1. One High School, grades 10-12, with an enrollment of 2,484 students;

2. Two Junior High Schools, grades 7-9, with 1,242 students each;

3. Four Elementary Schools, K-6, with 629 students each.

Thus, there are 5,032 students at the elementary level, and 4,968 at the secondary level.

Due to a district-wide program of inservice training in alcohol/drug abuse concepts, in each bulding there are staff members familiar with the distinct target groups above, especially the first three, and with the prevalence estimates for each. Staff members in each of the seven buildings applied these prevalence rates to their enrollments, and arrived at the data displayed in Table 3.2, and Table 3.3, the latter of which summarizes the data.

As mentioned before, to an unknown extent the three target groups—affected family members and abusing/chemically dependent students—overlap. Thus, if the two groups overlap completely, at least 25%, or 2,500 students are in the first three target groups discussed above. If these groups do not overlap at all, then 34.9%, or 3,493 students are among the more severely affected by their own or someone else's drug abuse. Finally, if half of those who abuse drugs are also affected family members, then nearly 30% or 3,000 students, are in these highest risk groups. These figures do not include students who are experimenters or even regular users of alcohol or other drugs.

Thus, the single, "quick fix" that the Midville Public School District was hoping would address the drug-related problems of its young people evaporates in the face of the facts. Not only are many more students involved than the few who become the most visible, they have very different individual needs. Clearly, assuming that Midville has decided that it cannot continue on as before, it must begin to think through, in a careful and complete way, what its role in resolving such problems may be, what changes it needs to make to play any effective role at all, and what sort of organized response to such problems it wishes to take.

Table 3.2

DETAILED PREVALENCE ESTIMATE: MIDVILLE PUBLIC SCHOOLS

GRADE LEVEL	ENROLL-MENT	ALCOHOL/DRUG EXPERIENCE		AFFECTED OTHERS [25%]
		ABUSE [15%]	DEPENDENCY [5%]	
K	638			160
1	662			166
2	670			168
3	783			196
4	772			193
5	748			187
6	761			190
7	776	116	39	194
8	805	121	40	201
9	846	127	2	211
10	876	131	44	219
11	850	128	42	212
12	815	122	41	203
TOTAL	10,000	745	248	2,500

The prevalence rates above are based on applying the following assumptions to enrollment data:

- 20% of students aged 12-17 are abusing alcohol and/or other drugs;

- 5% of students aged 12-17 are chemically dependent;

- 25% of all school-aged youth are affected by parental chemical dependency.

Table 3.3

PREVALENCE SUMMARY:
MIDVILLE PUBLIC SCHOOLS

GRADE LEVEL	ENROLL-MENT	ALCOHOL/DRUG EXPERIENCE		AFFECTED OTHERS [25%]
		ABUSE [15%]	DEPENDENCY [5%]	
K-6	5,032			1,258
7-12	4,968	745	248	1,242
TOTAL	10,000	745	248	2,500

The prevalence rates above are based on applying the following assumptions to enrollment data:

- 20% of those aged 12-17 are abusing alcohol and/or other drugs;

- 5% of those aged 12-17 are chemically dependent;

- 25% of all students are affected by parental chemical dependency.

Chapter 3 | # Supplement 3.1
Defining Target Groups:
AODA Prevalence Estimates

Figures 3.1 and 3.2 permit a school district to estimate the number of students in each of the three major target groups discussed in Chapter 3: (1) students who are chemically dependent, (2) other students who are abusing alcohol and other drugs, and (3) students who are children of alcoholics, or "affected family members."

These worksheets may be completed by persons in individual school buildings, or in individual grade levels (e.g., K-6, "middle school," etc.). The results can be compiled into a single, detailed school-district-wide estimate similar to the one depicted in Chapter 3, Table 3.3.

Note that there is room for the individual to indicate upon what statistical assumptions the prevalence estimate is based: e.g., upon those in this manual, upon actual student survey results, national survey results, etc.

If a school district conducts a student AODA survey of its own, it will obtain a set of results which lends itself to tabular presentation. Even so, it may be useful to employ these statistics in defining "target groups," and in completing the worksheets that follow.

Figure 3.1
DETAILED PREVALENCE ESTIMATE WORKSHEET

GRADE LEVEL	ENROLL-MENT	ALCOHOL/DRUG EXPERIENCE		AFFECTED OTHERS [___%]
		ABUSE [___%]	DEPENDENCY [___%]	
K				
1				
2				
3				
4				
5				
6				
7				
8				
9				
10				
11				
12				
TOTAL				

The prevalence rates above are based on applying the following assumptions to enrollment figures:

- ____% of those aged 12-17 are abusing alcohol and/or other drugs;

- ____% of those aged 12-17 are chemically dependent;

- ____% of those aged _____ are affected by parental chemical dependency.

Figure 3.2
PREVALENCE SUMMARY WORKSHEET

| GRADE LEVEL | ENROLL-MENT | ALCOHOL/DRUG EXPERIENCE | | AFFECTED OTHERS [___%] |
		ABUSE [___%]	DEPENDENCY [___%]	
TOTAL				

The prevalence rates above are based on applying the following assumptions to enrollment figures:

- ____% of those aged 12-17 are abusing alcohol and/or other drugs;

- ____% of those aged 12-17 are chemically dependent;

- ____% of those aged _____ are affected by parental chemical dependency.

What is a Student Assistance Program?

One day the husband of a woman whose portrait was being painted by Picasso called at the artist's studio. "What do you think?" asked the painter, indicating the nearly finished picture. "Well...," said the husband, trying to be polite, "it isn't how she really looks."

"Oh," said the artist, "and how does she really look?" The husband decided not to be intimidated, "Like this." he said, producing a photograph from his wallet.

Picasso studied the photograph. "Mmmm...," he said. "Small, isn't she?" (From Charles Hampden-Turner, Maps of the Mind p. 8)

Inescapably, any school system's plans to embark on an affirmative approach to helping its young people resolve their alcohol/drug-related problems will be based on either conscious or unconscious philosophical orientations and general intentions (i.e., "goals"). As the anecdote above illustrates, the form of the 'product' will depend heavily on the biases of those involved in planning, producing, and observing it. This chapter will consider some of the major philosophical bases that underlie the present description of the Student Assistance Program model.

The Role of the School

The issue of the school's role in addressing the AODA-related problems of youth is a philosophical concern large enough to merit its own discussion. One most often hears the issue raised in black-and-white terms: schools should or should not be involved in such activity. Most often, however, the question is not decided on the basis of whether or not the school has a role to play, but on what the nature and scope of its role should appropriately be.

Limitations. In any deliberations over whether or not to implement a student assistance program the school should keep the idea of limitations firmly in mind. The notion of limitations, as persons, as professionals, and as a system, is not a negative concept. It is, in the first place, realistic: no person or system can be all things to all people, nor does either possess unlimited resources. Secondly, the recognition of limitations permits energies and resources to be focussed more intensely in a few areas rather than being dissipated on an infinite field.

To return to the "family illness" analogy of Chapter 1, the concept of limitations has another application in terms of the role of the school system. While many spouses or parents of chemically dependent persons are successful in shedding feelings of responsibility (i.e., guilt) for causing a loved one's drug problem, they often re-invest their energy in feeling responsible for that person's lifetime recovery. In other words, they often trade feeling responsible for causing to feeling responsible for curing.

Schools often encounter the same pitfall early in their efforts to implement student assistance programs. Feeling responsible for eradicating drug problems entirely arises naturally out of concern; it is often reinforced by parents, police, and even by some of the more zealous and evangelistic among its staff. The truth of the matter is that a school system does not cause drug problems any more than a family does. Neither, then, is the school system solely responsible for eradicating them. At best, the school system has a role, not the role to play.

Opportunity. In general, the nature of that role relies on the fact that schools have an ideal opportunity —rather than obligation—to help. Further details of the school's role will be discussed in Chapter 6, as the basic functions which a student assistance program must carry out. For now, the following are among the most obvious arguments in favor of the school, whether public or private, having a role to play in addressing the AODA-related problems of young people.

1. The school has an obligation to create an environment which is not conducive to fostering the development or continuation of alcohol and other drug-related problems among youth. Put another way, schools have a responsibility to create environments which support healthy growth and development.

2. The school setting is the most practical setting within which to implement intensive AODA preventive and interventive programs, because of the opportunity it has for observing student behavior.

3. Student Assistance Programs have a positive impact on academic performance: i.e., addressing AODA issues allows schools to carry out their primary mission of education.

4. Student Assistance Programs also have a positive impact on general school performance. Alcohol and other drug abuse have been implicated as causative factors in truancy, absenteeism, classroom misconduct, vandalism, tardiness, drop-out rates, etc.

5. The school system performs a dual function, as a reflection of community values and attitudes, and as a change agent. Therefore, if a community is concerned about youthful alcohol/drug problems, the school is one segment of society in which healthful values can be reinforced as well as initiated.

6. There is ample precedent for schools to become involved in health problems that threaten large numbers of young people as well as the community as a whole. School involvement in public health problems has included everything from providing childhood innoculations against infectious diseases such as polio to enforcing state laws requiring children to have physicals or to visit the dentist once a year.

'Broad Brush' or AODA-Specific?

As if to recapitulate the evolution of the Employee Assistance Program, student assistance programs appear to exist in one of two forms. Some are AODA-specific, concentrating primarily if not entirely on student alcohol/drug-related problems. Other programs describe themselves as "broad brush" in character: they are designed to help any student with any problem, and they deal with general wellness strategies as well as problems such as pregnancy, suicide, family violence, and sexual abuse in addition to drug problems. There are number of good reasons, however, for preserving a strong AODA emphasis within a student assistance program, despite the fact that students indeed have other problems as well. There are also good reasons for the school district to take time to ensure that the assertion of "broad brush" needs is not a form of resistance to acknowledging alcohol and other drug abuse.

Prevalence. The prevalence of alcohol and other drug abuse and their related problems is one of the major reasons for preserving an AODA-focus in SAP's. Between 25% and 35% of all students in a given school system are affected by their own chemical use or that of a family member. More students are harmed by alcohol and other drug abuse than by all other problems combined.

AODA as a contributing factor. It has been demonstrated that alcohol and other drug abuse are involved in most instances of these other student problems as a contributing if not a primary factor. Alcohol-related car accidents are the leading cause of death among 18 to 24 year old males. Since the 1960's, the rate of suicide among young people aged 15 to 24 has increased dramatically, by 250 percent in young women and 300 percent in young men. As a group, alcoholics are 15 times more likely to commit suicide than the general population. The majority of teenage suicides occur when the victims are intoxicated or have a history of some drug abuse. Some studies show that 95% of teenage pregnancies occur when one or both partners are under the influence of intoxicants. There is also a high incidence of drug abuse in families where violence or sexual abuse occur. Some studies report alcoholism in 38% of the child abuse cases investigated. Alcoholism is implicated in between 45 percent and 60 percent of spouse abuse cases. Moreover, the rate of separation and divorce among alcoholic families is seven times that of the general population, and 40 percent of family court cases involve alcoholism in some way. The majority of juveniles in correctional institutions committed their offenses while high. Historically, programs aimed at these other problems have ignored or been blind to the fact that alcohol and other drug abuse at times causes other problems, aggravates them, or prevents their successful resolution. *See Social Consequences of Alcohol Use and Alcoholism.* Alcohol Health and Research World. (Fall, 1984), pp. 33-37).

The school context. With rare exceptions, these other problems do not occur in school, but in the students' homes or in the community. On the other hand, students routinely engage in the possession, use, delivery, or sale of alcohol and other drugs while in school or at school-sponsored activities. Thus, the school system has an immediate need to address those problems which occur within its locus of control; it is not in a position to have as great an impact on student behavior that occurs elsewhere. Moreover, drug abuse is "contagious": it is passed on through strong environmental influence, not only to students' age-mates, but to younger and younger children. The same is not generally true, or true in the same way, of the other problems cited above.

Similarly, one rarely hears of school staff routinely ignoring instances of rape, sexual abuse, or suicide within the school building. It is a commonplace, however, for school staff to ignore on a daily basis the most overt alcohol/drug use by students and its related behavior.

Effectiveness. In general, if a school becomes effective in recognizing and in dealing with AODA-related problems effectively , the same skills and structures will enhance its effectiveness in dealing with other problems which students face. History demonstrates that the reverse has not been true. Schools have aggressively implemented various counseling and pupil services programs over the decades, only to remain relatively ineffective at managing AODA-related problems. The competencies that sensitize it to the dynamics of shame and resistance, and that permit it to motivate students and families to get help for highly resistant problems also empower it to deal with non-AODA problems as well. In fact, one of the criticisms that staff will often direct toward its student assistance program is that "we never had all of these other problems until you started this program."

Staff awareness. It is also true that no other problem affects the staff of a school district as much as do alcohol and other drug-related problems. Routinely, at least 50 percent of teachers, counselors, and administrators in AODA training sessions indicate that they are "affected family members" who have been affected by alcohol/drug abuse in parents, siblings, spouses, or other close family members. Many others admit to concern for colleagues in the school system. School districts do not appear to be spared from sharing in an incidence of alcoholism among their staff of approximately 10 percent. And, most school districts will have to examine, as part of establishing an effective student assistance program, the drinking and drug abuse patterns of the staff.

All of the above argue for a Student Assistance Program model that is "broad brush" in conception and scope but which also recognizes the appropriate dimensions of AODA-related issues. The argument, in short, is not whether or not the SAP model is or is not "broad brush" or whether a given program should be. In point of fact, most existing programs have begun with a strong AODA focus—because it is where the greatest need was originally perceived to be—only to develop into broader programs soon afterward. This is essentially the history of the EAP model.

As in many areas, school officials and consultants would be wise to eschew the extremes. Few would argue that only alcohol/drug problems should be addressed, and that we should ignore all others. Likewise, it is wise to examine the extent to which vociferous arguments for a "broad brush" model represent denial in a more sophisticated guise. In any case, the pragmatic needs of students rather than abstract models should guide programming.

Other Philosophical Issues

It would be impossible to list all of the philosophical issues which are behind the Student Assistance Program model, described generally below, and in more detail in Part Two. However, the following is a partial list of some of the major premises upon which this perspective on student assistance programming is based.

- Alcohol and other drug use, abuse, and dependency affect, at the very least, between 25% and 35% of the nation's school-aged youth.

- The problems associated with alcohol and other drug abuse, chemical dependency, and the stress of living in a chemically dependent family environment represent the most serious and prevalent threat to the health and welfare of the nation's youth.

- Any harmful involvement with alcohol and other drugs—as the 'afflicted' or the 'affected' person—affects the whole person, impairing relationships and physical, social, emotional, intellectual, spiritual, and academic development.

- The recreational use of mood-altering drugs by under-age youth does not enhance, maintain or promote healthy growth and development. Consequently, all use of mood-altering chemicals should be proscribed on developmental grounds alone.

- The aim of a student assistance program is thus not to promote "responsible drinking" or other drug use, but to promote responsible decisions and behavior concerning alcohol and other drugs. This includes promoting responsible behavior toward those with alcohol and other drug-related problems, by students, staff, the school, and the community as a whole.

- Adolescents and pre-teens can and do develop chemical dependency with sufficient severity as

to require referral to a continuum of screening, assessment, treatment, and aftercare resources.

- While chemical dependency is always preceded by drug use and abuse, the latter do not always lead to the former. Therefore, a student assistance program must always be able to distinguish between these varieties of drug experience, and to recognize the unique needs of individuals so affected.

- Alcoholism and other chemical dependencies are most accurately regarded as primary, autonomous illnesses which can be effectively treated when those affected are identified early, treated appropriately, and are provided with appropriate aftercare support.

- Drug-involved youth and their families possess the necessary resources to recover from chemical dependency and other AODA-related disabilities.

- Alcohol and other drug abuse, while not "the school's problem," do represent a problem in and for any school, impairing its ability to carry out its educational mission. AODA-related problems have long been demonstrated to be both causal and contributive factors in vandalism, absenteeism, tardiness, disciplinary problems, classroom disruptions, declining academic performance, drop-out rates, etc.

- School systems possess the necessary resources to recover from the ways in which they have been affected by alcohol and other drug abuse.

- The school setting is the most effective one within which to deal with alcohol and other drug-related problems as they affect youth. Schools contain a cross-section of youth representative of the community as a whole, and are the only place where behavior can be monitored and evaluated by minimal standards of accceptable performance which are uniformly applicable.

- The diagnosis and direct primary treatment of chemical dependency falls outside the proper role of the school, as does the treatment of any other illness.

- While a student assistance program is intended to serve any student with any problem, it must also take into account the unique characteristics of chemical dependency as it affects youth and their families if it is to effectively assist those students who are so affected. Thus, the areas of policy and procedure, program design, and staff training must be appropriate to the demands which drug-related problems present.

- A student assistance program is a joint school/community effort. Meeting the drug-related needs of youth is neither the sole responsibility of the school nor its primary one. The co-involvement of school systems, human service agencies, and the community at large is necessary at all stages of a program's development, including design, implementation, operation and maintenance.

- A student assistance program represents a long-range commitment by the school to deal with AODA-related issues of students, of staff, and of itself as an organization. That is, a program is not conceived of as a short-term, band-aid solution, or as "the program of the year."

- A student assistance program is rooted in "ownership" and self-sufficiency. Its program belongs to the school, not to any outside agency. Thus, the responsibility for meeting the needs of youth are the school's. The program's success, continuation, or failure should not depend on outside funding, or upon staffing by any outside agency.

- In designing, implementing, operating and maintaining a student assistance program, as much attention is focussed on addressing the school environment within which drug-related problems persist as on specific services designed for students. Thus, a program fosters an accepting, facilitative, supportive atmosphere for effectively helping students who are harmfully involved with alcohol and other drugs.

- A student assistance program is a comprehensive, joint school/community effort, recognizing that the school has a role to play in each of the crucial areas of identifying, assessing, referring, and supporting AODA-affected students at all grade levels, and in serving students who are affected by their own drug use, who are affected by others' drug use, and who are recovering from chemical dependency. Thus, a student assistance program is not narrowly focussed solely on secondary school students, on refering students to treatment, on "primary prevention," etc.

- The responsibility for the implementation, operation, and maintenance of a student assistance program is not lodged solely with one person, but is supported by the energy, enthusiasm, and committment of teams of individuals within the school system. Thus, while an individual may coordinate or direct program efforts at the building and/or district-wide levels, ownership, roles, and responsibilities are broadly shared.

"There are also good reasons for the school district to take time to ensure that the assertion of 'broad brush' needs is not a form of resistance to acknowledging alcohol and other drug abuse."

From the foregoing, student assistance programs can be seen to be quite comprehensive and complex strategies designed to cope with an individual and social problem that is even moreso. To summarize, an effective response is necessarily comprehensive in several ways. First, the Student Assistance Program model requires that we see alcohol/drug problems as complex: Chapter 3 identified at least six different target groups, each with a very different experience of alcohol/drug-related problems. Secondly, any program must successfully perform each of five major functions with respect to each group as well as each student: early identification, assessment, referral, support, and case management. Third, a range of school staff must be involved: there are several roles within the school whose obligations with respect to these functions must be defined. Fourth, it is unlikely, again, that any single activity is going to address the focal needs of each student. A continuum of services, both within the school and out in the community, will be required.

Before each of these is addressed in Part Two as concrete program design issues, it is necessary to examine one more aspect of the ecology within which alcohol and other drug problems is found: "enabling" in the school setting.

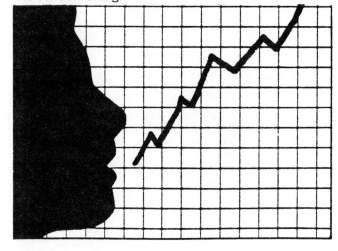

Chapter 4 | # Supplements

Most of the statements in Chapter 4 are "philosophical" in the sense that they are not statements of fact but statements of belief. It is important for a school district embarking on a student assistance program effort (1) to make conscious the belief system within which it is beginning, (2) to expand and even idealize that belief system to one which will support its SAP efforts, and (3) to seek a consensus of views shared by key individuals in the planning and implementation of the program.

Supplement 4.1 provides a structured method by which any group can examine aspects of its belief system regarding the issues discussed so far. It can be used to generate the "philosophy statement" that is an essential component of student assistance program policy language. The process can be utilized, or repeated, at any point in the implementation, operation, or maintenance of a student assistance program, and with many different types of groups.

Supplement 4.1

PROGRAM PHILOSOPHY:
A CONSENSUS-SEEKING TASK

I. GOALS:

A. To allow participants to discover components of their belief system regarding alcohol and other drug abuse and the school's role in coping with AODA-related problems;

B. To seek a consensus of beliefs shared by the group;

C. To promote the development of a belief system which will support an effective student assistance program;

D. To promote team-building and cohesiveness in a planning group.

II. PARTICIPANTS:

The process works well, within the time constraints allowed, with a group of approximately 20 persons. The task can be presented to several different types of groups: school staff, Boards of Education, a community task force, or a joint school/community group. For the purpose of the exercise, assume a joint school/community group is meeting to examine the form a student assistance program should take for its school. The group might be constituted as follows:

> Board of Education members (2)
> Superintendent of Schools
> Director of Instruction
> Director of Pupil Services
> High School Principal(s)
> Junior High School Principal(s)
> Elementary School Principal(s)
> Guidance Counselor(s)
> School Social Worker(s)
> School Psychologist(s)
> Teacher(s)
> Parents
> Student(s)
> Alcohol/drug agency representative(s)
> Police Officer(s)
> Clergy

It is advisable to have persons familiar with the field of alcohol and other drug abuse, and with student assistance programming, in attendance as resource persons who can provide information and clarification to committee members. One person must function as "chairperson" for the meeting. The chairperson or another can function as recorder (see below).

III. TIME:

Approximately one hour is needed for each Phase, with a half-hour break between.

IV. MATERIALS:

For Phase I, booklets should be made up for participants, consisting of each of the statements on the Sample Statements Worksheet, one per page. For Phase II the group should have access to a typewriter and a copy machine.

V. PHYSICAL SETTING:

The most effective meetings occur with participants seated around tables or desks arranged in a large circle or square.

VI. PROCEDURE:

Phase I. The chairperson of the meeting begins by explaining the goals of the meeting. The purpose is to seek those areas where the group is in agreement, and/or to phrase ideas in ways that maximize consensus. The goal is not to decide "right or wrong" positions.

The chairperson distributes one of the Statements tablets to each participant. Everyone is to read through the statements one at a time and indicate on each page whether they agree or disagree with the statement as it is written. If they disagree with it, they are to re-word the statement so that they are in agreement with it where possible. Group members should be cautioned to rephrase items so they can support or agree with them, and not so that others will.

When everyone has finished, the chairperson goes through the tablet, one item at a time, and asks for a raise of hands of those agreeing and disagreeing. (1) If everyone expresses agreement, the chairperson notes that on her copy. (2) If one or more people express disagreement, they express their revised language. The goal is to arrive at language which the entire group can agree with or agree to support. The chairperson notes the changes in language on his copy. (3) If everyone disagrees with a statement, or if consensus on language for a particular item cannot be reached, the chairperson notes that the item is to be "rejected" on her copy.

When all the items have been covered, the chairperson or recorder takes the master copy and types up the accepted statements in their final form. He may type them as a list, or may want to group related items together in paragraph form.

Phase II. When the "accepted" statements have been retyped, copies are made and distributed to each participant. The group is asked to read the document (or the chairperson may read it aloud).

Following the reading, group members are to suggest additional changes in wording, vocabulary, or order for the statements. The chairperson keeps track of suggested changes on his copy, and includes only those agreed to by a consensus of the entire group. The document is re-typed and copies made for each participant.

VII. PROCESS:

The role of the leader, or chairperson, is to promote the movement of the group toward consensus on each item, and on the final form and "flavor" of the document which emerges in Phase II. She should watch time carefully, and should move on to the next item if a consensus does not develop.

Alcohol/drug resource people, or others in the group with specialized backgrounds should be consulted to answer questions when they arise with respect to individual items (e.g., "What is chemical dependency?" or "Do we know how many kids are smoking marijuana?").

Lengthy or heated debates should be avoided in favor of seeking the minimal common ground upon which group members can initially agree.

The document or list which emerges is often used as a component of policy language which is subsequently developed for the student assistance program. Often it is possible to append to the document specific recommendations or conclusions.

VII. VARIATIONS:

As an alternative to trying to accomplish both phases in one meeting, group members can be given the statements and directions beforehand. More group time may then be spent in processing consensual items.

Group members may also be invited to submit additional comments for reaction by the entire group as a part of Phase I.

The process can be adapted to any set of "statements," and to any meeting where group consensus is an important prerequisite to group action.

SAMPLE STATEMENTS WORKSHEET

The following are sample statements which may be printed on individual pages of a booklet for distribution to group members. Many statements could easily be added.

****

---

1. The use of alcohol and other drugs leads to alcoholism or other chemical dependencies.

    [   ] Agree   [   ] Disagree

---

2. The role of the school is to teach responsible drinking.

    [   ] Agree   [   ] Disagree

---

3. The _____ School District recognizes that the use of alcohol and other drugs is becoming increasingly commonplace among students.

    [   ] Agree   [   ] Disagree

---

4. The _____ School District believes that it has the major responsibility for helping students with alcohol and other drug problems.

    [   ] Agree   [   ] Disagree

---

5. Alcoholism and other chemical dependencies are illnesses which are most successfully treated when identified early and given appropriate treatment.

    [   ] Agree   [   ] Disagree

---

6. From 25% to 35% of _____ School District's students are affected by their own harmful chemical use or by that of people close to them.

    [   ] Agree   [   ] Disagree

---

7. The problems associated with youthful drug abuse and the stress of living in a chemically dependent family represent the most serious and prevalent threat to the health and welfare of the nation's youth.

    [   ] Agree   [   ] Disagree

8. Since only a few students get into trouble with their drug use, some drug use by students can be condoned as responsible, mature or healthful.

[   ] Agree   [   ] Disagree

9. The school should apply its limited resources toward prevention rather than toward problems that have already developed.

[   ] Agree   [   ] Disagree

10. The school should apply its limited resources toward intervening with those kids in trouble, rather than toward those without problems.

[   ] Agree   [   ] Disagree

11. It is proper for the school system to become trained in the treatment of alcohol/drug problems to provide this service to students in school.

[   ] Agree   [   ] Disagree

12. The major responsibility for the drug problems in this community lies with parents and the police.

[   ] Agree   [   ] Disagree

13. The major focus of an alcohol/drug program should be on the high school. Such problems do not affect children in the elementary grades.

[   ] Agree   [   ] Disagree

14. The best solution to our drug problems is to hire a drug expert to solve them in the high school.

[   ] Agree   [   ] Disagree

15. The school should endorse some drinking by students if the alcohol is provided by parents and if the drinking is supervised.

[   ] Agree   [   ] Disagree

<table>
<tr><td>Chapter 5</td><td># Enabling
In the Educational Setting</td></tr>
</table>

No one dies from chemical dependency without the (unwitting) help of at least one other person.

* * * * *

Only to the extent that an organism (person, family, institution, or community) becomes aware of itself will it know how to change.

It has been known for a long time but not often appreciated that if one's goal is to make an impact on "the drug problem," it is not enough to focus attention on the chemically-involved student alone, nor on such young persons as a group. The drug-related problems of youth—taken individually or collectively—neither begin nor progress in isolation. Any attempt to cope with such problems which consciously avoids addressing their environmental context is both shortsighted and inadequate. In general, the Student Assistance Program model can be thought of as being aimed primarily at the environment as the best direct means of helping the individual.

The two quotations above contribute to a crucial point, then: if one's attempts to cope with the AODA-related problems of youth are to go beyond the accidental and piece-meal, as much if not more attention must be paid to the nature of the contexts within which they occur as to the individual signs, symptoms, and dynamics involved. Those involved in successful student assistance programs discover from the beginning that to help kids they must change certain aspects of the school setting. Or, after such a program has been in place for awhile, they are surprised to discover the ways in which the act of helping itself has changed the school system. The focus of this chapter is thus on the school context as a significant component of the "enabling system" which allows drug-related problems to progress.

The Concept of 'Enabling'

While the use of the term "enabling" has unfortunately acquired a negative connotation in the field of alcohol/drug abuse, dictionaries would indicate otherwise. Standard definitions note that "to enable" means "to empower, to give power to, to allow or permit, to make possible or easy." To enable a device means to turn it on. The term has even crept into the language of the clergy recently, who are exploring ways of spiritually enabling, or empowering, their parishioners.

In the AODA field, however, the negative connotation of "enabling" derives from its application to illness rather than health. In an application of the term that is consistent with its general usage we ask "what are the factors that allow or give power to drug abuse and/or dependency?" It is important to bear in mind that the concept of "enabling," used in this way, is not a description of causation, but only a description of permission. Thus, the absence of a specific law does not cause the commission of a specific crime, although it may be one factor among many that makes it easy. Similarly, the enabling system does not cause drug abuse or dependency, but merely (!) strengthens the dynamics of such problems or makes it easy for them to develop. Enabling, like drug abuse itself, is a complex and fascinating phenomenon, as illustrated by the following definition:

> *The enabling system consists of those ideas, feelings, attitudes, and behaviors which unwittingly allow drug problems to continue or worsen by preventing the drug user from experiencing the consequences of his/her condition, in order to enhance, maintain, or promote the enabler's sense of well-being.*

Unlike some other definitions which focus only on chemical dependency and the behavioral components of enabling, the above suits all chemical experience and the range of environmental enabling factors involved as well. In general, one can identify any aspect of the environment which does not promote "chemical health" as an enabling factor. Thus, even the chemically dependent person's denial functions as a part of their own enabling system.

There are at least four major components of this definition. "Enabling" (1) is a complex environmental system; (2) it consists of a system of cognitive, emotional, attitudinal, and behavioral components; (3) it functions by withholding awareness of the consequences of one's condition; and (4) it is motivated by the enabler's desire to maintain his/her own sense of well-being. Each of these requires more detailed explanation before the concept can be applied to the school setting.

Ideas, Feelings, Attitudes, and Behaviors

There is a significant cognitive component in enabling. In terms of conceptual knowledge, lacking accurate information or possessing inaccurate information regarding alcohol/drug abuse gives a firm foundation to the enabling system. Inaccuracies (e.g., "Only adults—not kids—can become alcoholic") often contribute to our failure to recognize problems or their scope in the first place. This is also the major way in which stereotypes contribute to enabling. One's stereotypes about who can and cannot be using drugs, or of who can and cannot be chemically dependent, will literally affect vision. Preconceived notions about the "typical drug abuser" result, in practical terms, in the failure to identify and thus help the majority of students who fail to fit these stereotypes.

More often, however, it is the absence of accurate information that is most harmful and most easily addressed. For example, in the absence of knowledge to the contrary it is common to regard drug use/abuse as a singular, uniform phenomenon. In this view, aside from differences of degree, all drug use is the same, individual experiences and needs are the same, and the same response will suit all students (e.g. there is a 'magic' curriculum).

What many are unaware of is the qualitative difference in alcohol/drug experience for many, including adults. If, for example, I am unaware that an individual lacks control over her chemical use, I may become involved in ineffective strategies to help her do so: threats, rational arguments, appeals to biology, religion, or the law, etc. When chemical use continues, I frequently feel frustrated and inadequate, and whatever negative attitudes I may have brought to the situation will be reinforced. In the end, the student's drug use continues and perhaps progresses to later and more serious stages. Thus, what I know and don't know can prevent a student from receiving appropriate help.

What we do with feelings is also a powerful and important enabling dynamic. It is fair to say that concrete feelings of some sort are nearly always involved in one's experience with drug-involved students, individually or as a group. The nature of these feelings is as important as whether or not they are recognized and expressed, and how they are heard by the student(s) involved. The fact that I am concerned or even fearful is a consequence of a student's condition which he will not experience if I am not aware of it or if it is not expressed to him. Thus, individual "ego defenses" can be seen as part of the enabling system. One can even express appropriate anger over student conduct. If, however, it is heard as judgement, resentment, or blame, the effect is to strengthen those defenses which block awareness. Thus, how feelings are expressed has much to do with whether or not students ask for help or accept it when it is offered.

The place of attitudes in the enabling system is similar. Stereotypes can be construed as attitudes: as predispositions, or habits, of feeling and—most importantly—of judging. Judgemental attitudes toward alcohol/drug use, abuse, dependency, and those with such problems, contribute most to the enabling dynamic. Put most simply, if a student senses that an admission of drug involvement, or even of a drug problem, involves accepting that she really is a bad person, she will be unlikely to ask for our help, or accept it when offered.

We enable most visibly through the ways in which these ideas, feelings, and attitudes manifest themselves in our behavior—through things we do or fail to do. There are many sins of commission in this regard: covering up, excusing, taking punitive action without offering help, to name only a few. More often than not, the enabling environment is characterized by what it fails to do: recognize AODA problems, talk about such problems openly, confront drug abuse, enforce consequences, and so on.

Even more importantly, everyone in the school system must thoroughly examine his or her own relationship to alcohol and other drugs. Do we tolerate the abuse of alcohol, for example, rather than healthy patterns of use? Do we fail to help members of the staff who have obvious problems? Aside from enabling through the behavior we model, we are likely to regard as acceptable student alcohol/drug behavior which is milder than our own.

Consequences

By definition, "problem use" of alcohol or other drugs means "use that is causing personal and/or social problems" for the individual involved—i.e., there are consequences for alcohol/drug use. Briefly put, one of the best ways to promote drug abuse is to make it clear that there are no consequences for it. By not having consequences for alcohol and drug-related behavior, we fail to let young people learn about their limits and boundaries. By having but not enforcing consequences we do a great deal more harm. First, we deny students the opportunity to learn: they will never have to make healthy decisions—or any at all—about alcohol/drug use if they do not experience consequences for those decisions they are already making. Experiencing the consequences of behavior is also essential to the development of responsibility by any definition. Finally, by having consequences which are rarely enforced, we contribute to students' cynicism and lack of respect for the school system. They become convinced of our insincerity.

It bears saying again that, aside from these more procedural factors, the feelings and attitudes that a students' AODA experience occasions are just as "factual" as the policies students may violate. Our failure to communicate these emotional consequences to them prevents them from experiencing the consequences of their condition as well as of their behavior. In all of these ways we deprive students (and others) with AODA-related problems of the information and experience they need if they are ever to make an enlightened decision that they need to modify their chemical behavior or that they require help to do so.

"It is frequently more useful to expose students to the concept of 'enabling' in place of 'peer pressure.' In other words, how do they help to provide an environment in which other students' drug problems can develop and/or worsen?"

The Motivation behind Enabling

Enabling is almost always unwitting and well-intentioned. This point cannot be stressed too much. It is often pointed out that no one consciously says "I think I'll help someone get sick(er) today." Just as enabling does not cause drug abuse, there is no blame attached to enabling, either. In assisting individuals and systems to examine their enabling dynamics, it is vital to accept the principle that "Everyone does the best they can with what they know." Enabling arises and acquires the force it does for just these reasons: we do what we can with inadequate or inaccurate information, we are unaware of the consequences of specific ideas, feelings, etc., and we behave with good intentions. We want to take care of, to protect, to "help."

Enabling, however, can be just as resistant to

change as the drug-using behavior of the chemically dependent student, and for much the same reasons. In the first place, the dynamics involved often result in good feelings for the enabler. It feels good to think I am "helping" by protecting, or it feels safer to sit on feelings or perceptions rather than take the risk of talking about them. All attempts to change our own enabling behavior, or those of a system, require taking the dual risks of self-examination and behavioral change. The strongest statement that can be made is that no significant impact on the enabling system (or on the problems associated with youthful alcohol and other drug abuse) can be made unless the various dynamics mentioned above are examined by individuals and the systems of which they are a part, and changed.

The System of Enabling

The first part of the definition stresses the systematic nature of enabling. As a "system" it consists of those discrete components described earlier; these, however, function to create a whole that is greater than their sum. While it is easy to recognize how the cognitive, emotional, and behavioral elements result in actions or inactions that shield students from the consequences of their drug use, abuse, or dependency, it is also necessary to appreciate that the collective postures of administrators, counselors, teachers and other staff can make up a powerful environmental system that unwittingly allows AODA-related problems to continue.

Finally, to the enabling dynamics of the school as an institutional setting we can add the enabling dynamics of parents and students, as well as of other systems (law enforcement, the church, etc.) to get an idea of just how powerful the contextual variables are, and how necessary it is to address them on a community-wide basis if significant progress is to be made in helping students with AODA-related problems.

Enabling in the School Setting: Role-Related Issues

Supplement 5.1 represents an attempt at a comprehensive list of specific enabling patterns common to those in the school setting among others. Because a student encounters educators in different ways, depending on their roles, some enabling dynamics are more relevant to some roles than to others.

The Classroom Teacher. Since classroom teachers have access to students and student behavior on the most frequent and regular basis, they have one of the most crucial roles within a student assistance program (see Chapters 6 and 7). It stands to reason then, that for troubled students to be managed effectively, enabling at this level needs to be identified, understood, and addressed. In general, enabling most frequently involves failure to identify or recognize students' AODA involvement, combined with the failure to report or refer. The following are some enabling patterns which classroom teachers have identified in themselves:

1. Avoiding places in the school building or its grounds where students are known to use alcohol and other drugs;

2. Failing to recognize or confront apparent exchanges of money and/or drugs in classrooms, halls, cafeteria, etc.;

3. Ignoring unacceptable behavior in the classroom;

4. Ignoring apparent intoxication of students in the classroom or other areas or supervision;

5. Ignoring, or supporting, students' verbal announcements in class about drug use;

6. Having unclear standards of acceptable academic performance or classroom conduct;

7. Failing to report incidents of observed student alcohol/drug use to those designated to handle such issues;

8. Failure to refer students suspected of AODA involvement, who have a pattern of unacceptable performance or conduct, to those designated to handle such problems;

9. Attempting to affect the AODA-related behavior of individual students by "counseling" them one's self;

10. Believing that a given student couldn't possibly be alcohol/drug-involved because she gets good grades, is an athlete, is a "good kid," etc.

The Pupil Services Worker. School counselors, social workers, psychologists, and other pupil services specialists are those who traditionally are in a position to discover the nature and scope of student problems, and presumably, of their AODA involvement. While to some degree the "counselor" is susceptible to the same enabling dynamics as those above, some aspects of enabling relate specifically to the screening/assessment function these educators are called upon to perform. Pupil services workers have identified the following as among the enabling factors that most frequently prevent the identification and successful management of AODA-related problems in students:

1. Making decisions or taking action without formal training in alcohol/drug concepts and skills;

2. Failing to include AODA-related questions as a routine part of discussions with troubled or problem students;

3. Regarding some alcohol/drug use by students as acceptable (i.e., to be 'condoned' rather than 'expected');

4. Believing, prior to investigation, that a given student could not possibly have an AODA-related problem, or that chemical use has no role in a student's problems in school or at home;

5. Attempting to affect students' AODA behavior by oneself;

6. Failing to involve others, especially administrators, classroom teachers, and parents, in managing the AODA-involved student;

7. Failing to refer to community AODA agencies those students who do not respond to in-school services:

Administrators. Principals and assistant principals become involved in the enabling process primarily by virtue of their roles in enforcing school policies (e.g., administering corrective discipline) and in providing administrative support for others dealing with students with AODA-related problems. In addition to the pattern of beliefs, feelings, attitudes, and behaviors mentioned earlier, administrators themselves frequently identify the following as concrete enabling behaviors:

1. Taking action without formal training in AODA issues;

2. Taking disciplinary action without consulting other professionals;

3. Taking disciplinary action without ascertaining the nature or degree of a student's alcohol/drug involvement;

4. Taking disciplinary action to punish rather than to provide students with choices that involve their addressing their unacceptable AODA-related behavior;

5. Failing to take disciplinary action on AODA

issues for fear of parent or community reaction, or the lack of administrative support from others;

6. Failing to openly admit the nature and scope of alcohol/drug use to protect one's position or the image of the school;

7. Believing that "cleaning up" drug problems is really the responsibility of counselors, the police, or parents;

8. Failing to support the recommendations of counselors and teachers regarding the management of students with AODA-related problems;

9. Believing in or relying upon over-simplified responses to the "drug problem" (e.g., ridding the school of drugs by renting police dogs to sniff lockers)

10. Enforcing a "get tough" policy which does not also include provisions for assessment or remediation of student AODA problems.

Similar lists could be devised for anyone else in the school setting who works with students in a specialized way: coaches and athletic directors, club advisors, coordinators of special programs, and so on.

"When a teacher makes a referral, and someone fails to 'ask the chemical question,' student drug use at best will not change, and at worst will progress to more serious stages."

At least two other groups, however, deserve formal mention in any discussion of enabling in the school setting: students and parents. Drug problems in students progress in part due to parental enabling (see Supplement 5.2) which begins with the overwhelming need to protect first the child, and second the family, from the intrusion of judgement from the outside. All of the dynamics mentioned above apply exquisitely to parents in a more emotionally intense form. Especially where drug use has progressed to abuse or dependency, in the family setting denial and enabling become hopelessly intertwined, which accounts for the resistance that many educators encounter when attempting to help the AODA-involved student.

Finally, adolescents spend most of their time not with parents or teachers but with each other, frequently within a well-defined peer culture. As we become involved in student assistance programming it becomes necessary sooner or later to ask how students themselves manifest the complex of beliefs, feelings, attitudes, and behaviors which allow drug problems to progress in their peers (see Supplement 5.3), and to provide a way for them to become aware of and change these patterns. It is frequently more useful to expose students to the concept of "enabling" in place of "peer pressure." In other words, how do they help to provide a environment in which other students' drug problems can develop and/or worsen?

Finally, it is also necessary for those in the school system to ask themselves how they enable with respect to children of alcoholics or other students affected by someone else's chemical use. By its reluctance to talk about such problems openly, the school staff only reinforces the "no talk rule" students have learned at home, and exaggerate the sense of shame which these students feel. By not talking, too, we do not permit students to discover that they are not alone and that as many as one out of four of their classmates (and half of their teachers) have the same problems. On occasion students are given misinformation that only exaggerates the symptoms of their family illness. More than one child has been told by a well-meaning teacher or counselor that perhaps if he got better grades, kept his room clean, or helped around the house "maybe your mother wouldn't drink so much." In these and other ways we can enable the family illness as well as students' own alcohol/drug use.

Enabling in the School Setting: System Issues

For the teacher who is observant and does report, for the counselor who does AODA assessments, for the principal who seeks to relate discipline and correction, for anyone who is addressing the personal and role-related enabling issues, another dynamic becomes apparent: the enabling factors that seem to have become institutionalized, that seem to have become part of the woodwork itself. To get at this context one could ask the same general questions of the system, such as "how are various enabling beliefs, feelings, attitudes, and behaviors reflected in our collective behavior? There are at least three areas of enabling at the system level that require comment: (1) policy and procedures, (2) program focus, and (3) support.

Clearly, not having a formal alcohol/drug policy and procedure is one of the best ways of keeping the school district incompetent to handle such problems. However, even though most school districts have some sort of AODA policy, even having one can contribute to the enabling system if, among other things—

1. The policy is widely promoted but widely unenforced (which communicates an unmistakable message to everyone in the school system);

2. The policy is too narrow, focussing only on "dealing," or on intoxication in school, or on "prevention," etc.;

3. The policy is so punitive in tone that students, teachers, and parents alike are afraid to cooperate with it;

4. The policy does not integrate clear consequences for violations with provisions for assessment and referral.

Likewise, the absence of clear and well-understood procedures, or taking for granted that AODA matters somehow "get handled," contributes to the school's inability to manage AODA issues successfully. Most simply put, the absence of procedures often means that even if a student does come to our attention, no one is assured of what options are available for the next steps, or who should be involved.

Secondly, the absence of a clear focus for AODA referrals often undermines effective effort. If dealing with AODA problems is not the designated responsibility of an individual or a team, it is easy for all staff to simply take for granted that these issues are routinely dealt with. Most often, they are not. When a teacher makes a referral, and someone fails to "ask the chemical questions," student drug use at best will not change, and at worst will progress to more serious stages. The effect on the staff is more pervasive: they stop referring.

All of the above speaks to the issue of support. Fragmentation of effort is the opposite of support and mutually assured responsibility: the guarantee that if one person takes step X, then others will take steps Y and Z. Classroom teachers must be made confident that if they take the risks to refer a student, the counseling staff will address the chemical issues. And counselors must be assured that if they need administrative support it is there. Administrators need to be able to trust that counselors will not work to get kids "off the hook" by protecting them from disciplinary consequences; counselors need to trust that "consequences" does not mean "punishment." Finally, everyone needs to know that the board of education and the community are aware of and support the firm enforcement of a school policy that couples consequences with help.

Addressing Enabling

One way or another, everything about the Student Assistance Program model has to do with changing the nature and scope of enabling in the school setting. The first step in dealing with enabling in individuals is education about it. A great deal of enabling is often eliminated as soon as those involved have a framework with which to examine their behavior. The next step is awareness: the opportunity to discuss the dynamics of enabling with others, and to do so in a safe environment where no blaming occurs. Educators at all levels must learn to confront enabling in themselves as well as in others. Finally, there must be a supportive atmosphere for the changes that are required. In large part, changing one's enabling behavior almost always entails risk: to one's sense of well-being, to one's relationships with students and parents, and sometimes to one's position. It is difficult to adopt new ways of dealing with AODA-related problems unless there is support for the changes from others. As individuals within the system begin to find ways of supporting individual changes, the system-wide changes become possible and workable.

Conclusion

"Enabling" is a concept with wide application. The concept can be applied in examining individual as well as collective behavior. We can also examine the various ways in which enabling dynamics have become institutionalized in the components of systems themselves. Moreover, it is a useful exercise to ask not only how other institutions enable (law enforcement, social services, the church, etc.) but also how their interaction, or non-interaction, constitutes a further, more global manifestation of enabling. Or even further, how do we 'enable' others' enabling? What patterns of beliefs, feelings, attitudes, and behavior strengthen and perpetuate the enabling components in other individuals and systems?

"Enabling can be thought of as failure or absence of 'prevention.'"

This approach to enabling and the problems associated with alcohol/drug abuse is admittedly "ecological": it stresses the mutual interaction between the drug-involved student and an environment that unwittingly, and often despite good intentions, allows such problems to continue. Drug abuse will continue unless and until the environment addresses its enabling and begins the recovery process that empowers health. To change, the system and those within it need to become aware of this concept and its implications as a prerequisite to consciously examining its manifestations. Because it is one of the most effective means of changing the enabling dynamic, training plays a crucial role in the implementation of student assistance programs.

It is also helpful to speculate on the relationship between "enabling" and "prevention." This relationship tells us more about the latter than the former. Enabling can be thought of as the failure or absence of "prevention." Taken as a neutral concept, "enabling" can refer to a continuum, with those factors which "give power to" alcohol and other drug abuse at one extreme and those which empower health on the other. The concepts in Chapter 1 can be viewed as describing "prevention" as "recovery." Here, "prevention" can be viewed as the process of moving from one extreme toward the other, by examining and changing those belief systems, feelings, attitudes, and behaviors that allow drug problems to begin, continue, and to worsen.

Thus, the concept of enabling has immense heuristic value, too: it permits those interested in ameliorating alcohol/drug problems in a thorough way to ask the most useful questions. And, in view of the second quotation that opened this chapter, to the extent that individuals and systems become fully aware of themselves they will know how to change. For the issue really is, once we recognize the enabling characteristics of the environment that "give power to" the disease process, what will we give power to instead, and how? Chapter 1 supplies an answer to the first question: we want to enable recovery. The remainder of this manual examines how this can be accomplished.

| Chapter 5 | # Supplements |

The supplements that follow list many specific examples of the "enabling system": thoughts, feelings, attitudes, and behaviors. The list concerning PROFESSIONAL ENABLING is lengthy, but not exhaustive. The worksheet can be used in its entirety, or items from it can be selected for use with given populations, such as coaches, counselors, district administrators, and so on.

Supplement 5.2, PARENTAL ENABLING, is a similar exercise which focuses on some additional enabling dynamics as they pertain to parenting. It can be useful for parent education efforts, or it can be given to specific parents with whose child the school is working.

Supplement 5.3 deals with STUDENT ENABLING. It, too, can be a useful adjunct to educational efforts around alcohol and other drug abuse whether in the classroom or the counselor's office.

Readers may also wish to experiment with utilizing the checklists in a pre/post-test manner. The STUDENT ENABLING worksheet, for example, lends itself to use at the beginning and end of a support group. Similarly, the results of administering the PROFESSIONAL ENABLING worksheet at the beginning of the school year could be compared with those administered near the end of the year, following AODA inservices, etc.

The worksheets are generally intended to be employed as self-administered checklists that can aid in teaching and discussion about enabling.

There is no formal provision for scoring the checklists, although those who wish to may assign numerical values to the responses (e.g., "NO" = 0; "SOMETIMES" = 1; "YES" = 2). In general, the items are worded in such a way that a higher numerical score indicates a greater incidence of enabling.

Supplement 5.1
PROFESSIONAL ENABLING

The statements below describe elements of belief systems, feelings, and behaviors which can contribute to the complicated system of enabling. For each statement indicate the degree to which it is applicable to your experience of student alcohol and other drug problems.

YES   NO   SOMETIMES

[ ]   [ ]   [ ]   1. I overlook obvious problems in students.

[ ]   [ ]   [ ]   2. I oversimplify problems related to alcohol or other drug abuse.

[ ]   [ ]   [ ]   3. I make decisions or take actions without formal training in the field of alcohol and other drug abuse.

[ ]   [ ]   [ ]   4. I view chemical dependency and other drug abuse primarily as a moral issue.

[ ]   [ ]   [ ]   5. In the staff lounge I gossip about the alcohol/drug problems of students.

[ ]   [ ]   [ ]   6. When I speak about those with alcohol/drug problems my tone is accusatory.

[ ]   [ ]   [ ]   7. I typically view the chemically dependent person as "one of those people."

[ ]   [ ]   [ ]   8. I feel strangely uneasy, tense, or anxious after handling a situation involving alcohol/drug abuse.

[ ]   [ ]   [ ]   9. I focus blame for student drug problems somewhere other than on alcohol or other drugs.

[ ]   [ ]   [ ]   10. I lack clear and definite standards of performance and conduct for students.

[ ]   [ ]   [ ]   11. I have gradually lowered my expectations for acceptable student performance.

[ ]   [ ]   [ ]   12. I avoid confronting students' alcohol or other drug problems.

[ ]   [ ]   [ ]   13. I am uncomfortable bringing up the subject of alcohol or other drug use when working with a student.

[ ]   [ ]   [ ]   14. I feel that if I were more adequate as a professional I would be able to solve a student's alcohol/drug problems.

YES	NO	SOMETIMES	
[ ]	[ ]	[ ]	15. I do not report observed or suspected instances of student alcohol/drug use.
[ ]	[ ]	[ ]	16. I take disciplinary action without consulting other professionals in the school.
[ ]	[ ]	[ ]	17. I hesitate to involve others in a student's AODA problems out of fear that the student or the situation will be mishandled.
[ ]	[ ]	[ ]	18. I hesitate to take action on a student's AODA problem out of fear that I will not be supported by the school district.
[ ]	[ ]	[ ]	19. I do not take action on student alcohol/drug use because I fear a student will be mistreated.
[ ]	[ ]	[ ]	20. I am fearful of parent or community reactions if I take action on a student's alcohol/drug-related problems.
[ ]	[ ]	[ ]	21. I set a healthy example for students with respect to my own use of alcohol and other drugs.
[ ]	[ ]	[ ]	22. My own chemical use has resulted in behavior that I am not proud of.
[ ]	[ ]	[ ]	23. I wait for problem behavior to change by itself. I "endure."
[ ]	[ ]	[ ]	24. I protect a student from experiencing consequences by minimizing the seriousness of problems.
[ ]	[ ]	[ ]	25. I fail to admit the scope of drug abuse to protect the school system's image in the community.
[ ]	[ ]	[ ]	26. I think that I alone am in the best position to handle a troubled or AODA-involved student.
[ ]	[ ]	[ ]	27. I hesitate to confront a student with AODA-related problems for fear of jeopardizing my relationship with him/her.
[ ]	[ ]	[ ]	28. I verbally support some use of alcohol or other drugs by students.
[ ]	[ ]	[ ]	29. I consider their alcohol/drug use only as a last resort in helping troubled students.
[ ]	[ ]	[ ]	30. I attempt to control a student's alcohol/drug use through 'proofs,' appeals to logic or threats.
[ ]	[ ]	[ ]	31. I look the other way when students are using alcohol/drugs at school-sponsored functions.
[ ]	[ ]	[ ]	32. I believe that "cleaning up" alcohol/drug problems is what school counselors are supposed to do.

YES	NO	SOMETIMES	
[ ]	[ ]	[ ]	33. I believe that the kids I work with are really "above" alcohol/drug-related problems.
[ ]	[ ]	[ ]	34. I try to put distance between myself and those about whom I am worried.
[ ]	[ ]	[ ]	35. When students disclose AODA problems in family members, I fear the consequences of taking action.
[ ]	[ ]	[ ]	36. Discussions of, or involvement with, alcohol/drug problems are "too close to home."
[ ]	[ ]	[ ]	37. I fear my own position might be jeopardized by acting to address student AODA problems or issues.
[ ]	[ ]	[ ]	38. I regard some degree of student alcohol/drug use as acceptable.
[ ]	[ ]	[ ]	39. I make excuses for, cover-up, and even defend student drug use or other unacceptable behavior.
[ ]	[ ]	[ ]	40. I become frustrated at my inability to effect change in a student's behavior.
[ ]	[ ]	[ ]	41. I sometimes compromise my own value system in dealing with student alcohol/drug use.
[ ]	[ ]	[ ]	42. I maintain the "no talk rule" concerning alcohol/drug problems in students or their families.
[ ]	[ ]	[ ]	43. I believe that all students can stop using alcohol/drugs by themselves if they really want to.
[ ]	[ ]	[ ]	44. I believe that student AODA-related problems should be kept secret to protect their privacy.
[ ]	[ ]	[ ]	45. I avoid places in the school building or grounds where I know students use alcohol or other drugs.
[ ]	[ ]	[ ]	46. I fail to take action on AODA problems because I fear I will not be supported by others.
[ ]	[ ]	[ ]	47. I minimize or excuse student alcohol and other drug use.
[ ]	[ ]	[ ]	48. I believe there is no reason for the school to be involved in solving students' alcohol/drug problems.
[ ]	[ ]	[ ]	49. I have purchased alcohol or other drugs for students, or allowed them to use them in my presence at school-sponsored activities.
[ ]	[ ]	[ ]	50. I have ignored the AODA-related problems of staff.

Supplement 5.2

PARENTAL ENABLING

Each statement below describes a thought, feeling, attitude, or behavior which can be a small part of the complicated system of enabling. For each statement, indicate the degree to which it is applicable to your experience with a child who may have an alcohol/drug-related problem.

YES   NO   SOMETIMES

[ ]   [ ]   [ ]   1. I have discovered supplies of alcohol or other drugs, but have been afraid to say anything to my child (or spouse).

[ ]   [ ]   [ ]   2. I have avoided talking to people in school or in alcohol/drug agencies out of fear of the stigma.

[ ]   [ ]   [ ]   3. I no longer trust my child.

[ ]   [ ]   [ ]   4. I doubt my own perceptions—I think maybe I am making something out of nothing.

[ ]   [ ]   [ ]   5. I think that if I had been a better parent I could have prevented this: it is my fault.

[ ]   [ ]   [ ]   6. I feel inadequate as a parent.

[ ]   [ ]   [ ]   7. I increasingly feel angry.

[ ]   [ ]   [ ]   8. I am fearful when my child leaves the house.

[ ]   [ ]   [ ]   9. I don't think my child knows or cares how I/we feel.

[ ]   [ ]   [ ]   10. I excuse my child's behavior by attributing it to adolescence—he/she will "grow out of it."

[ ]   [ ]   [ ]   11. I exert more control ("As long as you are living in this house you'll do what I say").

[ ]   [·]   [ ]   12. I have tried to become more understanding of the pressures he/she is under.

[ ]   [ ]   [ ]   13. I believe my child could not have a drug problem because he/she does not fit my image of such people.

[ ]   [ ]   [ ]   14. I maintain a "no talk rule" by not discussing painful events, feelings, or the possibility of a drug problem with other family members.

YES	NO	SOMETIMES	
[ ]	[ ]	[ ]	15. I blame my child's drug use on his/her friends.
[ ]	[ ]	[ ]	16. I attempt to control his/her behavior by becoming more strict.
[ ]	[ ]	[ ]	17. I focus blame for my child's drug use on the school, the police, or others.
[ ]	[ ]	[ ]	18. I endure: I think they will eventually grow out of it if I am patient.
[ ]	[ ]	[ ]	19. My spouse and I (or I and other family members) have become closer in attempting to cope with this problem.
[ ]	[ ]	[ ]	20. My spouse and I (or I and other family members) disagree concerning how to handle this problem.
[ ]	[ ]	[ ]	21. I excuse my child from participating in the usual family gatherings (holidays, dinners, picnics, vacations, etc.), or make excuses for him/her to others.
[ ]	[ ]	[ ]	22. I and other family members do chores that were formerly his/her responsibility.
[ ]	[ ]	[ ]	23. I/we prevent our child from experiencing the consequences of their behavior by "bailing them out" when they get in trouble with police, school, etc.
[ ]	[ ]	[ ]	24. I keep other family members from knowing of my concerns or of facts I have.
[ ]	[ ]	[ ]	25. I protect other family members from knowing about problem situations or incidents.
[ ]	[ ]	[ ]	26. I and/or my spouse tolerate some use of illicit drugs by our children.
[ ]	[ ]	[ ]	27. I and/or my spouse use illicit drugs ourselves.
[ ]	[ ]	[ ]	28. I and/or my spouse serve alcoholic beverages to our children or their friends.
[ ]	[ ]	[ ]	29. Our children have seen me or my spouse drunk.

Supplement 5.3

STUDENT ENABLING

Each statement below describes a thought, feelings, attitude, or behavior which can be a small part of the complicated system of enabling: of unknowingly helping someone's drug problems to continue or get worse. For each statement, indicate the degree to which it applies to your experience with another student who may have an alcohol/drug problem.

YES	NO	SOMETIMES	
[ ]	[ ]	[ ]	1. I would prefer that a student keep on using rather than have them become involved with a drug counselor in school.
[ ]	[ ]	[ ]	2. I have introduced another student to alcohol or other drug use.
[ ]	[ ]	[ ]	3. I have been concerned about another student's alcohol or other drug use but have been afraid to talk to them about it.
[ ]	[ ]	[ ]	4. I have been concerned about another student's alcohol or other drug use but haven't talked to a teacher or counselor about it.
[ ]	[ ]	[ ]	5. I am afraid that if I share a concern with another student I will lose his/her friendship.
[ ]	[ ]	[ ]	6. I am afraid others would think I'm a "narc" or that sharing a concern about another student would harm my reputation in school.
[ ]	[ ]	[ ]	7. I blame other things or people for a student's drug use or drug problem.
[ ]	[ ]	[ ]	8. My own use of alcohol or other drugs has resulted in behavior I am not proud of.
[ ]	[ ]	[ ]	9. I have protected, covered up, or lied for a student who uses, or who has an alcohol/drug problem.
[ ]	[ ]	[ ]	10. I try to avoid being around those that I am worried about.
[ ]	[ ]	[ ]	11. I believe that anyone can quit using on their own if they really want to.
[ ]	[ ]	[ ]	12. I keep secret those drug problems or incidents that I know about.

Part Two

Program Design

In a very real sense there is no such thing as the "Student Assistance Program." The term is intended to describe a model, an abstraction. In part it describes a set of basic functions which any assistance program must accomplish with respect to young people's alcohol and other drug-related problems. It also refers to a set of structures from which any individual school system may select in designing its program. In this sense, the manner in which any given school district realizes the model should differ from that of others. The only "real" program, then, is the one that you are creating. In another sense, too, we should be speaking of a Student Assistance Process rather than of a "program." While it is relatively easy to describe a model, creating any realization of the model is very much an ongoing process.

With these qualifications in mind, PART TWO examines the structural and procedural components of the Student Assistance Program as a model. It describes varying aspects of how to implement change on the system level — or, in terms of the questions in PART ONE, "What aspects of the system need changing (a) in order to help more kids, (b) in order to improve the process, and (c) in order to remove obstacles to (a) and (b)?"

Chapter 6 introduces the fundamental elements of designing a student assistance program. First, a program must perform certain basic functions to provide adequate help to students with AODA-related problems: identification, assessment, intervention, support, and case management. The school system must also define its relationship with alcohol/drug treatment agencies. Second, a school must clarify the roles which existing staff are to have in the program, and define some additional roles. Third, the program model requires some additional stuctures if these roles and functions are to be carried out effectively. Chapters 7 through 12 deal respectively with identification, assessment, intervention, treatment, support and case management issues. Program roles, structures, and procedures are described as they relate to each of the basic functions.

Chapter 7 explores in detail the various mechanisms and strategies for identifying students in need of help. It includes discussions of the role of the classroom teacher, the role of other staff, criteria for identification, procedures, and the promotion of student self-referrals.

Chapter 8 describes the nature and complexity of the assessment process within the student assistance framework. The major task, following identification, is (1) to discover the nature of students' AODA involvement and its role in causing and/or complicating other problems they may have, and (2) to arrive at a decision as to the proper type of help required. As the most complex of all the program functions, assessment will involve designing some program-specific structures and procedures and will often require the cooperation of many staff over a period of time. Chapter 8 emphasizes that assessment is not a task that is accomplished in a one-hour interview with a student.

Intervention, or the referral of students to appropriate help, is taken up in Chapter 9. Individual students may need assistance that can be provided with the school or they may require AODA-related services in the community — or a combination of the two. While many referrals will be simple, others will require the school to put more effort into motivating students and/or family members to accept the need for help. Referrals of this type will often require some strategies unique to the Student Assistance Program model, and clarity in school district policies and procedures.

In Chapter 10 the role of the school with respect to the actual treatment of alcohol/drug problems is defined. Chapter 10 examines the relationship of the school to the continuum of care, including screening services, evaluation and diagnostic services, and primary treatment. Although the direct primary treatment of diseases lies outside the scope of the school's responsibility, an effective student assistance program will have established working relationships with adolescent treatment facilities.

The nature of "support" for students engaged in developing healthier lifestyles relative to alcohol and other drug problems is covered in Chapter 11. Support for the individual student can be available in varying degrees, and can exist at several levels within the school system. It can be as minimal as having a counselor who is knowledgeable about alcohol/drug problems and who is consistently available, as complex as the array of in-school support groups, and as broad as a supportive, nurturing school climate.

Chapter 12 looks at the issue of case management, or how the program monitors itself as well as individual students. Once a student is identified the program assures students, parents and staff of due process. Case management and program coordination at the building level go hand-in-hand, and both depend crucially on the fact that a student assistance program has designed a clear and definite sequence of procedures.

Introduction to Program Design: Functions, Roles, and Structures

No concept is true. A concept is always a partial perception. A good concept simply allows me to see more than before. (Prather [1980], p. 17).

In designing its student assistance program a school system should begin from its awareness of target groups, or the description of the various ways in which students can be affected by alcohol and other drug abuse and the unique needs associated with these experiences. Six different target groups were identified in Chapter 3; the first five are our major concern in this chapter:

1. Students who are chemically dependent: those who are most seriously affected by their own alcohol/drug use;

2. Students who are not dependent, but whose use of alcohol and other drugs is causing them problems in their daily lives;

3. Students who are affected by and/or concerned about someone else's alcohol/drug abuse;

4. Recovering students who are returning to the school setting from an alcohol/drug treatment program;

5. Non-using or non-abusing students who need support for their decision to remain chemically free.

The design of a comprehensive student assistance program that will meet these needs will depend on how the district answers four broad questions:

1. What functions must the program perform on behalf of each student in each target group in order to bring about change?

2. What roles must be clearly identified for key school staff and for those in the community?

3. What in-school and community services will be required, and what are the respective roles of each?

4. What procedures will assure that students receive the help they need?

Program Functions

Six basic functions need to be performed and coordinated to help troubled or problem students, whether the problem is related to drug abuse or something else: (1) early identification of those in need, (2)assessment of the problem's nature and degree of severity, (3)intervention, including referral to appropriate sources of help, (4) treatment for the problem, (5) support for individuals engaged in making changes in their lives, and (6) case management to assure that the other functions are being performed. These program functions are components of a continuum of care. In designing its program, the school must define the nature and extent of its involvement in each of these functions. To be effective, a student assistance program must assure that all six functions are performed for any given student; to be comprehensive, it must assure that all six functions are performed for students in all five target groups.

Early Identification. "Identification" refers to the process by which students with AODA-related problems come to the attention of appropriate school staff and thus "enter" the program. Programs should be designed to promote the identification of students to the program staff through all of the following avenues:

— Staff Referral (e.g., teachers, principals, coaches, nurses, etc.)

— Self-referral (voluntary requests by students for help or information)

— Peer Referral (students seeking information or help on behalf of another student)

— Parent Referral (parent contact for information or help for a child)

— Community Referral (contacts through clergy, police, juvenile justice authorities, social services, etc.)

Another program design consideration concerns to whom referrals will be directed. It is vital that the program have a central focus for receiving referrals or contacts. Referrals are most often received and handled through the role of Student Assistance Coordinator/ Counselor, or are managed by the Core Team members within individual school buildings.

For staff referrals it is also important to distinguish between referrals made on the basis of *witnessed* alcohol/drug behavior and referrals made on the basis of *suspected* alcohol/drug involvement. "Witnessed Use" referrals typically result from firsthand observations by staff of violations of statutes or school policies which forbid the "manufacture, possession, use, delivery, or sale" of alcohol or other drugs in school or at school-sponsored activities. "Suspected Use" referrals are based on the observations of staff that a student is exhibiting a pattern of behavior which is unsatisfactory and which may or may not be alcohol/drug-related.

To be comprehensive, a program cannot limit itself to identifying students harmed by their own drug use alone. The school system must also develop a method for identifying students concerned about others' alcohol/drug abuse as well. Furthermore, the program will also have to clarify the process by which it will identify students who are in treatment so that an appropriate re-entry process can be followed.

Assessment. As used here, the term "assessment" refers to the process of gathering and interpreting information in order to discover the target group to which a student belongs once she comes to the attention of focal people in the school. More specifically, assessment is the process of gathering information regarding student behavior, and deciding on the nature of the particular student's needs, taking into account possible AODA-involvement. As such, the term denotes a continuum. At one extreme lies the type of "assessment" typically done by the classroom teacher: e.g., noting a pattern of decline in a student's classroom performance and deciding that the student should see a counselor. At the other extreme lies the type of assessment, usually referred to as "diagnosis," done by a chemical dependency treatment program in the community: deciding, on the basis of patient data, that the student is in the late stages of chemical dependency and requires hospitalization followed by long-term care in a halfway house.

While the school should avoid diagnostic responsibilities it does have a clear role to play in lesser degrees of assessment. Thus, the decision does not involve whether or not to do assessment, but what degree of involvement it will undertake. The decision will often depend on the availability and quality of AODA screening, assessment, and diagnostic resources that are available in the community.

Finally, assessment takes time and nearly always involves more than one person in the school building. Almost everyone within the school could be involved in the assessment process for a given student because they have valuable information concerning the student's behavior. In student assistance programs, the difficulties presented by distinguishing what is normal adolescent behavior from what is caused by drug abuse have been eased by designating teams of individuals as responsible for coordinating the assessment process and the information it produces.

Intervention. Stated most succinctly, intervention refers to the process of interrupting a harmful pattern of alcohol/drug-related behavior. As such, it applies to students who are abusing drugs, to students who are affected by parental alcoholism, or to recovering students who may be showing signs of relapse. The typical goal of intervention is to have the individual involved accept her need for help. The outcome of the intervention is always a referral to some source of assistance. Thus, having identified a student and having formed an idea of the nature and extent of a student's problem, the program must define the process for referring the student to appropriate care in school or in the community. Intervention and referral can consist of a simple recommendation of a source of information to parents. It can be as complex and time-consuming as orchestrating a formal interventive process, involving several key individuals from the school, the family, and the community. Formalized, concerted interventive strategies are usually required where students are chemically dependent and where the associated denial system is strong.

Note that assessment and intervention are inextricably linked: one cannot gather information without making some kind of recommendation; the decision to act must be based upon and guided by a decision as to what the student needs. The formal, intensive training that prepares school staff to implement and operate a student assistance program must appropriately address these two crucial areas.

"District-wide organization is also an obvious reflection of the fact that the program is conceived of as district-wide in scope; it is not a small-scale effort of a few individuals on behalf of a minority of students."

Treatment. The school has a legitimate role in providing direct services to students in each of the function areas above, with the exception of treatment. Professional treatment, whether for chemical dependency or other illnesses, has traditionally been regarded as being most appropriately delivered by community agencies outside of the school setting.

In the area of chemical dependency, primary treatment is typically provided on either an inpatient/residential basis, or on an outpatient/nonresidential basis.

The results of professional assessment, done by an agency in community, determines the type of care required. The proper role of the school at this point lies in contributing the information it obtains at its level of assessment to those working on the "diagnostic" end of the assessment continuum.

Thus, an important phase of program design involves the school in clarifying its working relationship with AODA diagnostic and treatment resources in the community. This involves identifying and evaluating such resources, learning how to communicate with them within the bounds of confidentiality, and providing information about students to treatment programs to aid in diagnosis. The school must also clarify these working relationships on behalf of students who are in treatment and are about to return to the school setting, in order to develop a re-entry process which will support these students during the early and most critical phases of their recovery. Treatment and assessment programs which are unwilling to work with schools in these ways should be avoided.

Support. In general, all students who become involved with the student assistance program will be engaged in changing either their own chemical behavior, or their behavior toward others who have such problems. Since such problems are extremely resistant to change, and since young people often lack the skills necessary to cope with them successfully, it is unrealistic to expect kids to change patterns of attitudes or behavior through educational presentations alone, or as the result of a few sessions with a school counselor. Many, if not most, will require some form of additional support for the changes we are asking them to make. The more severely affected the child, and the less supportive the environment (at home, in school, or in the community) the greater will be the need for support services.

For example, a clear case can be made for providing support services to the recovering student, who is either returning from an inpatient treatment program, or who is involved in an outpatient program and attending school at the same time. Most, for example, will need help in severing a harmful relationship with alcohol or other drugs in an environment where peer pressure to use them remains intense. Similarly, making healthy adaptations to living in an alcoholic family is a monumental task without some form of support from others.

Support can be provided in a number of ways by a student assistance program. It can range from having trained staff available to listen to student concerns, to implementing specific support groups, to taking steps to change the attitudes and knowledge of the staff at large and making the school climate in general more supportive of those with AODA-related problems.

Case Management. Many schools err in seeing "case management" as an organizational issue that is not directly related to helping kids. However, the importance of case management, or "coordination," cannot be overstressed. A program must identify a means for assuring that it is indeed functioning successfully for each student—that students are getting what they need. More specifically, it refers to the necessity, again, of having a program focus. Someone—a person and/or a team—needs to be aware of where a given student is along this continuum of program functions, and of what steps need to be taken next.

The coordinative, management function plays another crucial role by promoting the program's credibility with staff without which it cannot work. The value of this function is most often appreciated when it fails or when it is omitted in program design. Those for whom we define roles in a program will stop participating if they do not see clear results. Teachers, for example, will stop referring students if they are not assured that definite steps will be taken and that they will be kept informed (within the limits of confidentiality) of a student's progress. They will not make referrals for suspected drug problems if the counselors or other resource persons are not defined as being responsible for assessing drug involvement and appropriately trained to do it. In disciplinary matters, a principal will stop seeking information about a problem student's alcohol/drug involvement if the student "drops out of sight."

In short, the fact that attention to the coordination of the program does ensure its smooth operation supports its role in assuring that students and staff are both appropriately served.

This is an appropriate point at which to introduce the notion of levels of application. The description of program functions up to this point has been student-centered, emphasizing the fact that each function must be performed on behalf of the individual student in need of help. The program functions also apply to the emerging design of the program at several other levels as well. The student assistance program carries out these functions in successively wider contexts. As indicated above, one can ask how the functions will be performed for each target group; one must also ask how each will be carried out at the building level, and at the district-wide level. One should even ask, in the community-wide context, "Who else is in an ideal position to identify students in need of help with AODA-related problems?" "How are young people assessed for alcohol/drug abuse?" (or, "Are they assessed?") "Is appropriate drug treatment or help available, and do students get referred to it?" What support systems are available in the community for young people coping with AODA-related problems?"

All of the program design issues which follow—clarifying roles, developing program services, designing structures and procedures—relate to realizing the basic program functions outlined above.

Traditional Staff Roles in a Program

It should be clear from the foregoing that the school system will need to clarify the role which various staff persons (as well as parents, students, and others) will be expected to perform in identifying, assessing, referring, and supporting students who have AODA-related problems. Nearly everyone in the school building—including students themselves—can play a role in each.

Relationships and a Cycle of Action. For school staff members to move students along this continuum successfully they must understand that at any given time they might be either in a supervisory or a facilitative relationship with the troubled student. In general, those in a supervisory relationship with students are those:

(a) who are in a position to observe student conduct and performance;

(b) who have and uphold clear standards of acceptable student behavior or performance;

(c) who can offer students choices among alternative courses of action;

(d) who can take disciplinary action or enforce certain consequences aimed at correcting or improving student conduct or performance.

The facilitative relationship, on the other hand, generally consists of "counseling-like" activities. One is in a facilitative relationship when one is:

(a) forming an interpersonal relationship with a student

(b) attempting to discover the nature, extent, and cause of personal problems;

(c) providing help and/or support designed to assist in the resolution of personal problems.

Most people combine these two modes in their day-to-day interactions with students. It is necessary, however, to bear in mind that it is frequently not possible or effective to blend both styles in working with an individual student who is troubled or who is having problems. Thus, while the individual teacher, counselor, or principal may work with a student in both ways in a given encounter, the program must recognize and distinguish these in the roles it formalizes. It is not reasonable for a principal to apprehend students for being high in school and then expect them to be forthright about how much they are using and how often. Similarly, a counselor must be able to establish trusting interpersonal relationships to discover the extent of a student's problems without the student fearing punishment because she describes illicit drug activity. Clearly, though "supervisory" and "facilitative" relationships can be combined, the design of the program must distinguish these two styles in how it defines various individual responsibilities.

"It is vital that the program have a central focus for receiving referrals or contacts."

The classroom teacher provides a good example of how these two relationships are combined, and of how they relate to the role the teacher can perform in the program. The teacher, for example, is in an ideal position to observe student conduct and performance and to notice changes that frequently indicate that a student needs help. The teacher is also likely to become involved in the assessment process by contributing significant information to those engaged in discovering the nature and extent of a student's drug involvement. Several teachers may be invited to participate in a formalized intervention process to facilitate the referral to a treatment program outside of the school. And finally, in many programs teachers volunteer to take on the additional role of group facilitator by acquiring the necessary training to lead one or more support groups.

Moving a student along the program functions also requires defining a cycle of action within which traditional staff roles are also defined. To provide students with adequate help, the school, and individual staff, will continually be taking action based on an assessment/intervention cycle, depicted in Figure 6.1. Thus, "assessment" entails gathering and evaluating information; "intervention" entails recommending and taking action. The process is cyclical since the outcome of each typically leads into the other. Each can have up to four components.

Thus, a coach might (1) notice that an athlete's performance is slipping and the student is missing practices. He (2) begins to document these facts and (3) realizes that these lapses represent not only a change but also an increasingly frequent pattern. He (4) decides

the problem is serious enough to talk to the student about, and he will ask the student to see a Student Assistance Program Counselor. When talking to the student privately, he (5) expresses his concern over the changes and (6) shares the specific facts legitimizing this concern. He indicates that he (7) would like the athlete to see a Student Assistance Program Counselor and that (8) he will be seeing the counselor himself about these concerns. Regardless, however, the student's attendance at practices must improve in order not to jeopardise the athlete's eligibility to play.

Note that this describes eight discrete steps, and that the coach is essentially performing an identification function: bringing the student's behavior to others' attention. Similarly, if the student sees the counselor, she will begin the process again at the next level: gathering additional information, evaluating it, deciding on a course of action, etc.

In general, then, roles of traditional staff (teacher, principal, counselor) can be seen in terms of the relationship typical of each and in their use of the assessment/intervention cycle in moving a student from identification, through assessment and intervention, to support.

Figure 6.2 summarizes the continuum of six functions and the roles of staff within each. Virtually everyone can participate in the early identification of troubled students. Figure 6.2 also indicates that everyone in a school can contribute to each function, but may have a primary role to play in only one based on their supervisory/facilitative relationship. Counselors and other pupil services staff will naturally have an important additional role in assessment. Principals and other administrators will be crucially involved in intervention.

New Program Roles

In addition to encouraging staff to participate effectively, for a program to succeed it must also meet further requirements:

1. The program must have a focus; referrals must be focussed on one or more persons;

2. Persons involved in the program must be specifically trained in dealing adequately with the AODA-related needs of students;

3. The program must monitor the process of delivering services to students within each school building on a district-wide basis;

4. The program must assure staff as well as students that services offered by policies and procedures are indeed being delivered.

Figure 6.1
THE ASSESSMENT/INTERVENTIONS CYCLE

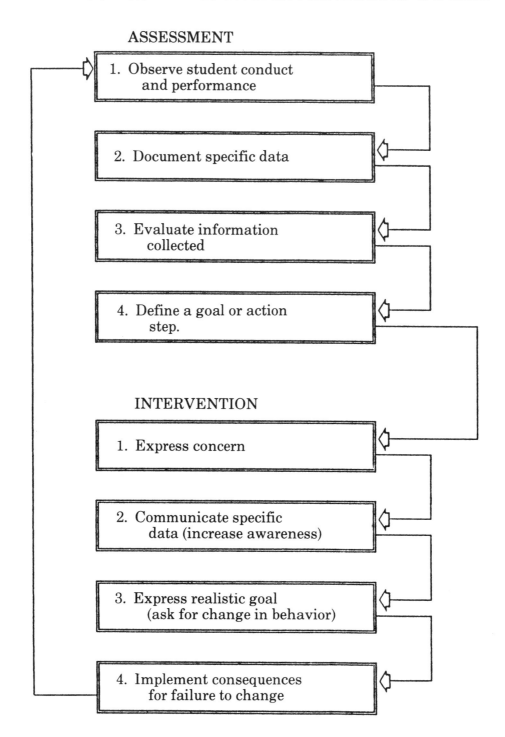

ASSESSMENT

1. Observe student conduct and performance

2. Document specific data

3. Evaluate information collected

4. Define a goal or action step.

INTERVENTION

1. Express concern

2. Communicate specific data (increase awareness)

3. Express realistic goal (ask for change in behavior)

4. Implement consequences for failure to change

Figure 6.2

BASIC PROGRAM FUNCTIONS

IDENTIFICATION	ASSESSMENT	INTERVENTION	TREATMENT	SUPPORT
STAFF REFERRALS -*Teachers, aides* -*Coaches, Nurses* -*Librarians* -*Principal* -*Assistant Principals* -*Counselors* -*School Social Workers and Psychologists* **SELF REFERRALS** **PEER REFERRALS** **PARENT REFERRALS** **AODA AGENT REFERRALS** **COMMUNITY REFERRALS** -*Police* -*Juvenile Justice System* -*Clergy* -*County Social Services* -*Physicians and Hospitals* -*Other Youth and Family Services Agencies*	*Major Roles:* *SAP Counselor/ Coordinator* *Core Team Members* Input From: *All school Staff* *Students* *Parents* *AODA Agencies* *Community Agencies*	*Major Roles:* *SAP Counselor/ Coordinator* *Referral Team* Involvement of: *Other school staff* *Concerned Students* *Parents* *AODA Agency Staff* *Community Agency staff* Referral to: *In-school Resources* -*Counselors* -*Support Groups* *Community Resources* -*Screening* -*AODA Assessment* -*Treatment or Counseling*	Community Resources: *AODA Services:* -*Screening* -*Assessment/ Evaluation* -*Inpatient Treatment* -*Outpatient Treatment* *Self-Help Groups:* -*Alcoholics Anonymous* -*Narcotics Anonymous* -*Cocaine Anonymous* -*Alanon* -*Alateen* -*Alatot* *Non-AODA Services*	Major Roles: *SAP Counselor* *Group Facilitator* *In-School Services:* -*One-to-One Counseling* -*Support Groups* -*Education*

The Student Assistance Coordinator. To achieve the necessary degree of program focus it is usually necessary to designate an existing staff person—typically a counselor or other pupil services staff person—as the "Student Assistance Coordinator" in a given high school, middle school, or elementary building. This is the primary coordinative role within the individual buildings. To the extent that this role remains a coordinative one, the responsibilities of the person fulfilling it involve monitoring individual students' progress in the program, chairing the building-level Core Team, evaluating the program's effectiveness on a regular basis, serving as a liaison between the school building, its local community area, and the larger district-wide Core Group (see below). This individual is frequently responsible for coordinating the various program implementation tasks prior to its actual operation. (Supplement 6.1 contains a detailed listing of the responsibilities of the SAP Coordinator).

The Student Assistance Counselor. Many tasks, especially those involving assessment and intervention, involve face-to-face contact with individual students. Those who have acquired the appropriate training in alcohol and other drug abuse fulfill the role of Student Assistance Counselor. In some schools, those in this role have been named "Drug Resource Persons," "AODA Specialist," and so on. They are typically counselors or other pupil services staff members with formal training in counseling skills. General counseling backgrounds are not sufficient, however. A person is selected to work with students on alcohol/drug problems, and to function in this role, because he (1) is perceived by students as a caring, trustworthy person, (2) has received intensive training in alcohol/drug abuse issues, and (3) fully supports the school district's student assistance program philosophy, policies and procedures. Furthermore, if she is involved in leading support groups she should have formal training not only in general group process but also in the specific problems associated with leading AODA groups in the school setting. Her chief duties fall within the assessment, referral, and support functions as a member of the building Core Team (Supplement 6.1).

In smaller secondary schools the functions of Student Assistance Program Coordinator and SAP Counselor are combined in one individual who carries out some of the counseling functions with students and also coordinates the program within the building. In other cases, a staff person is designated to function as the building Coordinator at some percentage of their time—usually between 25 and 50 percent. Counseling functions are then performed by existing, appropriately trained pupil services staff.

Support Group Facilitator. The role of support group facilitator is not limited only to those with formal counseling backgrounds. Anyone, whether a school district employee, AODA agency staff person, or community volunteer, can become a group facilitator if they acquire appropriate training and meet the requirements established by the school system. In most cases, classroom teachers find that leading a support group is an excellent means of becoming involved with the program. Further information on AODA-related support groups is covered in Chapter 11, and in PART THREE.

The Student Assistance 'Contact Person.' The relatively informal role of 'SAP contact person' is often carried out by classroom teachers and others who do not have formal counseling or pupil services backgrounds. This role is intended to promote student self-referrals and peer referrals in larger school settings.

The contact person should be a non-threatening resource person whom student may seek out voluntarily for information about the program, about alcohol/drug issues, or about help for themselves, friends, or family members. The contact person's role is basically limited to being a good listener, supplying basic information, and encouraging students to see the Student Assistance Counselor(s) for additional help. Contact persons are formally identified as such in brochures and other promotional materials given to students as part of the active promotion of the program. They require formal training in all fundamental aspects of alcohol and other drug abuse, and so are to be involved in the training programs for Core Team and Core Group members (See PART FOUR).

Students may also be solicited and trained for this role. In this capacity they, too, function as a safe entry into the program for concerned students. Their role is not to counsel or advise but to listen, answer basic questions within the limits of their training, and encourage students to seek additional help through other school staff. Students in the role of contact persons have been variously referred to as "peer counselors," "peer leaders," "peer resources," etc.

Program Structures

A number of structures have been mentioned previously which are either unique to the Student Assistance Program model or to the school system: the Core Team, the Screening Team, the Referral Team, and support groups.

The Core Team. The Core Team is the primary organizational unit of the Student Assistance Program model at the level of the individual high school, middle school, and elementary school. As the primary focus of the program it plays a role in many areas of the program, including its implementation, day-to-day operation, and ongoing maintenance. During the implementation phase, for example, the Core Team in each building should be involved in the design of the program, the formulation of policies and procedures for recommendation to the Board of Education, the identification of key staff for Core Team AODA training, and so on. It helps with program maintenance by collecting program data and recommending revisions, expansions, and improvements as part of the evaluation process.

Most of the operational activities of the program are focussed in Core Team members. At the building level, the Core Team collectively oversees the case management of individual students. The Core Team basically is formed around the mandatory participation of administrators and pupil services workers. At minimum the Core Team must consist of representatives from the administration (principal, assistant principals, deans of students), pupil services (counselors, psychologists, social workers), and other interested staff (coaches, health educators, etc.). The SAP Coordinator, SAP Counselor(s), Group Facilitators, and Contact Persons are all considered to be Core Team members. Thus, "membership" in this rather amorphous body is open to anyone who wishes to get involved in the program in any way. Core Team members should all receive extensive training during the implementation process, and additional AODA training as members' needs are identified. Since one of its key tasks is to expand its membership by involving others, it may eventually be constituted as in Figure 6.3.

The Screening Team. While many persons within the school are in a position to observe student behavior and to refer to the program, many students may not be identified because a given staff member is in a position to see only a portion of the student's behavior. Similarly, a single incident overlooked as being an isolated occurrence takes on significance when set along side of data from other people. Thus, a team approach to assessment is a compelling suggestion in most secondary school settings.

In smaller school systems, the Screening Team consists of the Core Team as a whole; in larger schools it is an ad hoc subgroup of a larger Core Team. Its primary function is to assist with the data collection and evaluation that are an essential part of the assessment process for individual students. In view of the complexity of assessing the nature and severity of student AODA-related problems, this often means dividing up, among several Core Team members, the various data collection tasks once students are identified: (interviewing students, contacting the student's other teachers, reviewing performance records, contacting parents, contacting community agencies, etc.).

A Screening Team would minimally consist of a principal, the Student Assistance Coordinator, Student Assistance Counselor(s), the school nurse, and attendance clerk(s). A helpful addition would be a staff member from a local AODA agency or treatment program. In some schools, members of this team meet regularly, once a week, to compare notes on students referred to each member, to pool information they have collected, and to make recommendations for further steps. This structure allows many different types of information—disciplinary problems, attendance and tardiness data, counselors' interview information, teachers' observations—to be brought together.

The Referral Team. The Referral Team is also an ad hoc group made up of Core Team members as well as others who have firsthand information regarding a student's AODA-related problems and needs. The team is usually organized whenever a formal intervention strategy is necessary in order to bring about a successful referral of a student to a chemical dependency treatment or assessment program. Members of such a team are those who have become concerned about the student, who have critical information about his conduct, who are willing to become involved on a personal level, and who are adequately trained or prepared to take part appropriately.

Program Services

The six program functions constitute intrinsic services which the school, as part of its student assistance program, will make available to students and/or parents. In addition, many programs have found it necessary to offer specific services for AODA-related issues as well as others.

Education. An important part of any student assistance program involves providing students with concrete alcohol/drug information. In some cases this is already provided to a degree by formal curricula that are part of health classes or other courses. In many student assistance programs, however, the SAP staff have found it necessary to educate about alcohol and other drug abuse in additional ways through formal classroom presentations by Core Team members. These presentations have the function of giving students appropriate information on how mood-altering chemicals interact with lifestyle to create real or potential problems, on how they can identify when they or others begin developing problems, and who they can go to for help. The presentations also help to introduce and/or promote the program in its early stages, and allow students to ask questions about it.

Education is also provided to staff members through periodic inservices conducted by Core Team members and/or AODA specialists from the community. Parents and other segments of the community are also invited to informational meetings designed to increase public awareness of student alcohol/drug-related problems and the school as well as the community's attempts to address them. SAP Counselors and Contact Persons provide individual students with information as they seek out the programs's resources. Finally, some schools have gone beyond the brief educational experiences discussed above, or which form a part of a broader curriculum, by implementing alcohol/drug education courses at the secondary level. Students may take such courses on an elective basis for credit. The course is typically a semester class which meets at least twice each week, alternating with other classes. (See Chapter 16 for additional information on educational groups and courses).

Support Groups. AODA-specific support groups of various types (see Chapter 13) have emerged as virtually obligatory services offered by an effective student assistance program. Support groups represent the most effective means of helping students to cope with AODA-related problems. The groups are designed to meet the needs of students in the three familiar, broad categories: (1) non-chemically dependent youth who are affected by their own drug abuse, (2) recovering students returning from a chemical dependency treatment program, and (3) students concerned about or affected by others' chemical use. The groups aim at improving school performance and personal functioning, providing accurate, personally meaningful information about alcohol and other drugs, and supporting changes in AODA-related behavior.

As a program design task, the district must consider the types of groups it will implement, the timetable for their implementation, the resources it will need to commit to support groups, and the specific policies and procedures that support groups will require. Each of these is explored in greater detail in PART THREE.

Procedures

Explicit and often detailed procedures for managing students with AODA-related problems are a major component of student assistance program design. Procedures, as opposed to policies, serve the following ends:

1. They integrate the target groups, program functions, roles, structures, and services that are to be provided to individual students.

2. They assure due process to students and parents in the implementation of school board policy on alcohol/drug-related problems.

3. They assure due process to the staff: any staff person can ask about the outcome of a particular procedural step taken on a student's behalf, knowing what should have come before, and what should come next.

4. They reflect "decision points" along the program functions: no student exits the program without the knowledge and consent of members of the Core Team.

Thus, procedures need to define the sequence of steps that follow identification, taking into account the circumstances under which the student is identified and the nature of the referring person. For example,

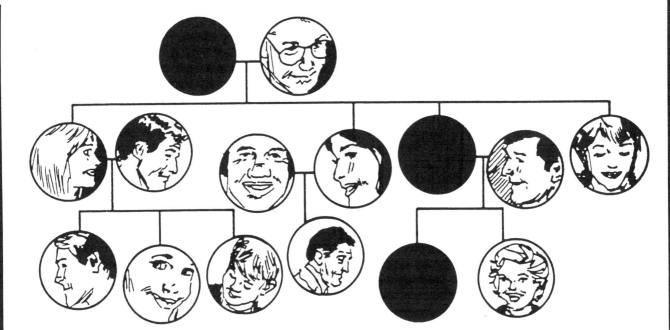

Figure 6.3

THE BUILDING-LEVEL CORE TEAM

STUDENT ASSISTANCE PROGRAM COORDINATOR

CORE TEAM MEMBERS

*Principal   Coach(s)
*Assistant Principal(s)   Nurse
*Counselor(s)   Interested Teachers
*School Social Worker(s)   Students
*School Psychologist(s)   Parents

ROLES

SAP Coordinator
SAP Counselor(s)
SAP Contact Person(s)
Group Facilitators

STRUCTURES

| Screening Team | | Referral Team |

* Indicates necessary membership in the building-level Core Team.

procedures will have to distinguish between "witnessed" violations of statutes and school policies and "suspected" drug involvement based on a pattern of declining school performance or other behavioral indicators. The issue of "dealing," or the delivery of controlled substances, often requires distinct procedures. Similarly, self-referrals are typically handled differently than "mandated" referrals. It is easy to foresee a host of other issues that require clear and definite procedural guidelines: the interaction at school-wide AODA policies with athletic codes, confidentiality for self-referrals, coping with in-school drug overdose situations, and so on (see Chapter 12).

District-wide Organization

Seldom will an effective program arise spontaneously from a district-wide organizational chart. More often, the organizational structure emerges as the program is on its way. However, in designing the program it is useful to have some idea of its global nature. In the most effective programs, district-wide organization achieves a consistency within the program that is balanced by a considerable degree of autonomy and freedom at the individual building level. District-wide organization is also an obvious reflection of the fact that the program is conceived of as district-wide in scope: it is not a small-scale effort of a few individuals on behalf of a minority of students.

As illustrated in Figure 6.4, the major district-wide structure is the Core Group; the major district-wide role is that of the Student Assistance Program Administrator or Program Director.

The District-Wide Core Group. The Core Group can be thought of as comprised of two blocks of people: (1) the individual Core Teams in each building, and (2) community representatives: parents, clergy, juvenile justice officials, youth services workers, AODA agency staff, and other interested and concerned citizens. In larger school districts, relevant members of the district-wide administration may also be included. The major functions of the District-wide Core Group are (1) to oversee the implementation, operation, and maintenance of the program, (2) to evaluate the program's effectiveness and recommend changes and expansions, and (3) to provide a link to the community as a whole within which community-wide responses to AODA problems can be initiated. Through the activities of the district-wide Core Group the program achieves its joint school-community character. For example, in one community the funding for the Student Assistance Program was shared equally by a Chemical People organization, the school board, and the village board.

The SAP Program Administrator/Director. The role of SAP Program Administrator in a small school district may be performed by an existing staff person; often it is someone in a position which already has district-wide responsibility for curriculum or pupil services. In a larger district, especially following the program's initial implementation, it may require creating a new position.

The SAP Program Administrator/Director bears the same relationship to the district-wide Core Group as the SAP Coordinator bears to the Core Team, but has responsibilities relating to the program as a whole. She may, for example, be primarily involved when issues affecting the district-wide functioning of the program arise, including funding decisions, presentations to the Board of Education, representing the program to the community at large, preparing annual evaluation reports, arranging for staff training, etc. (See Supplement 6.2).

In conclusion, it is true that anyone working with students will be conscious of their role in building a trusting relationship as well as in upholding standards of satisfactory conduct and performance. However, one of the principles behind the design of the student assistance approach is the recognition and separation of the supervisory and facilitative roles, embodying each in formal program structures. If it is possible to bifurcate the program, it would be into those roles and structures that are responsible for implementing school policy regarding AODA-related problems, and those engaged in forming the safe and trusting relationships with students that are necessary for bringing about an acceptance of the need for help. The former upholds standards of conduct and enforces consequences; the latter offers the help required to meet those standards. Once segregated, however, everything else about the program must be directed to harmoniously integrating these two roles to carry out the program's six basic functions.

Figure 6.4

THE DISTRICT-WIDE CORE GROUP

STUDENT ASSISTANCE PROGRAM ADMINISTRATOR

BUILDING-LEVEL CORE TEAMS

HIGH SCHOOL CORE TEAM(s)	*MIDDLE SCHOOL CORE TEAM(s)*	*ELEMENTARY SCHOOL CORE TEAM(s)*

MEMBERS FROM DISTRICT ADMINISTRATION

Superintendent
Board Member(s)
Directors of Instruction, Guidance, Special Education, Elementary Education, Secondary Education, Athletics, etc.

COMMUNITY REPRESENTATIVES FROM:

Area Clergy
Alcohol/Drug Agencies
Juvenile Justice System
Police and Sheriff's Departments
County Human Services Agencies
Community Recreation Services
Service Clubs and Organizations
Parent Organizations
Community Alcohol/Drug Task Forces, Etc.

Chapter 6 | Supplements

Supplement 6.1,"Role of the SAP Counselor/ Coordinator," describes the responsibilities associated with this role at the individual building level. The SAP Counselor typically has responsibilities involving face-to-face contact with students identified and referred to the program by others. This role will usually be taken on by existing pupil services staff who are appropriately trained to cope with AODA-related issues. In many schools, however, any appropriately trained individual may be designated one of several "SAP Counselors." The SAP Coordinator's role is more often limited to overseeing various tasks during the implementation, operation, and maintenance of the program within the individual building. In smaller school systems, the two sets of tasks are frequently combined within a single individual. In larger school systems, one individual takes on the program management tasks, and shares other functions with one or more members of the Core Team designated as SAP Counselors.

Supplement 6.2, "Role of the Student Assistance Program Director," describes the basic responsibilities of the Student Assistance Program Director at the district-wide level. As noted in the text, in smaller school systems this role, too, is often performed by an existing staff person who already has district-wide responsibilities. In larger systems, a new position is often created to coordinate this program.

Supplement 6.1

ROLE OF THE SAP COUNSELOR/COORDINATOR

The role of SAP Counselor/Coordinator, as the title implies, combines counseling and coordinative functions. In smaller school systems or school buildings a single individual frequently performs all the functions listed below. In larger school settings the building level SAP Coordinator retains the program management functions, and the remaining tasks are carried out by one or more individuals designated as SAP Counselor(s). The SAP Coordinator and those designated as SAP Counselors are always members of the building's Core Team and participate in its tasks during the program's development and maintenance as well. If, however, all of the responsibilities of the Student Assistance Program Counselor/Coordinator could be the province of a single individual in a school building, they would include counseling, education, and program management functions as follows:

COUNSELING TASKS:

1. Consult with school staff who are considering the referral of a student to the SAP to clarify the nature of the student's personal and/or performance problem and the appropriateness of a referral to the student assistance program;

2. Receive referrals (from the referral sources identified in Figure 6.2) of students who are suspected of having AODA-related problems;

3. Participate in the process of assessing the nature and scope of a student's AODA involvement by gathering data concerning the student through one or more of the following:

    - reviewing the student's school performance records
    - interviewing teachers concerning the referred student
    - consulting other school staff
    - interviewing the student on a one-to-one basis
    - contacting parents or significant others
    - contacting community agencies or professionals who may have information regarding or contact with the student;

4. Recommend a course of action to the student and/or others in the school (e.g., principal, coach, Core Team, etc.) based on data collected as part of the preliminary assessment;

5. Meet with the student (and with parents and school staff when necessary) to make referrals to in-school services, AODA agencies in the community, or to non-AODA-related sources of help;

6. Work with treatment agencies by providing them with information, attending meetings of treatment program staff, and facilitating the re-entry process for students returning to the school setting;

7. Provide appropriate feedback to referral sources on the recommendations and disposition of referred students;

8. Assist in screening students for appropriate placement in support groups

9. Function as a co-facilitator in one or more support groups.

EDUCATION TASKS:

1. Disseminate information about alcohol and other drugs and their related problems to students as part of the assessment process or through routine one-to-one counseling sessions;

2. Educate students about AODA-related problems, the Student Assistance Program, its policies, procedures, and staff, through classroom presentations;

3. Participate in the design and delivery of appropriate staff inservice presentations regarding student AODA-related problems and the school's program;

4. Participate in the design and delivery of appropriate educational programs for parents and the community regarding alcohol and other drug abuse and the school's student assistance program.

PROGRAM MANAGEMENT TASKS:

1. Monitor individual students' progress in the program;

2. Ensure that procedures are being followed for individual students;

3. Evaluate the effectiveness of procedures within the building;

4. Keep statistics on the utilization of the program at the building level, including its impact (how many students are served), and its effectiveness (how students are better as a result);

5. Function as chairperson of the Core Team;

6. Report to the principal and other staff on the program's effectiveness;

7. Monitor the functioning of support groups including the selection, training, and performance of support group facilitators;

8. Identify additional training needs of those with formal roles in the program (e.g., SAP Counselors, group facilitators, etc.);

9. Serve as liaison to local parent or community groups within the school building's attendance area;

10. Work with the building administrator to identify and allocate staff and budgetary resources for the program in the building;

11. Serve as liaison between the building Core Team and the district-wide Core Group.

Supplement 6.2

ROLE OF THE STUDENT ASSISTANCE PROGRAM DIRECTOR

The district-wide Student Assistance Program Director coordinates all aspects of the student assistance program's functioning, during the phases of design and implementation, daily operation, and maintenance (Part Four). She frequently functions as the chairperson of the district-wide Core Group. In smaller school systems, the SAP Director may perform all of the functions identified alone. In larger school systems, the Program Director assures that the tasks are carried out but shares responsibility for them with other members of the Core Group. If they were embodied in one individual, the responsibilities of the Program Director during the operation and maintenance of the program would usually include the following:

1. Functioning as chairperson of the district-wide Core Group;

2. Monitoring the implementation of the district-wide AODA policies and procedures;

3. Meeting regularly with building-level SAP Counselor/Coordinators, Core Teams, and group facilitators;

4. Scheduling regular meetings of the district-wide Core Group;

5. Identifying building-level and district-wide issues for inclusion on the agenda of Core Group meetings;

6. Assisting in the design and implementation of a process for evaluating the program, including:

   - formulation of consistent, district-wide goals and objectives for the program and its various services (e.g., support groups)
   - design of data collection instruments
   - collection of data from individual, building-level components of the program
   - preparation of periodic and/or annual evaluation reports based on information collected from SAP Counselor/Coordinators and Core Teams

7. Overseeing the programs's budget, including

   - identifying budgetary needs at the building level for personnel, materials, and training;
   - preparing budget reports and requests for the Board of Education
   - identifying other sources of funding in the community
   - seeking funding through grants

8. Reporting regularly to the Board of Education and District Administrator on the status of the Program;

9. Serving as liaison with the rest of the community and as spokesperson for the school's program;

10. Developing and maintaining effective working relationships between the school and alcohol/drug abuse service providers.

11. Maintaining contacts with other school systems which have implemented student assistance programs;

12. Coordinating the involvement of other members of the Core Group in the tasks above.

Chapter 7 | Early Identification

The identification of students who have AODA-related problems is obviously a necessary though not a sufficient condition for any successful assistance program. In addition, students must be identified in proportion to their numbers, and identification should occur as early as possible in the development of problems. On the individual level, in order to identify a student as being in need of assistance one must have a clear idea of identification criteria (what to look for), must know the procedure to utilize, and must possess certain skills in bringing the student to the attention of building AODA specialists (i.e., SAP Counselor/Coordinator, Core Team members, etc.). At the program level, the school must cultivate a variety of identification resources (as in Figure 6.1). It must also bear in mind that students may be identified as needing help because of their own chemical use, because of concern about someone else's, or because they are in the process of early recovery from chemical dependency. The degree to which the school integrates these two levels, within each building as well as on a district-wide basis, will determine how successful it is in carrying out the identification function.

It is also vital to identify students who have AODA-related problems as early as possible for several reasons. The earlier students are identified, the less they will have been damaged by their own chemical use or by that of family members. Also, since the severity of denial progresses along with the disease, the earlier students are identified the less resistant they are to accepting the need for help. Early identification is also associated with a greater motivation to make use of the assistance services that are offered.

Early identification is best achieved by (1) promoting wide staff involvement at all levels in reporting suspected as well as witnessed AODA problems, (2) by promoting student self-referrals and peer referrals, and (3) by promoting referrals fom parents. The first can be achieved by defining all school staff as having a role in early identification and providing them with the necessary identification and referral skills. The latter two are achieved, over time, as students and families begin to perceive the school's student assistance program as a credible one: as safe, confidential, and helpful.

Consequently, this chapter will concentrate on the specific role of school staff and other referral sources in early identification and on the procedures for identifying students who are affected by their own chemical use or by concern over another's. In general, students are identified to the SAP Counselor/Coordinator or other members of the Core Team, as in Figure 7.1.

The Role of Instructional Staff

As the person in the best position to observe and note changes in student conduct on a regular, daily basis, the classroom teacher plays the most vital role in the early identification of students who may have AODA-related problems. In large part, the role of the classroom teacher as well as of other staff will depend on the school's ability to distinguish between witnessed and suspected instances of student alcohol/drug involvement in its policies and procedures.

Witnessed Use

The role of the staff member is clearest in the case of "witnessed use," or the firsthand observation of instances where students are violating school policies (and state, federal, and local ordinances) against

> *the manufacture, possession, use, delivery, or sale of alcohol or other mood-altering drugs on school grounds or at school-sponsored activities.*

Thus, if a staff member witnesses a violation of such a policy during the school day, he should take a number of steps, including the following:

1. Obtain the student's name;

2. Inform the student of the apparent violation;

3. Note any others in the area who may also have witnessed the student's behavior or conduct;

4. Confiscate the chemical and/or any evidence of its use;

5. Escort the student to the office of the principal or her designee;

6. Document and report details of the incident to the principal and/or her designee.

Should the incident occur outside the school building or after the normal school day (e.g., at a football game, on a marching band trip, etc.), the staff member would do all except step 5. In either case, as Figure 7.1 indicates, the principal would take the standard disciplinary steps as spelled out in the school's alcohol/drug policy as soon as possible. The SAP Counselor/Coordinator and/or the Core Team members need to become involved immediately to begin the assessment process (Chapter 8). Disciplinary action alone seldom has a corrective impact on alcohol and other drug abuse.

Students who are heavily intoxicated or who are incapacitated (e.g., who are unable to walk or who are incoherent) may be suffering from a drug overdose. Such intoxication should always be regarded as a medical emergency and responded to in the same manner as other medical emergencies. The staff member should follow existing procedures by involving other staff members, who should arrange for transportation to emergency medical services, including detoxification. Appropriate disciplinary action and subsequent assessment by the Core Team would be mandatory follow-up steps.

Suspected AODA Involvement

In most school settings, students in either of the situations above will be in the minority compared to the numbers of students who are harmfully involved with alcohol and other drugs. Thus, an essential aspect of early identification involves not waiting for students to exhibit overt, unmistakable alcohol/drug violations in school. Just what to look for instead has not always been clear.

In the past, staff members have often received inservice training on the "signs and symptoms" to look for in identifying drug-involved students. Many have been instructed to look for telltale signs of dubious validity, including students who habitually wear sunglasses (to hide bloodshot eyes or dilated pupils), or who habitually wear long-sleaved shirts (to cover needle marks). One early publication admonished teachers to be alert for student who have green tongues, caused by the use of breath mints to cover the smell of alcohol on the breath. On the more rational side, teachers have also been asked to look for more realistic physical signs of alcohol/drug use, such as slurred speech, dilated or constricted pupils, staggering, incoherent speech, and so on.

Aside from the absurdity of some of these examples, such an approach to identification suffers from two common flaws. In the first place, concentrating on such physical signs is prone to error because they are not necessarily connected to drug abuse: they may frequently indicate the existence of other medical prob-

Figure 7.1
EARLY IDENTIFICATION

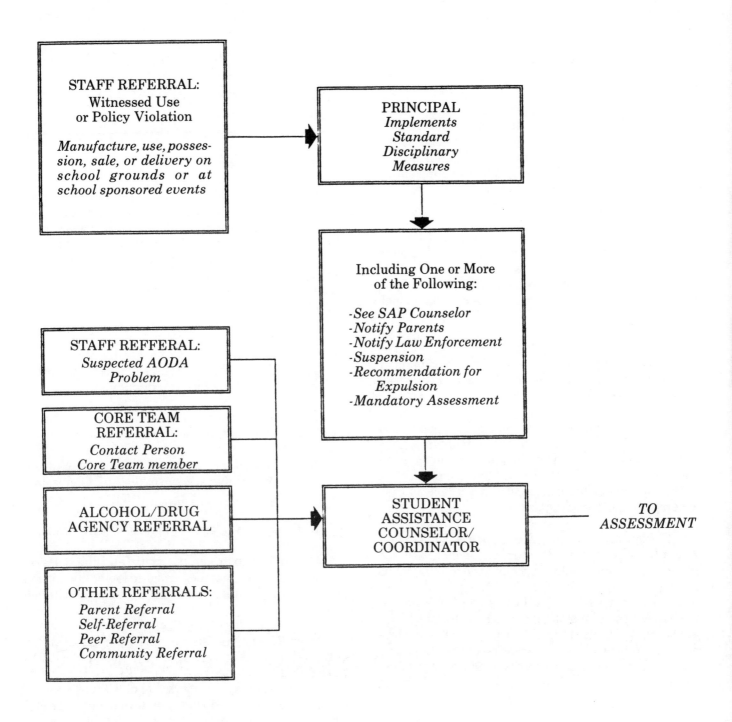

lems as well. Secondly, if these are indeed signs of intoxication they are most likely to be late indications of alcohol/drug use. In other words, by the time students are exhibiting physical symptoms which are apparent to the lay person within the school, they have most likely been involved with alcohol or other drugs for some time—frequently for several years. Moreover, in many of these instances there are other signs which would have indicated a problem within a few months of the onset of chemical use: school performance indicators.

Thus, early identification involves being alert to any unexplained change in the pattern of a student's behavior, conduct, and/or academic performance—especially where such changes represent a decline. Most schools implementing student assistance programs forsake the reliance on the "signs and symptoms" approach in favor of the "school performance" approach, often utilizing a form (similar to Supplement 7.1) to enable teachers and other staff to observe and document such patterns of performance.

Note that a student may be identified by a definite and repeated pattern of behavior and not on the basis of a single incident, such as "sleeping in class." Teachers are routinely expected to deal with students by using normal corrective measures for isolated incidents rather than referring the student to the student assistance program. The referral form also recognizes that there are some overt signs of harmful alcohol/drug involvement, but that these are relatively few in number and will usually be accompanied or preceded by other behavioral changes.

Note, too, that a student's behavior problems may be the result of living with a family member who is chemically dependent. The stress of living in a chemically dependent family can cause the same patterns of decline in school performance in a student as may accompany her own drug use.

Finally, just by utilizing a form such as Supplement 7.1, or by referring a student to the student assistance program staff, the teacher is not labeling the student as having a "drug problem." In fact, the school performance approach eliminates the need for "labeling," or the expectation that staff members need to "diagnose" the student. At this stage, the only "problem" the student has is his inability to perform satisfactorily. The referral form is used solely to document observations, to facilitate the referral to the SAP staff, and to begin the data collection that is part of the assessment process.

As Chapter 6 pointed out, "assessment" and "intervention" are inter-related. In what has been described thus far, the staff person can be thought of as

having performed a very rudimentary level of assessment: she has gathered information about a student's behavior and decided that it represents a problem. To bring that information and/or the student himself to the addention of others—to make referral—is an interventive step.

"As the person in the best position to observe and note changes in student conduct on a regular, daily basis, the classroom teacher plays the most vital role in the early identification of students who may have AODA-related problems."

The Referral Process

Generally, the school must develop a referral process based on the expectation that staff will refer. Beyond this minimum expectation, that process should also allow the individual staff member to define the nature and degree of his own participation. Once a staff member becomes aware that a student's behavior is unusual or unacceptable she can take one or more alternative courses of action:

1. Do nothing at all;

2. Utilize standard measures to correct the problem in performance or conduct;

3. Confer with the SAP Counselor/Coordinator if the unacceptable performance continues;

4. Complete and submit a Student Assistance Program Referral Form to the SAP Counselor/Coordinator;

5. Conduct a referral interview with the student.

Figure 7.2 illustrates the steps and the decision process that staff members may follow in identifying and referring students to the student assistance program.

Step 1. The first step involves the identification criteria discussed above as part of making a decision regarding a "suspected use" referral. The step involves recognizing specific behaviors that constitute a behavior or performance problem, a pattern of behavior that represents a change, and/or specific AODA-related facts. Becoming aware of a performance problem presupposes that the individual has clear standards of performance and a clear notion of what constitutes responsible behavior on the part of students.

Figure 7.2

STAFF REFERRAL PROCESS: "Suspected Use"

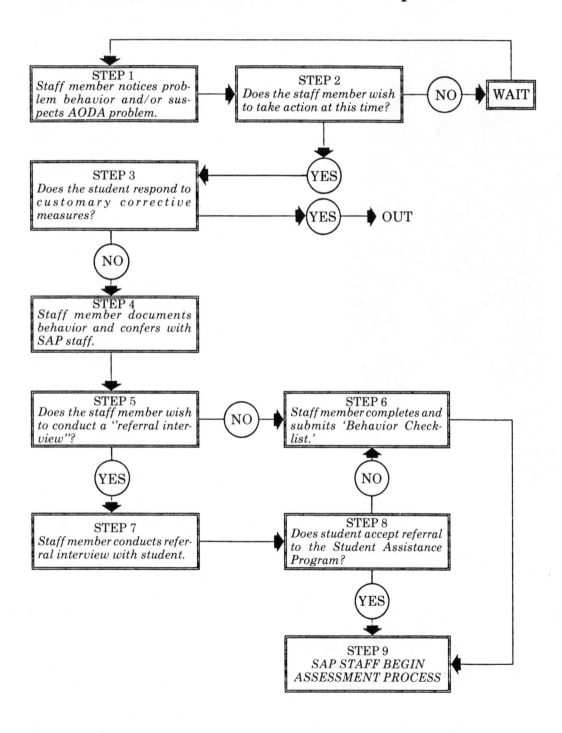

Step 2. The next step requires a decision as to whether or not to take any action. In some cases that staff member may decide not to act out of fear of getting involved, fear of the consequences of taking action, or out of indifference. At times a decision is made to postpone immediate steps in order to gain more information.

Step 3. In Step 3 the staff member takes usual and customary corrective measures. It typically includes conferring with the student, explaining in what ways his behavior and/or performance is unacceptable, stating the consequences for failure to improve, and discussing strategies for making improvements. If the student responds, and performance and behavior improve, no further action may be necessary. If the staff member has factual evidence that the student is harmfully involved with alcohol or other drugs, she may go on to the next steps.

Step 4. Some students, however, are unable or unwilling to change their behavior in response to these measures. Sometimes other problems, including alcohol and other drug abuse, render them incapable of changing by themselves or of maintaining changes for any period of time. If students fail to respond to the usual, conventional corrective measures at the staff member's disposal it is necessary to begin involving other people. At Step 4 one makes a decision to refer the student to the student assistance program, using either a referral form or a referral interview. The student has now demonstrated a pattern of unacceptable performance and an inability or unwillingness to change. Conferring with SAP staff members allows one to convey information, verify one's perceptions, and plan an additional course of action.

Step 5. Step 5 involves the staff member in a decision as to whether he wishes to confront the student again in a "referral interview" which is designed to motivate the student to accept help via the student assistance program. Staff members are not obligated to hold such referral interviews with students. There are many understandable reasons for not wanting to become personally involved any further at this point. Sometimes the student-teacher relationship has deteriorated to the point where a confrontation would be unproductive. Other staff members might feel that they lack the skills to carry out such an interview. Conducting the confrontation is also optional since there are other avenues for bringing about the referral.

Step 6. Whether one decides to hold a referral interview or not, it is necessary to relay documentation concerning the problem behavior to the SAP Counselor/Coordinator. Supplement 7.1 provides a typical format which teachers can use to communicate their concerns and observations regarding troubled students to the SAP staff.

Step 7. The referral interview is a brief meeting, perhaps no longer than five or ten minutes, between the staff member and the student. In conducting a successful referral interview it is important for the staff member to have a clear agenda in mind and to adhere to it. The major components of such an agenda include (1) communicating care and concern, (2) sharing the specific factual data that has led to one's concern, (3) expressing a realistic goal for the student, and (4) indicating what consequences will follow failure to bring performance or behavior up to acceptable levels. Supplement 7.2 summarizes the "DO's and DON'Ts" of the classroom teacher's role in early identification and the referral interview.

Step 8. Step 8 is actually part of the referral interview. By its close, the student should have indicated whether or not she accepts a referral to the SAP Counselor/Coordinator. It is important to remember that the success of the interview does not depend on whether or not the student accepts or rejects the referral (i.e., agrees to see the SAP staff), but rather upon the staff member's decision to involve other people in the process from this point on.

Step 9. Step 9 is actually the beginning of the assessment process. Whether or not the student accepts the referral, the staff member formally submits his data and the SAP staff begin the process of gathering additional information to discover the nature and scope of a student's alcohol/drug involvement, if any, and the services most likely to be of help.

"Schools which have taken steps to minimize the stigma associated with alcoholism and to break the "no talk rules" surrounding it regularly discover that 20 percent of the student body comes forward voluntarily to seek information, assistance, or placement in an "affected others group."

Affected Family Members

Compared to the identification of students in trouble because of their own drug use, the identification of students who are affected by others' use of alcohol or other drugs can be made relatively simple. Staff referrals are often precipitated by self-disclosures which students make about their home lives to trusted teachers. Suggesting that the student see the SAP staff, or bringing this information to the SAP staff would be routine steps. Staff members can also be sensitized to children of alcoholics issues and in what to look for in classroom behavior. All staff should be made aware of the fact that approximately 25 percent of students in their classrooms are children of alcoholics. Inservice time should also be spent in alerting staff to the typical behavioral responses of children to alcoholism in a parent and in explaining the process by which they can make referrals to Core Team members of students exhibiting such behaviors (e.g., patterns of compulsive overachievement, marked withdrawnness, rebelliousness and acting out). Many of the behaviors listed in Supplement 7.1 are typical of children of alcoholics, so referral to the program through this avenue is possible.

However, most students at any age level who are concerned about the alcohol/drug use of family members can be identified through self-referral if the school takes appropriate steps to attract them. Among such steps would be the following:

1. Providing brief classroom presentations on the nature of drug use, abuse, and dependency, and their affects on families;

2. Informing students that there are many others with such problems, that they are not alone, and that it is not their fault;

3. Announcing the availability of safe and confidential services in the school for students who want help or more information (e.g., support groups);

4. Providing students with a confidential mechanism for indicating their interest in joining a group or talking to a student assistance program counselor;

5. Creating an open, accepting, and nonjudgemental atmosphere in the classroom and elsewhere in the school.

Schools which have taken steps to minimize the stigma associated with alcoholism and to break the "no talk rules" surrounding it regularly discover that 20 percent of the student body comes forward voluntarily to seek information, assistance, or placement in an "affected others group." The response is generally greater at the elementary level. In any event, the identification of students concerned about or affected by others' chemical use is far more effective if it occurs through self-referral. Relatively few cases will be identified through formal staff referral mechanisms if the school has taken steps to permit students to feel safe in asking for help.

Identification by Other Staff

While they play perhaps the most important role, the task of early identification of students who have AODA-related problems does not fall solely on instructional staff. Principals, counselors, and other pupil services staff frequently have contact with students who come to their attention for a variety of reasons, which initially may appear unrelated to alcohol/drug problems. The major issue here is to be aware that the behavior being presented may or may not be related to a student's alcohol/drug use or to that of family members. Given the prevalence of alcohol and other drug abuse, assuming that it may be a factor in students' problems is safer than assuming that it is not.

Thus, principals, counselors, and other pupil services workers must become willing to include alcohol/drug questions when they interview or work with troubled or problem students who come to their attention. If a student is involved with alcohol and/or other drugs, a referral to the appropriate Core Team members should become routine.

Similarly, principals should seek the involvement of other Core Team members whenever alcohol/drug use is clearly involved in disciplinary problems. They should also become increasingly willing to take steps to identify the AODA-related experiences of any problem student as a part of the disciplinary process. For many students, alcohol/drug involvement or the related family problems will render the school's corrective disciplinary measures ineffectual unless and until these issues are addressed as well. In most instances, principals and pupil services staff will be members of the Core Team, making formal referral unnecessary.

The advent and increasing use of mini and microcomputers within school systems permits another avenue of early identification which does not rely upon waiting for students to become visible. Many school systems now routinely utilize computers to keep track of easily quantifiable student data, such as grades, attendance and absence patterns, tardiness, teachers' performance evaluations, and so on. When such data has been entered into a school's computer it is a relatively simple matter to discover baseline data that reflects the averages for the student body or the student population within a given building, and to search the file for those students whose behavior materially deviates from these norms. For example, if the average absenteeism rate is six per cent, the student attendance data base can be searched for those students whose absenteeism rate is above this point. The same can be done for other indicators. Even more powerful searches can be conducted involving the conjunction of several criteria: e.g., for students whose records indicate a higher than normal absenteeism rate, and a higher than normal tardiness rate, and whose grade point average is below 2.2, and whose teacher evaluations are below a certain score, etc.

Students whose names arise through these means need to be interviewed to discover what factors in their day to day lives, including alcohol and other drug abuse, might be causing these performance problems. It is also advisable to note whether currently unacceptable performance represents a change compared to previous performance levels.

Self, Peer, and Parent Referrals

Identifying students who have AODA-related problems on the basis of self-, peer, and parent referrals is important for several reasons. First, students who come to our attention through these avenues are typically identified earlier still in the disease process than through staff referral: those closest to the troubled student are in a better position than staff members to detect changes. Second, a milder degree of denial usually accompanies earlier identification. And third, self and family referrals indicate a greater degree of motivation to accept help and to change. Finally, self-, peer-, and family referrals usually mean that those who surround a student have become willing to get involved in helping them.

Initially, few students may be identified through these avenues because friends, parents, and students themselves are understandably reluctant to raise sensitive issues in an environment whose safety is uncertain. However, student assistance programs which have been in operation for two or more years typically report high rates of student self-referral, contacts by concerned peers, and referral by concerned parents or family members. In some schools, as many as 70 percent or more of all referrals to the program come through these channels. As noted above, most students with concerns about chemical dependency in family members seek help voluntarily in a successful program.

Self-, peer, and parent referrals will become frequent to the degree that the school's student assistance program has achieved credibility with these groups during the implementation, operation, and maintenance phases (see Part Four).

Self-Referrals. Before students will utilize the program they must first be made aware of its existence, of its services, of its policies, and of its personnel. Self-referrals occur when students voluntarily seek information or assistance from the SAP Counselor/Coordinator, SAP contact persons, or other members of the Core Team. They must be assured that these initial contacts are confidential: parents will not be notified immediately (if at all), the police will not be contacted, their disclosures will not result in a suspension from school, and so on. In general, effective policies contain assurances that students will not be punished or penalized for behavior that occurs prior to the point of self-referral.

Upon referral, the SAP Counselor/Coordinator meets with the student on a regular basis, as part of the assessment process, in order to discover the nature and extent of a student's alcohol/drug involvement, or the nature of their concern for another's drug use. The SAP Counselor/Coordinator can then recommend one or more definite courses of action for the student, as spelled out in the student assistance program's procedures (see Chapter 12).

Peer Referrals. Peer referrals often occur when students seek the advice of the SAP staff regarding another student. They may be concerned about another student's drug use or about a student's family situation. In working with such referring students the Core Team members will need to assure the student that her contact will be kept confidential. Often it will be necessary to explore with a student the difference between "narcing" and "helping" before she is comfortable in revealing information about a peer.

The SAP Counselor/Coordinator has two tasks at this point: beginning the data collection process that is part of assessment for the referred student, and working with the referring student on how she might continue to interact with her friend. A principle to be honored is "the person who comes to me is my client." Thus, the referring student frequently needs help in how to talk to her friend about her concern, information about "enabling," and help in identifying and expressing feelings about the friend in trouble.

Parent Referrals. To the extent that they know of the program and perceive it to be credible, safe, and confidential, parents will also contact the school for information and assistance in dealing with a child. Parents often do not risk contacting the school unless there has been a crisis or they have been involved with the SAP staff beforehand. Following initial contacts the SAP staff again has two tasks. The first is to begin collecting data on the student as part of the assessment process within the school. The second is to work with the parent or family member to discover the nature and extent of the student's AODA-involvement and related behavior at home. This will frequently entail first educating parents about the possible effects of their child's alcohol/drug abuse, about behavioral signs and symptoms (Supplement 7.3), and about parental enabling (Supplement 5.2).

AODA Agency and Community Referrals

To the extent that they are also aware of the school's program and its policies, services, and contact staff, a student may be referred to the school from local alcohol/drug agencies or from other segments of the community. Chemical dependency treatment programs will naturally refer students who are in treatment back to the school, identifying those recovering students who are likely to benefit from a support group. Local agencies that perform screening, assessment, or education services for alcohol and other drug abuse will recommend the school's services to families only if they know of and trust them. Establishing these referral and working relationships requires the school's SAP staff to do considerable outreach. Often it is the school that must initiate and cultivate these contacts with the AODA service community.

Aside from AODA agencies, students often become identified or referred to the school's student assistance program from other segments of the community. Members of the local clergy are continually working with families and individuals in distress, and a great proportion of these individual and family problems are alcohol/drug-related. The same is true of police departments, departments of social services, mental health centers, and other counseling services. All of these are in a position to refer children and families to the school's student assistance program services as additional sources of help. The working relationships which result in joint school/community referral arrangements are best initiated and cultivated during the early stages of program implementation.

Every school can identify those few students whose alcohol and other drug-related problems have grown so severe as to become unavoidable. The task is to identify AODA-involved students in proportion to their numbers, to identify not just the harmfully involved students but also those concerned about or affected by others' drug use, and to identify all of them as early in the progression of problems as possible. This entails the development of identification strategies that focus on all school staff as well as on students, families, and the community at large. Students will be identified to the program through these avenues only to the degree that referral sources are made aware of the program, of its services and contact personnel, and of the process for getting involved. Finally, the school must take steps to build the program's credibility with students, staff, and parents if they are to participate in identifying troubled students.

| Chapter 7 | # Supplements |

Supplement 7.1, "Student Assistance Program Referral Form," is an example of the type of behavior checklist which school staff can utilize in documenting their observations of unacceptable student conduct and in making a formal referral to the school's student assistance program. Note that it is not intended to be used to refer students on the basis of a single behavioral incident but to document the pattern of behavior that represents a change over time.

The form itself can be used to develop a generic behavior checklist which can be utilized in the identification of any student with any problem. Such a generic form may have a place for the referring staff member to indicate the type of program they have in mind for the student (e.g., student assistance program, dropout prevention, gifted and talented, etc.). Some schools have found that a short, half-page form is just as useful if it allows the staff member to indicate the general categories of behavior that precipitates the referral.

Supplement 7.2, "Referral Interview Guidelines," summarizes the concepts describing the classroom teacher's role in referring students who have been identified as needing help.

Supplement 7.3, "For Parents: Signs of Problem Use," is a lengthy list of behavioral signs that may be associated with adolescent drug use that has progressed to serious stages. It is intended to assist parents in identifying the signs and symptoms which may indicate a serious problem. School SAP staff may find it a useful tool in educating the parents of students about whom the school has developed a concern. It can also lead parents to gather important data as part of the assessment process.

Supplement 7.4, "Staff Referral Feedback Form," is one example of the mechanism for responding to staff referrals. Something of this sort is necessary, as staff frequently need to know that a student is receiving help and that their referral has been successful.

Supplement 7.1

STUDENT ASSISTANCE PROGRAM REFERRAL FORM

Referral of troubled students must be based upon behavior which you have actually observed. As a rule, an isolated instance of poor or unsatisfactory performance will not be grounds for referring a student to the Student Assistance Program. However, whenever a student exhibits several of the following, or when there is a definite and repeated pattern of behavior in an unacceptable direction, a referral to the SAP staff is appropriate.

Please give this form to the Student Assistance Program Coordinator in your building.

Student _____ Grade_____

Referral Date _____ Referred by _____

PLEASE CHECK RELEVANT ITEMS and COMMENT:

I. ACADEMIC PERFORMANCE   *COMMENTS*
_____ Decline in quality of work
_____ Decline in grade earned
_____ Incomplete work
_____ Work not handed in
_____ Failing in this subject

II. CLASSROOM CONDUCT   *COMMENTS*
_____ Disruptive in class
_____ Inattentiveness
_____ Lack of concentration
_____ Lack of motivation
_____ Sleeping in class
_____ Impaired memory
_____ Extreme negativism
_____ In-school absenteeism (skipping)
_____ Tardiness to class
_____ Defiance; breaking rules
_____ Frequently needs discipline
_____ Cheating
_____ Fighting
_____ Throwing objects
_____ Defiance of authority
_____ Verbally abusive
_____ Obscene language, gestures
_____ Sudden outbursts of temper
                                                    COMMENTS
_____ Vandalism
_____ Frequent visits to nurse, counselor
_____ Frequent visits to lavatory
_____ Hyperactivity, nervousness

III. OTHER BEHAVIOR

_____ Erratic behavior day-to-day
_____ Change in friends and/or peer group
_____ Sudden, unexplained popularity
_____ Mood swings
_____ Seeks constant adult contact
_____ Seeks adult advice without a specific problem
_____ Time disorientation
_____ Apparent changes in personal values
_____ Depression; low affect
_____ Defensiveness
_____ Withdrawal; a loner; separateness from others
_____ Other students express concern about a possible problem
_____ Fantasizing; daydreaming
_____ Compulsive overachievement; preoccupied with school success
_____ Perfectionism
_____ Difficulty in accepting mistakes
_____ Rigid obedience
_____ Talks freely about drug use; bragging
_____ Associates with known drug users

IV. POSSIBLE AODA-SPECIFIC BEHAVIORS

Witnessed	Suspected	
[ ]	[ ]	Selling; delivering
[ ]	[ ]	Possession of alcohol, drugs
[ ]	[ ]	Possession of drug paraphernalia
[ ]	[ ]	Use of alcohol, drugs
[ ]	[ ]	Intoxication
[ ]	[ ]	Physical signs, symptoms
[ ]	[ ]	Others?

What actions have you already taken? (E.g., shared concern and data with student, initiated consequences, parent contact, etc.).

What actions do you contemplate taking?

Supplement 7.2

FOR STAFF:
'REFERRAL INTERVIEW' GUIDELINES

On any given day, concerned teachers working with unrealistic expectations or vague guidelines attempt to confront students who they suspect have alcohol or other drug-related problems. In most cases such confrontations do not go well. Despite good intentions, the teacher often does not have a clear agenda in mind, or it may be an inappropriate one. Without a clear agenda, the anxious student and the uneasy teacher will both be led about by their defenses. Both often leave such interviews feeling uneasy at best; at worst, students feel angry and abused, and teachers feel inadequate and abused. On other occasions, teachers may think that they are obligated to contact parents about an alleged "drug problem," only to encounter a frightened, angry, and defensive family. Many staff members have had such experiences, which confirm their view that it is not their job to get involved in student alcohol/drug problems or student problems in general.

Because of the crucial role which teaching staff can play in the early identification of students with AODA-related problems, it is important to examine the ways in which such referral interviews, or confrontations, can be structured so that they have more constructive outcomes for both students and staff.

The most important factor in determining the success of a confrontation with a student is to scrupulously adhere to a concrete agenda which one has in mind beforehand. The following describes such an agenda and the common pitfalls to avoid in referring the troubled or problem student to the school's student assistance program staff. The most effective agenda consists of (1) expressing care and concern, (2) sharing specific, documented facts that legitimize concern, (3) expressing an appropriate and realistic goal, and (4) providing appropriate consequences for failure to improve performance or conduct.

CONCERN

The expression of care and concern in the interview is important as a means of setting its tone. Many students may expect judgement, blame, punishment, or anger on the basis of their past interactions with school staff or because they are themselves aware that their performance has been unacceptable. The fact that a teacher likes a student, is worried about changes, and is concerned about what may be going on with them will, in many cases, reduce a student's anxiety, defensiveness, and denial. In any event, any student deserves to be treated with respect and dignity.

SPECIFIC DATA

Specific information should be shared which legitimizes both the staff member's concern and her decision to confront the student. In most cases such information will not consist of an isolated incident but of a pattern of behavior which reflects a change in an unacceptable direction. Such information could refer to grades, attendance, classroom conduct, attitude and demeanor, or to any other facts of which the staff member is aware.

Especially useful, where it is true, is the fact that the current pattern of behavior represents not just a change in a negative direction, but a change from what the student used to be like. Any alcohol/drug specific information should also be included. The staff member should avoid communicating rumors, hearsay, or opinions as these invite denial and argument. It is also wise to avoid labeling (or "diagnosing") the student as having "a drug problem" or any other. The only "problem" about which the staff member can be certain consists of the facts themselves.

APPROPRIATE GOAL

In confronting students about problem behaviors, many staff will either not have a clear goal in mind or will become engaged in asserting an inappropriate one. A goal is inappropriate if it does not result directly in a student receiving help, or if it expects students to make changes of which they are incapable. Especially where alcohol and other drug abuse are concerned, the following are typically inappropriate as intended outcomes of the brief referral interview:

- wanting to "fix" the student
- wanting to control the student's behavior
- wanting to elicit an admission or confession of drug use
- expecting to stop or reduce the student's drug use
- expecting to gather information in order to diagnose the student
- wanting to gather information to gain certainty that there is a problem

As goals, these are usually beyond either the student or the staff member's control (e.g., stopping drug use). Often they will be irrelevant to bringing about a change in behavior. For example, even if a student did admit to drug use or to having a drug problem, something in addition would have to be done. The fact of the matter is, this "something else" can be done without such an admission. Pursuing unrealistic or inappropriate goals is one of the major factors which can contribute to an unsatisfactory outcome for the referral interview.

Especially where the staff member intends to get an admission of drug involvement and consequently to reduce or eliminate it, many staff members will resort to strategies to motivate students in this direction. Some of the more common and ineffective motivational strategies include:

- threats ("quit or else")
- appeals to the law ("don't you know it's illegal?")
- appeals to students' values ("it's immoral, evil;" "drugs are bad")
- appeals to reason (arguing, debating)
- appeals to the positive in students ("you're too smart to be using drugs;" "you're a good kid")
- appeals to the student/teacher relationship ("I know I can trust you to stop")
- eliciting promises to quit

Threats usually result in increased defensiveness. Appeals to laws, values, or intellectual issues merely invite arguments or debates ("marijuana is less harmful than alcohol," "what about your own drinking?") which sidetrack the interview and put the teacher on the defensive as well.

Thus, the absence of a clear, appropriate goal most often contributes to the unsuccessful outcome of such interviews, and also to the feelings of inadequacy, incompetence, powerlessness, and resentment on the part of the staff member.

The only appropriate goal for this type of referral interview is "I would like you to see Mr. Smith or Ms. Jones"—the Student Assistance Counselor/Coordinator. This is something which the student can do; it is a decision she can make. To assert this goal the staff member does not need to justify his perceptions, solicit admissions, or debate the relative merits of various drugs. Admissions, denials, and arguments are irrelevant.

CONSEQUENCES

Having shared her concern, the facts which precipitate it, and the request that the student contact the SAP staff, the staff member should then state two types of consequences. First are the usual corrective consequences which any staff member can assert and enforce if performance or classroom conduct does not improve within a specified period of time. Second, however, is the consequence that the staff person is going to speak with Mr. Smith or Ms. Jones about her concerns immediately. In other words, one consequence of the student's behavior is that the teacher is going to involve others—regardless of the student's decision to seek help or ability to improve his conduct. The goal and consequence are often expressed together: "I'd like you to see Mr. Smith or Ms. Jones, and I will be seeing them about my concerns later this afternoon."

If the student agrees to see the SAP Counselor/Coordinator the interview has succeeded. If the student does not agree, the interview has also succeeded: the teacher will report her concern to the appropriate SAP staff person, who will proceed with the assessment process (Chapter 8).

Adhering to or returning to this basic agenda increases the likelihood of a successful referral and of a respectful dialogue. For example, if a student interrupts, challenges, questions, accuses, debates, etc., the staff member can permit these reactions, always returning to the agenda to restate his concern, the specific facts behind it, the request that the student contact the SAP staff, and the information that he will be contacting the SAP staff about the matter anyway.

SUMMARY

FOR THE REFERRAL INTERVIEW:

1. Be observant. Note individual behaviors or patterns that you have seen and document them.

2. Be sensitive to unexplained changes in the student's behavior over time, and especially to a pattern of decline in performance.

3. Report evidence of concern to the SAP Counselor/Coordinator or other members of the Core Team, whether you confront a student personally or not.

4. Have a clear agenda in mind for the interview beforehand, and return to it whenever the conversation is diverted.

5. Express care and concern. Remain a sympathetic, nonjudgemental listener.

6. Explain that you need the student to know that you will be contacting the SAP staff about your concerns regardless of what the student decides to do.

7. If students voluntarily confide personal information regarding their own alcohol/drug use or that of friends and family, find an appropriate way of preserving the confidence as well as of protecting yourself. That is, whenever you are unwilling to accept responsibility for a student's unsafe situation or conduct, involve other people. Explain your need to do so in advance of making such a report. Confidentiality is never to be maintained when students are in actual or potential danger.

AVOID:

1. "Diagnosing" students. Few schools will have staff who are certified alcohol/drug counselors and who are qualified to diagnose whether a student is chemically dependent or not and what type of service he requires. Thinking that she must first "diagnose" a drug problem before anything can be done often prevents referrals or interferes with the referral interview.

2. "Counseling" students, or attempting to solve their problems by yourself. Alcohol/drug-related problems are among the most complex and resistant problems which young people can face. Attempting to resolve them oneself is a frequent instance of "enabling."

3. "Labeling" a student as a "drug abuser," "alcoholic," or "chemically dependent." Avoid judgemental terms such as "burnout," "junkie," "addict," etc. Aside from communicating negative attitudes, use of such terms places the staff member at risk of legal liability.

4. Contacting parents to inform them that their child has a "drug problem." Such information is more appropriately shared with SAP staff, who can decide when and how to involve parents once a referral has been made.

5. Becoming responsible for a student's drug-related problems (see number 7, above).

SUPPLEMENT 7.3

FOR PARENTS:
SIGNS OF PROBLEM USE OF ALCOHOL OR OTHER DRUGS

Adolescence can be a troubling, confusing time for both young people and their family members. In becoming alert to the possibility of an alcohol/drug problem, it is necessary to attempt to separate those adolescent behaviors which are transitory indications of the struggle to "grow up" from those which often indicate the presence of alcohol/drug abuse.

The following are offered as signs which may alert parents to potentially serious alcohol/drug involvement.

DECLINE IN SCHOOL PERFORMANCE:

[   ] An atypical decline in grades during the past year;
[   ] A rapid, recent decline in grades
[   ] Failure to inform parents of school events, including requests for parents to meet with teachers, suspensions, etc.
[   ] Loss of interest in school activities, including dropping out of athletics, clubs, or other extracurricular activities
[   ] Contacts from the school regarding truancy, tardiness, dropping classes, vandalism, fighting, thefts, or other unacceptable conduct

PROBLEMS WITH LAW ENFORCEMENT:

[   ] Arrests for driving while intoxicated (DWI)
[   ] Arrests for drinking/drug use at parties or in public places
[   ] Arrests for possession, delivery, or sale of alcohol or other drugs
[   ] Curfew violations
[   ] Other illegal acts which only occur when he/she is under the influence of alcohol or other drugs

PROBLEMS WITH FINANCES:

[   ] Involved in thefts
[   ] Family members begin missing money or valuables from the home
[   ] Frequent borrowing of money from family members or friends
[   ] Quitting a job and/or job loss due to unsatisfactory job performance
[   ] Inability to save money or to pay bills despite having a job or allowance
[   ] Sale of clothes, records, stereos, or other possessions
[   ] Appears to have sufficient spending money despite not having a job
[   ] Appears to have more spending money than allowance or job would provide
[   ] Is often seen exchanging money with friends

PERSONALITY CHANGES, EMOTIONAL PROBLEMS:

[   ] Frequent, extreme highs and lows
[   ] General change in mood toward a more depressed and negative or critical outlook
[   ] Withdrawal from family members

[ ] Is more secretive; stays physically isolated in room, withdraws into music
[ ] Increasing dishonesty; frequent lying; elaborate stories or excuses
[ ] Is increasingly defensive when asked about personal problems, when confronted with irresponsibility, etc.
[ ] Avoids communication with family members; spends a lot of time alone
[ ] Is increasingly angry, defiant
[ ] Is verbally and/or physically abusive
[ ] Exhibits general loss of energy, initiative, motivation, interest, or enthusiasm; is increasingly apathetic
[ ] Daily routine becomes inverted: frequently stays out late and sleeps late in the morning
[ ] General psychological impairment: inability to reason; memory loss; inability to think logically; feelings of paranoia

PHYSICAL PROBLEM:

[ ] Appears run-down; has frequent colds, flu, or other illnesses due to decreased immunity
[ ] Loss of normal appetite
[ ] Decline in personal hygiene; bathes infrequently, doesn't change clothes, etc.
[ ] Drastic weight gain or loss
[ ] Complexion appears unhealthy: is sometimes pale or flushed, has bloodshot eyes, face looks puffy
[ ] Has frequent injuries or bruises which may or may not have a satisfactory explanation (e.g., 'I just fell down')
[ ] Has self-inflicted tatoos, cigarette burns, scars
[ ] Suffers from insomnia or other sleep disturbances; or, chronic fatigue, tiredness;
[ ] Chronic dry cough
[ ] Changes in menstrual cycle

ALCOHOL/DRUG-SPECIFIC INDICATORS:

[ ] Adolescent vehemently asserts his/her right to drink or to get high
[ ] Smell of alcohol on the breath, or of marijuana on clothing
[ ] Bloodshot eyes, dilated or constricted pupils
[ ] Blackouts: inability to remember events which occur while out or while intoxicated
[ ] Presence of drug paraphernalia: roach clips, "bongs," cellophane bags, drug-related posters, cocaine spoons, cigarette papers, pipes, bottles, etc.
[ ] Discovery of unidentified pills or powders; discovery of alcohol, drugs, or paraphernalia among personal effects, especially when effort has gone into hiding them
[ ] Smell of incense in room or on clothing (to hide odor of marijuana)
[ ] Clothing with drug-related themes; drug-related drawings on books, clothing, or body
[ ] Returning home intoxicated; staggering, slurred speech, incoherence
[ ] Talks freely about getting high and uses a vocabulary typical among regular drug users
[ ] Family liquor supply dwindles, disappears, or gets watered-down
[ ] Medications begin disappearing from family medicine cabinet

DISRUPTION OF FAMILY RELATIONSHIPS:

[ ] Increasing irresponsibility in the family; fails to do chores, carry out normal tasks
[ ] Defies family rules without regard to consequences
[ ] Avoids or decreases participation in family social gatherings and rituals, such as holiday gatherings, vacations, meals, church activities, etc.

[   ] Increasingly feels like a stranger to the rest of the family
[   ] Behavior incites or aggravates increasing tension between parents
[   ] Is verbally or physically abusive to parents or siblings
[   ] Family members become more fearful of the adolescent
[   ] Stays out late or does not return home at all despite increasingly stringent consequences
[   ] Blames problems on parents and/or other family members;
[   ] Avoids contact with family members; goes immediately to room when returning home; is secretive about friends, phone calls, activities, or whereabouts
[   ] Family members become increasingly preoccupied with the adolescent as the center of their anger, apprehension, and suspicion, or of their care and concern.

SUPPLEMENT 7.4
STAFF REFERRAL FEEDBACK FORM

One of the ways to effectively build the credibility of the program is to provide adequate feedback to staff members who refer students to it. The SAP Counselor/Coordinator and other members of the Core Team need to steer a path midway between providing information which violates a student's rights to privacy and providing no information at all by invoking a narrow doctrine of "confidentiality." Rather than protecting a student's privacy, the latter more often reinforces the aura of secrecy that surrounds drug problems and isolates the program staff from the rest of the school. At worst, staff stop referring students to the program because they never find out what, if anything, was done.

While classroom teachers will rarely need to know personal information regarding a student, they do have a right to know that their referral was appropriate, that the program staff are in fact taking the steps they are supposed to take according to SAP policies and procedures, and that students are, in short, getting help.

The following is a sample form which SAP staff or Core Team members can utilize to provide referring staff members with useful and appropriate feedback regarding students. It should complement, not take the place of, face-to-face contacts between the referring staff member and SAP team members.

Note that nowhere does the form identify a student as having a "drug problem" or any other.

STAFF REFERRAL FEEDBACK FORM

TO:

FROM:

DATE:

RE: Status of your referral of _____ to the Student Assistance Program.

The following indicates the status of the student named above within the Student Assistance Program:

[   ] The in-school assessment process has begun, involving input from other staff;

[   ] A home contact has been made;

[   ] The student is involved in regular counseling interviews with _____ ;

[   ] The student has been referred to a support group in school;

[   ] The student has been referred for formal assessment and/or evaluation by a community agency;

[   ] The student has been referred to a treatment/rehabilitation program and should be returning to your classroom by _____ .
Please contact me regarding those assignments on which he/she may be working until returning to school.

[   ] Our assessment indicates no need for further action at this time;

[   ] Other: _____
_____ .

I will be happy to provide you with whatever additional information I can within the limits of privacy and confidentiality. I can be reached at_____ or in room_____ .

Chapter 8

Assessment

"If you hear hoofbeats going down the streets of your city, think "horses," not "zebras."

-Proverb

Of all the tasks which a student assistance program must perform, assessment is frequently the most misunderstood, difficult, time-consuming, and complex. Becoming clear about the meaning of the term and its application to managing students with AODA-related problems is a crucial step in designing a student assistance program.

In one school system, for example, the principal suspended three ninth grade boys for smoking marijuana in the hallways after school. The parents of all three complied with his requirement that each have an assessment done at a local AODA agency as a condition of being reinstated in school. Each did return, and each had a letter from the certified alcoholism counselor stating that he could find no alcohol or other drug problem in the boy concerned. The principal, angered by the report, telephoned the counselor and demanded how he could possibly have reached such a conclusion, since each boy had a history of frequent absenteeism, tardiness, poor grades, expressions of concern from staff, and belonged to a drug-using peer group. The counselor's only response was that he didn't know any of that information, and that if he had he would have come to a very different conclusion.

Examples such as this, illustrating only one of the difficulties involved in "assessment," can be multiplied indefinitely. Misconceptions about the meaning of "assessment" make it difficult to clarify the proper role of the school and its student assistance program in this process. It is not difficult to find people making a wide variety of claims about the term:

- "Assessment" refers to a single, brief counseling event;

- All of the information one needs in order to "do an assessment" can be gathered in a single "assessment interview." A student goes to a school counselor or to an outside agency and "has an assessment;"

- "Assessment" is the responsibility of one person in the school;

- "Assessment" means "diagnosis," or deciding that a student is or is not alcoholic or dependent on other drugs;

- The role of the school is to conduct a complete "assessment" in order to refer students directly to appropriate treatment programs;

- The school has no role in "assessment;" its role is, at most, to identify students and refer them immediately to community resources.

The major consequence of these misconceptions, taken alone or in combination, is that the school is often prevented from effectively managing students with AODA-related problems. It is typically impossible, for example, to determine in a brief one-hour interview whether a student is or is not likely to be chemically dependent. Moreover, many individuals, both within the school and on the outside, have frequent daily contact with students and thus have meaningful information regarding their behavior, which is vital to the assessment process. The amount of information, and the success of the process, is severely limited if assessment is the responsibility of only one individual. Furthermore, few school systems will have staff members with the clinical background, training, and skill to *diagnose* chemical dependency. On the other hand, all schools must gather some information in order to make a decision as to whether a referral to an appropriate community agency for a more in depth evaluation is called for.

To some extent the misconceptions about "assessment" result from semantic ambiguities; to some degree they stem from falsely dichotomizing the role of the school and the role of community AODA agencies. While the school's role in early identification is clear-cut, its role in the assessment process varies according to the availability of good AODA assessment services in the community.

The following definition of "assessment" is offered as a means of clarifying how the term will be used here:

> *Assessment is the process by which members of the SAP staff (a) gather information about referred students in order to determine the nature and scope of their AODA-related problems and their needs for help and (b) evaluate it in order to identify appropriate sources of help.*

No matter how the term is construed, adequately assessing the nature of students' alcohol/drug-related problems is further complicated by other factors. First, the nature of childhood and adolescent development makes the assessment of drug abuse and dependency more difficult in adolescents than in adults. Most adolescents lack stable, permanent patterns of values and of job, family, and social life, the interruption of which by drug abuse makes the assessment process comparatively simple in adults. Moreover, problem behavior may be due to drug abuse, to other problems, or may be a normal part of the adolescent's struggle for independence. Second, perhaps the most difficult assessment task is distinguishing between the adolescent who is abusing drugs and the one who shows definite signs of being chemically dependent. And yet the ability to make this distinction is vital to getting a student the appropriate help. Third, the presence of denial in students and their family members further complicates both the assessment and the intervention process by limiting the amount and nature of information the school can obtain. Finally, these obstructions are frequently augmented by the lack of appropriate knowledge and training in key staff members, and by poor communication between those systems (school, family, and community) which have meaningful data about students at risk.

The Role of the School

If the first function of a student assistance program is to find out *who* needs help, the assessment function seeks to discover *what* they have (the nature of the problem) and what they *need*. As used in Chapters 6 and 7, assessment can be thought of simply as the process of gathering and interpreting information; thus, even early identification involves assessment-like activity. In general, then, the term "assessment" really refers to a rather broad continuum of activities, with simple day-to-day observations on one extreme and clinical diagnosis on the other.

Three major tasks are involved in helping the school to clarify its role in the assessment process as part of its student assistance program. First, the school system will need to discover to what degree a continuum of AODA assessment services exist in the community. Discovering the boundary between it and these AODA services both defines the role of the school and clarifies the cooperative working relationships it must develop with these agencies. The parable of the principal and the three boys cited earlier illustrates that each institution had but a partial role to play in assembling sufficient information about students to know what form of help they required. Second, the school system and those with formal roles in its student assistance program will need to appreciate assessment as a process and not as a discrete counseling event.

The assessment interview is but one service or one source of information about a student in a process that involves many other people and which can take place over a period of months. Third, designing a program which effectively performs the assessment function entails providing key staff with appropriate training in alcohol and other drug abuse issues against which they can interpret the information they collect about students who are referred to the program.

The Assessment Continuum

The nature of this "assessment continuum" is depicted in Figure 8.1. Following identification, the next step in the assessment process can be thought of as "screening:" gathering enough additional information about the student in order to decide whether there is a significant problem of any type and whether or not the student is using alcohol or other drugs. Many community mental health centers, counseling clinics, and private practitioners perform this screening function. They will interview students and families and refer them to the appropriate source of help for what emerges as the focal "problem." They may refer to other programs or to their own services for this primary care. Obviously, it is crucial that screening agencies be skilled at dealing specifically with AODA-related problems (see Supplement 8.1, "Adolescent Assessment Services Checklist"). Thus, screening appropriately lies within the role of the school, can also be accomplished by community agencies, or can be done through cooperative working relationships between the two.

If there is reason to believe that alcohol or other drug abuse appears to be a major factor in a student's problems then the next step is AODA assessment proper: gathering information about the nature and scope of the student's alcohol/drug use and/or the degree to which he is affected by the drug abuse of someone else (typically a parent or sibling). Furthermore, the assessment staff (whether in the school or an outside agency) will need to evaluate the student's strengths, or his willingness and/or ability to change his behavior on his own or through the services available in school or the community. Many communities have a number of AODA assessment services available to them: local councils on alcoholism and drug abuse, AODA information and referral services, or AODA programs in county social services departments.

More formal or intensive "evaluation" services may be required, especially if students prove unable or unwilling to modify their behavior in response to services made available to them up to this point. Many chemical dependency treatment programs, for example, offer adolescent evaluation programs lasting several days. Such services are distinct from the treatment program itself. The data collected as a result of this more intensive evaluation are usually sufficient to determine whether formal treatment for chemical dependency is necessary or not.

While Figure 8.1 depicts the assessment continuum as a linear sequence, the process itself is more often cyclical. Each institution or agency essentially recapitulates the assessment process of the last, gathering additional information and interpreting it in order to recommend an appropriate next step, which may be a recommendation for a stronger variety of "assessment." The diagram also indicates that increasingly strong assessment services are required as drug abuse progresses and that school and agency roles may well overlap. The "I" indicates those points where intervention strategies may be required, again emphasizing that assessment and intervention form halves of a cyclical process. The existence of this continuum also clearly implies the need for case management, since someone needs to monitor where a given student is in this process.

Figure 8.1

THE ASSESSMENT CONTINUUM

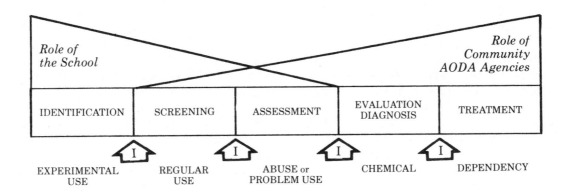

Figure 8.1 also demonstrates that it falls within the role of the school to do *some degree of assessment* short of actual diagnosis and/or treatment. How much assessment activity it engages in depends in large part on whether adequate AODA screening, assessment, or evaluation services exist in the community. To the extent that these services are not appropriate or conveniently available, the school system may have to define the roles of SAP staff more broadly or implement more sophisticated assessment services (e.g., use-focussed groups).

The Major Assessment Questions

Whether the focal point is the assessment continuum as a whole, the school system, the assessment agency, or the individual SAP Counselor working with an individual student referral, the assessment function can also be viewed as the process of gathering sufficient information about a student in order to answer a number of basic questions, as depicted in Figure 8.2:

1. *What is the nature and severity of a student's "problem?"* The first task following identification and referral to the SAP staff involves discovering the degree to which personal, family, social, and school behavior indicate that a student is indeed "troubled." At this point, assessment focuses on general lifestyle information. In part, this allows the SAP Counselor to evaluate the appropriateness of the referral: was the referral precipitated by an isolated incident ('sleeping in class') or are there reasonable grounds to continue exploring the student's situation? This initial "screening" allows the SAP Counselor to gain a sense of whether the unacceptable behavior is transient, a normal part of adolescent testing ('a bad case of the sixteens') or is representative of a more serious difficulty. The counselor can also gain a sense of whether other non-AODA-related problems are present: child abuse, sexual abuse, depression, suicidal tendencies, and so on.

2. *What is the nature of the student's alcohol/drug use?* Though all students who come to the attention of pupil services staff should be questioned regarding their alcohol/drug use, regardless of the presenting problem or the nature of the referral, this is a mandatory obligation of the SAP Counselor. Someone has to "ask the chemical questions." Initially, one is interested in whether or not the student has any experience with alcohol or other drugs. Insofar as possible at this point, specific information about the kinds of drugs, amounts, and frequencies of use should be sought. Where there is no evidence of alcohol or other drug use, other problems identified can be pursued. Where the student discloses alcohol or other drug experiences, the SAP Counselor will need to pursue additional information about them.

3. *What is the scope of the student's alcohol/drug involvement?* Where alcohol/drug use coexists with other problems an attempt must be made to discover the relationship of chemical use to these other difficulties. Drug use and problems can be related in a number of ways: life problems can be either the causes or the consequences of drug abuse. Drug abuse can complicate other problems the student is having, or can interfere with their resolution. Wherever chemical use has progressed beyond experimentation or places the student in unsafe situations it is advisable to focus attention on it as a primary problem and initiate attempts to modify it in the direction of abstinence.

4. *To what degree is the student willing or able to change his alcohol/drug behavior?* As part of the data collection process it is necessary to form a sense of the strengths in the student and her environment—those personal, social, family, and school factors that will support a change in the student's chemical use. Where the student appears capable of modifying his chemical use "by himself," utilizing in-school services, these would be appropriate recommendations. Where the student is involved in serious drug abuse, where there is considerable denial, where the personal and environmental supports for change appear to be lacking, or where the school does not provide services to address these issues, a referral to outside AODA agencies is the logical recourse.

Concerns about family members are typically disclosed during initial interviews or early in the assessment process. The same set of Major Assessment Questions is applicable to working with students who are concerned about or affected by the drug problems of family members or friends.

Sources of Information

What has been said makes clear that in order to adequately discover what an individual student needs, those in the school setting will have to gather considerable information, often utilizing services from outside the school system as well as from within. It is also clear that "assessment" as a process is not to be confused with the "assessment interview" as a single event. Especially when dealing with students who have patterns of significant alcohol or other drug use or who may be chemically dependent, a sizeable volume of data must be obtained from many sources. Many sources may have to consulted, over a period of months, in order to gain information sufficient to support an assessment decision that outside evaluation or treatment is needed and to enhance the likelihood that such an intervention will succeed (see Chapter 9). Once a student is identified and referred to the student assistance program the SAP staff should begin the

Figure 8.2

THE MAJOR ASSESSMENT QUESTIONS

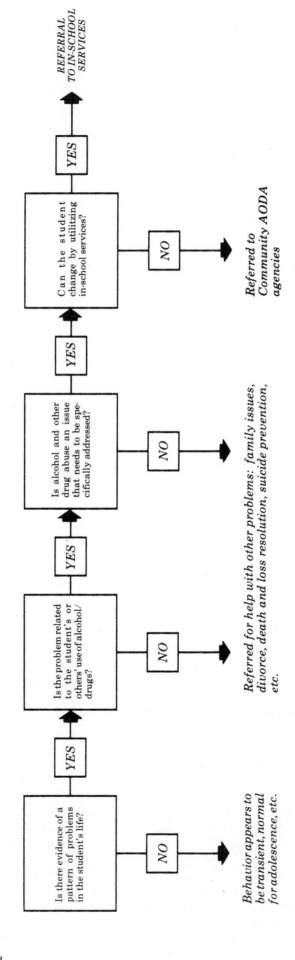

process of gathering data from *archival, personal,* and *environmental* sources.

Archival information consists of data stored in student records of one type or another. From cumulative files, for example, the SAP Counselor can obtain valuable information: grade and achievement history; absenteeism, tardiness, and class-cutting histories; the number and nature of disciplinary referrals; the incidence of school policy violations (including prior AODA policy infractions), history of prior suspensions; loss of athletic eligibility; history of other extracurricular involvements, etc. Archival information often indicates whether current behavior continues a trend in a negative direction or represents a change from acceptable behavior in the past. Anecdotal comments by teachers and other staff often indicate whether current behavior has antecedents.

Examining the student's records is often one of the first steps an SAP Counselor will take after receiving a referral and prior to interviewing the referred student. This information provides the SAP Counselor with a behavioral context within which to evaluate information collected from the student or from other sources. The archival data is frequently summarized with other data as in Supplement 8.4.

"There is increasing agreement that the root cause of chemical dependency lies in the idiosyncratic way in which the chemically dependent person metabolizes alcohol and other drugs when compared to nondependent persons."

Personal information is obtained through the SAP Counselor's firsthand experiences with the student in a number of ways. At the very least, personal information is collected through one or more interviews with the student. The purpose of such initial interviews generally is to gather information concerning all areas of a student's life in order to arrive at answers to the first two Major Assessment Questions above. For all except self-referrals, these initial interviews are also used to express concern to the student and to relate, in a general way, the nature of the information the SAP Counselor has collected thus far and which legitimizes his concern. (Supplement 8.3 summarizes some basic information about the AODA screening interview).

Support groups—specifically the use-focussed groups (Chapter 16)—provide an additional source of personal information where it is not possible to gain, through one or more initial interviews, enough data to enable the SAP Counselor to form an adequate picture

ot the severity of the student's alcohol/drug involvement. To assess the relationship of chemical use to other problems in a student's life may take considerable time and requires getting to know the student fairly well. For students who are in the most trouble with chemicals, denial and resistance will reduce the the amount of information the counselor will be able to obtain. Observing the student's behavior in a use-focused group typically allows the SAP staff to answer the last two Major Assessment Questions.

Finally, waiting and monitoring the student's school conduct and performance over time is also an assessment strategy. Many SAP Counselors will utilize behavioral contracts with students when other sources of information or help are inappropriate or are refused. (See Kanfer (1975) and Moursund (1985) in the *For Further Reading* section at the end of this chapter). In these circumstances students agree to behavioral contracts aimed at modifying their chemical use in the direction of abstinence. The contracts are reviewed regularly with the SAP Counselor over a period of a month or more. Inability to keep an abstinence contract provides important assessment information: it frequently indicates that the student needs additional help beyond what the school can provide. A history of such contract failure may be good evidence of loss of control over chemical use (see below).

Environmental information is collected from others who have firsthand experience with the student. Teachers, coaches, extracurricular activity advisors, and other staff represent some of the best sources of environmental information. Thus, in most student assistance programs the SAP Counselor will, immediately upon receiving a formal referral, contact all staff who see the student on a regular basis, asking them to report any behaviors from the recent past that may have been of concern to them. Such requests for information are handled either through a form (such as Supplement 8.2) or through informal conversations. In addition, where such information is not in files available to the SAP Counselor, she should contact pupil services staff—counselors, psychologists, social workers—to see if they have had prior or current contacts with the student and/or his family.

Parents are also contacted as soon as is practical and possible, depending on the manner in which the student is referred to the program and in accordance with school policy. Where students have violated policies against the use of alcohol or other drugs in school or at school-sponsored events, parents are always notified as a matter of course, and become immediately involved in the assessment process. For students referred by staff because of suspected AODA involvement or because of performance problems, parents may be contacted at a later stage in the assessment process. The purpose of contacting parents at this stage is not to intervene formally or to inform them of a problem but to indicate that some concerns have developed and to ask if they have any information which may be of help to the SAP Counselor.

In the case of self-referrals, parents are rarely notified as part of the assessment process, although their involvement in anything of an interventive nature would be mandatory. (As a general rule, with the exception of referrals generated by policy violation, parents need not be notified as long as the student is making satisfactory progress in the student assistance program: i.e., is following recommendations and is changing his behavior). It is often necessary to begin educating parents at this point in the nature of drug use, abuse, and dependency, and to inform them of telltale signs for which they may begin to look. Often, too, siblings attending the same school can provide useful information. Former and current friends of the referred student can also yield pertinent information if they understand that the source of the information is kept confidential and that the information will be used to help—not to punish.

Community agencies can also provide meaningful assessment data if they have had prior contact with the student and if they have permission to disclose the data they have: juvenile justice authorities, probation and parole officers, clergy, social workers, private practitioners, etc. Depending on local statutes, for example, police and sheriff's departments may be permitted to notify the school of alcohol/drug violations that occur in the community—drunk driving incidents, drug busts, arrests for dealing, etc.—provided the information is not used by the school to discipline or punish the student involved. In some communities such information is provided by police and is not deemed to fall within the laws assuring the confidentiality of juvenile court records.

Having a certified alcohol/drug counselor from a local AODA agency meet with the student and his parents in school can also be a vital step in the assessment process. Timing is important in involving this resource person. The AODA counselor can provide the meaningful information to the school, the student, and to parents after the school has gathered ample assessment information already, dealt with the student's and parents' initial denial and resistance, and begun to educate parents about alcohol and other drug abuse. The AODA counselor's interview often forms a bridge between assessment and intervention, since he typically becomes involved when the student's prior conduct demonstrates the need for a more professional opinion.

Assessment Recommendations

It is surely not enough to collect and interpret information alone. Viewed as a cyclical process, each level or episode of assessment activity should have an outcome: something specific should happen, or a specific decision should be made by the SAP staff. Often these decisions or outcomes take the form of one or more recommendations for further action. At the earliest stages of assessment the recommendation usually involves taking steps to gather additional information.

Recommendations of whatever sort should always be documented (see Supplement 8.5) and communicated to the student (and to parents as appropriate). In addition, all staff members should be made aware of the range of assessment outcomes so they can seek appropriate feedback about referrals they have made. Such feedback should also be routinely provided by the SAP Counselor for referrals made by other school staff members (e.g., see Chapter 7, Supplement 7.4).

For example, at the conclusion of a given counseling session with a student, the SAP Counselor might conclude that one or more of the following recommendations are appropriate, necessary, and possible:

1. There is no apparent personal or performance problem at this time; no further action is necessary at this time;

2. There is no apparent AODA-related problem; however, referral to other sources of help is appropriate for other problems identified;

3. Further assessment interviews with the SAP Counselor are needed;

4. The student needs to contract for specific behavioral changes in AODA-related behavior, to be monitored by regular meetings between the student and the SAP Counselor;

5. The student needs to participate in an in-school information or use-focussed group for a specified period of time, after which additional recommendations may be made;

6. The student needs an in-school assessment, conducted by a certified alcohol/drug counselor from an approved AODA agency in the community;

7. The student needs the professional AODA assessment, evaluation, or diagnostic services of an approved AODA agency in the community;

8. The assessment information supports the need for referral to primary treatment for chemical dependency through a community-based inpatient or intensive outpatient AODA program;

9. The student needs involvement in other community services (e.g., Alateen, Alcoholics Anonymous, Narcotics Anonymous, Cocaine Anonymous, etc.).

10. Wait and continue to monitor the student's school performance

The assessment recommendations, if carried out, represent interventive steps and illustrate the handshaking that occurs between the assessment and intervention functions. These recommendations also indicate that assessment can be a long-term process. Theoretically, the same student could be involved in many contacts with the SAP staff who make increasingly stronger recommendations based on the data gathered through prior steps.

Thus, the initial screening phase of the assessment process can be reduced to five general steps which the SAP Counselor/Coordinator should take after being notified of the referral of a student to the student assistance program:

1. **Gather archival information**, primarily to review current school performance data and ascertain whether it is unsatisfactory and/or represents an unexplained change in a negative direction;

2. **Gather environmental information** from all of those who have first hand information and/or concern about the student's conduct in the recent past. Parent or family contact may be possible or mandatory, depending on the nature of the referral;

3. **Gather personal information through one or more interviews** with the referred student, including data on alcohol or other drug use and possible concerns about others' use (as in Supplement 8.3);

4. **Review the information** (perhaps summarized as in Supplement 8.4) and arrive at a provisional recommendation for the next steps;

5. **Present the information** to the Core Team or its Screening Team and arrive at one or more recommendations, supported by the team and the building administrator (Supplement 8.5). The recommendations should be presented to the student, and to parents if appropriate.

Appropriate feedback should also be given to the referring staff member concerning the outcome of the initial screening/assessment.

Assessing for Alcohol and Other Drug Use, Abuse, and Dependency

To return to the terminology introduced in Chapter 3, a primary assessment task is to determine the target group to which the referred student appropriately belongs. Students can be categorized initially as being affected either by their own chemical use or someone else's. Though the assessment of the degree to which students are affected by others' chemical use is comparatively simple, the same is not true of students actively using drugs themselves. Most students who have not progressed beyond experimental or irregular/infrequent drug use are fairly open with counselors about these patterns. Many factors, however, have been mentioned which limit the amount of information the SAP staff is likely to obtain from students concerning more serious patterns of drug use. To denial and the impairment caused by chemical use itself one could add the natural reticence of a student confronted by an authority figure and the fact that all chemical use by adolescents is illegal behavior.

However, even if the staff can gather comprehensive information regarding a student's relationship to alcohol or other drugs it is still necessary, in the assessment process, to filter that information through one's own experience, values, attitudes, and belief system. Comparing the data one has collected with what one knows about the dynamics of alcohol and other drug use is what makes answering the Major Assessment Questions possible. At the very least it is necessary to be aware of the distinctions that have been traditionally drawn between *experimentation, regular use, drug abuse ('problem use'), and chemical dependency.*

The following describes briefly the salient features of these four varieties of chemical experience. Each represents increasing risk of personal harm due to chemical use, and increasing risk of developing chemical dependency. Figure 8.3 summarizes some of the major risk factors of which it is important to be aware during the assessment process. In addition, the term "abuse" is used here with a systematic ambiguity. In broad conceptual terms, all drug use by students should be construed as "abuse," constituting either a real or potential threat to human growth and development. As an assessment category, however, the term is used more specifically to denote the use of chemicals in a way that produces actual harm as it becomes apparent to the assessment staff.

Figure 8.3

SUMMARY OF MAJOR RISK FACTORS

RISK FACTOR	*Experimentation* / *Regular Use* LOW RISK	*Problem Use* MODERATE RISK	*Chemical Dependency* HIGH RISK
Age of First Chemical Use	16 years of age or older	14 to 15 years of age	13 years of age or younger
Number of Drugs Currently Used	1 drug, typically alcohol	2 drugs, typically alcohol and marijuana	3 or more drugs
Lifetime Prevalence	1 drug	2 to 3 drugs	3 or more drugs
Frequency of Current Use	1 time per month or less	2 to 3 times per month	Weekly to daily use
Amounts Typical of Current Use	Typically uses only up to point of effect	Some reverse in tolerance; use to point of intoxication	Always uses up to or past physical limits
Motivation	Experimentation, curiosity	Use is an incidental correlate of social activity	To avoid problems; to medicate emotional pain; to escape; postpone withdrawal
Consequences	No incidents of harmful consequences	Infrequent episodes of drug use interferring with personal life	Pattern of harmful consequences in school, home, social life
Quality of Drug Relationship	Little emotional attraction to drugs or their effects	Experiences mild euphoria	Drug use is intensely rewarding, pleasurable
Incidence of Family Dependency	No alcoholism in parents or siblings	Has 1 biological parent who is chemically dependent	1 or both parents dependent; dependency in a grandparent
Presence of Essential Symptoms	No indicators for any essential symptom	Indicators for one essential symptom	Indicators for 2 or more essential symptoms

Experimentation and Regular, Infrequent Use

The term "experimentation" is aptly employed to describe the first few episodes of chemical use by adolescents or pre-teens. The experimentation stage is usually short-lived, lasting only a few weeks or months. In this phase students are literally engaged in the process of discovering what alcohol and other drugs are, what they do, and how they used. They discover that alcohol, marijuana, cocaine, or other drugs are in fact mood-altering: their characteristic effect is to alter the way one feels. For adolescents struggling with complex internal and social changes in a complex and frightening world, learning that one can change the outside by changing the inside can be a significant discovery. Moreover, those who repeat the drug experience or who experiment with additional drugs frequently discover that the effects are predictable and reliable: drugs do what they do every time they are used. They can be trusted.

These discoveries should not be taken lightly in view of the fact that first drug use is occurring at earlier and earlier ages. Drugs become not only a source of feeling good but can take on functional significance as well: they help to medicate the stresses, strains, and struggles of adolescents who, developmentally, are engaged in the traumatic task of encountering the world in a realistic, semi-independent way for the first time. If an adolescent has learned that chemicals will resolve problems easily, quickly, and work 100 per cent of the time, then he has little reason to experiment with other coping strategies. Or, he may have already discovered that these do not work as well or as predictably as chemicals do. Thus, chemical use should not be deemed harmless because it is "experimental." The use of alcohol or other drugs can begin to impair adolescent development from the beginning, depending on how attractive chemicals become for the student and what decisions he is led to make about their place in his life.

While many adolescents and preteens, for a variety of reasons, will make conscious decisions not to continue chemical use, many others decide that they will continue. "Regular Use" thus denotes a stage where a pattern has begun to emerge in a student's relationship to alcohol or other drugs. While they may or may not be conscious of them, students evolve "rules" which consist of *their* perceptions about what constitutes safe, "acceptable," or "responsible use of alcohol or other drugs. Drug use at this stage tends to be infrequent but regular, students rarely get into any obvious trouble, and seldom over-use, or use to the point of incapacitation. The primary motivation behind chemical use is to experience the mild "high" a drug can produce, usually in a social setting with peers. Drug use is incidental and peripheral to other activities; it is not the primary focus of peer and social interaction.

The outstanding feature of "regular use" as a stage is the absence of overt, clear, definite harmful consequences to the student. There are no obviously discernible problems with parents or peers, school performance, with the law, or with physical and mental health—even though the student is at risk for developing such problems later. Many students make conscious decisions at this stage also. Many will decide to limit their chemical use to alcohol alone, having experimented with several other drugs as well. Others will confine drinking or other drug use to parties and will develop clear limits on their intake.

Abuse, or 'Problem Use'

While all chemical use by students should be regarded as "abuse," for the purpose of assessment the term "abuse" can be applied to chemical behavior which now results in a pattern of overt, visible, demonstrable problems, or which represents real dangers to the student. Thus, the student's age becomes a factor in interpreting the significance of assessment data. Few counselors would be alarmed to find that a high school junior is drinking once a week. The same behavior in a sixth grader should be cause for alarm.

Most students at this stage are using several drugs simultaneously, and on a regular basis. The frequency of drug use also increases as a rule. Students exhibiting abusive patterns of chemical behavior typically use on at least a weekly basis or more frequently. Chemicals are used not just for the mild mood-altering effects but to the point of impairing functioning—drinking to get drunk, for example. Many of the personal and social signs listed in Supplement 7.4 begin to become apparent as drug use affects school performance, emotional stability, family relationships, social functioning, etc. Alcohol and other drugs are less an incidental accompaniment to social interaction and more frequently become the primary reason for socializing. Solitary drinking and/or other drug use becomes more frequent and typical. For many, the early signs of chemical dependency may appear: blackouts, preoccupation, loss of control, tolerance, and a pattern of harmful consequences. Denial progresses beyond the normal reticence to talk about such matters and is now strengthened in order to protect the student's relationships with chemicals from outside interference or intervention.

Chemical Dependency

It is widely noted that chemical dependency is one of the most complex of all human pathologies, affecting the victim's physical, social, familial, mental, emotional, and spiritual well-being. The search for a singular cause for chemical dependency has been abandoned in the face of enlightened research demonstrating the multidimensional character of its etiology. At the very least a number of psychological, social, and physiological factors predispose persons to alcoholism and/or dependency on other drugs. There is increasing agreement that the root of chemical dependency lies in the idiosyncratic way in which the chemically dependent person metabolizes alcohol and other drugs when compared to nondependent persons. Although there is no "alcoholism gene," a combination of anatomical, physiological, and biochemical substrates can all be passed on genetically (see NIAAA, 1985; Topel, 1985).

While the knowledge of how chemical dependency is caused in a given student lends no information of value to the assessment process, becoming clear on the complexities of causation does improve that process. It is first of all necessary to realize that many different factors may be causally related to drug use. At various times, curiosity, stress management, and peer pressure have been among the factors alleged to cause drug use. It is also necessary to recognize the interaction of various causal factors with different varieties of drug use. The factors that precede experimentation differ from those that appear to cause continued drug use, and these differ from the factors responsible for the progression to drug abuse or for the transition from abuse to dependency. Familiarity with these facts does have a bearing on how student AODA problems in general are managed. It makes no more sense to send a student who is experimenting with drugs to treatment than it does to teach an actively chemically dependent youth how to resist peer pressure.

It is beyond the scope of this book to give a detailed account of chemical dependency or to attempt to synthesize the various meanings attached to this term (see, for example, the definition of "chemical dependency," "alcoholism," "addiction," "habituation," and related terms in the Glossary). Most definitions describe chemical dependency as a primary, progressive, chronic, and fatal disease characterized by loss of control, the development of tolerance and a tendency to increase the dose, preoccupation, harmful personal and social consequences, and powerlessness—or an inability to stop using despite persistent consequences.

Chemical dependency is a *primary* disease in that drug use has progressed to an autonomous, independent status, regardless of the factors which may have precipitated drug use initially. The disease is *progressive* in that it always gets worse if it is not interrupted and treated appropriately. Harmful consequences become more frequent and more severe over time. Moreover, the disease progressively affects the functioning of the whole person. We now know that chemical dependency progresses far more rapidly in adolescents than in adults. If drinking, for example, begins in young adulthood, it takes from seven to 14 years for alcoho-

lism to develop in the adult. When the average age of first use is 11 or 12, however, chemical dependency in adolescents develops within six months to two years. Thus, the typical adolescent cocaine addict begins using cocaine at the age of 14 years and seeks help within 1.5 years, or by the age of 16 (Gold et al., 1985).

Because chemical dependency is incurable, it is a *chronic* illness. If it were curable, the recovering alcoholic could safely return to normal, social drinking. The experience of clinicians as well as of members of Alcoholics Anonymous, Narcotics Anonymous, and Cocaine Anonymous teaches that recovery must be based on abstinence from all mood altering chemicals. Finally, dependency is fatal in that it always leads to premature death, if not from direct medical consequences of drug use then from accidents, homicides, suicides, etc.

"In a small survey of adolescent deaths from suicide, 66% had an alcoholic parent." (Biek, p. 111)

One of the hallmark symptoms of chemical dependency is *loss of control*. From the onset of chemical dependency the drug user gradually loses the ability to predict the outcome of drug-using episodes once the chemical use begins. For example, the teenager who goes to a party intending not to get high or to have only two beers and who ends up having a blackout and drinking to the point of incapacitation may be experiencing loss of control. As the disease progresses such episodes become more frequent and troublesome.

The development of *tolerance* to the mood-altering effects of alcohol or other drugs develops at different rates in different people prone to addiction. Tolerance in part describes a metabolic adjustment of the body to the continuing presence of the chemical. The body becomes more efficient at metabolizing the drug, lowering the amount in the bloodstream that is available to exert mood-altering effects. Consequently, there is a tendency to gradually increase the dose. Subjectively, the dependent adolescent is not experiencing a greater "high," even though drugs are objectively present in the body in higher concentrations, increasing the physical, personal, and social impairment.

Preoccupation can begin with the adolescent's first few alcohol/drug using experiences. For this reason it is wise to ask students about their first experiences with chemicals. Those at comparatively greater risk for being or becoming dependent will typically describe these initial experiences as highly rewarding and significant; episodes of first use are often described with the considerable enthusiasm which accompanies preoccupation. The adolescent who has become more preoccupied with alcohol or other drugs devotes increasing amounts of mental and emotional energy to all aspects of their use: thinking about when, where and how to obtain chemicals, planning parties, fantasizing about what the experience will be like, making certain enough is on hand ("protecting the supply," having a "stash"), etc. Preoccupation is also evidence that the adolescent has a strong, pathological emotional commitment to drugs and their highs. More and more aspects of the student's lifestyle begin to revolve around repeating this significant, welcome experience to the exclusion of others.

Chemical dependency is always characterized by the presence of *harmful consequences* directly related to the use of drugs: problems with family relationships, school performance, peer relationships, forming appropriate intimate relationships, maintaining acceptable social conduct, and so on. The continuation of chemical use beyond the point where its harmful consequences are apparent even to the drug user is evidence that the student is indeed dependent and is *powerless* to maintain abstinence without outside intervention and support.

In addition to the qualitative dynamics above the SAP Counselor should be alert to a number of quantitative aspects which are not diagnostic indicators but which can indicate students who are at increased risk of being or becoming dependent. In addition to the nature of first using experiences the SAP staff should note the age at which students first begin experimenting. Similarly, the number of drugs a student has tried in her lifetime is an indicator of relative *commitment* to drugs and their effects: a student who has tried four or five different drugs is at greater risk than one who has tried one or two. Similarly, the number of drugs currently used on a regular basis is significant. We know, for example, that the average adolescent in treatment began using chemicals at age 11, has used six drugs in his lifetime, and was regularly using four drugs at the time of admission to treatment. While such quantitative indicators are not diagnostic by themselves they can help the SAP Counselor form an educated opinion about the likelihood of dependency.

In gathering information to assess the likelihood that chemical dependency is present it is also necessary to distinguish between the accidental signs and complications of dependency and its essential symptoms, as described by McAuliffe and McAuliffe (1975a,b). As noted above, the kinds, amounts, and frequencies of drugs used have no necessary connection to dependency. The development of tolerance and presence of blackouts do not occur in everyone. These are accidental signs that are not diagnostic. Similarly, complications—such as family problems, job loss, problems with friends and school—though they are commonly the

effects of chemical dependency need not be present. Nor does their presence indicate that a student is dependent: pneumonia always causes a fever, but a fever is not by itself diagnostic of pneumonia.

Many counselors have found that the description of chemical dependency in terms of eight categories of "essential symptoms" provides benchmarks more useful in making assessment judgements about adolescent drug abuse and dependency. The eight "essential symptoms" which follow are those whose presence always indicates the presence of the disease (see McAuliffe and McAuliffe, 1975a, b, for a complete description).

1. Psychological Dependency or Need is characterized by having a drug-oriented lifestyle: alcohol and/or other drugs become the center or focus of day-to-day living, rather than incidental factors at its periphery. Drugs are involved in most if not all activities: hobbies, work, school, social and recreational activity, sex, choices of friends and peer group, etc. The degree of emotional commitment to obtaining and using drugs is also a measure of the centrality that they assume.

2. Mental Obsession is nearly synonymous with "preoccupation," or a strong cognitive compulsion where a major portion of a student's mental energy is spent in thinking about all aspects of the chemical and its effects. Protecting the supply (having a "stash") reflects a concern over maintaining the drug's availability and the fear that would accompany its absence. Many of the factors listed in Supplement 7.4 indicate mental obsession with chemicals: talking frequently and openly about drugs, surrounding oneself with drug-related music, literature, posters, and symbols, and so on. Conversely, other areas of life suffer from inattention: loss of interest in drug-free friends, dropping out of extracurricular activities, loss of concentration on school and family matters, etc.

3. Emotional Compulsion refers to the emotional side of "preoccupation," or the intense emotional urgency to use alcohol or other drugs. Emotional compulsion is often indicated by the manner in which drugs are used: using several drugs simultaneously, using frequently, and in large amounts are all signs of emotional compulsion. The dependent student also becomes increasing defensive when the drug relationship is questioned or threatened. Using when one did not intend to, or using more than one intended are instances of loss of control that often indicate the presence of this essential symptom. Continuing to use chemicals even despite one's own disapproval is often a late-stage indicator: using after attempting to control or promising to quit, using despite disapproval of harmful consequences, using despite judgements that one's chemical use is "bad for me," and so on.

4. Drug-Induced Low Self-Esteem indicates that chemical use is a direct *cause* of low self-worth. Chemical use results in behavior that the dependent person herself would judge as immoral or against her own standards and values. Behavior which violates this personal code of conduct always erodes self-esteem and creates mounting feelings of guilt and shame. Dishonesty may manifest itself overtly by stealing drugs or stealing money or objects with which to buy them, or it can be more covert as in lying to cover up drug use and its consequences. Harming the relationships that one values—with friends, family members, lovers—also erodes self esteem further. Excuses and other denial mechanisms are used to defend the chemical use despite these consequences. In later stages, depression, anxiety about self-image, and feelings of inadequacy and shame become overt indicators of low self-esteem caused directly by chemical use.

5. Rigid Negative Attitudes become characteristic of the chemically dependent student as the personality changes from a hitherto normal outlook to one that is typically pessimistic, hostile, negative, rejecting, and blaming. Negative thoughts, feelings, and behaviors become part of a rigid pattern of conduct directed against the self but also against others who threaten the drug relationship. Many people comment that a characteristic feature of chemical dependency is its ability to bring about a radical transformation in the personality in this negative direction. Open rejection of and resentment toward "good kids," drug-free students, drug education efforts, or the student assistance program go beyond the superficial resistance one might often see in a normal adolescent.

6. A Rigid Defense System develops to protect all aspects of the chemically dependent student's relationship with alcohol and/or other drugs. Denial is one of its major manifestations, whether of drug involvement and its extent, of drug abuse, of individual episodes of drug use or consequences, or of personal feelings. Blaming, minimizing, rationalizing, excusing, theorizing, justifying, and other defense mechanisms are chronically present in discussions about any aspect of alcohol/drug involvement.

7. Delusion about the nature of the chemical relationship and its consequences is also a direct consequence of chemical dependency. Defenses and delusion are the two major components of the denial system that evolves. Defenses arise to protect the relationship with the drug and one's self-esteem; delusion arises from many sources and serves to impair a student's conscious awareness about the effects of alcohol and other drug use on his life. Consequently, much of what appears to be denial is *sincere delusion*—a sincere lack of awareness that other symptoms are present. The student appears not to appreciate the extent to which she is preoccupied with chemicals, has a drug-centered lifestyle, is experiencing negative consequences, has low-self esteem caused by chemical use, is protecting her relationship with drugs, and so on. Statements that drug use is "under control," or "I can quit any time I want," are frequently sincere expressions. The extent of delusion can be appreciated when such statements indicate that the student is unaware that they are inconsistent with other facts.

8. Powerlessness describes the dependent adolescent's inability to freely accept, recognize, or remedy his condition or to manage the increasingly troublesome effects of chemical use. Powerlessness is typically reflected in the student's inability to stop using or to control the effects of drug abuse even though he may wish to. He may wind up getting high despite intentions, promises, or efforts to stay straight. The inability to keep abstinence contracts, for example, even while struggling sincerely to do so or in the face of severe consequences is often evidence that the adolescent is powerless to control chemical use by himself. The major implication of powerless is that outside help is needed.

Assessing for Affected Family Member Issues

The single largest target group consists of children and adolescents who are concerned about alcohol or other drug abuse in someone else; most often, these are children affected by parental alcoholism. It is estimated that 25 per cent of all students are directly affected by parental alcoholism. Perhaps another 10 percent are affected by the drug-related problems of siblings or close friends.

Generally speaking, assessing for concerned person issues is relatively simple compared to assessing for personal drug problems and follows the same process outlined earlier. Depending on the steps taken by the student assistance program for identification of such children, the majority will be identified on the basis of self-referral. Many students, however, who are referred for school performance problems may exhibit concerned persons issues in addition to problems related to their own chemical use. Thus, the inclusion of family drug behavior questions in assessment screening interviews is necessary for all referrals.

Useful assessment data can be contributed by classroom teachers and other environmental sources. To the extent that all staff and the assessment staff are aware of the behavioral effects of parental chemical dependency on children they will be provisionally able to identify students exhibiting these often characteristic patterns: the "family hero," "lost child," "scape-goat," "mascot," and so on (see Wegscheider, 1981). The school nurse may also be a valuable source of information. In her excellent study of adolescent patients at the Teenage Clinic of the University of Wisconsin's Department of Pediatrics, Joan Biek (1981) discovered that 57 per cent were affected by a parental drinking problem. These patients also reported twice as many somatic complaints as did adolescent patients who did not have problem-drinking parents. A high percentage of the concerned persons patients reported tiring easily, shortness of breath, stomachaches, concern about weight, frequent headaches, and sleeping problems.

The major assessment task for concerned persons consists of answering, with this issue in mind, the Major Assessment Questions: (1) Does the student seem to have problems in living? (2) Is the student concerned about another's alcohol/drug use? (3) To what degree is the student affected by another's alcohol/drug use? and (4) Is the student willing to make use of in-school or community resources? Although the SAP staff should make use of as many sources of information as possible, parent contact is often delayed since it rarely provides assessment information that cannot be gotten in another manner, it may jeopardize a child's safety in the home, and may frequently discourage students from answering questions freely.

Consequently, the most valuable information for the assessment of concerned person issues is likely to come from the interview held with the individual student. Despite the presence of denial, many researchers have found that reports by students of parental drinking or other drug-related problems are reliable and valid if handled correctly. O'Malley et al (1986, p. 433) notes that students' reports of parental drinking practices were highly valid and that "reports of their parents' drinking practices can be used with some degree of confidence without obtaining the data directly from the parents." Similarly, Sher (1986) found that there was a high degree of reliability between siblings regarding student self-reports of parental alcoholism. The highest agreement between siblings occurred with reference to specific, overt behavioral consequences of a parent's drinking: e.g., drunk driving, seeking help, being arrested. Finally, DiCicco et al (1984b) and Biek (1981) have discovered highly effective ways of obtaining accurate information from students in one-to-one interviews.

Rather than trying to infer the presence of drug abuse or dependency in a parent or other family member these authors have found it is best to approach the subject as directly as possible. As part of her research, Joan Biek developed a "semistructured interview" for obtaining relevant information through a series of eight questions (1981, p. 113). These have been adapted below to include other drug use as well. For example, following questions which get at general information about current living arrangements, the first two questions the SAP Counselor might ask are:

1. Do you know any teenager who has ever had difficulty because of either parent's use of alcohol or other drugs? [Yes, No] and

2. Have you ever known either of your parents to drink or use other drugs? [Yes, No]

Following a "no" response to item 2, the assessment interview can turn to exploring other areas. A "yes" response can be followed up with the remaining questions:

3. At any time in your life has the drinking or drug use of either parent created problems between him/her and the other parent or relative? [Yes, Sometimes, No]

4. Have friends or relatives ever thought that either parent has a drinking or drug problem? [Yes, Sometimes, No]

5. Have you ever worried because of either parent's use of alcohol or other drugs? [Yes, Sometimes, No]

6. Have you ever felt hurt, angry, or scared because of either parent's drinking or drug use? [Yes, Sometimes, No]

7. Has the drinking or drug use of either parent ever caused problems for you? [Yes, Sometimes, No].

Following "No" responses to items 3 through 7 the assessment interview can also proceed to other areas. "Sometimes" responses are allowed because they are less threatening positive responses and because they "may elicit information of an infrequent or single occurrence" (Biek, p. 111). Items 3 and 4 address the extent to which a parent's chemical use has affected others. Items 5 through 7 indicate the extent to which chemical use has become an emotional concern of the child. "Yes" or "Sometimes" responses to any of these should be pursued by asking the student to describe a specific incident. Thus, if a student answered "Yes" to question 6, the SAP Counselor could respond with "Tell me about the last time that happened."

The same information can be obtained in a more informal way by asking a student "Have you ever wished that someone would stop using alcohol or other drugs, and if so, who?" (DiCicco et al, 1984b). An affirmative reply can reliably be taken to indicate that someone's chemical use has progressed beyond what is normal or acceptable and has resulted in problem behavior on enough occasions to create at least a mild concern: normal drinking or drug use does not make people wish a person would stop. More specific questions can then be asked, such as "Has this person's drinking or other drug use ever made you feel angry? (or worried, ashamed, guilty, afraid). "Yes" responses to any of these should be followed by asking the student to describe a specific incident, such as the last time that happened.

Based on students' responses to these interviews, the SAP Counselor should gain sufficient information to form a notion of whether or not the student is a "concerned person" or an affected family member, and of how severely he is affected. This information will allow the SAP staff to make an appropriate recommendation for help, either through in-school services or through those available in the community.

In designing its student assistance program the school system must focus a great deal of attention on its role in the assessment process, on its place in the community's continuum of care for alcohol and other drug abuse-related problems, and on clarifying the roles of SAP staff with regard to this process. It is also clear that for most students assessment will be a process and not a single discrete event. Nonetheless, in addition to other sources of data the interview will typically yield the most useful information, and this requires that all of those with assessment roles in the student assistance program have appropriate training in the dynamics of alcohol and other drug abuse.

Just as clearly, establishing an assessment process of whatever scope will precipitate issues involving case management and school policy. The process that evolves will have to take into account the manner in which students are identified and referred to the SAP staff. Self-referrals, for example, may be handled differently with regard to confidentiality and parental contact than referrals from school staff. Similarly, some assessment activities will be handled differently based on whether a student is referred on the basis of witnessed alcohol/drug violations of policy, suspected AODA involvement, or because of an in-school drug overdose. (These procedural issues and others relating to the assessment process will be dealt with in more detail in Chapter 12).

In any event, the major outcome at various points of the assessment process is that the SAP staff will have sufficient information in order to judge the nature and scope of a student's AODA-related problems, to understand what the student needs to develop a healthier manner of living, and to recommend appropriate sources of help in the school or in the community.

Intervention is the process of actually getting the affected student to accept this help.

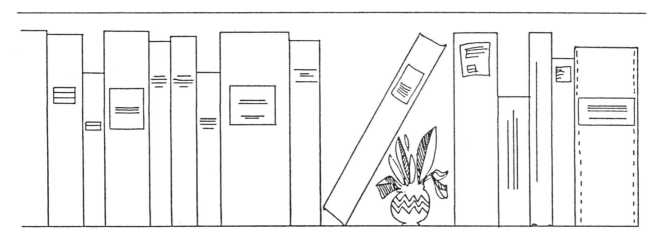

FOR FURTHER READING

The following are but a few of the references which will be of value to those engaged in assessing alcohol and other drug-related problems in adolescents.

ALCOHOL/DRUG ABUSE AND DEPENDENCY:

Alibrandi, Tom. *Young Alcoholics*. Minneapolis, MN: Comp Care Publications, 1978. This comparatively early work is valuable as a study of adolescent *alcoholism* as opposed to alcohol abuse. It contains a number of valuable checklists and inventories, some with a high degree of reliability and validity, useful in assessing the nature and scope of student alcohol use.

Johnson, Vernon. *I'll Quit Tomorrow*. New York: Harper and Row, 1980. Johnson's book is one of the best descriptions of the nature and progression of chemical dependency, the dynamics of denial, the process of intervention, and the components of recovery.

Krupski, Ann Marie. *Inside the Adolescent Alcoholic*. Center City, MN: Hazelden, 1982. Krupski's book provides an excellent, detailed discussion of denial as it occurs in adolescent alcohol abusers and alcoholics. She provides concrete guidance for understanding and responding to denial for counselors who work with youth.

Mayer, J.E. and W. J. Filstead. "The Adolescent Alcohol Involvement Scale." *Journal of Studies on Alcohol*. 40 (1979): 291-300. While intended for use as a survey instrument rather than as a diagnostic tool, the AAIS has shown itself to be a useful assessment device that is easy for students to take and easy for counselors to score and interpret.

McAuliffe, Robert M. and Mary Boesen McAuliffe. 1975a. *The Essentials of Chemical Dependency.*

Volume I. Minneapolis, MN: The American Chemical Dependency Society, 1975. This book and its companion volume (below) describe chemical dependency as a pathological relationship to mood-altering chemicals. The authors describe the progression of the illness in terms of eight categories of "essential symptoms." Over 400 symptoms associated with the presence of chemical dependency are described with numerous helpful checklists.

———. 1975b. *Essentials for the Diagnosis of Chemical Dependency. Volume II*. Minneapolis, MN: The American Chemical Dependency Society, 1975.

Milam, James R. and Katherine Ketcham. *Under the Influence*. Seattle: Madrona Publishers, 1981. Milam's book provides one of the better descriptions of alcoholism as a metabolic, physiologically-based disease caused by abnormal biochemical responses to alcohol in those with a predisposition to develop chemical dependency.

COCAINE

The following are among the most useful descriptions of the nature, dynamics, symptoms, prevalence, and consequences of cocaine use among adolescents:

Gold, Mark S., M. D. *800-COCAINE*. New York: Bantam Books, 1984.

———, et al. 1985. "Adolescent Cocaine Abusers: Confronting the Epidemic." *Seminars in Adolescent Medicine*. (December, 1985).

———, et al. 1986. "Cocaine Update: From Bench to Bedside." *Controversies in Alcoholism and Substance Abuse*. (1986): 35-60.

Newcomb, Michael D. and P. M. Bentler. "Cocaine Use Among Adolescents: Longitudinal Associations with Social Context, Psychopathology, and Use of Other Substances." *Addictive Behaviors.* 11 (1986): 263-273.

Moursund, Janet. *The Process of Counseling and Therapy. Englewood Cliffs*, New Jersey: Prentice-Hall, Inc., 1985.

CHEMICAL DEPENDENCY AND THE FAMILY

Below are some basic references for professionals engaged in identifying and assessing children and youth who are affected by alcohol/drug use and dependency in parents and other family members. (Additional references can be found in the "For Further Readings" Section of Chapter 14).

Biek, Joan, R.N. "Screening Test for Identifying Adolescents Adversely Affected by a Parental Drinking Problem." *Journal of Adolescent Health Care.* 2: (1981): 107-113.

DiCicco, Lena et al. 1984b. "Identifying the Children of Alcoholic Parents from Survey Responses." *Journal of Alcohol and Drug Education.* 30:1 (1984): 1-17.

Pilat, Joanne M., and John W. Jones. "Identification of Children of Alcoholics: Two Empirical Studies." *Alcohol Health and Research World.* (Winter, 1984/1985): 27-33.

Wegscheider, Sharon. 1981. *Another Chance: Hope and Health for the Alcoholic Family.* Palo Alto: Science and Behavior Books.

While there are many texts and articles relating to basic counseling techniques and skills in working with adolescents, the following represent a few specialized topics which may be of interest:

Altman, Kerry Paul. "The Role-Taking Interview: An Assessment Technique for Adolescents." *Adolescence.* 20:80 (1985): 845-851.

Kanfer, Frederick H. "Self-Management Methods." In Kanfer, Frederick H. and Arnold P. Goldstein, eds. *Helping People Change.* New York: Pergamon Press, Inc., 1975, pp. 309-356.

Marks, S. J., Leslie H. Daroff, and Samuel Granick. "Basic Individual Counseling for Drug Abusers." In Friedman and Beschner, eds. (1985), pp. 94-111.

McHolland, James D. "Strategies for Dealing with Resistant Adolescents." *Adolescence.* 20:78 (Summer, 1985): 349-368.

Chapter 8 | **Supplements**

Supplement 8.1, the "Adolescent Assessment Services Checklist," describes a number of characteristics for which the school system should look in identifying and establishing working relationships with local AODA screening and assessment agencies or services.

Supplement 8.2 is a modification of the staff referral form often used to identify students to the student assistance program. Immediately upon receiving a student referral, the SAP Counselor would send this form, or something much like it, to teachers and to any staff members who deal with a student on a regular basis. It is used to begin the data collection process prior to personally interviewing the referred student.

Supplement 8.3, "Guidelines for the AODA Screening Interview," outlines some fundamental aspects of the screening and drug assessment interview(s). It describes general interview content areas, specific AODA-related questions, and offers suggestions for the SAP Counselor's role in conducting the interview(s).

Supplement 8.4, the "Student SAP Screening Summary" is a sample form which can be used to collect the data gathered from archival, personal, and environmental sources. Such data is necessary to support the assessment recommendations and may form the basis for formal intervention strategies.

Supplement 8.5, the "SAP Student Services Plan" summarizes this data more briefly and focuses more attention on the general and specific recommendations for help designed to assist the student in changing his AODA-related behavior. Many schools utilize or require such a document only for students who are referred to the student assistance program because of violations of the school's AODA policies. Documentation of this sort is typically necessary to support recommendations for expulsion and to ensure the student and his family of due process.

Finally, Supplement 8.6 lists some of the major findings of "Drug Abuse Correlates" research. Care must be taken not to regard the correlates as causative or diagnostic factors. They often help to validate the school system's perceptions of a student's behavior by indicating the degree to which it fits a general profile.

Supplement 8.1

ADOLESCENT ASSESSMENT SERVICES CHECKLIST

1. What is the assessment program's philosophy regarding drug use, drug abuse, and chemical dependency? Since one of the primary purposes of assessment is to direct adolescents and their families to appropriate care, much depends on the agency's philosophical orientation. Whether or not it utilizes such language as "disease concept," an assessment agency should recognize the unique needs presented by chemical dependency and the fact that it is a primary, progressive, chronic condition. Even those services which regard drug use as a "symptom" should be sophisticated enough to determine when such a "symptom" has been elevated to the status of an autonomous pathology which will aggravate or complicate existing problems or prevent their resolution, and which will resist attempts to treat its "underlying" causes. The program should also be able to distinguish between those young people who will be able to change their behavior in response to education, improved parenting, or firmer expectations for more responsible conduct, and those who will require primary treatment for chemical dependency.

2. What is the program's philosophy regarding adolescent alcohol and other drug use? Assessment programs which espouse a "responsible drinking" philosophy for underage youth, or which hold that some degree of experimentation or use of "recreational drugs" is acceptable should be avoided at all costs. There is less confusion for student, family, and school where agencies support abstinence as a norm for adolescents. There is a difference between expecting a certain degree of adolescent experimentation and actively condoning illegal, irresponsible, and often dangerous behavior. These permissive attitudes toward drug use should often prompt curiosity as to the degree of training the staff has had in AODA concepts as well as curiosity about the drug-using habits of the program's staff itself. It is not unreasonable to inquire about the agency's policy regarding staff alcohol/ drug use.

3. What are the major components of the program's assessment process? An appropriate assessment or drug evaluation program will involve more than a single interview with the adolescent and/or her family. It will tacitly recognize assessment as a process in which a great deal of data must be collected from a variety of sources. A good assessment program will also include an alcohol/drug education component for the adolescent as well as for family members.

4. Does the program require parent/family involvement? The diagnostic or evaluation judgements of a program are only as sound as the collected data upon which they are based. Therefore, if either the family or the school system is ignored, two of the most important sources of information will be lost. The assessment process will either be prolonged, or the staff are likely to return evaluations of "no chemical dependency" based on inadequate data.

5. What is the length of the assessment process? A formal assessment program, as opposed to an agency advertising "assessment," will be structured over a period of time. Many programs are organized into "phases" which involve an intake procedure, an education component, individual counseling, conjoint student/family sessions, group counseling, etc.

6. What range of assessment/diagnostic judgements does the program and/or its staff recognize (e.g., "abuse," "dependency," "high risk without abstinence," etc.)? To be valuable to the student, the family, and the school an assessment program will offer a broad range of evaluative judgements between the two extremes of "no drug problem" and "is chemically dependent and needs inpatient treatment." It should be capable of assessing the adolescent's strengths and weaknesses and those of his environment in order to ascertain how supportive of change that environment will be. The program should also be able to recommend a wide range of courses of action appropriate to a range of diagnostic judgements supported by the data it collects.

7. What is the staffing pattern? Does the adolescent and/or the family interact with more than one person? In general, the more individuals who have an opportunity to see and work with an adolescent and his family, the greater will be the depth of the assessment.

8. What is the process for admission to the program? A good rule of thumb is to refer to a person, not to a program or an agency. It is advisable to identify those who see the student and/or family members first, and those counselors or therapists who seem most accepted by and successful with adolescents. There is nothing wrong with telling students and families to "insist on seeing Ms. Jones" if she does the most trustworthy work.

9. What is the nature of the working relationship between the assessment agency or service and the school system? The agency should be eager to establish not only referral relationships but day-to-day working relationships as well. An effective assessment program or service will appreciate the amount of information the school can contribute to the assessment process and the degree of support the latter can provide for the student engaged in making healthy changes in his behavior. It will not irrationally assert "confidentiality" when approached by the school, but will routinely seek releases of information in order to enable staff to communicate with the school system. It will also assist the school in seeking such releases of information from families when the school refers them to the agency.

10. Is the agency specifically approved, licensed, and/or certified by the state to provide alcohol/drug services? While many agencies in a given community may present themselves as assessment resources, not all will have the expertise or experience in dealing appropriately and competently with alcohol and other drug-related problems. Not all AODA-specific agencies are adept at working with adolescents. All things considered, however, in AODA matters those agencies which are subject to regular survey by the state for compliance with state mandates for alcohol/drug services should be preferred over general counseling centers, mental health centers, or private practitioners.

11. What are the qualifications of the staff? Are they certified alcohol/drug counselors? What is the experience of the staff in working specifically with adolescent AODA problems? Alcohol and/or drug certification and experience in working with drug-involved youth should be the two minimum qualifications of the staff in any program or agency offering adolescent AODA assessment services to the school. The formal certification process at least assures that the counselor or therapist has satisfied the minimum educational, skill, and practicum requirements of the state certification body. Experience in working with adolescent as opposed to adult drug abusers enhances the counselor's appreciation of the unique problems presented by the interaction between drug abuse and adolescent development.

12. Does the assessment agency also operate a residential or outpatient program for the primary treatment of chemical dependency? Does the agency refer clients to other treatment programs? How many such referrals have taken place in the past year? If the assessment program also provides primary treatment for chemical dependency it is wise to inquire about its diagnostic and referral statistics. Diagnosing a high percentage of incoming clients as chemically dependent can be a reflection of a bias. (It can just as easily indicate that the agency receives a disproportionately high number of referrals of young people who are likely to be heavily involved with alcohol or other drugs). Similarly, referring to one's own treatment program when others are accessible or comparable in cost may also reflect a conflict of interest. The fact is, no 10 adolescents will benefit equally from the same program. The treatment field has evolved sufficiently to provide a wide range of programs suited to individual differences in adolescent patients.

13. To what other agencies or services does the assessment program refer?- For example, how many adolescents were referred to AA, NA, or CA, to other therapists in the community, to the school's services, etc.? A good assessment program will recognize that adolescents and families will frequently have many more problems than those presented by alcohol or drug abuse alone. It will also appreciate the value of self-help groups in the community for both the adolescent and his family.

14. What is the cost of the assessment program? Is the program eligible to receive third-party insurance payments? Are fees based upon ability to pay? Assessment programs will vary in their services, their funding sources, and in their fee systems. Publicly funded programs are often free, at least in part, or have a nominal fee for services beyond a set number of sessions. Even private agencies seek third-party payments and arrange for public assistance for families in financial need. Its is necessary for the school to have such information at hand when referring families to assessment services.

ADOLESCENT ASSESSMENT SERVICES CHECKLIST

1. *What is the assessment program's philosophy regarding drug use, drug abuse, and chemical dependency?*

2. *What is the program's philosophy regarding adolescent alcohol and other drug use?*

3. *What are the major components of the program's as essment process?*

4. *Does the program require parent/family involvement?*

5. *What is the length of the assessment process?*

6. *What range of assessment/diagnostic judgements does the program and/or its staff recognize (e.g., "abuse," "dependency," "high risk without abstinence," etc.)?*

7. *What is the staffing pattern? Does the adolescent and/or the family interact with more than one person?*

8. *What is the process for admission to the program?*

9. *What is the nature of the working relationship between the assessment agency or service and the school system?*

10. *Is the agency specifically approved, licensed, and/or certified by the state to provide alcohol/drug services?*

11. *What are the qualifications of the staff? Are they certified alcohol/drug counselors? What is the experience of the staff in working specifically with adolescent AODA problems?*

12. *Does the assessment agency also operate a residential or outpatient program for the primary treatment of chemical dependency? Does the agency refer clients to other treatment programs? How many such referrals have taken place in the past year?*

13. *To what other agencies or services does the assessment program refer?*

14. *What is the cost of the assessment program? Is the program eligible to receive third-party insurance payments? Are fees based upon ability to pay?*

Supplement 8.2

STUDENT ASSISTANCE PROGRAM
REQUEST FOR INFORMATION

TO:

FROM:

REGARDING: Student _____ Grade _____

DATE:

The above student has been referred to the Student Assistance Program. In order to assist us in assessing the nature of help the program might provide, please indicate on the form below any behavior you might have noticed within the past 3 months or concerns you may have about the student. Please feel free to make comments where appropriate.

Please return this form to _____ as soon as possible.

PLEASE CHECK RELEVANT ITEMS and COMMENT:

I. ACADEMIC PERFORMANCE COMMENTS   COMMENTS
_____ Decline in quality of work
_____ Decline in quality of work
_____ Decline in grade earned
_____ Incomplete work
_____ Work not handed in
_____ Failing in this subject

II. CLASSROOM CONDUCT COMMENTS   COMMENTS
_____ Disruptive in class
_____ Inattentiveness
_____ Lack of concentration
_____ Lack of motivation
_____ Sleeping in class
_____ Impaired memory
_____ Extreme negativism
_____ In-school absenteeism (skipping)
_____ Tardiness to class
_____ Defiance; breaking rules
_____ Frequently needs discipline
_____ Cheating
_____ Fighting
_____ Throwing objects
_____ Defiance of authority
_____ Verbally abusive
_____ Obscene language, gestures

_____ Sudden outbursts of temper
_____ Vandalism
_____ Frequent visits to nurse, counselor
_____ Frequent visits to lavatory
_____ Hyperactivity, nervousness

III. OTHER BEHAVIOR   COMMENTS
_____ Erratic behavior day-to-day
_____ Change in friends and/or peer group
_____ Sudden, unexplained popularity
_____ Mood swings
_____ Seeks constant adult contact
_____ Seeks adult advice without a
      specific problem
_____ Time disorientation
_____ Apparent changes in personal values
_____ Depression; low affect
_____ Defensiveness
_____ Withdrawal; a loner; separateness from others
_____ Other students express concern about a
      possible problem
_____ Fantasizing; daydreaming
_____ Compulsive overachievement;
      preoccupied with school success
_____ Perfectionism
_____ Difficulty in accepting mistakes
_____ Rigid obedience
_____ Talks freely about drug use; bragging
_____ Associates with known drug users

IV. POSSIBLE AODA-SPECIFIC BEHAVIORS
Witnessed   Suspected
  [   ]   [   ]   Selling; delivering
  [   ]   [   ]   Possession of alcohol, drugs
  [   ]   [   ]   Possession of drug paraphernalia
  [   ]   [   ]   Use of alcohol, drugs
  [   ]   [   ]   Intoxication
  [   ]   [   ]   Physical signs, symptoms
  [   ]   [   ]   Others?

What actions have you already taken? (E.g., shared concern and data with student, initiated consequences, parent contact, etc.).

Supplement 8.3

GUIDELINES FOR THE AODA SCREENING INTERVIEW

PURPOSE

It typically falls outside the role of the school system to diagnose chemical dependency. The purpose of the AODA screening interview for students referred to the student assistance program is to begin to answer the first two major assessment questions: what problems the student seems to have in his life, and the degree to which the student's use of alcohol or other drugs is involved. The screening interview typically occurs only after the SAP Counselor has gathered some preliminary data from other sources: chiefly from school records and from other school staff. Often the goal at this stage is either to discover if a referral to a specific service is called for (e.g., a support group), or if more data needs to be collected.

GENERAL INTERVIEW AREAS

Since one purpose of the screening interview is to identify what if any problems the student may be experiencing it is necessary to gather information about many areas of his life. Many SAP Counselors feel more comfortable asking about family life, social and peer relationships, physical health, school performance, work and/or financial status, and attitudes toward self before addressing AODA-specific behavior. Others integrate alcohol/ drug questions into these areas as they go along. The National Drug Abuse Center for Training and Development, in "Assessment Interviewing for Treatment Planning (1978), suggested that screening interviews gather information in the categories of student relationships, rationality, and resources as follows:

Relationships:

1. Family relationships

2. Current home life

3. Closest relationships

4. Sexual relationships

5. Group relationships

Rationality

1. Extreme mood swings

2. Suicidal tendencies

3. Control of strong feelings

4. Potential for violence

5. Denial or defensiveness

Resources

1. Employment

2. Skills and competencies

3. Leisure, fun

4. Home

5. Legal problems

6. School

7. Financial resources

8. Use of other agencies

AODA-SPECIFIC INTERVIEW AREAS

At this stage it is generally only necessary to find out if students have any experience with alcohol or other drugs at all (most will), and to form an opinion about whether there is reason to explore chemical issues in more detail later. In the initial AODA screening interviews it is unlikely that the SAP Counselor will obtain much more information than what is listed in Figure 8.3, "Major Risk Factors." A typical sequence of questions might consist of the following:

1. In my experience students your age have tried alcohol, and many have tried other drugs as well. Have you ever tried alcohol or other drugs?

2. What drugs have you tried? [*Lifetime Prevalence*]

3. How old were you when you first tried _____? [*Age of First Use*]

4. Tell me about the first time you tried _____? [*Quality of Drug Relationship*]

5. What drugs do you use most often now? [*Current Drug Use*]

6. How often would you say you use _____? [Frequency of Current Use]

7. How much would you say you drink/use on a typical occasion? [*Amounts Typical of Current Use*]

8. Of all the drugs there are, which one do you think you would most like to take? Why?

9. Which of the things you have tried do you prefer to use? Why?

10. Have you ever been bothered by anyone else's alcohol or other drug use? [*Incidence of Family Dependency*].

Questions 3 and 4 are repeated for each substance the student identifies experimenting with in question 2. Questions 8 and 9 get at the issue of "drug of choice." Students will often reveal how sophisticated their knowledge of drugs is by how they respond to Question 8. The counselor may be able to get a sense of the subtle dynamics like commitment to drugs by how students answer question 9. Obviously, an affirmative answer to question 10 should lead to an exploration of family drinking and drug use if these issues have not arisen earlier as part of the general content areas.

TOOLS and TECHNIQUES

It is not difficult to locate many so-called "assessment instruments" for alcohol and drug abuse (e.g., see Alibrandi, 1978, for some good examples). While useful in some ways, they are often inappropriate for initial data gathering for several reasons. As a rule, counselors find that surveys, checklists, and instruments based upon lists of "yes/no" questions are of little use in initial AODA screening interviews because they tend to be intimidating and impersonal. Furthermore, most are alcohol-specific, and rewording them to include other drugs makes them awkward and cumbersome to interpret. Many questionnaires also utilize jargon (e.g., "Do you ever have blackouts?") which a student is unfamiliar with or can misunderstand. Frequently the questions will expect students to utilize sophisticated mental processes if they are to respond accurately. For example, "Does your drinking cause problems with your parents?" asks the student to recall many episodes of drinking, to identify those that resulted in difficulties with parents, and to attribute the trouble directly to chemical use rather than some other factor—all in a few seconds. Finally, even if a questionnaire avoids these faults it often provides only a raw numerical score which can be above or below a danger point: information which may be interesting for the counselor but which is unlikely to help the student change his behavior at this point.

Assessment instruments do however, have value. They are typically most useful as an aid for the SAP Counselor rather than for the student. Following one or more interviews, for example, a review of a typical questionnaire helps the SAP Counselor to organize and document his perceptions. Some SAP Counselors have adapted AODA questionnaires for use in a "card sort" strategy. Each question is typed on a card. At the beginning of the interview the counselor might ask the student to sort the deck into "yes" and "no" piles. This is less intimidating than an interrogation, and the counselor gets a good idea of the student's AODA experience just by the size of the "yes" pile. Furthermore, he can gain more useful information by focusing discussion on the "yes" cards: "I see you put 'I have missed school because of drinking' in the "yes" pile. Tell me about the last time that happened." (Some schools are even experimenting with putting questionnaires on a minicomputer to take advantage of students' increasing computer literacy and the interactive nature of computers. Programs to present and score questionnaires can easily be written in Basic, and the results can be immediately printed out for documentation.)

While they often have limited value as data collection tools, such instruments can be better used later in the assessment process, after the student has discussed his chemical use in some depth and has received some education regarding alcohol and other drug abuse. AODA assessment instruments can then reveal to the student what his drug-related behavior means.

GENERAL AODA INTERVIEW GUIDELINES

Obviously, the SAP Counselor or others involved in the screening process should be skilled interviewers and should be comfortable dealing with alcohol and other drug abuse issues with kids. Many for whom the role of SAP Counselor is new have found that both skill and comfort come with practice. Clearly, building rapport and trust is also basic to the success of any counseling relationship, and may take several sessions. The following are among the basic guidelines for subsequently bringing up the subject of alcohol and other drug abuse with students early in the screening/assessment process:

1. Clarify how the student happens to be seeing you. For the student who self-refers, ask what brings her to you specifically. Often a friend has suggested she speak to someone, or a troublesome incident has precipitated a desire to get some information. For students referred formally by a staff member, review the circumstances that led up to the referral: "All of your teachers have expressed some concern about your absenteeism and declining grades," etc.

2. Clarify your role in the student assistance program. Ask if the student has heard of the student assistance program, how it works, and what services it offers. Let him know that your role is to help him figure out what is going on, whether he is happy with it, and what you can do together to change it. Be very clear that there is nothing punitive about the program or your role.

3. Explain confidentiality. Let the student know that what she discloses in the interviews is entirely confidential (i.e., will not be reported to parents, the principal, or to police). It is also vital to let the student know that if what you learn leads you to fear for her health, safety, or welfare you may need to involve other people, and that you will let her know when that happens.

4. Be clear about what is going to happen. Let the student know that in order to discover what is happening with him you will have to talk about many areas of his life. Because there is a lot to discuss, you may not get to everything today, and it may even be necessary to meet several times a week for a couple of weeks. Students accepting referral to the program because of AODA policy violations also need to know what consequences there are for failing to follow through.

5. Be clear about the need to discuss alcohol and drugs. Let the student know that in addition to the other areas you will explore you will need to ask about her alcohol and other drug use: "I know that most kids your age have at least used alcohol, and many are using marijuana and other drugs. Some kids get confused about that or get into trouble without knowing it. A lot of kids are worried about their parents' drinking or drug use, too. A lot of kids need help figuring all that out."

6. Acknowledge that the student has some responsibility for what happens in the screening. Express the hope that the student feels safe enough about talking to you that he will be honest about what is going on. Giving the student permission to say "I'd rather not answer that," often prevents minimizing or other dishonest answers.

7. Ask specific, open-ended questions. Avoid "yes/no" questions in favor of more open "when/how" questions. Whenever possible, ask students to describe episodes of behavior rather than patterns. A "yes" answer to a question should often be followed up with "Tell me about that," or "Tell me all about the last time that happened."

8. Be aware of the forms which denial may take. In the initial screening it is often not useful to confront denial directly: the purpose is to gather information, not to change behavior. Consequently, vague answers can be pursued with more specific questions (e.g.,"I don't drink that often" can be followed by "How many times did you drink in the last month"). Hostility or anger may indicate a need to change the subject to a safer area which can still provide useful information: What do you like to do to have fun?" (Does having fun typically involve drug use?) The fact that a student is rather defensive about drug use and relatively open about other areas is useful assessment information in itself.

9. Be aware of the ways in which you can "get hooked." Especially where the counselor has strong beliefs about adolescent alcohol and other drug use he can sometimes be drawn into arguing about the merits of drugs, defending school policy, defending his own drinking, theorizing about whether drugs should be legalized, upholding moral standards, excusing some drug behavior as justifiable, and so on.

10. Educate about alcohol/drug use where appropriate. Explaining the difference between experimenting, abuse, and dependency helps students to see their own and others' behavior in a conceptual context. Sometimes giving appropriate feedback is "educational:" express your concern about the student's simultaneous use of alcohol and other depressant drugs simultaneously, about driving while intoxicated, experiencing blackouts, having an increase in tolerance, and so on.

11. Provide appropriate feedback to conclude the interview. There has to be an outcome for each discrete stage of the assessment process: either the decision that a specific recommendation for help is needed, or that one must gather more information to make this decision. At the end of the interview the SAP Counselor should summarize what the student has told him and check with the student to see if it is accurate. The counselor should also give the student his estimation of the information's significance: e.g., "I'm a little concerned about some of the things you have told me, and I think we should meet again to discuss them further."

RECORDS

As a rule, few records of a student's participation in the student assistance program should be kept, and never as a part of his cumulative file or files which are open to other staff members. It is usually necessary to keep records of some sort, to assist in program evaluation, to monitor student progress, and to provide documentation for any formal intervention strategies which may ultimately become necessary. School boards, for example, often require certain documentation for students who violate school AODA policies and who may subsequently become subject to expulsion hearings.

Supplement 8.4 provides examples of forms which can be used to summarize the results of the screening interview along with other data which the SAP staff has collected. This information is often taken to the Core Team or to those members constituting the "Screening Team."

The Screening Team, upon reviewing the results of the preliminary screening summarizes assessment recommendations by describing an individualized services plan and student outcomes monitored over time. Supplement 8.5 is an example of how such information can be documented.

Supplement 8.4

STUDENT SAP SCREENING SUMMARY

Student: _____ Referral Date _____

ENVIRONMENTAL SOURCES:

Summary of Staff Observations:

Academic Performance:

Classroom Conduct:

Other Behavior:

Possible AODA Behavior:

Witnessed:

Suspected:

Other Comments by Staff:

Summary of Other's Observations (parents, peers, etc.)

ARCHIVAL SOURCES:

_____ Unexcused absences   COMMENTS:
_____ Frequent excused absences
_____ In-school absenteeism
_____ Tardiness
_____ Suspensions
_____ Disciplinary referrals
_____ Loss of athletic eligibility
_____ Increasing noninvolvement in activities
_____ Home problems
_____ Job problems
_____ Legal problems
_____ Others:

SCREENING INTERVIEW SUMMARY

Interviewer: _____ Date(s) _____

RELATIONSHIPS:
- Family constellation
- Quality of home life
- Closest relationships
- Sexual relationships
- Group relationships

RATIONALITY:
- Extreme mood swings
- Suicidal tendencies
- Control of strong feelings
- Potential for violence
- Denial/Defensiveness

RESOURCES:
- Employment
- Skills and competencies
- Leisure, fun
- Home support
- Legal problems
- School performance
- Financial resources
- Use of other agencies

AODA-SPECIFIC AREAS:
- Stage of chemical use
- Risk Factors
- Family concerns
- Denial:

INTERVIEWER'S RECOMMENDATIONS:

Supplement 8.5

CONFIDENTIAL

STUDENT SAP SERVICES PLAN

Student _____ ID No. _____

School _____ Grade _____

Parent _____

Address _____

City/State/Zip _____ Home Phone _____

CORE TEAM RECOMMENDATIONS:		
DATE	*RECOMMENDATION*	*OUTCOME*

Agreed to by:

Student _____ Date _____

SAP Counselor _____ Date _____

Parent(s) _____ Date _____

Principal _____ Date _____

Core Team Members present:

_____ Date _____

_____ Date _____

_____ Date _____

_____ Date _____

_____ Date _____

_____ Date _____

_____ Date _____

_____ Date _____

Supplement 8.6

DRUG ABUSE CORRELATES

Research has established that a number of factors bear both positive and negative correlations with youthful drug abuse (NIDA: 1976, 1979). The results of drug abuse correlate research, however, have to be interpreted with great caution. First, it is vital to bear in mind that none of the following have been shown to have causal relationships to development of chemical dependency; most, in fact, have been shown to have no causal connection. Second, the dozens of studies upon which correlates are based vary widely in the number and nature of subjects studied and in the circumstances under which the data was collected. Thus, a study of 25 young heroin addicts in a psychiatric unit will yield different correlates that a study of 950 adolescents in a chemical dependency treatment program. Yet the results of many such studies at and between these two extremes are pooled to yield the "correlates" below. Finally, few correlate studies are longitudinal in nature. Rather, they constitute state descriptions, or descriptions of traits of drug abusers during active drug use, or during or shortly after treatment. In such research it is likely that personality and social traits are effects of chemical use rather than its causes.

For a more detailed description of correlate research see Ardyth Norem-Heibesen and Diane Hedin, "Adolescent Problem Behavior: Causes, Connections, and Contexts of Drug Abuse," in Adolescent Peer Pressure: Theory, Correlates, and Program Implications for Drug Abuse Prevention. (Washington, DC: National Institute on Drug Abuse, 1981. Publication No. (ADM) 81-1152.

Drug abuse has been positively correlated with:

- knowledge of drugs and their effects
- accepting attitudes towards drugs
- intentions to experiment or use
- use of other drugs
- impulsivity
- feelings of alienation, disillusionment
- excessive personal stress
- boredom, sensation seeking, need for stimulation and novelty
- assertiveness
- antisocial tendencies
- low sense of psychological well-being
- low self-esteem
- running away from home
- general feelings of rejection
- reliance on peer group for drug information
- skepticism about school drug education programs
- skepticism about media prevention efforts
- peer support for and approval of deviant behavior
- pro-drug attitudes and behavior in peers
- sexual promiscuity
- having a close friend with a drug problem
- parental use of alcohol and/or other drugs

- parental chemical dependency
- parental use of medications
- lack of parental concern
- parental permissiveness
- childhood stress and trauma
- absence of a parent
- family instability and disorganization
- poor quality of family relationships
- over- and under-dominated by parents
- harsh physical punishment
- feelings of rejection by parents
- negative attitudes toward school
- low achievement in school
- disciplinary problems in school
- rejection of traditional values

Drug use has been negatively correlated with:

- high self-esteem
- liking of school
- grades and achievement in school
- decision making skills
- self-reliance
- feelings of belonging
- religious beliefs
- optimism about the future
- humanistic environment in the school
- alternative education programs for dropouts and underachievers
- involvement in community institutions and programs addressing youth problems
- clear, consistent child rearing practices
- parent religiosity
- parental intolerance of deviance
- presence of controls and regulations in the home
- presence of an extended family

Chapter 9 | Intervention and Referral

To the extent that people or systems are not fully aware of what is happening with them, they will not know what they need to do in order to change.

Another major function which a student assistance program must perform is intervention. Once students have been identified and some degree of preliminary assessment has occurred, the school system must be prepared to take steps to get the student to appropriate help. At times in-school services will be sufficient; at others referral to outside agencies will be necessary. The nature of appropriate interventive strategies and services offered to a student will depend largely upon the nature and scope of his AODA-related problem and the degree to which he has the personal, social, and family resources to support changes in his behavior. Interventive strategies appropriate for students who are experimenting with alcohol and other drugs will typically be ineffective for those who are abusing or who are chemically dependent. Moreover, some students who are abusing alcohol or other drugs may be able to change their behavior in response to a given strategy while others may not.

Thus, in designing its student assistance program the school system will need to understand intervention and its mutual interaction with assessment, develop a repertoire of intervention services and strategies, appreciate intervention as a process, and clarify the roles of various staff members in this intervention process.

Intervention and "Prevention"

"Prevention" is a term which has gained such currency in the language that most people have an intuitive sense of what it means. For the purposes of designing a student assistance program, however, it is necessary to clearly distinguish between prevention and intervention as terms and as program elements for many reasons, not the least among which is the fact that one often encounters arguments within a school as to which is "better," which is a priority, or in which one the school should be investing its resources.

Although intervention and prevention are usually regarded as polar but mutually exclusive activities, there is not always widespread agreement among experts as to the exact distinction between the two. Prevention, for example, is sometimes described as consisting of those activities which keep a problem (such as alcohol/drug abuse) from developing or from progressing to later and more serious stages. In this global sense, virtually *every* activity on behalf of any student with any degree of AODA involvement is a prevention activity, and student assistance programs are primarily prevention programs. In this view, intervention activities are reserved for those who are chemically dependent and consist of strategies for getting people into treatment. (Some definitions of "prevention" are so broad as to include even treatment, since it prevents chemical dependency from progressing to its severest consequences).

Even specific activities are often labelled exclusively "prevention" activities (AODA information and education programs, alternatives programs, rewriting policy language, etc.) whereas others are exclusively "intervention" (e.g., referring people for treatment). These either/or perspectives falsely dichotomize activities and strategies and fail to recognize that education can just as easily lead students to stop using drugs as they can prevent students from beginning to use them.

In a very fundamental sense, however, a given activity becomes either preventive or interventive depending on the nature of the student to whom it is applied, and the nature of her AODA involvement. In this view, the distinction between prevention and intervention activities must be both student-centered and outcome-based. Thus, at the risk of adding yet another set of distinctions to those already current, the following definitions are offered as a means of understanding the nature of intervention as a basic program function:

> *Intervention consists of those purposeful activities by which meaningful persons or segments of the environment strengthen the individual and his environment in order to interrupt existing harmful AODA-related behavior in a manner intended to bring about a change in a positive direction.*

In contrast,

> *Primary prevention consists of those purposeful activities designed to strengthen those aspects of the individual and the environment which will preclude the onset of harmful AODA-related behavior.*

Both definitions share some common points. Each recognizes that alcohol and other drug abuse occur within both an individual and an environmental con-

text, and that the respective activities are purposeful and planned—designed to bring about specific AODA-related changes. The definitions differ in only one crucial way: the appropriate target group for primary prevention activities consists of students who have not yet begun to use alcohol or other drugs. Intervention activities are those applied to students after they have begun chemical use. Thus treatment can be thought of as the most concentrated form of intervention (but one which lies outside the scope of the school system) because it continues the process of interrupting harmful dependence on alcohol or other drugs. Perhaps paradoxically, a support group for recovering students becomes a prevention activity. Moreover, activities directed toward children of alcoholic parents can simultaneously be both preventive and interventive in character: they interrupt the harmful effects of alcoholism on children and can prevent such children from beginning to abuse alcohol or other drugs.

The Progressive Intervention Continuum

While it is risky to proceed too far from a too general principle, the process of intervention may be characterized in something like the following terms. People often fail to change their alcohol/drug-related behavior because they are insufficiently aware of its nature or personal implications. Denial can be thought of as a complex of factors (biological, psychological, emotional, social) which impair this awareness-factors which prevent people from having the information they need in order to know that they need to change and how they need to do it. (Tarter, *et al.*; 1984, 1985 contain the best descriptions of the complex of factors involved in the denial system). Though the major outcome of intervention is to interrupt harmful AODA-related behavior, its major function is to counteract denial. Thus, intervention can be regarded as the process by which significant aspects of the environment enhance awareness.

The National Institute on Drug Abuse (NIDA) and the National Institute on Alcohol Abuse and Alcoholism (NIAAA) recognized seven AODA program activity areas which enhance awareness, counteract denial, and are thus important to the intervention process: information, education, alternatives, intervention, treatment, environmental change, and social policy change (French and Kaufman, p. 4-6). A number of things are noteworthy about the list. First, each activity area can have either a preventive or an interventive effect, depending on the nature of the problem presented by the individual student upon whom the activity is focussed. Secondly, the list includes activities, the locus of whose action is either the individual or the

Figure 9.1

CONTINUUM OF PROGRESSIVE INTERVENTION

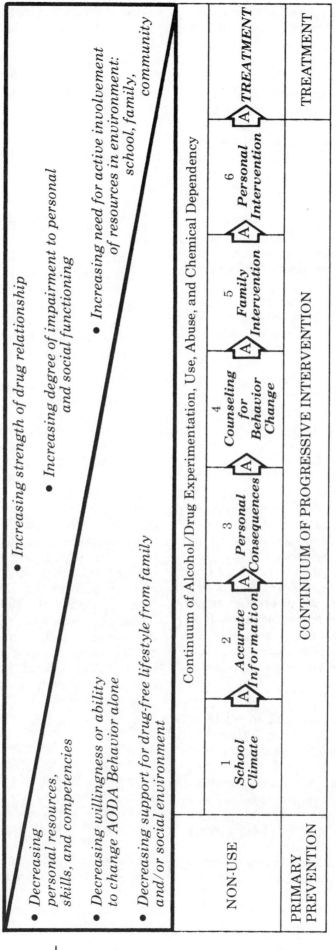

- Increasing strength of drug relationship
- Increasing degree of impairment to personal and social functioning
- Increasing need for active involvement of resources in environment: school, family, community

- Decreasing personal resources, skills, and competencies
- Decreasing willingness or ability to change AODA Behavior alone
- Decreasing support for drug-free lifestyle from family and/or social environment

Continuum of Alcohol/Drug Experimentation, Use, Abuse, and Chemical Dependency

NON-USE	1 School Climate	2 Accurate Information	3 Personal Consequences	4 Counseling for Behavior Change	5 Family Intervention	6 Personal Intervention	TREATMENT
PRIMARY PREVENTION	CONTINUUM OF PROGRESSIVE INTERVENTION						TREATMENT

 Indicates assessment activities which precede intervention steps.

environment. Third, the arrangement of activities on the list seems to reflect a progression from mildest intervention strategies (i.e., "information") to more concerted (i.e., "intervention" proper).

Like assessment, the intervention program function within the Student Assistance Program model is best considered to be a process, not an individual event. Figure 9.1 depicts this continuum. For the purposes of this discussion the NIDA/NIAAA program areas can be analyzed into six different intervention activities which lie along a progressive intervention continuum. Students may be thought of as being arranged along this continuum according to the nature and severity of their relationship with alcohol or other drugs. In general, as one moves progressively to the right in the figure, drug-involved youth are found to have fewer personal resources, skills, and competencies due to the impairment of alcohol and other drugs, a decreasing willingness or ability to change AODA-related behavior, and a decreasingly supportive family and social environment. Similarly, the drug relationship becomes increasingly strong, the impairment caused by alcohol/drug use increases, and there is an increasing need for more active involvement in the intervention process from key resources in the student's environment: school, family, and/or community.

In an effective student assistance program, a repertoire of intervention services and strategies will be available to the staff and to the student and they will be appropriately employed. Appropriateness is determined by the nature of the individual student's AODA-related problem, by the quality of the data collected during the assessment process, and by whether the student's behavior has changed to acceptable levels based on assistance made available to him earlier in the process. At key points along this continuum of progressive intervention the student and/or his family may be referred to in-school services or to those within the community. Note that additional assessment typically accompanies the utilization of a stronger intervention strategy.

Thus, Figure 9.1 identifies six components of an intervention process, progressively arranged to reflect their general relationship to a student's increasing need for outside help. Many students are able to stop using alcohol or other drugs in response to the development of a *school climate* which supports drug-free lifestyles. Others may change their behavior upon being given *accurate information* about alcohol and other drugs and their effects. Some students will need to experience *personal consequences* for violations of school standards or policies in order to make healthier decisions about chemicals. Still others will require *counseling for behavioral change*, or the opportunity to work through their AODA-related problems through a one-to-one or group experience. Those students who are unwilling or unable to improve school performance and/or modify their alcohol/drug behavior in response to education, consequences, and counseling may require *intervention with the family system* which may be unwittingly enabling drug-related problems to continue. Finally, a formal, well-orchestrated *personal intervention* may be necessary for those few students who do not respond to these strategies, with referral to treatment programs in the community as the primary goal.

School Climate

School climate is one of the intervention components which focuses on the quality of the environment in which students find themselves. School climate has generally been defined as those qualities of the school and the people in it which affect how people feel while they are there. More specifically, a school climate can be one which unwittingly fosters alcohol/drug use and their related problems, one which promotes, supports, and maintains drug-free lifestyles, or one which is indifferent to the issue.

In many ways we teach about alcohol and drug abuse far more by example than by precept. As Chapter 5 pointed out, many aspects of the school system—from individual behavior to punitive policies or the absence of consequences—can contribute to a climate which unwittingly allows AODA-related problems to continue or to worsen. For example, the degree to which the possession, use, or delivery of alcohol/drugs by students is open and *visible* to other students certainly contributes directly to a climate which communicates to students that drug use or abuse is a norm. When students typically see others' drug-related behavior as incurring no overt consequences it is often interpreted as tacit permission to use. When the dire predictions implicit in drug messages based on "scare tactics" fail to materialize, students learn to distrust or discount the underlying message that alcohol and other drug use is harmful.

Students also frequently express contempt for the inconsistent, preferential treatment given some groups of students regarding alcohol/drug abuse issues. The school staff, for example, may see athletes as somehow a "special" group which it often expects to live up to higher standards than other students. Students must perceive as unjust or capricious a system where drug use by athletes or student council representatives goes unnoticed or excused when others are suspended from school, further fragmenting the school into hostile cliques.

Furthermore, the discovery that the use or abuse

of alcohol or other drugs is routinely part of staff social and recreational activities at best creates skepticism about any anti-drug education by the school and at worst promotes cynicism about the school as an institution with values worthy of respect. Students do notice the failure of the school to recognize and intervene respectfully and humanely with staff members whose AODA problems have become obvious, and must conclude that having such problems is either acceptable, that dealing with them is not, or that helping others with these problems is somehow unsafe.

In a more positive school climate there is open, visible, and clear support for a drug-free lifestyle by students, for responsible behavior with respect to alcohol and other drugs by adults, and for responsible behavior toward people with problems by everyone. Developing and enforcing, uniformly and fairly, policies against the use of alcohol or others drugs not only assists an individual student so involved but begins to remove such behavior from daily visibility. Most schools keeping statistics in these areas note that the number of disciplinary referrals and suspensions for AODA-related conduct decreases after an enlightened school policy is developed and enforced. While a policy does not magically reduce student drug use, it does drastically reduce it within the school setting.

Drug education efforts that are consistent across different grades, school buildings, and staff members contributes to a school climate that supports chemical health. In building this climate it is important not only to communicate accurate information about alcohol and other drugs but also to communicate the values according to which the school has decided that alcohol/drug use is harmful or dangerous to students. A positive school climate communicates the fact that the school and its staff members care enough about students to invest themselves in helping those with AODA-related problems. Part of the success of the "Just Say No" effort lies in the degree to which it builds a visible, vocal climate of positive peer support for staying drug-free. Many students, however, will require more than just a slogan: accurate information, personal support, communication skills, and an opportunity to discover personal values.

The school can be warm, friendly, caring, and physically and emotionally safe, with students and staff working together to take the risks that are often necessary in solving painful problems. In a school whose climate supports chemical health people care about one another, demonstrate their respect for each other, and trust each other. In a cohesive atmosphere, where students and staff feel safe and accepted for who they are, there is less need for defensiveness and denial to protect self worth. There is a sense that rules, policies, and procedures are person-centered and designed to uphold humane values rather than to exert control or maximize the opportunity to punish.

While climate is admittedly a global characteristic it does have a direct and concrete impact on student and staff behavior. With respect to alcohol/drug issues, school climate is a significant interventive as well as preventive component. Many students who begin experimenting with chemicals are able to make decisions to remain drug free as a result of the degree to which the school environment promotes and supports such decisions and the values upon which they are based. Changes in school climate are often more the effect of a student assistance program rather than its precursor. The climate changes as the SAP staff promotes awareness of the program and as students who benefit from the program talk to others about it.

Accurate Information

Many students are able to change their AODA-related behavior upon being given appropriate, accurate information about alcohol and other drugs. For example, Tables 2.1 and 2.9 (Chapter 2, Supplements) depict the slight decreases since 1979 in the use of alcohol and marijuana among high school seniors and among 12 to 17 year olds. Although it may be due in equal measure to developing, enforcing, and informing students about school alcohol/drug policies, many experts attribute the change in part to the impact of more appropriate curricula and to drug education programs. Appropriate alcohol/drug education provides consensual information which avoids the extreme positions which can come from a single piece of research. It presents accurate, honest, timely information about the effects of alcohol and other drugs on the whole human system, not just on the body. Students need to know about the different varieties of chemical experience, the signs and symptoms of each, and the effects of drug use, abuse, and dependency on human lives.

Students also need information about and an opportunity to examine the impact of chemical use on their own lives: how chemicals can interfere with the tasks they face—forming rewarding relationships, finding acceptance, solving problems and taking risks, developing goals, and taking steps to achieve them. Thus, appropriate education is generic as well as AODA-specific. Its activities often focus on critical life skills such as decision making, problem solving, interpersonal communication, coping with stress, and identifying values.

Accurate information can be provided to all students through either a commercially available or a district-devised comprehensive K-12 curriculum. Staff members are invited to develop alcohol/drug units where they are relevant to the subject matter of their courses. In some school systems the SAP staff develop a semester course on alcohol and other drug abuse which covers the areas indicated above and which is offered to students as an elective. Classroom presentations by the SAP staff on basic AODA issues is also frequently one of the steps in implementing a student assistance program (see Part Four).

"When students typically see others' drug-related behavior as incurring no overt consequences it is often interpreted as tacit permission to use."

On a more individual level, accurate, personally relevant information can be provided to students through counseling sessions. The SAP staff and/or appropriately trained pupil services staff can provide significant information through pamphlets, handouts, and discussions in regular meetings with a student. The safety of the counseling relationship enables students to discuss their personal experience with alcohol and other drugs and to examine at greater depth its effects on their lives and decisions. Many self-referrals to the student assistance program consist of students who want more information and the assistance and support of a trusted adult in adopting a drug-free lifestyle.

Support groups which focus on students' own chemical use are another setting within which appropriate alcohol/drug information may be utilized by students in changing their behavior (see Chapter 11 and Chapter 16). In a *Drug Information Group* lasting only four to six weeks, students with relatively non-severe patterns of alcohol/drug use can be given information about drugs and their effects on individuals and families, the progression from experimentation to dependency, how to know if someone has a drug problem, how to talk to them about it, and where to get appropriate help.

Thus, accurate information is an important interventive as well as preventive component of a student assistance program, provided to students on a global as well as individual basis, including both an AODA-specific as well as a generic focus.

Personal Consequences

The development and visible enforcement of improved policies regarding students with alcohol/drug-related problems is a component of school climate and is part of the information conveyed to students through drug education efforts. Many students possess the personal skills, competencies, and motivations enabling them to modify their alcohol/drug behavior in response to these measures. For others, the experience of specific, direct, personal consequences for AODA-related behavior—whether in the school, in the family, or in the community—is an important step in intervening in their chemical use.

By allowing the student to experience direct personal consequences for alcohol/drug use or related behavior the school prevents him from evading the awareness that the decisions he is making have logical outcomes and often have effects on others. A student can learn *about* decision making through information; he learns how to *make decisions* by experiencing and evaluating their consequences. Allowing the student to experience consequences also provides the school with the opportunity to specifically explain the expectations it has for acceptable behavior and the beliefs and values which underlie those expectations. Consistently experiencing consequences for unacceptable behavior also lets the student know that he is not invisible, that people in the school environment are watching, and that they care. None of this has anything to do with punishment. Punishment teaches students about the misuse of power and control; experiencing consequences rooted in clear expectations teaches them about responsibility.

As a component of the school intervention process, students can experience direct personal consequences for their behavior in a number of ways. As pointed out in Chapter 7, early identification is also early intervention and requires that all staff members be clearly in touch with their standards for acceptable performance in and out of the classroom. Communicating these expectations to students when their school performance becomes unacceptable can form the basis for referral to the student assistance program if behavior fails to improve. Referring a student to the program is itself one early means of allowing her to experience one consequence of her behavior.

With respect to school AODA policies, there is substantial agreement that not only must the policy delineate a clear schedule of consequences for school-related alcohol/drug behavior but that students actually be allowed to experience them. Referral to in-school or community services should be offered at the time consequences are imposed (e.g., suspension) but the latter should not be used in lieu of consequences. Many policies do contain provisions by which a student can reduce consequences by utilizing school and/or community services to change her behavior. Thus, policy language may state that alcohol/drug use and participation in extracurricular activities are incompatible, but that a student may continue in these activities if she successfully participates in the student assistance program: i.e., changes her behavior through counseling, a support group, referral to a community AODA agency, etc. This allows students to experience consequences and to make here-and-now decisions about their AODA-related behavior.

Students may also incur and experience consequences, not just for policy violations, but for failure to change their behavior. It is conceivable, for example, that a student becomes involved with the student assistance program through a self-referral or peer referral. Depending on the school's policy and the individual student's circumstances, the SAP staff may decide to defer notifying and involving parents. The universal exception to confidentiality allows the school to involve other people whenever it has reason to fear for the student's health, safety, or welfare. Contacting and involving a student's parents is a legitimate consequence of the student's unwillingness or inability to eliminate his chemical use or significantly modify it in a healthy direction.

Thus, students can experience direct personal consequences for their general school performance, for violations of school policy, or for failure to modify their behavior in accordance with expectations placed upon them within the student assistance program.

Counseling for Behavioral Change

As Figure 9.1 also indicates, some students' relationship with alcohol and/or other drugs strengthens to the point of causing significant impairment in personal and social functioning. Students who begin chemical use early in adolescence may suffer from impairments to the normal development of decision making skills and other personal competencies. The abuse, or 'problem use,' of chemicals presents the student and the SAP staff with clearly visible, demonstrable situations where drug use is causing a pattern of problems in the student's life. Whatever the cause, some students will be unable to change their alcohol/-drug behavior without more concerted intervention in the form of counseling which has specific expectations for behavior change.

For some students, alcohol and other drug abuse agencies in the community may be the appropriate setting for this counseling. Some agencies' formalized assessment programs consist of education and individual and group counseling for students who have more than experimental patterns of drug use. These programs, which most often involve parent participation as well, can bring about significant changes in the behavior of students who are not chemically dependent. Where appropriate education and counseling services are unavailable, many schools incorporate similar services into their student assistance program. Counseling for behavioral change typically occurs on a one-to-one basis with the SAP staff or through the student's participation in one of the use-focussed support groups.

Whether through individual counseling or a use-focussed group, the appropriateness of this type of interventive strategy depends on the student's willingness to participate. The student might be motivated by a sincere desire to make changes, or by a desire to avoid other consequences at home or in school. Clear, specific goals for individual change emerge early in the process. The primary goals of this intervention strategy are for students to identify their chemical use *as a problem*, and to make significant changes in the direction of abstinence. More intensive education about alcohol/drug use, abuse, and dependency is combined with the expectation that students examine their alcohol and other drug involvement as fully as possible by discussing specific personal experiences. Students learn what denial is and how it is exhibited in their behavior. Most individual SAP Counselors and facilitators of use-focussed *Personal Change Groups* (Chapter 16) employ contracts as a significant tool in bringing about the reduction or elimination of chemical use (Kanfer, 1975; Moursund, 1985). Students are expected to discuss breaches of week-to-week contracts, for example, and to make use of the skills given them to keep the contracts in the future.

Students typically become involved in this intervention strategy because they choose it in lieu of a more stringent consequence in school or at home. They have more severe patterns of chemical use and a higher degree of denial and resistance than other students. It is understood at the beginning that at any time they might be referred to more appropriate sources of help at an outside agency if their progress becomes unsatisfactory. It is rare for parent contact to have been deferred until this point, so parent contact, education, and support is typically involved in counseling for behavioral change.

Family Intervention

Working with the family is a significant area of environmental change according to the NIAAA's intervention criteria. Parents or significant others may become involved at any point in the assessment/intervention process, depending on the circumstances of the student's referral to the program, the student's willingness to change, and the assessment by the SAP staff of the likelihood of parental support. Thus, the issue is not so much a matter of whether parents will become involved as when.

It is often necessary to intervene in the family system in order to bring about or support further intervention in the student's AODA-related problems. Many parents are unaware that their child is using alcohol or other drugs; they may have seen no changes in his behavior or noticed no overt signs of chemical use. Others become worried and confused by erratic or problem behavior but attribute it to adolescence in general or to specific sources of stress rather than to alcohol/drug use. Still others may have direct knowledge of alcohol or other drug involvement but may be afraid to acknowledge it as being harmful and dangerous, or to identify their child as having a "drug problem." Some families may even conclude that the student does have a serious problem but may be afraid to ask for help in the community or the school system. Finally, a parent's chemical dependency often prevents the family from recognizing or addressing a student's own use or abuse of chemicals.

"A student can learn about decision making through information; he learns how to make decisions by experiencing and evaluating their consequences."

The school can intervene in the family system in a number of ways. Most parents will require accurate information about alcohol and other drug abuse, enabling, and denial. They often need specific guidance in what to look for as a means of bringing into focus behavior they have already seen or identifying new indications that a student may be in trouble with drugs. The data the school has collected in the early phases of the assessment process is often what they need to validate their own perceptions. They may also need help in clarifying their own expectations for acceptable conduct by the student and information on effective parenting skills. While it is beyond the scope of the school's role to intervene directly in a parent's alcoholism, it can work with the codependent spouse or other family members to the point where they will accept a referral to a community agency, Al-Anon, Alateen, etc. Some school systems implement parent information and support groups, help in building parent networks, and provide workshops in parent effectiveness training as components of their student assistance programs. Others refer parents to Parents Al-Anon and Tough Love groups in the community. In some cases it may become necessary to refer the family to an AODA screening/assessment agency or directly to a chemical dependency treatment program.

In the vast majority of cases, where a student is not chemically dependent, the joint, cooperative efforts of the school and the family are sufficient to bring about changes in the student's chemical use.

Personal Intervention

In most instances the previous intervention strategies, undertaken either in school or in the community, will either result in the drastic improvement in a student's AODA-related problems or in a referral to an appropriate counseling or treatment agency. On relatively rare occasions, however, severe drug abuse or chemical dependency is coupled with few personal, social, and family resources supportive of change. In these cases it becomes necessary for those in the student assistance program to enlist many different resources within the school in a more formalized, highly structured, and deliberate personal intervention strategy. The personal intervention represents the strongest type of environmental change along the progressive intervention continuum.

The decision to utilize a personal intervention strategy is most often based on the likelihood that a student is chemically dependent and the probability that she and/or her family will not accept referral to professional help without considerable motivational power. Personal intervention may also be advisable if it unlikely that the student or family will follow through with professional recommendations or remain in treatment without the impact of this technique.

Those involved in organizing and conducting the intervention should be appropriately trained in intervention skills and in the basic principles of alcohol and other drug abuse which underlie them. First developed as a technique to be used in clinical settings by alcoholism specialists (Johnson, 1980, 1986), the major stages in the process can be effective in the school setting if organized with deliberate care. (See Supplement 9.1, "Arranging a Personal Intervention").

One of the first steps in the preparation process requires the SAP Counselor/Coordinator in the building, and other members of the Core Team, to review the data that has been collected regarding the student, including the "Major Assessment Questions" and the history of the student's failure to change despite services already provided within the school and/or the community. Once the decision is made to proceed with a personal intervention strategy, the Core Team begins to identify who will be effective members of the Referral Team—those who will be present at the intervention event. The Referral Team typically consists at least of the building administrator, the SAP Counselor/Coordinator, the student's group leaders, and staff members with key firsthand information about the student. In individual cases others may have crucial roles to play: a coach, police or probation officer, an AODA counselor, family members, and even other students.

The next step—selecting a realistic, appropriate goal for the intervention—usually entails identifying a referral resource in the community. In many cases the appropriate service will be a chemical dependency treatment program. Occasionally the Referral Team will recommend that the student and his family go to an assessment agency and follow its recommendations. In selecting the goal, other factors in addition to the possibility of chemical dependency need to be considered. Referral to a psychiatrist, for example, may be appropriate for the student who is depressed or who presents evidence of suicidal tendencies. It is wise for the school, however, when considering non-AODA-specific services, to identify those resource persons and agencies which nonetheless have a professional understanding of chemical dependency. All members of the Referral Team will need to agree in advance to support the same goal when the intervention meeting is held.

Those on the Referral Team must also arrive at and be prepared to communicate to the student the consequences of his failure to accept referral and/or to improve his behavior. Many types of consequences are possible. The school often has consequences in the form of suspension and expulsion, loss of eligibility for extracurricular activities, and so forth. Other key members of the Referral Team (e.g., family members, juvenile justice authorities, etc.) may have consequences appropriate to their experience with the student.

Finally, significant attention needs to be devoted to planning a specific agenda for the intervention meeting: deciding on a chairperson, determining the order in which data will be presented, and anticipating the student's resistances, among others. One of the overriding concerns in conducting the intervention meeting is that those involved express their data in a nonjudgemental, caring, yet firm manner.

The major purpose of the personal intervention strategy is to enhance the awareness of the student and his family to the point that denial is minimized long enough for the student to agree to get help. An admission of chemical dependency is not only inappropriate but unnecessary.

Few school systems will want to conduct such meetings without ample preparation, the guidance of a professional AODA counselor from the community, and the involvement and cooperation of parents at the earliest point. In some cases, however, where parents have resisted previous attempts at intervention, the focus of the intervention meeting is perhaps on parents more than upon the child. Some principals, for example, have explained to parents that their child has a terminal illness, for which they are denying their child treatment, and that unless they admit the student to a treatment program within 48 hours, the school will be obligated to file a report of suspected child abuse or neglect according to state statutes. This rather extreme but justified approach is only possible where members of the Core Team and Referral Team are well trained, have gathered significant data about the student's condition, and are acting within a firm but enlightened school policy actively supported by the Board of Education.

These various components of the progressive intervention continuum can also be visualized as an elaborate series of "filters," with school climate at the top, and personal intervention and referral to community services at the bottom. Those students who do not or cannot respond to the previous attempt to change their behavior pass on to the next. While referral to community agencies may occur at any point it usually becomes the mandatory recommendation by the time personal intervention strategies are called for.

Clearly, the assessment and the intervention processes are interrelated and form the heart of the Student Assistance Program model. Figure 9.2 depicts this mutual interaction. In general, the results of the initial screening form the basis for the Core Team's decisions about what source of help may be appropriate to the student and what steps to take. Actual referral recommendations are made to the student (and to parents when they become involved) by one or more members of the Core Team. If the student accepts the referral recommendations, her behavior is monitored to see if it improves to acceptable levels. The failure to accept referral to in-school or community resources, or the failure to improve school performance may result in standard disciplinary measures. The SAP staff continues to monitor the student's behavior as a new assessment/intervention cycle begins.

Figure 9.2

GENERAL INTERVENTION PROCESS

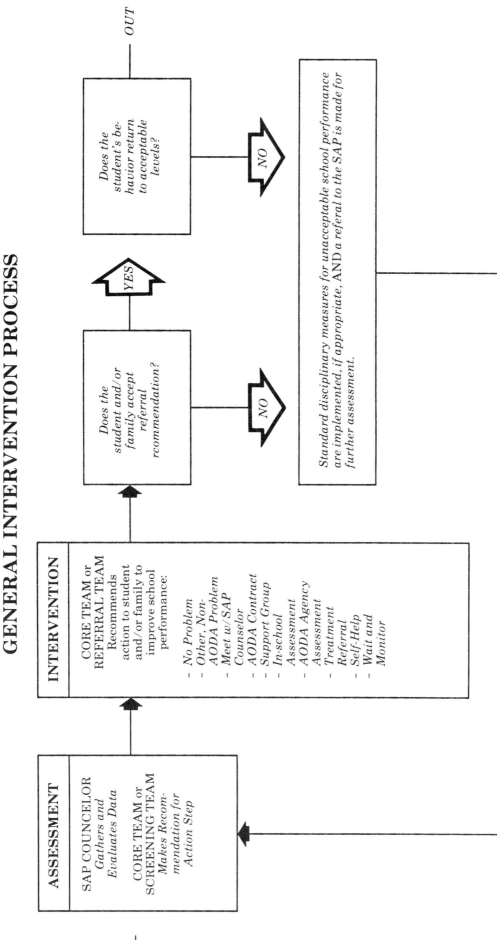

(Outcome of intervention provides input for next level of assessment.)

FOR FURTHER READING

Fatis, M. and P. Konerko. "Written Contracts as Adjuncts in Family Therapy." *Social Work*. 28, (1983): 161-163. The authors describe the aspects of written contracts which the couselor can use to assist the student and other family members in solving problems.

Johnson, Vernon E. *I'll Quit Tomorrow*. New York: Harper and Row, 1980. The techniques for personal intervention in chemical dependency were first described in this book.

_____. *Intervention: How to Help Someone Who Doesn't Want Help*. Minneapolis: The Johnson Institute, 1986. The technique of intervention in chemical dependency is examined as a step-by-step process of gathering information, arriving at a goal for the intervention, discovering consequences, anticipating defensive reactions, and finalizing a clear agenda for the intervention meeting.

McHolland, James D. "Strategies for Dealing with Resistant Adolescents." *Adolescence*. 20:78 (Summer, 1985): 349-368. A number of different styles of denial and resistance in adolescents is described from a developmental perspective and a wide variety of specific counseling strategies for coping with them is suggested.

Potter-Effron, Patricia and Ronald T. "Treating the Family of the Chemically Dependent Adolescent: The Enabling Inventory and Other Techniques for Responsibility." *Alcoholism Treatment Quarterly*. 3:1 (1986): 59-72. The Potter-Effrons present four clinical techniques for working with families with chemically dependent adolescents including the family intervention and the home contract.

Chapter 9 | **Supplements**

Supplement 9.1, "Arranging the Personal Intervention" summarizes some of the basic steps involved in assembling the Referral Team and preparing for the personal intervention meeting.

Supplement 9.2, "Referral to Community Agencies," describes some of the factors of which the school and the SAP staff need to be aware when referring students and parents to out-of-school resources.

Supplement 9.3 is the "General Consent Form" for the release of information. Most alcohol and other drug abuse agencies are severely constrained by federal legislation as to what information they may disclose to persons outside their program. Schools, too, are subject to state statutes governing the confidentiality of general student records. The General Consent Form, signed by a student and/or his parent, permits the school and AODA agencies to share information which will improve the care or management of the student.

Supplement 9.1

ARRANGING THE PERSONAL INTERVENTION

The SAP Counselor, in consultation with the members of the Core Team will normally conclude that a formal intervention strategy is needed based on the following considerations:

1. There are general behavioral indicators of a problem (i.e., grades, attendance, conduct) from several sources (staff, parents, screening interviews, support group participation);

2. There is evidence of alcohol and/or other drug abuse;

3. It seems possible that chemical dependency or chronic drug abuse is at the root of a student's behavior problems or complicates attempts to correct them;

4. The student has been unwilling or unable to change his behavior utilizing other strategies and resources;

5. It is unlikely that the student and/or family will accept referral to professional help without the motivational power of a formal intervention;

6. It is unlikely that the student and/or family will follow through with professional recommendations (e.g., for chemical dependency treatment) without the motivational power of a formal intervention.

In arranging the intervention meeting the SAP Counselor/Coordinator should exercise care to select appropriate participants who are properly trained in intervention skills and who have been properly prepared for this specific meeting. This Referral Team is typically composed of key members of the Core Team as well as others who have significant information about the student or who have an important relationship with him. In preparing for the referral or intervention meeting, the SAP Counselor/Coordinator should take into account a number of criteria for participants:

1. Who are the most meaningful and/or influential persons surrounding and familiar with the student? (E.g., The SAP Counselor/Coordinator, the building administrator, concerned teachers, a coach or advisor, other students, family members, community agency representatives, police, clergyman, etc.)

2. Does everyone have personal, firsthand experience of the student's behavior and/or alcohol/drug use?

3. Can everyone assemble in your office to prepare for the personal intervention meeting?

4. Do all the members of the Referral Team understand enough about the nature of alcohol and other drug abuse or dependency, and the student's history, to accept the need for personal intervention?

5. Do the participants understand the intervention process and their proper roles within it?

6. Are the participants emotionally adequate to the intervention? Can they participate with care and concern and without judgement or blame?

7. Who will be the moderator, or leader of the intervention session: The SAP Counselor/Coordinator, building administrator, agency AODA Counselor, etc.?

8. Is there a need for training or consultation from an AODA agency counselor in preparing for and conducting the personal intervention?

The preparation process may take several weeks. When members of the Referral Team have been identified, the staff member(s) in charge of preparing for the personal intervention should assure that as individuals and as a team they are prepared for the intervention meeting:

1. Are all the participants generally prepared for the session? Do they understand the agenda, what will happen?

2. Are participants specifically prepared for the session. Do they have written lists or documentation of behavior, incidents, or patterns which legitimize their concern? Is there sufficient data to make the intervention successful?

3. Have various alternatives for referral been considered by the members of the intervention Referral Team? Will everyone agree to support the same referral goal?

4. Have the pertinent Referral Team members considered and decided upon appropriate consequences for the student's and/or family's failure to accept referral and improve in the areas of concern?

5. Have the Referral Team members anticipated the student's and/or family's defensive responses and discussed ways of responding to them appropriately?

6. Is there a moderator for the session? Is he or she aware of their role in:

   a. introducing the meeting; stating why everyone is here and how they got together;
   b. establishing "ground rules;"
   c. keeping the meeting on track;
   d. closing the meeting by summarizing the group's concern and offering the referral recommendations agreed upon by the Referral Team in advance?

7. Have members of the Referral Team decided upon an order of presentation of their information?

8. Does anyone need to be added to or eliminated from the Referral Team?

Supplement 9.2

REFERRAL TO COMMUNITY AGENCIES

In referring students who have AODA-related problems to outside agencies it is wise to observe some general guidelines:

1. Discover what agencies or practitioners the student or family may already be involved with. It may be necessary to inquire whether AODA issues are being dealt with, and to inform the agency that the school is referring to another community resource.

2. As a rule it is unwise to refer students to agencies without the knowledge or consent of parents or legal guardians. Even though many states have "minor's consent for treatment" legislation, the agency typically needs to contact parents at a certain point in the counseling or treatment program. Many AODA agencies will not accept adolescent referrals without parent involvement and willingness to receive help for themselves.

3. Wherever possible it is a good idea to present parents with a choice between two or more equivalent AODA services, assuming several equally good agencies are available or convenient. The SAP staff should research available resources and recommend only those that are philosophically consistent with its program and willing to develop good working relationships with it.

4. In recommending a choice of agencies or services to parents, the SAP staff should be sufficiently familiar with the services to answer questions about the program and to explain its functions and limitations.

5. In most cases the SAP staff should allow the student or parent to make appointments and arrangements themselves.

6. Be sure to designate someone within the school to serve as a contact person between the school and the agency, and to inform the agency of who this person is.

7. Wherever possible, secure a written "General Consent Form" for the release of information, signed by the student and/or parent (Supplement 9.3). The release of information can permit the school to communicate with the agency and vice versa. Consult state statutes to determine under what conditions and at what age students can consent to the release of information.

Supplement 9.3

GENERAL CONSENT FORM
FOR THE RELEASE OF INFORMATION

I, _____
            (student or parent/guardian name)

authorize _____
            (name of person/school disclosing information)

to disclose to _____
_____
_____

*(name or title of person/organization
to whom information is to be disclosed)*

the following identifying information from my records: (specify the extent or nature of information to be disclosed)

_____
_____
_____

The purpose or need for such disclosure is _____

_____
_____
_____

This consent to disclose information may be revoked by me at any time except to the extent that action has already been taken in reliance thereon.

This consent (unless expressly revoked earlier) expires upon

_____
(specify date, event, or condition upon which it will expire)

SIGNATURE OF STUDENT: _____ Date _____

SIGNATURE OF WITNESS: _____ Date _____

SIGNATURE OF PARENT, GUARDIAN,
LEGAL REPRESENTATIVE: _____ Date _____

_____
(specify relationship)

| Chapter 10 | # Treatment |

The program functions considered thus far—early identification, assessment, and intervention—all point toward treatment for at least 5 per cent of the nation's secondary school students. It has been repeatedly emphasized that the direct, primary treatment of youthful chemical dependency lies outside the province of the school system. Treatment for chemical dependency is, however, a crucial need of many students and is a vital program function. Although the school system does not provide treatment, it is necessary for those within its student assistance program to become familiar with a number of treatment issues.

For example, to the extent that they will not just be recommending treatment but services appropriate to the needs of a given students, those within the school's student assistance program will need to become aware of the variety of treatment modalities available and of the factors which make each one appropriate for given students. Those within the program will also need to have some understanding of the treatment and recovery process and its implications for adolescent patients. The outcomes of treatment can vary from program to program locally, and there is considerable variation among programs nationwide. Finally, the most important task of the school system entails the development of effective working relationships with those treatment programs in which its students are likely to participate.

Types of Treatment:
The Continuum of Care

The field of chemical dependency treatment has evolved to the point where the dependent teenager and his family as well as referring agencies are faced with varied services and diverse modalities from amongst which to choose. Adolescents with a diagnosis of chemical dependency are successfully treated within a variety of residential and nonresidential settings. The setting most appropriate for a given adolescent is contingent upon the severity of drug abuse, the types of drugs being abused, the adolescent's personal strengths (i.e., health, mental state, lifestyle), and environmental supports (i.e., family relationships, quality of home life, nature of peer group, status in school, etc.).

Hospital-based residential programs are appropriate for adolescents whose chemical dependency presents serious medical hazards due to the risk of overdose, the presence of physical addiction, the risks involved in withdrawal, and/or the medical complications of prolonged drug use: nutritional deficiencies and generally poor health. The need for medically supervised detoxification is nearly always present in adolescents with patterns of frequent use of multiple drugs, or with histories of heavy use of drugs such as amphetamines, cocaine, opiates, barbiturates, or alcohol. The restrictive regimen of a hospital-based program may be indicated for those who are at a high risk for accidental overdose, for those for whom suicide is a significant threat, and for adolescents with serious mental or emotional problems in addition to chemical dependency.

Non-hospital-based residential programs are appropriate for adolescents who require a highly structured, 24-hour program. Both hospital and nonhospital programs contain a structured and controlled environment to counteract a lack of internal motivation and self-direction, and the absence of strong family supports. Most of the treatment day consists of structured time spent in activities which include lectures, large and small group therapy, physical and recreational therapy, one-to-one counseling sessions, and orientation to the principles of AA, NA, or CA.

Longer term residential treatment can be conducted through therapeutic communities or group homes which specialize in chemical dependency. Some of these long-term programs can last from three months to a year or more. Traditionally, residential treatment programs have been short-term, with an average length of stay of between four and six weeks. Increasingly, however, adolescents are being effectively managed and successfully treated through a combination of short-term residential treatment and intensive outpatient care.

Alfred Friedman (1985, pp. 65-69) has summarized many of the factors which lead to a recommendation to inpatient or residential treatment. Hospital and nonhospital programs are typically appropriate for:

1. Adolescents who require detoxification in a controlled medical environment;

2. Adolescents who require hospitalization for medical or psychiatric reasons such as toxicity, risk of suicide, potential death from overdose, severe affective disorder;

3. Adolescents who show extreme, frequent, compulsive multiple drug abuse;

4. Adolescents who demonstrate a lack of self-control, self-direction, potential for violence toward others, or a need for external controls;

5. Adolescents with a poor home climate or little family support;

6. Adolescents who can benefit from a brief separation from their usual home or school environment;

7. Adolescents who can benefit from structure: limit-setting, rules or expectations for behavior, a system of rewards and consequences for behavior, and emphasis on personal responsibility skills;

8. Adolescents who need to have their access to alcohol or other drugs blocked via residential placement for a short period of time;

9. Adolescents who can benefit from having the opportunity to interrupt and examine harmful patterns of social interaction;

10. Adolescents who generally lack the support of home, family, school, job, or nondependent peers

Intensive outpatient programs are nonresidential modalities suited for adolescents with less severe patterns of chemical abuse: those who have been using for relatively short periods of time, whose drug use is more intermittent, or who are unlikely to experience severe withdrawal symptoms. Students with intact and supportive families are most often responsive to intensive outpatient programs, as are those who possess relatively well-developed personal and social competencies and support systems.

Intensive outpatient programs involve adolescents and family members in a treatment regimen for several hours a day, three to five days a week, for several weeks. The primary treatment components involve lectures, small group therapy, and individual and conjoint counseling for the adolescent as well as the family. Sessions may be held during the day or the evening. Evening programs have the advantage of interfering less in the adolescent's school attendance and family members' occupations.

Tables 10.1 and 10.2 give some idea of the characteristics of adolescents in treatment on a nationwide basis. The figures are derived from the federal CODAP system ("Client Oriented Data Acquisition Process), which contains the largest data base of drug patients in treatment programs. The statistics in Tables 10.1 and 10.2 are taken from the 52,510 adolescents who were in federally sponsored treatment programs in 1980. The vast majority—81.5 per cent—were admitted to drug-free outpatient programs; 11.4 per cent were in residential, nonhospital-based programs. Only a small number were treated through intensive hospitalization or intensive outpatient or alternative school programs—2.8 percent and 4.3 per cent, respectively.

Youth in these programs cited many reasons for entering a treatment program. Problems in the family and in school are what caused most adolescents to agree to seek treatment. Almost half, or 48.5 per cent, cited problems with family members as an important factor precipitating their admission. Another 39.5 per cent indicated that problems in school were the significant factor. Legal and medical problems were almost as common: 35.3 per cent gave legal problems as a reason for entering treatment; 32.7 per cent had experienced a previous drug overdose episode. Emotional problems were cited by 27.7 per cent; 15.9 per cent had previously attempted suicide. Approximately one in five (20.4 per cent) had been in a treatment program previously.

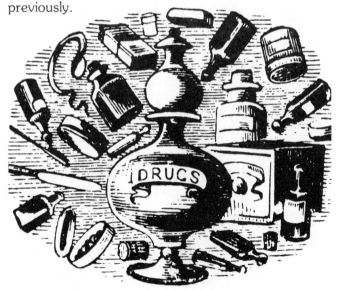

Table 10.1 indicates that use of marijuana is the primary drug of abuse among males in both residential and drug-free outpatient programs. It also indicates that males and females in inpatient programs differ somewhat in drug-of-choice. Males are most often treated for primary dependence on marijuana, depressants, and alcohol. Female adolescents are most often dependent upon depressants, followed by marijuana and amphetamines. Marijuana also seems to be the most frequently used drug among adolescents in outpatient drug-free programs.

Table 10.2 describes the pattern of drug-taking typical of inpatient and drug-free outpatient adolescents during the year before admission to treatment programs. Again, marijuana and alcohol form the core of drug abuse for the greatest number of patients in both treatment modalities, with the exception of inpatient female adolescents for whom the weekly use of other multiple non-narcotics was most prevalent (39.3 per cent).

Aftercare counseling on an outpatient basis should not be confused with outpatient services as primary treatment. While one individual or group counseling session per week may be sufficient to sustain and support recovery, it is typically not sufficiently intensive as primary treatment. Aftercare services of many kinds, however, are nearly always recommended for the adolescent and her family members. Some adolescents may require placement in group homes, in halfway houses or other transitional living environments for recovering persons, or in foster homes. The need for this additional support for recovery skills discovered in treatment may be due to a hostile family environment, to the absence of family support for recovery, or to the need to strengthen personal skills through a longer period of "enforced" sobriety.

Most aftercare programs will entail less restrictive services, typically involving individual and family counseling sessions once or twice a week, supplemented by attendance at AA or Al-Anon. Aftercare may last from four weeks to two years depending on the program and the motivation of the student and her family members.

Familiarity with this continuum of care enhances the school system's student assistance program by permitting it to develop appropriate working relationships with various treatment agencies and to make better and more appropriate referral recommendations for individual students. Understanding the treatment process of different modalities may assist the school in recognizing that a given student's apparent failure in one may indicate a need for a more restrictive program or for involvement over a longer term.

The Process Of Treatment and Recovery

Regarding "treatment" as a quick fix, a cure for drug abuse, or a magical solution to a student's problems is one of the pitfalls facing anyone who is close to or who is working with the chemically dependent adolescent. It is necessary to distinguish between treatment as a relatively brief event and the extended process of recovery. For adolescents as well

Table 10.1

PRIMARY DRUG OF ABUSE
IN THE YEAR BEFORE TREATMENT:
Adolescents Under Age 18

PRIMARY DRUG	RESIDENTIAL TREATMENT		OUTPATIENT DRUG-FREE	
	Males	Females	Males	Females
Marijuana	33.3	19.7	44.0	28.4
Tranquilizers, sedatives barbiturates	12.1	27.9	5.4	13.5
Alcohol	11.6	4.9	3.6	2.8
Hallucinogens	8.0	4.9	2.8	3.6
Other drugs	5.3	9.8	2.6	2.8
Cocaine	4.4	8.2	2.0	2.1
Amphetamines	4.3	11.5	2.8	9.2
Heroin or Opiates	4.3	3.3	0.4	0.7
No problem	16.7	9.8	36.4	36.9
TOTAL:	100.0	100.0	100.0	100.0
N =	138.0	61.0	250.0	141.0

Source: Adapted from Hubbard *et al.*, p. 50.

Table 10.2

PATTERN OF WEEKLY DRUG
USE IN THE YEAR BEFORE TREATMENT:
Adolescents Under Age 18

PRIMARY DRUG	RESIDENTIAL TREATMENT		OUTPATIENT DRUG-FREE	
	Males	Females	Males	Females
Alcohol/marijuana	27.5	11.5	60.0	41.8
Mult. non-narcotics	25.4	39.3	7.2	10.6
Single non-narcotics	19.6	26.2	14.0	22.7
Narcotics	16.7	9.9	6.0	7.8
Minimal	8.0	3.3	12.4	17.0
Heroin, no narcotics	1.4	8.2	0.4	0.0
Heroin and narcotics	1.4	1.6	0.0	0.0
TOTAL:	100.0	100.0	100.0	100.0
N =	138.0	61.0	250.0	141.0

Source: Adapted from Hubbard *et al.*, p. 53-54.

Heroin and Narcotics: weekly use of both heroin and other narcotics

Heroin, no narcotics: weekly use of heroin but less than weekly use of other narcotics

Narcotics: weekly use of narcotics other than heroin

Multiple non-narcotics: weekly use of two or more of the following: tranquilizers, barbiturates, sedatives, amphetamines, cocaine.

Single non-narcotics: weekly use of one non-narcotic drug listed above.

Alcohol/marijuana: weekly use of alcohol and marijuana only

Minimal: none of the above drugs used weekly or more often.

as adults, recovery—or the process of learning how to live and grow without mood altering chemicals—may begin in treatment but will last a lifetime. A fairly clear pattern of benchmarks associated with early recovery has emerged, regardless of the treatment modality, and which extends past the patient's discharge. It is useful to see the recovery process in terms of four stages: admission, compliance, acceptance, and surrender.

Admission is one of the first hurdles in the treatment and recovery process and refers to the mental and emotional dynamics involved in allowing the recovering person to identify herself as being "chemically dependent." The stigma surrounding chemical dependency and the associated shame and guilt can make this a difficult admission. In the initial stages of treatment, most patients experience feelings of depression, helplessness and hopelessness, guilt, and low self-worth. The intervention resulting in treatment, even if done with care and respect, frequently leaves the adolescent demoralized, angry, or with free-floating negative feelings. Denial is strong and affect is inappropriately flat. In this early phase of treatment or recovery, the goals are to assist the adolescent to learn the symptoms of chemical dependency and to recognize them in her past conduct, to identify with others who have experienced similar symptoms, and to begin to see the extent of denial. During the admission phase, the recovering adolescent gains an initial awareness of self-defeating behavior and sees her feelings as being the result of the illness. Education about the disease of chemical dependency and discussions of behavior in group therapy promote the ability to identify oneself as being chemical dependent, at least at a cognitive level.

"The fact that many publicly-funded treatment programs apparently do not regard alcohol as a drug should alarm even the layperson."

Compliance follows the admission of chemical dependency. The recovering adolescent is starting to feel good physically and emotionally for the first time in several years; initial fears about what treatment is like have not been borne out. Compliance is characterized by verbal and behavioral acknowledgement of the fact that one is dependent, but without emotional acceptance at any depth. Problems become externalized rather than internalized. The approach to recovery is based on changing superficial lifestyle or situational habits. Remaining drug-free may be seen as depending on changing the external world. The patient often concludes that "this can be beaten" by the exertion of will power and vigorous attempts to keep oneself and others under control. In formal treatment settings, patients often become more manipulative. The primary task

becomes "What do I have to do to get out of here?" They will pick up and use "treatment jargon," obey the rules mechanically, and attempt to appear to others that they are ready to leave. Complacency about abstinence and the feeling that one can stay straight by oneself are also typical of the compliance phase.

Acceptance has been described as moving from suspicion of others to suspicion of self, and accepting the disease and its past, present, and future implications at some emotional depth. Defensiveness is markedly reduced as a result of additional education, self-examination, and sharing with others in a safe way. The adolescent patient begins to accept greater responsibility for past behavior, and the implications of the chronicity of the disease for the future. Having learned that denial is insidious and sincere, he realizes that support from others will be an important part of ongoing recovery. The adolescent becomes more open to self-evaluation, more trusting of others, and more positively committed to change.

Surrender was identified very early as a crucial recovery phase by Dr. Harry M. Tiebout (see Tiebout, 1953, 1954). Surrender is often defined as a thorough emotional identification with the chronicity of the disease and its implications for the future. Most observers, casual and clinical, note that surrender is characterized by a major transformation of the individual from a pattern of negative to a pattern of positive thinking, feeling, and behaving. While difficult to describe in clinical terms, there a number of outward behavioral indicators of the surrender phenomenon. Denial and defensiveness disappear as the individual becomes more open and honest with himself and with others. Acceptance of self increases as the individual places himself in a proper perspective with others. He exhibits a willingness to change and an enthusiasm for a sober lifestyle. Many exhibit a definite sense of gratitude.

Whether in residential or nonresidential programs, progress through various recovery steps is facilitated by many program components, including education, small group therapy, large group meetings, individual counseling sessions, and family sessions. The most effective treatment programs are those which have recognized the validity of the Twelve Steps of Alcoholics Anonymous (and the related programs of Narcotics Anonymous, Cocaine Anonymous, etc.) as a guide to recovery, and the necessity for involvement in such self-help groups following primary treatment.

This description may appear deceptively simple. In fact, the recovery process is as complex and as incompletely understood as is the disease. The progress through the phases listed above does not occur within the confines of a 30-day treatment program, but can take two years or longer for the individual actively engaged in recovery. Moreover, it can take up to two years for physiological processes to normalize after severe chemical use ceases.

For adolescents the tasks of recovery are complicated by the fact that many leave primary treatment at the compliance stage, without having had the time necessary to arrive at the emotional acceptance of the ramifications of the disease and the recovery process. Many will verbally acknowledge the fact that they are chemically dependent and will endorse their need to remain abstinent. In the early months of recovery there may frequently be little emotional commitment to these aims. Many adolescents, because of the developmental impairment caused by chemical dependency, will also possess fewer personal and social competencies with which to accomplish the rest of the initial recovery tasks.

The school system that appreciates the difficulties of the recovery process faced by adolescents will recognize that an important part of its student assistance program will entail providing recovering students with short-term, in-school support services. This support can help students to remain drug-free long enough so that the remaining recovery tasks can be accomplished. (See Chapter 15).

Treatment Outcome

For the family of a chemically dependent adolescent as well as for the school system's SAP staff the answer to the question "Does treatment work?" is an important one. Unfortunately, it is not an easy question to answer. We are accustomed to hearing specific "recovery rates" for many behavioral/medical problems and their related procedures: e.g., heart disease and coronary artery bypass surgery, leukemia and chemotherapy, etc. It is not possible to generalize with any meaningful statistics about treatment success or recovery rates in the field of chemical dependency for many reasons. First, there is significant variation across the country in how chemical dependency is regarded. While most effective treatment programs regard chemical dependency as an illness, many still do not. This is not just a philosophical debate, as treatment methods and goals proceed directly from what one construes the nature of an illness to be. Not all programs, for example, define dependency as a chronic condition, the recovery from which must be based on abstinence. The professional literature still contains debates about whether "controlled social drinking" is possible for alcoholics, and about the efficacy of abstinence as a treatment goal. Secondly, there is not uniform agreement on how to define or evaluate recovery itself. Some programs measure recovery by improvements in patients' general living circumstances. Others define recovery in terms of periods of continuous sobriety. Still others use both criteria to define treatment success. Finally, adolescents and adults are not always segregated in separate programs. All of these variables, and many others, lend meaning to the "recovery rate" reported by an individual treatment program and make it impossible to delineate "recovery rates" for treatment in general.

Table 10.3, for example, illustrates some of the treatment outcomes for adolescents in federally sponsored treatment programs. The figures are based on the Treatment Outcome Prospective Study (TOPS). The TOPS study was "a long-term, large-scale longitudinal investigation of the natural history of 11,750 drug abusers who sought services in publicly funded drug abuse treatment programs" from 1979 to 1981 (Hubbard et al., p. 49). Adults and adolescents were combined in the treatment programs, outcomes for both were included in the study, but Table 10.3 separates the results for each group.

In terms of drug-specific outcomes, some reduction in rates of chemical use were demonstrated for adolescents as well as young adults. The greatest reduction was in daily marijuana use. At one year following discharge from treatment, the number of adolescents using marijuana daily was reduced by almost 50 per cent (62.68 per cent versus 32.08 per cent). Smaller decreases are noted for heavy alcohol use, weekly use of other drugs, and any drug-related problems. In terms of the data reported in Table 10.3, the greatest impact of the treatment programs was measured by the reduction in suicidal thoughts or attempts and in the involvement of adolescent clients in full-time work—measures of general life improvement.

Somewhat paradoxically, in outpatient drug-free programs 54 per cent of the clients under age 17 reported daily marijuana use *after* treatment, as opposed to only 48 per cent *before* treatment. An additional finding of the TOPS research was that only 35.2 per cent of adolescents were involved in heavy alcohol use *before* outpatient treatment, but that 36.6 per cent were thus involved *during* treatment. What is most revealing about these findings is reflected in the researcher's conclusions: *"While the drug user is clearly the target of drug abuse treatment programs, programs need to recognize and treat the extensive alcohol use reported by young clients....Unfortunately, drug abuse treatment programs do not seem to identify problems related to alcohol use, or treat the problems, or have much impact on alcohol consumption patterns"* (Hubbard et al., p. 54).

These are not optimistic reports concerning publicly funded treatment programs, and point up not only the difficulties in generalizing about treatment effective-

Table 10.3

NATIONAL TREATMENT OUTCOMES FOR YOUTH

BEHAVIOR VARIABLE	AGE	
	Less than 18	18-19
Daily Marijuana Use		
Before Treatment	62.68	51.80
After	32.08	23.85
Heavy Alcohol Use		
Before Treatment	51.05	38.55
After	35.68	34.45
Weekly Use of Other Drugs		
Before Treatment	58.08	62.10
After	38.40	34.88
Any Drug-related Problem		
Before Treatment	85.25	87.25
After	47.03	46.13
Suicidal Thoughts or Attempts		
Before Treatment	49.85	50.43
After	18.03	20.90
Predatory Illegal Acts		
Before Treatment	58.13	60.45
After	48.18	42.83
Full-time Work		
Before Treatment	5.02	15.53
After	22.43	20.78
N =	132.0	133.0

Source: Adapted from Hubbard *et al.*, p. 63. Figures represent changes identified in patient groups in both residential and outpatient drug-free programs, comparing behavior in the year before treatment and at one year after termination. Figures indicate the per cent of adolescents exhibiting the behavior variable listed.

ness but also the variability in quality and nature of chemical dependency treatment. The fact that many publicly-funded treatment programs apparently do not regard alcohol as a drug should alarm even the layperson.

Fortunately, many programs operate within the belief system regarding chemical dependency which has been presented in this book: that it is a primary, progressive, chronic illness and that recovery is based on—but not limited to—abstinence from all mood altering chemicals. Programs operating within this framework can demonstrate the greatest success in treating adolescent chemical dependency.

Hazelden, located in Center City, Minnesota, has enjoyed one of the loftiest reputations as a chemical dependency treatment program for over three decades. Its residential treatment program for adults and adolescents is centered on the disease concept, a respect for the spiritual components of the illness and the recovery process, and an unwavering commitment to the principles of Alcoholics Anonymous and its namesakes. Its 1982 report on patient admissions in 1979 demonstrates what have emerged as excellent recovery rates within the field of alcohol and other drug abuse (Laundergan, 1982).

For example, with respect to abstinence from alcohol, 66.3 per cent of those responding to follow-up questionnaires report continuous abstinence at six months; 48.5 per cent report abstinence at one year. Some patients experience what is called the "therapeutic relapse:" a brief episode of drinking or drug use that is followed by a return to abstinence and involvement in a recovery program. Over 72 per cent of the young adults reported continuous abstinence or one occasion of drinking at six months following treatment; 57 per cent fit this pattern at one year (Laundergan, p. 12).

The effectiveness of this treatment program is even greater when rates of abstinence from other drug use is examined. Continuous abstinence, drug use on only one occasion, or drug use for medical reasons was typical of 79.2 per cent of young adults at six months; the same pattern was true for 80.7 per cent of patients responding after one year (Laundergan, p. 14). It is significant that at six months 82.7 per cent were attending Alcoholics Anonymous once a month or more. This percentage had dropped to 68.2 per cent after one year, accompanied by the decreases in abstinence noted above.

Finally, since recovery rates are usually reported in percentages, it is important to inquire of a program how it calculates this rate if it advertises one. It is necessary to know what the recovery rate is a percentage of. Hypothetically, suppose 100 adolescents are admitted to a given treatment program, 60 complete the program successfully, and 45 respond to a follow-up questionnaire. Of these, 30 report life improvements, and 20 report continuous sobriety for one year. How is the recovery rate to be determined? First, the recovery rate could include the 30 reporting improvement, the 20 reporting abstinence, or the union of the two. Secondly, if recovery is based on the 20 patients reporting abstinence, how is the rate calculated? The 20 abstinent patients represent 20 per cent of admissions, 33 per cent of those completing the program, 44 per cent of those responding at follow-up, and 66 per cent of those reporting some improvement as a result of treatment.

While recovery statistics only lead us to ask specific questions about specific programs, research has demonstrated some general characteristics which as an aggregate increase the likelihood that the adolescent patient will be able to respond to treatment with a good chance for lifetime sobriety. The odds for favorable treatment outcomes are increased if the adolescent completes the program satisfactorily, if the program segregates adolescents from adults, if parents become involved in both treatment and aftercare, and if the adolescent becomes involved in aftercare. Moreover, the most significant factor increasing the likelihood of one year's continuous sobriety is involvement in Alcoholics Anonymous, Narcotics Anonymous, or Cocaine Anonymous. After the first year, the greatest predictor of future sobriety is the length of continuous sobriety in the past. The majority of those who can maintain sobriety for one year will able to maintain it for two. There is some evidence that those who can maintain continuous sobriety for five years have an excellent chance of maintaining lifetime sobriety.

Treatment and the School

While it is important to become familiar with the range of treatment services available, their appropriateness for a given student, the usual process of recovery, and reasonable outcomes, the most important task of the school vis-a-vis its student assistance program is to establish effective working relationships with those programs which its students and families are likely to be utilizing. The school system is likely to encounter the school/treatment boundary as it refers students to treatment and as it integrates them back into school upon their return.

As pointed out in Chapter 9, once it believes chemical dependency is at the root of students' problems, it is wise for the school to either refer students and families to assessment agencies (which will subsequently refer on to treatment programs) or to provide families with a list of three or more treatment programs from among which to choose. Providing such a list presupposes that the school and its SAP staff have identified and researched various treatment programs. Supplement 10.1 contains a checklist of criteria by which the school system can evaluate those treatment programs it identifies in its community or elsewhere. By gathering such information on programs the school is also better prepared to answer the questions of students and parents at the time of referral. Within the perspective of this book, those programs are to be preferred (a) which operate within the illness or disease concept of chemical dependency, (b) which are adolescent-specific programs, (c) which endorse abstinence as a goal of treatment and a condition for recovery, (d) which actively support patients' involvement in self-help programs, such as AA, and (e) which are willing to make a significant effort to develop a cooperative working relationship with the school system and its student assistance program staff.

In some cases the school system may have to take the activist role in developing these working relationships. As it is beginning its student assistance program the school may send a letter to those treatment facilities which may have its students as patients. The letter may announce the program and express the school's desire to work cooperatively to enhance the treatment process and support the student in his recovery. It may also name those on the SAP staff in each school building who are designated to work closely with students who have been in treatment. Supplement 10.2 is an example of one such letter.

Often a student will go to a residential treatment program during the summer, or will be admitted without the participation or knowledge of the school. A wise treatment program will obtain the appropriate release of information, will contact the school, and invite its involvement. Some programs may neglect to contact the school; a few may avoid such contact. In these instances, it is permissible for the school to contact parents to let them know that the SAP staff is appropriately trained and eager to support the student and the family in the recovery process. The letter should urge family members to invite the school to become involved in the discharge planning process (see Supplement 10.3).

Finally, as with the other program functions, the treatment of chemical dependency in students can entail policy decisions which many schools do not struggle with until their student assistance programs have been in operation for some time.

"It is not difficult to make a case that these students are learning more while in treatment than they would during a comparable period in their school."

Discussions over confidentiality may arise when a student is admitted to a treatment program and those in the student assistance program begin to wonder what teachers, other staff, and students should be told about the student's absence and whereabouts. While alcohol and drug treatment programs are heavily constrained by federal confidentiality statutes, schools are not so constrained as a rule. The development of intricate and detailed policies does not seem appropriate, either. Moreover, the grapevine soon discovers and communicates whatever the school would seek to protect anyway. Common sense rather than guidelines should govern the school's response. If school policy states that chemical dependency is an illness or disease, and that student's with it will be treated in the same manner as students with any other illness, then the issue is taken out of the legalistic realm. Respect for the family's privacy should enable the school to steer a middle course between adherence to rules and a Pyrrhic secrecy.

Another issue that soon arises involves the returning recovering student and credit for accomplishments in treatment. In many cases the school performance of students prior to admission to treatment will have deteriorated to the point of threatening their continuation in school or their ability to graduate on time. For some others, missing four to six weeks of class might jeopardize an otherwise acceptable record. It is important for the school to arrive at a policy regarding whether or not to award students credit or to acknowledge the things they learn or accomplish while in treatment.

The typical treatment program will consist of frequent lectures on scientific, social, and psychological aspects of chemical dependency, exercise programs, sex therapy and education, art therapy, physical or occupational therapy, group discussions, etc. It is not difficult to make a case that these students are learning more while in treatment than they would during a comparable period in their school. Moreover, other things being equal, those treatment programs are to be preferred which contact the school, ask for assignments, provide teachers during the treatment day, and regard school work as part of the recovery program.

Supplement 10.4 is an example of a form used by De Paul Rehabilitation Hospital's Adolescent Treatment Program. (De Paul Rehabilitation Hospital in Milwaukee, Wisconsin, specializes solely in the treatment of chemical dependency and other addictive disorders). The form is sent to the school of every adolescent in the treatment program. While the treatment program may not be able to grant credit for activities student/patients engage in, it can provide the school with an itemized list of the hours spent in various activities, and encourage it to utilize the information to grant credit for work accomplished while in treatment.

Developing this relationship not only assists in referring students to treatment but eases the re-entry process (see Chapter 15). Moreover, professional AODA counselors and other treatment staff are among the most valuable resources the school can discover. Most are eager to work with the program as advisors, co-leaders of support groups, and trainers. Establishing and clarifying good working relationships with chemical dependency treatment programs and other related community AODA services is an important task in the design and implementation of a student assistance program.

Chapter 10 | Supplements

Supplement 10.1, "Adolescent Treatment Program Checklist," contains a number of questions the SAP staff should utilize in identifying those chemical dependency treatment programs which it will recommend to parents. Many of the criteria are similar to those the school would employ in evaluating AODA screening and assessment programs for adolescents (Supplement 8.1).

Supplement 10.2 is a sample of a letter which the school might send to a treatment program upon learning that one of its students has been admitted. It requests that the school be involved in the discharge process, especially if the student is to be returned to the district.

Supplement 10.3 is an example of a letter which the school might send to the parents/guardians of a student who has been admitted to a treatment program which has failed to involve the school in the treatment process.

Supplement 10.4 is an example of a format within which a treatment program can report to a school concerning the hours student/patients spend in various program activities. The school can utilize such information in acknowledging the relevance of some work done in treatment to course work the student might have missed. Some such accounting will in most cases be necessary for granting students credit for work done while in treatment.

Supplement 10.1
ADOLESCENT TREATMENT PROGRAM CHECKLIST

PART I: TREATMENT PROGRAM:

1. What is the treatment philosophy of the program?

2. What are the major program components?

3. What is the staffing pattern?

4. What is the typical daily/weekly schedule?

5. What are the criteria for admission to the program?

6. What constitutes the assessment/evaluation phase of treatment?

7. What is the admissions process?

8. Who are the admissions counselors?

9. What is the average length of stay?

10. What is the cost?

11. What is the nature of the program's involvement with Alcoholics Anonymous, Narcotics Anonymous, and other self-help groups?

12. What are the professional qualifications and credentials of the treatment staff?

13. Is the program certified to provide alcohol/drug abuse treatment by the State?

14. What are typical requirements or recommendations for aftercare?

15. What provisions does the program make for dual diagnoses?

16. How does the program serve the needs of adolescent patients who have learning disabilities, are emotionally disturbed, suicidal, etc.?

17. Under what circumstances are adolescent patients discharged against staff advice (ASA)? (i.e., what constitutes a poor prognosis or unsatisfactory progress in the treatment program?)

18. Under what conditions are adolescent patients expelled from treatment?

19. What are the program's statistics on treatment outcome/effectiveness for adolescents? How does it define "recovery"?

20. What are the patient characteristics (demographics) for the program for the past year or more?

21. Is the treatment program specifically designed to treat adolescents?

PART II: WORKING RELATIONSHIPS WITH SCHOOLS:

1. Does the treatment program contain an educational component?

2. Does the program actively seek student assignments from the school?

3. To what degree are school staff involved in the data collection or assessment process in the treatment program?

4. To what degree are school staff involved in discharge planning?

5. Does the treatment program routinely seek releases of information allowing it to communicate with school staff?

6. Does the treatment program provide information to the school on the student/patient's participation in various activities during treatment?

7. Is there a general willingness by the treatment program to establish a cooperative working relationship with the school system?

Supplement 10.2

SAMPLE LETTER TO CHEMICAL DEPENDENCY TREATMENT PROGRAMS

March 1, 1987

Mr. Director
Adolescent Treatment Program
1234 Lane
Midville, USA

Dear Mr. Director:

We are gratified to learn that one of our students, _____ ,
has been admitted to your treatment program. As concerned educators, aware of the
problems presented by alcohol and other drug abuse, we feel good when one of our
students takes this difficult and affirmative step.

We are eager to be included in your efforts as _____
progresses in treatment. As you may know, the Midville Public School District has
implemented a Student Assistance Program. We have trained individuals on our staff
who can ease _____'s re-entry into the school system, and we
have implemented a Recovery Support Group to assist students returning from treatment.

We invite your staff to utilize us as a concerned resource. Our major interest is that the
progress made at your facility be maintained and supported by jointly planning for
_____'s return to school.

We would especially appreciate having the opportunity to participate in the discharge
planning process. Please notify either of us to arrange a conference time once the student's
departure from your program appears imminent.

Sincerely,

Daniel Webster
SAP Coordinator
Midville High School

Henry Clay
Principal
Midville High School

cc: parents

Supplement 10.3

SAMPLE LETTER TO PARENTS

March 1, 1987

Mr. and Mrs. Parent/Guardian
1234 Drive
Midville, USA

Dear Mr. and Mrs. Parent:

We are aware that your son/daughter _____ has been admitted for treatment at _____. We wish you to know that we support you and your child in this difficult but positive step.

At the conclusion of the treatment process there is a discharge conference called by the treatment program for the purpose of planning for your child's aftercare. You and the treatment staff may be glad to learn that we have support groups and staff trained in alcohol and drug abuse concepts as part of our Student Assistance Program. Since we are eager to do whatever we can to support your child upon his/her return to school, it is important that we be aware of the recommendations discussed during the discharge conference. At that time we can review what support services we can provide and how we can ease your child's return to school.

You as parents/guardians have a right to invite concerned individuals to this discharge conference. If the treatment program does not take steps to do so, we are hopeful that you would extend an invitation to us to attend. Our goal is make your child's re-entry into the school a positive and supportive experience, with care taken to protect your family's privacy.

If we can be of any assistance whatever, please contact either of us at 555-1000.

Sincerely,

_____   _____
Daniel Webster   Henry Clay
SAP Coordinator   Principal
Midwville High School   Midville High School

cc: treatment program

Supplement 10.4

RECORD OF STUDENT INVOLVEMENT
IN TREATMENT ACTIVITIES

Name: _____

Admission Date: _____

Discharge Date: _____

The student named above was a patient at De Paul Rehabilitation Hospital between the dates shown. During that time he/she spent time in various activities as noted below:

1. SEMINARS: (_____ Hours) Lectures by a variety of staff (medical, clergy, counselors, etc.) on various aspects of addiction and recovery.

2. GROUP THERAPY (_____ Hours) Small group sessions conducted by a Chemical Dependency Counselor focussing on problem identification, self-disclosure, confronting defenses that prevent self-growth and acceptance of dependency, behavior change, and personal growth (six patients).

3. EXPERIENTIAL GROUP (_____ Hours) Conducted by an Occupational Therapist, this group focuses on assertiveness training, self-concept, social skills, peer relations, and alternatives to drug use.

4. CRAFTS (_____ Hours) Supervised experience in mastering ceramics, leatherwork, string art, macrame, etc.

5. EXERCISE (_____ Hours) Supervised physical activity in the weight room, gymnasium, or running outside. Competitive and noncompetitive activities are included.

6. SEX EDUCATION (_____ Hours) Conducted by a Health Nurse, the focus is on education and values clarification.

Homebound School Courses   Grade

_____   _____

_____   _____

_____   _____

_____   _____

_____   _____

Chapter 11 | **Support**

"I understand that I am not alone and a lot of kids have the same problems as me."

"I understand there are other people who are hurt—not JUST me."

"I have learned that when I am feeling bad not to let that spoil my day."

"Now I don't worry as much."

"I feel like this group is sort of a family to me."

"I don't get angry as easy as I used to, and I'm doing better in school."

"I have learned how to express my feelings and talk about problems."

(Student comments on their support group experience. Courtesy of Ms. Carol Troestler, Student Assistance Program Coordinator, Sauk-Praire Public Schools, Sauk Prairie, Wisconsin).

"Enabling," as we have seen, consists of the ways in which all aspects of the system unwittingly lend support to unhealthy styles of relating to mood-altering chemicals and those with such problems. The task is not, strictly speaking, how to stop enabling, but how to begin to enable—or empower—chemical health.

Formalized services offering support to students who are coping with AODA-related problems are needed for at least two basic reasons. First, the problems caused or complicated by alcohol and other drug abuse are typically serious and even in their milder forms are highly resistant to change: students do not stop using chemicals or start feeling better about their alcoholic parents just because we tell them they should. Secondly, as noted above, students function in a school, family, and community environment that is often not supportive of either chemical health or changes in that direction. Consequently, students with AODA-related problems will need various forms of support for the changes we are expecting them to make.

In designing its program a school system will have to examine how its various components work together to provide support for these changes. In general, this will entail providing knowledgeable and supportive individuals who will be accessible to students, creating an atmosphere or climate within the school that supports healthy alcohol/drug-related attitudes and behaviors, and providing specific support services to those students demonstrating a need to change. With respect to the individual student, the services that are likely to have the most immediacy and impact will include counseling and support groups.

Rationale for Support Groups

Implementing support groups in the school setting, whether they deal with alcohol/drug-related issues or others, requires a considerable expenditure of time, effort, and other resources by the school system and by individuals directly involved in facilitating them. Aside from the resources spent in identifying students, leading the groups, and working with staff and parents, considerable time and energy is required in the planning stages for individual groups, and for the implementation of support groups in general. Many decisions need to be made on a district-wide basis concerning, for example, such issues as parental consent, confidentiality, and the qualifications of group facilitators to name just a few. Even when well-planned, energy must continually be invested in maintaining good working relationships between group leaders, students, classroom staff, parents, building administrators, and others. Furthermore, questions about the school systems's proper role in dealing with such problems arise again. Support groups, after all, appear to come perilously close to crossing the boundary between school and "treatment."

In view of the fact, then, that support groups do not represent a casual commitment on the part of a school system, there must be fairly clear and compelling reasons for deciding to implement them. In some early student assistance programs, support groups were considered to be an optional service to students, the school limiting its role to identifying students in need or in trouble and referring them to appropriate help in the community. In recent years, however, student support groups have emerged as essential components of a comprehensive, effective approach to student AODA-related problems for a number of reasons.

The arguments in favor of implementing support groups fall into three major categories: groups are efficient, they provide a developmentally appropriate context for changing behavior in children and youth, and they are effective in dealing with AODA-specific issues.

Efficiency

A primary reason for implementing AODA-related support groups has to do with the fact that drug use and related problems are extremely resistant to change. Whether they are recovering from chemical dependency, are struggling with their own drug abuse, or dealing with the stress of living with a chemically dependent family member, the promotion of healthier and more constructive behaviors in students requires considerable education, illustration, and support. Changing resistant behavior requires an environment that is safer and more supportive of change than that provided by a student's routine associations with other students, family members, and even staff members.

One of reasons why constructive change is difficult is that the behavior required is both new and risky. Thus, from a more pragmatic standpoint, whether the issue is confronting a family member with a drinking problem, expressing a feeling, or resisting peer pressure, the group provides an opportunity for students to experiment with and practice new behavior in group before trying it out in the "real world." Enlisting the ideas and suggestions of group members also provides the student with many realistic alternative behaviors that he would typically have been unable to come up with by himself.

Once a school district has a fairly clear idea of how many children and youth are affected by their own or others' drug-related problems it is faced with the problem of how to reach all of those students in need, or at least of how to reach them to a significant degree. Consequently, one argument in support of implementing groups has to do with numbers. Hypothetically speaking, a group leader or counselor can accomplish with eight students in one hour what would take eight hours if each was seen individually. Moreover, leading three support groups each week enables a counselor to work with 24 students. In some average-size high schools it is not uncommon to find 10 or 12 support groups operating during the week, attended by 70 or 80 students over a period of nine weeks. Because the support groups are sometimes facilitated by classroom teachers (and often by outside volunteers), more students can be helped than would normally be possible for the average high school counselor.

Just as research on class size shows, however, the number of students seen is not as important as the quality of the time spent. The small, problem-focussed group permits counselors and others who lead groups to bring about changes that would be difficult or next to impossible to accomplish in a comparable number of one-to-one meetings with students. The small group permits an intensity of interaction that is often the most conducive to helping kids deal with difficult problems.

Finally, aside from being helpful to students, support groups can help the school system to perform the basic program functions more effectively. Data collection, for example, is an important assessment task. By listening to and observing students in use-focussed groups a counselor can acquire a more thorough and intuitive notion of the nature and severity of a student's relationship with chemicals than would be possible in one-to-one interviews alone. Similarly, this type of support group can provide invaluable data for a formal intervention as well as leading a student to respond to it more readily.

Developmental Appropriateness

Most drug-related behavior occurs within and is supported by a fairly strong and cohesive peer group that does not readily sanction individual independence, even if the adolescent is developmentally equipped to resist peer group pressures. For the children of alcoholics, the family represents a "group" setting which is even more intense and less accepting of changes that can involve the open recognition of an AODA problem, violation of the "no talk rules," or the reduction of enabling behavior by the affected child or adolescent. The support group, made up of other children or adolescents facing similar problems and tasks, thus provides a developmentally appropriate context within which to discover, examine, and experiment with change and still do so in an environment that is both emotionally "safe" and made up of one's peers.

Similarly, students struggling with their own chemical use are not responding to "peer pressure" to use drugs so much as they are responding to an intense need to belong and to avoid behavior that would precipitate their rejection by their peers. Groups focussing on drug use provide a controlled and directed peer setting within which individual students can examine "peer pressure" and ways of rejecting drugs that are based on affirming positive aspects of themselves and that do not involve rejecting other adolescents as people. Groups provide opportunities to explore such issues and practice behaviors to a degree that one-to-one counseling relationships do not provide as readily.

Finally, groups are even more developmentally appropriate for the recovering student who is faced with internal pressures to return to chemical use, and an external family, school, and peer environment that at best often does not understand the magnitude of the task of staying straight. At worst, the environment actively promotes the return to chemicals. For these students more than others, the support group provides an environment of peers who are struggling with the same issues.

Alcohol/drug-Specific Issues

Perhaps the greatest benefit of support groups is their particular efficacy in addressing the needs of children and youth as they are specifically affected by alcohol/drug-related problems. Yalom (1975, pp. 3-69) has identified a number of "curative factors" of psychotherapy groups, for example, which also uniquely describe the ways in which the brief problem-focussed support groups in school are effective in dealing with alcohol/drug-specific needs of students.

Inclusion. Regardless of whether their concern is with their own alcohol/drug experience or with another's, most children and adolescents have been forced to deal with these problems in isolation. Most feel that they are the only ones who feel the way they do, that no one else has similar problems, and that others would judge them harshly if they knew. The strength of the "no talk rules" and society's general unwillingness to be open about family alcoholism leads most affected children to think they are the only ones facing such problems. Few young people who are abusing alcohol or other drugs discuss their pain with each other. The student in treatment also often feels isolated and "different," convinced that no one else could possibly share her problems.

"The arguments in favor of implementing support groups fall into three major categories: groups are efficient, they provide a developmentally appropriate context for changing behavior in children and youth, and they are effective in dealing with AODA-specific issues."

One of the things which the brief, problem-focussed group accomplishes better than anything else is allowing students to discover that they are not alone. Students discover that they are not alone in feeling guilty for causing their parent's drinking, in feeling confused and scared about their own drug experiences, or about their struggle to stay straight. The feeling of isolation diminishes immediately upon entering the group room for the first time, and often disappears entirely as the group develops.

Hope. Many students with AODA-related problems have lost hope. The child of an alcoholic parent often feels that nothing can change, or that things will only get worse. Drug abusing and drug dependent youth also feel hopeless and helpless to bring about changes in their lives.

Groups offer hope. In support groups students not only have the opportunity to identify with the problems of others, but to witness change and progress in themselves and other group members. As they see other students recovering and growing, they realize that they can, too. In every session, the support group offers members concrete examples of hope as an antidote to the hopelessness that frequently characterizes their experience with their own drug-related problems or those of people they care about.

Self-worth. Low self-worth has consistently been discovered to be one of the correlates of alcohol and other drug abuse, and is frequently a problem for affected others. Sometimes low self-worth arises from unsatisfactory family experiences. Other times it is the result of a pattern of alcohol and drug-related harmful consequences. In many cases it is part of a normal process by which adolescents question and explore their personal adequacy. For many, feelings of low self-worth will precipitate initial experimentation with alcohol or other drugs, and will render earlier experiences attractive enough to repeat.

Support groups offer students the opportunity to experience themselves as helpful to others, and hence as inherently valuable human beings. This sense is all the stronger because it comes from other youngsters in the group. It is common to hear students say to each other, in one version or another, "What you said in group last week really helped me." In addition to experiencing themselves in a new way, the support group itself provides students with a support system that most have not previously had available to them. Or, to the extent that all groups build trust, they provide an opportunity for asking for and receiving help.

Information. Children and youth, like our culture as a whole, suffer from belief systems that render them ill- or under-informed about alcoholism, drug dependency, or other forms of drug abuse. Much of the suffering of children of alcoholics stems from their mistaken belief that they are somehow the cause of their parent's drinking, and most lack the "information" that they are far from alone in their experience. Similarly, students actively using drugs actually know far less about them than adults think they do. Street wisdom and amateur chemistry are superficial knowledge in comparison to the awareness of how chemicals affect students' relationships, development, and day-to-day lives. Even recovering students, who gain explicit

knowledge about chemical dependency in treatment, often lack specific information on the recovery process or the symptoms of relapse.

There is ample research illustrating that merely the presentation of didactic information alone can effect positive changes in group members. In all groups some teaching must occur because knowledge itself has "curative" value. Imparting information promotes healthy changes in three ways. First, teaching about alcohol and other drug abuse provides students with a set of concepts and a vocabulary that allows them to discuss their experiences. Secondly, acquiring such a "language" helps to explain and clarify students' experience. Accurate information often reduces anxiety and confusion students may have concerning their own use or that of friends and family members. Finally, information regarding the dynamics of relapse is frequently new to the recovering adolescent and helps to demystify the difficult task of maintaining sobreity.

Groups as "families." Almost without exception, students with AODA-related problems have unsatisfactory family experiences. For children of alcoholics, this is nearly always so. The most severely affected may have experienced physical violence or sexual abuse. Most will suffer from the absence of the chemically dependent parent and the unavailability of the remaining one. For the drug abusing student, poor relationships with parents and/or siblings may precede chemical use, or else such relationships deteriorate because of it. The recovering student, too, typically has a history of extremely painful family relationships prior to treatment. Moreover, there is increasing evidence that at least half of all chemically dependent youth have at least one chemically dependent parent, and so are affected family members, too.

Groups have an advantage over one-to-one counseling in permitting students to experience a surrogate "family" in a significant sense of the word. The group experience often allows students to work through problems in a way that would be difficult or impossible within their real families. And for many, the group's leaders will represent their first experience with adults who exhibit consistent nurturing and emotional availability, mixed with an ability to establish and enforce fair and firm limits.

Skill Enhancement. To the extent that drug use or parental chemical dependency impacts on social skills, most AODA-affected children will exhibit some degree of difficulty in communicating and interacting with others. For teenagers, drug-related difficulties are compounded by the struggles of adolescence itself. Many have little access to information about themselves based on how others see them. Most recovering and drug abusing students are functioning at an emotional and social level at least two or three years lower than their chronological age. This means that they lack many personal and social skills they would have acquired if normal development had not been interrupted by drug abuse.

By definition, however, the successful support group will provide students with new and greater opportunities for social interaction. It may provide the first occasion for them to receive accurate interpersonal feedback from other adolescents as well as from the adult leaders. The group also provides a safe place to experiment with new behavior, with problem-solving skills, and with solutions. Groups, for example, are an ideal setting within which to employ role-playing, which has been demonstrated to be one the of the most effective techniques for assisting young people to acquire new behaviors.

Vicarious Learning. Drug use, abuse, or dependency, in themselves or others, often insulates young people from witnessing the growth and development that is occurring in their peers. Drug-related problems frequently result in an isolation that prevents students from witnessing how others disclose problems, struggle openly and honestly with them, or practice solutions.

Groups provide opportunities for such vicarious learning. Evidence shows that even the group member who appears not to be participating actively in the group session still benefits by observing and imitating the behavior of other group members. Students frequently comment that they have responded to situations in ways they heard other group members exploring previously. Groups expand the behavioral alternatives of each member by providing him with the vicarious experiences of others in the group.

Acceptance. Feelings of alienation are one of the most frequently reported correlates of drug abuse and dependency in young people. To some extent, such feelings are a normal accompaniment of adolescence. In addition, however, many young drug abusers report feeling as though they do not belong and are not accepted by parents, peers, the school, or society in general. Children affected by parental alcoholism experience the additional isolation caused by the stigma attached to alcoholism in the family.

Within the group that is even marginally successful, however, some degree of cohesiveness develops. Yalom describes cohesiveness as 'the attractiveness of the group for its members.' In a cohesive group, students begin to feel accepted by the group for who they are. The group promotes a sense of belonging. Group members discover that acceptance is achieved through risk-taking, self-disclosure, accepting the need for help, and demonstrating acceptance of other group mem-

bers. Acceptance supplies students with the strengths to experiment with personal change.

Openness. It is also widely acknowledged that drug-related problems produce emotional defensiveness: an isolation from one's own feelings. Children raised in chemically dependent families frequently learn that they should not have or express feelings such as anger, guilt, fear, loneliness, or hurt. For other students, a sophisticated denial system as well as chemical use itself insulates them from painful feelings. Consequently, many drug-affected youth have become unable either to identify or to express strong emotions, especially those they have learned to judge as negative or "bad." Moreover, chronic emotional distress leads many to develop a catastrophic fear of their feelings: they fear that by expressing feelings they may lose control, or they will harm themselves or others.

Groups provide an environment and an opportunity for identifying and expressing strong feelings. More important than the expression itself, however, is what students learn by expressing feelings. Group members learn that they need not be afraid of their feelings and that they will not be overwhelmed by them. Students learn that their feelings are normal, that they are not harmful to them or others, and that the expression of powerful emotion does not alienate them from other people. Groups frequently provide an opportunity for emotional openness that is not available to them among peers, their families, or even counselors.

"Groups focussing on drug use provide a controlled and directed peer setting within which individual students can examine 'peer pressure' and ways of rejecting drugs that are based on affirming positive aspects of themselves and that do not involve rejecting other adolescents as people."

Realism. Drug abuse often exaggerates the tendency toward "magical thinking" that to some extent characterizes adolescence in general. "Magical thinking" denotes the tendency to believe that there are simple, and immediate solutions to problems or pain, that one shouldn't have problems, that there are ways of escaping pain altogether, or that everything can be fixed once and for all. Many young people discover that chemicals are the ideal solution to pain—a solution that is far more reliable, predictable, and available than solutions involving contact with other people.

Just by clarifying problems, however, the group experience teaches that life experience is more complicated than it may appear to be. It also teaches that although there are solutions to problems, life is sometimes unfair and unjust, that new problems will arise from time to time, and that students do have the ability to survive them and survive them well.

All of the above indicate that support groups are not only effective settings within which children and adolescents can learn to cope with problems, but that they are also ideal for addressing many of the AODA-specific issues affecting young people.

Types of AODA-Related Support Groups

It has frequently been emphasized in previous chapters that not only do students have several different varieties of chemical experience, but that each of these results in unique needs. The various types of support groups that have evolved as part of the Student Assistance Program model represent, consequently, ameliorative services in the school setting that are tailored to meet such needs uniquely. It follows that the types of AODA-related support groups bear a relationship to the AODA target groups identified earlier. Moreover, support groups can be differentiated according to which of two primary purposes they are intended to achieve: "initial groups" which promote change in students, and "maintenance groups" which support the constructive changes students have already begun to make.

The following discussion outlines the major types of AODA-related support groups that are possible as components of a comprehensive student assistance program. Lest their variety and number appear intimidating, it should be understood that not all of the groups are required by every program, nor would all of these groups necessarily be operating simultaneously even if they all were implemented. The point is that groups are designed and implemented not based on the requirements of a model but on the requirements of students.

Figure 11.1 illustrates the basic AODA-related support groups and the principles behind their classification. The groups are classified according to the target group each is designed to serve, the severity of students' AODA-related problems, and whether the group initiates or maintains change.

In designing AODA-related support groups, the first step is the recognition that students who are affected by their own chemical use have needs for help that differ in some respects from those of students who are affected by others' chemical use. (Some students,

of course, will be dually-affected: many young people who are abusing chemicals come from families where one or both parents are chemically dependent). The second step involves noting that students within each category will be affected to varying degrees of severity. Finally, a student's first group experience is generally intended to initiate changes in behavior, either in their own chemical use patterns, or in their response to the AODA problems of others. Many students, however, will at some point later on need a group experience to maintain or support them in the changes they have made.

A note on group "names" is probably in order. Many individual group names have gained currency in various school systems: "Use/abuse Group," "Insight Group," "Mirrors Group," "Chemical Health Group," etc. In any two programs, the same name may be used for different groups, or vice versa. The terms used below, however, are suggested as labels for generic types of groups for purposes of classificiation and discussion, and are not intended as names that a school might give to its actual groups.

Used-focussed Groups

The first major category consists of group services that focus students' attention on their own relationship with mood-altering chemicals. Among those students affected by their own chemical use, a distinction must also be made between those who are diagnosed as chemically dependent and who have been or are involved in a treatment program, and those students who are not chemically dependent, or who have not yet been diagnosed as such. This division is necessary on both theoretical and practical grounds. First, drug abuse differs conceptually as well as clinically from drug addiction or dependency. Secondly, the "recovery" issues for students in each group will consequently differ significantly. Abstinence, for example, is the prevailing treatment goal for dependent youth, whereas it is not a lifetime necessity for non-dependent youth.

The distinction between "recovering" and other drug-involved youth also makes sense for the school from a procedural point of view. There will be many students who may in fact be chemically dependent but who have not yet been so diagnosed through referral to assessment agencies. As was pointed out in Chapter 8, a use-focussed group is often the device by which the school can gather enough meaningful information about a student's drug involvement to justify as well as bring about a successful referral. Moreover, it would be highly inappropriate to mix students who have elected a use-focussed group in lieu of suspension with students who have returned to the school from a treatment program.

Figure 11.1
TYPES OF AODA-RELATED SUPPORT GROUPS

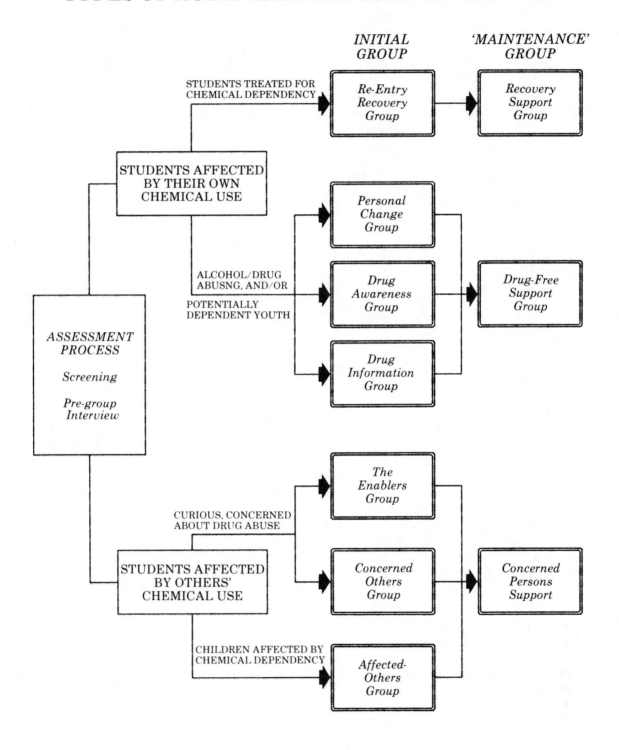

Figure 11.1 also illustrates two varieties of use-focussed groups for recovering students. *The Re-entry Support Group* is for students who are chemically dependent and who have recently returned from an inpatient or residential chemical dependency treatment program. It is also appropriate for students actively involved in an outpatient treatment program, AA, or NA, and who are concurrently attending school. The group is intended to help those students struggle honestly with their need to stay drug-free, especially given the pressures students will experience within the school setting itself. Such a group is suited to students with insufficient recovery skills and who are at the highest risk for relapse. It is not intended to provide therapy as such, or to take the place of either aftercare services or self-help group involvement in the community. In fact, the simultaneous use of such ancillary support systems is encouraged if not expected. The basic norm of the group is abstinence. The group focusses specifically on the problems faced by students early in their recovery process: re-entry into the school system, understanding and coping with peer pressure, and learning to make use of a support system.

It is possible to distinguish further between the Re-entry Support Group and the *Recovery Support Group*. The Recovery Support Group, is a maintenance group for students who have made it past the first few critical months of sobriety and who hopefully have reached a degree of stability in their daily lives following treatment. The emphasis in this group is placed upon reinforcing the student's support system outside of school and identifying and dealing with those dynamics that lead to relapse.

To a great extent, the distinction between these two varieties of the recovery group is an arbitrary rather than a necessary one. A good case can be made for not separating students in early recovery from those with a more stable sobriety. It is frequently useful for the newly returned student to be exposed to students who have been able to acquire the skills to stay straight for long periods of time. The distinction is intended to illustrate the degree to which the school can exercise its creativity in discovering the needs of students and in designing services to meet them.

The remaining use-focussed groups are more complex. They have a combination of prevention, intervention, and assessment functions, and they recognize that students will lie along a continuum of alcohol/drug involvement ranging from curiosity and early experimentation to severe drug involvement and chemical dependency. The major goal of such groups is to modify students' chemical use in the direction of abstinence by providing them with the requisite information and skills, or to discover students who are unable to modify their alcohol/drug use without professional help. Figure 11.1 illustrates the possibility of implementing at least three such groups, based on how severely the student is affected by her alcohol/drug involvement.

The *Personal Change Group* is designed for those students whose chemical use is most severe. They will most often be involved in frequent, multiple drug use, have longer histories of drug involvement, and will demonstrate a pattern of problems in their daily lives that are either caused or aggravated by their drug use. Most will elect to be in the group as a result of violations of school policies on drug use. These students will usually bring to the group a high degree of denial and defensiveness. In such groups the leaders promote a great deal of group interaction and are more aggressively confrontive. These groups provide accurate information on alcohol/drug use and require students to examine the place of chemical use in their lives. Students are also required to engage in behavioral contracts aimed at reducing or eliminating their chemical use. The group also enlists students in making definite decisions regarding their future drug involvement at its conclusion. At this point group leaders may elect to refer for evaluation or treatment those students who appear unable to make healthy changes.

The *Drug Information Group* lies at the other extreme. Such a group is designed for students who are curious about the decisions they must make regarding drug use, who want more information, or who have not progressed beyond initial experimentation. This group is frequently brief (four to six weeks) and is basically informational. Topics would include the dynamics of drug use, abuse, and dependency, its affects on the family, how to talk (intervene) with someone about whom one is concerned, sources of help in the school and the community, and personal experiences of those in a recovery process. Students appropriate for this group (who constitute the majority of adolescents) typically have not experienced serious problems because of their drug involvement. Most will enter the group through self-referral or at the suggestion of a school counselor or family member. Although the focus is still on leading students to healthier choices and behaviors with respect to alcohol and other drugs, the emphasis in this group can be more informational given the relative absence of denial in students with milder drug histories.

The *Drug Awareness Group* represents the middle ground: students who have gone beyond curiosity or experimentation, who are at some risk due to their chemical use, but who demonstrate—on the basis of the initial assessment—little or no evidence of chemical dependency. These students seem to possess the personal and environmental strengths to be able to change their drug use patterns given appropriate information and the opportunity to examine their behavior in a group of their peers.

Many students will emerge from their experience in one of these groups having made a decision to remain drug-free. Many will be able to sustain a drug-free lifestyle themselves due to personal strengths, a positive peer group, and a supportive family environment. Others, however, may feel the need for further support in discovering and solidifying what they have learned regarding alternatives to drug use, coping with peer pressure, and so on. The *Drug-Free Support Group* is a maintenance group providing support to those students who have been in one of the use-focussed groups, who have made a decision to remain drug-free, who are motivated in that direction, and who have been able to identify to the SAP staff a need for support.

Affected-Others Groups

The criteria "concerned about someone else's chemical use" also describes a continuum of severity along which children can be arranged according to their degree of "affectedness." Some students will ask to be members of an affected others group out of curiosity, others out of concern for a family member or friend, and still others because of their experience with chemical dependency in a parent or sibling. It is possible, given the size of the school and its group leadership resources, to design and implement discrete groups geared specifically to such degrees of concern.

Many students who are curious or concerned about someone else's alcohol/drug use may be appropriate for the Drug Information Group discussed above rather than for a specific affected others group. The agenda for this group (see Chapter 14) could be designed in such a way as to be appropriate to students in either of the two major classifications. Figure 11.1 depicts three additional support group services for affected-others.

A *Concerned Others Group* would be appropriate for students who have some personal experience with people who have alcohol/drug-related problems. The emphasis in such a group is not necessarily on chemical dependency but on defining for students the difference between drug use, drug abuse, and dependency, allowing them to identify and express feelings about their "person of concern," and providing them with skills in how to talk to someone about their concern. This type of group is often more appropriate for younger children who are worried about older siblings, or for adolescents worried about boyfriends and girlfriends.

The *Affected Others Group* is designed for students who live closer to and have been more severely affected by chemical abuse or dependency. As indicated elsewhere, such students frequently suffer from developmental deficits, difficulties in academic perfor-

mance or conduct, problems with relationships, and feelings of anger, fear, guilt and shame associated with parental chemical dependency. The Affected Others Group is intended to allow students to address these issues in a more intensive manner and to provide them with a greater degree of support.

The *Enablers Group* is included here as an example of how creative the school can be in designing group structures as circumstances might require. In one school, for example, the entire basketball team was "busted" at a weekend drinking party involving several hundred youth. The school was faced with only two choices, neither of which seemed appropriate. One was to do nothing, and the other was to enforce the athletic code to the letter and suspend the entire team for the season. Instead, they suspended the team for the season, but indicated that the suspension would be limited to only one game for those who agreed to satisfactorily complete a support group. The group they designed was The Enablers Group, which focussed members' attention on student enabling: a more accurate term for "peer pressure." The implementation of this group not only expanded the alternatives of the school, but also allowed the student athletes to experience reasonable consequences for their conduct and the opportunity to change. It is included here as an affected others group because it dealt with the ways in which students are involved in others' drug use. It could, of course, just as easily be identified as a use-focussed group.

As with the use-focussed groups, some students will need more than a single group experience. For children in the Affected Others Group especially, circumstances and crises may arise several years following their initial group experience that will precipitate the need for support. The Concerned Persons Support Group is a maintenance group for kids who identify such a need and who are willing to utilize the group for specific purposes.

Other Groups. The groups discussed above are AODA-specific, even though other issues will unavoidably be raised in students' discussions: suicide, depression, physical and sexual abuse, death and loss, separation and divorce, and so on. To the extent that a student assistance program is "broad brush"—is for any student with any problem—there is nothing to prevent the school from implementing support groups to deal specifically with these issues as well.

Support groups represent an effective in-school service which the school can make available to students and families as an important part of its student assistance program. The scope of the school's involvement in support groups will depend on how it defines its role in addressing AODA problems and on the limitations of its resources. Each of the groups above, and the planning issues surrounding their implementation, is discussed more fully in Part Three.

| Chapter 12 | # Case Management and Program Integration |

It should be plain from the previous five chapters that much is required if students who have alcohol and other drug-related problems are to be successfully helped. They must be identified as early as possible, and can exhibit a wide variety of AODA-related concerns. A significant amount of information must be gathered from staff, parents, and school records as well as from students themselves. The decision as to the type of help which is most appropriate to the child's situation and from which the student might benefit most can be a painstaking and lengthy one. Acquiring AODA-specific training and skills is necessary if staff are effectively to motivate students and their families to accept the appropriate help. It is also necessary to identify, evaluate, and develop good working relationships with those agencies which are likely to be providing direct services to students and their families. Support within the school for students-in-change can range from one-to-one counseling to support groups. Moreover, as we have seen, for the program functions to be performed effectively many expectations have to be placed upon the classroom teacher, the administrator, and the pupil services worker. It is also advisable to focus some new expectations in persons and structures with roles specific to the Student Assistance Program model: the SAP Counselor/Coordinator, the Core Team, the Screening and Referral Team, and so on.

The student assistance program functions were defined as those services or program components which were necessary (a) in providing the individual student with what he needs to ameliorate an AODA-related problem and (b) in assuring that each target group is effectively served. The first five program functions relate specifically to student needs; the last program function—*case management*—assures that the individual student is appropriately served and that the process is working smoothly. Thus, "case management" can be defined as *those activities which bring students, parents, staff, and other resources together within a planned framework of action intended to achieve individual goals.*

Attending to case management as a program function in the design of its student assistance program will involve the school system once again in clarifying the roles of various staff, devising concrete procedures, and integrating procedures and critical policy issues (Chapter 19) such as parent involvement, drug abuse consequences, and confidentiality.

Review of Program Roles

Anyone within the school system could conceivably become involved in the identification, assessment, intervention, treatment, and support of a student who has an AODA-related problem. The student assistance program, if it is to be successful or long-lived, must not be the sole province of a few individuals. Rather, steps must be taken during implementation to communicate to everyone the basic expectations which define the nature of their participation in the program.

Traditional Staff Roles

Expectations of All Staff. While there are many additional roles and responsibilities characteristic of the process of implementing a student assistance program, the following represent some basic expectations of all school staff during the program's operation. In general, staff can be expected to cooperate with the program's policies and procedures in the following minimal ways:

- Report instances of witnessed alcohol/drug use;

- Develop clear standards for acceptable student behavior and performance;

- Be alert to unexplained or persistent changes in performance or behavior;

- Confer with members of the SAP regarding potential student referrals;

- Document patterns of unacceptable behavior or performance;

- Refer students to the SAP staff when appropriate;

- Participate in the assessment process by providing SAP staff with information when requested;

- Participate in intervention meetings;

- Participate in re-entry meetings held on behalf of students returning to school from treatment;

- Respect students' rights to privacy and confidentiality.

- Facilitate the involvement of students in short-term support groups.

The Role of Building Administrators. As the source of leadership within the individual school building, the administrator's role is chiefly concerned with actively supporting various aspects of the program and its policies and procedures:

- Be an active member of the building's Core Team;

- Provide vocal support for the student assistance program, its procedures and its staff within the school building;

- Acquire proper training in fundamental AODA concepts;

- Refer to the SAP those students involved in disciplinary action and who are suspected of being AODA-involved;

- Uniformly enforce the school system's AODA policies;

- Chair meetings between school staff and the parents of AODA-involved youth;

- Participate actively in other Core Team activities, such as Screening Teams and/or Referral Teams.

- Participate in the development of policies and procedures which facilitate the functioning of support groups.

The Role of Pupil Services Staff. School counselors, social workers, psychologists, and other pupil services staff members are frequently in contact with students and/or families over issues ranging from minor problems to crises. In most cases pupil services staff members should be obligatory members of a school building's Core Team, and may be identified formally as individual Student Assistance Program Counselors (see Chapter 6, Supplement 6.1). In any case, a few basic expectations define the role of the pupil services staff person in the student assistance program in general:

- Acquire proper training in alcohol/drug skills and concepts.

- Include alcohol/drug questions in any interview with students;

- Include alcohol/drug issues in all assessment activities regarding students and/or their families;

- Refer students with potential AODA-related problems to the SAP staff/Core Team;

- Be an active member of the building's Core Team, Screening Team, and Referral Teams;

- Participate in the assessment/screening process;

- Participates in the data collection phase of screening and assessment;

- Reviews and evaluates all data collected during assessment;

- Makes recommendations for referral and/or intervention;

- Monitors the progress of individual students and reviews outcomes;

- Coordinates the leadership, scheduling, and functioning of support groups.

Summary of Program Roles

The roles of SAP Counselor/Coordinator, the Core Team, the Screening and Referral teams, and of Group Facilitators are specific to the Student Assistance Program model. One of the major reasons for the creation of these roles and structures is to insure that the program indeed accomplishes the program functions for each student in need and for each of the AODA-related target groups.

The SAP Counselor/Coordinator. An outline of the responsibilities of those in either of these roles has already been presented in Chapter 6. For the purposes of this chapter it is necessary only to stress that one of the major responsibilities of those in these roles is "case management:" monitoring a student's progress through the program's procedures and his attainment of individual goals. In general, this function may be carried out by the SAP Coordinator in her capacity of chairing Core Team meetings and Screening Team meetings. The individual SAP Counselor is responsible for the individual case management, or integration of program services, for those individual students on her caseload.

Supplement 12.2, the "SAP Referral Record," is an example of one of the tools which can be developed to assist the SAP staff and the program in monitoring individual students within the program.

The Core Team. Members of the Core Team are responsible, as a group, for the operation of the program at the building level. In larger school systems and secondary school buildings the Core Team may be the primary guarantor of case management as it reviews all referrals to the program and their status. While the Core Team may have other responsibilities during the early design and implementation stages of the program, the following summarizes its major functions during program operation. The Core Team:

The Screening Team and Referral Team, as ad hoc components of the Core Team, function as assessment and intervention structures, respectively. Drawing the membership of these two groups from the larger Core Team increases the likelihood that all will be familiar with a given student's history and will have sufficient training in AODA issues to enable them to perform adequately.

Group Facilitators. In addition to their obvious role in leading support groups, group facilitators should also be involved in the management of a student before, during, and after her placement in the group. While the SAP Counselor/Coordinator, perhaps in conjunction with other Core Team members, recommends a support group as a service, the support group leaders ideally should be involved in the screening and selection of students for their particular group. Thus, the following would be among the duties of group facilitators which relate to case management functions:

- Becoming aware of the circumstances under which the student accepts referral to a support group;

- Interviewing each student recommended for or expressing a desire to be in a support group;

- Selecting individual students on the basis of their compatibility with others in the group;

- Communicating with classroom teachers as needed and within the boundaries of confidentiality concerning the student's progress in group;

- Informing the SAP Counselor/Coordinator of the student's progress, especially his failure to comply with minimal group expectations.

Integrating Parent Contacts

Parents play a crucial social and political role in the implementation and maintenance of a school system's student assistance program. In fact, in a few school districts the student assistance program has been arrested or discontinued because parents were left uninformed and uninvolved. These issues, however, will be taken up in Part Four.

As we have seen, parents can and should be involved more specifically in each of the previous five program functions. They have a critical role to play in everything from early identification and assessment to intervention, treatment, and the involvement of their children in support groups. As the definition of "case management" above indicates, parents and other family members are one of the resources which need to be integrated into any planned strategy for helping students to change their AODA-related behavior. Thus, part of the process of designing its student assistance program must involve the school in devoting some attention to why, when, and how it will involve parents in the day-to-day management of individual students. The decisions it comes to will have implications for policy as well as for procedures.

In addition, the student assistance program often provides to parents services similar to those it provides to students, including support groups, education, and referral information. Some schools implement support groups, led by SAP staff in conjunction with local AODA agency staff, which function to provide parents with alcohol/drug information and the support of other parents who are coping with AODA-involved children. The school is often the catalyst behind the formation of support groups which proceed to operate independently: Families Anonymous, Tough Love, and Parents Al-Anon groups (see Nurco *et al.*; York *et al.*).

Why Involve Parents?

For many reasons it is wise for the school to involve a student's parents or guardians as early as possible. Legal obligations may make parental involvement mandatory. In many states the school is obligated to inform parents and/or seek consent for any type of counseling services provided to a student on anything more than a casual or infrequent basis. Situations are foreseeable where the school might be held liable for failing to pass along to parents information about their child's potentially dangerous behavior, including alcohol and other drug abuse. Some states also have legislation which makes parents legally responsible for their child's behavior.

Increasingly, too, parents are demanding to be involved in the patterns of relationships which grow up between their children and the school as an institution. Many parents would assert their right to know about problems their children are facing, especially in an area such as alcohol or other drug abuse, which involves illegal as well as dangerous behavior. Parents should be involved by the school out of its respect for the family as an institution which can cooperate in any attempts to help children achieve happier and healthier lifestyles. The school can only facilitate change which must, to some degree, be supported by the family.

The family, as we have seen, also plays a crucial role at various points in the assessment and the intervention process. Family members frequently possess critical information about a student's behavior which illuminates the data the school staff has been able to collect based only on its own experience with the student. Similarly, the involvement and active support of the family is usually required to support the changes in behavior that are the intended outcomes of the various steps in the intervention continuum.

Nonetheless, the why, when and how of involving parents in the student assistance process is frequently one of the more emotional and troublesome aspects of designing a student assistance program. Rational, legal, and practical considerations appear relatively straightforward, but do little to overcome the personal resistance of many educators to working with individual parents around the highly charged issue of drug abuse. In many cases, the resistance imputed to parents may be a projection of the fears, uncertainties, and discomforts of the staff itself in addressing these issues or in confronting denial. Training and a willingness to examine one's own AODA-related attitudes helps not only in actually working with parents but in devising appropriate policies and procedures for their involvement in the student assistance process.

Denial. Thus, one of the more important reasons for working with the family and for involving it early in the process has to do with denial. That the progression of denial in family members progresses along with alcohol/drug abuse and denial in the student has repeatedly been emphasized. It is safe to say that nearly everyone in the school who has had to confront a parent about a student's drug abuse has encountered denial in any of its many forms. Especially where chemical dependency is concerned, drug abuse in an adolescent child has a tremendous impact on the entire family, which often demonstrates serious maladaptations to the dependent child's behavior. It is equally safe to say that working with parents as early as possible in the progression of a child's drug-related problem makes working with denial that much easier. In any event it is necessary to understand and anticipate the presence of denial in family members.

For many families, alcohol and other drug use by a child can itself represent a major crisis, compounded by the contact by and involvement of the school. Feelings of fear, panic, anger, guilt, shame, and embarrassment will often be provoked by the school's initial contact. This confusion of feelings can be further aggravated by the family's initial, impulsive reactions to what it feels is the school's intrusion into its privacy. These reactions can range from cooperation or compliance to defiance and anger. Parents may blame the school, the child, or both for this threat to individual self-worth and the public image of the family. A given family may manifest all of these reactions at different points in its work with the school staff. It is important for the SAP staff to understand the nature of these reactions and to deal with them accurately, firmly, appropriately, and compassionately.

Denial can take many forms, depending on the seriousness of the drug-related problem and the stage in the school process at which parents become involved. Overt denial often greets the first suggestion that alcohol or other drug abuse is involved in the student's difficulties. The parents may make negative comments about the school, the student assistance program, or about the counselor. They may request a second opinion, accept the adolescent's excuses and alibis, or search for other explanations for the student's behavior problems.

Ann Marie Krupski (982) provides one of the most complete discussions of the manner in which parents may manifest denial as their youngster is encountering the assessment/intervention/treatment process. Comparing this to the stages involved in the grieving process, Krupski identifies the following as some predictable manifestations of parental denial:

• Verbal outrage at the counselor, when his suggestions that the child has a drug problem conflict with parents' distorted stereotypes of 'drug abusers;'

• Acceptance of the adolescent's distortions of the assessment process and the school's student assistance program services;

• Sabotaging the school's process by terminating counseling or support group involvement, asking for a new counselor, refusing to attend meetings, changing community agencies; going to the Board of Education and politicizing the issue;

• Self-blame, manifested by guilt over what parents could have done better or differently.

The most important factor for the school staff to remember is that the major function of denial is to protect self-worth, and that parents will manifest the greatest denial to the extent that they feel—as individuals, as parents, and as a family—inadequate, threatened, and judged. Bearing in mind that the school's involvement often adds to the stress already created by the adolescent's drug use, *how* the school staff communicates with parents is probably more important that the facts it conveys. The most important thing is not to provoke an adversarial relationship while still standing firm regarding the needs of the child and the policy and procedural obligations of the school.

When Should Parents Become Involved?

A number of principles guide the school in determining when parents should be contacted and informed of their child's involvement in the student assistance process. It is most important, first, to avoid the extreme positions in devising its stance. Automatically and immediately informing parents whenever a student becomes identified and referred to the program is likely to discourage patterns of self-referral and peer-referral upon which *early* identification, program credibility, and a climate of safety are based. On the other hand, never informing parents increases the risks to the school in terms of legal liabilities, is likely to have political ramifications later, and subtly undermines parental authority, responsibility, and family integrity. Where, then, is the middle ground?

A number of situations can be integrated into the school's procedures and embodied in its policy language. First, parents should always be contacted whenever and as soon as the SAP staff fears for the student's safety or welfare, or the safety and welfare of others. Secondly, parents will always be contacted, immediately and automatically, when a student violates school policies against the use, possession, or delivery of alcohol or other drugs on school grounds or at school-sponsored events. Finally, parents should be assured that they will be specifically informed of their student's involvement in the student assistance program at some point, either through contact with the SAP staff, through the student's self-disclosure, or a combination of the two.

Accordingly, the situation of the individual student will most often determine how soon parents become involved. They will typically become involved immediately in circumstances surrounding policy violations, somewhat later for staff referrals for suspected AODA-related problems, and later still in the case of self-referrals and peer-referrals. In the latter cases, one of the responsibilities of the SAP Counselor is to strengthen the student to the point where she can confront her parents with the fact of her drug use and the progress she has made in the program.

A willingness to become personally involved in working toward a solution is the major criterion for determining whether a confrontation is appropriate—whether of an individual or a family. Thus, it is also important for the SAP staff to recognize that involving parents is not a discrete event but is the beginning of what may very well turn out to be a long-term process for the parents as well as for their child. The SAP staff should have clear goals and expectations in mind before each incident of parent contact. For students with relatively serious AODA-related problems (e.g., policy violations, serious deteriorations in school performance) the initial meeting with parents is utilized primarily to communicate to them the seriousness of the behavior, the fact that it violates school policy, and that the school—with the support of the community—has instituted procedures which must be followed and services which may be of help. Subsequent meetings with parents and/or other family members are typically devoted to conveying accurate information about alcohol and other drug abuse, helping parents to change enabling behavior, assisting in improving parenting skills, discussing in-school and community options for referral, and so on. Thus, involving and working with parents is an important component of case management—bringing together in a planned way the resources necessary to support individual change. Working successfully with parents frequently requires all of those in the student assistance program to bring to bear all that they know about alcohol and other drug abuse and all of their skills in its sensitive management.

Procedures

The development of a clear statement of procedures is another critical factor contributing to effective case management of individual students and of the various AODA target groups. A statement of procedures should be developed, agreed to by members of the Core Team within each building (procedures can vary between buildings), and communicated to all staff members. The Board of Education should also be well-aware of the step-by-step process for handling individual cases. Such a clear and well-understood procedure statement accomplishes a number of things:

- As a document, it integrates program roles, functions, and services, with the needs of kids in the various target groups;

- Procedures are a means of assuring due process to students and parents: individual cases will not be handled capriciously;

- Procedures assure the staff that due process will be followed. Any staff member aware of the program's procedures can inquire about a student's

progress, or about the stage of the process he is in, and whether certain things have or have not been done;

- Procedures reflect decision points within the student assistance process. In other words, no student 'drops out of sight,' or exits the program unless as a result of a conscious decision by those coordinating the program. Even the student who is not engaged in a group or in counseling may still be being monitored by the program staff.

Procedure Language

Formal, written procedure statements can become complex in view of the many different factors they need to take into account: the nature of the referral (e.g., self, staff, etc.), the nature of the "problem" (e.g., witnessed use, suspected use, family concern), program functions (procedures for identification, for assessment, for intervention), and the services available (in-school versus community). Procedures are also necessarily dependent upon policy language and the decisions behind it. Confidentiality, the timely and appropriate involvement of outside AODA Counselors, parent involvement, information, and consent, and the co-curricular consequences for drug abuse are but a few of the issues that often need to be integrated into procedure as well as policy language.

Procedures for identification have been discussed elsewhere (Chapter 7). Supplement 12.1 represents an example of a statement of procedures organized primarily by the nature of the referral source, and the process to be followed after the student has been identified to the SAP staff.

Figures 12.1 and 12.2 represent some examples of how a school's procedures might be diagrammed. In addition to the factors already mentioned, the diagrams indicate that developing procedural statements which are complete is complicated by the nature of consequences for first and second offenses.

Record-Keeping

As a general rule, in the student assistance program few records on individual students should be kept. The following guidelines should govern those that are maintained:

- Only the minimal information which documents that the program's procedures and services are being appropriately offered to the individual student should be maintained;

- Records should be maintained which will provide the minimal information necessary to evaluate the program's effectiveness;

- Records should document the summaries, conclusions, recommendations, and actions of the staff and/or student;

- Records should not be "client notes," which reveal confidential, personal information which the student has disclosed or related to the SAP staff about himself or others;

- SAP records, like other records relating to medical problems, should never become part of a student's cumulative file;

- The program staff should designate what records will be maintained by which program staff;

- Records should be regarded as "personal notes" which are the property of the individual staff;

- In devising a record-keeping and information management system, the staff should make it consistent with state laws which most restrict access and disclosure of records to others.

Supplement 12.2 contains an example of a "Student Assistance Program Referral Record"—a single form on which most of the relevant information concerning an individual student can be summarized. Many schools adopt a form, of which Figure 12.3 is a facsimile, which enables them to track a student's progress in the program and to collect the minimal information which will be useful in evaluating not only the student's individual progress but the effectiveness of the program as a whole (see Part Five).

It is neither possible nor desirable to diagram or draft complete procedure language which anticipates each "what if" and the uniqueness presented by each student. The examples offered in this chapter are intended to be illustrative only. Regardless of the ultimate form of a school's procedure statements, the core of its student assistance program will be the effective case management of students through the assessment, intervention, and support processes once they come to the attention of those in the program.

Chapter 12 | **Supplement**

Supplement 12.1, "Sample Student Assistance Procedures," is one example of how a school system might wish to organize a statement of its program's procedural components. The procedures are organized loosely according to how a student becomes identified to the program: i.e., by STAFF REFERRAL, ("witnessed use," suspected AODA-related problem,), AGENCY REFERRAL ("recovering students"), and OTHER REFERRAL SOURCES discussed in Chapter 7. Supplement 12.2 is to be taken as an *example* only; the actual form of the procedures a school system develops will depend greatly on concrete local policy matters.

Supplement 12.2, the "SAP Referral Record," contains an example of a form which the SAP Counselor/-Coordinator may need to develop in order to facilitate the case management of students in the program. It can also be utilized to facilitate the collection of raw data for evaluation purposes, such as the number of referrals, the pattern of referrals, the pattern of disposition of students within the SAP, the impact of the student assistance program's services on school performance, etc.

Supplement 12.1

SAMPLE PROGRAM PROCEDURES

As the focal person in the school building who is adequately trained in handling AODA-related problems, the SAP Counselor/Coordinator must manage each student referral appropriately. Appropriately managing a given student requires assuring that the student is offered the appropriate form of help and monitoring his behavior to see if it returns to acceptable levels. Decsribing these apparently simple tasks can become complicated by the source of referral (e.g., staff, family, peer, self, community), the nature of the AODA problem (e.g., policy violation, performance problem, suspected family dependency), and the in-school services available to the student (e.g., support groups, one-to-one counseling, seeing a Certified AODA Counselor).

Moreover, procedures within the student assistance program occasionally will need to be coordinated with disciplinary action. The sample which follows does not differentiate between first and subsequent offenses, whereas the policy language upon which it is based probably would. Essentially the same procedures would be followed, but specific recommendations might vary at key points. Thus, if a recommendation for expulsion would accompany a second offense involving *witnessed use*, the Core Team's deliberations/recommendations (1.1.6(d)) would typically be communicated to the student and family as well as being forwarded to the school system's expulsion review committee.

Supplement 12.1 is intended to be illustrative only. Schools may prefer to be more or less detailed in specifying individual procedures for a variety of different circumstances.

Figures 12.1 and 12.2 are examples of how a district might illustrate its procedures graphically, based on the procedures below.

STUDENT ASSISTANCE PROGRAM PROCEDURES

1.0 STAFF REFERRAL. Staff members who witness instances of the violation of the alcohol/drug policy, who encounter an alcohol/drug overdose situation, or who suspect the existence of an AODA-related problem should be governed by the following procedures:

1.1. *Witnessed AODA Policy Violation:* The staff member witnesses a violation of school policy and/or local, state, or federal regulations against the possession, use, delivery, transfer, or sale of alcoholic beverages and/or other mood-altering chemicals, committed in school, on school property, or at a school-sponsored event:

1.1.1. *The staff member will take the following steps:*

a. Inform the student of the observed violation;
b. Obtain the student's name;
c. Ask the student to accompany him/her to the principal's office, to a police officer, or to the official in charge of the event;
d. Confiscate the chemical and/or evidence of its use;
e. Take note of others who many have witnessed the behavior;
f. Report the incident and details relating to alcohol/drug use to the building administrator, documenting the incident appropriately.

1.1.2. *The Building Administrator will take the following steps:*

a. Suspend the student in accordance with school policy for first or second offenses, pending a reinstatement conference with the student and parents;
b. Notify parents of the suspension and schedule a reinstatement conference;
c. Explain to parents any conditions for reinstatement;
d. Notify the SAP Counselor/Coordinator of the suspension, of the circumstances involving chemical use, of staff witnessing the incident, and of the reinstatement conference.
e. Notify local law enforcement authorities of the alleged violation, turning over to them confiscated materials.

1.1.3. *The SAP Counselor/Coordinator will begin the initial screening process by taking the following steps within ____ days:*

a. Contact the staff member making the referral;
b. Contact other staff who work the student on a regular basis;
c. Review the student's performance records, including any past history of AODA offenses or contact with the SAP;
d. Contact parents and/or other family members
e. Contact other community agencies with whom the student and/or family may have been involved
f. Review data with members of the Core Team
g. Make recommendations to the appropriate administrator;
h. Help the administrator plan the reinstatement conference.

1.1.4. *The Building Administrator will take the following steps:*

a. Notify concerned persons of the reinstatement conference and encourage them to attend, including the SAP Counselor/Coordinator, the student, parent(s), other concerned persons from the school or community;
b. Chair the reinstatement conference;

c. Explain to parents and the child the school's policy on chemical use.

d. Explain to parents and the child the conditions for reinstatement, which could include taking part in an assessment process in the school and/or in the community and agreeing to follow initial recommendations.

e. Explain to the student and parents the conditions under which suspension or expulsion will be held in abeyance, or under which extra curricular privileges will be restored.

f. (If the student/parents reject referral to the SAP, implement standard disciplinary measures and proceed to 1.2.2 for long-term follow-up.

g. Notify the coach and/or other advisors of extracurricular activties in which the student may be involved;

1.1.5. *The SAP Counselor will conduct one or more personal screening interviews with the student and will propose one or more of the following recommendations:*

a. No apparent personal or performance problem at this time; no further action necessary at this time;

b. No apparent alcohol/drug-related problem at this time; however, referral to other services or agencies is appropriate;

c. Further assessment interviews with the SAP Counselor are needed;

d. Student needs to contract for specific behavioral changes in AODA-related behavior, monitored through regular meetings between the student and the SAP Counselor;

e. The student needs to satisfactorily complete an in-school use-focussed support group, after which additional recommendations may be made;

f. The student requires an in-school assessment, also involving parents, by a Certified AODA Counselor from an approved AODA agency in the community;

g. The student requires referral to an approved AODA agency for a professional assessment;

h. The assessment information supports the need for referral to primary treatment for chemical dependency through a community-based residential or an intensive outpatient program;

i. The student needs involvement in other community services such as Alateen, Alcoholics Anonymous, Narcotics Anonymous, Cocaine Anonymous, etc.

1.1.6. *The SAP Counselor/Coordinator will hold a Core Team Assessment Conference in order to take the following steps:*

a. Review assessment recommendations and formulate a SAP Student Services Plan (Supplement 8.5);

b. Decide on the necessity of formal intervention by the Referral Team;

c. Inform building administrator, if not involved, of recommendations for course of action;

1.1.7. *The SAP Counselor/Coordinator and Core Team members will conduct a Referral Team Meeting in order to meet with the student, parents, (and other concerned persons) to convey recommendations.*

a. If the Referral Team's recommendations are accepted, proceed to 1.1.8.

b. If the Referral Teams's recommendations are rejected, return to 1.1.4(c).

1.1.8. *The SAP Counselor/Coordinator will maintain an accurate record of the student's progress in the program through the following, (depending on whether or not the student accepts help):*

a. Remaining in contact with parents regarding the student's progress;
b. Remaining in contact with support group leaders to monitor student's progress;
c. Remaining in periodic contact with other staff who see the student regularly;
d. Remaining in contact with community agencies to which the student and/or family has been referred.

1.1.9. *The SAP Counselor/Coordinator will inform the Building Administrator, members of the Core Team, and extracurricular advisors of the student's satisfactory or unsatisfactory completion of and compliance with program recommendations.*

1.1.10. *Failure to follow through with recommendations or to improve conduct to acceptable levels may require returning to step 1.1.4(e).*

1.2. *Suspected AODA-Involvement:* The staff member notes a pattern of school performance representing a change in an unacceptable direction and which usual and customary corrective measures have failed to remedy:

1.2.1. *The staff member will take one or more of the following steps:*

a. Confer with the SAP Counselor/Coordinator about student's behavior;
b. Complete and submit a Student Assistance Program Referral Form;
c. Conduct a referral interview with the student.

1.2.2. *The SAP Counselor/Coordinator will begin the initial screening process by taking the following steps: ("*" indicates optional step)*

a. Contact the staff member making the referral;
b. Contact other staff who work with the student on a regular basis;
c. Review performance records;
d. Conduct one or more screening interviews with the student;
*e. Contact parents and/or other family members;
f. Contact other community agencies with whom the student and/or family may have been involved;
g. Review data with members of the Core Team.

1.2.3. *Following the initial screening process the SAP Counselor/Coordinator will propose one or more of the following recommendations:*

a. No apparent personal or performance problem at this time; no further action necessary at this time;
b. No apparent alcohol/drug-related problem at this time; however, referral to other services or agencies is appropriate;
c. Further assessment interviews with the SAP Counselor are needed;
d. Student needs to contract for specific behavioral changes in AODA-related behavior, monitored through regular meetings between the student and the SAP Counselor;
e. The student needs to satisfactorily complete an in-school use-focussed support group, after which additional recommendations may be made;
f. The student requires an in-school assessment, also involving parents, by a Certified AODA Counselor from an approved AODA agency in the community;
g. The student requires referral to an approved AODA agency for a professional assessment;

h. The assessment information supports the need for referral to primary treatment for chemical dependency through acommunity-based residential or an intensive outpatient program;

i. The student needs involvement in other community services such as Alateen, Alcoholics Anonymous, Narcotics Anonymous, Cocaine Anonymous, etc.

1.2.4. The SAP Counselor Coordinator will conduct a Core Team Assessment Conference in order to take the following steps:

a. Review assessment recommendations and formulate a SAP Student Services Plan (Supplement 8.5);

b. Decide on the necessity of formal intervention by the Referral Team;

c. Inform building administrator of recommendations for course of action;

1.2.5. The SAP Counselor/Coordinator and Core Team members will conduct a Referral Team Meeting in order to meet with the student (* and parents or other concerned persons) to convey recommendations.

1.2.6. Failure to follow through with recommendations or to improve conduct to acceptable levels may require parent contact and a return to step 1.2.2.

1.2.7. The SAP Counselor/Coordinator will maintain an accurate record of the student's progress in the program through the following:

a. Remaining in contact with parents regarding the student's progress;

b. Remaining in contact with support group leaders to monitor student's progress;

c. Remaining in periodic contact with other staff who see the student regularly;

d. Remaining in contact with community agencies to which the student and/or family has been referred.

1.3. Suspected Family Concern: The staff member becomes concerned that a student is affected by someone else's AODA-related problem.

1.3.1. The staff member will take one or more of the following steps:

a. Confer with the SAP Counselor/Coordinator about student's behavior;

b. Complete and submit a Student Assistance Program Referral Form;

c. Conduct a referral interview with the student.

1.3.2. The SAP Counselor/Coordinator will take the following steps:

a. Contact the staff member making the referral;

b. Contact other staff who work the student on a regular basis;

c. Review the student's performance records;

d. Conduct one or more screening interviews with the student;

e. Determine whether or not any members of the family have been involved in a recovery process (i.e., treatment, AA,Al-Anon, etc.);

1.3.4. Following the initial screening process the SAP Counselor/Coordinator will propose one or more of the following recommendations:

a. No apparent personal or performance problem at this time; no further action necessary at this time;

b. No apparent alcohol/drug-related problem at this time;

however, referral to other services or agencies is appropriate;

c. Further assessment interviews with the SAP Counselor are needed;
d. The student needs to contract for specific behavioral changes in AODA-related behavior, monitored through regular meetings between the student and the SAP Counselor;
e. The student needs to satisfactorily complete an in-school support group, after which additional recommendations may be made;
f. The student requires referral to an approved AODA agency for additional information or help;
g. The student needs involvement in other community services such as Alateen or Al-Anon.

1.3.4. The SAP Counselor Coordinator, in consultation with the Core Team, will take the following steps:

a. Review assessment recommendations and formulate a SAP Student Services Plan (Supplement 8.5);
b. Inform building administrator of recommendations for course of action;
c. Meet with the student to convey recommendations;
d. Inform the referring staff member of the student's status through the Staff Referral Feedback Form.

1.3.6. The SAP Counselor/Coordinator will maintain an accurate record of the student's progress in the program through the following:

a. Remaining in contact with support group leaders to monitor student's progress;
b. Remaining in periodic contact with other staff who see the student regularly;

1.4. Alcohol/drug Overdose: The procedures to be followed when a student appears to be experiencing an alcohol/drug overdose or acute alcohol/drug intoxication will be the same as those to be followed for any other medical emergency.

1.4.1. The staff member confronted with a possible alcohol/drug overdose or acute intoxication will immediately observe the following guidelines:

a. The staff member will not leave the student alone, seeking the assistance of other staff or students;
b. Contact the school nurse and the building administrator immediately;
c. Administer resuscitation if needed;
d. Attempt to calm and reassure student;

1.4.2. The building administrator and/or the school nurse will determine additional needs and will take the following steps:

a. Remove the student from the building for emergency medical attention (i.e., contacting emergency medical services, paramedics, police, or ambulance services);
b. Contact parents and/or guardian to inform them of circumstances and of facility to which student has been taken;
c. Following emergency care, the school will follow the policy and procedure for "STAFF REFERRAL: Witnessed AODA Violation" (1.1).

2.0. OTHER REFERRAL SOURCES. Students may also come to the attention of the Student Assistance Program Staff through self referral, or through referral by parents, peers, or community agencies.

2.1. Self Referral. In general, for students who first become involved in the program by voluntarily contacting the SAP Counselor/Coordinator or other members of the Core Team, or who are referred by the other sources above, the procedures for "Suspected AODA-Involvement" (1.2.2 - 1.2.6) will be followed by the SAP Coordinator/Counselor, with parent involvement optional at the SAP Coordinator/Counselor's discretion.

2.2. Peer Referral and Parent Referral. In general, the SAP staff will follow the procedures for "Staff Referral: Suspected AODA-Involvement," (1.2.2 - 1.2.6), regarding the peer or parent as the referral agent. The SAP Counselor/Coordinator may wish, upon initial contacts, to explore resources which might be helpful to the referring person(s) (e.g., a concerned person's group, Al-Anon, etc.).

2.3. Agency Referrals. The school will be contacted by community agencies working with AODA-involved youth most frequently because of a witnessed use situation or because the student is returning from a treatment program.

2.3.1. If school policy was violated, the SAP staff will proceed according to "Witnessed Use" procedures (1.1.2 - 1.1.8). If the chemical use did not involve a violation of school policy, the referral would be handled as "Suspected AODA-Involvement" (1.2.2 - 1.2.6).

2.3.2. For students returning from a chemical dependency treatment program, the SAP Coordinator/Counselor will take the following steps:

   a. Seek to be involved in the discharge planning process or to have access to its recommendations;
   b. Conduct a re-entry meeting with the student's classroom teachers to clarify short-term and long-term expectations for school performance;
   c. Meet with the student and/or parents to clarify their expectations upon the student's return to school;
   d. Communicate to the student and family the school's recommendations for a support program (e.g., attendance in a Recovery Support Group, simultaneous use of AA/NA/CA in the community, follow-up with aftercare counseling, etc.).

Figure 12.1
THE BASIC PROCESS

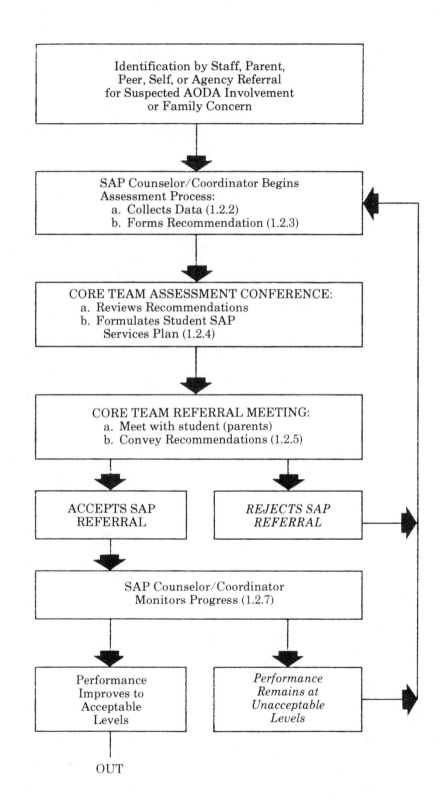

Identification by Staff, Parent,
Peer, Self, or Agency Referral
for Suspected AODA Involvement
or Family Concern

SAP Counselor/Coordinator Begins
Assessment Process:
  a. Collects Data (1.2.2)
  b. Forms Recommendation (1.2.3)

CORE TEAM ASSESSMENT CONFERENCE:
  a. Reviews Recommendations
  b. Formulates Student SAP
     Services Plan (1.2.4)

CORE TEAM REFERRAL MEETING:
  a. Meet with student (parents)
  b. Convey Recommendations (1.2.5)

ACCEPTS SAP
REFERRAL

*REJECTS SAP
REFERRAL*

SAP Counselor/Coordinator
Monitors Progress (1.2.7)

Performance
Improves to
Acceptable
Levels

*Performance
Remains at
Unacceptable
Levels*

OUT

Figure 12.2
WITNESSED USE PROCEDURES

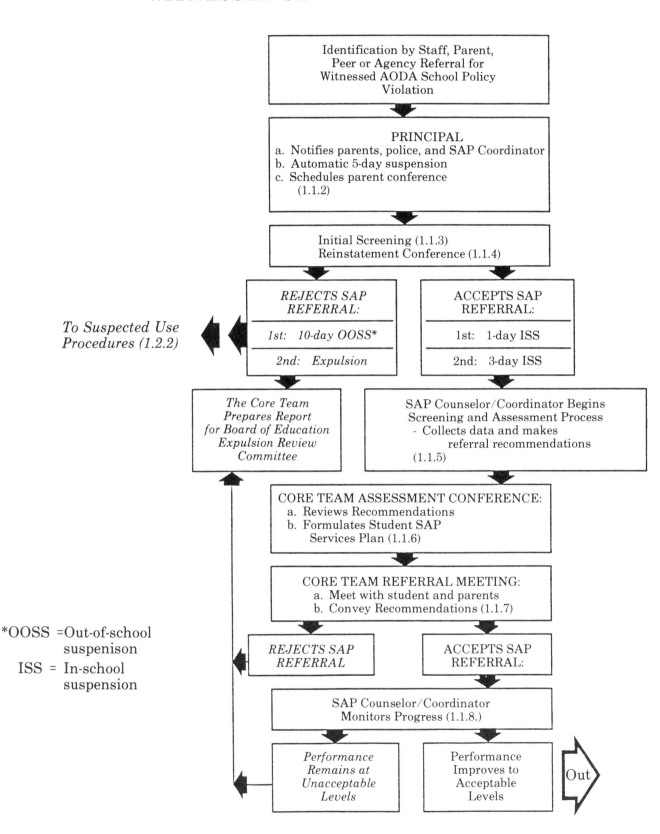

Identification by Staff, Parent, Peer or Agency Referral for Witnessed AODA School Policy Violation

PRINCIPAL
a. Notifies parents, police, and SAP Coordinator
b. Automatic 5-day suspension
c. Schedules parent conference
   (1.1.2)

Initial Screening (1.1.3)
Reinstatement Conference (1.1.4)

REJECTS SAP REFERRAL:

1st: 10-day OOSS*

2nd: Expulsion

ACCEPTS SAP REFERRAL:

1st: 1-day ISS

2nd: 3-day ISS

To Suspected Use Procedures (1.2.2)

The Core Team Prepares Report for Board of Education Expulsion Review Committee

SAP Counselor/Coordinator Begins Screening and Assessment Process - Collects data and makes referral recommendations (1.1.5)

CORE TEAM ASSESSMENT CONFERENCE:
a. Reviews Recommendations
b. Formulates Student SAP Services Plan (1.1.6)

CORE TEAM REFERRAL MEETING:
a. Meet with student and parents
b. Convey Recommendations (1.1.7)

REJECTS SAP REFERRAL

ACCEPTS SAP REFERRAL:

SAP Counselor/Coordinator Monitors Progress (1.1.8.)

Performance Remains at Unacceptable Levels

Performance Improves to Acceptable Levels

Out

*OOSS =Out-of-school suspenison
ISS = In-school suspension

Supplement 12.2

THE SAP REFERRAL RECORD

A number of forms have been discussed in Part Two which assist those in the student assistance program to gather information and to document decisions made along the way. The "SAP Referral Form" (Supplement 7.1) may be used by school staff to identify students to the program. Similarly, the "Request for Information (staff)" (Supplement 8.2) is used by the SAP Counselor/Coordinator to request input from staff once a student has been referred, and can be used to summarize the comments received. The "Student SAP Screening Summary" (Supplement 8.4) allows the SAP Counselor Coordinator to pull together the results of staff observations, student records, the comments of others who know the student, and of personal screening interviews, resulting in the formation of the "Student SAP Services Plan" (Supplement 8.5) in consultation with the Core Team.

The SAP Referral Record

Figure 12.3, the "SAP Referral Record," is a facsimile of a form used to summarize all of this relevant information. The form serves the purposes of both case management and of evaluation. Thus, it allows anyone examining it to ascertain where the student is in the program, what services have been provided at what dates, and brief clues as to the outcome. It also indicates the degree to which the student's participation in the program has had any impact on such quantifiable indicators as attendance, tardiness, grades, and conduct. (This data can also be condensed even further for purposes of program evaluation. See Part Five).

The form, or one similar to it, is completed and maintained by the SAP Counselor/-Coordinator to whom an individual is referred as a result of identification.

Student Information. This brief section contains the student's name and identification number. It is wise to assign an identifying number to each student referred to the program, primarily for the purposes of confidentiality. When records are summarized, only ID numbers need be used. The student name section can easily be blotted out if records need to be duplicated. The student's sex, age, and grade provide information which will allow comparisons later. The name of the SAP Counselor/Coordinator who receives the referral is necessary to distinguish between individuals responsible for given students.

Referral Source information documents how the student was identified to the SAP staff. The date of the referral is written under the appropriate heading and indicates the *date of entry into the program.* "Administrative" referrals can be those which come from building administrators who encounter students because of "witnessed use" policy violations. In addition, an administrator may be working with a student on other disciplinary grounds, and may refer him to the SAP because of a suspicion that alcohol and other drug use is involved in the student's behavior problems. "Staff" referrals are those coming directly from other school staff, including teachers, guidance counselors, and other pupil services staff. Family, peer, and self-referrals are similarly coded. "Community" can indicate that the referral came from an AODA agency, a clergyman, the police or sheriff's office, the juvenile justice system, etc. Additional blanks can be used to separate these referral sources.

Referral Category distinguishes between alcohol/drug-related referrals and non-AODA referrals. Obviously, this information is coded after initial screening. Non-AODA referrals would include students judged to have no significant AODA involvement but some other categorical problem: child abuse and neglect, suicide, teenage pregnancy, etc.

Assessment Recommendations provides a brief log of the recommendations of the Core Team as follows:

Step:
A numeral (i.e.,"1," "2,") indicates the order of recommendations and actions taken. Some students may remain in the program for some time, working their way gradually through the assessment/intervention continuum.

Recommendation:
A shorthand description of the assessment recommendation of the Core Team and the date of acceptance is entered, perhaps from those listed in Supplement 12.1, step 1.2.3. (e.g., 'No problem at this time,' 'Meetings with SAP Counselor,' 'Behavior contract,' 'In-school AODA Assessment,' etc.).

Referred To:
Documents the specific in-school or community service to which the student accepted referral. (E.g., 'Mr. Jones,' 'Affected Others Group,' 'Midville Council on Alcoholism,' etc.).

Outcome:
A brief statement of the outcome and its date, indicating whether the student's behavior changed or not, whether the support group was completed satisfactorily, the results of a formal assessment, etc. In some cases, the outcome indicates the need for further action by the Core Team, leading to another entry as "Step 2."

Evaluation provides minimal statistical documentation of the degree to which the program's services resulted in quantifiable changes in the student's behavior. "Termination Date" records the date when the student exits the program. The exit point can be difficult to define. For some it could be the point at which the student refuses services and accepts disciplinary consequences. It would obviously include the point at which the student leaves school. It could also indicate the point at which the student is referred to community services for primary care (i.e., chemical dependency treatment). In any case, for evaluation purposes it will be necessary to define and document the entry and exit points for each student.

This section also provides for a comparison between certain baseline indicators prior to program referral, during the student's program involvement, and after termination from the program. Figure 12.3 is based on a general notion of "marking period," which could be quarters of the school year, semesters, and so on. It provides for comparing school performance for two such periods pre- and post-program involvement.

The "Other" category is provided to allow variation in indicators not used by all students or by all school buildings. For example, some schools may wish to develop a numeric indicator of level of alcohol/drug use and record changes, if any, as a result of the student's participation in the program. Some schools also utilize objective measures of teachers' evaluations of students' cooperation, behavior, and attitude which can also be compared pre- and post-program. It is even possible to record scores on certain tests of alcohol/drug knowledge, psychometric tests of self-concept, and so on.

Finally, while Figure 12.3 is designed as a written form, the data it contains is easily adaptable to entry in a microcomputer. Categorical items, such as Referral Source and Referral Category are easily translated into number codes that can be entered in a single field. The Assessment Recommendations discussed in Chapter 8 can also be assigned numerical codes and entered in a single field. Computerizing data has the advantage of permitting many different reports to be generated. Most file handling software permits the user to protect files with passwords. Even single fields, such as student names, can be omitted from visual or printer output unless the user has access to the password.

Figure 12.3
SAP REFERRAL RECORD

I. STUDENT INFORMATION:

STUDENT NAME:	ID #	M/F	AGE	GRADE	SAP Counselor

II. REFERRAL SOURCE AND DATE OF REFERRAL:

ADMIN	STAFF	FAMILY	PEER	SELF	COMMUNITY		

III. REFERRAL CATEGORY:

ALCOHOL/DRUG-RELATED:				NON-AODA:			
Witnessed	Suspected	Concerned	Recovering				

IV. ASSESSMENT RECOMMENDATIONS, DISPOSITION, AND OUTCOMES

STEP	ASSESSMENT RECOMMENDATION	DATE	REFERRED TO:	OUTCOME	DATE

V. EVALUATION:

Termination Date:	MARKING PERIOD				
	Prior to Referral		During Program Services	After Program Services	
INDICATORS	2nd	1st		1st	2nd
Attendance Ratio (%)					
Tardiness Ratio (%)					
Disciplinary Incidents (#)					
Grade Point Average (dec.)					
Other:					
Other:					
Other:					

Attendance Ratio: Number of days absent/possible attendance days;
Tardiness Ratio: Number of times tardy/possible attendance days;
Disciplinary Incidents: Number of referrals for behavior problems;
Grade Point Average: Expressed as a decimal;
Other: Measures of alcohol/drug quantity and frequency.
                               teacher evaluations. scores on self-concept tests,
                               etc.

PART THREE | # Basic Support Groups

Whether their purpose is to support adolescents in recovery, to intervene, to prevent further AODA problems, or to help children of alcoholics cope more successfully—brief, problem-focussed support groups have emerged as obligatory components of an effective, comprehensive student assistance program.

Building on the general description of AODA-related support groups in Chapter 11, Chapter 13 focusses on the issues surrounding their implementation within the school setting. While it is certainly possible to conduct a successful support group without the entire structure of a student assistance program, implementing groups on the scope required by the prevalence of AODA-related problems quickly forces the school system to recognize and define its limitations. To be maximally effective, considerable attention must go into the planning process for the individual support group and for groups in general. Chapter 13 also examines some of the policy issues involving the support groups and which require consistent policies on a district-wide basis. Finally, Chapter 13 reveals that the implementation of AODA-related support groups is not without its pitfalls.

The remaining chapters explore the nature of each of the major types of groups. The needs of students in each target group, the goals for the respective support groups, and representative activities for each are described. Chapters 14, 15, and 16 examine, respectively, the Affected Other Groups, the Recovery Support Groups, and Other Use-Focussed Groups.

| # Implementing Support Groups

There is an old Hassidic story about the Rabbi who had a conversation with the Lord about Heaven and Hell. "I will show you Hell," said the Lord and led the Rabbi into a room in the middle of which was a very big, round table. The people sitting at it were famished and desperate. In the middle of the table was a large pot of nourishing stew. The smell of the stew was delicious, and the people around the table were holding spoons with very long handles. Each one found that it was just possible to reach the pot to take a spoonful of stew, but because the handle was so long, he could not get the food to his mouth. The Rabbi saw that their suffering was terrible.

"Now I will show you Heaven," said the Lord, who led the Rabbi into another room exactly the same as the first. There was the same large table and the same large pot of stew. The people were, as before, equipped with the same long-handled spoon. But here they were well-nourished and plump, talking and laughing.

At first the Rabbi did not understand. "It is simple, said the Lord. "You see, here they have learned to feed each other." (Yalom (1975), pp. 13-14).

Upon deciding to implement AODA-related support groups as a service of the student assistance program, one is faced immediately with the task of defining their limits within the school setting. The fact is, "groups" now come in a bewildering variety of forms: informational, "rap," and activity therapy groups; behavior modification, sensitivity, and encounter groups; human relations training, assertiveness, and transactional analysis groups; guided interaction, psychoanalytic, and confrontation groups; Gestalt, sensory awareness, cathartic, and primal scream groups; psychodrama, self-directed, self-help, and leaderless groups, and many others defined by problem focus (e.g.,marriage encounter), therapeutic orientation of the leader (e.g., reality therapy group), or the client population (e.g., delinquent youth).

Limitations of Support Groups

"Support" versus "Therapy." It has been stated on several occasions that the school is wise to think through the difference between its role in making the means of assistance available to students and actually providing therapy. Thus, one of the primary tasks of the school—as well as of the individuals leading support groups—is to distinguish as clearly as possible between the "support group" as a part of a student assistance program and "group therapy." Neither the technical manual nor the dictionary provide much clarity here, but some guidelines can be suggested which help the system as well as the group leader in defining the differences operationally.

It is possible to differentiate between many types of groups based on the professional qualifications (requirements) of the group leader or therapist, the degree of responsibility they assume for changing group members' functioning, the intensity and duration of the group, and the general aims and goals of the group. Groups as therapeutic tools can thus be seen as arranged along a continuum based on these criteria. At one extreme would be the "psychotherapy" or "treatment" group; at the other would be the "support group." Between these two extremes lie many types of groups, based on the qualifications and responsibilities of group leaders, the intensity of the group's focus on problems, and the group's goals.

In psychotherapy or treatment groups, for example, leaders are highly trained, professionally certified therapists with maximal skills in diagnosis and the provision of direct, primary treatment for presenting problems. The therapist takes on the primary responsibility for achieving the goal of treatment—the complete resolution of diagnosed problems. Such therapy-oriented groups are often utilized in residential settings. Participation in the group is typically long-term (one to two years) or is indeterminate. "Patients" leave treatment only when they are judged to have been restored to effective functioning. Patients initially seek out or are accepted into such a regimen because they have demonstrated an inability to function in normal social environments independently.

At the opposite extreme we would place the "support group." In such groups the leaders, or "facilitators," possess basic knowledge concerning group dynamics and of the problems group members identify. Their role is not usually defined by requirements for professional licensure, and they are often uncertified. Facilitating ("making easy") peer interaction within the group is more important than professional direction. Diagnosis is irrelevant to the general group goal of providing information, problem clarification, interpersonal support, and/or referral to more treatment-like services. Strengthening the individual, providing information, and enhancing her general coping skills are more important than the complete resolution of problems. These groups are consequently time-limited, and brief in comparison to psychotherapy groups. The type of support group provided by a student assistance program should clearly be of this latter type.

A similar means of clarifying the limitations of the "support group" as opposed to "therapy" is through defining the purpose and goal of such groups in general. The general intent or purpose of SAP support groups should be to improve rather than to cure. All AODA-related support groups should have two general goals: (1) to promote, enhance, or maintain students' abilities to cope healthfully and constructively with AODA-related problems in themselves and/or others, and (2) to enable students to make use of those resources available in the environment, where the "environment" is the group, the school, the family, or the community.

Finally, the individual group facilitator can define the "therapy/support group" boundary on immediate, subjective grounds that have to do, again, with maintaining a clear sense of both personal and professional limitations. One might refer to this as the "out of my depth" test. In short, whenever the group facilitator feels that what the student is dealing with is severe, critical, or beyond the leader's level of preparation, it is time to involve other people or to make a referral to those who are professionally qualified to work with the student in the customary, "therapeutic" role.

Planning to Implement a Support Group

Clearly, considerable planning and preparation must accompany the decision by the school system to implement support groups in general, and by the individual group facilitator preparing to lead a specific one. Support groups within a student assistance program are more structured than might be supposed. They have clear and definite objectives limited by the size of the group, the length of time it meets, and the qualifications of the group facilitators. They require careful planning. Common practice has revealed that the following are among the more important planning issues that should precede the implementation of any individual group:

Define the Target Group. The first step in planning to implement an individual group must be the definition of the target group whose needs the support group is intended to meet. This refers to designing a group that will address the general needs of recovering students, affected others, and so on. It is also necessary to recall that even within these broad target groups, students will lie along a continuum which describes the degree to which they are affected by a given variety of drug-related problem. Awareness of the different needs of students will either require designing and implementing different types of groups or adapting a given group to the needs of those students the group leader selects for inclusion.

Identify Goals and Objectives. Defining the intended benefits or outcomes for students in the group is another crucial planning step. The group leaders should devote considerable time to defining specific goals and objectives that they intend the group meet. For any of the groups, outcome objectives should be developed in at least three general areas: (1) improvement in general personal and interpersonal functioning (e.g., trust, self-disclosure, decision-making skills), (2) improvement in school performance (e.g., grades, attendance, classroom conduct), and (3) improvements in specific AODA-related indicators (e.g., patterns of alcohol/drug use, coping with parental drinking, etc.). In setting goals, group leaders should bear in mind that the general purpose of the student assistance support group is to improve rather than to cure, and that what realistically can be accomplished in the group will be limited by time, number of sessions, number of group members, and other factors.

"It is impossible to lead a group without endorsing, implicitly or explicitly, a set of values about groups in general, about the nature of being a human being, or about the nature of AODA-related problems."

Decide Basic Questions of Setting and Structure. There are a number of concrete decisions that need to be made regarding group structure, size, frequency, duration, and location. The following is a description of the lines along which most student assistance programs have made these decisions:

1. Number of sessions. Groups are usually time-limited rather than open-ended. A given group functions best when it is defined as consisting of a definite number of sessions. A group could be defined as meeting for 4, 8, 12, or 15 sessions: the number of sessions is arbitrary. Limiting the number of meetings can allow more children to be served, can limit the number of group leaders needed, and can permit students to experience all phases of normal group development, including closure.

2. Structure. The most effective groups are not "rap," or "drop-in, drop-out" groups which students can attend or not as they wish. Students accepted for participation in a group make a formal commitment to attend all sessions. Even in more open-ended "maintenance" groups students should contract to attend a given number of consecutive sessions.

3. Frequency. Meeting groups once a week has emerged as the typical, and traditional, pattern. Here, as elsewhere, however, student assistance program staff have demonstrated their creativity and the flexibility of the support group. Some groups, such as Affected Others Groups, for example, meet twice a week to assist students to cope with stressful weekends in their families. In one case, a school held a weekend "marathon" group session because a number of students violated the alcohol/drug policy two weeks before school was out. In another, the elementary school's daily schedule permitted only 25-minute meetings, so group leaders adapted by meeting groups three times a week.

4. Duration. The typical group meeting lasts for a class period, which is usually less than an hour, depending on the realities of the daily schedule. It is a responsibility of group leaders not to allow the group to disrupt the routine of students or other staff by continuing the group beyond a class period or the established group time limit. Occasionally, exceptional circumstances present themselves which demand that the group run overtime, but group leaders should educate their group members to raise difficult issues before the end of the meeting.

5. Meeting Schedule. Groups meet during the school day rather than before or after school. This prevents problems around transportation, interference with extracurricular activities, or parental consent. It also conveys the message to students as well as to staff that the student assistance program is a significant fixture of day-to-day school life. Meeting during the school day also presents scheduling problems of its own, however, and the solutions that first might present themselves often turn out to be the least feasible. It is nearly impossible, for example, to schedule the group when all members will be in a study hall or in otherwise unscheduled time. Likewise, scheduling a group during the preparation time of the teacher co-leader creates unpredictability for students, and forces them to miss the same class each week.

The optimal solution that has emerged involves establishing one day of the week as "group day," and staggering the group meeting throughout the day over several weeks in a predictable way: the first meeting is held first period, the second meeting falls during second period, etc. This means that a given student will miss, say, only one third period English class every eight or nine weeks. It does, however, involve finding ways of covering the class of the teacher who may be co-leading the group.

6. Location. The location of group meetings frequently presents problems, especially if finding unused space is difficult. Space issues, aside, however, groups should be held in areas that protect personal privacy. Groups should not be located in areas where others can overhear students when they are expressing powerful feelings, for example. Many times, however, prospective group leaders confuse privacy with confidentiality and secrecy. Confidentiality protects what is said and done in group, not the fact that a student is in a support group. Likewise, attempts to hold groups in secretive, out-of-the-way places only reinforces the secrecy that surrounds such problems. Aside from privacy considerations, support groups should be located in plain view to reinforce the acceptability of participating in the school's program.

7. Size. A group size of from six to eight members appears to be the ideal for most groups. Again, larger or smaller group sizes are possible. Some Drug Information groups can have 10 to 12 students or more, for example. Adjusting the group's size simply requires the group leaders to adjust their goals and expectations for the group accordingly. Larger groups permit less interaction and are more didactic and discussional than smaller ones.

Closed versus Open Groups. Groups are typically closed rather than open. That is, the same students begin and end the group together. The major advantage of the closed group is that it minimizes the interruptions to group trust caused by the entry of new group members, or the departure of others. The major disadvantage of the closed group is that students who have need of a group must wait until a new one begins. Even within the open group, however, students make a commitment to attend a given number of consecutive sessions. As group leaders become more experienced they often change their closed groups to an open structure. Most maintenance groups are open in character.

Ground Rules. Group leaders will need to develop a set of a few basic ground rules that will form the basis for group interaction. The most basic rules define what will be regarded as responsible conduct within the group, and the rights and responsibilities of group members. Initial rules thus relate to confidentiality, promptness, attendance. Additional ground rules help define respectful conduct, and state that everyone in the group "belongs," that scapegoating or name-calling are not allowed, and that although "passing" is allowed, everyone must participate in the group in some way. Group leaders should also develop ground rules, or expectations, that relate to specific AODA-related behavior. Recovering students, for example, are expected to attend AA, NA, or aftercare meetings; chemically-involved students will be expected to contract for reduced drug use.

Definition of Values and Beliefs. It is impossible to lead a group without endorsing, implicitly or explicitly, a set of values about groups in general, about the nature of being a human being, or about the nature of AODA-related problems. To a large degree, group ground rules are statements about values. In leading AODA-related groups, however, it is also vital to be clear about one's beliefs concerning drug abuse and dependency, about the effects of drug use on children and youth, and on the nature of "recovery." Finally, it is crucial that the values, beliefs, and norms which will be upheld by group facilitators be consistent with those propounded by the school system in its philosphy and policy language regarding student alcohol/drug use.

Clarifying the Selection Process. Most students will have participated in a selection process as a result of their initial assessment—i.e., discovering what type of AODA-related problem they have. Group leaders should ideally participate in an additional screening process by which individual students are selected for and oriented to a particular group. Before entering a group students need to be made aware of the nature of the group, its goals, activities, and its ground rules. Thus, group leaders should meet with students in pre-group interviews designed to address the following areas:

1. What brings the student to the group? Is the group the student's idea or someone else's?

2. Is the student motivated to make changes in the direction of improvement?

3. Will this student be "alone" in the group? Is the student compatible with others already selected or already in the group?

4. Does the student understand the purpose for and expectations of the group?

5. Is this the student's first group experience?

6. Does the student possess the personal strengths and social and verbal skills necessary to be in this group at this time?

Curriculum. The most complete group proposal would contain explicit statements concerning the issues discussed here, and would also include a session-by-session outline of the group's activities. Preparing a group "curriculum" presupposes that group leaders can identify sequential objectives for group members and that they are able to integrate these with what they know about the stages of group dvelopment. Group leaders should also prepare materials, activities, and exercises to be utilized as needed. Experienced group leaders often find it helpful to develop for students a "group handbook" or workbook containing most of the materials that will be used.

Evaluation. Evaluating the group is necessary to discover if goals are being met (i.e., if students are improving), to assist group leaders themselves, and to provide information to others concerning the effectiveness of the groups. Group leaders will need to develop a simple evaluation plan which is consistent with other groups to some degree. The simplest evaluation designs will include subjective student self-reports, archival data from student records, and objective tests, rating instruments, or surveys.

Policy Issues

Although many people are leading individual groups every day, the implementation of such a broad spectrum of groups inevitably leads to the need for developing district-wide policies and procedures. Such policies permit the school to communicate about groups more effectively to students, staff, parents, and the community; they assure students and their families of due process; and, they assure consistency from one group to another and from one building to another in crucial areas. The following are a few of the areas in which it is wise to develop support group policies.

Co-leadership of groups. Although it requires more group facilitator resources, co-leadership of groups is to be preferred. It makes the leadership of all groups easier, provides an effective means of training additional group leaders, and promotes creativity in the design and actual leadership of groups. In many instances, groups are co-facilitated by a school employee and by an appropriately trained volunteer from the community or from a local AODA agency.

Compensation for group facilitators. In many schools, classroom teachers and other staff, in addition to pupil services staff, are invited to become group facilitators. Many do so voluntarily, at least initially. It is important, however, to devise some mechanism for recognizing and/or compensating those who do lead groups over the long run. Compensation can involve, for example, paying an hourly wage, adjusting a teaching assignment or contract, and/or hiring substitutes to cover classes.

Selection of students. The procedures by which students are identified and selected for a particular group need to be clarified. In general, students should not just appear in a group without having been interviewed at least once by the group facilitator(s), who should be empowered to make final selections of specific students for their group. This assures that both students and group leaders are clear, before the group begins, about the nature of the group, expectations of students, and the nature of students' decisions to become involved.

Parental consent/information. It is wise to have a policy that definitely states the school's stance on parental information and/or consent for their children's involvement in support groups. Such policies, of course, must be consistent with local statutes. Some schools prefer to see support groups as essentially extracurricular activities; as such, parental consent is not sought, but parents are informed of their child's desire to be in a support group. Other schools choose to regard the support group as another counseling service, and accordingly seek parental consent. In either case, there are rarely good reasons for retaining a child in a support group against the expressed wishes of parents.

Children at risk. Students in support groups will frequently make disclosures involving child abuse and neglect, incest, sexual abuse, suicide, and other problems placing them at great physical risk. Policies for group leaders must spell out that they will be required to observe the same legal requirements for reporting these incidents as other staff in the school system.

Confidentiality. Policy language needs to be developed clarifying for everyone the fact that "what is said in group stays in group," except in circumstances where children are in danger or at risk. Confidentiality usually precludes disclosures as to the specific type of group a student is attending, although not the fact that they are in a support group in general. As with other areas of the program, care has to be taken not to confuse children's rights to confidentiality and privacy with secrecy.

Group attendance. The realities of scheduling frequently dictate that students will be taken out of classes to attend support groups. Thus, at least within each building, it is wise to have a clear and firm stance regarding students' attendance in groups. Such statements should clarify the respective responsibilities and obligations on the part of students, group leaders, classroom teachers, and building administrators.

Working relationships with staff. Working with students in groups necessarily involves other staff, whether classroom teachers, other counselors and pupil services workers, members of the Core Team, or parents. Policies on confidentiality should not be used to prevent all communication between group leaders and others who also work with students on a regular basis. Leaders of use-focussed groups, for example, will need to maintain contact with a principal if a student is in the group in lieu of a suspension or some other disciplinary consequence. Coaches will want to be kept informed of whether student athletes are complying with group expectations. Similarly, counselors and other pupil services workers may be working with a student and/or his family, requiring sharing of information between them and the group leader on the student's behalf. The group leaders may often have useful suggestions for classroom teachers who are worried about a given group member's classroom performance. Feeling a need to protect students from others in the school will breed the mistrust that quickly undermines the success and continued existence of support groups.

Evaluation. Individual support groups, as well as the support group component of a student assistance program in general, should be evaluated as to their impact, effectiveness, and process: how many students are we seeing, how are they different because of their group experience, and how are our procedures working? Evaluation need not be a cumbersome or expensive endeavor. Simple means of gathering both subjective and objective data are available. Evaluation, however, to be meaningful, should be consistent across individual groups and across the district as a whole. The Core Team, through a subgroup made up of group facilitators, should decide on consistent, district-wide evaluation criteria, data collection instruments, and the process for collecting, interpretting, and disseminating the evaluation information.

"Policies on confidentiality should not be used to prevent all communication between group leaders and others who also work with students on a regular basis."

Staff support. "Burnout" can often become a major problem after only one or two years if no attention is paid to the issue of "who helps the helpers?" The leadership of support groups requires not only staff time but considerable emotional investments in students dealing with serious and often tragic issues. Support groups for group leaders should be established. Regular utilization of such a support system should be among the requirements for becoming and remaining a group facilitator.

Criteria for the selection of support group leaders. There is no formal or uniform credentialing or licensing process for support group leaders in student assistance programs. In addition, possession of a counseling certificate or therapist's credential does not automatically qualify one as a support group leader. Moreover, support group leadership is open to anyone: it is not restricted to counselors or other pupil services workers in the school system alone. Nor is being a recovering alcoholic or affected family member to be construed as a credential.

Consequently, the school system must devote some attention to defining a set of criteria for support group leaders to assure that they are adequately prepared to lead groups and to assure that they work with students appropriately and in conformance with school policies and procedures. Criteria must be developed in at least three general areas: (1) assuring adequate formal training in basic AODA issues, (2) assuring formal training in the specifics of leading AODA-related support groups in school, and (3) assuring that group leaders demonstrate responsible and healthy conduct with respect to their own alcohol/drug experience.

Supplement 13.1 is a representative example of a policy and procedure statement for group facilitators that a given school system might adopt.

Pitfalls

Implementing support groups as part of a student assistance program is not without difficulties. Experience has shown that there are a number of potential problem areas that can undermine the effectiveness of an individual support group or of the effort in general. If they are aware of them in advance, those involved in the design and implementation of a student assistance program can take steps to avoid the most common pitfalls.

1. Burnout. Regardless of the compensation mechanism a district employs, the stress of exposure to the pain and problems of AODA-affected youth invariably takes its toll. The phenomenon of "burnout" can express itself physically (somatic complaints, sickness) and emotionally (depression, feelings of inadequacy). It is often a major cause of high rates of turnover for group facilitators.

A major strategy for preventing or "treating" staff burnout involves encouraging group facilitators to define their personal limitations. The support group for group leaders is an effective means of providing facilitators with an opportunity to reassess the limits of the groups as well as of themselves, to share successes and failures, and provide each other with mutual support. Staff support groups can meet as infrequently as once a month or as often as once a week. In a large school district, several staff support groups may be meeting regularly, and may be facilitated by a community professional.

Regular involvement in organizations such as Al-Anon is also highly recommended, utilizing the rationale that AODA group facilitators unavoidably become affected by others' alcoholism or drug abuse. Restricting the number of groups a person may lead, either simultaneously or consecutively also helps to prevent turnover.

2. Dependency on the group. Since one of the primary goals of the groups is to strengthen the student, everything possible should be done to prevent students from relying on the group or its leader(s) as their sole source of support. In individual meetings, group leaders are wise to promote students' reliance on each other for support during the group and between meetings by developing group members' skills in asking for and and giving and receiving help. Older students should also be made aware of sources of help in the community and urged to utilize them. Group leaders may be available to students outside of group meetings, but only in cases of emergency, and only after students have tried to utilize other supports. The support group should never take the place of help available through formal counseling or self-help groups in the community.

In the successful group, participants and facilitators alike will be aware that the group typically will not be available during the summer, and certainly not after graduation. Facilitators, especially, must be aware that the group's function is at least twofold: to provide support, and to teach students how to make use of the support that is available from each other and from the environment.

3. Inadequate support from administration. For the groups to function smoothly, the support of the building administrator is vital. As Supplement 13.1 illustrates, many issues that allow groups to exist depend on administrative involvement in and endorsement of the student assistance program in general and of the groups particularly. Many concrete, day-to-day problems involving scheduling, releasing students from class, communicating with parents, and so on, can be resolved by the active support of the building administrator.

4. Isolation. When a program begins to function actively, there is often a tendency to identify the program with the support groups rather than seeing them as only one service. Furthermore, inappropriate attention to "confidentiality" frequently results in "secrecy," and in the perception by others that the groups are isolated "cliques." Those involved in group facilitation must take steps from the beginning to coordinate their activities with other members of the Core Team, and to communicate frequently about the groups to other staff and to students.

5. Failure to recognize limitations. Most of those directly involved in the SAP will bring to it a high degree of enthusiasm, commitment, and energy at its initiation. Although knowing better, many will expect the program, and the groups particularly, to eradicate drug-related problems in the school altogether. Goals may be set unrealistically high. Some may, for example, expect recovering students to maintain permanent sobriety because of the Recovery Support Group, only to feel frustrated or inadequate when they experience periodic relapses. Similarly, many leaders of use-focussed groups expect students who are heavily drug-involved to emerge from their groups drug-free. Unless group leaders and others involved in the student assistance program meet periodically to define and redefine the limitations of the groups, and even of the school's role in dealing with drug problems, the program is likely to be seen as a failure, and group leaders are likely to drop out.

6. Facilitator conflicts. Group facilitation requires considerable emotional investment in the group and its process. Co-leadership requires investment on another level. Invariably, co-leaders will differ on how incidents should be handled, on their respective roles within a group meeting, and even on the appropriate goals for their group. They may even have differing views on the nature of AODA-related problems, and have different personal experiences with such problems. Many have commented that successful coleadership is more like a marriage than it is like any other relationship. As such, it is vital that when, not if, conflicts and differences arise the individuals involved be willing to resolve them cooperatively. The failure to resolve differences undermines the co-facilitation relationship and is ultimately destructive to the group itself.

Thus, the implementation of the individual group and of support groups in general do not represent a casual or haphazard decision on the part of the school system. It must devote time to clarifying the limitations of groups and of the school system in dealing with AODA-related problems. Group leaders should be selected based on many criteria, including their acceptability to students, and must be appropriately trained. Considerable attention needs to be invested in planning the individual group as well as in developing the policies and procedures that will support the effort. Finally, even with the most careful planning, all of those involved in the student assistance program need to be prepared to deal with the problems that will inevitably arise.

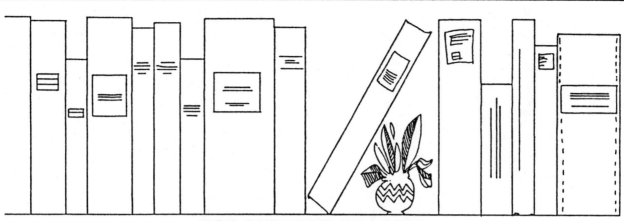

FOR FURTHER READING

The following books and articles are but a few of many excellent resources on small group process and/or on leading groups with adolescents:

Anderson, Joseph. *Counseling through Group Process.* New York: Springer Publishing Company, 1984.

Berkowitz, I., ed. *Adolescents Grow in Groups.* New York: Brunner/Mazel, 1972.

Brandes, N. *Group Therapy with Adolescents.* New York: Aronson, 1973.

Group Skills for Alcoholism Counselors. Rockville, Maryland: National Institute on Alcohol Abuse and Alcoholism, 1980.

Hargrave, Mary C. and George R. "Groupwork with Preadolescents: Theory and Practice." *Child Welfare.* 62 (1983) 31-36.

Kanfer, Frederick H., and Arnold P. Goldstein. *Helping People Change.* New York: Pergamon Press, Inc., 1975.

MacLennan, B. and N. Felsenfeld. *Group Counseling and Psychotherapy with Adolescents.* New York: Columbia University Press, 1968.

Raubolt, Richard R. "Brief, Problem-Focussed Group Psychotherapy with Adolescents." *American Journal of Orthopsychiatry.* 53 (1983) 157-165.

Wolf, Sidney. "Counseling—For Better or for Worse." *Alcohol Health and Research World.* (Winter, 1974) 27-29.

Yalom, Irvin D., M. D. *The Theory and Practice of Group Psychotherapy.* New York: Basic Books, Inc., 1975.

There are many collections of exercises and structured experiences for use in groups of all types. With few exceptions, these can easily be modified to be used in AODA-specific support groups. The following are among the more familiar sources of group activities:

Canfield, Jack and Harold Wells. *100 Ways to Enhance Self-Concept in the Classroom.* New Jersey: Prentice-Hall, Inc., 1976.

Clarke, Jean Illsley. *Leader's Guide: Who Me, Lead a Group?.* Minneapolis, MN: Winston Press, Inc., 1979.

Egan, Gerald. *The Skilled Helper.* Monterey, CA: Brooks/Cole Publishing Co., 1975.

_____. *Exercises in Helping Skills.* Monterey, CA: Brooks/Cole Publishing Co., 1975.

_____. *Training the Skilled Helper.* Monterey, CA: Brooks/Cole Publishing Co., 1979.

Johnson, David. *Reaching Out.* New Jersey: Prentice-Hall, 1981.

_____, and Frank P. Johnson. *Joining Together.* New Jersey: Prentice-Hall, 1982.

Pfeiffer, J. William and John E. Jones, eds. *A Handbook of Structured Experiences for Human Relations Training.* La Jolla, CA: University Associates, 1969. Vols. I-VII.

Stevens, John O. *Awareness: Exploring, Experimenting, Experiencing.* Moab, Utah: Real People Press, 1971.

Chapter 13 | Supplements

Supplement 13.1, "Sample Policies and Procedures for SAP Group Facilitators," is an example of the policy areas which should be addressed relating to the implementation of support groups.

Supplement 13.2 provides a sample "group contract" for a use-focussed group. Such contracts are useful for all types of AODA-related support groups as they reinforce basic ground rules (e.g., confidentiality), spell out the minimal expectations for responsible group member behavior, and are useful during the process of preparing individual students for group participation prior to the first session.

Supplement 13.3 provides a "Sample Information Letter to Parents," informing them of their child's decision to be in a support group. The letter can easily be reworded to seek parental consent in accordance with the school district's policy.

Finally, Supplement 13.4 provides a means for estimating the number of children in need of support groups and the number of groups and facilitators likely to be required. Figures 13.1 through 13.4 are worksheets that are helpful in calculating estimates of need.

Supplement 13.1

SAMPLE POLICIES AND PROCEDURES FOR STUDENT ASSISTANCE PROGRAM GROUP FACILITATORS

Many issues arise during the early stages of implementing support groups as part of a student assistance program—issues which require joint decisions by group facilitators, school administrators, and other student assistance program staff. School systems are encouraged to formalize statements of policies and procedures for support groups for several reasons.

First, policy development helps to ensure building-wide and district-wide consistency in the way groups are implemented and in the way certain group issues are handled (e.g., confidentiality). Second, such a statement helps to give the school some principled means of deciding who may become a support group facilitator. It also helps to orient new or prospective group leaders to their roles and responsibilities. Third, a formal policy statement defines for other school staff what the groups are about and how individual students are to be managed. Finally, such statements are often valuable in communicating to parents and the community the dimensions (and limits) of the school's role in offering support groups.

The following is a hypothetical example, intended to be suggestive only, of the types of issues a school might include in a policy statement on support groups that are part of a student assistance program.

MIDVILLE PUBLIC SCHOOLS

POLICIES AND PROCEDURES FOR AODA SUPPORT GROUP FACILITATORS

1. *CO-FACILITATION.* Co-leadership will be the preferred method of facilitating student support groups. At the district and building levels steps will be taken to ensure that problems arising out of limited resources of qualified personnel and staff time are resolved in favor of co-leadership of groups. Co-facilitation arrangements will be voluntary, not assigned, subject to the approval of the Core Team and/or the SAP Counselor/Coordinator in each building.

2. *COMPENSATION.* Staff time spent leading support groups will be recognized by the district in one or more of the following ways:

   a) Payment will be made at the rate of   per hour. Group leaders will be compensated for one additional hour for each hour of direct face-to-face group contact.

   b) A substitute will be hired to replace a teacher who must lead a support group during a scheduled class.

c) Group leadership may replace other assignments (e.g., supervision)

d) Group leadership will be compensated for by individual contract (e.g., 10% group facilitation, 90% classroom teaching)

e) A group leader will be compensated after the manner of others leading extracurricular activities (e.g., drama, coaching, student council advisor, etc.).

3. **SELECTION OF GROUP MEMBERS.** Students will be screened by counselors or other SAP staff persons and recommended for the group, at which time they will be interviewed by the appropriate group facilitator(s). No student will be accepted into a particular group without having been seen by at least one of the group facilitators for at least one screening or orientation interview. The purposes of the pre-group interview include:

a) Assessing the appropriateness of the student for the group in question;

b) Informing the student of the nature of the group, its general goals, ground rules, and requirements;

c) Assisting the student to define preliminary goals;

d) Assessing the student's motivation for entering the group;

e) Securing the student's agreement to comply with the expectations of a basic group contract (See Supplement 13.2)

4. **PARENTAL INFORMATION AND CONSENT.** All parents will be informed of their child's desire to participate in one of the Student Assistance Program's support groups through one or more of the following means:

a) A general informational brochure will be mailed to all parents, describing the school's Student Assistance Program and its services, including support groups;

b) An informational letter (see Supplement 13.3) will be sent to parents of children wishing to be in a group, inviting parents to contact SAP staff for further information [no consent];

c) A letter will be sent to parents seeking their written permission for their child to participate in a support group [parental consent];

d) Parents will not be informed of their child's participation in a support group, but the student will be urged to make or consent to that disclosure as soon as is practicable and in the student's interest.

No student will be kept in a support group against the expressed wishes of parents.

5. **CHILDREN AT RISK.** School system employees who are facilitating support groups and who are designated reporters of child abuse/neglect and sexual abuse under State statutes will comply with State laws and established school procedures for reporting such cases, Persons leading groups who are not designated reporters will also be required to comply with the above.

6. CONFIDENTIALITY. Students will be informed of the group facilitator's responsibilities regarding confidentiality prior to entering group. Group leaders will safeguard the confidentiality of what students say and do within the group. Exceptions to this general policy are as follows:

    a) Whenever the group facilitator becomes concerned for the health, safety, or welfare of the group member or others, he/she may need to involve other school district and/or community agency staff. Students will be informed of these steps in advance of their being taken.

    b) Students' names may be reported to attendance secretaries as part of item 7, below.

    c) Confidentiality extends to all facets of students' conduct within the group. However, group leaders may disclose to other SAP staff, without violating confidentiality, their conclusions, recommendations, and/or assessment of student progress based on their experience of the student in a group.

    d) The fact of a student's participation in a group may be disclosed to parents according to item 4.

7. GROUP ATTENDANCE. It is the policy that students attending a group session that occurs during one of their scheduled classes will report directly to their group room at the beginning of the period instead of to the scheduled class. A list of students attending groups, listing only students' names, names of group leaders, room number, and time, will be furnished to the office and to classroom teachers. Attendance will be taken in group. Tardiness and in-school absenteeism will be reported and handled according to existing school policies prohibiting this behavior for normal classes. Students are responsible for making arrangements in advance with teachers to make up work they might miss by being in group on a particular day.

8. WORKING RELATIONSHIPS WITH STAFF. For the support groups to be effective it is necessary for group leaders, teachers, and administrators to work cooperatively on behalf of students. Group leaders and other school staff will make every effort to establish appropriate communications between each other to assure that student problems in group and/or in the classroom can be resolved successfully and cooperatively.

9. EVALUATION. It is necessary to collect some information regarding the impact of the support groups (i.e., the numbers of students involved) and their effectiveness (i.e., their benefits or outcomes) at the level of the individual group, the school building, and the district. Thus,

    a) Group leaders will participate in the development of simple, consistent evaluation materials to measure student outcomes in school performance, student attitudes toward their group experience, and the impact of the group on specific AODA-related behaviors.

    b) Student identifying information may be furnished to those engaged in data collection or research, who will be bound by school policies governing confidentiality of the information collected.

    c) Results of evaluation will be shared periodically with the student body, the staff, the Board of Education, and the community.

10. **SUPPORT FOR GROUP FACILITATORS.** A support group for group facilitators will be formed and will meet monthly or more frequently. The primary purpose of the support group will be to provide group facilitators with mutual personal and professional support. It may also engage in planning, designing of materials, policy review, and evaluation activity.

11. **CRITERIA FOR SELECTION OF GROUP FACILITATORS.** Group leadership is not the sole province of any single professional group within the school district. Groups may be co-facilitated by teachers, pupil services staff, administrators, other district employees, students (with supervision and training) parents, or other members of the community. Eligibility of prospective and current group leaders will be determined by the building-level SAP Counselor/Coordinator according to the following criteria:

   a) Persons wishing to become group facilitators are required to complete an assessment at a local State-approved AODA agency by a certified Alcohol/Drug Abuse Counselor, and to follow through with any recommendations for personal recovery. Results of the assessment will be released to the building SAP Counselor/Coordinator and will remain confidential.

   b) The group leader will have a minimum of 40 classroom hours of formal training in general AODA concepts, including signs and symptoms, assessment issues, family dynamics, intervention skills, the dynamics of personal and family recovery, and school SAP policies and procedures.

   c) The group leader will have a minimum of 40 classroom hours of formal training in the facilitation of AODA-related support groups in the school setting and/or will have co-leadership experience in two group sequences supervised by a trained and experienced AODA group facilitator.

   d) Group leaders will acquire additional training, approved by the building SAP Counselor/Coordinator, in their specific group area of interest (e.g., affected other group, recovery support group, use-focussed group, etc.).

   e) Group leaders will be familiar with and abide by all school policies and procedures relating to the Student Assistance Program and to working with students with AODA-related concerns.

   f) Group leaders will become familiar with and abide by all policies governing the facilitation of support groups.

   g) Group leaders will demonstrate personally and socially constructive conduct with regard to mood-altering chemicals at all times.

   h) Group leaders who do have personal experience with alcohol and other drug-related problems should demonstrate involvement in a recovery process.

   i) Group leaders will be expected to regularly participate in the support group for group facilitators.

Supplement 13.2

SAMPLE SUPPORT GROUP CONTRACT
FOR USE-FOCUSSED GROUPS

Student _____

Group _____

Facilitator _____

I Understand:

_____ That I have made a commitment to attend the group for consecutive sessions;

_____ That attendance will be taken in group and it is my responsibility to report to the group room and be ready to begin on time;

_____ That it is my responsibility to make arrangements in advance with classroom teachers for any work that I may miss by being in group;

_____ That it is my responsibility to keep what others say and do in group confidential;

_____ That the group leaders will also keep confidential what I say and do in group, involving other people only when they become concerned for my health, safety, or welfare.

_____ That all school policies regarding acceptable behavior apply to group, including tardiness, absenteeism, and drug use;

_____ That I am responsible for completing all assignments that are part of the group;

_____ That at any time I may be referred to other in-school or community services;

_____ That I will at some point be expected to make a contract with the group, aimed at modifying my chemical use in the direction of abstinence.

Signed: _____ Date: _____
                          (student)

Supplement 13.3

SAMPLE INFORMATION LETTER TO PARENTS

October 15, 1986

Dear Parent:

Your student, _____ , has expressed an interest in being involved in one of our Student Assistance Program groups. These groups are for any student who wishes more information on how alcohol and other drug abuse affects them and other people. The groups are available to every student in the district, and participation is voluntary.

The groups meet once a week and will allow your child to meet with from six to eight other interested students. The groups are led by trained facilitators who are skilled in promoting the development of a safe atmosphere within which students can examine healthy ways of avoiding alcohol and other drug-related problems. In order to create a safe atmosphere, the basic ground rule in the groups is strict confidentiality.

Students involved in groups may miss a class once a week, and have agreed to make arrangements in advance to remain current in their class work.

If you would like further information on the Student Assistance Program or the services it offers to children and their families, please feel free to contact me at 555-1100.

Ms. Mary Smith
Student Assistance Program Coordinator
Midville Junior High School
Midville, USA

Supplement 13.4

NEEDS ASSESSMENT: Support Groups

During the process of implementing a student assistance program many find themselves moving between two paradoxical fears. One is the fear that the school will invest the time and energy in a comprehensive program and only a handful of students will participate. The other is that the school will begin advertising its program's services and the staff will overwhelmed by the numbers of students requesting or accepting help. Experience has taught that the latter is most likely to occur. Consequently, during the program design phases of implementation (see Part Four) those planning the program will need to develop some estimates of the number of groups and group leaders that are likely to be required at various times.

While there is no way to determine exactly how many students will utilize support groups in a given school year, applying arithmetic to some simple assumptions will yield a working estimate. Determining the number of support groups one will need depends on a number of steps: (1) defining the nature and scope of the target group, (2) estimating the program's probable impact on that target group in a given period of time, and defining the number of students who can be helped in a single group experience. Figure 13.1 formalizes the process, which is described below.

Prevalence. For example, our hypothetical school system—Midville Public Schools—has determined that it will offer "Affected Others Groups" for children who are affected by others' alcohol/drug abuse or dependency. It has estimated the size of this target group (according to Table 3.1 in Chapter 3) by assuming that 25 percent of its students are affected in this way (prevalence rate). Thus, in one junior high school, with an enrollment of 1,242 students in grades 7-9, approximately 310 students are potential members of an Affected Others Group or Concerned Persons Group in that building.

"Penetration Rate." The staff also realizes that it is neither reasonable nor possible to meet the needs of all of these students in a single school year. The Core Team members decide that if they could reasonably expect to identify about 80 per cent of such students, and about one-sixth of these each year, then 80 per cent of all affected students could theoretically be served by the time they graduate. Thus, they assume a "penetration rate"—or rate at which all of those in need can be impacted in a given time period—of 16.6%, or 41 students per year. Note that these assumptions amount to statements of goals and objectives.

Group Size. Finally, if each group is limited to only 6 participants, Midville Junior High School should plan to operate seven of these groups each year (41 divided by 6). Some quick mental arithmetic discloses that if each group meets for 12 weeks, the school will need to have three groups running concurrently. Finally, depending on how it allocates its group leadership assignments, between two and six facilitators will be needed to co-lead these groups.

Figure 13.1

SAMPLE SUPPORT GROUP NEEDS ASSESSMENT

Type of Group: <u>Affected Others Group</u>

Grade Level: <u>*7th through 9th*</u>

A. Enrollment: . . . . <u>1,242</u>

B. Percent in target group: . . . . <u>25%</u>

C. Total in need of support services: (B x A) . . . . <u>310</u>

D. Rate of Impact on C: . . . . <u>80%</u>

E. Penetration Rate per year: . . . . <u>16.6%</u>

F. Annual impact on target group: (C x D x E) . . . . <u>41</u>

G. Size of support group: . . . . <u>6</u>

H. Number of groups needed annually: (F divided by G) . . . . <u>7</u>

The same process can be used to estimate the number of use-focussed groups and recovery support groups which will be needed during a given school year. The school will want to examine the need for each type of group in each of its buildings. Figure 13.2 exemplifies how Midville Public Schools might arrive at an overall estimate of the need for support groups on a district-wide basis.

Figure 13.2

DISTRICT-WIDE SUPPORT GROUP NEEDS ASSESSMENT

TYPE OF GROUP	GRADE LEVEL	A ENROLLED IN GRADE	B PERCENT IN TARGET GROUP	C TOTAL IN NEED (A x B)	D RATE OF IMPACT	E PENET. RATE	F ANNUAL IMPACT (C x D x E)	G	H NO. OF GROUPS (F/G)
Affected Others	k-12	10,000	25%	2,500	80%	8.3%	166	6	28
Use-Focussed Groups	7-12	4,968	15%	745	80%	16.6%	99	6	17
Recovery Support	7-12	4,968	5%	248	50%	16.6%	21	7	3

Figure 13.3
SUPPORT GROUP NEEDS WORKSHEET

Type of Group: _____

Grade Level(s): _____

A. Enrollment .... ☐

B. Percent in Target Group .... ☐

C. Total in need of support services (A x B): .... ☐

D. Rate of impact on C: .... ☐

E. Penetration rate per year: .... ☐

F. Annual impact (C x D x E): .... ☐

G. Number of students in each group: .... ☐

H. Number of groups needed annually (F/G): .... ☐

Figure 13.4

DISTRICT—WIDE SUPPORT GROUP NEEDS ASSESSMENT SUMMARY

TYPE OF GROUP	GRADE LEVEL	A ENROLLED IN GRADE	B PERCENT IN TARGET GROUP	C TOTAL IN NEED (A x B)	D RATE OF IMPACT	E PENET. RATE	F ANNUAL IMPACT (C x D x E)	G	H NO. OF GROUPS (F/G)

Chapter 14

The Affected Others Groups

By far the largest target group of children with AODA-related problems is made up of those student concerned about or affected by someone else's alcohol or other drug abuse or chemical dependency. Personal experience, local school surveys, and research all point to the fact that at least 25 per cent of school-aged youth are children of alcoholics; another sizeable percentage are concerned about the drinking or drug use of family members or friends. In an early application of the "Children of Alcoholics Screening Test (CAST)," for example, Pilat and Jones (1984) found that a cutoff score of 6 or more "reliably identified 100 per cent of the clinically diagnosed children of alcoholics." When the test was administered to 174 10-12th graders in a school setting, 27 percent were identified as children of alcoholics, and an additional 17 per cent were identified as being affected by problem drinking in a parent (p. 30). To the extent that these results apply to students generally, up to 44% of students may be affected by parental drinking alone, not to mention other drug abuse by parents or chemical abuse problems in friends.

More important even than identification, perhaps the greatest need of these children is to have the nature, scope, and implications of familial chemical dependency recognized and appreciated by educators as well as by health care professionals in all fields. It was not uncommon, until relatively recently, for alcoholism as a topic to have been absent at conferences on divorce, child abuse and neglect, family violence, or sexual abuse. Within education, discussions of family alcoholism were once difficult to find in programs on children with special educational needs, dropout prevention, discipline problems, teenage pregnancy, and so on. The problem of teenage suicide has most recently captured the attention of the public and the professional community, yet there is little discussion of the frequency with which teenage suicide is related to student alcohol/drug abuse or family alcoholism. While general awareness always lags behind the discovery of problems, much of the reticence to deal with the relationship between alcoholism or other drug dependencies and other student problems should be traced to denial in the professional community. Pilat and Jones also found, for example, that 33 per cent of therapists taking the CAST were determined to be children of alcoholics; a total of 49 per cent had been affected by parental problem drinking (Pilat and Jones (1984), p. 31).

Needs of 'Affected Others' Children

There is now a vast body of literature on the effects of parental drinking and drug use on children of all ages, including "adult children of alcoholics." Several excellent full-length books have been written describing the dynamics and effects of familial alcoholism, the needs of affected children, and effective strategies for education, treatment, and support. (See "Resources for Educators" at the end of this chapter). It is within the scope of this chapter to briefly recount only some of these issues and the appropriateness of Affected Others Groups in the school setting for addressing these needs.

Risk for Developing Drug Abuse. Children of alcoholics represent the largest group of students at the highest risk for developing patterns of drug abuse by adolescence, and chemical dependency by young adulthood. It has long been known that alcoholism runs in families: between 40 percent and 60 per cent of recovering alcoholics identify themselves as children of alcoholics, and the genetic basis of the intergenerational transmission of the disease is becoming increasingly well understood. Children of alcoholics are from two to five times more likely to develop the disease than children of nonalcoholics (NIAAA (1985)).

Dr. Sheppard G. Kallam of Chicago's Social Psychiatry Research Center has been able to correlate adolescent drug abuse with first-grade behavior in a longitudinal study. More than one third of first-grade students exhibited patterns of shy, aggressive, or shy-aggressive behavior. Of these, between 56 percent and 78 percent went on to drink alcohol or use other drugs as adolescents. What is interesting about these findings is that the behaviors and their incidence are identical to what is displayed by children of alcoholics, although the study did not explicitly address this issue.

Physical Complaints. Children of alcoholics suffer from a greater number of physical illness and complaints than children from nonalcoholic families. Fetal Alcohol Syndrome (FAS) has, of course, been identified as the source of physical deformities and mental, behavioral, emotional, and psychological abnor-

malities in children born to alcoholic mothers. Hyperactivity and minimal brain dysfunctions also appear more frequently in children of alcoholics. Adolescent children of alcoholics also report a higher incidence of asthma, insomnia, ulcers, headaches, and stomach aches. Diseases associated with chronic stress and lifestyle (e.g., "Type A" personalities) are also more common among adult children of alcoholics: heart attack, hypertension, cancer, and ulcers.

Relationships. It has been estimated that approximately one third of the children of alcoholics will wittingly or unwittingly chose an alcoholic spouse. Alcoholic families often become socially isolated due to embarrassment and shame. The unpredictable behavior of the alcoholic parent and/or the nondependent spouse often prevents children from developing the ability to trust. Some children will have difficulty forming friendships or intimate relationships. Social interactions at school and in the community take on the quality of social interactions developed to deal with alcoholism within the family.

Dysfunctional Families. Even in its least severe forms, chemical dependency usually results in some degree of emotional or physical neglect of children. The dependent parent becomes physically and/or emotionally unavailable to children as harmful consequences, preoccupation, and abdications of responsibilities escalate. Preoccupation with the behavior of the dependent person often renders the remaining spouse equally unavailable to children as well. Those children are least resilient in those families where the mother is alcoholic, where a another sibling is born within the child's first two years of life, and where there is conflict between parents during the child's first two years (Werner, p. 37). In many cases, however, the consequences of parental dependency are more severe. When both parents are dependent, both sources of physical and emotional support are missing. In more than half of all alcoholic families there is some degree of physical abuse and family violence; some researchers report a rate of incest as high as 30 per cent. Children of alcoholics are more often placed in foster homes and are involved in delinquent behavior than children without alcoholic parents.

Psychological/Emotional Impairment. Inconsistencies, unpredictabilities, and physical and emotional absence can have a serious and lifelong impact on a child's psychological and emotional development. There is tendency to think that young children and adolescents are least affected by parental alcoholism: the former because they are not aware of what is happening, and the latter because they are more mature and better able to cope. The evidence suggests that first graders and adolescents manifest the most symptoms (Bosma, 1975). Feelings of fear, anger, guilt, loneliness, shame, and hurt commonly accompany individual incidents which occur in the dependent family. The lack of permission or overt prohibition to talk about feelings and the development of ego defenses often result in a diminished capacity to have, identify, or express these emotions. Feelings can become systematically repressed or denied.

Children of alcoholics as a group manifest a greater incidence of mental illness, depression, psychosomatic complaints, poor self-concept, impaired sense of reality, isolation, emotional detachment, inappropriate affect, social aggression, suicide, teenage pregnancy, and running away. Many of these symptoms are not due just to distress in the family: children of alcoholics manifest these symptoms to a greater degree than children with parents who are chronically mentally ill or hospitalized for psychiatric care.

Sharon Wegscheider (1981) and Claudia Black (1981) have also described some of the common survival behaviors which children of alcoholics can adopt. Birth order, innate personality traits, and the needs of the family are among the factors affecting a child's choice of behavioral strategies. Often these behavioral strategies will cluster into compulsive, stereotypic "roles:" the Family Hero, the Scapegoat, the Lost Child, the Mascot, etc. The survival behaviors/roles frequently become compulsive, choiceless, and self-destructive. The survival behaviors are learned as ways of coping with the distress brought on by active chemical dependency, but are carried into adulthood where they can disrupt relationships where no chemical dependency exists.

School Performance. Research on the impact of parental alcoholism on children's school performance has been contradictory at times, due to variations in the survival behaviors which children adopt. Many children react to familial dependency by doing well in school in an effort to bring self-esteem to the family. Others become popular and accomplished in an attempt to cover deep-seated feelings of inadequacy. Some schools report that over 40 per cent of their athletes are children of alcoholics, for whom athletics provides a source of self-esteem, and frequent excuses for spending time away from the home. On the other hand, many children act out their pain and anger through disruptiveness in the classroom, poor attendance, tardiness, poor grades and dropping out. Special education teachers routinely admit that the majority of the students in their programs are children of alcoholics.

Developmental Deficits. In terms of Erikson's stages of personality development, parental alcoholism can significantly impair the healthy accomplishment of developmental tasks in early life. Perhaps the cornerstone of a healthy personality is the development, during infancy, of a sense of trust: the feeling that the environment of other people is warm and nurturing, and that basic needs for physical and emotional safety will be met. Later, children acquire autonomy, or the sense of self-control and confidence in one's ability to take risks and explore new behavior. A feeling of initiative develops as a child's curiosity, playfulness, and risk-taking is met with affirmation and appropriate limitations by parents. Feelings of industry, or that one is useful, valuable, and can have a constructive impact on one's life, are consolidated by adolescence.

Where there is parental alcoholism, these developmental issues can be resolved in a more negative direction. The unavailability of parents and the absence of nurturance fosters a basic mistrust of other people and of the environment in general. Personal shame, doubt, and inadequacy may develop as a child experiences punitive or restrictive parenting. Guilt may develop if a child's innate curiosity is repressed, ignored, or criticized by a parent. In alcoholic homes the child receives validation for himself and his behavior only because of its impact on the alcoholic's behavior. Feelings of personal inferiority frequently develop as children feel they can do nothing right. Often they experience the failure of their attempts to control a parent's drinking, concluding that the drinking is their fault.

Particularly tragic is the fact that many children of alcoholics will reach adolescence —and its vital task of discovering "Who am I?" — with a developmental base of mistrust, shame and self-doubt, guilt, and inferiority. Since little information about this illness is typically conveyed to children and adolescents, most assume that they alone have this problem, that no one else can understand, that the drinking or drug use is somehow their fault, and that the environment is unsafe — it is not safe to talk about such problems, to be vulnerable, or to ask for help.

Planning the Affected Others Group

Recovery from such problems is a lifelong process. Increasingly, treatment programs and self-help groups arise to treat the problems of adult children of alcoholics who carry the effects of their childhood experience into their adult lives. While it is neither possible nor appropriate for the school take on the sole task of helping children of alcoholics to resolve all of these issues, it is in an ideal position to begin early the process of prevention, intervention, and treatment. As described in Chapter 11 and 13, support groups are among the most ideal formats within which to begin to deal with these problems. As with all support groups, it is important to stress once again that the role of the school — and of the support groups — is not to provide therapy or treatment but to provide information and support. The major goal is to facilitate improvement, not to effect a "cure" or resolution of problems which

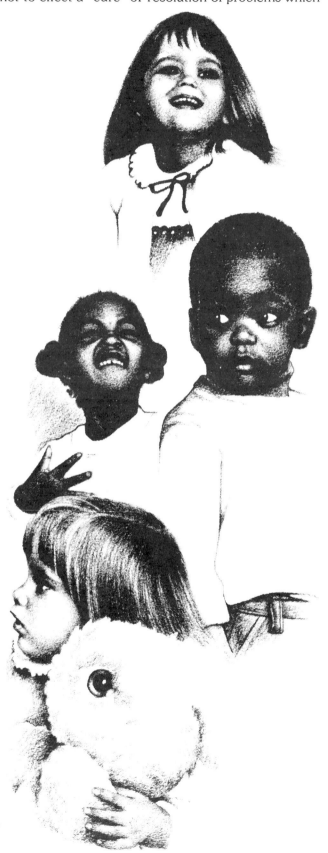

does require the skill and experience of the trained clinician in a treatment setting.

In clarifying its role and in planning and implementing groups for children affected by or concerned about others' chemical use, the school staff need to make decisions in many areas. The SAP staff who facilitate the support groups should have a clear understanding of the target group, the specifics of group structure and setting, their role in the selection process, the goals and objectives for the group, a curriculum, and an evaluation scheme.

Target Group. By definition, the support groups for kids affected by others' chemical use are designed specifically to assist children in understanding and coping more successfully with these problems: they are considered here to be homogeneous groups. Although other issues and problems may surface in the group itself, facilitators and students should be clear that the primary purpose of the group is to focus on their responses to the AODA-related problems of others.

Even so, the school and its student assistance program staff need to be aware that children will lie along a continuum of concern. Especially where students are identified in large numbers through strategies which encourage self-referral, students will indicate an interest in a support group of this type for several reasons. Some, more frequently at the elementary level, will have no hint of AODA-related problems in their families but will be "curious." Others, especially at the secondary level, will indicate an interest in the group out of concern for a peer. At all levels, students will present themselves for the group because of intimate contact with alcoholism in an adult in their family. Thus, in planning for these groups in general the SAP staff may wish to implement at least the two varieties discussed in Chapter 11: an Affected Others Group for students affected by another's chemical dependency, and a Concerned Others Group for those less severely affected. Such a division is certainly not obligatory. In most cases students with both degrees of concern will work well together in the same group. The point is that the group facilitators should be prepared to alter the content of the group to suit the nature and severity of the needs students bring to it.

Structure and Setting. There is considerable variation concerning the specifics of implementing and integrating Affected Others Groups into the school routine. For example, in some schools Affected Others Groups meet weekly for half the school year. Though there are no hard and fast rules, groups most often meet for at least eight to ten sessions. Students wishing to be in the group make a commitment to attend all sessions consecutively. The groups are most successful — i.e., efficient at meeting specific goals — if they are not "rap" or "drop-in" groups.

Most Affected Others Groups are "closed:" the same students begin the group together and end after a given number of sessions. Rarely will a student come to the attention of the SAP staff who has an urgent need to be in a support group immediately. In most cases interest outstrips the group leadership resources of the school, and a waiting list is established. Although groups can function well with from four to fifteen members, for the aims we wish to achieve the optimal group consists of five to seven members. Group size and group goals are directly related. If a group is intended to be more informational and discussional, more students can be accommodated. If one wishes to concentrate on interpersonal learning and behavior changes, smaller numbers are required.

Although schools have experimented with holding groups before, during, and after school, the most effective design seems to involve integrating the groups into the normal school day. For elementary children especially, holding groups during the school day produces less inconvenience for transportation. Perhaps more important, integrating support groups into the normal routine communicates the importance of the groups to students and staff.

Groups typically meet once a week for an hour or less and are scheduled so as to correspond to the usual breaks of the daily bell schedule. Some schools have found it beneficial to have Affected Others Groups meet more frequently at the elementary level, and for less than a full hour.

Finding an appropriate location for these groups is often problematic in schools where space is at a premium. Ideally, a separate room is designated the group room and is furnished appropriately -bean bag chairs or pillows, posters, carpeting -to convey warmth and maximize the opportunities for varied interactions. A counselor's office, a meeting room in the library, or the back of a classroom can do just as well. As a rule, however, settings which do not require sitting at desks promote more effective interaction and group process. It is most important that the location for the group insures the privacy of group members but does not reinforce secrecy. The more public and visible the group room can be, the more the school communicates that there is no shame or stigma attached to AODA-related problems. At the same time, the room should permit students to interact in the group without being seen or overheard by others.

The Selection Process. The process of screening and assessing students who are affected by others' chemical use was described in some detail in Chapter 8. In many cases the person doing the initial screening and assessment, the SAP Counselor/Coordinator, may also be a facilitator for a Concerned Others or an

Affected Others Group. Selecting students for his support group would occur naturally as part of this assessment process. In most cases, however, the persons who conduct initial screenings are not those leading the groups. Thus, it is important that the facilitators of the Concerned/Affected Others Groups develop and participate in a secondary selection process. The overriding principle is that no student enters a support group without having been seen at least once first by one of the co-facilitators. It is worth emphasizing that for concerned and affected students, this selection process accomplishes a number of things:

- It permits facilitators to do "triage," or sorting of students according to the nature of their interest and need;

- It permits facilitators either to select students whose needs are consistent with the group as designed, or to adapt the group to the needs of the students;

- It allows facilitators to explain the goals, activities, and content of the group;

- It permits facilitators to explain to students the basic ground rules and expectations of the group: e.g., confidentiality, promptness, participation;

- It allows students to ask questions and become comfortable with their decision to be in a group;

- It allows facilitators to explain the conditions under which parents (a) will be sent a letter requesting their specific permission/consent, (b) will be contacted by letter or telephone informing them generally of the student's participation in a support group, or (c) will not be involved at all.

Goals and Objectives. Given the nature and scope of affected children's needs, the numbers of students in need of help, the brief amount of time the group will meet, and the limitations of the school's role, developing appropriate and realistic goals and objectives is a vital component of the success of Affected Others Groups. In general, goals are statements of the general intentions of what the facilitators wish the group to accomplish; objectives refer to more specific, measurable outcomes for students with respect to the general goals (see Part Five). Goals should be formulated in each of at least three areas: (1) AODA-specific knowledge, attitudes, and behavior, (2) general personal and interpersonal functioning (e.g., enhancing self-esteem, and (3) strengthening school performance if necessary. A general goal, for example, might be "To let students know that they are not alone in having AODA-related problems." A specific, related objective might be stated as follows: "By the end of the group, 85 per cent of the group members will indicate on evaluation forms that they learned other students have the same kinds of problems."

In general, the goals of the Affected Others Group revolve around (1) education—helping students to understand the nature of chemical dependency, (2) work with feelings—identifying and expressing feelings about AODA-related behavior, (3) support—discovering that help is always available in various forms, and (4) personal responsibility—discovering that one can take positive action on one's own behalf. Supplement 14.1 contains an extensive list of goals commonly associated with the Affected Others Group.

Curriculum. Goals and objectives contribute most to the planned, structured character of the Affected Others Groups, and imply the existence of an equally definite curriculum with which to carry them out. Building an effective curriculum depends on group leaders' understanding of the needs of affected children and of the stages and dynamics of group growth. Initial sessions are devoted to getting acquainted, discussing ground rules and expectations, and teaching about basic AODA concepts. Final sessions are devoted to closure: acknowledging progress, solidifying accomplishments, reinforcing the needs for ongoing support, and saying good-bye. The middle, or working phase, consists of building trust in the group, promoting risk-taking, and encouraging changes in behavior.

The "For Further Reading" sections following this chapter contains a number of references which can guide group leaders in establishing an agenda for a given Affected Others Group. There is room for great individual variation. Some group leaders are most comfortable with a clear agenda for the entire sequence of meetings, with detailed activities, exercises, and structured experiences. Others are more comfortable allowing students to determine the content of each meeting by the concerns they bring in, making certain that group work is focussed on the group's primary purpose.

Legal Issues. The primary legal issue which arises regarding the Affected Others Groups relates to parent involvement. Parent involvement for other support groups presents few if any problems. Most parents would be gratified to know their children are gaining more information about drugs in a use-focussed group. Parents of recovering teenagers welcome their child's involvement in a support system. Even at the secondary level, the school staff is less concerned about parent involvement than at the elementary level.

There is as yet no national standard or legal precedent which will help the individual school in formulating a policy on seeking parental consent for a child's participation in a student assistance program support group of any kind. Decisions need to be consistent with state guidelines. Much will depend on how the school defines the groups and their role in the SAP. Where groups are defined as primarily educational in nature, consent is not usually required. If the group is defined primarily as a counseling function, then parental consent is often a must.

The consent issue can be complicated by varying state laws regarding minor's consent for treatment. Even if the groups are regarded as a counseling or therapeutic function, in some states minors can consent to mental health, medical, and alcoholism/drug abuse treatment at a certain age and within certain constraints. In these areas, the "information-consent-nothing" dilemma is focussed primarily on the elementary level.

As a general rule, it is wise to adopt a policy stating that parents of children in Affected Others Groups will at least be informed of their child's decision or wish to participate. At minimum, parents may be informed through a letter (e.g., Supplement 13.3) or a telephone call from the SAP Counselor/Coordinator. These contacts should generally describe the purpose of the group in educating students about alcohol and other drug abuse. Communications with parents must avoid

labeling the child or the family as having any specific "problem." Sometimes including a copy of a general group agenda answers most parents' questions about the groups.

In no case should a child be admitted or retained in a group against the specifically expressed wishes of parents. However, even where a parent denies permission the SAP staff has options for continuing to provide the child with some degree of support. Occasional one-to-one meetings with the student are certainly possible, where much of the educating, talking about alcoholism, and support typical of the group can still occur. Some counselors seek to involve other children in the group with the child who cannot attend, encouraging them to interact socially and to provide a support network outside of school. In many cases it is possible to obtain permission for a child's group involvement from the nondependent spouse. Finally, the school may wish to pursue legal avenues or formal referral of the family to social service agencies if it suspects child abuse or neglect and has the courage to utilize 'suspected alcoholism' as the basis for the referral.

In any case, an important issue for planning the Affected Others Group involves becoming aware of the state and local statutes governing parental consent, minors' consent and clarifying the school's policy language in these areas.

Evaluation. It is important to conduct some sort of formal evaluation of the Affected Others Groups for many reasons. Given the resources and risks required to implement these groups as part of a student assistance program, the school system should have some way of demonstrating that the groups do effect changes in a healthy direction in participants. To be useful, group evaluation need not be time-consuming, expensive, or sophisticated. Simple questionnaires can be developed which permit students to respond to true/false questions about how the group helped them. Allowing students to respond with subjective impressions and comments also gives the facilitators and other SAP staff useful information. In some cases, group leaders may wish to supplement these more informal evaluation mechanisms with formal tests or surveys of self-concept, personal and social functioning, etc. Finally, as part of its *program evaluation*, the student assistance program staff will want to able to compare school performance indicators of students on a pre- and post-group basis.

DiCicco *et al.* (1984a, pp. 24-25) provides some examples of results typical of Affected Others Groups. The following are some examples of student responses to true/false group evaluation items:

- 76.6% "I said things in the group about myself and my family that I usually don't tell people;"

- 68.1% "Since I have been in the group I have felt less lonely;"

- 64.6% "I have talked to the leaders about things that are bothering me;"

- 79.7% "Things said in the group are so private that you really can't repeat them outside of group;"

- 70.8% "I learned that one of my parents is probably an alcoholic;"

- 95.8% "I learned that other kids have the same kinds of problems at home as I do;"

- 74.5% "The group made me feel that I should deal with problems in my home differently than I have been doing;"

- 89.6% "I learned things in this group that I can really use;"

- 57.4% "Since I have been in the group, I have felt less angry at my parents."

Evaluation data can often be most effectively used in communicating to others about the program. Reporting to the staff often about these types of outcomes helps to keep the program visible and lets the staff know that the groups do have concrete accomplishments. Frequent reports such as these also prevents the support groups from being seen as isolated, secretive components of the program. Publishing such data in the student newspaper can do nothing but attract others to the program.

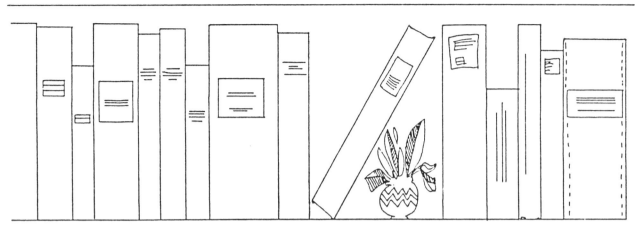

For Further Reading

RESOURCES FOR EDUCATORS:

A Growing Concern: How to Provide Services for Children from Alcoholic Families. Rockville, MD.: National Institute on Alcohol Abuse andAlcoholism, 1983.

Ackerman, Robert J. 1978. *Children of Alcoholics: A Guidebook for Educators, Therapists, and Parents.* Holmes Beach, FL: Learning Publications, Inc.

Black, Claudia. *It Will Never Happen to Me.* Denver: M. A. C., Printing and Publications Division, 1981.

Black, Claudia. *My Dad Loves Me, May Dad Has a Disease.* Newport Beach,CA.: ACT, 1979.

Bosma, W. G. "Alcoholism and Teenagers." *Maryland State Medical Journal.* 24:6 (1975): 62-68.

Brown, K., and J. Sunshine. "Group Treatment of Children from, Alcoholic Families." In Altman., and R. Crocker, eds. *Social Groupwork and Alcoholism.* New York: Haworth Press, 1982.

Canfield, Jack and Harold Wells. *100 Ways to Enhance Self-Concept in the Classroom.* Englewood Cliffs, NJ: Prentice-Hall, Inc., 1976.

Cork, Margaret. *The Forgotten Children.* Toronto: Addiction Research Foundation, 1969.

Deckman, J. and B. Downs. "Group Treatment Approach for Adolescent Children of Alcoholic Parents." In Altman., and R. Crocker, eds. *Social Groupwork and Alcoholism.* New York: Haworth Press, 1982.

Deutsch, Charles. *Broken Bottles Broken Dreams.* New York: Teachers College Press, 1982.

DiCicco, Lena et. al. 1984a. "Group Experiences for Children of Alcoholics." *Alcohol Health and Research World.* (Summer, 1984): pp. 20-24.

Friel, John C. "Co-Dependency Assessment Inventory." *Focus on Family.* 8:3 (May/June, 1985): 20-21.

Gazda, G. M. *Theories and Methods of Group Counseling in Schools.* Chicago: Charles C. Thomas, Publisher, 1969.

Gravitz, Herbert L. and Julie D. Bowden. "Recovery Continuum for Adult Children of Alcoholics." *Focus on Family.* (May/June, 1985): 6-7.

Hawley, N. P., and E. L. Brown. "Use of Group Treatment with Children of Alcoholics." Social Casework. 62:1 (1981): 40-46.

Hope for Children of Alcoholics. New York: Al-Anon Family Group Headquarters, 1980.

Lawson, Gary, James S. Peterson, and Ann Lawson. *Alcoholism and the Family.* Rockville, Maryland: Aspen Systems Corporation, 1983.

McCabe, Thomas R. *Victims No More.* Center City, MN: Hazelden. 1978.

Pilat, Joanne M. and John W. Jones. "Identification of Children of Alcoholics: Two Empirical Studies." *Alcohol Health and Research World.* (Winter) 1984: 27-33. *Services for Children of Alcoholics: Research Monograph No. 4.* Rockville, MD: National Institute on Alcohol Abuse and Alcoholism, 1981.

Wegscheider, Sharon. 1981. *Another Chance: Hope and Health for the Alcoholic Family.* Palo Alto: Science and Behavior Books.

Wegscheider-Cruse, Sharon. 1985. *Choicemaking.* Pompano Beach, FL: Health Communications, Inc.

Werner, Emmy E. "Resilient Offspring of Alcoholics: A Longitudinal Study from Birth to Age 18." *Journal of Studies on Alcohol.* 47:1 (1986):34-40.

West, Peg. *Protective Behaviors.* Madison, WI.: Madison Metroplitan School District, 1982.

Woititz, Janet G. *Adult Children of Alcoholics.* Hollywood, FL.: Health Communications, Inc., 1983.

BOOKS FOR KIDS:

Black, Claudia. *It Will Never Happen to Me.* Denver: M. A. C., Printing and Publications Division, 1981. Black, Claudia. *My Dad Loves Me, May Dad Has a Disease.* Newport Beach, CA.: ACT, 1979.

Brooks, Cathleen. *The Secret Everyone Knows.* San Diego, CA: The Kroc Foundation, 1981.

Donlan, Joan. *I Never Saw the Sun Rise.* Minneapolis, MN: CompCare, Inc.,1977.

If Your Parents Drink Too Much. New York: Al-Anon Family GroupHeadquarters, 1974.

Melquist, Elaine. Pepper. Frederick, MD.: Frederick County Council onAlcoholism, 1974.

Snyder, Anne. First Step. New York: Holt, Rinehart, and Winston, 1975.

What's Drunk, Mama? New York: Al-Anon Family Group Headquarters, Inc.,1977.

ART THERAPY WITH CHILDREN OF ALCOHOLICS

Baruch, D. W., and H. Miller. "Developmental Needs and Conflicts Revealed in Children's Art." *American Journal of Orthopsychiatry.* 22 (1952):187-203.

Black, Claudia. "Children of Alcoholics." *Alcohol Health and Research World.* 4:1 (1979).

Cohen, F. "Introducing Art Therapy into a School System: Some Problems." *Art Psychotherapy.* 2:2 (1974): 121-136.

Denny, B. "Art Counseling in Educational Settings." *Personnel and Guidance Journal.* (October, 1969): 119-124.

Gantt, L. and M. S. Schmal. *Art Therapy—A Bibliography.* 1940-1973. DHEW Publication No. (ADM) 74-51. Washington D. C.: U. S. Government Printing Office, 1974.

Gardner, H. *Artful Scribbles: The Significance of Children's Drawings.* New York: Basic Books, 1980.

Isaacs, L. D. "Art Therapy for Latency Age Children." *Social Work.* (January, 1977): 57-59.

Kellog, R. *Analyzing Children's Art.* Palo Alto, CA: National Press Books,1969.

Chapter 14 | **Supplements**

Supplement 14.1 is a representative list of the types of goals which the leaders of an Affected Others Group may wish to accomplish. The selection of goals will depend on the type of group one is designing or leading, or upon the needs of the students in the group. Thus, a Concerned Others Group may focus more on educational goals and less intensively on some behavioral goals. Similarly, a maintenance group for affected others would assume a certain level of knowledge in its members, and would typically be devoted to helping students further change behavior.

Supplement 14.2 is a summary of the planning issues discussed in Chapters 13 and 14. It can be used as an outline for preparing a formal proposal to implement a specific type of group as an SAP component in the school. Such a proposal would often be submitted to the board of education, the building administrator, and/or the building Core Team.

More specifically, the checklist can assist the individual group facilitator in planning the specific group he will lead.

Supplement 14.1

GOALS AND OBJECTIVES
FOR AFFECTED OTHERS GROUPS

The needs of children who are concerned about or affected by the chemical abuse or dependency of someone close to them are many and varied. The school in general and the support groups in particular cannot be expected to meet all of these needs. The following represents a list of the general goals from which those leading Affected Others Groups or Concerned Persons Groups may select. Most of the goals relate to children who are living with or affected by chemical dependency in a parent or other close family member. They can be easily modified to reflect less severe patterns of concern. Although the list may look extensive, it is not impossible to partially accomplish most of them in this type of brief problem-focussed group.

GOALS:

1. To educate students about the dynamics of alcohol and other drug use, abuse, and dependency. Students need accurate information about the distinction between alcoholism/drug dependency and other forms of chemical use. The disease concept, the progression of the illness, its characteristic symptoms, and the nature of denial are all important concepts which help students to understand the dependent person as well as their experience of him or her.

2. To educate students about alcoholism/drug dependency as a family disease. Students need to understand that everyone in the family is affected in predictable ways, and that they can change the way they act and feel.

3. To help students to deal with ambivalent feelings toward their person-of-concern. Many students will be confused by loving and hating a dependent parent at the same time. One of the virtues of the disease concept is that it helps students to see that the dependent person is not bad, just sick. Separating the person from the disease, and the person from his behavior, allows children to begin to see that they are loved even though the dependent person is not always able to show it.

4. To help students to understand, identify, and express feelings. Students need an environment in which they can break the family rules against having feelings, especially painful ones such as guilt, shame, anger, loneliness, and sadness. They need to understand that such feelings are normal given their experiences, and that nothing bad happens when they are expressed.

5. To build confidence, self-esteem, and a more confident and optimistic outlook. The self-esteem of many students will have been eroded by their belief that drug use is their fault and that they alone have such problems. Many need to be validated for their own behavior and for themselves, not because of the impact their behavior has on the drug-using person.

6. To foster less compulsive reactions to the person-of-concern's behavior. Concerned and affected students often will need help in changing their behavior from reactive to more choiceful and healthful patterns. They can be encouraged to identify self-destructive and disruptive defenses.

7. To identify alternative ways of responding to events in the alcoholic family. Students need help in identifying ways of responding to stressful events which do not place them in unsafe situations, exaggerate stress in the family, or strengthen their isolation.

8. To confront the child's denial system. While many children, especially at the elementary level, will openly admit to their concern and recognize the problem as alcoholism or chemical dependency, others will not. Others will have difficulty admitting that they have any negative feelings or that their behavior is at times self-destructive. While it is never the purpose of the group to encourage students to label the person-of-concern as "alcoholic" or anything else, it is necessary to enhance students' awareness of how they have been affected and to support them in taking responsibility for changing their own behavior.

9. To encourage students to develop and use a support system outside of the group. The group lasts only a few weeks. The need for information and support extends throughout the day and will continue past June and graduation. It is important that the group process be utilized to promote students' discovery and use of outside supports. Initially students can be encouraged to make use of other people: group members, other students, a trusted teacher, or other family members. For older students, attendance at Alateen should be encouraged if not made a group expectation.

10. To let students know that they are not alone.

11. To let students know that the chemical use is not their fault — they are not blame for the chemical use or for what is happening in their family or to their relationships.

12. To encourage and strengthen self-responsibility. Students need to know that there is hope, and that they can feel better even if their person-of-concern does not stop using chemicals or get help.

13. To assist students in resolving developmental deficits. In general, the group should address, where they exist, mistrust, guilt and shame, and self-doubt through activities which promote trust, autonomy, initiative, and industry.

14. To help students understand their own confusion. Affected and concerned students need to know that their confusion is normal and that they are not "crazy." The unpredictable and contradictory behavior of the dependent person is part of the disease, as is his or her denial. For example, teaching about blackouts helps students to understand that what the user might deny really did happen.

15. To help students understand their powerlessness in a useful way. They did not cause the drug problem, nor can they cure it. They are innocent victims but not helpless victims. They can do positive things for themselves which will help them to feel better.

16. To help students to understand, identify, and change their enabling behavior. Students need to know about enabling and how to change it in ways that are intentional, constructive for them, and safe. The primary motivation for changing enabling should be that it helps kids to stay safe, be more responsible for themselves, and feel better. Its effects on the using person is only secondary. Group leaders should guard against portraying enabling in such a way as to let students feel responsible for "curing" the dependent or abusing person.

17. *To increase self-protective behaviors.* Students who are in unsafe environments need to be taught that there are things which they can do to help them stay safe: finding escape routes in case of fire, staying with a neighbor if the house is locked, avoiding trying to keep parents from fighting, telling a grown-up when someone touches them in a place that makes them uncomfortable, etc.

18. *To assist students in contracting for specific, simple behavioral changes.* As stated above, new behavior should be intentional, constructive, and safe. One good way of bringing about changes is to ask individual students, week-to-week, to agree to try a new behavior and report to the group about it. One of the best strategies involves having students contract to talk to each other about their experiences and feelings outside of group during the week.

19. *To help students focus on making progress and having fun. A group can become heavy and serious if the focus in every session is upon problems and painful feelings.* It is easy to lose sight of progress that has been made in only a few meetings. The fact that students are attending, are talking, and are expressing feelings may represent major steps for them. In addition, many children of alcoholics do not know how to have fun. Leaders should take time to focus on progress and to engage group members in noncompetitive play.

20. *To help students understand, identify, and express anger toward other family members.* Children of alcoholics will often feel more angry and confused about the nondependent spouse or older siblings than they do about the dependent person. Students may believe that these family members are responsible for the drug use. Sometimes they are angry with family members who did not protect them from the dependent person's behavior. Understanding chemical dependency as a family illness helps children to separate the person from the disease with respect to all members of the family.

21. *To inform students of their high risk for developing chemical dependency.* Many students will claim that they will "never be like Dad." They need to know that they have a high risk of developing chemical dependency if they use alcohol or other drugs. It is completely unrealistic to expect students at any age to make responsible, informed decisions about drug use in the absence of this information.

22. *To help students see that nothing bad happens if they talk.* Most children of alcoholics, aside from feeling isolated, believe that catastrophic things will happen if they share their experiences. One of the major outcomes of the Affected Others Groups for students is their discovery that talking about such problems is safe and that they can identify safe, supportive persons in their environment with whom to share.

23. *To facilitate the involvement of the family in professional help and/or treatment.* While it is not the goal of the school staff to intervene directly in the chemical dependency in the family, they should be alert to opportunities to work with any members of the family who are willing to get involved. Group leaders should be prepared to refer family members to agencies which can deal appropriately with chemical dependency.

Supplement 14.2

GROUP PLANNING CHECKLIST

1. Define the Target Group. (What AODA-specific target group is the group intended to assist? What, in general, are the needs of students for whom the group will be designed? Are there any distinctions in terms of degrees of severity?)

2. Identify the general goals of the group for participants. (What AODA-related areas of student knowledge, feelings, and behavior will the group address? E.g., "To educate students about the disease of alcoholism;" To let students know that they are not alone.")

3. Develop specific, measurable objectives for participants for each goal. (E.g., "by the end of the group 90 per cent of the students will be able to identify 5 symptoms of alcoholism;" "By the end of the group 80 per cent of the students will indicate they feel less alone with this problem.")

4. Decide the basic questions of structure and setting. (When will the group meet? Where will the group meet? How often will the group meet? How many sessions will the group last? How many participants will the group be limited to? What is the meeting schedule — i.e., "Every Tuesday during third period?).

5. Will the group be "open" or "closed?"

6. Develop a set of initial ground rules, or expectations, for group members. (E.g., What is said in group stays in group; No put-downs or scapegoating; No "gossip", or talking about people who aren't here; Be ready to start on time; etc.).

7. Define the values and beliefs within which you will operate. (What are your beliefs about alcoholism and other drug abuse? What will you teach? What are your beliefs about "acceptable" levels of drug use by kids? What are your values concerning what is valuable and important about students, which will guide you in defining ground rules and group norms?)

8. Clarify the selection process for group members, the criteria by which they will be selected for the group, and your role in the selection process.

9. Develop a curriculum, or outline of the group.

10. Prepare or select materials to be used in the group.

11. Plan for evaluation. (How will you know if what you have done has brought about any changes in students? To whom will evaluation data be communicated?)

12. Clarify your working relationships with other staff.

13. Develop a clear policy and procedure for informing parents of their child's involvement in the group. Clarify a process for responding to parent concerns or requests for information.

Supplement 14.3

OUTLINE FOR AFFECTED OTHERS GROUPS

The needs of children who are affected by or concerned about others' use of alcohol and other drugs are many and varied. Some children will be living with active parental chemical dependency. Children at the elementary and secondary levels will have slightly different needs as well as different competencies with which to deal with their concern.

There will also be varying degrees of intrafamily support for the child and any patterns of behavior he may be changing. The content and activities of an Affected Others Group will have to be suited to the needs, ages, and degree of concern in participating students.

A review of Affected Others Groups in student assistance programs as well as of community-based clinical programs for the treatment of these issues reveals the following broad topic areas to be among those most commonly addressed. The outline is intended only to suggest how a group might proceed. Most such groups progress from (1) general information about alcohol and other drug abuse to (2) an examination of students' feelings and behaviors in response to it in their lives, and to (3) examining positive changes in coping behavior, including the use of resources.

Lecturettes, role plays, discussion, and art work are the most often-used techniques. Art work — the use of drawings or collages — is an appropriate tool for all age groups. Projective techniques often reveal significant information to group leaders, and permit group members to interact in non-verbal ways: many students will have learned to use language as a defensive rather than as a problem-solving tool in their families.

Session 1: Group Formation

The first sessions are devoted to getting acquainted, establishing minimal group ground rules or expectations, explaining the purpose of the group, having students indicate what brought them to the group, and explaining in broad terms what the group will be about.

Secondary students may be asked to identify relatively specific goals upon which they wish to work, or ways in which they would like to group experience to be of help them. Identification of specific goals should always be an initial activity in a maintenance group for students who have already been in an Affected/Concerned Others Group.

Sessions 2 and 3: Alcohol/Drug Abuse and Dependency

All students in their first Affected Others Group will need accurate information about the nature of alcohol/drug use, abuse, and dependency conveyed in developmentally appropriate terms. At the elementary level, basic concepts around the progression from use, to abuse, to dependency can be conveyed through a 10 minute film such as *A Story About Feelings*, exercises from Claudia Black's *My Dad Loves me, My Dad Has a Disease*, through the use of flashcards, etc. At the secondary level, the "feeling chart" (Johnson, 1980) is an effective way of presenting the same concepts to adolescents. Brief knowledge tests and attitude surveys can also be given around which discussion may be centered.

Art work can be used with students at all ages as part of the education process. Students might be asked to draw a picture illustrating a particular symptom (e.g., "blackouts") or what it is like when their person-of-concern drinks or uses drugs. Sharing drawings with group members promotes talking, trusting, and feeling, and underscores particular concepts.

Sessions 4 and 5: Chemical Dependency and the Family

Films such as *Soft Is the Heart of a Child* seem to be effective, for students in the fourth grade and above, for teaching about the effects of chemical dependency on family members. Information about "survival roles" may be presented only to the extent that it allows students to identify specific defensive and behavioral ways in which they have reacted to another's chemical use.

Art work is again an effective means of both teaching and promoting identification and discussion of the ways children have been affected by parental chemical dependency.

Sessions 6, 7, 8, and 9: Feelings and Behavior

Exercises and activities are devoted first to identifying feelings as opposed to thoughts. Group members are then encouraged to identify and express feelings associated with another's chemical use. Often, a general assignment might be to "draw a picture of how it feels when someone you care about drinks," followed by sharing the drawing with the group. Other group members are encouraged to indicate whether they have ever felt the same way, or had the same experiences.

Discussion proceeds to focus upon how group members react to the drinking or drug abusing person. For example, as a student describes feelings associated with an event, group leaders might ask about what the student did when that happened. Many students will describe behaviors that are unsafe (attempting to break up arguments) or which further their isolation (hiding in their bedroom). Group leaders may then ask the student and the group to suggest other things the group member could do instead that are safe and constructive. Students may be encouraged to "contract" to try these new responses during the week.

Sessions 10 and 11: Positive Coping and Resources

Aside from the more individualized positive coping steps which emerge as students discuss personal experiences, group time is spent on discussing additional coping strategies and resources. Students might roleplay problems which have occurred in their families or with their person-of-concern. Exercises can focus on identifying choices, "do's and don'ts," confrontation skills, stress reduction techniques, and self-concept enhancement.

Discussion should always focus upon how and when to involve others, and how to build a support network. These discussions often signal the beginning of the "closure" phase of the group by asking students how they will take care of themselves after the group's conclusion. A group assignment to attend an Alateen meeting together would be appropriate for older students. The group needs to consider many resources for continued support, including maintaining a telephone list, talking to each other after the group is over, attending Alateen, contacting other community resources, and utilizing other in-school services.

Session 12: Closure

The final session is used to allow group members to evaluate their own and other's progress in the group, to evaluate the group itself, and to say good-bye to each other as group members. Evaluation activities should acknowledge progress and encourage students to continue making use of supports and skills they have learned in the group.

The Recovery Support Group

"I can't dance sober."
- Recovering student

*"Childhood is a nightmare.
But it is so very hard to be
an on-your-own, take-care-
of-yourself-cause-there-is-
no-one-else-to-do-it-for-
you grown-up."*
(Sheldon Kopp, p. 224)

Nearly everyone who works in a secondary school and who has had students return to school from a chemical dependency treatment program is aware, from personal experience, that unless such students are provided with and make use of a support system they often have difficulty staying drug-free for longer than a week or two. The support groups for recovering students have proven to be one of the most effective ways of easing recovering students' re-entry into the school and of allowing them to achieve a stable period of sobriety.

Students returning to school from a chemical dependency treatment program find themselves caught in the middle of the interplay of many powerful and confusing forces. The individual recovering student is in the very early stages of a major change in lifestyle as she makes the transition from the treatment to the school environment. Treatment was a relatively safe environment where abstinence was the norm, actively supported and protected by all treatment staff and program activities. The school, on the other hand will be perceived as a frightening environment where chemical use or abuse is not only the norm but is accepted, expected and promoted.

The treatment team has access to much information concerning the student's progress while in treatment and his prognosis. In cooperation with the student they also will have formulated a discharge plan, consisting of specific, short- and long-term objectives. Such behavioral change goals reinforce the progress made while in treatment and describe things the student will need to do in order to stay straight. Most adolescent treatment staff are also aware that the environment to which the student must return is often hostile to recovery in many ways. The chemical dependency counselor may often think, "I know what this young person needs to do to stay straight, but I doubt they can do it once back in their home or school environment."

The school, on the other hand, is typically unfamiliar with the dynamics of chemical dependency. Within its walls are many staff with a multitude of conflicting expectations of the recovering student—both realistic and unrealistic—regarding everything from school attendance to personal appearance. Many classroom teachers are also unsure about basic issues such as how they should respond to the student in class. Thus, a common response of the educator might be, "I know what this student needs to do in school, but I don't know how to relate to her problem."

The demands on the time of the recovering student frequently complicate a student's recovery in additional ways. Many will be expected—in addition to attending school, keeping current, and making up past work—also to be attending outpatient therapy as well as Alcoholics Anonymous or Narcotics Anonymous regularly. Many will have difficulty managing school, aftercare, and AA, and still have time for homework, family relationships, a social life, and perhaps even a job.

Clearly, coping with the attitudes and behavior of school staff, peers, and family members complicates recovery even further. And since chemical dependency routinely interrupts adolescent development, these young people are faced with many more expectations than their peers and yet will lack the very personal and interpersonal skills and strengths that will enable them to live up to them as well as their peers do.

Thus, it is a major problem to remain drug-free and forge a new lifestyle in the midst of a host of external and internal pressures to resume chemical use. While it is true that all adolescents struggle—at some level—with similar problems, recovering students have more at stake.

"We have only ourselves, and one another. That may not be much, but that is all there is."
(Sheldon Kopp, p. 224).

Recovering students suffer from an arrested but chronic illness: a return to chemical use constitutes relapse and the return of the problems and personal pain that originally accompanied the illness and which prompted the need for treatment. Moreover, maintaining sobriety, or deciding to remain a "non-user," requires skills and competencies that have been impaired by chemical dependency but which a student's peers possess to a greater degree. Compared with their nondependent peers, recovering students have a much greater task and less with which to accomplish it.

Expectations of the Returning Recovering Student

The recovering student also faces a myriad of expectations placed upon him by school staff. While understandable, such expectations taken as a whole are contradictory, confusing, and unrealistic. When asked how they expect the student returning from a chemical dependency treatment program to be different, a large cross-section of educators has identified the expectations below:

General behavior: Many staff members expect newly recovered students:

- to exhibit better coping skills,
- to show a lessening of the "tough kid" attitude, to exhibit greater honesty,
- to display conduct typical of a "model citizen,"
- to show general improvement in all areas of their personal lives;
- to be "fixed," or "cured".

Personal Appearance: Many expect the returning students:

- to look alert,
- to be clean and neat,
- to dress "normally,"
- to get haircuts,
- to wear less makeup (girls),
- to get rid of earrings (boys), and
- to improve their personal hygiene in general.

Relationships: Many will expect recovering kids:

- to develop boy/girl relationships where they have had none,
- to be better at handling relationships,
- to have more "mature" relationships,
- to change peer groups (i.e., give up old "using" friends and make new, healthier friendships), and
- to have improved family relationships.

School Performance: Understandably, many will have clear expectations that recovering students' school conduct will improve. The student is expected:

- to be cooperative,
- to engage in extracurricular activities ('that they should have been participating in the first place'),

- to be apologetic for their former disruptiveness.
- to hand in all their assignments completed and on time.
- to make up all work they missed while in treatment, and work they did poorly on before treatment.
- no longer to be absent or tardy, cut classes, or have disciplinary problems.

Emotional Well-being: Many staff will expect that treatment will have a profound impact on a student's emotional stability. The student:

- will no longer be moody,
- will be more emotionally open and honest,
- will have better self-acceptance,
- will be more accepting of criticism,
- will be more in control of his feelings.

Expert Drug Resources: Often recovering students are seen as having crossed an invisible boundary; they are now 'on our side.' They are expected:

- to be "experts" on drug issues,
- to speak in classes,
- to disclose the identities of all the drug dealers in town,
- to "narc" on other students using drugs,
- to "convert" or "save" other drug users.

Abstinence: The greatest expectation, of course, is that students survive their re-entry into the real world without returning to the use of those mood-altering chemicals that they have learned will 'make all problems go away.'

No Difference: Not all staff share these optimistic if unrealistic expectations; many have expectations exactly opposite those above. Students will not change, they will be as bad as before, and they will fail in their efforts to stay straight. Still others expect that these young people will be more emotionally fragile, that they will be apprehensive and fearful upon re-entering the school, and they will be depressed and resentful, lonely, overwhelmed, self-righteous, or "brainwashed." The list above applies solely to the school system's expectations that will greet the returning student. An additional set of expectations is placed upon recovering kids by their parents and families, and by their peers. More broadly still, there is a cultural expectation that these students also be engaged in the process of "growing up:" making progress on the normal developmental tasks of adolescence, including developing a healthy sense of identity, setting lifelong goals, attaining independence from their families, achieving financial independence, and so on.

From all of this a number of straightforward conclusions can be drawn. First, taken as a whole, such expectations are unrealistic and overwhelming for any adolescent, much less one who is in the earliest stages of recovery from an illness which has impaired the whole person. Secondly, all of these expectations are to some degree present among the staff as a whole. Third, the student will unavoidably discover these expectations because the staff will communicate them either explicitly or implicitly through their attitudes and behavior. Finally, the student will also experience contradictory expectations at different times and from different people throughout the day.

The *"post-treatment high"* also represents a major risk factor which jeopardizes the adolescent's recovery process and which recommends the need for in-school support. Since the beginning of formal treatment programs, clinicians and AA members have been aware of the "post-treatment high" phenomenon, as true of adolescents as it is of adults. Many recovering adolescents will return from treatment with intense feelings of well-being, optimism, relief, and enthusiasm for sobriety, supported by a belief that all of their major problems have been solved by their treatment experience. Ironically, this unrealistic commitment to sobriety often leads students to deny the need for ongoing support or participation in an in-school recovery group. In addition, during this short-lived period which lasts only from one to three months, some of the unacceptable school performance behaviors which precipitated the need for treatment reappear: tardiness, unexcused absences, failure to complete classroom assignments, and so on. For such students, these lapses in school performance represent relatively minor, insignificant problems when compared, in their own minds, to those they have dealt with during treatment.

Such behavior can be confusing to classroom teachers as well as the Student Assistance Program staff unless they are aware of it, anticipate it, and understand it. When the "high" wears off students no longer feel special and the realities of day-to-day living return, making the need for ongoing recovery support even more vital. Thus, it is important for program staff to acknowledge the "post-treatment high" phenomenon—to students—and to involve students immediately in the Recovery Support Group.

The above represent only a few of the issues which point to the need for the school system and the chemical dependency treatment community to become better acquainted on behalf of their patients/students. Thus, the problems of recovering students returning to school from a treatment program dictate the need, first, for establishing clear and cooperative working relationships between school districts and treatment programs. Second, the school system needs to develop an explicit re-entry process so that no student, following a month's hospitalization, will just show up at the front door on a Monday morning. Finally, these and other demands on a recovering adolescent are among the best arguments in favor of the need for a recovery-focussed support group.

The Re-Entry Process

The development of a clear re-entry process has been demonstrated to increase the likelihood that students returning from chemical dependency treatment programs will achieve extended periods of continuous sobriety. At least four components of such a re-entry process can be identified: (1) clarifying the school's working relationship with the treatment program, (2) clarifying the expectations of school staff regarding the returning student, (3) clarifying the expectations of the returning student, and (4) providing specific, appropriate in-school support services.

Step One: Working With Treatment

The SAP staff will need to take steps to develop a good working relationship and communication with the chemical dependency treatment programs in its area. The Student Assistance Program Counselor/-Coordinator should have as much information as possible about the recovering student prior to his return to school. The most important information would include the date on which a student is due to be discharged, information concerning his progress in treatment, the prognosis (e.g., "good, fair, poor"), and the discharge plans (or "aftercare objectives") which the student, family, and treatment staff have mutually discussed and agreed to.

The knowledge that a Recovery Support Group is available in school permits the treatment staff to incorporate attendance at such a group into the discharge plans. In some cases, the availability of such a group may determine whether or not the treatment staff recommends a return to the home environment as opposed to a halfway house or other services in the extended continuum of care. The information above can be communicated to the school in writing, assuming that either the school, the treatment program, or both have obtained the necessary prior written consent (see the Supplements in Chapter 9).

Ideally, the SAP Counselor/Coordinator, or someone designated to work with recovering students, should seek to be invited to the discharge staffing which reputable treatment programs hold shortly before the adolescent is discharged. Here the school contact person can gain information which will be useful in developing a support system for the student, such as the diag-

nosis and the pattern of the student's chemical abuse, the degree of cooperativeness in treatment, significant issues which emerged, the degree of damage to intellectual, emotional, and social functioning, the nature and degree of family involvement in treatment, the general prognosis for post-treatment recovery, and specific recommendations for aftercare: AA involvement, attendance at an aftercare group, continuing therapy for other problems, etc. (See Supplement 15.1).

Step Two: Clarifying Expectations of School Staff

It is helpful for both the recovering student and those who will work with her on a daily basis to have a clear idea of what can realistically be expected of the returning student. A second step in the re-entry process should thus be a meeting of the SAP Counselor/Coordinator and all teachers or others who are likely to have firsthand, regular experience with the student. Such a meeting can be brief—30 minutes at best—and should be convened shortly before the student's first day back in school. Classroom teachers, the student's guidance counselor, and the assistant principal should be invited to bring to the meeting specific expectations, both long- and short-term, that they will have for the student. In such a meeting, staff members individually share their expectations with the group. What often emerges is an awareness on the part of all concerned of how unrealistic or contradictory their initial expectations are. In fact, some schools have discovered that placing the most resistant or punitive staff member last in the order often has a moderating influence on his attitudes toward the recovering student.

The function of the SAP Coordinator/Counselor will be to share with the group, within the limits of confidentiality, the information gained from the treatment center concerning its assessment of the student's real competencies. This information can be utilized to modify the expectations of the staff in a more realistic direction. The group should arrive at a modest set of short-term and long-term goals which will be reviewed with the student and monitored by all those involved. The SAP Counselor/Coordinator may also utilize the meeting to educate staff concerning chemical dependency and to address their specific concerns about how to respond to the student on a daily basis.

Thus, the purposes of the re-entry meeting are fivefold: (1) to discover staff expectations, (2) to moderate expectations in a realistic direction, (3) to develop specific, individual goals for the student, (4) to encourage moderation of attitudes, and (5) to convey information about the student learned from the treatment program.

Step Three: Clarifying Students' Expectations

As difficult as the return can be for staff, it is always far more so for the student who confronts a confusing, frightening, and ultimately new experience upon his return to the school. Students are often aware that past performance has placed their graduation in jeopardy, or that just by being in treatment they have fallen further behind. They often fear the reactions of staff members in whose classes they have been disruptive. They are often fearful that other students will suspect them of "narcing" on them in treatment or to school officials. They are nearly always fearful of their ability to stay straight in an environment where much of their former drug-related behavior took place: getting high, planning to get high, buying or selling drugs, talking about drug experiences, and so forth. And most will have been told in treatment that they will have to give up old drug-using friends and make new, straight friends.

Thus, a vital step in the re-entry process is the meeting between the SAP Counselor/Coordinator and the returning student, since one of the purposes of such a meeting is to allow the student to discuss what he expects the return to school to be like. Many of these expectations are exaggerated, catastrophic fears; just talking with a knowledgeable person removes some of the anxiety. Others, however, are based on real problems the student will face. The re-entry meeting with the student allows the counselor and student to gain a more realistic view of problems and to discuss ways of coping with them.

Another purpose of the meeting is to communicate to the student the short-term and long-term expectations that were arrived at in the staff meeting discussed above. Students may be relieved to discover that they will not be expected to turn their school careers around overnight, and to have concrete goals to work toward during their first few weeks or months back in school. Many counselors have discovered that the use of explicit, written behavioral contracts, specifying expectations with regard to attendance, conduct, and academic performance, are a useful tool in assisting recovering students to be clear about the school's expectations of them.

Step Four: Offering Support

Finally, the re-entry meeting is also a time when the SAP Counselor/Coordinator discusses specific in-school support services that are available. Most immediately, the recovering student should be given permission to seek out the SAP Counselor/Coordinator (or the relevant staff person who works with recovering students) whenever she feels in danger of returning to drug use or whenever she feels under extreme emotional pressure during the school day. In addition, students should be strongly urged to make a commitment to attend the Recovery Support Group for a specified period of time. If the school has developed the kind of working relationship with treatment discussed above, students may already be aware of the support group and will have agreed to attend it as part of their discharge meeting.

As the availability of intensive outpatient chemical dependency treatment programs increases, a growing number of students may be in treatment while remaining in school. For these students, the school should adhere to the same principles as above, although a less rigorous structure is called for. Of most importance will be the communication between the treatment staff, the SAP staff, the student, and parents. Such students may also participate in the Recovery Support Group concurrent with their treatment.

The Recovery Support Group

The re-entry process, the availability of a knowledgeable support person, and the presence of a sensitive staff are all parts of a general support system that surrounds the recovering student. More concrete support is offered by the Recovery Support Group.

The Recovery Support Group differs from the other types of support groups in a student assistance program in a number of ways. First, most Recovery Support Groups are "open" in order to accommodate students returning from treatment at various times during the year. Group members, moreover, are much more knowledgeable about and experienced in group process as a result of their treatment experience. They bring to the group a familiarity with the basic group ground rules, an awareness of the importance of confidentiality, and skills in self-disclosure, confrontation, and group problem-solving. Little explicit teaching about alcohol and other drug abuse is needed due to recovering students' knowledge about drugs gained while in treatment or on the streets. Group facilitators can also rely on the fact that students entering the group will understand, to some degree, the nature of the recovery process and what staying straight will require. Finally, the Recovery Support Group does not have a specific curriculum, since the students typically determine the agenda by the problems they bring to the group week-to-week.

While these factors may appear to make this an easy group to lead, they actually require facilitators of the Recovery Support Group, and the school system in general, to be as well-prepared as for other support groups. The discussion above has dealt with many re-entry issues of which the facilitators of the Recovery Support Group should be aware with respect to each student in the group. Practically speaking, it is thus a good idea for the group leader(s) to be involved in the re-entry process itself. In addition, a number of specific issues arise relating both to the process and the content of the Recovery Support Group.

The Role of the Facilitator

Perhaps because students themselves determine the day-to-day agenda of the Recovery Support Group, group leaders must be very clear about their role, the purposes of the group, the various challenges to the integrity and success of the group, and their knowledge of the dynamics of recovery and relapse.

Group Purpose and Norms. Stated most accurately, this group is for students who are chemically dependent, and who are willing to struggle honestly with their need to stay alcohol/drug-free. The most immediate, specific goal would be to help students maintain continuous sobriety. Other goals include allowing students to identify with each other's problems, allowing students to discover that they are not alone or unique in experiencing threats to their sobriety, and generally strengthening the progress made while in treatment. The basic norm of the group is abstinence from the use of all mood-altering chemicals, regardless of the student's "drug of choice" in treatment.

'Credentials.' Group leaders also need to be prepared for the inevitable challenges regarding their own current use of alcohol or other drugs, or questions as to their "credentials" as recovering persons themselves. As Vannicelli (1980, p. 21ff) has pointed out, questions such as "Do you use drugs?" or "Are you a recovering alcoholic/addict?" most often mask the question students may not know how to ask any other way: "Am I going to get what I need from you?" Leaders should direct the discussion to this latter issue, often by asking why such information is important to students. In any event, facilitators should be prepared to answer direct questions concerning their own chemical experience honestly at some point.

Limitations of the Group. Facilitators should be clear themselves that the Recovery Support Group

must not take the place of either outpatient aftercare or attendance at Alcoholics Anonymous, Narcotics Anonymous, or other self-help groups in the community. Leaders should be clear about how their support group differs from the former. They should also reinforce the expectation that students make use of these other support systems in addition to their in-school group.

"All of the significant battles are waged within the self."
(Sheldon Kopp, p. 224).

Outreach. "Cutting," or missing a support group meeting may often be an important sign of an incipient relapse. Therefore, when a student is absent from the group the facilitators should immediately contact the student and determine the reason for her absence. Sometimes students will cut the group because they have already had a relapse which they are afraid to disclose to the group. At other times they will indicate that they were "feeling OK" and did not feel the need for the group on that day. In this case they need to be reminded that they have contracted to attend a given number of consecutive sessions, and that attendance is a responsibility issue as well as a health issue.

Communication. Moreso than the leaders of other support groups, facilitators of the Recovery Support Group need to maintain communication linkages with parents and with the counselors of those students who are simultaneously involved in aftercare. Parents may need to be informed, for example, when a student misses a group meeting, when he drops out of the group altogether, or when he suffers a relapse. Parents should also be encouraged to contact support group leaders when they experience problems at home that jeopardize the student's recovery. Similarly, the outpatient-aftercare counselor should be informed of any interruptions in the student's group participation or recovery, and these counselors should be invited to share relevant information with group leaders in school. These communications are not designed to involve the support group leaders in the student's therapy in any direct way, but to alert group leaders, parents, and aftercare counselors to threats to the student's recovery.

Such communications constitute only apparent violations of the general rule of confidentiality that must exist within all groups. Group leaders should explain to incoming group members that such communications are possible under certain circumstances. The circumstances governing communications outside the group are the same as those applied to other groups and other students: leaders will involve other people whenever they learn of behavior or circumstances that jeopardize the student's health, safety, or welfare.

Dealing with Relapse

The greatest threat to the individual student and to the integrity of the Recovery Support Group is the return to chemical use, or relapse. The group leaders must be prepared to deal with the individual relapse episodes, and must also engage recovering students in "relapse prevention" by teaching them how to recognize and deal with the early signs of relapse before chemical use returns.

The most basic rule or group expectation around relapse is that it must be talked about in the group when it occurs. Other group members or the leaders should make such disclosures themselves when they have information regarding a given student. Group leaders can reinforce the expectation of talking about relapse by inquiring, at the beginning of each session, as to whether students are going to their AA meetings, attending their outpatient meetings, and are staying straight. Students will often be reluctant to disclose the fact that they have had a relapse out of fear that they will be kicked out of the group, fear of the judgements of other group members and the leaders, out of guilt or shame, or out of a feeling that "all is lost." Therefore, the relapse should be handled in a way that does not confirm these fears.

The general response of leaders should be to reinforce the chronicity of the disease—that it is incurable and is subject to relapse—and to explore the notion of the "therapeutic relapse." All is not lost; the relapse experience can be turned into a positive experience by examining the circumstances surrounding the episode and exploring skills involved in responding to such situations in a more constructive manner. The group as a whole can brainstorm specific "prevention" steps. Group leaders will often solidify suggestions by contracting with the student involved to take specific action steps for the next few weeks. Thus, the relapse event itself is never grounds for automatic exclusion from the group—it is the reason for the group's existence in the first place.

Beyond these general responses to relapse, the group leaders need to be prepared to deal with specific relapse situations. Vannicelli has outlined a number of these that are particularly applicable to the school-based Recovery Support Group (Vannicelli, pp. 30-33).

Coming to Group "High" or Intoxicated. On rare occasions a group member may come to group high or intoxicated. If the fact that the student has been using is immediately obvious to group leaders, the situation should be treated according to existing school policies against in-school alcohol/drug use. That is, it should be dealt with as an example of "witnessed use," with one of the leaders escorting the student to the principal's office for immediate disciplinary action. The remainder of group time must be spent processing other group members' feelings. In most cases, the student will return to group the next week, where the incident needs to be discussed again.

Clandestine Use. Frequently students will begin using alcohol or other drugs and will not acknowledge it as a relapse and will not bring it up in group. In this case, the leaders or other group members who may have information regarding the student's conduct outside of group will need to raise the issue. They may need to confront the student with facts, or with their perceptions of his/her behavior that lead them to suspect a relapse has occurred. Group leaders need to reinforce the basic norm of abstinence and assess the student's willingness to continue to work toward that goal. Whenever the leaders have information that chemical use is continuing and is still not being discussed, they should consider a number of options, including (1) contacting parents and/or the aftercare counselor involved, (2) planning an additional level of intervention, or referral to community treatment services, or (3) removing the student from the group on the grounds that the group does not seem to be appropriate for them at this time. A pattern of relapses—not the relapse itself—and an unwillingness by the student to honestly cope with it is ground for exclusion from the group.

Verbal Compliance. In some cases students may verbally support the group norm of abstinence and the rules about discussing relapse incidents in the group. At some point, however, it may become clear to the group leaders as well as to other members that a student's compliance is verbal only: they fail to demonstrate a willingness to make use of the preventive and supportive systems the group provides. When a pattern of such unwillingness appears, or when chemical behavior does not change, the group leaders should respond according to the options above.

Open Defiance. Occasionally students will not even demonstrate a willingness to comply with basic group expectations. They may become re-involved in former patterns of drug use, may begin using drugs they previously had no experience with, or may start using drugs they say gave them no trouble. They may openly discuss and justify their chemical use in the group: "I can handle it now," "I was treated for marijuana—I never used speed before," or "Alcohol got me into treatment; marijuana isn't addicting." Group leaders should bear in mind that if a student remains involved in the group, some part of them probably wants to keep coming. As above, however, at some point the group will no longer be appropriate for them, their continued chemical use will undermine the basic group norm, and they will have to be removed. The leaders' responsibility to protect the health of the group as whole dictates that a pattern of relapse cannot be allowed to continue beyond two or three sessions without excusing the student from the group.

Relapse Prevention

The causes and dynamics of relapse are as complex as the disease itself. Some of the factors leading to relapse are biochemical in nature: in many students the process of returning to metabolic normalcy may take two years. Another factor contributing to relapse is the intense stress of daily living. Some research indicates that chemically dependent persons have nervous systems which "augment," or amplify incoming stimuli, leading them to be more sensitive to anxiety-provoking situations. The fact that most chemically dependent adolescents have less sophisticated coping skills and less experience in their use is another contributing factor. Years of reliance upon mood-altering chemicals places these students in the position, relative to their peers, of having more problems to cope with, and yet fewer competencies with which to meet them.

In addition, many young people will emerge from treatment programs in a state of verbal compliance with treatment concepts, with little in-depth emotional acceptance of the disease and its future implications. A student may, for example, state out loud "I am chemically dependent and must remain chemically-free forever," while saying to themselves "But only because that's what they told me in treatment." For most adolescents, the process of accepting at some emotional depth the chronicity of the illness and its implications for their future conduct will require one or two years of continuous sobriety and consistent involvement in self-help groups as well as aftercare in the community.

Still others will find recovery difficult because the environment itself is hostile to or unsupportive of their recovery. For reasons cited earlier, the school and one's peers often represent the two most significant impediments to abstinence. For a majority of chemically dependent adolescents, however, recovery is complicated by the fact that they have at least one chemically dependent parent who most likely has not yet undergone treatment. Even in families where a parent is not chemically dependent, many residual or preexisting problems may persist which provide rather chronic sources of stress and distress for the family as well as the recovering adolescent.

Concerted attention has only recently been focussed on what AA members have known for fifty years: that relapse is predictable, rarely accidental. It is usually possible to identify a set of progressive signs and symptoms of relapse that recapitulate the initial progression of the disease. The return to chemical use is typically only the last symptom of the disease to return. Leaders of Recovery Support Groups will need to be aware of the indications of relapse to assist them in identifying students in danger of returning to chemical use. They will also need to teach explicitly about the relapse progression so students can take specific preventive measures. (For various discussions of the dynamics of relapse see Budenz (1979), Crewe (1974), Daley (1986), Gorksi (1980), Gorksi and Miller (1982), and Milam and Ketcham (1981).

For the individual student a number of concrete steps are involved in the relapse prevention strategy:

1. Become aware of the major symptoms of relapse

2. Identify high risk situations and factors in one's own life

3. Develop a list of alternative behaviors or responses to high risk situations

4. Practice skills involved in coping with high risk situations and factors

5. Have group members contract to utilize one or more relapse prevention skills over the short-term (e.g., one to three weeks)

6. Review the behavior contract with the group each week.

Supplement 15.2 identifies some of the relapse symptoms associated with one's feelings, attitudes, behavior, and belief system. While recovering students bring to their support group a measure of knowledge and sophistication which members of other groups may lack, they also bring a set of needs unique to themselves. It is vital that leaders of the Recovery Support Group have a thorough knowledge of what happens in chemical dependency treatment, of the stages of recovery, and of the dynamics of relapse. They should also become as familiar with Alcoholics Anonymous and Narcotics Anonymous and the Twelve Steps as they would be with insulin therapy if they were leading a support group for diabetic youth. And, they must continually bear in mind that as fragile as recovering youth might appear at times, they need to be constantly reminded that they do possess the resources to stay straight and to take charge of their own lives.

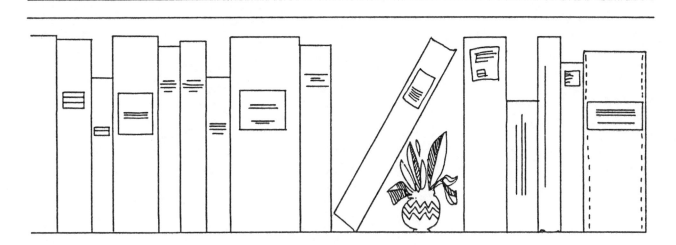

FOR FURTHER READING

Alcoholics Anonymous. New York: Alcoholics Anonymous World Services, Inc. 3rd Edition.

Daley, Dennis. *Relapse Prevention Workbook.* Holmes Beach, FL: Learning Publications, Inc., 1986.

Gorski, Terrence and Merlene Miller. *Counseling for Relapse Prevention.* Independence, MO.: Independence Press, 1982.

Kurtz, Ernest. *Not-God: A History of Alcoholics Anonymous.* Center City, MN: Hazelden, 1979.

Marshall, Shelly. *Young, Sober, and Free.* Center City, MN: Hazelden, 1978.

Small, Jacquelyn and Sidney Wolf. "Beyond Abstinence." *Alcohol Health and Research World.* (1978): 32-36.

Vannicelli, Marsha. "Group Psychotherapy with Alcoholics: Special Techniques." *Journal of Studies on Alcohol.* 43:1 (1982), 17-37.

Chapter 15 | Supplements

Supplement 15.1, "The Discharge Summary," is a checklist which can be used by the SAP Counselor/-Coordinator (or other person designated to work with treatment programs) in gathering information about students soon to return from a treatment program. The information can be shared, in summary form, with those staff involved in the re-entry meeting to assist them in formulating realistic expectations and goals for the recovering student. The information can also help leaders of the Recovery Support Group to understand the areas in which students may need support and to recognize signs of a return to former drug-related behavior patterns that can signal relapse.

The information should never become part of a student's permanent or cumulative file, and must be handled in strict conformity with the confidentiality requirements of the treatment program from which the data is obtained. To the extent that such records are retained, they should only be kept until the student graduates or leaves school, and then destroyed. They should also be maintained by the SAP Counselor/-Coordinator and retained separately from all other usual student records.

Supplement 15.2 is a "Relapse Prevention Checklist," or summary of many warning signs of relapse. The information is useful to group leaders in identifying students at risk of relapse. The information should also be shared with group members, who can become involved in brainstorming ways of preventing or coping with these symptoms when they occur.

Supplement 15.3 reprints the 12 Steps of Alcoholics Anonymous, which have become the basis for the "12 steps" of most other self-help recovery groups: Al-Anon, Alateen, Narcotics Anonymous, Overeaters Anonymous, Gamblers Anonymous, Families Anonymous, Neurotics Anonymous, Cocaine Anonymous, etc. It is vital that leaders of the Recovery Support Group become well-versed in the 12 Steps, their meaning, and their relevance to the recovery process.

Supplement 15.4 is a brief description of the goals and activities of the Recovery Support Group.

Supplement 15.1
THE DISCHARGE SUMMARY

The following is a partial list of the information which the treatment program can make available to the school concerning an adolescent's treatment experience. The information should be obtained under consent provisions of federal and state guidelines governing confidentiality of patient alcohol and other drug abuse records. General information should be shared only with those who will have day-to-day contact with the student. Counselors and leaders of the Recovery Support Group may find that more detailed information assists them in supporting the returning student.

1. What was the diagnosis?

2. What was the student's pattern of chemical use (kinds of drugs, amounts used, frequency of use, "drug-of-choice")?

3. What is the assessment of the treatment staff regarding the student's level of participation and cooperation in treatment?

4. What is the general prognosis for the student upon leaving treatment?

5. What are likely to be the major obstacles to the student's ability to maintain continuous sobriety in the first six months (or year)?

6. What does the treatment staff recommend regarding an appropriate level of involvement in school upon the student's return (i.e., reduced schedule, etc.)?

7. What specific problem areas will the student need to work on within the next year?

8. What specific aftercare recommendations will the treatment staff make (e.g., outpatient counseling, attendance at AA/NA, family therapy, etc.).?

9. What are the specific recommendations of the discharge plan?

10. What is the degree of the student's involvement in and commitment to the recommendations in the discharge plan?

11. What is the degree of the family's support for the student's recovery goals?

12. What are the major strengths which support the student's recovery?

Supplement 15.2
RELAPSE PREVENTION CHECKLIST

Relapse is a progressive process. Persons who have experienced relapses commonly report that, in retrospect, they can identify antecedents of which they were predominantly unaware prior to the return to chemical use.

Below is a list of specific signs or symptoms of relapse in the areas of attitudes, emotions, behavior, and belief system. Within each category, symptoms are placed in a general early-to-late order. At any given time, a student may identify the presence of one or more symptoms. Identifying one or more symptoms in each of the categories is more frequently indicative of serious trouble.

ATTITUDES. Attitudes may be thought of as predispositions to think, feel, or react to situations in a predetermined way rather than in ways appropriate to individual circumstances. They are mental and emotional "habits." The attitudes that accompany relapse lead one to be negatively prejudiced toward events, people, or one's day-to-day experience. The following are some indicators of attitudes associated with relapse:

[　] 1. Apprehension: Apprehensions, fears, or anxieties about one's ability to stay drug-free "forever;" preoccupation with the future instead of focussing on the "one day at a time" philosophy of AA/NA.

[　] 2. "Tunnel Vision:" Seeing aspects of one's life or experience in small, isolated fragments; becoming preoccupied with either positive or negative events rather than seeing events in a more realistic perspective.

[　] 3. Mild despair: feeling that problems cannot be solved, that one cannot take action that positively changes one's circumstances; feeling that "I've tried my best and nothing is working."

[　] 4. Indifference: apathy or indifference toward other people or events, often hiding feelings of anger or fear.

[　] 5. Powerlessness: a helpless dissatisfaction with one's life; an inability to initiate action; scattered thinking or concentration; loss of self-confidence; a mindset that justifies a return to chemical use because things are so bad.

[　] 6. Resentments: extreme anger or hostility toward the world in general, toward the group or group members, toward the school or family members. Resentments often appear when anger with oneself is utilized to scapegoat or blame others.

EMOTIONS. Many of the painful emotions associated with the progression of chemical dependency—anger, hurt, guilt, shame, loneliness, fear, etc.—also return during recovery. To the extent that defenses block the awareness and expression of feelings, they remain unidentified and unresolved. The accumulated emotional pain often makes the return to chemical use seem an attractive alternative to the risk-taking inherent in sharing feelings with others. Some common emotional components of the relapse dynamic include:

[   ] 1. Vulnerability, fragility: feeling emotionally vulnerable and unprotected; fearing that occasional mood-swings will lead to chemical use.

[   ] 2. Denial: The denial system reasserts itself in response to stress, anxiety, and painful emotions that the student judges as "bad." The denial patterns are similar to those that served adolescents when they were actively using alcohol or other drugs.

[   ] 3. Defensiveness: in addition to protecting feelings, defensiveness arises to protect the student's sense of well-being when he feels vulnerable. Defensiveness is also encountered when discussing specific problems or recovery in general.

[   ] 4. Depression: in mild forms, depression manifests itself in listlessness, apathy, flat affect, oversleeping, failure to live up to school and family responsibilities, or poor nutrition. In later stages, periods of depression are more severe, frequent, and long-lasting. Students demonstrate the "HALT" phenomenon: hungry, angry, lonely, and tired. They become more isolated, complaining that no one cares.

[   ] 5. Self-pity: students see and portray themselves as helpless victims of circumstances; the "poor me" syndrome may be used to gain attention in school and in group.

BEHAVIOR. Most behavioral factors associated with relapse involve returning to behavior patterns that were typical of the student while actively using chemicals. Students place themselves in high-risk situations, become less responsible or structured in their daily living, become more socially isolated, and ultimately withdraw from their support systems or reject outside help. Among the more common behavioral signs of relapse are the following:

[   ] 1. Compulsiveness: adherence to strict, rigid, repetitive patterns of behavior or routines; an avoidance of new situations or encounters in favor of routines that represent "safe" or risk-free interactions with people.

[   ] 2. Impulsiveness: overreactions to problems or stressful circumstances that are often self-destructive; making impulsive decisions without considering alternatives or consequences; making impulsive decisions to skip group meetings, AA meetings, or aftercare appointments, sometimes with the justification that "things were going OK."

[   ] 3. Isolation: as uncertainty, loss of self-confidence, and painful feelings build up, students begin to isolate themselves from others in their family, in school, and/or in group, either by emotionally withdrawing or actively avoiding interaction. Periods of loneliness increase.

[   ] 4. Unmanageability: students begin to experience failure. Impulsive acts or decisions result in failure due to poor planning, lack of consideration to alternatives, details, or consequences in the pursuit of unrealistic goals. Failures increase anxiety, stress, and feelings of low self-worth.

[   ] 5. Rejection of friends: recovering students may become increasingly angry with and resentful of friends, fellow AA members or support group members as these begin to confront increasingly erratic and dangerous behavior.

[   ] 6. Loss of structure: adherence to daily routine and structure begins to deteriorate; students may overeat or skip meals, substitute junk food for good nutrition, experience periods of insomnia and oversleeping, return to patterns of absenteeism and tardiness in school, begin missing assignments, etc.

[   ] 7. Erosion of formal support systems: Attendance at AA/NA meetings, support group meetings, or aftercare counseling session become sporadic. Students may claim the groups are boring, or they fail to do any good.

[   ] 8. Dishonesty: students may be conscious of their own rationalization and denial, but seem unable to help themselves.

[   ] 9. Open rejection of help: completely dropping out of support systems; openly rejecting those students, school staff, and/or family members who begin confronting irresponsible behavior or who express concern; increasing isolation and withdrawal.

[   ] 10. High-risk situations: students begin placing themselves in situations that are associated, for them, with a high risk for returning to chemical use: association with former "using" friends, going to bars, parks, or friends' homes where they formerly used alcohol/drugs, hanging around other kids who are "high," etc.

BELIEF SYSTEM. A number of components of one's belief system are associated with the return to chemical use, many of which involve an insufficient grasp of the nature of the disease or the implications of the fact that it is chronic:

[   ] 1. Stubborn commitment to sobriety: a rigid and often vocal pronouncement that "I will never drink/use again" sounds good. Often the fact that a student has made a decision "once and for all" makes pursuing a daily program of recovery less necessary or important.

[   ] 2. "I can do it alone:" the general stance that one can, by oneself and by exerting enough willpower, remain straight, makes it difficult to accept the need for help or support from any outside source.

[   ] 3. Intolerance: intolerance of others' drinking or drug use, or attempting to impose one's own judgements on others; placing the blame on society in general, on those in the school who allow drug use, or on other students. Focussing attention on the outside world removes the focus from one's own behavior.

[   ] 4. Magical thinking: daydreaming and wishful thinking, fantasies of escape from problems or rescue by unlikely circumstances ("Maybe a storm will cut off the electricity and I won't have to take the history test"); the "If only..." syndrome; an immature wish to be happy or free of problems without careful thought to specific goals; inability to constructively plan; diminished skills at problem-solving, decision-making, attention to details.

[   ] 5. Thoughts of "social" use: euphoric recall of previous, positively colored drug experiences reminds the student that drugs could normalize or medicate their feelings of confusion and pain;

[   ] 6. Thoughts of control: rationalizing a return to chemical use by thinking "I can handle it now," or "Now I know the danger signals and I'll stop when I have a blackout," or "I'll use drugs I never got into trouble with before."

Supplement 15.3

THE TWELVE STEPS OF ALCOHOLICS ANONYMOUS

1. We admitted we were powerless over alcohol—that our lives had become unmanageable.

2. Came to believe that a Power greater than ourselves could restore us to sanity.

3. Made a decision to turn our will and our lives over to the care of God *as we understood Him.*

4. Made a searching and fearless moral inventory of ourselves.

5. Admitted to God, to ourselves, and to another human being the exact nature of our wrongs.

6. Were entirely ready to have God remove all these defects of character.

7. Humbly asked Him to remove our shortcomings.

8. Made a list of all persons we had harmed, and became willing to make amends to them all.

9. Made direct amends, except when to do so would injure them or others.

10. Continued to take personal inventory and when we were wrong promptly admitted it.

11. Sought through prayer and meditation to improve our conscious contact with God *as we understood Him,* praying only for   knowledge of His will for us and the power to carry that out.

12. Having had a spiritual awakening as a result of these steps, we tried to carry this message to alcoholics, and to practice these principles in all our affairs.

Supplement 15.4

GOALS AND ACTIVITIES FOR THE RECOVERY SUPPORT GROUP

PURPOSE: *To help recovering students struggle honestly with their need to stay straight.*

GOALS:

1. To assist recovering students in maintaining abstinence—maximal periods of continuous sobriety;

2. To provide emotional and interpersonal support for staying straight;

3. To prevent relapse by teaching students to identify and cope with the signs of relapse before it occurs;

4. To assist students in recovering from relapse episodes when and if they occur;

5. To help students alter behaviors that have been immature or self-destructive;

6. To provide support for improving school performance (grades, attendance, conduct);

7. To reinforce the need for students to make use of simultaneous supports: Recovery Support Group, AA/NA, outpatient aftercare, etc.

8. To provide a social or peer group which aids students in making the transition from a drug using peer group to one that is more supportive of their recovery;

9. To assist students in identifying and exploring "alternative highs;"

PREPARATION OF GROUP LEADERS: In addition to basic training in alcohol and other drug abuse, and special training in the leadership of AODA-related support groups, it is vital that those leading the Recovery Support Group become as familiar as possible with chemical dependency treatment and with Alcoholics Anonymous (as well as Narcotics Anonymous and Cocaine Anonymous), since most of the goals of the Recovery Support Group relate to reinforcing the need for abstinence and the need for outside support. Additional workshops or inservices may be available from local AODA agencies or chemical dependency treatment centers.

"Professional days" that otherwise might be spent at conferences can be used to spend several days at a treatment center. Attendance at open meetings of AA/NA/CA is one of the best ways to acquire additional knowledge about the recovery process from those actively engaged in it.

GROUP ACTIVITIES. Of all the support groups, the Recovery Support Group is the least structured. It is rarely necessary to have a formal curriculum for the entire group series. The agenda for individual sessions is often determined by the kids themselves, although group leaders need to be prepared to deal with special topics as the need arises (e.g., relapse prevention, coping with peer pressure, etc.). As in the self-help groups, one of the 12 Steps may be used as a topic.

Many group leaders have found that the following is a good way to open each group:

> *I need to hear from everyone how your week has gone, whether you are going to your meetings, whether you have been staying straight, and who wants time today.*

This acquires the status of an opening ritual after a few weeks, reinforces the norm of abstinence and the use of AA, NA, etc., and enhances students' responsibility for self-care.

Virtually any group activity or exercise that enhances personal growth—trust building, risk-taking, communication skill, etc.—is appropriate for the Recovery Support Group.

Other Use-Focussed Support Groups

"If drug education does indeed seek to promote more deliberate and rational decision making, then it is fairly apparent that students must gain a wide variety of competencies that transcend the mere recall and understanding of cognitive drug information." (Winkelman and Harbet (1985), p. 18).

Between those students concerned about another's chemical use and those recovering from their own chemical dependency there lies as vast and complex territory. Reliable estimates put the number of secondary students involved in "problem use" or abuse at 20 per cent; half of all high school students have used marijuana by their senior year, and over 90 per cent use alcohol. The use of cocaine by the same age group is becoming increasingly frequent (see Table 2.2). The motivations for chemical use are many, ranging from simple curiosity to the relief of extraordinary personal distress and emotional pain. Patterns of involvement can vary, as we have seen, from experimentation and occasional regular use to abuse, alcoholism, and other chemical dependencies. There are also great differences between students in terms of the numbers, kinds, and amounts of drugs used, their commitment to the rewarding drug "high," and the frequency and severity of problems caused by chemical abuse. These factors and more imply that different students will require different strategies in order to adopt positive, healthy changes in their own alcohol/drug use.

The brief, problem-focussed group is often an appropriate and effective setting within which to address these needs and their variety. As the name implies, the use-focussed group in any of its forms focuses students' attention on their own chemical behavior in a manner intended to bring about change in the direction of abstinence. Use-focussed groups also accomplish some purposes for the school system. As pointed out earlier, these groups can assist the school in effectively assessing and intervening in students' own chemical use. Some of the groups can be effective when integrated into policies and procedures. As indicated in Figure 11.1, it is possible to recognize a number of different types of use-focussed groups, depending on the needs and size of the school and on how narrowly one wishes to specialize the groups, and on the manner in which the school and the AODA services in the community divide up the continuum of care. The primary rationale for discriminating between different types of use-focussed groups is the appreciation that students are affected by their own chemical use along a continuum of severity.

While most of the issues surrounding Affected Others Groups and the Recovery Support Groups are relatively straightforward, no such unanimity exists regarding how to design or conduct the use-focussed groups. Any of these groups can be involved, simultaneously, in prevention, assessment, intervention, and support for students involved in chemical use. Three of the groups mentioned in Chapter 11 will be described in more detail below — the Drug Information Group, the Personal Change Group, and the Drug-Free Support Group — along with suggestions for group topics and strategies. As with the other AODA-related support groups, a number of issues need to be taken into account in planning to implement use-focussed groups.

Some Topics for Use-Focussed Groups

In all support groups some explicit teaching must occur. Students either need more information, more accurate information, or information of a different type than they have. The following is only a partial list which briefly describes some of the broad topic areas that would traditionally be among those addressed in a use-focussed group. The amount of time spent on various topics will naturally depend on the type of use-focussed group, the length of the group, and the personal needs of the students within it.

Alcohol/Drug Information. This does not refer to teaching students about the types of drugs and their respective effects on body systems. More relevant to most students' immediate situations will be information about the continuum of drug experience: the differences between alcohol/drug use, abuse, and chemical dependency. Students need to know that there are qualitative differences between various ways of using chemicals, and that there are predictable symptoms of each, leading up to the disease of chemical dependency. Students also need to be taught about the nature, causes, functions and manifestations of denial. The effects of alcohol and other drug abuse on others — chiefly family members — is also an important topic.

Other specific topics can be addressed as appropriate to the concerns of a given student or a specific session. Curiosity about physiology, genetics, drug laws, etc., should always be acknowledged by facilitators, who can share the information they have, make a commitment to gather information for the next meeting, or assign one or more students to do some research and report back to the group.

Personal Communication Skills. Many have used devices such as the Johari Window to introduce concepts involving self-disclosure, giving and receiving feedback, leveling and confrontation. Interpersonal communication skills and concepts relate both to group process and to alcohol and other drug abuse. The use of chemicals frequently interferes with or impairs perceptions of self, perception of others, and the identification and expression of feelings.

Consequences. A certain amount of time needs to be devoted to describing and discussing the fact that alcohol and other drug abuse can have various harmful consequences. Attention should be focussed, at the appropriate time in the group's development, on consequences which have attended the student's individual chemical use experiences. Discussions of consequences do not consist of threats or preachments by facilitators, or predictions that "if you continue using, this will happen." Talking about consequences allows students to see that more is involved in drug use than just the temporary euphoric feelings it produces. Consequences may be subtle or overt, mild or severe.

Alternatives. Much has been written about alternatives to drug use for youth. Any group focussing on students' own alcohol/drug use must address the issue in some manner. Alternatives, especially when suggested by adults, are often thinly disguised attempts to distract kids from alcohol/drug use. In fact, realistic alternatives represent experiences and personal investments that are discovered to be as good or better than the satisfactions offered by drug use. As such, the best alternatives are those which are suggested or discovered by students themselves. The discussion of alternatives should lead naturally to assignments to discover and employ them. Alternative activities may include techniques for stress management, the development and use of personal support systems, social/recreational activities, or opportunities for self-investment. In many cases the latter should involve a brief assignment to do some type of volunteer work in the school or the community, which involves contact with other people.

"Economics" of Drug Use. Most students, regardless of their chemical experience, are not consciously aware of the degree to which they invest personal resources in alcohol/drug use. Many exercises can be created which focus students' attention on how much money they spend in getting and using alcohol or other drugs in a given week. Time is a more subtle resource, and the study of its relationship to drug use can be very revealing. For example, students can be assigned to create a list of things they do during a typical week, later coding it according to which activities involve getting or using alcohol or other drugs. Many students are surprised to find out the number of hours they spend in activities where alcohol or other drug abuse is directly or indirectly involved.

Peer Pressure. The subject of "peer pressure" is invariably raised, if not by students then by facilitators. In discussing peer pressure, facilitators should be wary of using the term as an excuse, or accepting "peer pressure" as an excuse for students' behavior. The discussion should revolve around "peer refusal" strategies and skills. Most students do not experience peer pressure as a global influence on their behavior, but rather in discrete episodes of behavior where refusing to go along with what they perceive to be group expectations jeopardizes their self-esteem and sense of "fitting in." Consequently, group time should be devoted to discussin,g identifying, and practicing ways of refusing to use alcohol or other drugs which are self-affirming and other-affirming. Virginia Satir's analysis of communication patterns as manipulative roles has proven to be a useful framework within which to examine "peer pressure" as a communication issue (Satir, 1972: pp. 59-95). Facilitators may also find it useful to reframe the topic of peer pressure as "student enabling."

Decisions and Decision Making. In any use-focussed group some time must be devoted to explicitly analyzing decisions and decision making. The process can be informative, but the intention is to let students know that their behavior indicates that they are making decisions, that they can make new ones, and that they don't have to live with a decision forever. The final meetings of use-focussed groups are typically devoted to having students make conscious their decisions regarding their alcohol/drug involvement. Such decisions should be formally written out and discussed with the group. These decisions may often take the form of a contract covering alcohol/drug behavior for a short time in the future (e.g., 3 months). Decisions can also involve plans students create to assemble support systems to help them keep such contracts.

In the less interactive, more didactically oriented information groups, these topics may only be addressed briefly and with fairly superficial discussion. In the more intense groups which concentrate on behavioral change, more time would spent in each area (as well as others), and in developing skills and competencies.

Some Strategies for Use-Focussed Groups

Topic areas need to be integrated with group techniques and strategies to the extent that behavioral change is an expected outcome. As the quotation opening this chapter observes, the recall of information alone is not sufficient. While many techniques, tools, and strategies are possible to employ in the use-focussed groups, the following have become the most commonplace. Again, they would be employed to a greater or lesser degree depending on the type of use-focussed group one is conducting.

AODA Self-Knowledge. In all use-focussed groups students must be expected, as early as possible, to discuss their own alcohol and other drug use. It is important to tell prospective group members "This group is not about drugs - it is about your drug use." Expecting students to discuss some aspect of their own chemical use in the first meetings reinforces this expectation as a norm.

Students' own alcohol/drug use can be examined in a natural progression. For the reasons discussed in Chapter 8, it is advisable to have students begin talking about their drug involvement by relating their first drug experiences. Students should be encouraged to describe episodes in some detail. These are usually "safe" for students to talk about, allow them to discover that there are no bad consequences for talking about them, and they allow the group leaders to gather important information about group members. Over several meetings the discussion should progress to a discussion of current drug use, changes in the pattern since their first experiences, and harmful consequences that may have occurred. Group leaders amass information about individual students which will be useful in developing contracts aimed at reductions or abstinence.

Alcohol/Drug Use Contracts. There are good reasons for utilizing, in all use-focussed groups, individual contracts for reducing or eliminating chemical use. Such behavioral contracts may be employed in a wide variety of ways:

- They may, for example, be implemented at any point in the group: some are used from the first meeting on, while others are implemented at the midpoint, after students have discussed many aspects of their chemical use;

- Contracts can be individualized for each student or can require abstinence for all group members;

- Contracts can be for abstinence or for substantial, specific reductions in chemical use;

• Contracts can be verbal, written, or both.

A typical written contract might read as follows: "*I agree to abstain from the use of all mood-altering chemicals for the next 8 group meetings. I understand that I am responsible for bringing up in group problems I have in keeping the contract as soon as they occur.*"

The purpose of the contracts is not to control students' chemical use. The only consequence of a particular failure to keep the contract is the expectation that the student discuss it in group the next time. (Groups are then begun by facilitaors asking how students have done with their contracts in the past week). Instead, behavioral contracts can help the group's leaders and students discover specific risk situations and pressures to get high. Alternatives can then be examined, or specific skills for resisting pressures to use can be practiced. Another reason for implementing contracts is that the group succeeds to the extent that members are aware of their feelings and are able to express themselves openly. Chemical use, even during the week, usually impairs these abilities to some degree.

Contracts also allow students to conduct "experiments." They discover that they can go for various periods of time without using, that they do have the competencies to stay straight. Contracts also reinforcer the basic group norm and school philosophy on abstinence. Finally, how well students keep the contracts or how willing they are to apply themselves to them yields valuable assessment information for group leaders. The student who is unwilling or unable to keep an abstinence contract, for example, despite the resources of the group, may require intervention and referral to treatment.

Role Playing. Role playing has been shown to be one of the more effective strategies for problem solving and for teaching and strengthening new skills. Many issues which arise in the use-focussed groups lend themselves to role playing strategies. Peer pressure, or student enabling, is often most effectively examined using this strategy. For example, group members can role play various "pusher/pushee" situations, allowing them to get more accurately in touch with the feelings on both sides. The same technique can then be used in practicing more effective refusal scripts: those which enhance and affirm self-worth and self-esteem in both sender and receiver.

Role playing can be employed to help students analyze almost any interpersonal situation and practice better coping skills. When a student discloses the failure to keep a contract, for instance, group leaders should inquire about the circumstances. The situation leading up to an episode of drug use often points to the use of a role play to practice better refusal strategies. Or, some students may fear the reactions of parents if they told them they were in the group, or told them about their drug use. Role playing such a student/parent interaction removes some of the catastrophic fears and may strengthen the student to the point where they can make the appropriate disclosures.

Confrontation. Confrontation as a strategy is employed in the use-focussed groups in a number of ways. First, leaders must teach group members about confrontation: what it is, how it is effectively and appropriately done, and why. Group members should be encouraged to confront denial and defenses in each other, since dishonesty is a threat to the group itself. Second, group leaders must be prepared to confront denial in students in appropriate ways, and when the group has matured enough to understand and support this type of interaction.

Logs and Journals. Week-to-week assignments to make journal or log entries can be an effective tool in helping students to carry over group issues throughout the week. Assignments should be specific. They should focus students' attention on a specific topic, feeling, situation, or skill relevant to the group. Students might be asked to write one paragraph each day describing the times they felt like getting high, examples of peer pressure, circumstances surrounding specific feelings, etc. Journals are usually not collected, but leaders should check to see that assignments are being followed. Sharing material from the week's journal entry may often become a group ritual.

Self-Inventories. Some group leaders have had great success in adapting the fourth and fifth steps of Alcoholics Anonymous for the closing phases of the longer use-focussed groups. This two-part assignment requires students to make a list of all the times when their own chemical use has harmed them or others, and to confidentially disclose the contents of the list to another adult. Several group meetings are spent in discussing the nature of the assignment and how it turned out. Such a process often helps students to "own" at a deeper emotional level the nature and consequences of their own drug abuse and to make more emotionally and developmentally sound decisions regarding their future involvement. Obviously, care must be taken by facilitators to establish the process: identifying "safe" adults in the community with whom the assignment may be shared, informing them of the ground rules, and so.

The Drug Information Group

The Drug Information Group addresses the need to provide certain students with accurate AODA information, a safe environment within which they can discuss their drug use and its place in their lives, and an opportunity to examine their own decisions regarding chemical use.

Target Group. The Drug Information Group is designed to be appropriate for students who are at lowest risk for developing serious, consequential patterns of alcohol and other drug abuse (see Figure 8.3). These students are at the extreme of drug use that is more experimental and infrequent. Experimentation has probably not progressed beyond the use of alcohol and marijuana, so their alcohol/drug use can be characterized as non-severe. As depicted in Figure 8.1, drug use has not significantly impaired the personal and/or social functioning of students appropriate for this type of group. For most, the school, peer, and family environments will be personally supportive, relative to students at the other extreme. This group will have the most benefit for students who do not suffer from the deficits and absence of personal competencies and skills that render changing patterns of chemical abuse more difficult in other students.

Structure. The Drug Information Group is typically a closed group, accommodating between 5 and 15 students, which meets weekly for from four to eight sessions. As with most groups, the closer together in age the group members are the more effective their interactions will be. The Drug Information Group permits the greatest variation in numbers of students and the length of the group because the group goals tend to be more educational and the group can rely upon less intense personal interaction. Some schools have informational groups which last only four or five sessions and which are primarily "classroom" experiences. Others last longer and require a greater degree of inter-member participation and discussion.

Although its success depends on some significant degree of member participation and interaction, of all the groups the Drug Information Group tends to be the most didactic. Leader involvement is typically higher compared to many other groups. Participants exhibit greater motivation and interest in being in the group, with a correspondingly low degree of denial or defensiveness. Confrontations by group leaders or other group members are rarely needed or as intense as in the Personal Change Group, for example.

Selection of Group Members. The leaders of the Drug Information Group should have an opportunity to interview prospective group members and to participate in the selection process. This enables facilitators not only to describe the group and its ground rules, expectations, agenda, and activities to prospective members but also to exercise some choice, where necessary, in selecting members appropriate to the group's goals and purpose. In general, students are appropriate for the Drug Information Group —

- who self-refer to the student assistance program;

- who express interest in the group due to parent or peer referral;

- who accept referral to the group based on identification through "suspected use" procedures;

- who accept the group in lieu of loss of extracurricular privileges;

- who appear, from the initial screening and assessment process, to have a relatively mild degree of alcohol/drug involvement;

- who are likely to be able to change their AODA-related behavior based on education about alcohol and other drugs;

- or, who can benefit from AODA education prior to being placed in another group (e.g., a Concerned Persons/Affected Others Group).

---

*"It is important to tell prospective group members 'This group is not about drugs — it is about **your** drug use.'"*

Generally speaking, those students will be inappropriate for a Drug Information Group who have severe patterns of drug abuse or who elect the group in lieu of suspension, or expulsion.

Since the focus of this group is on specifically changing alcohol/drug use, general group contracts are a good way of making this goal explicit. The individualized group contract is also a good method of formulating, with students, a set of individualized goals upon which they will work while in the group. The major item on any group contract for a use-focussed group will be a non-use contract.

Goals and Objectives. The major purposes of the group for the school system include providing a service to students for whom referral to an AODA agency is unnecessary or inappropriate, having a service to offer students to reduce consequences, and having a method of providing concentrated AODA education to particular students in addition to the school's general AODA prevention curriculum. As with other AODA-related groups, goals and objectives for the use-focussed groups fall into three major areas: (1) changing AODA-related behavior, including knowledge, attitudes, and patterns of drug use, (2) enhancing general personal and interpersonal functioning, and (3) enhancing or maintaining acceptable levels of school performance. Within these broad areas group leaders or those designing a Drug Information Group as a component of the student assistance program must be careful to suit the goals and objectives of the group to the needs of the students who will be selected to be in it. Among the major goals of this more informational group would be the following:

- To modify students' chemical use in the direction of abstinence;

- To provide information on the nature of alcohol/-drug use, abuse, and dependency; the dynamics and symptoms of progression; the dynamics of enabling and denial;

- To provide information on the effects of chemical use, abuse, and dependency on others, including friends and family members;

- To increase students' awareness of the dynamics of intervention;

- To enhance students' communication skills in relating their concern about others' chemical use;

- To familiarize group members with the AODA-related resources available in the school and in the community (e.g., other support groups, the SAP staff, local AODA information, assessment, and referral agencies, community treatment programs, Alateen and Al-Anon, etc.);

- To familiarize group members with the potential impact of alcohol and other drug abuse on behavior, feelings, goals, growth and development (not just physiology);

- To examine the process of making decisions about alcohol/drug use;

- To examine the dynamics of peer pressure and other forms of student enabling behavior;

- To provide support, skills, and competencies for students opting for a drug-free lifestyle.

Objectives should be more specific and measurable. The following are be examples of objectives which group leaders might devise for a given Drug Information Group:

- "By the end of the group, 80 per cent of the members will demonstrate reductions in the frequency and amounts of alcohol/drug use, as measured by pre- and postgroup scores on the STADUS survey;"

- "By the end of the group, 80 per cent of the members will be able to list 5 symptoms of chemical dependency on an objective test."

With the use-focussed groups especially, it is important for group leaders and the school in general to develop goals and objectives which are realistic. Unfortunately, for many students it is unrealistic to think that in four to ten hours over as many weeks some information and discussion will result in abstinence in every group member. It is, however, completely reasonable to expect the group to have some degree of impact on students' alcohol/drug use. Failure to keep goals and objectives realistic is one of the sources of group leader burnout, especially for those who have high expectations of students and strong personal feelings about student drug abuse.

Misconstruing the purposes of the Drug Information Groups can lead to a different kind of failure. Some schools have stopped conducting them because "some students were incapable of responding to the groups: their drug use was worse during and after the groups than it was before." Aside from screening and selection issues, which come to mind first, it is also likely that this is exactly one of the more valuable outcomes. Discovering that a given student is unwilling or unable to comply with group expectations is a useful piece of assessment and intervention information.

Curriculum. The discussion of topics and strategies above gives a fairly good notion of what the curriculum of a use-focussed group might contain. To the extent that a specific Drug Information Group remains basically brief and informational, the more behavior-oriented goals cannot be realistically addressed: e.g., goals relating to decision making, communication skills and resisting peer pressure, and so on. In the briefer, more informational groups there is typically not time to devote concerted attention to discussing patterns of students' own drug experience either. The goals of a group functioning within these parameters would need to be adjusted accordingly.

Evaluation and Follow-up. The major rationale for conducting some degree of evaluation for use-focussed groups is, of course to determine whether they are effective. It is one thing to be able to say that 75 students were in such groups in a year; it another to be able to say that they were different as a result. Group leaders, other SAP staff, and the administration need to know that this type of group is instrumental in impacting on a certain variety of AODA-related behavior. Secondly, evaluation provides the SAP staff with information which can be useful in promoting others' awareness of the program: students, staff, parents, and the community as a whole.

On the individual group level, for example, such groups have been shown to be effective in addressing both general personal functioning and student drug abuse behavior. Botvin (*et al.* (1985)) has shown that a 20-session group of this type for 239 seventh graders produced significant reductions in alcohol abuse compared to controls who did not receive the group. At evaluation, those in the group reported less frequent drinking, less drinking per occasion, and fewer episodes of drunkenness (p. 550). On a broader program level, Wisconsin's Department of Public Instruction has been able to demonstrate that SAP program services result in a reduction in students' alcohol and marijuana use (Anderson *et al.* (1986), p. 74).

The areas to be evaluated are the same as the areas within which goals have been developed. Evaluation, however, does not have to be sophisticated or time-consuming. Self-report surveys of alcohol/drug use are easy to develop, administer, and score. The comparison of group members' school performance variables pre- and postgroup is a routine task which may not even involve the group facilators. Finally, student self-reports on their subjective estimates of the group's value also provide useful information. Such a group evaluation would be natural and consistent with group closure activities, and could ask for students' responses to items as simple as:

- What did you like most about this group?

- What did you like least about this group?

- Would you improve or change the group?

- If they asked, what would tell a friend this group provided for you?

- Would you recommend this group to other students?

- List at least three things you found out about yourself.

- How did the group affect your use of alcohol or other drugs?

- What decisions have you made about your use of alcohol and other drugs?

Some type of individual follow-up with students is necessary for all types of use-focussed groups. Follow-up activities for students in the briefer Drug Information Groups tends to be short-term. In some cases group leaders will have suggested to students the possibility of referral to other groups (e.g., an Affected Others Group), or students may have entered into short-term contracts for abstinence. Group leaders may wish to see students individually once a month for three months, just to see how they are doing. A "reunion" of the group on the same basis is also possible.

The Personal Change Group

The Personal Change Group offers a more intense and often more long-term group experience for students who are unlikely to change their AODA-related behavior without such intensive involvement. In some communities such services are offered outside of the school by an AODA agency. More often these groups are offered in school as part of the student assistance program's services. They are frequently co-facilitated by a school staff member and an alcohol/drug abuse counselor from a community AODA agency. Of all the in-school support groups that are part of the student assistance program, these groups can be the most intense, taxing, personally challenging and yet rewarding to become involved with.

Target Group. The Personal Change Group is designed to be appropriate for students who have serious AODA-related problems or who are at high risk for developing chemical dependency. These students have progressed beyond experimentation and regular use, and are experiencing a pattern of problems in their daily lives due to alcohol/drug abuse. Again, as illustrated in Figure 8.1, their chemical use has often impaired their personal and social functioning to some degree. Relationships in school, with peers, and perhaps even in the family do not provide these students with the supports they need to stay straight. Many of the students at this extreme will not have the personal and social competencies to develop and maintain a drug-free lifestyle. In addition, most will not define their drug use as a problem.

Structure. To be effective, this group functions best within more limited boundaries. Between five and seven students constitutes the optimum number. Most people find that a greater number of sessions are needed in order to have significant impact on the denial and the severity of AODA-related problems students bring into this group. Many Personal Change Groups meet for from 12 to 18 sessions. Again, meeting twice a week is sometimes desirable from a group standpoint, although it multiplies problems with staff.

The Personal Change Group is often a closed group: the same students begin and end the group together. Because a school policy violation may precipitate a student's entry into the group, there may be pressure to create a more "open" format. Opening the group has unique advantages and disadvantages. The open group permits the new group member to experience others at more advanced stages of group growth and individual progress. Seeing students interacting openly about their own drug use, for example, has a moderating influence on the new group member's resistance and denial. The open group also permits group leaders to accept new group members as soon as they are identified; there is no pressure to start a new group or to put students on a lengthy waiting list. The major disadvantage to an open format is the effect on group process of members entering and leaving. As a rule, such comings and goings always disrupt the group process and erode group trust, which takes time to rebuild. In addition, group leaders must be more attentive to where individual students are in their group participation: students still contract to attend a given number of consecutive sessions.

Regardless of the structure, the Personal Change Group is often the most intensively interactive of the groups. Leader participation may be highest in initial meetings, but soon group members take on the major responsibility for group interaction. Leaders must, however, be prepared to confront denial in its various forms and to educate group members in how to confront each other appropriately. Denial and defensiveness are typically strongest in the Personal Change Group, as most students' participation is to some degree coerced.

Selection of Group Members. Leaders of the Personal Change Group often have little opportunity to select members for inclusion in the group: many are referred because of school AODA policy violations, for example. If more than one Personal Change Group is being held, however, group leaders will have more ability to select compatible group members. In any event, the facilitators must interview all students prior to their placement in the group for all of the reasons discussed above regarding the selection process generally. In addition, however, the leaders of the Personal Change Group need to know the circumstances which bring the student to the group. Leaders also need to know what consequences, if any, the student avoids by completing the group satisfactorily or inherits by dropping out, etc. These considerations should all be part of the formal group contract which *every* member of a Personal Change Group should sign before the group begins (see Supplement 13.2).

In contrast to members of the Drug Information Groups, the Personal Change Group group tends to be designed for students —

- who become identified to the student assistance program because of "witnessed use" violations of school AODA policies;

- who accept referral to the group to minimize con-

sequences for unacceptable school performance: i.e., suspension, expulsion, loss of extracurricular privileges;

- who are referred to the school group by police, courts, or other components of the juvenile justice system;

- who are unlikely to be able to change their AODA behavior without a group incorporating confrontation, clear behavioral expectations, and intensive interaction;

- who appear, from the initial screening and assessment process to have a comparatively severe degree of AODA involvement;

- who may be chemically dependent but about whom the SAP staff needs more information in preparation for more and more formal personal intervention.

Goals and Objectives. The purposes of the Personal Change Group, from the school's perspective, are the most complex of the support groups. It functions as an aid to the assessment process; it helps to gather information which may legitimize a formal personal intervention strategy; it can reverse students' chemical abuse problems or prevent them from worsening; and it can provide a supportive atmosphere for students struggling to change. Also, it can accomplish simultaneously, in any given session, the prevention, assessment, intervention, or support functions for various group members.

Student-centered goals for the Personal Change Group are consistent with those outlined above for the Drug Information Group. There is perhaps a crucial difference. Student enter the Drug Information Group with a variety of backgrounds and motivations; many students ask to be in the group just out of curiosity. By definition, however, students enter the Personal Change Group because they are involved in problem use, or abuse. Thus, the two most important goals involve allowing students to begin to define their own alcohol/drug use as a problem, and consequently giving them the knowledge, skills, competencies, and support necessary to modify their chemical use in the direction of abstinence. Comments above regarding developing realistic expectations apply to the Personal Change Group even more critically. It is important for leaders to appreciate the nature and scope of personal, environmental, and historical forces with which they are competing in attempting to affect adolescents who exhibit the more severe patterns of drug abuse.

Curriculum. The Personal Change group thus tends to be more intense, interactive, and lengthy compared to the more information-oriented use-focussed groups. This is due primarily to the fact that students enter the former with greater denial, more severe problems and fewer competencies and resources with which to deal with them. Consequently, the agenda for the Personal Change Group is more complex, frequently incorporating all of the topics and strategies discussed earlier.

Evaluation and Follow-up. As with the informational groups, evaluation needs to be conducted to determine whether the group is having any effect on students and on their alcohol or other drug use in particular. The methods adopted to evaluate the Drug Information Group will apply to the Personal Change Groups as well.

Follow-up with individual students tends to be more long-term. To the extent, for example, that the outcome of the group for an individual student was intervention and a referral to treatment, leaders and other SAP staff will be maintaining regular contact with the student for some time to come. For other students, maintaining regular follow-up contacts with the facilitators or with the SAP Counselor/Coordinator is important. All students should be required to translate individual decisions made at the end of the group experience into a contract stating their intentions regarding future alcohol/drug use and what steps they will take to help them keep the contract. One-to-one meetings between the group leaders and former group members, on a bi-weekly or monthly basis, is one way of monitoring behavior changes and providing support when needed.

Other Use-Focussed Groups

Two other types of groups bear mention, each designed, again, to address students with somewhat different AODA-related needs.

Figure 11.1 depicted a third type of use-focussed group, the Drug Awareness Group, in order to acknowledge the fact that there are many students who lie in the middle of the continuum, who have gone past experimentation but who are not at risk for dependency and who are not in serious or visible trouble. Rather than designing and implementing a third group, the Drug Awareness Group is mentioned to make the point that groups need to be designed with the needs of students in mind. Students who are midway on the continuum can function equally well in a group designed for either extreme, provided group leaders adjust the goals, objectives, and curriculum of the group to make it more appropriate to students selected to be in it. On the other hand, larger school districts and high schools may very well be able to identify sufficient numbers of students as to justify the design and implementation of all three different types of initial use-focussed groups.

The fourth type of group, the Drug Free Support Group, is a *maintenance group*. Similar to the Recovery Support Group, this group is designed to provide support to students who have already made a decision to remain drug-free, and yet who need additional information, skills, and support in maintaining a drug-free lifestyle. Students will most commonly enter this group either as a result of self-referral to the SAP staff, or as a result of previous participation in one of the other groups (i.e., Affected Others, Drug Information). If previous group experience and AODA education can be taken for granted, then most of this group's activities revolve around coping with peer pressure and discovering meaningful alternatives to drug use. As with all groups, the group leaders must not allow it to become a merely a club or clique for kids who feel alienated because of their decision to remain drug-free. Students must be able to identify, perhaps with the help of leaders, specific goals and change objectives which they wish the help of a group in attaining. A major goal of the group, then, entails providing students with the skills in developing or broadening support systems which will decrease their reliance on a formal support group. Even such "maintenance groups" should be brief (six to twelve weeks) and time-limited.

Effective leadership of the use-focussed groups requires considerable personal preparation, including a thorough knowledge of fundamental alcohol/drug abuse concepts and experience in leading this type of AODA-specific group. Facilitators must be comfortable in encountering adolescents' resistance to being in the group and must be prepared to deal with it in a firm but caring manner. The Personal Change Group, especially, requires leaders to exhibit nonjudgemental but nonpermissive attitudes toward adolescent drug use. They must be able to set and enforce limits as to what constitutes acceptable behavior in the group. They must be prepared to confront student denial and defensiveness in a way that respects the strategies a student has had to adopt in order to survive, and which also communicates their care and concern for his safety, welfare, growth, and happiness. They must be comfortable in leveling with a student — giving him appropriate emotional feedback about his condition, his behavior, and his disclosures in the group. In all of this, the leaders must always strive to define and redefine their own personal and professional limitations and those of the support group.

Chapter 16 | # Supplement

Supplements 16.1 and 16.2 describe outlines for Drug Information Groups and Personal Change Groups, respectively. The outlines are intended only to be suggestive of the broad sequence of topics and activities typical of the groups at either extreme of the AODA continuum.

Supplement 16.1

OUTLINE FOR DRUG INFORMATION GROUPS

The Drug Information Group is intended for students at or near the experimentation end of the drug use continuum. As pointed out in Chapter 16, students frequently enter the group on the basis of self-referral and are in general more motivated to examine and change their alcohol/drug use on the basis of information and some personal sharing.

Some Drug Information Groups are abbreviated to consist of only four to six sessions, concentrating mainly on basic AODA information. (Sessions marked with an asterisk ("*") would be typical of such an abbreviated, didactic group). With only slight modifications, the agenda for the Drug Information Group can also be used for Drug Free Support Groups, placing more emphasis on topics related to alternative activities and peer refusal techniques.

Session 1: Group Formation (*)

The first session is devoted to getting acquainted, establishing the minimal group ground rules or expectations, review of a group contract if one has been required, and having students describe what brought them to the group. Leaders should explain in broad terms what the primary purpose of the group will be and provide an overview of the remaining sessions.

Session 2: Alcohol/Drug Use, Abuse, and Dependency (*)

Students are given information on the differences between drug use, abuse, and dependency, and the symptoms and dynamics typical of each stage. Johnson's "feeling chart" (Johnson, 1980) has shown itself to be an effective vehicle for presenting such information. A "names of drugs and what they do to the body" approach should be avoided. Instead, the leaders should stress the effects of alcohol and other drugs on the whole person: physical, mental, emotional, social, spiritual, etc.

Session 3: Self-Assessment (*)

Students are asked to describe and evaluate their own alcohol/drug use.

Students are assigned to complete a simple Drug History Questionnaire at the end of session 2. The questionnaire might list the various types of drugs along the left-hand margin; across the top are columns labeled "Date First Used," "Circumstances," "Current Frequency," and "Last Used." Students briefly describe their first and current experience with the various drugs listed.

Session 4: Self-Assessment, continued

The purpose of the session is to help students answer the question, "How do you know if someone has an alcohol/drug problem?" Drug histories are followed-up with questionnaires or assessment tools designed to allow students to evaluate the nature and severity of their alcohol/drug use. A number of sources contain assessment tools that can be utilized (e.g., Mayer and Filstead (1979), Alibrandi (1978)). Students complete questionnaires and discuss with the group what they discover.

Session 5: Drug Abuse and the Family (*)

The effects of chemical dependency on families and family members is presented, including descriptions of typical defensive patterns and enabling. Students are encouraged to identify ways in which others family members, peers, and/or school staff have enabled them.

Students' own enabling behavior toward other students are also discussed.

Students are also encouraged to discuss the degree to which they might be concerned about or affected by someone else's chemical use.

Session 6: Confrontation

The rationale behind the need to confront those about whom one has developed a concern is addressed. Denial and defenses may be discussed using a framework such as the Johari Window (Luft, 1966). Students often practice how to confront with care and concern in role plays.

Sessions 7 and 8: Peer Refusal Strategies

Responding to peer pressure is a concern of most students who are attempting to modify their chemical use or who have made a decision to remain drug-free. Situations in which students feel pressured to use chemicals are role-played to discover the feelings engendered by various refusal scripts which are defensive and involve blaming, placating, withdrawing, or preaching (Satir: 1972, pp. 59ff). Students identify and practice refusal strategies which are self- and other-affirming.

Session 9: Resources (*)

Additional sources of help, both within the school and the community, are reviewed. In-school resources most often consist of SAP Counselors and other support groups. Community-based AODA agencies are described, in addition to self-help groups such as AA, NA, CA, and Alateen. A panel presentation by students who have made use of these services is often part of this session.

Session 10: Goals and Decisions

The focus of the final session, in addition to group closure activities, is on having students formulate and verbalize specific short-term goals and decisions relating to their alcohol or other drug use. Students are also required to identify a plan of action for supporting them in achieving their goals. Group leaders often need to provide students with feedback regarding the appropriateness of these decisions.

Supplement 16.2

OUTLINE FOR THE PERSONAL CHANGE GROUP

The Personal Change Group can be the most complex and challenging of the AODA-related support groups. The students bring to the group a more severe pattern of alcohol/-drug abuse and higher degree of denial. The group achieves a mixture of prevention, intervention, and assessment outcomes. A group of this nature may exist as often in the community as it does within the school setting. This group typically consists of more sessions than other groups. Most vary between 12 and 18 meetings; many meet more than once per week.

As a use-focussed group, the Personal Change Group's primary purpose is to modify group members' alcohol drug use by focussing student's attention *intensively* on the place of alcohol and other drugs in their lives. This requires students to discuss their alcohol/drug experiences. Group leaders need to provide students with appropriate information about the use/abuse/dependency progression against which they can interpret their own and others' behavior. Leaders also need to educate the group concerning communication skills, confrontation, denial, and defenses in order to promote appropriate group interaction.

In view of the complexities of this group, many activities and agendas are possible. The most workable formats follow a logical progression. Attention is first focused on student's drug experiences, accompanied by lectures on the signs, symptoms, and dynamics typical of each stage. Discussion of drug experiences deepens gradually as the group develops, and attention to communication skills enhances member interaction. Reduced use contracts are often introduced at the beginning, becoming abstinence contracts by the fifth session. Discussion of contracts introduces each session. The final stages of the group are devoted to assisting students to take greater personal responsibility and ownership of their chemical use, through some combination of self and/or peer evaluation activities. The group concludes by focussing on conscious decisions for reduced use or abstinence. Group leaders present group members with feedback which may include recommendations for additional intervention steps.

The following outline is at best illustrative of activities which might comprise a Personal Change Group.

Session 1: Group Formation

The first session is devoted to getting acquainted, establishing minimal group ground rules and expectations, a review of the basic group contract (see Supplement 13.2), and outlining the general purpose and format of the group. Group members should describe the circumstances which brought them into the group. Leaders should reinforce the fact that even though some students may be in the group in lieu of other consequences, they nevertheless have chosen to be there. The Drug History assignment is explained.

Session 2: Initial Alcohol/Drug Experiences

Leaders may give a brief lecture on the progression of chemical use from experimentation to regular use. The purpose of the session is to have students begin to make disclosures about their alcohol/drug experiences. Each student briefly describes first experiences with each of the major mood altering chemicals, according to a Drug History Questionnaire each has completed. Students are assigned to complete a similar questionnaire, describing current alcohol/drug use.

Session 3: Current Drug Use

The focus is on current alcohol/drug use, as described in the assignment. Students describe current use patterns (kinds, amounts, frequencies, circumstances) and how these have changed since their first alcohol/drug experiences.

Session 4: Harmful Consequences

Leaders present a brief lecture on the stages of abuse and dependency. Students describe incidents when chemical use has resulted, to some degree, in consequences which they now judge to be harmful, painful, or unplanned. Discussion centers around occasions when chemical use has interfered with relationships with parents or other family members, friends, physical and emotional well-being, attainment of goals, school performance, job performance, etc. While no attempt is made to label a student as having a "drug problem," leaders underscore incidents demonstrating a direct relationship between chemical use and negative consequences.

Session 5: Contracts

Abstinence contracts may be introduced at this time. Leaders explain the purpose of contracts and ground rules surrounding them (e.g., the obligation to discuss in group difficulties in keeping the contracts). Students ask other group members to serve as an informal support system when they feel inclined to break the contract. Peer pressure and high risk situations may be discussed. Students sign formal, written contracts.

Session 6 and 7: Feelings and Defenses

Two sessions may be devoted to a more focussed discussion of interpersonal communication. The Johari Window (Luft, 1966) has proven to be an effective metaphor for discussing defenses, self-disclosure, denial, and confrontation skills which enhance knowing and being known. Role-playing student/counselor, student/parent, and other confrontational situations foregrounds feelings and introduces effective confrontational strategies.

Session 8: Drugs and Lifestyle

Discussion centers around the amount of time and other resources students invest in obtaining and using alcohol and other drugs. Exercises such as "Twenty Things You Love to Do" (Simon et al., p. 30) can be adapted to include coding for activities where drugs are used (DU). A similar exercise (or journal assignment) can be developed which asks students to indicate the amount of time they spend in various activities. Attention is focussed on how significant alcohol and other drugs are to a student by noting the proportion of time and other resources that is directly involved in their use.

Session 9: Alternatives

The preceding activity leads to an examination of alternative ways of achieving personal rewards which do not involve drug use. Students should contract to try alternative activities in succeeding weeks. Some group leaders have found that effective alternatives involve students in personal investments in and contact with other people — i.e., volunteer work.

Session 10: Recovery Panel

The session is devoted to listening to a panel made up of young people who are either recovering or who have made decisions to stay drug-free. Panel members describe the circumstances which led up to their decision to remain drug-free and how they maintain abstinence, and respond to group members' questions.

Sessions 11 and 12: Personal Assessment

The personal assessment is more intensive than that carried on in the Drug Information Group. A number of strategies adopted from the treatment community have proven to be useful.

First, Sessions 11 and 12 can incorporate two assignments adapted from the fourth and fifth steps of Alcoholics Anonymous. The "Personal Inventory" assignment requires students to make a list of all of the times, places, and occasions when their chemical use has harmed themselves or others, including the feelings that the incidents aroused. The next assignment, "Disclosure and Ownership," involves students in sharing their concern about their own chemical use, contained in the lists they have drawn up, with another adult outside of the group. Sessions 11 and 12 are used to explain the assignments and to discuss the results.

Second, Sessions 11 and 12 can utilize the "peer review" strategy commonly used in treatment programs. Students take turns presenting to the group their conclusions regarding the nature and seriousness of their alcohol/drug use and what they need to do differently. Leaders and other group members are allowed to ask questions. Each group member responds to the student with his or her own assessment and recommendation.

In groups consisting of more session, both strategies may be used. In any case, these techniques require considerable preparation by the group leaders.

Session 13: Resources

Session 13 is devoted to a discussion of resources for further help that are available in the school and the community.

Session 14: Decisions and Closure

The final session is utilized to allow students to acknowledge what has happened in the group, and to announce their intentions and decisions regarding the future as it relates to their alcohol/drug use. Specific verbal commitments for abstinence or reductions in use are discussed, as well as plans for support. Group leaders and group members provide each group member with appropriate feedback and recommendations. Goup leaders may need to see some students on a one-to-one basis, especially where a recommendation for formal assessment or treatment emerges from their experience of the student in the group.

Part 4

The Process of Program Implementation

Thus far we have examined the Student Assistance Program Model by defining the needs of those it is intended to assist, the essential program functions it must perform, and some characteristic structures, roles, procedures, and services that permit the school system actually to provide help to students who have AODA-related problems. In Part Four, The Process of Program Implementation, we will focus on the process of bringing such a program into being. Chapter 17 introduces the major tasks in the implementation process, each of which is described in more detain in Chapters 18 through 23.

The implementation process can be analyzed into at least six major tasks. Planning and organizing activities result when the initial awareness of student AODA-related problems by a minority of persons in the school district begins to be expanded to include others. One of the more crucial steps requires the development of a new philosophy and policy language which will establish the direction of the program and will organize and integrate its roles, structures, and procedures. Next, many practical program design decisions need to be made, based on analyzing needs, developing a budget and an implementation timeline, securing final Board of Education Approval, and the development of goals and objectives. Training of Core Teams and Core Group members gives substance to the form which has evolved out of the planning process. A program can usually be though of as operating when the policy legitimizing it has been enacted, the roles and procedures have been defined, and when key staff receive training enabling them to perform their roles effectively. Promoting the program, or increasing student, staff, parent, and community awareness of it and the issues it is to address is often the next important step. Finally, effort has to be invested in evaluating the program's impact on the numbers of those in need, its effectiveness at bringing about change, and the efficiency of its processes.

An Overview
of The Implementation Process

The scope of any particular school system's realization of the Student Assistance Program Model should be apparent from what has been discussed thus far. The program will have an impact on the school system and the various subsystems of which it is most immediately composed: students, teaching staff, pupil services staff, building administrators, central administration, and the Board of Education. It will also have an impact on parents, local AODA agencies, law enforcement, the juvenile justice and social services systems, and various other segments of the community. Just as apparent is the fact that the school system will be able to implement, operate, and maintain its program to the extent that it has the cooperation and support of all of the groups involved. The process of implementing such a comprehensive, joint school/community effort is also likely to be complex. Before examining some of the discrete tasks involved in implementing a student assistance program, a look at some general considerations is in order.

The Implementation Cycle. For purposes of exposition the implementation tasks are arranged here in an order that is logical, but not necessarily chronological. The order of the major tasks and their associated activities is not necessarily rigid. If anything, the implementation process is more cyclic than linear in several ways. While these steps constitute those which must be accomplished in order to have a well-made program, the school system may begin the process at almost any point. In one school system, for example, the process might begin by providing a staff inservice on alcohol and other drug abuse and asking interested staff to join in the formation of a "Core Committee." In another, the process could begin with school staff going around to community groups to enlist their support. In still another, routine revisions of AODA policy language may initiate the rest of the process. In many school systems, an intensive Core Group training workshop provides the impetus and background information around which the initial planning and organization occur.

The implementation process is also cyclical in that it does not end. Implementation consists of three stages: initial implementation, program operation, and program maintenance. Each corresponds in a very general way to first, second, and third year activities. Thus, many school systems will accomplish all of the basic tasks during the first year of initial implementation activity. The program should be examined, during its operation, with the same tasks in mind. Similarly, the implementation tasks represent an evaluation checklist which may guide the district in the subsequent years of program maintenance.

Gradualism.

School systems are well-advised to take their time in implementing a student assistance program. Not only may the accomplishment of various tasks take time, but the changes the program seeks to make among those in the school environment will be even more gradual. For example, to the extent that full utilization of the program's services depends on its credibility with staff, students, and parents, it may take several years for this credibility to be earned.

"Re-inventing the Wheel."

In other words, a school district cannot have another district's student assistance program. The success of another district's program may provide the impetus, but each district must evolve its own realization of some basic model. No model will ever suit exactly the unique context provided by each community. Moreover, the SAP acronym should probably stand for "Student Assistance Process." In some key ways, the process a school district goes through is probably more important than the model or structure at which it ultimately arrives.

School District A, for example, has had a student assistance program for seven years. In its initial years its focus was primarily upon alcohol and other drug abuse. In the intervening years, District A has significantly eliminated many of the dynamics of denial, enabling, and resistance in staff, students, and the community. As it gained experience and was able to take for granted that AODA issues would be handled competently, District A's program was gradually expanded to include other problems: teenage pregnancy, suicide, child abuse, and other children-at-risk issues. District A now refers to its "broad brush" Student Assistance Program.

District B hears about District A's program and wishes to implement one just like it. District B, however, only has immediate access to the outward manifestation and final product of a process which took several years to evolve. District B does not have any immediate access to the District A's history. Basing its program notions only on District A's current practice is like wanting a college degree without attending four years of school. Or, in terms of the analogy of Chapter 1, a school system cannot have another district's recovery: it can discover its own recovery process on the way to its own program.

Recovery Entails Conflict.

As painful and dysfunctional as the chemically dependent family can become, it and its members still organize their resources to maintain an equilibrium which will allow it to function. The recovery of the dependent person or of only one family member significantly disrupts this equilibrium. It frequently replaces old conflicts with new ones, as family members learn how to readjust their behavior to new circumstances. Health requires dropping old defensive patterns, replacing enabling with being responsible for oneself, taking risks, and so on.

The process of implementing a student assistance program will, to a similar degree, disrupt the equilibrium of the school system and the community. It may foreground dysfunctions in subsystems previously hidden or thought to be resolved. Old mistrust issues, turf issues, blaming, placating, withdrawing, and other defensive postures which may have acquired the force of habit and the guise of normalcy are now exposed. Paradoxically, individuals, groups, and the system as a whole may feel less "safe" while implementing a program than they did before. What are voiced, for example, as concerns about legal liability or confidentiality are often projections of more personal and deep-seated fears, or statements that it is not safe to take risks here.

It is important that those involved in the implementation process appreciate the degree to which the implementation of a student assistance program can disturb this status quo. Such personal and emotional issues are not resolved by board policy or an administrator's decree. Program implementers need to recognize and address the conflicts foregrounded during the process with the same sensitivity and respect with which they would treat the same issues in a recovering family.

Implementation as Recovery.

Thus, there at least two complementary ways of looking at the implementation process. On one hand, as presented in Chapter 1, the implementation, process can be regarded as a series of "recovery" steps, involving (1) the decision to recognize the nature and scope of the AODA problem, (2) acquiring accurate AODA information, (3) enhancing the district's climate and self-image, (4) examining the ways in which the school system unwittingly enables AODA-related problems to continue, (5) changing a variety of enabling dynamics in terms of policy, structure, and behavior, (6) learning to confront problems appropriately, and (7) defining and acccepting personal, professional, and institutional limitations in addressing students' AODA-related problems.

On the other hand, as described in the remaining chapters of Part Four, the process can be regarded as a series of tasks or steps — a somewhat mechanical sequence involving (1) planning and organizing, (2) drafting philosophy and policy language, (3) making program design decisions, (4) training key school staff and community members, (5) promoting the program to students, staff, parents, and the community, and (6) evaluating the program's effectiveness. These two parallel processes are clearly related, the first addressing the personal, affective, and behavioral changes which need to occur, and the latter describing major organizational tasks which need to be accomplished. While the discussion below is devoted to examining the mechanical, "cookbook" steps of program implementation, at each step in the implementation process those implementing programs will need to bear in mind the more affective recovery issues as well.

Planning and Organizing

To borrow an analogy from classical drama, the "inciting moment" — or event which precipitates the dramatic action — occurs early in the play and can come from a variety of unexpected sources. The initial impetus for the development of a student assistance program can also arise from many sources in a number of ways. Often the impetus arises from within the school. One or more staff members may become aware of the Student Assistance Model through a conference, workshop, or training event. Frequently school districts hear of the SAP model as a result of another district's promotional activity. Most recently, the federal government has once again focussed national attention on student drug-related problems. Sometimes a critical incident — a drug bust, an overdose, a suicide — captures everyone's initial attention. The source of interest can also come initially from the community. Local parent AODA task forces, community AODA advisory committees, Chemical People groups, or service clubs may begin to focus attention on coping with such problems within the school setting. Occasionally the initial contact with the school or the community may come through a consultant from an AODA agency.

In general, the first major implementation task involves broadening the scope of initial awareness in order to begin planning and organizing activities in preparation for the remaining implementation tasks. Regardless of the source of initial awareness, one of the first activities consists of expanding initial awareness on the part of key personnel in the school system of the nature and scope of student AODA-related problems, and of the availability of a more effective alternative or complement to what may already be going on: a comprehensive student assistance approach.

Many of the activities at this stages are simultaneously devoted to increasing the number of people involved and providing them with appropriate and accurate information about the nature and extent of student AODA-related problems and the nature of a more effective and comprehensive response. The following are thus among the activities typical of the planning and organizing stage:

• Conducting a preliminary needs estimate (as opposed to a formal needs assessment) which more accurately reflects the scope of student alcohol/drug use and related problems;

• Meeting with representatives of the administration and pupil services staff to present these needs and the SAP model as a response to them;

• Forming an initial "Core Committee," "Implementation Group," etc., made up of administration, pupil services staff, members of the Board of Education, and other interested persons, in order to examine feasibility of implementing a student assistance program;

• Making presentations to staff, parents, AODA agencies, and service clubs, and other community groups to enlist their involvement and/or support;

• Identifying local AODA resources for screening, assessment, and treatment of students;

• Identifying potential sources of SAP training, and consultation.

• Making presentations to the Board of Education, securing its permission to proceed with exploring the SAP model and to return with a formal proposal at a later date.

Ideally, as a result of activities aimed at widening the sphere of initial awareness, a group of key school personnel will have been assembled which can take the leadership in planning and directing the remaining implementation steps. The "Core Committee" is often the nucleus around which the SAP Core Group gradually forms. Community involvement in the student assistance implementation process is important, and should be sought as early as possible.

Policy Development

The district needs to develop policy language which deals effectively with student AODA-related problems. The Core Committee or a working subgroup, including Board of Education representation, often takes responsibility for

- Examining current AODA policies;

- Evaluating the effectiveness and appropriateness of current policies

- Examining current patterns of enforcement of AODA policies;

- Looking at examples from other districts with student assistance programs;

- Drafting new policy language to be recommended to the Board of Education later.

The development of an appropriate policy statement can be a time consuming task, given the complexity of AODA issues, student needs, legal implications, community standards, internal values, and the climate of the school board.

Many issues have to be examined and resolved to arrive at appropriate policy language. Consensus needs to be arrived at regarding, among other things,

- A schedule of consequences for first and subsequent AODA offenses;

- Conditions under which suspension and expulsion will be recommended or held in abeyance;

- The interaction of violations of school AODA policies with referral to the student assistance program;

- Provisions for self-referral;

- Confidentiality, as it covers students and parents in addition to referral sources;

- The involvement of law enforcement;

- Provisions for parent information and/or consent for students' involvement in support groups;

- The interaction of the student assistance program, school AODA policy, and athletics.

Many schools are now adopting co-curricular codes as part of a student assistance program. Co-curricular codes recognize that consequences for alcohol and other drug use should extend to all students who are involved in extracurricular activities, and should not be limited just to athletes.

Many other issues currently face those attempting to develop more effective policies against student alcohol and other drug abuse. While not immediately germane to the student assistance program in its entirety, discussions around school policy will invariably touch on the conditions for legitimate search and seizure activity. As this is being written, pressure is mounting for drug testing of students.

In addition to its policy stance, it is also recommended that the school system devote some time to developing a statement of its philosophy regarding student alcohol and other drug abuse. Whereas policy language consists mainly of "if/then" statements, philosophy language is a statement of the school system's values and beliefs. Development of a brief philosophy statement involves key school representatives in an examination of basic beliefs and values upon which many aspects of their student assistance program will be based: the role of the school, the nature of drug abuse as opposed to the disease of chemical dependency, abstinence from alcohol and other drug use as the norm for school-aged youth, and so on. The philosophy language is important because it allows the school another vehicle for communicating about the program later to students, staff, parents, and the community.

It is wise for the school district to provide for several levels of review of the suggested philosophy and policy language by administration, staff, students, and parents. Emerging from the policy development process should be a provisional document which is shared with as many other key segments of the school system as possible for input: teaching staff, students, parent representatives community groups, youth-serving agencies, etc. This provisional language is ultimately submitted to the Board of Education for its examination and approval.

Program Design

Although a good idea of the form of its program develops as result of the activity thus far, many specific decisions still need to be made. The roles of various persons in the program need to be clarified and formalized, the needs assessment process is carried further, decisions are made regarding support groups and procedures, and the remaining implementation steps are laid out. Thus, among the major activities characteristics of the program design phase would be the following:

- The needs assessment process is often carried further to develop realistic estimates of the prevalence of student AODA-related problems.

- The needs assessment is also focussed on evaluating the school system in terms of the basic program functions: how are students currently identified, assessed, referred for community services? What treatment services exist in the community and what is the quality of their working relationship with those in the school system? What support services will be made available to students?

- Specific student-centered goals and objectives for the program are written for each target group;

- The identification of the members of Core Teams should take place if it has not already done so. Core Teams in each building should be established, consisting minimally of the building administrators and pupil services staff members. Others who express an interest in becoming involved may be included: interested teachers, coaches, etc. (See Chapter 6).

- The designation of building-level SAP Coordinator(s) and definition of their roles;

- The designation of building-level SAP Counselors and definition of their roles;

- The designation of a district-wide SAP Program Administrator;

Support groups typically involve a host of additional decisions:

- Who will lead support groups? How many groups will be needed in each building? Which groups will be implemented will first?

- How many group facilitators will be needed? How will group leaders be selected? What are the training needs of support group facilitators?

Goals also need to be developed for the remaining implementation steps, including

- A timeline for the remaining implementation tasks;

- A three-year budget for the program.

Often, the major product of the program design stage is a formal proposal to the Board of Education, with a request that it formally endorse the philosophy and policy language and the student assistance program. This proposal may be a comprehensive written program description, a grant request to another funding source, or a simple implementation proposal.

Core Group Development

Throughout this process, the school may have been gradually identifying, expanding, and formalizing its district-wide Core Group, made up of the members of the various building-level Core Teams as well as community representatives. Training in various degrees may also have occurred at previous points. The major task of Core Group development, however, involves training for all of those who will have key roles to play in the program. Training for Core Group members involves a number of decisions:

- Identifying participants for Core Group Training from the school system and the community;

- Identifying training objectives;

- Identifying, evaluating, and selecting training resources;

- Developing an agenda for onsite Core Group Training in consultation with training resources;

- Scheduling and conducting Core Group Training;

Core Group Training should lead to a clear understanding among participants of their respective roles in the student assistance program. Initial training should be comprehensive, covering basic three major areas:

basic alcohol/drug concepts and competencies, skills related to various roles in the student assistance program, and opportunities to assess personal experiences and attitudes. Aside from providing a common basis in AODA concepts for participants, one of the major purposes of Core Group training is team development. It should thus provide opportunities for interaction which will enhance the functioning of individual Core Teams and the Core Group as a whole.

The process of Core group development also involves the identification of additional training needs: e.g., for support group facilitation skills, assessment and intervention skills, etc., for persons who will have such specialized functions within the program.

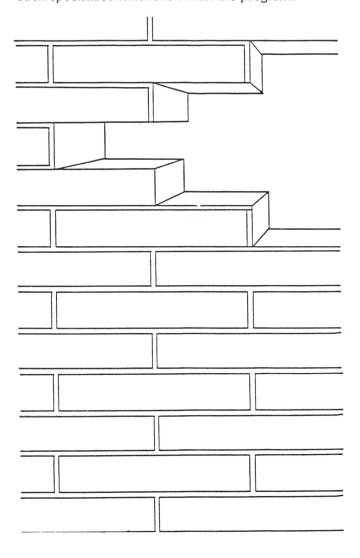

Program Promotion

Formal Board endorsement of the policy and the program, followed by intensive Core Group training, often constitute the major benchmarks of program implementation, after which a program can be considered operational, or ready to begin offering services to students.

To further widen interest and participation specific steps aimed at enhancing the awareness of the program among students, staff, parents, and the community also need to be taken:

- The program needs to be formally announced to **students**. They will also need to be informed of the specifics of the program: its policies and procedures, its staff, and its services (e.g., support groups). Informal classroom presentations by members of the building Core team can also be used as an opportunity to provide students with minimal education in basic AODA concepts and an opportunity for them to ask questions. A special brochure describing the program is distributed to students as well.

- The program needs to be formally announced to all **staff**. Staff inservices typically cover basic information on alcohol and other drug abuse, the program's policies, procedures, and services, explanations of the staff member's role in the program, and directions on how and when to refer students.

- The program needs to be formally announced to **parents**. An informational cover letter, together with the school's AODA philosophy and policy statement, are often mailed to all parents. Many schools design and distribute student assistance program brochures to students and parents alike. Workshops, seminars, or information nights for parents can supplement written announcements.

- Various segments of the **community** as a whole need to be informed about the school's student assistance program. A series of evening seminars covering basic topics from Core group training are frequently offered to enhance alcohol/drug awareness as well as to promote the school's program. Individual members of the Core Teams or the Core Group should also seek to meet personally with service clubs and community agencies to further promote the program.

Program Evaluation

Evaluation activities occur throughout program implementation, operation, and maintenance. As part of its plan submitted to the Board of Education, for example, those planning the program will have identified a time line for implementation. Such a timeline is an explicit statement of goals and objectives for the implementation *process*. Later, during the program's initial operation, specific, measurable goals and objectives for various program components will have to be evaluated. In addition to process objectives, for example, the school will need to develop specific goals concerning the program's *impact*, or the number of students it will serve in relation to the number of students identified as in need. It will also need to develop objectives which deal with the program's *effectiveness*, or ways in which students are different as a result of their participation in the program.

"A school system cannot have another district's recovery: it can discover its own recovery process on the way to its own program."

The results of evaluation are used in two major ways. Evaluation data leads to defining and redefining goals for the remaining maintenance phase of the program, including ways in which the program needs to be expanded, cut back, or changed. More generally, the data the program generates is used to continue communicating with others about the program. Results are regularly presented to the Board of Education, students, staff, and the community to maintain the program's visibility and to enhance its credibility with each group.

Thus, the following are typically involved in program evaluation activities:

• Clarifying annual goals and objectives involving measurement of process, impact, and effectiveness;

• Designing a data collection system, including forms, evaluation criteria, and a collection process;

• Collecting data periodically;

• Meeting regularly to analyze and interpret program data;

• Preparing reports on the program's progress for the staff and the Board of Education;

• Utilizing evaluation data in continued promotional activity to students, staff, parents, and the community;

• Utilizing evaluation data to plan revisions in the program.

The paramount task facing those seeking to implement a student assistance program involves constantly seeking to enlarge their numbers, increasing participation from as many segments of the school and community as possible, and providing them with the information they require in order to accomplish these implementation steps.

Chapter 17 | # Supplements

The Program Implementation Activities Checklist on the following pages can be used for a number of purposes. On the one hand, it can be viewed as a partial list of the tasks that typically are accomplished in the course of implementing a Student Assistance Program. The list of 12 categories is presented in a somewhat logical, or idealized, sequence and corresponds roughly to the major implementation steps discussed in Chapter 17. The list should not, however, be construed as prescribing any necessary chronological order.

On the other hand, the checklist can be seen as a partial list of suggested ways in which staff and community members can become involved if they were not originally part of a program's implementation or operation. Activities typical of the Initial Implementation, Operation, or Maintenance phases of implementation are keyed "I," "O," and "M," respectively.

Supplement 17.1

PROGRAM IMPLEMENTATION ACTIVITIES CHECKLIST

*Or, A Partial List of the At Least 1000 Things
That Need Doing*

I. PLANNING and INITIAL AWARENESS

I   [ ]   1. Review Student Assistance Program efforts of other districts.

I   [ ]   2. Collect written program descriptions of Student Assistance Program models.

I   [ ]   3. Form an ad hoc concept committee, "Core Committee," "interest group," etc. (administrators, counselors, etc.)

I   [ ]   4. Perform preliminary needs assessment (prevalence estimates, etc.)

I   [ ]   5. Prepare for an initial presentation of the student assistance program concept to Board of Education.

I   [ ]   6. Present initial proposal to BOE; secure permission to proceed and return with a formal proposal.

I   [ ]   7. Present initial proposal to community groups (service clubs, church groups, local government, business leaders, parents groups, staff, etc.)

II. PHILOSOPHY AND POLICY

I O M   [ ]   8. Become a member of the Core Group

I O M   [ ]   9. Review existing policies regarding alcohol and other drug abuse

I O M   [ ]   10. Review existing athletic codes regarding alcohol and other drug use

I O M   [ ]   11. Examine existing procedures for managing students with AODA-related problems

I O M   [ ]   12. Analyze specific "case histories" of how students were treated in the past year to evaluate effectiveness of existing policies and procedures

I   [ ]   13. Review model policies, or policies of other school systems

I M   [ ]   14. Prepare draft of revised AODA philosophy and policy

I M   [ ]   15. Prepare draft of new procedures for AODA problems

III. PROGRAM DESIGN

I   [   ]   16. Identify building Core Teams

I O M   [   ]   17. Identify additional Core Group members

I O M   [   ]   18. Identify potential "contact persons"

I   [   ]   19. Identify district-wide SAP Program Director and define coordination responsibilities for program implementation

I   [   ]   20. Identify building-level SAP Coordinator(s) and define coordination responsibilities for program implementation and operation

I   [   ]   21. Designate building-level SAP Counselors and "contact persons" and define their roles in program operation

I O M   [   ]   22. Become familiar with AODA agencies and their services

I   [   ]   23. Develop goals and objectives for program implementation

I O M   [   ]   24. Develop specific student-centered goals and objectives for each AODA-related target group

I O   [   ]   25. Plan implementation of support groups (who will be leaders, which groups first, at what grade levels, etc.

I   [   ]   26. Prepare an implementation timeline

I   [   ]   27. Prepare a budgetary estimate covering at least one year for implementation and two years of program operation

I O M   [   ]   28. Identify other funding sources, including state and local government grants, corporate grants, etc.

I O M   [   ]   29. Write grants

I   [   ]   30. Make presentation to Board of Education for its approval, including:

- Needs for program
- Draft of policy and procedures
- Goals and objectives
- Budget implications
- Funding sources
- Endorsements

IV. CORE GROUP DEVELOPMENT

I O M   [   ]   31. Identify persons to be trained, including:

- Building-level Core Teams and other interested staff
- School Board members
- Community task force members
- Supportive parents
- Interested students
- AODA agency staff
- Social services agency staff
- Criminal justice system personnel

                                    - Clergy
                                    - Community leaders
                                    - Business leaders
                                    - Service club representatives
                                    - Media (TV, Radio, and press)

I O M [ ] 32. Identify training objectives

I O M [ ] 33. Identify potential training resources

I O M [ ] 34. Select training resource and determine training agenda, location, etc.

I O M [ ] 35. Schedule Core Group Training

I O M [ ] 36. Advertise Core Group Training

I O M [ ] 37. Hold Training

V. STUDENT SUPPORT GROUPS

I   [ ] 38. Identify suitable locations for groups in various buildings

I O M [ ] 39. Identify Group Facilitators

  O M [ ] 40. Co-lead a concerned-person group

  O M [ ] 41. Co-lead a recovery support group

  O M [ ] 42. Co-lead a "use-focussed" group

I O M [ ] 43. Assist in the development of group materials

I O M [ ] 44. Assist in the development of a group handbook for students

I O M [ ] 45. Assist in the development of a group information packet for staff

I   [ ] 46. Write group policies and procedures (e.g., confidentiality, release
                    from class, reporting abuse and neglect, parent information/
                    consent, etc.)

I O M [ ] 47. Substitute for group facilitators who are classroom teachers

I O M [ ] 48. Develop goals and objectives for groups

I O M [ ] 49. Design an evaluation system for groups

I O M [ ] 50. Design evaluation forms and/or instruments

  O M [ ] 51. Collect evaluation data on groups

  O M [ ] 52. Compile evaluation data

  O M [ ] 53. Analyze group evaluation data

  O M [ ] 54. Write evaluation reports

O M [ ] 55. Coordinate with district-wide program evaluation efforts

O M [ ] 56. Communicate results on group outcomes and effectiveness to staff, students, Board of Education, and community

I O M [ ] 57. Assist in classroom presentations on support groups

O M [ ] 58. Assist in the screening of students for support groups

I O M [ ] 59. Establish contacts with AODA agencies for referrals from groups

I O M [ ] 60. Establish contacts with local self-help groups (e.g., Alcoholics Anonymous, Narcotics Anonymous, Al-Anon, Alateen, etc.)

VI. CASE MANAGEMENT

O M [ ] 61. Interview students referred to the program

O M [ ] 62. Contact or interview parents of referred students

O M [ ] 63. Collect background data on student referrals (review records)

O M [ ] 64. Interview staff concerning referred students

O M [ ] 65. Screen students for support groups

O M [ ] 66. Belong to school assessment team

O M [ ] 67. Maintain contacts with AODA education, assessment, and treatment agencies

O M [ ] 68. Attend discharge staffings for students in treatment

O M [ ] 69. Meet with school staff to clarify expectations when students re-enter school from treatment

O M [ ] 70. Conduct re-entry interviews with recovering students and parents

I O M [ ] 71. Clarify school policies and procedures for reporting child abuse and neglect

I O M [ ] 72. Maintain minimal records of student participation in student assistance program activities

I O M [ ] 73. Participate in districtand/or building-level evaluation efforts

O M [ ] 74. Review progress to redefine goals, assess procedures, etc.

VII. WORK WITH AODA AGENCIES

I   [ ] 75. Contact AODA agencies in initial stages of program planning for support

I O M [ ] 76. Identify and evaluate AODA consultation resources

I O M [ ] 77. Identify and evaluate AODA training resources

I O M [ ] 78. Identify, visit, and evaluate AODA assessment resources for students and families

I O M [ ] 79. Identify, visit, and evaluate AODA treatment resources

　O M [ ] 80. Determine availability of AODA agency staff for training, in-school assessments, consultation, etc.

I O M [ ] 81. Develop contacts with self-help groups in the community

VIII. PROGRAM PROMOTION: STUDENTS

I O M [ ] 82. Introduce program through classroom presentations

I O M [ ] 83. Integrate relevant AODA concepts into classroom curriculum

I O M [ ] 84. Work with district-wide AODA curriculum committee

I O M [ ] 85. Work with students to design promotional posters

I O M [ ] 86. Assist student newspaper in publishing AODA program-related articles

I O M [ ] 87. Work with student council on ways to promote the program

I O M [ ] 88. Explain program and policies to school clubs

I O M [ ] 89. Participate in informational sessions for all students who are participating in extracurricular activities and their parents

I O M [ ] 90. Develop a list of books, pamphlets, etc., for school library

I O M [ ] 91. Write or purchase AODA pamphlets for students and help with distribution

IX. PROGRAM PROMOTION: STAFF

I O M [ ] 92. Work with school inservice committee to plan AODA inservices

I O M [ ] 93. Conduct periodic staff inservices on AODA

　O M [ ] 94. Lead support groups for interested staff

　O M [ ] 95. Periodically report on program to staff

I O M [ ] 96. Prepare articles for district newsletter

I O M [ ] 97. Write, edit, and/or assist with the printing and distribution of a "Student Assistance Program Newsletter"

X. PROGRAM PROMOTION: PARENTS

I O M [ ] 98. Speak to parent organizations on AODA issues and program progress

O M　[ ]　99. Form and/or facilitate parent support group along the lines of Al-Anon, Tough Love, or Families Anonymous

I O M　[ ]　100. Assist with design, printing, and fund-raising for a brochure which advertises the program to parents

I O M　[ ]　101. Prepare a form letter to all parents as part of the initial announcement of the program

I O M　[ ]　102. Hold periodic "parent information nights" on AODA issues

I O M　[ ]　103. Maintain a list of parent-contact persons willing to speak to other concerned parents

XI. PROGRAM PROMOTION: COMMUNITY

I O M　[ ]　104. Give informational presentations to community groups (business organizations, churches, service clubs, local government, etc.)

I O M　[ ]　105. Serve on community task force, advisory committee, etc. for AODA issues

I O M　[ ]　106. Develop personal contacts within local media-radio, TV, press

I O M　[ ]　107. Prepare press releases announcing the program

I O M　[ ]　108. Plan and conduct an "AODA Awareness Week" for school and community persons

I O M　[ ]　109. Design and print a brochure explaining the program, and distribute to all local agencies serving youth

XII. PROGRAM EVALUATION

I　　　　[ ]　110. Identify persons to plan for program evaluation

I　　　　[ ]　111. Decide on scope of evaluation and prepare an evaluation plan

I O M　[ ]　112. Examine the feasibility of using computers to assist in evaluation

I O M　[ ]　113. Identify hardware and software requirements

I O M　[ ]　114. Identify goals and objectives of the program in areas of students, staff, parents, and the community

I O M　[ ]　115. Identify evaluation coordinator(s)

I O M　[ ]　116. Devise a data collection strategy (forms, etc.)

　O M　[ ]　117. Collect and analyze data

　　M　[ ]　118. Revise program activities, goals, and objectives in the light of data

　O M　[ ]　119. Prepare evaluation reports

O M [ ] 120. Report on program progress frequently to students, staff, parents, community, and Board of Education

I O M [ ] 121. Prepare news releases to media on program progress

XIII. MISCELLANEOUS

O M [ ] 122. Serve as a "contact person" for student self-referrals

I O M [ ] 123. Preview films and other audiovisual materialsappropriate for staff, student, and community

I O M [ ] 124. Compile directory of AODA resources and other resources in the community

I O M [ ] 125. Assist in fund-raising

I O M [ ] 126. Serve as a member of the school district's core group

I O M [ ] 127. Help to form and/or advise a school-based "speakers bureau" of persons (including students) who can speak to school and community groups

O M [ ] 128. Volunteer to drive students to aftercare meetings, or AA, NA, Al-Anon, and Alateen meetings

O M [ ] 129. Volunteer to be a staff advisor for a student/staff, 24-hour AODA telephone crisis line

O M [ ] 130. Recruit and coordinate a pool of parent volunteers to work with other parents or students

O M [ ] 131. Help to form an SAP Support Group for representatives from all local school districts engaged in SAP approaches

Planning and Organizing for Program Implementation

A parsimonious cowboy entered a harness shop and asked for only one spur.

"What use is one spur?" asked the clerk.

"Well," replied the cowboy, "I figure if I can get one side of the horse to go, the other side is likely to follow."

Family members can intervene on behalf of one of their members' chemical dependency in many ways. The most effective strategies rely on seeing the process of intervention and family recovery as being essentially the same. In part, preparing family members for a formal intervention strategy consists of strengthening them to become more emotionally adequate to the intervention process.

In the process of family recovery it is often one family member who initiates the recovery process by seeking outside help. As pointed out in Chapter 1, the first step in a family's recovery — *the decision to recognize* — can be a complicated one. This decision to recognize involves many factors: finally seeing alcohol and other drug as the focal problem, realizing that it has been going on for a long time, that it is getting worse and will not go away by itself, admitting that one's past attempts to deal with it have been inadequate, and deciding to get help. The next step — acquiring accurate information — often occurs after becoming involved with alcohol and other drug abuse resources such as a counselor, a local agency, or Al-Anon. Here, one or more family members receive appropriate information about what has been happening to the dependent person, to them, and to the family system: the nature of the disease of chemical dependency, its symptoms and progression, the nature of chemical dependency as a family illness, the dynamics of denial and enabling, what the recovery process involves, and so on.

At some point in these initial contacts the therapist or counselor will ask the family member two vital questions: (1) Who are the people around the dependent person who are most meaningful to him? and (2) Can you get them together in my office next time? The goal is to form an intervention team and prepare its members for a formal intervention event. At the same time the enabling factors of the environment, or family context, are addressed. With the support for active chemical use diminished, it becomes less possible for chemical dependency to continue.

In some ways the process of implementing a student assistance program parallels the process of intervening in chemical dependency in the family. Instead of the family being the intervention context and the dependent person its focus, our context is the school system, and the way in which it has been affected by alcohol and other drug abuse becomes the focus of intervention.

Thus, one or more individuals in the school system have also reached the "decision to recognize" point. They begin to see the nature and scope of student alcohol/drug-related problems; they acknowledge that is has been going on for a long time, is getting worse, and will not spontaneously go away by itself. They also recognize that past and current strategies have been ineffective, or are at least inadequate compared to the magnitude of the problem. They also discover that they need help. They begin the process of "acquiring accurate information, perhaps through a workshop, training seminar, or AODA conference. They may also discover that the Student Assistance model represents a workable and effective alternative.

At some point those initiating the student assistance process will need to ask themselves the same two questions that the therapist asks the newly recovering family member: (1) *Who are the key people in the school system "family?"* and (2) *Can we get them together, physically as well as conceptually, to begin the process of implementing the program?* Building this "Core Committee" is the first goal of the planning and organizing stage of program implementation. Its major tasks will involve conducting a preliminary needs assessment, discovering sources of training and consultation, and preparing an initial presentation to the Board of Education. The general objectives at the initial implementation stage consist of consistently expanding the numbers of people involved from various sectors of the school and community and enhancing their awareness of the nature and scope of AODA-related problems affecting youth and the school system.

As Chapter 17 pointed out, the impetus for change can come from any direction, both within and outside of the school setting. In one school system, for example, a high school counselor heard of the SAP model at a conference and described it to his principal. The principal suggested presenting the information to a meeting of other administrators and pupil services staff in the building. They accepted the idea and recommended that the counselor and principal present the information to a district-wide meeting of administrative staff. Members of this group also responded favorably and recommended approaching the superintendent. A meeting with the superintendent resulted in his convening a meeting of administrative and pupil services representatives from each building in the district, at which

the information was also presented. Out of this group an initial "Core Committee" was formed, with district-wide representation. Members of this group later made a presentation of initial findings to the school board and sought its permission to proceed with planning. At each step, more key people became involved and the presentations became more formal and informed.

In another case, the author made a workshop presentation at a conference for a women's service organization. One of the women in attendance was also a member of a local Chemical People organization, to whom she relayed the information about the Student Assistance Program model. Some members of The Chemical People organization were also school district staff, who began the process described above. Ultimately, the program was implemented with joint financial support from the school board, the Chemical People organization, and the village board.

Thus, the implementation process can begin anywhere in a community, and should ultimately extend throughout the community. For our purposes, however, we will focus solely on the process as it occurs internal to the school system, while acknowledging that the entire community is the context.

Forming the Core Committee

The Core Committee is thus the initial group which investigates the feasibility of the student assistance program. Its membership is gradually expanded throughout the various tasks of program implementation. It typically evolves into the district-wide Core Group. These initial activities may even be the stimulus for the formation of community-based AODA organizations. Given this crucial role, it is important that those beginning the process seek to involve key people in the Core Committee and appreciate its major functions in the initial phase of program implementation.

Membership

A number of principles should guide those who are engaged in forming the Core Committee. First, begin where there is already some degree of interest. The purpose of initial awareness activity is not suasive; major objections to the program, obstructions, resistance, and denial will need to be responded to but at a later time. Preoccupation with resistance at this stage only directs attention away from the larger base of interest and support.

Second, seek district-wide involvement from those working with all grades or age-levels. A common misconception is that "the drug problem" only affects the high school, that the elementary level is immune to such problems, and thus those at the elementary level need not be involved. Those at the elementary level, however, need at least to be aware of the nature and scope of the effects of parental chemical dependency on elementary children and of the program structures and activities appropriate to their level. They also need to appreciate the district-wide scope of the program.

Third, seek the involvement of "key" people from both the school and the community. The program will ultimately require major commitments on the part of the school district. The program will require staff time and financial resources, and the district will have to formally commit itself to many issues around philosophy, policy, and procedures. Involving key school district decision makers and those who deal with student problems on a daily basis is important from the beginning. Community representation (e.g., parents, representatives from local agencies and institutions, etc.) is equally important. At all stages of program implementation it will be important to communicate that responding to student AODA-related problems is not solely the school's responsibility. Active community involvement is also useful in supporting the school district in the policy stances it needs to take.

School District Administration. One of the major pitfalls in program implementation arises from insufficient administrative support, often because the participation of key administrators was not sought from the beginning. The support of the individual building principal is crucial to the ultimate implementation and operation of the program. He will be called upon to interpret and support the district's AODA policy and procedures, commit staff and staff time to AODA training, participate in case management decisions for individual students, and generally provide advocacy for the program at its most local level. Many programs have stalled or faltered because building administrators were not involved early in the process of their design and implementation. While the participation of all building administrators in building-level Core Teams will be sought later, seeking the involvement of key administrators is important in the formative stages.

In larger school districts the involvement of other members of the central administration should also be sought, especially assistant superintendents for instruction and pupil services, supervisors of elementary and secondary education, supervisors of special education programs, athletic directors, etc.

It is also important to seek the involvement and support of the district administrator, and/or his desig-

nee, as early as possible. The superintendent's open support for the program, or for investigating its feasibility, often helps to decrease initial resistance and to increase participation from other levels. He or she often serves to provide regular feedback to the Board of Education on the early steps of implementation.

"(1) Who are the key people in the school system 'family?' and (2) Can we get them together, physically as well as conceptually, to begin the process of implementing the program?"

Board of Education. Those assembling this ad hoc Core Committee should also seek the participation of one or more members of the Board of Education. An initial presentation to the Board could include a request that one or more members volunteer to participate in the Committee; Board members can also be sought out informally. Some degree of Board representation at least helps to insure that the Board will be informally kept informed of the Core Committee's activities prior to a formal presentation. In addition, the Board will be asked at some point to formally authorize the program, enact revised policy language, provide funding, and participate in training. Some degree of Board involvement prior to these steps helps it to make timely decisions, and prevents it from having to make them in the absence of information or perceived support from within the school as well as from the community. The Board's questions concerning the degree of community support can be partially responded to if some of its members have witnessed the degree of community participation in the Core Committee.

Pupil Services Representatives. Pupil services staff within the school building have a unique perspective on students and the nature and prevalence of AODA-related problems. They are also more acutely aware of the practical difficulties of dealing successfully with such problems in accordance with the school system's current policies and procedures. They can thus provide critical input to the initial awareness process. In addition, much of the day-to-day management of students with AODA-related problems will often be handled by existing guidance counselors, school social workers, psychologists, and other pupil services staff members. Since they will perform such crucial roles in the operation of the program which ultimately emerges, their input into its design is vital. The failure to involve appropriate pupil services staff members early usually creates or exaggerates conflict and mistrust over turf issues later.

Interested Teachers. An effort needs to be made to prevent the program from being seen primarily as an administrative mandate. No program can function adequately without the active support and participation of the classroom teacher. In the initial implementation stages the involvement of classroom teachers often provides yet another perspective on student AODA-related problems which is not widely available to those outside the classroom. Teachers are able to see the problem from the perspective of individual student behavior. They can also contribute feedback regarding existing problems in communication and cooperation between the instructional, pupil services, and administrative staff in handling specific cases. They can also provide useful input at later stages when specific roles and procedures are discussed. The involvement of key interested teachers also provides the Core Committee with an advocacy voice to the staff as a whole within individual buildings. In addition to interested staff, an effort should be made to identify teachers in key specific relationships with students, including health teachers and coaches.

Parents. It would not be difficult for any school system to identify parents who are concerned about student alcohol and other drug abuse and who wish to participate in preventive and interventive programing. Parent representatives on the Core Committee are often sought among existing organizations: parent task forces and advisory groups, Chemical People Groups, parent/teacher organizations, and so on. Often, parents of students who have received treatment for chemical dependency are eager to take part, and bring yet another unique perspective to the design and implementation of a program.

Community Groups. Soliciting members for the Core Committee from local community service clubs and organizations is also desirable in order to increase the base of support. Many community groups, such as the Lions, Elks, Kiwanis, Rotary, Jaycees, etc., seek specific youth-related and/or alcohol/drug abuse projects to sponsor. Furthermore, members of service clubs come from many walks of life in the community. Their involvement in the implementation process prepares them informally to educate others and to advocate for the program at all points during the remaining process. In the initial stages, existing members of the Core Committee often identify these community groups and organizations, contact them, and ask to be placed on the agenda for an upcoming meeting in order to describe the nature of student AODA-related problems and the need for a student assistance program, and to solicit their support.

AODA Professionals. Most school systems will want to identify and involve appropriate representatives from local alcohol and other drug abuse services such as prevention organizations, assessment agencies, and treatment programs. As specialists, they can provide meaningful technical assistance and consultation to the Core Committee on the nature and scope of student AODA-related problems. Furthermore, it is important to discover as early as possible whether or not these resources are available locally. The process of setting up a student assistance program is also frequently the vehicle for developing better working relationships with these agencies.

Other Community Agencies. Many other community-based agencies and institutions can provide useful input and support for the school system's efforts to implement a student assistance program. Representatives from the police department and sheriff's department should be invited to participate as well as others in the juvenile justice system: judges from juvenile court, probation and parole officers, juvenile intake workers, etc. Local departments of social services should also be contacted in an effort to involve those working in protective services for children.

Core Committee Tasks

As we have noted, one of the major functions of the Core Committee is to continue to expand its membership and promote further awareness of AODA-related problems and the district's efforts to respond to them appropriately. If a Core Committee has been formally established it will often devote some attention to identifying the remaining implementation tasks, forming subcommittees, etc. At the same time, however, it is devoting itself to a number of short-term tasks: (1) conducting a preliminary needs assessment, (2) investigating sources of consultation, technical assistance, and training, and (3) preparing an initial presentation for the Board of Education.

Preliminary Needs Assessment

In preparation for an initial presentation to the Board of Education, seeking its permission to continue investigating the feasibility of a student assistance program, members of the Core Committee will need to assess the needs for a program and the availability of resources in a number of areas. This information is also useful as the Core Committee makes presentations to other segments of the community to gather support and participation.

Student AODA Issues

A major part of the initial needs assessment involves preparing meaningful information justifying the need for the program itself: the nature and scope of student AODA-related problems. Prevalence data can come from applying national estimates to student enrollments, or from conducting surveys of the local student population.

Applied Prevalence Estimates. Many of the most recent findings in relation to student alcohol and other drug use have been summarized in Chapter 2. The Tables in Supplement 2.1 also present some detailed breakdowns by age, substance used, frequency, age of first use, "problem use," and so on. One approach to arriving at local prevalence is to apply these national percentages to local enrollments. In other words, to the extent that Midville High School's 2,484 students are characteristic of the nation's high school students, then: 124 students (5%) are smoking marijuana daily, 399 (16.1%) have tried cocaine, and 119 (4.8%) are daily drinkers (see Table 2.9). As pointed out in Chapter 2, regional and demographic variables often account for only relatively small variations in many prevalence rates.

However, as we have emphasized throughout, more useful and accurate than individual frequencies of drug use are the descriptions of varying target groups. The frequency of drug use is often informative only at the extremes: rates of non-use versus rates of daily use. Frequencies do not given an appropriate view of the

needs of students. In applying national statistics it is more useful to make assumptions concerning the prevalence of varieties of drug-related problems, as illustrated in Chapter 3. It is much more instructive to approach the community and the Board of Education with the information that approximately 993 (20%) of Midville's secondary students have problems because of drug abuse, that 248 (5%) are chemically dependent, and that 2,500 (25% of the entire student body) are negatively affected by parental alcohol/drug abuse or dependency (e.g., see Chapter 3, Tables 3.2 and 3.3). It is also important to stress that to these three target groups must be added students who are recovering from chemical dependency, who are involved in experimental alcohol/drug use, and who have other non-AODA-related problems — all of whom have different needs.

Student Surveys. Student surveys conducted in the local school system are also a means of arriving at prevalence data. Given the time and effort which must be invested in designing, conducting and analyzing student AODA surveys, they are best employed in a limited number of circumstances. First, student surveys are usually not the best means of "proving" that a problem of sufficient scope exists. Applied estimates can do so just as well. However, when there is serious doubt that national prevalence estimates apply, a small-scale student survey based on a random sample of students may indicate the degree to which national estimates, or assumptions about the prevalence of target groups, are accurate for a given community. One advantage to relying upon target group descriptions rather than on raw frequencies is that there may be considerable variation between communities with regard to specific indicators, but little variation regarding the size of target groups. For example, it is likely that 5 per cent of any community's adolescents will be chemically dependent, though the drugs most frequently used will vary with their availability and demographic differences between communities. Second, local surveys can also be useful in compiling baseline data against which the program will ultimately be evaluated, and where national survey results are useless. The STADUS survey in Supplement 2.2 is an example of one which allows school personnel to define and measure the size of target groups in addition to acquiring raw frequency data.

School Performance Indicators. It is also useful to compile a preliminary estimate of the degree to which student alcohol and other drug abuse impacts on other school behavior. It is also useful to know the extent to which alcohol and other drug abuse is involved in other school-related problems. Thus, if a school system wishes to reduce absenteeism, tardiness, or dropout rates it will need to appreciate the degree to which alcohol and other drug abuse contributes to these rates.

At this stage, the most easily obtained and quantifiable data is needed. It would be useful, for example, to know:

- the total number of suspensions which occurred in the past year and the number which were AODA-specific or AODA-related;

- the number of AODA-related expulsions which occurred, as a percentage of total expulsions;

- the numbers of students referred to assessment or treatment for alcohol/drug problems;

- a description of AODA-related "critical incidents" involving students, such as car accidents, overdoses, suicides, vandalism, drug busts, incidents of violence;

- the absenteeism and tardiness rates, and an estimate of how many are AODA-related;

- the dropout rate, and an estimate of how many students who drop out have AODA-related problems;

- an estimate of the degree to which alcohol and other drug abuse is related to other problems: unwanted pregnancies, child abuse/neglect, suicide, etc.

Supplement 18.2 gives an example of a format within which student AODA prevalence data can be summarized.

Opinions and Attitudes.

Some schools and communities embark on a needs assessment project of even larger scope, surveying the opinions and attitudes of staff, parents, and the community at large regarding the seriousness of AODA-related problems among youth, suggestions for appropriate responses, and their degree of support for specific school policy stances, for example. Such surveys are often conducted on a limited scale, through interviews with key segments of the community and the school. While not typical or necessary during the initial implementation steps, such surveys often provide useful information and support for the school system.

Community AODA Services

At some point in the implementation process the school will need to formally identify all of those agencies in the community which provide screening, assessment, diagnostic/evaluation, treatment, and aftercare services for students with AODA-related problems.

This type of needs assessment may reveal a variety of appropriate services for youth and their families. It may reveal that many such services are not locally available, do not focus specifically on youth or on alcohol/drug abuse, or are philosophically incompatible with the approach the school system wishes to take. To the extent that such services are available, identifying them may further the process of enhancing concrete working relationships between them and the school. To the extent that they are absent, the school system and members of the Core Committee may wish to begin the process of identifying more distant resources, planning to supply more services itself, or advocating for the development of a more adequate and appropriate local continuum of care. (Supplements 8.1 and 10.1 can help in the process of evaluating AODA screening, assessment, and treatment resources for youth).

Training and Consultation

Figure 18.1 depicts the implementation process not as a linear but as a cyclic process. Although the most extensive training typically occurs during Core Group Development, the figure indicates that some degree of training activity may be associated with many of the implementation tasks. Often, for example, it is exposure to relevant SAP training events which precipitates the development of a student assistance program. Similarly, some degree of training facilitates the development of appropriate policy language and program design for those involved in these tasks.

To the extent that training is a relevant issue during the early stages of implementation, members of the evolving Core Committee need to identify and evaluate training resources which are conversant with both alcohol and other drug abuse issues and the Student Assistance Program model. Preliminary AODA-related training is often available from local AODA resources.

Anticipating the need for more intensive and large-scale training during Core Group Development, the Core Committee should identify and evaluate potential training and consultation resources according to criteria such as the following:

- What is the philosophy or belief system of the training/consultation resource regarding alcoholism, the disease concept, permissiveness toward adolescent alcohol/drug use, etc.?

- To what degree does the training/consultation resource understand the dynamics of the school setting? What is the position of the resource regarding the proper role of the school?

- To what degree does the resource have a "model" of student assistance programs? Or, does the agency or resource propose merely to engage in undirected "community organization?"

- Are alcohol and other drug abuse appropriately emphasized in the SAP model of the training/consultation resource?

- Does the resource propose, emphasize, or rely primarily upon singular responses or "quick fixes?" (E.g., a curriculum, a get tough policy, hiring one of their staff members, etc.)

- Does the resource propose to do everything for the school system, or does it seek to promote the school's self-sufficiency?

- Does the resource rely primarily upon invasive strategies? (E.g., mandatory drug testing, locker searches, automatic expulsion of drug-involved students, etc.).

- Does the resource understand the necessity of involving many key segments of the community?

Figure 18.1
THE IMPLEMENTATION CYCLE

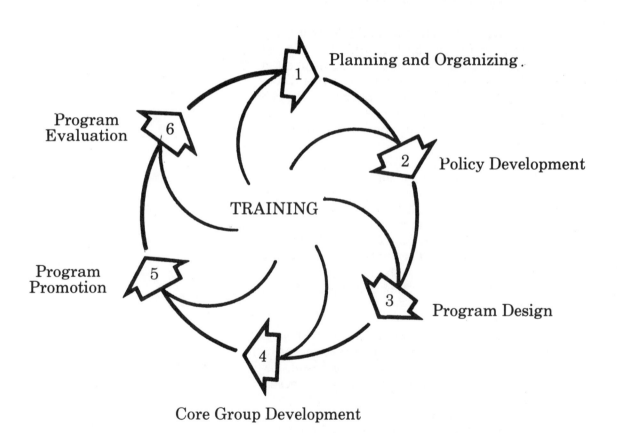

Planning and Organizing

1

2 Policy Development

Program Evaluation

6

TRAINING

Program Promotion

5

3 Program Design

4

Core Group Development

The Initial Presentation to the Board of Education

The Board of Education may be aware of the initial interest in a student assistance program because of previous, brief contacts by Core Committee members or informal reports by the district administrator. At some point, however, it is often useful to approach the Board of Education with a more formal presentation, summarizing the needs assessment data that has been collected, and describing the broad outlines of a program model. It is important that the Board understands that the SAP model is a comprehensive, joint school/community effort, with implications for policy, in-school services, training, etc. The goal of the presentation is often to seek the Board's permission to continue investigating the Student Assistance Program model with a view to returning later with a formal proposal.

In a brief presentation, there is time just to relay the information above in its most digested form. In many cases it is possible to obtain more time on a Board's agenda and to begin educating Board members on basic alcohol/drug abuse issues: historical trends in student drug use (e.g., Table 2.9), the different dynamics of drug use, abuse, and dependency, the nature of the disease concept, effects of parental alcoholism on children and families, enabling, and so on.

"In some ways the process of implementing a student assistance program parallels the process of intervening in chemical dependency in the family."

If they have not become involved beforehand, the initial presentation is an appropriate time to request formal participation by one or more Board members in the Core Committee. Similarly, if the initial Board contact is made before a formal Core Committee has been established, the meeting can be used to secure the Board's formal permission to constitute one and to proceed as above.

Thus, by the end of the Planning and Organizing stage a good deal of progress will have been made in involving key school and community persons in the implementation process and in enhancing their awareness of basic AODA-related issues. More people will have an appreciation of the general extent of the need for a comprehensive approach to student AODA-related problems and of the outlines along which such an approach might proceed.

The stance of those involved in this initial activity is also important. Just as in chemically dependent families, the process of beginning recovery significantly disrupts or threatens the status quo: comfortable beliefs and attitudes, the illusion that everything is going fine, and traditional ways of doing things. It is worth restating the one of the goals at this point is to seek the involvement of those in the school who are already interested and supportive. Resistance should be acknowledged and accepted, but should not preoccupy those involved in these initial implementation activities.

Chapter 18 | # Supplement

Supplement 18.1, "Implementation and Planning Checklist I," contains a list of the major activities involved in the initial planning and organizing stages of SAP implementation. It can be used to assist in forming the Core Committee and tracking its activities.

Supplement 18.2 represents an example of a "Needs Assessment Summary." It can be used to briefly summarize the preliminary data on the prevalence of student AODA-related problems. Data presented in such a format can be useful in initial presentations to the Board of Education.

Supplement 18.3 is an "AODA Agency Directory." It can be utilized in identifying and evaluating local sources of AODA assessment and treatment services, SAP consultation and training resources, and services specializing in the treatment of adolescent chemical dependency.

Supplement 18.1

IMPLEMENTATION CHECKLIST 1:
Planning and Organizing

TASK: *To begin planning and organizing for student assistance program implementation by widening the involvement of key school and community representatives and enhancing their awareness of AODA-related issues.*

IMPLEMENTATION ACTIVITY	RESPONSIBILITY OF:	RESOURCES NEEDED:	COMPLETION DATE:
A. Form an ad hoc interest group or Core Committee: 1. Present SAP concept to key building-level administrators 2. Present SAP concept to district-wide administration 3. Present SAP concept to pupil services staff 4. Secure training for Core Committee members B. Seek to widen Core Committee membership: 1. Identify service clubs and organizations, significant community institutions and agencies 2. Designate members of Core Committee to make presentations regarding SAP to interested community groups 3. Make presentations to community groups and seek their representation on the Core Committee 4. Define primary tasks of the Core Committee 5. Form appropriate subgroups, or subcommittees, to begin work on remaining implementation tasks (e.g., policy development) C. Conduct preliminary needs assessment 1. Prepare preliminary estimate of the prevalence of AODA-related problems among students 2. Prepare estimate of the relationship of student AODA to other problems (i.e., disciplinary and attendance problems, dropout rates, "critical incidents," etc.) 3. Conduct opinion/attitude survey of parents, school staff, and community members D. Identify and evaluate AODA resources 1. Prepare directory of AODA screening, assessment, diagnosis, treatment, and after-care services for youth 2. Evaluate appropriateness and adequacy of youth services in the AODA continuum of care 3. Identify and evaluate potential sources of AODA/SAP training, consultation, and technical assistance.			

IMPLEMENTATION ACTIVITY	RESPONSIBILITY OF:	RESOURCES NEEDED:	COMPLETION DATE:
E. Secure Board of Education (BOE) permission to proceed 1. Present results of preliminary needs assessment to BOE 2. Seek formal BOE recognition of the SAP Core Committee 3. Seek BOE representation on the Core Committee			

Supplement 18.2

PRELIMINARY NEEDS ASSESSMENT SUMMARY

The "Needs Assessment Summary" presented below is a sample format which can be utilized in preparing preliminary information on student AODA-related problems and the extent of the need for a student assistance program. A form such as Supplement 18.2 can be completed by those in each school building at all levels. Data can then be summarized on a similar form. Separate summaries may need to be prepared for elementary and secondary levels. The form is divided into three sections: (1) AODA Prevalence Estimate, (2) AODA-related School Performance Indicators, and (3) Critical Incidents.

AODA PREVALENCE ESTIMATES

The prevalence of student AODA-related problems can be discovered either through the application of national statistics to local enrollments, through a local student survey, or through a combination of the two. What is important is analyzing the data according to assumptions regarding the numbers of students in each target group, and the realization that those in each target group will have unique needs requiring different responses by the school system. Section I thus asks the preparers to make assumptions on the prevalence of chemical dependency, drug abuse, etc., for each age group or grade level, and to enter the total number of students so affected. The items in Section I likely to be of most relevance to elementary buildings are those estimating the prevalence of students who are "Affected Others" and those who are "Non-using."

AODA-RELATED SCHOOL PERFORMANCE INDICATORS

Section II allows those in each building to provide actual or estimated numbers of students whose behavior has been affected by alcohol and/or other drug use in some specific ways during a comparison period (e.g., the past year). "Suspensions" refers to the total number of suspension incidents in the past year for each grade level. It can be reported either in terms of numbers of incidents or numbers of students. The numbers of suspensions and expulsions that were AODA-specific should be indicated (i.e., disciplinary actions for possession, use, delivery, etc.). The "AODA-related" category may be used to indicate the number of suspensions where alcohol or other drug use was not directly involved, but where the staff suspects that students had AODA-related problems. This figure represents an estimated number. The last column indicates the percentage of suspensions and expulsions that were AODA-specific and AODA-related compared to the total. Thus, if there were 100 suspensions, 30 of which were AODA-specific and 40 of which are estimated to be AODA-related, the total percentage of AODA-involved suspensions would be 70 per cent.

Absenteeism, tardiness, and dropout rates can be handled similarly. Absenteeism can be reported in terms of the annual rate (e.g., "6% of students are absent on a typical day"), the total number of days missed during the year, or according to some other formula. Tardiness can be reported according to an annual rate (per cent of students tardy) or numbers of days or hours missed. As above, however, staff are asked to indicate the actual and estimated numbers of days/hours missed due to alcohol or other drug-related problems, and the percentage of AODA-involved incidents as a percentage of the total. The involvement of alcohol and other drug abuse in the number of students dropping out can be estimated similarly. There is room to indicate the school's annual dropout rate.

The final two categories ask for the number of students who were referred to alcohol/ drug abuse assessment services in the community, and the number of students who were treated for chemical dependency. The comparison of the total numbers assessed and/or treated with the numbers of students in need (e.g., chemically dependent) or having school performance problems can be instructive.

CRITICAL INCIDENTS

The final section allows preparers to give anecdotal information regarding AODA- related incidents which may have occurred in the building during the past year: incidents of vandalism, drug busts, overdoses, etc.

Supplement 18.2

NEEDS ASSESSMENT SUMMARY

I. AODA Prevalence Estimate: Numbers of students estimated to be in AODA-related target groups, based on [   ] *actual survey* [   ] *application of national prevalence data.*

Number of students estimated to be:	Grade Level	Per Cent	Total Number
Chemically Dependent			
Abusing Alcohol and Other Drugs			
Affected Others			
Recovering from Chemical Dependency			
Non-Using and Non-abusing Students			

II. AODA-Related School Performance Indicators:

Performance Indicator (past year):	Grade Level	Total	Number AODA-Specific	Number AODA-Related	% AODA of Total
Suspensions					
Expulsions					
Absentee Days					
Tardiness (hr/dy)					
Dropouts (%)					
AODA Assessments					
AODA Treatment					

III. Critical Incidents:

Supplement 18.3

AODA AGENCY DIRECTORY

The AODA Agency Directory should be compiled at some point early in the implementation process. It allows the members of the Core Committee to begin to evaluate the availability and nature of local assessment and treatment services, of prevention and intervention programming services, and SAP training, and consultation services.

The initial resource identifying information (agency name, address, telephone, contact person) can be recorded on the form below. The remainder of the form can be completed as a result of interviews with agency staff and/or site visits by Core Committee members. The "Services" key allows the preparers to indicate the types of service the agency provides: assessment, prevention and intervention programming, chemical dependency treatment, SAP consultation and training. The "Y" column indicates whether the agency's services are youth-specific. A local chemical dependency treatment program, for example, may not have a separate treatment program for adolescents. "Comments" allows Core Committee members to indicate general evaluations of the agency based on staff interviews and/or site visits.

AODA AGENCY DIRECTORY

AGENCY/Address	Contact Person	Services							Comments
		A	P	I	Tx	Y	C	Tn	

KEY: A = Assessment Services   Tx = Treatment Services
          P = Prevention Services   Y = AODA Treatment for Youth
          I = Intervention Services   C = SAP Consultation
                                   Tn = AODA/SAP Training

| Chapter 19 | # Policy Development |

"It is adventure and taking chances that make life worthwhile. Monotony is the awful reward of the careful."

The development of an appropriate statement of philosophy and policy language with respect to student drug and alcohol-related problems and the student assistance program represents one of two major benchmarks of program implementation, the second being Core Group Development (Chapter 21). The present discussion outlines some of the more important issues involved in philosophy language, policy language, and the process for their development.

Often, a school system's policy statement on alcohol and other drug abuse contains a mixture of philossophy language, policy language, and procedure language. There are some good reasons for keeping all three separate. Procedures, as described in Chapter 12, are essentially descriptions of the process which integrates roles and services with the student assistance program. Although they must be based upon policy language they are not often formally endorsed or enacted by the board of education, primarily because of the need to be able to alter them in the light of experience and because they may vary between local school buildings.

While most school districts have some kind of alcohol and other drug abuse policy, relatively few may have separate statements of their philosophy regarding these issues. The philosophy statement may thus be a component of the student assistance program which is new to the district. In developing a statement of its philosophy the school system examines its belief system and values regarding student drug and alcohol abuse problems and the school's role in their resolution. Philosophy language clearly must be supported by and formally adopted by the board of education.

The need to develop appropriate policy language is the most obvious, since it represents the primary "legal" document which guarantees students, staff, and parents due process in the school system's management of alcohol and other drug-related problems.

Among the many issues complicating the task of developing a new or revised AODA policy are the need to anticipate many legal issues and to make the policy broad, or co-curricular, in nature and scope of application. Finally, the process of developing appropriate philosophy and policy language should involve individuals from both the school and the community in order to maximize consensus, ownership, and support regarding the products which emerge.

Philosophy Language

The time and effort required to develop a philosophy statement concerning student drug and alcohol-related problems is justified considering the usefulness of the process and the product. One important reason for developing philosophy language is that it engages key school system personnel in a serious examination of the beliefs, attitudes, and values regarding drug and alcohol abuse, chemical dependency, and those afflicted with or affected by such problems. It engages the system in examining how these are manifested in individuals and in the climate of the school as a whole, and how they need to be changed.

An appropriate philosophy statement directly addresses some of the issues involving "enabling" in the educational setting (cf. Chapter 5). The philosophical language which results is a statement of the beliefs and values of the school system regarding the nature of such problems and the role of the school in attempting to help students to resolve them. The philosophy provides answers to questions such as 'Why should the school system get involved?' and 'If I have a drug problem is it safe to trust the school system for help?' A related reason for developing philosophy language is that all AODA policies and procedures will contain *implicit* statements of values and beliefs. The process of developing a philosophy statement makes such beliefs *explicit*, which can assist in the development of more appropriate policy language.

Philosophy language has another, more public function. One of the key implementation tasks is program promotion (Chapter 22), or informing students, staff, parents, and the community about the school's student assistance program. Copies of philosophy and policy language are typically sent to parents and community groups, and described to students and staff members. A statement of the school district's philosophy regarding alcohol and other drug abuse can thus materially affect how others perceive such problems as well as the program. One of the major functions of an appropriate philosophy statement is to counter the stigma, fear, and denial concerning such problems which prevent students and their families from asking for or accepting help.

Components. Supplement 19.2 contains an example of a hypothetical school district's philosophy language, illustrating some of the following suggestions for the development of an appropriate philosophy statement concerning the student assistance program and the school's role:

- The statement is positive in tone.

- It takes risks. It is not a reflection of a bland consensus, but makes statements and takes positions which may be new, unfamiliar, or even controversial in the community.

- It does not portray the program as a witch-hunt, nor lay blame for the existence of alcohol/drug problems in individuals or the school system.

- It does not deny the existence of drug and alcohol-related problems; it explicitly recognizes their existence, nature, and scope.

- It avoids simplistic perspectives by recognizing the complexity of AODA-related problems: the different needs presented by students affected by their own drug use, abuse, or chemical dependency, or by these problems in others.

- It upholds abstinence as a norm for children and adolescents by taking a firm stance against any youthful drug and alcohol use: the use of alcohol or other drugs for their mood-altering effects does not promote or enhance normal, healthy growth and development.

- It recognizes the need for the school system to examine and change its own environment.

- It acknowledges the necessity for community-wide ownership of drug and alcohol-related problems and responsibility for their resolution. The school has a role to play in addressing drug and alcohol problems, but it must have the cooperation and support of the community.

Process. Developing such a statement is not an easy task. It is essentially a consensus-seeking process which requires the input from many different segments of the school and the community. The initial Core Committee, made up of administrative, pupil services, and Board of Education representatives, is a proper group to begin the process of developing a philosophy statement, using input and advice from other concerned persons. The process is made easier if those involved have access to models or sample language, have previously acquired some appropriate training in alcohol and other drug abuse issues, or have knowledgeable AODA consultants available to them.

Developing a philosophy statement from scratch often increases the difficulty of the task. Sometimes having a model or an example from another school district helps to focus deliberations. Some schools approach the task in the manner presented earlier in Supplement 4.1. The statements listed there, or propositions drawn from the sample philosophy statement in Supplement 19.2 may be used as the starting point for group discussion. The Core Committee's draft language is typically submitted to student, staff, parent, and community representatives for their review and comment before a final draft is prepared for inclusion with the policy language presented to the Board of Education for adoption.

Policy Language

Where the philosophy statement is a discussion of values and beliefs, the policy statement describes "due process." It lists the ways in which the school system is predisposed to act in various circumstances. It consists essentially of a sequence of "if... then" statements. The policy statement at which the school system arrives should contain a number of components. In addition, in preparation for drafting the policy the school will need to examine a number of legal issues.

Components

The sample policy presented in Supplement 19.2 was developed to illustrate some ways of incorporating the following components in policy language.

No drug or alcohol use. The policy should contain a firm and clear statement of the unacceptability and illegality of student drug and alcohol use, both in school and at any school-sponsored activity. Most language will need to include provisions against the "manufacture, use, possession, delivery, transfer, or sale" of alcoholic beverages and other controlled substances. Existing policies regulating the use of over-the-counter drugs and prescribed medications may be incorporated into this broader language. Some schools include the use of tobacco products as well. (It is difficult, however, to firmly oppose student tobacco use while providing a designated smoking area on school grounds).

Consequences. The policy should spell out a schedule of consequences for witnessed violations of the non-use policy. In view of its illegality and the threat it poses to individual student development and the school climate as a whole, consequences for student drug and alcohol use should be rather strict. Most policies allow for different consequences for first and second offenses. There is little reason for providing students with a third chance.

It is crucial that consequences be imposed together with an offer of help. The message in consequences is two-fold: the school steadfastly regards drug and alcohol use as unacceptable behavior, and if students need help to bring behavior up to acceptable levels the school will make the means of help available — i.e., referral to the student assistance program. Even here there are two schools of thought. Some feel that referral should be offered in lieu of suspension or expulsion to increase the motivation to accept help. Others argue that consequences earned should be received, and that positive efforts to change behavior should be used as a criterion for reducing the severity or duration of consequences. Many administrators may wish to preserve some flexibility in their ability to respond to individual situations, and develop language that permits both options.

Co-curricular Consequences. The sample policy includes suspension from eligibility to take part in any extracurricular activity for 1 calendar year as a consequence for witnessed violations of the AODA policy, regardless of whether a student is involved in the student council, marching band, French club, or athletics. Students may return to participation to the extent that they accept referral to the student assistance program and make satisfactory progress within it. Athletics or any other extracurricular activity may wish to adopt more but not less stringent consequences. Specific procedures may also need to be developed to address the extracurricular component. The Core Team, for example, should be the arbiter of "satisfactory progress." Some schools may wish to experiment with allowing students to petition the Core Team when they feel they should be allowed to participate in extracurricular activities again.

Expectations of Staff. The policy makes it a clear expectation that all staff are responsible for observing student behavior, attempting to correct it through usual measures, and referring those students who are unwilling or unable to respond. The policy also states the Board will extend legal protection against liability only to the extent that staff comply with this and other policy expectations. In other words, staff incur the risk of liability by not complying with the policy.

Self-Referral. The policy should contain provisions which not only encourage self-referral but which will not punish students for voluntarily seeking help. Thus, students who self-refer do not risk disciplinary action for behavior which occurred prior to self-referral, unless the violation of school policy has already been reported. Students are expected, however, to maintain "satisfactory progress" in the program from that point on, which may entail keeping an abstinence contract.

Satisfactory Progress. The discussion in Part Two pointed out not only the degree to which AODA-related behavior is resistant to change, but also the need for a variety of assessment, interventive, and support strategies in order to bring about changes in the direction of abstinence. Upholding abstinence as a norm is necessary; realism dictates that some allowances need to be made for the time necessary for students to achieve stability in change. The policy thus requires "satisfactory progress" while leaving the decisions about it up to individual building administrators, SAP Coordinator/Counselors, and Core Team members.

Voluntarism and Responsibility. The sample contains language which states that everything about a student's participation in the student assistance program is voluntary, even though his involvement represents a choice between difficult alternatives. Students and parents alike are responsible for maintaining satisfactory levels of performance. Section (10e) of the sample illustrates the lengths to which the school can go when there is strong administrative support, backed by a thorough understanding of the nature and seriousness of chemical dependency. It essentially supports the building administrator in making a report of suspected child abuse and neglect when parents refuse treatment for a student whom the staff has good reason to believe is chemically dependent.

Records. While the SAP Coordinator/Counselor, other counselors, group facilitators, and Core Team members may keep minimal notes on a student's progress in the program, these should be kept to a minimum. Those records which are maintained should be kept separate from the student's permanent record or cumulative file. In addition, the policy should caution all staff against using diagnostic terms ("drug abuse," chemically dependent") as well as pejorative labels in writing and talking about a student to others.

Parent Involvement. When or whether to notify parents of a student's involvement in one or another aspect of the student assistance program is an issue which will be debated in most school systems. There are good reasons for adopting a board policy that all parents will be informed of their child's participation in the program *at some point*, while leaving some flexibility in this decision for individual cases. Informing parents that a child is in the program, including support groups, does not mean revealing the nature of a student's disclosures, which should nearly always be regarded as confidential. Furthermore, the SAP staff

should be able to document the reasons for postponing parent information and involvement. In most cases it will be possible to obtain the student's permission to contact parents once she is aware of what will and will not be disclosed, and once the SAP staff has an opportunity to strengthen the student to take part in the disclosure herself. Parents are always informed immediately of policy violations. Adopting an aggressive policy of involving parents avoids potential legal problems, and forces staff to confront what may be their own resistances to these contacts rather than according them to students.

Implementation Responsibilities. The policy should often contain statements describing the responsibilities for operating the program at the building level. Though Core Team members should be involved in the decision making process, the ultimate responsibility for implementing the policy with respect to individual students rests with the building administrator. The building administrator, or those whom he or she designates, is responsible for developing the procedures necessary to carry out the policy, and for providing training and inservice opportunities for key staff.

Many other issues could be addressed in the student assistance program policy. Issues involving the search of students, their lockers and possessions are most likely addressed elsewhere and can be referenced. In addition, some policies contain extensive definitions of terms, such as "drugs," "tobacco products," "mood-altering," "chemical dependency," etc.

While it is tempting to want to develop a complete, comprehensive, and landmark policy statement, it is useful to regard the task as a process which may take several years. For most schools implementing a student assistance program, many of the issues confronting them will be new. It is unlikely that every eventuality can be anticipated and resolved. Most school systems discover the need for additions, deletions, and changes in policy language during the first year of the program's operation. Attention to the issues above should provide a good foundation and minimize the need for wholesale revisions.

Legal Issues

Many of the issues above involve legal issues, or processes which at least have to remain within legal boundaries or administrative rules promulgated at one level or another. There are a number of legal issues which invite research or discussion in the process of developing more appropriate alcohol/drug policy language.

Controlled Substances Laws. Key people in the student assistance program as well as in the district as a whole should be as aware as possible of federal laws, state laws, and local ordinances governing the "manufacture, use, possession, delivery, transfer, or sale" of alcohol or other drugs by minors, including the statutory consequences for their violation. The staff should also be as familiar as possible with local and state laws and penalties governing drunk driving by teenagers.

Working Relationships. Core Team members should also be familiar with the procedures followed with local law enforcement agencies regarding the confiscation of drugs, rules of evidence, conditions for involving law enforcement in searches, procedures for turning over contraband to police officers, and so on. Collecting and keeping drugs, for example, places the staff member in illegal possession as much as the student. The SAP staff also needs to understand the limitations of law enforcement: turning over drugs and/or evidence of their use to law enforcement officials does not necessarily result in prosecution. The policy language contains provisions for contacting police, for example, primarily because it is a legal obligation and because it involves the resources of another community institution in handling an individual student.

Minor's Consent. The school staff should investigate whether the state has legislation permitting minors to consent to treatment for chemical dependency and at what age consent can be given. The legal as well as practical, limits of minors' consent should also be clarified. In some states, for example, which permit minors' consent for treatment, parental consent may be required for third–party payment. In others, minors can present themselves for treatment but cannot be given medication without parental permission. In still others, treatment agencies can provide a limited number of counseling sessions before seeking parental consent to proceed further.

Confidentiality, again. In examining the legal basis for the complex issue of confidentiality, it is necessary to bear several distinctions in mind. First, federal confidentiality regulations were intended to apply to federally funded alcohol and drug programs and forbid revealing the records of "the identity, diagnosis, prognosis, or treatment of any patient" without prior written consent. No information can be revealed. ("Confidentiality of Alcohol and Drug Abuse Patient Records," Federal Law Title — 42 Public Health; *Federal Register*, Volume 40, C. F. R. 27802, July 1, 1975). While this statute does apply to information concerning students in treatment programs, the applicability of the federal regulation to school systems and students in general is uncertain. Nevertheless, some states have adopted similar confidentiality provisions as part of their mental health or alcohol/drug abuse statutes. It is advisable for schools to contact state departments of health and social services for this information and an opinion as to its applicability to managing students in

school setting. (For further information on applicability of and compliance with the federal regulation, contact NIDA or NIAAA; see Appendix A).

Second, states may have adopted alcohol/drug-specific confidentiality statutes that apply to educators. In Wisconsin, for example, students and pupil services staff are prevented from disclosing information received from a student about the student's or another's drug-related problems unless (a) the student consents in writing to the disclosures or (b) the staff member judges that the student or another is in imminent danger and that disclosure will alleviate the danger. (*Laws of Wisconsin*, Title XIV, Section 118.126). The statute also grants pupil services staff immunity from civil liability for disclosing or failing to disclose such information "in good faith."

Third, the school should bear in mind the difference between confidentiality, privacy, and secrecy. The fact that a student is participating the program is not confidential, but may be a matter of privacy. Assuring parents of confidentiality is also a matter of respecting a family's privacy. On the other hand, the need to severely restrict any identifying information about students or their participation may be an unfortunate reinforcement of the secrecy which tends to shroud alcohol and other drug-related problems. Finally, the school can become too preoccupied with protecting confidences by trying to extend the notion of confidentiality to everyone: to the referring teacher or student, for example.

The Hatch Act. In 1978, the Hatch Amendment to Section 439 of the General Provision Act of 1974 was passed. In part it provides that "No student shall be required to submit to psychiatric examination, testing, or treatment without the consent of the student or in the case of an unemancipated minor without the consent of the parent" (*The General Education Provision Act*, 20 USC 123h, Sec 439, subsection (b).) Subsequent rules have defined "psychiatric or psychological examination" to mean "A method of obtaining information, including a group activity, that is not directly related to academic instruction and that is designed to elicit information about attitudes, habits, traits, opinions, beliefs, or feelings." "Treatment" is defined as activities which are "designed to affect the behavioral, emotional, or attitudinal characteristics of an individual or group." (United States Department of Education, public hearing on Proposed Rulemaking Implementing the Hatch Amendment, Orlando, Florida, March 23, 1984, p. 20).

The amendment and the administrative rules promulgated thus far would require parent permission for a minor's participation in counseling or support groups that "are not directly related to academic instruction." Unless and until more realistic rules are forthcoming, the Hatch Amendment seems to require that school's seek parental permission for a student's participation in nearly every component of its student assistance program. (For a more complete discussion of the Hatch Amendment and its implications, see Greene and Pasch (1986)).

The Process

Even more than philosophy language, policy language should be developed with the input and participation of as many key segments of the school and community as possible, and there should be opportunities for several levels of review before final language is submitted to the board of education for adoption. Supplement 19.1 summarizes the major steps in the development process. Here it is only necessary to observe that one of the activities involved in maintaining the student assistance program following its initial implementation is to reexamine and revise policy language in light of the first year's experience.

Aside from many of the details addressed above, those involved in developing philosophy and policy language should also be mindful of its tone of what it communicates to students, staff, parents, and the community regarding the school system's stance. In evaluating the language they finally arrive at, they should ask themselves a few additional questions:

- As a student, how comfortable do I feel with the program? Is it a sincere offer of help that I can make use of? Based on the tone of the philosophy and policy, would I ask for help voluntarily? Would I be inclined to accept help if it was offered?

- As a parent, how likely am I to seek information and assistance from the school, should I suspect that a member of my family has a drug or alcohol-related problem? Based on the tone of the philosophy and policy, would I accept the school system's help if it were offered?

- As a teacher or other staff member, how confident am I that students will receive appropriate help? Would I refer students I really cared about, or would I feel I have to protect them?

- In general, how well does the philosophy and policy begin to address the fears, suspicions, and negative attitudes which typically surround the subject of alcohol and other drug abuse?

Chapter 19 | # Supplements

Supplement 19.1, "Implementation Checklist II: Policy Development," lists the major activities associated with formulating a philosophy and policy statement to be submitted to the board of education for adoption.

Supplement 19.2 contains sample philosphy language and policy language that forms the basis for the student assistance program.

Supplement 19.1

IMPLEMENTATION CHECKLIST II: Policy Development

TASK: *To develop appropriate AODA philosophy and policy language.*

IMPLEMENTATION ACTIVITY	RESPONSIBILITY OF:	RESOURCES NEEDED:	COMPLETION DATE:
A. Form a philosophy and policy language subgroup of the Core Committee, made up at least of representatives from administration, pupil services, athletics, and the Board of Education.			
1. Examine and evaluate existing AODA policy language			
2. Examine existing extracurricular codes			
3. Examine sample SAP/AODA policies from other school districts			
4. Review federal, state, and local laws and ordinances proscribing possession, use, sale, etc., of alcohol and other controlled substances			
5. Clarify working relationships with local law enforcement			
6. Identify other legal issues which need to be addressed in school policy			
B. Prepare initial draft of SAP/AODA philosophy statement			
C. Prepare initial draft of new co-curricular SAP/AODA policy			
1. Submit draft of philosophy and policy for review by school district attorney			
2. Circulate draft of new philosophy and policy language for review and comment by Core Committee members, members of building Core Teams, and members of the Board of Education			
3. Circulate draft of new philosophy and policy language for review by student, parent, and community groups			
D. Prepare final draft of revised SAP/AODA philosophy and policy language			
1. Solicit review comments and recommendations from groups reviewing initial draft			
2. Write final draft			
3. Submit final draft to Core Committee for final endorsement			
E. Submit final draft fo the Board of Education for approval			
F. Submit approved philosophy and policy language to various community groups, agencies, and institutions for their endorsement			

Supplement 19.2

SAMPLE PHILOSOPHY AND POLICY LANGUAGE

To the considerable variation that exists in state and local laws and the unique climate and will of each community must be added the various ways of implementing the SAP model as factors which militate against creating a philosophy or policy statement of universal applicability. Thus, the sample philosophy and policy language below is intended to be illustrative only.

The sample policy omits statements regarding support groups and confidentiality. The individual school district may wish to develop a separate policy and procedure statement for SAP support groups, such as the example in Supplement 13.1, and merely refer to it in its Student Assistance Program or drug and alcohol policy. Alternatively, that language can certainly be incorporated in the example which follows.

Confidentiality is even a more complex issue, since it can be applied to many types of information, circumstances, and people. The school should avoid needless complications. In many cases, existing policies preserving the confidentiality of student records and self-disclosures would be construed to apply to students who have AODA-related problems as well. Where these are lacking or inadequate, specific references may need to be developed.

SAMPLE PHILOSOPHY STATEMENT

The _____ School District recognizes that the use of alcohol and other drugs and the problems associated with it are becoming increasingly commonplace in our society and among youth. One's own chemical use or that of a loved one can have serious and lifelong consequences.

The _____ School District also recognizes that the abuse of alcohol and/or other drugs often precedes the development of problems. At some point, an individual's use of alcohol or other drugs may be deemed destructive to him/herself or to others, causing problems in daily living. Where the capacity to make responsible decisions regarding alcohol and other drug use has been reduced or compromised, prompt and appropriate attention can help the vast majority of individuals involved.

The _____ School District recognizes that students often need education, assistance, and support because of their own drug use or because of drug-related problems in those they care about. Many students will require support for their decision to remain drug-free. Since chemical dependency is preceded by the abuse of alcohol or other drugs, the school system wishes to provide education and/or assistance to any student displaying signs of harmful involvement.

The _____ School District also recognizes that a person's use of alcohol or other drugs can lead to the illness of chemical dependency. Complete recovery is possible, however, if the illness is identified early and treated appropriately through referral to community agencies. The _____ School District regards alcoholism, drug addiction, and dependency as it does any other illness or chronic behavioral/medical problem. Our primary purpose is to be helpful, and to eradicate the judgements or blame which only continue to stigmatize those with such problems and make their recovery difficult or impossible.

The _____ School District believes that it is in the best interests of the community for it to take steps to promote, enhance, and maintain a drug-free school system and student body, and that along with parents and other segments of the community it has a role play in helping students to remain drug-free.

Whenever factors arise which interfere with a student's school performance, the _____ School District will mobilize its resources to convert the situation. Therefore, the _____ School District wishes to cooperate with all segments of the community in making the means of assistance available to all those individuals who develop alcohol or other drug-related disabilities.

SAMPLE STUDENT ASSISTANCE PROGRAM POLICY

The _____ School District establishes a Student Assistance Program to provide education, assistance, and support for students affected by their own or others' drug and alcohol-related problems along the following guidelines:

1. The possession, use, delivery, transfer, or sale of alcoholic beverages or controlled substances by students, while in school or at school-sponsored events, is expressly forbidden.

   a. FIRST OFFENSE: Parents and law enforcement will be contacted immediately upon verification of the violation. The student will be suspended for from ____ to ____ days, and will be ineligible for participation in all extracurricular activities for a period of 1 calendar year. The building administrator may reduce the suspension to ____ days and loss of extracurricular eligibility to ____ if:

      (1) The student agrees to see the SAP Coordinator/Counselor and follows his/her recommendations satisfactorily; OR

      (2) The student and family agree to a drug and alcohol assessment provided at a State approved alcohol/drug agency in the community and conducted by a Certified Alcoholism/Drug Abuse Counselor, and follow his/her recommendations;

   b. SECOND OFFENSE: Parents and law enforcement will be contacted immediately upon verification of the violation. A recommendation for expulsion will be made to the Board of Education. The building administrator, or the Board of Education Expulsion Review Committee, or the Board of Education may hold a recommendation for expulsion in abeyance if:

      (1) The student agrees to see the SAP Coordinator/Counselor and follows his/her recommendations satisfactorily; OR

      (2) The student and family agree to a drug and alcohol assessment provided at a State approved alcohol/drug agency in the community and conducted by a Certified Alcoholism/Drug Abuse Counselor, and follow his/her recommendations satisfactorily;

2. Because of the potential dangers to the student presented by his/her acute intoxication with alcohol or other drugs, students exhibiting evidence of acute intoxication, incapacitation, or a drug overdose in school or at school-sponsored events will be transported immediately to the local hospital or facility designated to provide detoxification services, followed by immediate notification of parents and police. Following his/her return to school, section 1 of this policy will be implemented.

3. Reductions in length of suspension or extracurricular ineligibility, or withholding of expulsion may be revoked whenever a student fails to demonstrate compliance with expectations of or satisfactory progress in the Student Assistance Program.

4. All school staff members are expected to refer to the appropriate Student Assistance Program staff:

a. Any student who they witness in violation of section 1, above;

b. Any student who exhibits a definite and repeated pattern of unacceptable school performance which does not respond to usual and customary attempts to correct it;

c. Any student exhibiting signs, symptoms, or indications of an alcohol or drug-related problem;

d. Any student whose self-disclosed alcohol/drug-related behavior places them or others at risk or in imminent danger.

Referral of a student to the Student Assistance Program by itself does not constitute an allegation that a student has an alcohol/drug-related problem.

5. Students may also be referred to the SAP Coordinator/Counselor through self-referral or referral by peers, parents, or community representatives.

6. An essential feature of the program is that students and their family members are encouraged to contact the building administrators and/or the SAP Coordinator/Counselors for help with alcohol and other drug-related problems, with the assurance that such contacts will be handled sensitively and confidentially.

7. Upon referral to the SAP Coordinator/Counselor, he/she may consult with the student, parents, and/or staff members in an attempt to assess the nature and scope of the student's problem. This initial screening will result in one or more of the following recommendations:

a. No apparent personal or performance problem at this time; no further action is necessary at this time;

b. No apparent alcohol/drug-related problem at this time; however, referral to other in-school or community services is appropriate;

c. Further assessment interviews with the SAP Coordinator/Counselor are needed;

d. The student needs to contract for specific behavioral changes in AODA-related behavior, monitored through regular meetings between the student and the SAP Coordinator/Counselor;

e. The student needs to satisfactorily complete an in-school support group, after which additional recommendations will be made;

f. The student requires an in-school assessment, involving the student, parents, and SAP staff, conducted by a Certified AODA Counselor from an approved AODA agency in the community;

g. The student requires referral to an approved AODA agency for a professional assessment;

h. Assessment information supports the need for chemical dependency treatment in an inpatient or outpatient program in the community;

i. The student requires involvement in other community services, such as Alateen, Alcoholics Anonymous, Narcotics Anonymous, etc.

8. Except for violations reported under section 1, a student who self-refers to the Student

Assistance Program and who is making satisfactory progress in following his/her recommendations will not be liable to suspension, extracurricular ineligibility, or other disciplinary action for behavior which occurs prior to self-referral unless:

a. The student discloses conduct already reported under section 1, as a witnessed violation, OR

b. The student fails to follow the SAP Coordinator/Counselor's recommendations or to make satisfactory progress in the Student Assistance Program.

9. Evaluations concerning "satisfactory progress in the Student Assistance Program" will be made by the building SAP Coordinator/Counselor in consultation with the building administrator, support group facilitators, and other members of the Core Team.

10. Participation in the Student Assistance Program is voluntary. At all times it is the prerogative of the student and/or parent to accept or reject referral to the SAP Coordinator/Counselor or to community-based services.

a. Regardless of whether a student accepts or rejects assistance, it remains his/her responsibility to bring school performance up to acceptable levels or face such corrective or disciplinary actions as may be warranted

b. If a student accepts treatment for chemical dependency, that fact will be regarded as it would for any other illness with respect to the student's rights, benefits, and privileges.

c. When either the student or parent(s) do not wish to cooperate in making needed assistance available, the student's status in school may have to be reevaluated, taking into account the best interests of the student, the nature of the problem, and the health, safety, welfare, educational opportunity, and rights of other students and staff.

d. Any student judged by the building administrator to present a risk of imminent danger to him/herself or others may be removed from the school pending the results of a professional evaluation.

e. The School District regards chemical dependency to be a chronic, progressive illness which is fatal if left untreated. Consequently, refusal by parents to seek treatment for a chemically dependent child will result in a report to the Department of Social Service for suspected child abuse/neglect under Section _____ of State Statutes.

11. No records of the student's participation in the Student Assistance Program will become part of the student's permanent record or cumulative file. Diagnostic labels such as "drug abuser" or "chemically dependent," in addition to pejorative labels, are never to be used in documents referring to a student or in conversation about the student with third parties by any staff member.

12. The use of prescription medications is to be construed as an exception to this policy when used *by the individual* for whom they are prescribed, when used in the manner and amounts prescribed, and when used in accordance with other school policies governing student medications.

13. Parents of all students participating in the Student Assistance Program will be specifically notified of their child's involvement at some point.

a. Parents will be informed of their child's involvement in the Student Assistance Program immediately in cases of violations of this policy.

b. In cases where students participate in the program through self-referral or other avenues (section 4), parents will be notified as soon as practicable. The SAP staff will document reasons behind their decision to postpone parent notification and involvement.

   c. Prior parent notification and consent will be required in all cases before student contact with any Certified AODA Counselor who is from an approved AODA community agency and who is not a School District employee.

14. The Board of Education's protection from liability will be extended to all staff to the extent that they act in accordance with this policy and observe the procedures consistent with it established within their respective buildings.

15. The responsibility for operating the Student Assistance Program will be in the hands of each building administrator (or his/her designee), who will interpret the district's policy to students, staff, parents, and the community.

   a. Final decisions regarding disciplinary action and the consequences of other violations of this policy will be made by the building administrator in consultation with the SAP Coordinator/Counselor and other members of the building Core Team.

   b. It shall be the responsibility of each building administrator (or his/her designee) to develop procedures consistent with this policy to and to permit the necessary staff training and inservice necessary for their implementation.

16. The Board of Education will make available resources sufficient for personnel and training necessary for the implementation of this policy.

| Chapter 20 | # Program Design |

A great many concrete decisions need to be made regarding the formal design of the student assistance program. Some are local, building-level decisions, others affect the district as a whole, and still others may involve the school system in activities impacting on the continuum of care for alcohol and other drug abuse in the larger community. In practice, of course, many program decisions are made throughout the implementation process. They are involved in the decision to investigate the Student Assistance Program model in the first place; a host of concrete decisions are implicit in the process of devising appropriate AODA policy language. Many of the issues described during the Program Design phase of program implementation will have been raised during the early deliberations of the Core Committee. To the extent that they are not, or need to be focussed upon in more detail, these activities will be treated here as belonging to a separate stage in the implementation process.

Whether as a continuation of the Planning and Organizing phase or as a discrete stage itself, the Program Design task engages school system staff in four major areas of activity: making decisions about the organization and coordination of the program at the district and building levels, expanding the needs assessment process to focus on how the six major program functions are currently accomplished, developing an ongoing implementation plan, and making a formal presentation to the Board of Education for its endorsement of the program.

Organization and Coordination

The formation of the Core Committee and the workings of a policy subcommittee represent the degree of formal organization which already exists. As mentioned earlier, widening the membership of the Core Committee is an ongoing implementation task. Additional organizational decisions need to be made at some point. These typically will involve assembling well-defined Core Teams, identifying and clarifying program roles (e.g., Student Assistance Program Coordinators), drafting program procedures (which are not typically endorsed by the Board of Education), and continuing the process of networking with community youth-serving and AODA-related resources.

Assembling Core Teams. The Core Committee will ideally be made up of at least one representative from each school building, and will be district-wide in scope. One of the tasks of each such representative will be to begin the process of forming building-level Core Teams. The Core Teams can be though of as reflecting the Core Committee in miniature. As described in Chapter 6, and depicted in Figure 6.3, at least building administrators and pupil services staff should participate, along with interested teachers and building-level staff in key relationships with students: the nurse, coaches, club advisors, etc. Parent and student representatives are also helpful.

Some work needs to go into educating Core Team members concerning the role of the Team in the various program functions: e.g., early identification, assessment and intervention, and support group facilitation. The functions of its possible substructures, such as the Referral Team and the Screening Team should also be considered where appropriate. Obviously, the assembly of building-level Core Teams relies on the degree of the school system's commitment to a team approach to operating a student assistance program.

Core Teams can serve a number of important functions during the design as well as operation phases of program implementation. As subgroups of a district-wide effort they represent the unique needs and character of individual buildings. Drafts of philosophy and policy language should be submitted to these groups for their review and input. Decisions on program coordination are also ultimately local. The Core Teams are in the best position to identify additional members of the district Core Group and participants in Core Group training. While policy language lends district-wide consistency to the program, specific procedures may need to reflect the autonomy accorded to individual buildings in its implementation. Similarly, inservice needs are frequently best defined and met within the individual high school, middle school, and elementary buildings. In short, the early formation of Core Teams provides the basis for how remaining implementation steps will be realized at the local level.

Program Roles. At some point in the implementation process, decisions need to be made on designating persons to fill various program-specific roles and on defining their responsibilities. A district-wide Student Assistance Program Director may have been designated as part of the initial Core Committee's formation. Her responsibilities at this point may have been defined as consisting of guiding and coordinating the implementation process. Additional responsibilities which relate to the operation and ongoing maintenance of the program may be defined later.

Within individual buildings, one or more persons need to be designated to fulfill the role of SAP Coordinator/Counselor(s). As described earlier, in some larger buildings these two roles may be separated into those functions which primarily involve coordination and those which primarily involve direct services to students. During the implementation phase, the building level SAP Coordinator/Counselor often chairs the Core team and coordinates its decision-making regarding the program's implementation at this level. He is often the major liaison person between the Core Team and the district-wide Core Committee or Core Group.

The Core Committee may also become involved in defining the role of "contact person" and identifying persons within the building who would be invited to participate in the Core Team in that role.

Procedures. The Core Committee, or the emerging Core Group, can draft a statement of procedures which integrate the school's AODA policy, program roles, and student AODA-related services. Such a draft document would outline the general philosophy and principles behind the effective management of students with AODA-related problems (e.g., Supplement 12.1). While the Board of Education may be informed of general procedures it typically does not formally endorse them since they may need to be altered repeatedly even during the program's first months of operation. A general descritpion of program procedures can be utilitzed by each building-level Core Team as a point of departure in drafting its own.

Networking. The school district, through its Core Committee, will need to continue to evaluate the community's continuum of care for those with AODA-related problems. The compilation of a directory of AODA services may have been completed earlier. The various AODA services may have been contacted and evaluated, either by site visit, questionnaire, or interview with agency staff. To the extent that these activities have not been completed earlier, they often become part of Program Design activities. If they have been completed, the scope is often then widened to include an investigation of the function of other community institutions with respect to student alcohol and other drug abuse: the police and sheriff's departments, the juvenile justice system as a whole, the department of social services, local hospitals and detoxification services, etc. The thorough analysis of the continuum of care often awaits the designation of roles within each building, since one of the goals of the analysis is to establish or improve school/agency communication and working relationships.

Continuing Needs Assessment

A preliminary assessment of the need for more effective programming for students with AODA-related problems will already have been done, at least in terms of the relative numbers of students likely to begin the various target groups. More in depth surveys may often have been delayed until this point. In any event, the school will need to conduct further needs assessment activity in several areas: evaluating the school regarding the program functions, evaluating the need for support groups, and drafting specific student-centered impact goals for each target group.

The implementation process has begun, and continued this far, because there is a perception that student needs outstrip the school's current response. There may be a general perception that what the school system has been doing is inappropriate, or that it isn't enough. In making specific decisions about the design of its student assistance program, the school system will have to examine itself more concretely regarding each of the basic program functions described in Part Two. In other words, to what degree does the district identify, assess, intervene, and support students with AODA-related problems, and work effectively with chemical dependency treatment programs in the community? The answers to this question are often intuitive, but specific attention needs to be focussed on it within each building as well as on a district-wide level. Focussing on some specific questions often reveals the patterns of philosophical, conceptual, attitudinal, and procedural factors which will need to be addressed in order to improve the ability of the school to manage students who have AODA-related problems more effectively.

Supplement 20.2, "Assessing Program Functions," contains a checklist of basic questions which can guide program implementers in making program design decisions. This assessment usually reveals that most barriers to effective program operation can be addressed by clarifying staff roles and procedures, enhancing the knowledge and skills of staff members, and clarifying the role of the school system with respect to the continuum of care - goals which must be addressed through the remainder of the implementation process.

Support Groups. AODA-related support groups are one of the major services which are unique to the student assistance program and which may not currently exist within the school system. As described in Chapter 11 and 13, the implementation of support groups cannot be casual. Decisions need to be made concerning the types of groups which will be implemented in each building, and according to what time schedule. Supplement 13.4 can assist Core Team and Core Committee members in estimating the number of groups and group leaders which will be required. Many policy issues, such as those described in Supplements 13.1, also arise: parent permission, criteria for selecting group facilitators, confidentiality, etc. While policy issues should be resolved on a district-wide basis, individual Core Teams will have to be involved in making local decisions about the nature and number of groups and the plans for their implementation.

Student-centered Goals. Establishing specific program goals provides direction for the program at the building as well as the district-wide levels, and anticipates activities in program evaluation — the final implementation task. Previous needs assessment activities should have resulted in realistic estimates of need, based at least on the numbers of students purported to be in the various target groups. The Core Committee, in preparation for its presentation to the Board of Education, should prepare a number of specific goals which relate specifically to these student needs. As *implementation* goals these amount to statements of intent, whereas during the first year of a program's operation, goals are usually more concrete and more outcome-oriented.

In our hypothetical school district, for example, Midville High School has 2,484 students enrolled in grades 10-12. As a result of its preliminary needs assessment activity the Core Team has settled upon 5 per cent, or 124 students, as a realistic estimate of the number who are chemically dependent. In addition, 15 per cent, or 372 students, are abusing alcohol or other drugs, and 25 per cent, or 621 students, are affected family members. The Core Team has also realized that all of these students cannot be assisted during the program's first year. It would be more reasonable to expect to identify and help one sixth of each of these students in each of their six secondary school years. Moreover, they would also be satisfied to identify and assist, or have an impact upon, only 75 per cent of those in need in their first year. In formulating some preliminary program impact goals, then, they conclude that they intend to identify and assist 15 chemically dependent youth (124 x 16.6% x 75%), 46 abusing students, and 77 affected family members.

Student-centered goals are ideally established by the individual Core Teams in the various school buildings, and summarized at the Core Committee level. Goals relating to the implementation process itself are also defined at this point.

The Program Implementation Plan

In preparation for the presentation of the program to the Board of Education, a more formalized implementation plan is also necessary. The minimal components of an implementation plan include (1) the general scope and design of the program, (2) a three year timeline for implementation and operation, and maintenance, and (3) an estimated budget for each year.

Scope and Design. It is important for the Board of Education to understand that the student assistance program is not just for a specific age group (e.g., high school students) or for a specific type of alcohol/drug problem (e.g., kids who get caught "dealing"). Its comprehensiveness in terms of target groups as well as grade levels must be stressed. The implementation process need not attempt to manage the complexities of the entire school district, especially in a larger community, all at one time. In some school systems, for example, the program is implemented on a pilot basis in one or more natural subsystems of the school district, and expanded to include the rest of the district in succeeding years. Sometimes programs are implemented vertically: they typically begin with the high school and are exported "downward" in successive years to the middle and elementary schools. Alternatively, some districts have implemented the program in school buildings which have a feeder relationship to

each other: e.g., one high school and its feeder middle and elementary schools. The program is then exported "horizontally" to other similar subsystems in succeeding years.

Pilot programs have a number of advantages. They require fewer staff and financial resources during the first year. The Board may be willing to take certain risks in approving new policy language, knowing that it is on a provisional, experimental basis. The pilot program strategy also lets school staff gain considerable experience which it can employ in assisting sister buildings in designing and implementing the program. Pilot programs do, however, have some disadvantages. Implementing the program on a such a limited basis may not create the broader atmosphere of district-wide and community-wide ownership which is necessary for successful student assistance programs. Moreover, the training, inservice, and promotional activities may be difficult to limit to only one segment of the school district. These disadvantages are not as problematic for vertically implemented programs, because these remain district-wide in scope.

The plan to proceed on either a district-wide or pilot program basis may have emerged early in the deliberations of the Core Committee. It is a major program design decision, however, which needs to be made as early as possible.

A Three-Year Plan. It is beneficial to plan the implementation of a student assistance program to occur over at least a three year period. This does not mean that initial implementation tasks need to be spread out over this time period. It merely indicates that the establishing an effective program involves maintenance.

Figure 20.1

MIDVILLE PUBLIC SCHOOLS
Program Implementation Timeline

IMPLEMENTATION TASK	1987 JAN	FEB	MAR	APR	MAY	JUN	JUL	AUG	SEP	OCT	NOV	DEC	1988 JAN	FEB	MAR	APR	MAY	JUN	JUL	AUG	SEP	OCT	NOV	DEC
1. Planning and Organizing																								
a. Form Core Committee	→																							
b. Needs Assessment		→	→																					
c. Presentation to BOE				→																				
2. Policy Development																								
a. Review Existing Policy			→	→																				
b. Draft New Policy					→																			
c. Review New Policy					→																			
3. Program Design																								
a. Form Core Teams				→																				
b. Designate Coordinator(s)					→																			
c. Continue Needs Assessment		→	→	→	→																			
d. Train Group Facilitators						→																		
4. Core Group Development																								
a. Expand Core Group			→	→	→	→																		
b. Train Core Group							→																	
c. Train Assessment Staff								→																
d. Train Group Facilitators								→																
5. Program Promotion																								
a. Circulate brochures									→	→														
b. Conduct Staff Inservice								→																
c. Conduct Student Inservice									→	→	→	→	→	→	→									
d. Conduct Community Education											→			→			→			→				
6. Program Evaluation																								
a. Develop Goals and Objectives								→																
b. Develop Data Collection										→														
c. Collect Data												→						→						
d. Prepare Evaluation Report																			→					

Planning that covers this time frame has a number of advantages. In educational circles it can become easy to discount each year's new initiative, program, project, or mandate as a phase which will pass, ultimately changing life in the school very little. Thus, getting others to think about the program in longer-range terms helps to prevent this "program of the year" syndrome. It also requires implementers to be consciously aware of the need for ongoing program promotional activity. The program, in other words, does not run by itself. A three year plan forces all involved to think in terms of initial implementation, program operation, and program maintenance tasks. Finally, presenting the Board of Education and other funding sources with a three year plan helps create the appropriate atmosphere for a long-term commitment to working to address student alcohol and other drug-related problems. The student assistance program does not represent just another "quick fix."

Figure 20.1 is a simple example of the type of timeline which Core Committee members may wish to include in their Board presentation. Such tables can easily be more detailed, breaking implementation tasks down into more specific activities. As the focus at this point is only upon the program implementation phase, a timeline is often need be made up for only the first year. It is difficult for Core Committee members to anticipate, with any degree of certainty, the specific program activities which will be needed three years hence. In some cases, however, broad program activities can be anticipated: broadening the implementation of support groups, expanding the program to other buildings, scheduling additional Core Training, expanding staff inservice programs in AODA, etc.

Note that a timeline is an implicit statement of specific goals and objectives of a *process* nature. It depicts which goals will be accomplished by what time. A more explicit statement of such goals and objectives is frequently a necessary part of the presentation to the Boards of Education

Budget. By the stage of program design, those planning the program and its implementation will have a fairly good idea of the resources which will be needed in terms of numbers of staff, amount of staff time, training needs, materials, etc. An initial decision regarding the scope of the program will have an impact on the amount of personal, material, and financial resources which will be required during the first and succeeding years of the program's operation. Supplement 20.3 is an illustrative example of a three year budget which our hypothetical school district might propose to the Board of Education. As indicated above, requesting budget authority for at least the first three years accustoms the Board and others in the district to think of the program as being long-term.

Presenting the Program to the Board of Education

Planning and organizing, philosophy and policy development, and program design tasks all point toward preparing a formal presentation to the Board of Education in order to seek endorsement of the program and its policies and funding for remaining implementation tasks as well as for its operation. If the Board has been kept informed of preliminary activity, and if Board members have been included on the Core Committee, it will be well-prepared to formally "enact" the student assistance program. Community involvement in the process will also allow Board members to perceive their actions as consistent with the community's will, energies, values, and support.

In some school districts, staff have gone to considerable lengths to prepare a formal program description which is submitted to the Board. The program description attempts to give Board members as complete a picture of the program as possible at this stage. The following are among the typical components of a formal program description:

- Statement of Need: trends in student alcohol/drug use; local prevalence estimates; description of target groups; description of existing services, policies, and practices;

- Policies and Procedures: recommended AODA philosophy and policy language; outline of procedures for managing various AODA-related problems; policy issues relating to support groups;

- Staffing Pattern: descriptions of the roles and responsibilities of the District Student Assistance Program Director, building-level SAP Counselor/ Coordinators, Group Facilitators;

- Program Services: a description of in-school information, counseling, referral, and support group services offered to students and parents;

- Goals and Objectives: a statements of the broad goals of the program, including how it is intended to impact on each AODA-related target group; statements of specific program objectives for the first year; a statement of implementation goals and objectives;

- Implementation Steps: a description of the remaining steps of program implementation, including a timeline for the first year;

- Program Budget: a request for funding for the first year of program implementation; an estimate of funding needs for the second year and third years (program operation and maintenance);

- Networking: a description of working relationships between the school's student assistance program and the community and between the school and community AODA resources;

- Endorsements: a list of supportive statements and/or letters from community agencies, parents' groups, service clubs and organizations, AODA agencies, etc., including pledges or contributions of financial support.

Despite its virtues, such a lengthy and complete document is not always necessary. And, in some cases, the presentation of the program to the Board of Education does not take place all at once. The Board may be presented with various components of the program -policy language, funding requests, position requests - at various appropriate stages of the implementation process.

By the end of the Program Design stage of initial implementation, the major decisions about the existence and broad outlines of the student assistance program have been made. The next major step in moving toward making the program operational is often securing appropriate AODA training for all of those with key roles in the school's program, and for significant community representatives.

Chapter 20 | # Supplement

Supplement 20.1, "Implementation Checklist III," summarizes the implementation activities typical of the Program Design phase.

Supplement 20.2, "Assessing Program Functions," is a checklist of questions regarding how each of the basic program functions early identification, assessment, intervention, treatment, support, and case management are currently carried out within the school system or individual buildings.

Supplement 20.3, "Sample Program Budget," provides a sample three-year budget estimate and detailed budgets for each of the program's first three years.

Supplement 20.1

IMPLEMENTATION CHECKLIST III:
Program Design

TASK: *To design a Student Assistance Program and secure Board of Education permission to implement it.*

IMPLEMENTATION ACTIVITY	RESPONSIBILITY OF:	RESOURCES NEEDED:	COMPLETION DATE:
A. Organization and Coordination 1. Assemble building-level Core Teams 2. Designate District SAP Director 3. Designate building-level SAP Coordinator(s) 4. Identify SAP "contact persons" in each building 5. Define roles of Program Director, Coordinator, and Contact Person 6. Identify potential support group facilitators 7. Draft procedure statements 8. Continue compiling directory of AODA services 9. Continue evaluating AODA continuum of care 10. Review proposed philosophy and policy language			
B. Continue Needs Assessment Activity 1. Assess current status regarding program functions 2. Assess need for various AODA-related support groups in each building 3. Determine plan for implementing support groups in each building 4. Identify proposed goals and objectives for various AODA-related target groups			
C. Develop Implementation Plan 1. Determine initial scope of program (i.e., pilot program or district-wide?) 2. Develop implementation goals 3. Develop 3-year timeline for remaining implementation steps 4. Develop a proposed budget for the program			
D. Present program to Board of Education for endorsement, including: 1. Statement of need 2. Proposed philosophy and policy 3. Staffing needs 4. Description of program services 5. Goals and objectives 6. Funding request			

Supplement 20.2

ASSESSING PROGRAM FUNCTIONS

As part of designing its student assistance program or of assessing the need for a different approach to student AODA-related problems, examining the school system with respect to the basic program functions can be instructive. The questions which follow can assist those involved in planning and designing a program to assess the degree to which the early identification, assessment, intervention, treatment, support, and case management functions are performed in each school building and throughout the district as a whole.

IDENTIFICATION

1. To what degree are school staff aware of qualitative and quantitative differences in students' AODA-related experiences? Are they aware of the different "target groups" of students and differences in their AODA-related needs?

2. To what degree is the school currently identifying students in each target group? Are students being identified in proportion to their numbers?

3. To what degree does the school employ several identification criteria: i.e., "witnessed use," "suspected use," "concerned other?"

4. To what extent are students identified by a variety of identification and referral sources: staff, peer, parent, self-, and community referral?

5. Are students currently identified accidentally and haphazardly? Is there a conscious and deliberate strategy?

6. What patterns of resistance or denial prevent the early identification of students abusing alcohol or other drugs? What patterns prevent the early identification of children of alcoholics and other concerned students?

7. How are such patterns of denial and/or resistance currently manifested in students, teachers, counselors, administrators, and parents?

8. How are referrals recorded or documented? Is there a need to devise or revise referral forms?

9. Do patterns of identification reflect any stereotyping of students? Are there generally accepted biases regarding students who "are probably on drugs" as opposed to students who "can't possibly be using drugs?"

10. To what degree does the general school climate promote or prevent identification of students with AODA-related problems? If you were a student with such a problem would you self-refer or accept help if it was offered?

11. To what degree do all staff members understand their role in early identification? Has their role been formally clarified? Do classroom teachers think it is their responsibility to "counsel" students themselves? To report suspicions about drug abuse to parents?

12. To what degree to staff fail to identify and refer because of perceptions that "nothing ever changes?"

13. Can the school's information system or student data base be utilized to identify potentially troubled or problem students?

14. What are some appropriate short- and long-term goals for enhancing the early identification process?

ASSESSMENT

1. How are students currently assessed for the presence of AODA-related problems? Is it the responsibility of one person? Is it taken for granted and loosely assumed to be done by all "counselors?"

2. How do you know that appropriate AODA assessment is being done? Can others depend on it being done?

3. Is the school clear about the continuum of care for alcohol and other drug abuse in the community? Have key school staff developed effective communication and working relationships with AODA agencies?

4. Is the school clear about its partnership with community AODA agencies regarding assessing student AODA-related problems?

5. What sources of data are used in the assessment process (e.g., student records, contacts with staff and parents, student interviews)? Are various resources available, such as one-to-one counseling, use-focussed groups, etc.?

6. Is the staff clear about the interrelationship between assessment and intervention as processes?

7. Is the staff clear about the limitations of the school's roll — that it cannot and need not diagnose drug-related problems?

8. Are staff members aware of a range of assessment recommendations?

9. Are those involved in assessing students appropriately trained in alcohol and other drug abuse issues? Do they know what to look for and what it means?

10. Is assessment done for all students in all target groups?

11. To what extent does the staff appreciate assessment as a process and not as a discrete, brief event?

12. Are there any philosophical stances in the staff which enhance or impede their ability to accurately assess students for AODA-related problems?

13. What records are maintained to document the fact that the assessment has occurred, its findings, and its recommendations?

14. What are some appropriate short- and long-term goals for enhancing the assessment process?

INTERVENTION

1. What is the pattern of interventive steps currently taken by the school? Does the school seem to choose between inpatient treatment and nothing?

2. Does everyone understand the continuum of progressive intervention? Do staff members appreciate the different levels of intervention appropriate to students with different degrees of AODA-involvement?

3. Does the staff understand intervention as a process and not as a discrete event?

4. Who are involved in the intervention and referral processes?

5. How do you know that a student who needs treatment for chemical dependency will get it?

6. What is the scope of the continuum of care for AODA problems in the community? What are the implications for the school in terms of expanding in-school services? Does the school need to advocate for changes in the community's service delivery system for AODA-involved youth?

7. What is the quality of the working relationships between the school and community AODA agencies? Is "confidentiality" used as an excuse not to cooperate or communicate?

8. At what point are parents involved in the assessment/intervention process?

9. Are relevant staff members knowledgeable about the process of intervention in alcohol/drug abuse and skillful in its use?

10. What school policies and procedures contribute to intervention? Are there appropriate consequences for AODA-related behavior? Are they appropriately enforced?

11. What biases impede intervention and referral (e.g., punishment alone will change behavior; all students can change by themselves if they want to)?

12. To what degree are school staff fearful of confronting students and/or parents when alcohol/drug issues are involved?

13. What are some appropriate short- and long-term goals for enhancing the intervention process?

TREATMENT

1. Is everyone clear about the appropriate boundary between the school's role in identification, assessment, and intervention, and the AODA agency's role in primary treatment of chemical dependency?

2. What treatment resources exist locally? Are treatment program appropriate for youth?

3. What factors inhibit the utilization of local chemical dependency treatment resources (e.g., inappropriate philosophical orientation, absence of AODA-specific treatment, absence of staff qualified to work with youth, etc.)?

4. What expectations do school staff have regarding the returning, recovering student? Are the expectations realistic and appropriate?

5. Does the school observe a formal process to ease the re-entry of student into the school system after treatment?

6. To what degree is the staff knowledgeable about the dynamics of chemical dependency and the recovery issues of young people?

7. What is the quality of the working relationship between the school and treatment programs?

8. Are there needs for additional treatment programs, or more appropriate treatment programs for youth, that are not being met in the community?

9. What are some short- and long-term goals which would enhance the school's participation in the treatment process? The availability of treatment?

SUPPORT

1. What sources of in-school support exist (e.g., knowledgeable counselors, support groups, etc.)?

2. Do all staff recognize the need to provide support for students engaged in changing resistant behaviors?

3. How supportive is the school climate for getting help or remaining drug free?

4. Does the school recognize the unique needs of each target group? Are there separate support services for recovering students, concerned others, and student affected by their own drug use?

5. To what degree does the administration support the need for and functioning of support groups?

6. To what degree does the teaching staff support students' participation in groups?

7. What, specifically, is the level of need for various support groups?

8. What is the level of need for support group facilitators?

9. Is there an adequate understanding of the rationale for and limits of the AODA-related support groups (i.e., that they do not provide therapy or supplant community self-help services)?

10. What barriers exist to the implementation of AODA-related support groups among students, staff, and administration, and the community?

11. What are some short- and long-term goals which would enhance the degree of support services fort students changing harmful AODA-related behaviors?

CASE MANAGEMENT

1. Are student AODA-related needs currently being met by "activities which bring students, parents, and other resources together within a planned framework of action intended to achieve individual goals?"

2. Do teachers, pupil services staff, and administrators understand their respective roles in identifying, assessing, intervening, and supporting students with AODA-related problems?

3. To what extent are AODA-related services considered to be the sole responsibility of one person in the school? To what extent is the participation in AODA-related services shared cooperatively?

4. Do AODA-related services have a focus, or is it just taken for granted that kids get helped?

5. What assurances are there that AODA issues will always be addressed and addressed appropriately? Is this, too, taken for granted?

6. Are there clear procedures which guide staff and assure due process to students, parents, and staff?

7. Do procedures distinguish between witnessed use, suspected AODA-involvement, affected others issues, etc.?

8. Do procedures promote or hinder self-referral?

9. To what degree are parent contacts avoided, feared, or postponed? To what degree are parents seen as allies in helping students to change?

10. To what degree is there a need to create specific program roles and structures? Is there a need for a "team" approach?

11. To what degree does staff document efforts to help students who have AODA-related problems?

12. What are some short- and long-term goals which would enhance the effective management of students with AODA-related problems?

Supplement 20.3
SAMPLE PROGRAM BUDGET

The sample budget which follows is a representative example of a three-year budget for the implementation of a student assistance program in our hypothetical school district, Midville Public Schools. The existence of many local variables render it impossible to develop a definitive budget. The two largest cost centers for the program are personnel and training. Thus, the various local decisions in these two areas will materially affected the magnitude of actual program costs. Thus, the examples on the following pages are merely intended to be illustrative of the major cost centers involved in the first three years of a program's implementation. Note that these are *planning* documents.

The three one-year detailed budgets are followed by a three-year summary.

BUDGET DETAIL

Personnel. The examples reflect certain assumptions concerning costs as well as decisions made during the Program Design phase of implementation. For example, Midville Schools has identified a District Coordinator and seven building-level SAP Coordinators. Existing staff persons will serve in these roles. During the first year, where each will be involved primarily in planning and implementation activity, each will be compensated at the rate of 10 per cent of their base salaries. Note that approximately 80 per cent of a full-time equivalent (FTE) position is involved initially; in the second and third years, coordination expands to 1.25 FTE.

During the second and third years, the District SAP Director's involvement remains the same, at 10 per cent. The secondary SAP Coordinator positions are expanded to 25 per cent to reflect the time spent in leading support groups and in assessment and intervention activities. Coordination at the elementary level also remains at 10 per cent of a full-time position. Most of this time is expected to be spent in leading support groups for Affected Others.

Note that the budgets do not contain an estimate of the costs for staff time spent in leading support groups. In the early planning stages of program implementation, it will seldom be possible to accurately estimate the number of groups which will be operational and the cost of facilitating them. Often, decisions regarding a method of compensating group facilitators has not been decided upon at this stage either.

Training and Consultation. Training costs will vary widely according to the source of training and the size of training groups. Midville Public Schools has decided to rely upon outside training resources specializing in the implementation of student assistance programs. Core Group Training is an intensive five-day workshop for approximately 60 Core Team members and community representatives. Substitutes for 20 staff members will be needed, at a cost of $45 per day for five days ($4500). Similarly, Group Facilitation Skills training for 18 potential support group leaders will require substitutes for approximately nine staff members for five days ($2025). Midville also plans to hold a three-day workshop on assessment skills for its secondary level Core Team members.

Consultation costs have been figured on the basis of 4 consultation days at $600 per day.

Printing and Mailing. Midville plans to design and distribute special brochures advertising the program to students, parents, and the community. Altogether, it estimates that it will print and distribute 13,000 brochures each year. Brochures are estimated to cost $.10 each for printing.

Miscellaneous. Midville plans to purchase three films for use in training students, staff, and parents during the first year. It will also purchase a number of reference books on alcohol and other drug abuse for Core Team members.

MIDVILLE PUBLIC SCHOOLS
Student Assistance Program
Three-Year Budget

ITEM/DESCRIPTION	FIRST YEAR	SECOND YEAR	THIRD YEAR
I. PERSONNEL			
A. District Coordinator	4,000	4,000	4,000
B. Building Coordinators	18,200	29,900	29,900
TOTAL:	22,200	33,900	33,900
II. TRAINING and CONSULTATION			
A. Training Costs			
1. Core Group	5,000	5,000	
2. Group Facilitation	6,500	6,500	6,500
3. Assessment Skills	4,000		
4. Inservice	1,000	1,000	
5. Miscellaneous			
6. Consultation	2,400	600	
B. Substitutes	7,650	2,025	2,025
TOTAL:	26,550	15,125	8,525
III. PRINTING AND MAILING	2,475	2,475	2,475
IV. MISCELLANEOUS MATERIALS	1,800	800	0
GRAND TOTAL:	53,025	52,300	44,900

MIDVILLE PUBLIC SCHOOLS
Student Assistance Program Budget
First Year Budget Detail

ITEM/DESCRIPTION	BASE SALARY	PER CENT TIME	FIRST YEAR TOTAL
I. PERSONNEL			
A. District Coordinator	40,000	10	4,000
B. Building Coordinators			
1. High School	26,000	10	2,600
2. Middle School 1	26,000	10	2,600
3. Middle School 2	26,000	10	2,600
4. Elementary 1	26,000	10	2,600
5. Elementary 2	26,000	10	2,600
6. Elementary 3	26,000	10	2,600
7. Elementary 4	26,000	10	2,600
TOTAL:			22,200
II. TRAINING and CONSULTATION			
A. Core Group Training			
1. Training Cost			5,000
2. Substitutes (20)			4,500
B. Group Facilitation			
1. Training Cost			6,500
2. Substitutes (9)			2,025
C. Assessment Skills			
1. Training Cost			4,000
2. Substututes (9)			2,025
D. Inservice Training			1,000
E. Miscellaneous Training			
F. Consultation			2,400
TOTAL:			22,200
III. PRINTING AND MAILING			
A. Student Brochure (5000)			500
B. Parent Brochure (6000)			600
C. Community Brochure (2000)			200
D. Staff Newsletter (750)			375
E. Mailing			800
TOTAL:			2,475
IV. MISCELLANEOUS MATERIALS			
A. Films (3 x @$500)			1,500
B. Books			300
TOTAL:			1,800
GRAND TOTAL:			53,025

MIDVILLE PUBLIC SCHOOLS
Student Assistance Program Budget
Second Year Budget Detail

ITEM/DESCRIPTION	BASE SALARY	PER CENT TIME	SECOND YEAR TOTAL
I. PERSONNEL			
A. District Coordinator	40,000	10	4,000
B. Building Coordinators			
1. High School	26,000	25	4,000
2. Middle School 1	26,000	25	6,500
3. Middle School 2	26,000	25	6,500
4. Elementary 1	26,000	10	2,600
5. Elementary 2	26,000	10	2,600
6. Elementary 3	26,000	10	2,600
7. Elementary 4	26,000	10	2,600
TOTAL:			33,900
II. TRAINING and CONSULTATION			
A. Core Group Training			
1. Training Cost			5,000
2. Substitutes			
B. Group Facilitation			
1. Training Cost			6,500
2. Substitutes (9)			2,025
C. Assessment Skills			
1. Training Cost			
2. Substututes			
D. Inservice Training			1,000
E. Miscellaneous Training			
F. Consultation			600
TOTAL:			15,125
III. PRINTING AND MAILING			
A. Student Brochure (5000)			500
B. Parent Brochure (6000)			600
C. Community Brochure (2000)			200
D. Staff Newsletter (750)			375
E. Mailing			800
TOTAL:			2,475
IV. MISCELLANEOUS MATERIALS			
A. Films (1 x @$500)			500
B. Books			300
TOTAL:			800
GRAND TOTAL:			52,300

MIDVILLE PUBLIC SCHOOLS
Student Assistance Program Budget
Third Year Budget Detail

ITEM/DESCRIPTION	BASE SALARY	PER CENT TIME	THIRD YEAR TOTAL
I. PERSONNEL			
A. District Coordinator	40,000	10	4,000
B. Building Coordinators			
1. High School	26,000	10	4,000
2. Middle School 1	26,000	25	6,500
3. Middle School 2	26,000	25	6,500
4. Elementary 1	26,000	10	2,600
5. Elementary 2	26,000	10	2,600
6. Elementary 3	26,000	10	2,600
7. Elementary 4	26,000	10	2,600
TOTAL:			33,900
II. TRAINING and CONSULTATION			
A. Core Group Training			
1. Training Cost			
2. Substitutes			
B. Group Facilitation			
1. Training Cost			6,500
2. Substitutes (9)			2,025
C. Assessment Skills			
1. Training Cost			
2. Substututes			
D. Inservice Training			
E. Miscellaneous Training			
F. Consultation			
TOTAL:			8,525
III. PRINTING AND MAILING			
A. Student Brochure (5000)			500
B. Parent Brochure (6000)			600
C. Community Brochure (2000)			200
D. Staff Newsletter (750)			375
E. Mailing			800
TOTAL:			2,475
IV. MISCELLANEOUS MATERIALS			
A. Films			
B. Books			
TOTAL:			0
GRAND TOTAL:			44,900

Chapter 21

Core Group Development

"History is 99 per cent the achievement of people who never made history."

Since the beginning of the program implementation process, involvement has been widening, from one or two individuals to the formation of a Core Committee, through the assembly of Core Teams in each school building in the district. Core Group development continues the process of expanding participation in the student assistance program and enhancing participants' awareness of and skill in dealing with AODA-related problems. Activities typical of the Core Group Development phase of program implementation culminate in the formation of a joint school/community Core Group whose members undergo intensive training which covers both alcohol/drug-related concepts and skills and the specifics of the student assistance program.

The School/Community Core Group

The district's Core Committee, or the group which begins the implementation process, often evolves into a group with broader representation. As the name implies, the school/community Core Group is a body made up jointly of school/community representatives. To the extent that the nucleus of the Core Group is made up of school district staff, its primary function, at least initially, is to oversee and support the implementation, operation, and maintenance of the school district's student assistance program. In most cases the Core Group itself will evolve into an organization which is active in many areas of effective response to AODA problems which extend beyond the boundaries of the school system to include the community as a whole. As mentioned previously, sometimes it is a community-based group, looking into the scope of drug and alcohol problems among youth, which provides the impetus for student assistance programming in the school. The directionality of school/community involvement is not important; we have arbitrarily chosen the school system as the starting point.

As depicted in Figure 6.4 in Chapter 6, the district-wide Core Group should consist of key school staff who will have roles in the implementation and operation of the program:

- Core Committee members;

- The district administrator (or his designee);

- Other key representatives from the central administration (e.g., the Director of Guidance or Student Personnel, the Directors of Elementary and Secondary Education, the Athletic Director, the Director of Instruction, etc.);

- School Board representatives;

- The Core Teams in each elementary and secondary building, consisting of building administrators, pupil services staff, teachers and other interested staff; interested students and parents from each building.

Obviously, the size of the district will have an impact on the size of school's representation on the Core Group. In our hypothetical district, with a K-12 enrollment of 10,000 students in seven buildings, the Core Group could easily consist of 35 or 40 school representatives alone.

Expanding school/community participation does not need to be delayed until any specific stage of program implementation. Rather, as indicated earlier, it is part of an ongoing process. However, to the extent that it has not yet involved key segments of the community, representatives from the following should be approached to become part of the Core Group:

- Local police and sheriff's departments;

- Youth-serving agencies (e.g., counseling centers, mental health clinics, etc.);

- Alcohol and other drug abuse services;

- The self-help groups, such as Alcoholics Anonymous, Al-Anon, Alateen, Narcotics Anonymous, Cocaine Anonymous, Families Anonymous;

- Juvenile court judges; municipal magistrates; juvenile intake workers and other participants in the juvenile justice system;

- Probation and parole officers;

- Members of the local or county department of welfare or social services, especially those who deal with child protection services, family violence, sexual abuse, etc.;

- Clergy;

- Electronic and print media;

- Parents groups and organizations;

- Existing alcohol/drug task forces, advisory groups, community action groups, Chemical People groups, etc.;

- Service clubs and organizations (e.g., Kiwanis, Optimists, Rotary, Lions, Jaycees, Junior League, etc.);

- Volunteer organizations (e.g., Big Brothers, Big Sisters, etc.);

- Municipal and county government;

- The medical community;

- Business and industry.

The formation, at some point, of a joint school/community Core Group becomes a necessary implementation task. With even minimal participation by school staff and the community representatives above, the Core Group can easily number above 60 persons. A group of this size will soon require some degree of organization. To the extent that the Core Group retains its school district focus, the SAP Program Director often chairs the Core Group; other "officers" may be elected.

The Core Group also needs a clear sense of direction and succeeds to the extent that it is task-oriented. Membership and participation in any community group typically subsides if members are merely subjected to films, information nights, and speakers. While alcohol/-drug awareness and training activities are needed to develop the Core Group, the Group and its members must have concrete tasks. The overall task of the Core Group is to provide school and community support for the student assistance program by facilitating the identification, assessment, intervention, treatment, and support of students with AODA-related problems utilizing the resources within the school and within the community.

In general, the Core Group assists with the remaining program implementation, operation, and maintenance activities. Often, the Core Group will need to recognize at least five major tasks and form working groups or subcommittees to carry them out.

Core Group training. A subcommittee is often charged with identifying and scheduling appropriate AODA-related training for all members of the Core

Group. This may entail developing a broad and long-range training plan designed to enhance the level of awareness of many in the school and the community of the drug and alcohol-related problems faced by young people. More often, the initial concern is with identifying local and/or non-local sources of intensive AODA-related training which will not only provide Core Group members with a uniform language and perspective but which will contribute to team building.

Membership and fund-raising. Often a number of individuals are identified who will meet individually with the community representatives listed above in order to acquaint them with the school system's efforts thus far and to solicit their participation in the Core Group. Members of the evolving Core Group routinely ask to speak to community groups, service clubs, and local business and industry leaders for the same reason. Additional sources of funding for the program or specific aspects of it are also sought at this point. Individuals and organizations will frequently contribute to the costs of initial training, purchase of films and materials, etc.

Community Awareness. As one of the implementation steps involves promoting the program to community, school and community members of the Core Group can share this task. This subcommittee can be responsible for making alcohol and drug presentations to community groups, scheduling community lecture series, film festivals, and awareness nights, developing and distributing brochures about the school's student assistance program, writing and distributing a SAP newsletter for students, school staff, and parents, distributing pamphlets to areas businesses, and so on.

Parent support activity. Many communities lack specific information and support services for parents concerned about how to prevent or cope with their children's alcohol/drug-related problems. Core Group members, following appropriate training, can hold parent education seminars dealing with alcohol and other drug abuse and effective parenting and communication skills oriented toward prevention. Other parents are concerned about patterns of drug abuse in a their children and need information about community resources, the school's services, and effective parenting skills for effective intervention. Still others may need support because of children who are abusing drugs or who are recovering. The Core Group can be instrumental in establishing Parents Al-Anon groups, Families Anonymous groups, or other parent support systems.

Community assessment. The school, through the Core Committee, may have done some preliminary work in identifying and evaluating the continuum of care in the community for children with AODA-related problems. In most cases this reveals that there are gaps in the service delivery system, duplications, or problems in cooperative working relationships. A subgroup of the Core Group, made up of medical, legal, social services, and AODA service providers together with school staff can address these areas more specifically on an ongoing basis. It can develop estimates of the need for assessment and treatment services for adolescents and families and compare these with the current availability and appropriateness of services and funding. It can recommend increases or changes in local AODA-related services. It may take the initiative in working with the self-help groups to develop young people's AA meetings. It can also address the effectiveness of local ordinances controlling the availability of alcohol, sale of drug paraphernalia, penalties for drunk driving and intoxication, and so on.

Thus far we have addressed the Core Group as a functional and organizational adjunct of the school system. In some communities, however, the Core Group (though it may be called something else) forms first in the community. It carries out the same tasks identified above, but with a view to facilitating the identification, assessment, intervention, treatment, and support of AODA-involved youth in any community "system:" legal, religious, employment, recreational, medical, and so forth. The school system becomes involved on a par with other systems in the community. In some cases, these community tasks forces have gone to some organizational lengths. Some incorporate as nonprofit agencies to facilitate their fund-raising activities.

Core Group Training

Regardless of the timing or mode of its formation, before the Core Group can perform its major functions effectively its members must receive extensive and intensive training in the fundamentals of alcohol and other drug abuse problems. Members of the Core Teams within the school system (i.e., those with roles in the student assistance program) also need training to enhance skills in identifying, assessing, intervening, and supporting students with AODA-related problems. Community representatives from other "systems" require the same information in order to enhance the ways in which they meet the needs of youth and families with these problems and in order to develop better cooperative relationships with the school. Core Group training is thus one of the major benchmarks of program implementation which enables, or "empowers," those in the school system and the community to respond effectively to AODA-related problems.

Thus, the Core Group needs to (1) identify participants for Core Group training, (2) identify and evaluate

Core Group training resources, (3) determine training objectives and an agenda, and (4) identify additional training needs of its members following the initial workshop(s). Some of the major criteria for evaluating training resources have been mentioned in Chapter 18, and Supplement 21.2 provides worksheet for assembling the Core Group training roster.

Core Group Training Objectives. Training for Core Group members needs to be extensive. Participants will need a basic understanding of the continuum of drug use, abuse and dependency, and the dynamics of the effects on individuals, families, and systems. Given the prevalence of "affected others" among professionals and the population at large, ample time must also be devoted to allowing participants to identify and discuss attitudes and personal experiences. The specifics of the student assistance program model also need to be addressed, in terms of the interaction between program roles, policies, and procedures.

The following, then, are recommended as objectives for Core Group training:

- To provide participants with an understanding of the continuum of alcohol and other drug use, abuse, and dependency;

- To provide participants with an understanding of the nature and progression of chemical dependency as it affects adults and adolescents;

- To provide participants with an awareness of the dynamics of denial as they are manifested in individuals, families, and systems;

- To provide participants with an understanding of the system of enabling as it is manifested in individuals, families, and systems;

- To provide participants with an awareness of the nature and progression of chemical dependency as a family illness;

- To provide participants with an awareness of the effects of parental chemical dependency on children and childhood development;

- To develop the understanding and skill of participants in preparing and participating in the assessment and intervention process with adults or adolescents;

- To explore the treatment and recovery process for chemically dependent persons, family members, and other systems;

- To provide participants with an awareness of the components of a comprehensive Student Assist-

ance Program;

- To examine the prevalence and needs of students in various AODA-related target groups;

- To provide participants with an awareness of the structures, functions, and implementation steps of a Student Assistance Program;

- To clarify the roles of administrators, pupil services staff, teachers, and other staff in the Student Assistance Program in the identification, assessment, intervention, treatment, and support of students who have AODA-related problems;

- To provide participants with an understanding of the types and purposes of AODA-related support groups and the issues surrounding their implementation;

- To allow participants to discover and experience their own feelings, attitudes and behaviors as these may relate to how youth and their families are affected by alcohol and other drug abuse.

- To develop a cohesive school/community team approach to the resolution of alcohol and other drug problems in the school and the community;

- To allow participants to develop joint school/community plans for developing more affective preventative/interventive strategies on a local level.

Structure and Agenda. The training required to achieve such objectives must be lengthy and intensive. These objectives can be accomplished in a Core Group training session of approximately 40 hours. Scheduling training can present a host of problems, not the least of which is releasing key staff from their normal school responsibilities to attend, and absorbing the cost of substitutes for those with classroom responsibilities. The most effective training, however, is concentrated within five or more consecutive days. Such a concentrated workshop enhances the intensity of training and the interaction between participants.

Many training institutions offer graduate credit for training of this scope and intensity. In order to encourage involvement in the training and the program, many school districts also award participants "board credit" or some other formal acknowledgement of participation and of the value of the material to one's normal role in the school.

Providing Core Group training "onsite," or in the community, obviously allows school and community representatives to participate together, although there are other alternatives. If key school and community participants attend courses or training events away from their communities, it is always advisable to attend as teams.

Core training is also complicated by the need to combine several instructional modalities: lectures, discussions, large and small-group experiences, role plays, task-oriented planning sessions, and so on. Supplement 21.3 represents a typical agenda for a Core Group training workshop. Even within a five-day structure, however, all of the relevant or useful information concerning alcohol and other drug abuse cannot be considered. Following Core Group training, school staff and other Core Group members will frequently identify further, more specialized training needs for those with specialized roles in the student assistance program. The sample budget (Supplement 20.3), for example, recognizes the need for pupil services staff and other Core Team members in individual buildings to receive additional training in assessment concepts and skills. Those leading support groups will also typically need formal training in group dynamics and the specifics of leading AODA-related groups in the school setting. Identifying these additional training needs is also a task of the Core Group.

Thus, Core Group training is designed for all those school and community persons who will be performing essential roles and functions within the school's student assistance program. The workshop provides an intense exposure to the basic concepts of alcohol and other drug use, abuse, and dependency, and how each of these in manifested in families and individuals — especially school-age youth. Moreover, the training is designed to relate topics to the policies and procedures of a school system's approach to substance abuse.

The general objective of the training is to provide key school personnel with the knowledge and skills which will allow them to effectively carry out their respective roles and functions within a Student Assistance Program. To the extent that members of the community and other concerned persons take part in the workshop, a secondary objective is to provide the same information to these supportive elements of the community.

With the formal endorsement of the program by the Board of Education, and the formation of a strong and active school/community Core Group, the program is all but implemented. What remains is to begin informing others — students, staff, parents, and the community — of the existence of the program and how to make use of it.

Chapter 21 | Supplements

Supplement 21.1, "Implementation Checklist IV: Core Group Development," lists the major activities associated with the expansion and training of Core Group members representing the school and the community.

Supplement 21.2, the "Core Group Participant List" is a simple form allowing Core Group members to identify and assemble a roster of people who will be taking part in Core Group training activities.

Supplement 21.3, "Sample Core group Training Agenda," is typical for an intensive five-day Core Group training workshop for school and community representatives.

Supplement 21.1

IMPLEMENTATION CHECKLIST IV:
Core Group Development

TASK: *To form joint school/community Core Group and conduct Core Group training.*

IMPLEMENTATION ACTIVITY	RESPONSIBILITY OF:	RESOURCES NEEDED:	COMPLETION DATE:

A. Form and/or expand school/community Core Group
 	
  1. Make presentation to community groups
  2. Identify additional Core Group members
  3. Identify tasks for Core Group
  4. Identify subcommittees for community awareness, membership and fund-raising, training, parent support, community assessment, etc.
 	
B. Arrange for Core Group training
 	
  1. Identify and evaluate training resources
  2. Identify participants for Core Group training
  3. Select appropriate training site
  4. Develop appropriate objectives and training agenda
  5. Schedule and conduct Core Group training
 	
C. Identify additional training needs
 	
  1. Identify potential group facilitators and provide appropriate training in AODA group leadership
  2. Provide training in assessment skills for Core Team members in each building
  3. Provide appropriate training for Core Team members and other staff at elementary level dealing with children at risk			

Supplement 21.2
CORE GROUP PARTICIPANT LIST

BUILDING	ADMINISTRATOR(S)	PUPIL SERVICES STAFF	OTHER CORE TEAM MEMBERS	OTHER INTERESTED STAFF

Community Representatives	Representing: (parents, police, AODA Agency, etc.)

Supplement 21.3
SAMPLE CORE GROUP TRAINING AGENDA

MIDVILLE PUBLIC SCHOOLS
Student Assistance Program
Core Group Training Workshop

AGENDA

Monday, July 20, 1987

9:00 am - 10:00 am

WELCOME AND INTRODUCTIONS
    Introduction of Participants; Expectations of
Participants; Workshop Goals

10:00 am - 12:30 pm

**DYNAMICS OF DRUG USE, ABUSE, AND
DEPENDENCY**
    Definitions; Experimentation; Social Use;
Dependency; Using to Feel Normal

12:30 pm - 1:30 pm

LUNCH

1:30 pm - 2:30 pm

DEFENSIVE POSTURES AND FAMILY SYSTEMS
    Formation of Families; Defensive Postures in
Family Communication; Role plays and discussion

1:30 pm - 4:30 pm

**CHILDREN'S ADAPTATIONS TO FAMILY
DRUG ABUSE**
    Film: "Soft Is The Heart of a Child;" Feelings;
Survival Behaviors

Tuesday, July 21, 1987

9:00 am - 10:00 am	THE DENIAL SYSTEM IN CHEMICAL DEPENDENCY The 4 Functions of Denial; Defenses and Awareness; The Delusionary Memory System
10:00 am - 11:10 am	ENABLING Definition of "Enabling;" Film: "The Enablers," Discussion
11:10 am - 12:30 pm	INTERVENTION The Stages of Family Recovery as Preparation for Intervention; Requirements for Intervention
12:30 pm - 1:30 pm	LUNCH
1:30 pm - 2:45 pm	INTERVENTION PREPARATION Constituents of the Chemically Dependent Family; Gathering Appropriate Data; Group Exercise: Writing Data; Group Exercise: Sharing Data
2:45 pm - 3:40 pm	PREPARATION, continued Selecting an Appropriate Goal; Group Exercise: The Goal
3:40 pm - 4:30 pm	CONSEQUENCES Defining Appropriate Consequences; Group Exercise: Consequences

Wednesday, July 22, 1987

9:00 am - 10:10 am	INTERVENTION: THE EVENT Structuring the Intervention Meeting; Deciding on a Moderator and an Order; Film: "The Intervention"
10:10 am - 12:15 pm	THE INTERVENTION EVENT, continued Intervention Role Play & Discussion
12:15 pm - 1:15 pm	LUNCH
1:15 pm - 2:15 pm	TREATMENT AND RECOVERY Components of Treatment; Phases of Recovery; Recovery and Self-Help Groups
2:15 pm - 3:25 pm	WHAT IS A STUDENT ASSISTANCE PROGRAM? Target Groups; The Basic Program Functions; Program Roles and Structures
3:35 pm - 4:30 pm	Film: "A Better Time a Better Place"

Thursday, July 23, 1987

9:00 am - 10:00 am   THE TEACHER'S ROLE IN A STUDENT
ASSISTANCE PROGRAM
Early Identification; Confronting the Troubled
or Problem Student; Other Referral Alternatives;

10:00 am - 11:10 am   THE ASSESSMENT/INTERVENTION PROCESS
Major Assessment Questions; Assessment Tools
and Techniques; Progressive Intervention

11:10 am - 12:15 pm   SUPPORT GROUPS
Rationale for Implementing Support Groups;
Types of AODA-Related Support Groups

12:15 pm - 1:15 pm   LUNCH

1:15 pm - 2:15 pm   THE RECOVERY SUPPORT GROUP
Common Staff Member Expectations of Recover-
ing Students; Steps in the Re-entry Process;
Issues in Recovery Groups

2:25 pm - 3:15 pm   THE AFFECTED OTHERS GROUPS
Needs of Children of Alcoholics; Identification
and Screening Issues;

3:15 pm - 4:30 pm   SMALL GROUP EXERCISE

Friday, July 24, 1987

9:00 am - 10:15 am   THE USE-FOCUSSED GROUPS
The Use, Abuse, Dependency Continuum;
Identification and Selection of Group Members

10:15 am - 11:30 am   STAGES OF PROGRAM IMPLEMENTATION
Planning and Organizing; Policy Development;
Program Design Issues; Core Group Development;
Program Promotion; Program Evaluation

11:30 am - 12:30 pm   SCHOOL/COMMUNITY PLANNING SESSIONS

12:30 pm - 1:30 pm   LUNCH

1:30 pm - 2:15 pm   SMALL GROUP CLOSURE

2:15 pm - 3:00 pm   FILM: Father Martin's "Guidelines For Helping
Alcoholics"

3:10 pm - 4:00 pm   LARGE GROUP CLOSURE
Evaluation

Chapter 22 | **Program Promotion**

The enactment of appropriate policy language and the training of persons who will have key roles within the student assistance program are the two major benchmarks of its implementation. Actively promoting the program is necessary in order to widen the scope of involvement in and support for the program, to enhance the level of alcohol/drug awareness among key groups, and to generate referrals to the program. Program promotion activities must be directed toward all staff, students, and the community, including parents.

Staff Awareness

The school must plan for and implement a number of strategies designed to increase the awareness of all staff members concerning the program and the issues it is designed to address.

Staff Inservice. A school's student assistance program is often formally inaugurated following a staff inservice specifically designed to orient all staff to the program. Core Team members often design and take the major responsibility for presenting the staff inservice. This initial inservice, typically lasting a full day, should address a number of principal areas.

First, it should address fundamental alcohol/drug issues. Basic information drawn from Core Group training, for example, provides the staff with a conceptual context within which to better understand student AODA-related problems and the workings of the student assistance program. If it has not been shared with them previously, the staff will need to know the basis for the need for the program the nature and scope student drug and alcohol use and related problems. The dynamics of drug use, abuse, and dependency and the symptom associated with each form the basis for understanding the needs of various target groups. The staff also should be exposed to information concerning the impact of chemical dependency on the family, and especially upon children. Subjects such as denial and enabling are also frequently addressed in an initial inservice.

Second, the inservice is often utilized to describe the program's basic structure, services, policies and procedures, and personnel. Building administrators and/or Core Team members review the major components of the new AODA policy language, and describe the procedures for self-referral, staff referral, and identification of students by parents, peers, and the community. The staff will also need to know about the types of support groups which will be implemented and about their purposes and limitations.

Finally, all staff members will need information clarifying their role in the program, chiefly in the area of early identification of students who may have drug and alcohol–related problems. The inservice should cover the criteria for identification and review referral procedures for suspected AODA-involvement and witnessed policy violations. Specific attention is often given to developing skills in conducting the confrontation, or "referral interview," with students (e.g., see Supplements 7.1 and 7.2). Many schools break up the staff into small groups in which student/teacher confrontations are role played.

In addition to orienting the staff to the program in fairly broad terms, the staff inservice should also stress a number of other issues. Frequently, involvement in the design and implementation of the program has been limited to relatively few staff within each building. The inservice is often a means of stressing the importance to the program of all staff members and of increasing their ownership. One of the major pitfalls that can develop in a program is allowing the staff to see the program as the province of only a small, isolated "clique" within the building. In addition, it is wise for inservice planners and presenters to anticipate the major fears and other forms of resistance which may be present among the staff and to address as many of these as possible. The issue of legal liability for making referrals and the degree of administrative (i.e., Board of Education) support are frequent themes. As noted before, however, the program staff should never expect 100 per cent support for the program nor allow preoccupation with small pockets of resistance to obscure the broader base of interest and support.

In addition to a major inservice program to inaugurate the program, additional inservices throughout the first year may be scheduled to deal with specialized topics in alcohol/drug abuse, child abuse and neglect, suicide, and other student problems. Many staff want additional information on chemical dependency treatment and recovery, the nature of support groups, the

AODA services available in the community, etc. Some schools conduct mini-sessions, or "bring your own problem" workshops, in which staff are encouraged to meet in small groups with the SAP staff to discuss ways of dealing with specific students or student problems. Staff awareness and participation can be continually encouraged by inviting them to become members of the building Core Team or District Core Group, to volunteer to become group facilitators, and to attend future Core group training sessions.

Other Promotion Strategies. In addition to the initial staff inservice and subsequent training, a number of other activities help to enhance the visibility of the program with staff:

- Development of a Student Assistance Program Handbook for staff, which summarizes policy and procedure language, identification criteria, an explanation of the staff member's role in the program, a description of various support groups, how to deal with parents regarding AODA issues, etc.;

- Regular reports at staff meetings concerning the progress of the student assistance program. These reports, often by the SAP Coordinator or other Core Team members should be brief and should concentrate on recent successes, program changes, opportunities for staff involvement, etc.;

- Preparation and distribution of a Student Assistance Program Newsletter for all staff in the district;

- Holding meetings with various departments on how staff can integrate AODA information into their individual course curricula.

Student Awareness

Considerable effort needs to go into informing students of the existence of the program. Students in all grades will need to be made aware of many of the same issues as the staff: the program's intent, its policies and procedures, services such as support groups, and the names of program staff and how to contact them. It is just as important to maintain the visibility of the program with students as it is with staff.

Student Inservice. Most schools have found that announcing the program to large groups in auditorium-sized meetings is not as effective as meeting with students in smaller groups. One of the more effective methods of announcing the program to students involves members of the Core Team in making presentations in individual classrooms. For example, Core Team members might go into secondary school classrooms on two occasions during the first year. On the first occasion, the goals are to provide basic information on drug use, abuse, and dependency, to explain the program's policies, procedures, and services, and to answer students' questions. It is very important to stress the confidential nature of the program, and the fact that the program is designed to provide help, not to detect or punish.

On a second occasion the staff goes into different classrooms to make a second presentation. This time, the effects of drug abuse and dependency on families is discussed. Films such as *A Story About Feelings* or *The First Step* are frequently shown to introduce affected others issues. Presenters also explain the support groups for Affected/Concerned Others. Often, students are asked to complete a film evaluation form, on which they can also indicate their desire for more information or their willingness to speak to a counselor or join a support group. At the elementary level, the SAP staff would typically meet with students only once to discuss the family issues and to explain the Affected Others Group.

Other Student Awareness Activities. Many schools utilize additional strategies for explaining the program further and for promoting the credibility and visibility of the program with students:

- Designing and distributing a brochure on the student assistance program written specifically for students. The brochure is a simple, one-page tri-fold description of the school's policy language and program services such as support groups. The brochure also should list the names of Student Assistance Coordinator/Counselor(s) and Contact Persons and where they can be located;

- Enlisting students in the design of posters to advertise the program;

- Making regular announcements over the public address system concerning how to get help for alcohol/drug-related problems, the availability of the SAP staff, when support groups will be meeting, etc.;

- Encouraging students in the program to write articles (anonymous if necessary) for placement in the student newspaper;

- Informing new students transferring into the building of the program;

- Continuing to provide classroom inservices to each incoming class (e.g., freshmen) in subsequent years.

- Implementing elective semester courses on alcohol and other drug abuse, covering topics similar to those dealt with in Core Group training;

- Acquiring appropriate fiction and nonfiction materials on alcohol and other drug abuse for the school library.

Extracurricular Activities. Many schools require student athletes and their parents to attend, prior to the start of the school year or a specific athletic season, an information session on alcohol and other drug abuse. The coaching staff and Core Team members also review training rules and the school's drug and alcohol policy. Parents and their athletes often jointly sign a document which explains the training rules as well as the consequences for failing to adhere to them. The staff also explains the interaction between the extracurricular activity and the school's student assistance program. More and more, schools are adopting co-curricular codes as part of their student assistance programs. These codes essentially extend the concept of "training rules" to all extracurricular activities, and are statements that eligibility for extracurricular activities is contingent upon remaining drug-free.

Parent and Community Awareness

Parent Awareness. Many school systems formally notify parents of the existence of the student assistance program through an announcement letter over the signatures of the district administrator and the president of the board of education. The letter usually contains a brief description of the program and its intent, and recognizes the joint/school community cooperation which has gone into its implementation. Parents wishing more information are invited to contact the relevant SAP Coordinator(s). The letter may be accompanied by a copy of the new school district policy on student drug and alcohol use. One of the reasons for seeking the endorsement of the policy and the program by various community groups earlier is that it helps to convey to parents the broad base of involvement and support for the student assistance program effort. Such endorsements should be included in information mailed to parents.

Many schools prefer the more informal and attractive image conveyed by a student assistance program brochure similar to the one developed for students but created specially for and mailed to parents. Others develop a *Student Assistance Program Handbook for Parents*. The handbook contains a digest of the program's policy and procedures, identifies members of the Core Teams in each building, explains the nature of various support groups. It frequently contains drug and alcohol information helpful to parents: warning signs of alcohol/drug abuse, how to talk to children and youth about drugs, community AODA agencies and support groups, etc.

In addition to printed materials announcing and explaining the program to parents, Core Team members may wish to hold a series of "information nights" for parents who have children attending the various school buildings. Core Group members may also wish to cooperate with parent/teacher groups and other parent organizations in the development of presenta-

tions about alcohol and other drug abuse and the school's student assistance program.

Community Awareness. Preparing a series of community education seminars is an effective means of both announcing the student assistance program and providing community members with appropriate drug and alcohol information. Announcing a series of five or six topics over a two month period usually promotes attendance. One of the more workable strategies enlists Core Group members in presenting key topics from the Core Group training agenda on successive evenings: the progression of drug use, abuse, and dependency, family dynamics, the nature of enabling and intervention, a panel of recovering students, community resources, a description of the student assistance program, etc.

During the program promotion stage the school system will also wish to establish or maintain contacts with those major segments of the community which have been mentioned previously. Core Group members will often ask to appear before service clubs and organizations to announce the program or to report on its progress. Continuing to meet with members of AODA agencies furthers the process of solidifying effective working relationships. In communities where the they have been involved in the Core Group and attended Core Group training, area clergy can begin offering alcohol/drug education programs to members of their congregations, pointing out the existence of the school's student assistance program in the process. Preparing periodic news releases for printed and electronic media also helps either to announce the program or to keep it visible.

Usually, with the announcement of the program to these major segments of the school and community the program can be considered to be implemented. Referrals from staff begin or increase, a small but growing number of students begin voluntarily seeking help, support groups are implemented. A great deal of school and community effort has gone into the accomplishment of this and the preceding steps, just to bring the program into being. Programs do not run themselves, however. Almost immediately, attention has to now be focussed on planning for and/or conducting an evaluation of the program's impact, effectiveness, and process must proceed in order to better direct efforts needed to maintain it.

Chapter 22 | # Supplement

Supplement 22.1, "Implementation Checklist V: Program Promotion," summarizes the major activities for this implementation task.

Supplement 22.2 contains reproductions of actual brochures used to promote the Student Assistance Program in two Wisconsin school districts.

Supplement 22.1

IMPLEMENTATION CHECKLIST V:
Program Promotion

TASK: *To promote the awareness of the existence of the student assistance program among staff, students, parents, and the community.*

IMPLEMENTATION ACTIVITY	RESPONSIBILITY OF:	RESOURCES NEEDED:	COMPLETION DATE:
A. Increase staff awareness of the student assistance program			
1. Plan and conduct staff inservice(s) covering AODA issues, the policies and procedures of the program, and the staff member's role;			
2. Develop written materials for staff			
3. Make regular presentations updating the program at staff meetings			
4. Identify additional topics for staff inservice and training			
5. Write SAP newsletter for all school district staff			
6. Make regular, brief presentations to the Board of Education			
B. Increase student awareness of the student assistance program			
1. Plan and conduct classroom presentations about the program for all students			
2. Develop SAP brochure for secondary school students			
3. Plan other promotional materials for students (e.g., posters, etc.)			
4. Announce program in student newspaper			
5. Plan presentations for students in extracurricular activities and their parents			
C. Increase parent awareness of the student assistance program			
1. Draft and mail to parents a letter announcing the program, containing philosophy and policy language and program endorsements			
2. Develop and distribute SAP brochure for parents			
3. Develop and distribute a SAP Handbook for parents			
4. Plan and conduct a series of "information nights" for parents at the level of each individual school building			
D. Enhance community awareness of the student assistance program			
1. Plan and conduct a community education series on drug and alcohol abuse and the student assistance program			
2. Continue making presentations on the program to local agencies, service clubs, and community organizations			
3. Prepare periodic press releases on the program for local media			
E. Implement support groups			

PREP

Your Future Depends on You

You and

Who To Contact?

Lakeland High School Personnel

Randy Nesbit, PREP Program Director	356-5252
Gerald Sislo, District Administrator	356-5252
Robert Ostazeski, Principal	356-5252
Nancy Krause, Administrative Asst.	356-5252
Paul Harshner, Guidance Counselor	356-5252
Mary Reeves, Guidance Counselor	356-5252
Mary Greschner, Teacher	356-5252
Ginney Neuman, Teacher	356-5252

PREP

Needs You and

Your Future

Depends

on

PREParation

PREP

Pupil Resource & Education Program

What Is PREP?

The Pupil Resource and Education Program is designed to increase students' knowledge of Alcohol and Other Drug Abuse (AODA) and related problems. PREP will also work as a referral service to assist students in obtaining help for their specific needs such as further assessment and possible treatment.

LUHS is one of the first schools in the Northern part of the State to establish a program such as PREP. It receives funding through a special grant provided by the State of Wisconsin.

The purpose of the school's PREP program is to initiate a Student Assistance Program under the direction of a trained AODA counselor. PREP will help in identifying and referring students directly being affected by AODA. Upon request educational materials on AODA will be provided to all Lakeland students, concerned parents, and community members. PREP also offers a number of educational and support groups. All PREP activities are conducted in strict confidence.

Why Have a Program?

National Statistics

Five percent of the students 7th through 12th grade are chemically dependent and in need of treatment.

Twenty percent of the students 7th through 12th grade are harmfully involved with alcohol or other drugs. This could indicate that because of their use of chemicals, they may be having problems with relationships with parents or friends, grades or school attendance, or emotional development.

Twenty-five percent of the students kindergarten through 12th grade come from homes where at least one person is abusing alcohol or other drugs. These students are often affected by this person as shown in their school performance or behavior.

Local Statistics

A local survey indicated that 83% of all students at LUHS consume alcoholic beverages and that 53% of all students have tried marijuana prior to graduation. These statistics along with the fact that 60% of all students find alcohol readily available and 34% find marijuana available

Reflecting on these statistics, over 50% of all LUHS students feel that Lakeland has an AODA problem.

Caring and Concern

LUHS has a responsibility and concern to care for the needs of its student body. As a result of the survey it was clear that LUHS does have an AODA problem and that the school and community has a responsibility to respond appropriately. Chemical dependency is a progressive illness that affects a person physically, emotionally, mentally, socially and spiritually. It not only affects the person abusing the chemical, but family and friends as well. The causes of chemical dependency are complex and may include an inherited pre-disposition, social attitudes and emotional stress.

It is believed that families and community resources share the responsibility of prevention and intervention with the school. A community Advisory Council has been established to increase awareness and help coordinate community resources.

What Groups Are Offered By PREP?

The groups meet once a week and consist of 6 to 12 students. They will meet the needs of people in the following situations and are guided by a qualified staff member. *Confidentiality is of utmost importance.*

Chemical Awareness

Education in these groups involves a non-judgmental environment that encourages the open discussion of attitudes, beliefs, and feelings. Students learn about chemical use and abuse, its effects on families and friends and skills for coping with difficult situations.

Concerned Persons

Students concerned about someone else's use of alcohol or other drugs are given the opportunity to discuss their feelings and concerns. They learn about chemical abuse, its effects on families and friends, and skills for coping with difficult situations.

Support groups are available for students who are chemically dependent or who are returning from treatment. These groups will give students support in their recovery from chemical dependency and an opportunity to discuss concerns.

Growth or Non-Users

These groups are for students who do not wish to use alcohol or other drugs and desire support and assistance in saying "no". These groups discuss self esteem, values, and drug information.

Lakeland Union High School, thru the concerned effort and support from students, counselors, teachers, and members of the community, are presenting thru "PREP" a chance to educate, expose, counsel, and in some cases, rehabilitate adolescents in regards to AODA (Alcohol and Other Drug Abuses).

I feel nothing but creative and constructive results from the implementation of "PREP" at LUHS, which in turn will bring longstanding results not only to LUHS, but also to our community and the society in which we live.

Ernie L. Rosenthal
Chief of Police, Woodruff

Drug and alcohol use plays a part in at least 90% of the Court cases tried in Oneida County.

Because of our concern over the problem of alcohol and drug use among our young people, we have started a program to inform people of the problem and to educate our youth so they understand the consequences and future problems that can come from abuses of drugs and alcohol. This must be a cooperative effort between the county, the school system, local units of government, the public and parents.

Hopefully, PREP will reduce the need for more enforcement and rehabilitative programs.

John Hogan
District Attorney, Oneida County

Support

STUDENT
ASSISTANCE
PROGRAM

Brookfield Central High School
Brookfield East High School
Elmbrook Middle School

Administration Building

District Coordinator: ***Richard Beth***
Supervisor — Psychological Services
(785-3900)

Robert G. Baxter
Pupil Personnel Services Director

Dr. Ronald Goedken
Superintendent of Schools
SCHOOL DISTRICT OF ELMBROOK

2430 North Pilgrim Road
Brookfield, Wisconsin 53005

Student Assistance Staff

Brookfield Central High School (785-3910)

Dru Munson, *Assistant Principal*
(building coordinator)
Robert Dixon, *Counselor*
(team coordinator)
Sheryl Kaczmarek, *English/Communications
teacher*

Philip Kuehn, *Social Studies teacher*
Mary Mayberry, *P.E. teacher*
Jerry Meythaler, *English teacher*
Debra Porter, *S.L.D teacher*
Roberta Prochaska, *English teacher*
Dave Steinbach, *P.E. teacher/Coach*
Rick Synold, *Health/P.E. teacher/
Coach*

Brookfield East High School (781-3500)

Burl Johnson, *Assistant Principal
(building coordinator)*
Walter Akert, *English teacher*
Pat Bardonner, *Nurse*
Mary Jo Bartel, *English teacher*
Linda Caldwell, *P.E. teacher*
Thomas Erickson, *English teacher*
Richard Foote, *Counselor*
Inez Lentz, *S.L.D. teacher*
Dave Roberts, *E.D. teacher*
James Treutelaar, *Science teacher*
Joan Whitman, *S.L.D. teacher
(team coordinator)*
Richard Wood, *Biology teacher/coach*

Elmbrook Middle School (785-3920)

William Zahn, *Assistant Principal
(building coordinator)*
Conrad Laska, *Science teacher
(team coordinator)*

Lee Glawe, *Social Studies teacher*
Robin McCarthy, *S.L.D. teacher*
Debra Patz, *S.L.D. teacher*
Steve Roecker, *Science teacher*
Linda Rogge, *S.L.D. teacher*
Gaylen Stoa, *E.D. teacher*
Ann Tavernini, *S.L.D teacher*

Elmbrook Philosophy

The administration, faculty and parents of the School District of Elmbrook recognize that alcohol and other drug abuse, chemical dependency, and the stress of living in a chemically dependent family environment represent a most serious and prevalent threat to the health and welfare of youth. The philosophy of the School District of Elmbrook is one of caring and concern for these students. Chemical dependency is a progressive illness that effects people physically, emotionally, socially, and spiritually. Alcohol and other drug abuse has too long been demonstrated to be a cause and/or a contributing factor in vandalism, absenteeism, tardiness, disciplinary referrals, classroom disruptions, declining academic performance, and drop-out rates. The school setting has been proven to be an effective environment for dealing with alcohol and other drug abuse, and dependency as they affect youth. The School District of Elmbrook recognizes its responsibility to provide prevention and intervention educational programs for the promotion of an increased awareness of the abuse and problems involved in chemical usage.

Program Description

The Student Assistance Program has been established at Brookfield Central High School, Brookfield East High School, and Elmbrook Middle School.

The program identifies, screens, refers, and assists students who may be affected by their own or someone else's use of alcohol or other drugs. Upon referral, the student is interviewed by trained staff. Recommendations are made to involve the student in an in-school educational group or a referral is made to a community resource.

All contact with the student is kept confidential. Involvement in the program is completely voluntary.

Services Offered

Screening

Referred students are interviewed by Student Assistance staff to determine the extent of the problem and make appropriate referral to in-school programs or outside agencies.

Individual Education

The referred student is put in contact with a Student Assistance staff member who provides information and assistance regarding the student's involvement or concerns.

Assessment Group

This small group is designed to provide specific education and assistance to those students who are minimally to severely involved in alcohol/drug abuse.

Concerned Others Group

This small group is designed to meet the needs of those students who are concerned about or affected by someone else's use of alcohol and other drugs. The concern may be directed toward another student, a parent, or other family member.

Recovering Students Group

This small group provides support for students who have returned from an inpatient treatment program or who are currently involved in outpatient care. The major goal of the program is to support the student in his/her attempt to maintain a drug-free life style. Involvement with AA or other treatment plans is recommended.

Referral Process

Parental Referral

Parents who are concerned that alcohol and other drug usage may be affecting their son or daughter are encouraged to contact the Student Assistance personnel in their respective building.

Student Self-Referral

A student who is concerned about his/her own use of alcohol or someone else's use of alcohol or drugs, may contact a Student Assistance staff member directly or a guidance counselor who can make the necessary referral.

Staff Referral

Teachers and other school staff have been alerted to the signs and symptoms of possible chemical use and misuse. They are encouraged to seek assistance from the designated Student Assistance personnel in their building.

All referrals to the Student Assistance Program are strictly confidential.

Program Evaluation

Decisions concerning the scope of program evaluation are often made during the program design phase of implementation. The scope of evaluation activity will vary from one district to another, depending on the size of the district and the program, the resources available to conduct program evaluation (including staff time and funding), and the extent to which the district wishes to identify and pursue more research-oriented questions regarding student drug and alcohol use.

Some degree of program evaluation typically must occur, and serves a number of purposes. First and most obviously, program evaluation allows the school system to discover if any changes are occurring and to document them. Evaluation also reveals how and where to make changes in the student assistance program's policies and procedures, services, staffing patterns, and resources. The products of program evaluation — the answers to these fundamental questions — are also useful in communicating to others about the program: students, staff, parents, and the community as a whole. Finally, some degree of program evaluation is necessary since sources of funding and other support typically require some degree of accountability.

Planning and conducting an evaluation of its student assistance program will involve the school district and the SAP staff in a numbers of activities during program implementation as well as its operation and maintenance phases. First, evaluation provides the answers to a number of basic questions: (1) to what degree is the program having an *impact* on the numbers of those determined to be in need, (2) to what degree do program *outcomes* show that people receiving services change in the desired direction, and (3) how well is the *process* set up to achieve impact and outcomes actually functioning? Second, program staff will need to develop specific goals and objectives in each of these areas. Goals and objectives will typically need to address both the school and community contexts. Thus, the program will need to examine its impact and effectiveness, for example, on students and staff (the school context) and on parents and other segments of the community (the community context). Finally, program evaluation requires the student assistance program staff to create a process for collecting and interpreting information.

Program Impact Outcome, and Process

Measuring the various dynamics of alcohol/drug programs can be exceedingly complex. (A rather complete discussion of evaluating AODA prevention programming can be found in French and Kaufman (1981), though the terminology and approach taken differs somewhat from that taken below). As indicated above, however, at its most simple the school will want to know about the impact of the program, it effectiveness, and its process.

Program Impact

Evaluating the impact of the program as a whole and its specific services is crucially related to the school system's estimates and definition of need. One of the fundamental necessities in designing and implementing the Student Assistance Program model is the recognition that the large and amorphous "drug problem" becomes more manageable with the identification of various target populations, each of which has somewhat different AODA-related experiences and different needs. Impact is often measured in terms of "penetration rate:" i.e., to what degree does the program, a specific activity, or service have an impact on the total number of those estimated to be in need?

At its most immediate level the program will need to examine its impace upon the AODA–specific student target groups identified earlier in Chapter 3, and modified slightly as follows:

- Students affected by their own patterns of alcohol and other drug abuse, including students who are chemically dependent;

- Students affected by or concerned about others' alcohol/drug abuse;

- Students who are recovering from chemical dependency;

- Students who do not use alcohol or other drugs, or who have not developed discernible AODA-related problems.

The program and its activities will also impact on the school staff, including administrators, teachers, and pupil services staff. The program will contain components having an impact on these target populations in terms of their knowledge, attitudes, and behavior with respect to students who have AODA-related problems. Program activities and services will also address the needs of parents and the wider community in the same areas. Evaluating the program's impact will thus require developing goals and objectives which refer to students, staff, parents, and the community.

Program Outcomes

Measurement of the student assistance program's outcomes provides an evaluation of its "effectiveness," or the degree to which the various target populations impacted upon demonstrate changes. Measures of outcome or effectiveness are measures of how people are different. It is one thing, for example, to discover that 80 out of 100 students thought to be abusing alcohol or other drugs took part in a use-focussed group (i.e., an impact or "penetration rate" of 80 per cent. It is another to demonstrate that, of these, 60 showed reductions in chemical use following their group experience (i.e., an effectiveness measure of 75 per cent).

The program's activities and services typically will have an effect on AODA-specific as well as nonspecific knowledge, attitudes, and behavior of those in the various target groups and populations. In developing and measuring the attainment of outcome-related goals and objectives for students, many indicators can be used. Indicators can be examined among specific groups (i.e., students in a use-focussed group) and/or among larger population (all students, those in the seventh grade, etc.). Among the alcohol/drug-specific indicators would be the following:

- Reductions in drug and alcohol use: reductions in the numbers of substances used, the frequency of use, amounts consumed per occasion;

- A decrease in the number of students intending to use alcohol or other drugs;

- Increases in the age of first use (i.e., delaying drug use);

- Increases in the total number of students who have never used ("abstainers") or of those who did use but who have quit;

- Increases in knowledge about alcohol/drug use, abuse, and dependency;

- Changes in attitudes toward alcohol and other drugs;

- Changes in attitudes toward those with AODA-related problems;

A number of indicators relate to changes in the consequences of alcohol/drug abuse:

- Improvement in family relationships;
- Improvement in peer relationships;
- Reduction of the incidence of school violence;
- Reduction of rates of absenteeism, tardiness, dropouts, disciplinary referrals, AODA-related suspensions and expulsions, vandalism;
- Improvement in grades, attitudes toward school, teachers' evaluations, and other measures related to academic performance;

A number of variables are thought to be "intermediate indicators" which have a correlation with alcohol and other drug abuse-related problems. The program could thus evaluate the effectiveness of it services regarding:

- Improvements in attitudes toward drug and alcohol abuse and dependency;
- Improvements in areas of personal development (i.e., self-concept, responsibility, moral development, feelings of alienation, decision making, locus of control, social interaction, achievement orientation, etc.);
- Improvement in family interactions
- Improvement in use of alternative pursuits
- More positive peer interactions, including the development of alcohol/drug refusal skills

The program will also wish to evaluate outcomes among staff in areas such as:

- Knowledge of fundamental AODA concepts (i.e., the use/abuse/dependency continuum, effects of family alcoholism on children, "enabling," etc.);
- Attitudes toward alcohol and other drugs and those with AODA-related problems;
- Knowledge of the program's policies, procedures, services, and staff;
- Numbers of staff members making formal referrals.

Inventories designed to assess changes in school climate, perceptions of the school system (e.g., Supplement 1.1), and patterns of enabling (e.g., Supplement 5.1) also address outcomes among staff. Similar

outcome goals and objectives can be developed for the community in terms of AODA-related knowledge, attitudes, and behavior.

Program Process

Program Process Evaluation of the program's process entails measuring the extent to which various services are performed, or the degree to which these services are integrated so as to achieve impact and outcome goals. A complete set of process goals and objectives would describe the program completely, and would enable someone else to replicate it. In general, impact objectives describe who the program is for, outcome objectives specify the changes the program intends to make, and process objectives enumerate those program components, resources, and services which achieve impact and outcome. Process goals and objectives are most often developed and examined in three major areas: program implementation, the performance of specific activities, and the operation of basic program functions (i.e., identification, assessment, etc.).

The proposal finally submitted to the board of education for approval will usually contain process goals and objectives in the form of an implementation plan and/or timeline (cf. Figure 20.1). The progress of program implementation thus implicitly involves process evaluation. Process evaluation provides continual feedback to Core Group and Core Team members which can be used to guide organizational decisions, the allocation of resources, scheduling of training, and revision of procedures. A complete listing of implementation process goals and objectives would allow someone outside of the program to see how it evolved. Thus, evaluation of the implementation process would include developing goals for initial planning and organizing, policy development, program design, Core Group development, program promotion, and evaluation.

Another type of process evaluation includes specifying the specific services which will be performed by the program and/or various staff persons. Forming Core teams in each building, implementing a given number of each type of support group in each building, providing classroom presentations, and developing a student/parent brochure are all specific services which the student assistance program will perform, and which could be identified as process objectives. Process evaluation can also be very specific to various positions within the student assistance program. A process objective could state that "By June 1, 1988, the Student Assistance Program Coordinator at Midville High School will have provided assessment services to 10 per cent of the student body."

Finally, evaluating the program's process literally

entails examining how well its various components are working. Supplement 20.2, "Assessing Program Functions," provides an initial opportunity to discover gaps in the school's ability to identify, assess, intervene, support, and manage students with AODA-related problems. Examining each of these areas after the program's first year of operation constitutes a further evaluation of process variables. The school will also want, for example, to keep track of sources of referrals to the program — administrative, staff, self, parent, peer, and community — as well as information about the proportion of AODA-related and non-AODA-related problems. A low incidence of self-referral, for example, would typically provide the impetus for the staff to devise strategies to enhance the program's credibility with students.

Effort and Efficiency

Impact, outcome, and process evaluation represent the minimal areas within which the school will wish to evaluate its student assistance program. Some districts, however, may wish to examine and evaluate their programs also from the standpoint of effort and efficiency. The evaluation of "effort" typically requires keeping track of the resources which are invested in providing services, impacting on target groups, and achieving outcomes. The major effort indicators are staff time, money spent, and individual "units of service." Effort evaluation requires keeping track of the total number of staff hours spent leading support groups, conducting assessment interviews, making classroom presentations, etc. Most programs quickly discover that actual time spent on the program exceeds what was authorized in terms of position authority or the budget — another way of saying that people are investing significantly more time and energy than they are being compensated for. The actual expenses of the program during a given accounting period is an explicit statement of financial resources devoted to the program. Finally, keeping track of the numbers of support groups, the numbers of community presentations, numbers of brochures distributed, and so on, while it says nothing about impact or outcomes, does demonstrate the level of activity occurring in the program.

Evaluation of the program's efficiency is a variety of "cost/benefit" analysis. It basically involves comparing the resources devoted to the program and the various measures of impact or outcome. Resources, again, can include staff time, monetary resources, "units of service," or other effort indicators. Benefits, or outcomes, can include numbers of persons seen, numbers of students reducing chemical use, numbers of students maintaining abstinence, and so on. While most schools will not need to evaluate the program in this detail, it might have some surprising results. Let us say that a student with a high risk profile for dropping

out of school is identified and treated for chemical dependency in 10th grade, and stays in school to graduate. If the school is reimbursed $3,068 per year, keeping him in school resulted in $9,204 in school aid, compared to the cost of 20 staff hours invested in his recovery.

Goals and Objectives

Developing goals and objectives is possible at several points in the implementation process, as well as throughout the student assistance program's operation. Individual school systems will vary according to the amount of time and energy they invest in formulating and formalizing statements of goals and objectives. Programs whose initial implementation is support by grants may need to prepare more detailed goals and objectives. To the extent that goals and objectives are planning tools and statements of the program's direction and intent, all programs should develop them to some degree.

The energetic evaluator or program planner could arrive at a list of goals and objectives at several levels, with those at each place in the hierarchy neatly supporting those above. Obviously, it is neither possible nor useful to develop detailed goals and objectives for each and every facet of the student assistance program. Nevertheless, in terms of the description above, the school may find it useful to develop goals and objectives in at least 12 areas: impact, outcome, and process objectives for each of at least four target populations students, staff, parents, and the community. Supplement 23.2 contains some examples of goal statements in each of these areas.

Goals. Goals are statements of broad or general intentions to bring about change. Goal statements are not typically measurable or quantifiable because they do not state variables (although they may assume them). Goals form the basis for the development of more specific objectives which do contain quantifiable variables. While there are many formats for goal statements, they should probably contain at least the following information:

- the direction of change ("To increase/decrease/maintain/initiate")

- the change variable or indicator ("drug use, absenteeism, drug and alcohol knowledge")

- the target group ("in AODA-involved students, among staff, in the community, in parents")

- the resources to be used ("through support groups, Core Team training, staff inservice, the implementation of a student assistance program

Perhaps the most general goal states the intention to develop a student assistance program: *"To reduce the incidence of AODA-related problems among students through the implementation of a comprehensive, K-12, joint school/community student assistance program."* A goal with intermediate generality would be one such as the following: *To increase awareness of the Student Assistance Program among High School students through classroom presentations."* And, most specifically, *"To reduce the rates of drug and alcohol use of student's referred to the SAP staff through the implementation of use-focussed support groups."*

Objectives. Objectives are more specific statements of change which logically grow out of goal statements. They are similar in form to the latter but are quantifiable, measurable, and definite. The quantifiers that are often added to goal statements to turn them into objectives include more specific statements of the expected levels of change in indicators or target groups, and a time frame for their accomplishment. The following is a representative format for objectives:

- time frame ("By June 1, 1988")

- the target group ("75 per cent of recovering students")

- expected direction or level of change in indicator ("will have maintained continuous sobriety")

- resources used: persons, services, activities ("through participation in Recovery Support Groups.").

Statements of goals and objectives are clearly related. Each goal should be accompanied by least one objective which measures its attainment; each objective should relate to the accomplishment of at least one goal.

Different sets of goals and objectives tend to be developed during program implementation as opposed to program operation. There are some understandable reasons why this should be so. First and most obviously, those implementing the program may initially have only general notions of what they wish the program to accomplish. Stating that "75 per cent of drug and alcohol abusing students will become abstainers as a result of use-focussed groups" is an understandable hope but may not be a realistic objective during the implementation stage, since many design decisions may not yet have been made. Secondly, goals and objectives that are more realistic can be developed within local buildings, where program design and procedures may vary from one building to another. Third, goals and objectives are more usefully construed as aids to program planning rather than as measurements of program success or failure. Thus, general goals and objectives may be developed at the district-wide level of the Core Group. The development of more specific goals and objectives — consistent with the district-wide plan — may be developed by the more local, building-level Core Teams.

Since the basic purpose of establishing a student assistance program is to meet unmet needs and bring about changes, these needs and the changes they indicate should be identified from the very beginning of the implementation process and expressed as goals and objectives.

Data Collection and Interpretation

The evaluation design for the student assistance program must also provide for the collection of relevant data which will verify the degree of accomplishment of goals and objectives, and which will provide descriptive information concerning various program components. The design of a data collection system typically awaits the formulation of goals and objectives, since these will determine what data will be relevant. Thus, members of Core Teams and the district-wide Core Group will need to make a number of decisions in the design and implementation of an effective data collection process.

Coordination. First, the responsibility for coordinating data collection at the building and district-wide levels needs to be clarified. In most cases, this can be a shared responsibility of the Core Team in each building, supervised by the building SAP Counselor/Coordinator. The amount of time required for sufficient program evaluation should be considered in developing the SAP Coordinator job description.

Materials. If the program is to be evaluated on a district-wide basis, some district-wide consistency must be sought in the development and use of evaluation materials as well is in the development of goals and objectives. It would be desirable, for example, for all school buildings to utilize the same "Student SAP Referral Record" (e.g., Supplement 12.3) so that information on referral sources, referral categories, and outcomes are comparable throughout the district. Similarly, measures of student alcohol/drug use (or other personal change indicators) before and after support group involvement should also be consistent between different groups within the same building, as well as between groups in different buildings.

Data Gathering. A process and a methodology for pulling together data from diverse program components should also be identified. In most cases the SAP Coordinator will have been designated as the person to whom various evaluation documents should be periodically submitted. In addition, the raw data will have to summarized or encoded in some meaningful way. A form, for example, can be used to summarize the data from the individual "Student SAP Referral Records" completed for each student referred to the program in each building.

Increasingly, schools will be able to make use of microcomputers as well as mainframes to record and analyze data from the student assistance program. If these facilities are to be utilized, a significant degree of attention should be devoted to planning for data entry, selection of appropriate software, designing types of output and reports, etc.

Interpretation. If data is well organized and consistent across buildings and age levels of students, interpretation can be relatively straightforward. At the simplest level, data is analyzed in order to discover the degree to which specific program objectives and goals were attained. Outcome data, especially, demonstrates the degree to which the program's services are able to change patterns of drug use and its consequences.

The data can also reveal significant patterns at work in the emerging program, and can lead the SAP staff to ask vital questions concerning the programs's operation. Again, the "Student SAP Referral Record" (Supplement 12.3) and the form on which its information is summarized can yield important information about the workings of the program. From Supplement 12.3, for example, one could compile the total number of referrals by age and sex, the distribution of referrals by referral source (i.e., administrative, staff, self, etc.), the distribution by presenting problem (i.e., AODA, Non-AODA) and correlations and cross tabulations among these variables.

From these rather simple tabulations, the school might ask itself a number of questions which can guide it in maintaining the program from year to year. For example:

- What is the total, number of students referred to the program from various sources? How does this compare with estimates of need, or goals and objectives?

- Do any patterns emerge in terms of the relative proportion of male versus female referrals? Of one age group to another? From one building to another?

- What is the rate of self-referral? Does it increase during the year, or from year-to-year? What steps need to be taken to increase it?

- Do any referral sources appear to be under-represented? (E.g., coaches, counselors, administrators, etc.) What steps need to be taken to increase their participation in the program?

- What assessment recommendations appear to be made most frequently? Least frequently?

Many individual programs, keeping only minimal statistics, have been able to demonstrate significant outcomes. As yet, however, there has been no attempt to gather information from the hundreds of student assistance programs in existence nationwide. In Wisconsin an attempt has been underway since 1983 to develop a standard evaluation and data collection model for student assistance programs (Anderson, Krebsbach, and Fredlund (1986, pp. 69-75). The data collected from local school programs in 1983-84 revealed the following findings:

- Alcohol and marijuana use decreased following participation in the SAP among student referred because of their own drug and/or alcohol use;

- Students referred because of their own alcohol/-drug use differed from students referred because of a concern over others' use. The former illustrated higher levels of drug use and lower levels of school performance (grades, attendance, and conduct) than the latter.

- Students referred for concerned persons issues show a reduction in their own alcohol use after involvement in the program, demonstrating the preventive as well as interventive nature of the program.

- New Holstein Public Schools, which received an Outstanding Program Award from the National Association of Student Assistance Program and Professionals in 1986, has documented a 25 per cent decrease in disciplinary referrals, a 30 per cent increase in attendance, and a significant increase in grade point average in 49 per cent of students participating in its program.

The analysis of data submitted from Wisconsin schools participating in the evaluation project in 1984-85 is currently in progress.

Research Issues. Every school system in the country is a fertile environment for meaningful research on the subject of student alcohol and drug-related problems. Those school systems which have or are in the process of implementing the Student Assistance Program model are in an excellent position to add to and expand the body of knowledge about this complex area. Whether to enhance its own programming or to contribute to the body of understand generally, individual school systems might wish to devote some energy to discovering the answers to some emerging questions:

- How many students present multiple AODA-related problems? (I.e., how many students are affected by their own chemical use as well as that of family members?)

- What is the degree of involvement of alcohol/drug abuse in other problems: suicide, unwanted pregnancy, dropout rates, child abuse, vandalism, etc.?

- To what degree do different subpopulations in the school demonstrate different patterns of AODA-related problems?

- While rates of alcohol and other drug use decrease, and school performance indicators increase, to what degree are the two directly correlated in individual students?

- What is the rate of relapse among recovering students in the student assistance program (i.e., a Recovery Support Group?) Do recovering students in these groups have lower rates of relapse compared to recovering students who do not participate?

- What is the age of first use for students in various target populations? What other variables contribute to a high risk profile for developing chemical dependency as opposed to drug and alcohol abuse?

- Can the development of subsequent AODA-related problems be predicted based on school performance in earlier grades?

Evaluating the student assistance program is clearly a significant step in its implementation, operation, and maintenance, and requires as much conscious attention as the preceding steps. A number of specific steps need to be taken to organize the evaluation effort. First, decisions need to be made concerning the scope of evaluation activity. Some evaluation designs are comprehensive, detailed, and resemble sophisticated research designs. Outcomes are measured by pre-and post-test instruments with documented reliability and validity; studies may be longitud-

inal, or comparisons may be made between to contemporaneous control groups. Other evaluation designs merely wish to describe program activity, impact, and outcomes in simple numerical terms. Second, decisions about the scope of the evaluation design form the basis for more specific decisions concerning the coordination of evaluation or measurement efforts. Persons within the school system should be designated to be responsible for coordinating evaluation activities. In addition, the descriptions of the roles and responsibilities of key SAP staff (e.g., SAP Counselor/Coordinator(s), group facilitators, etc.) should contain statements concerning their responsibilities for the implementation of the evaluation design at the local level.

Third, decisions need to be made regarding what will be measured in the areas of program impact, outcome, and process for the various target populations in the school and the community which the program will serve.

General goals and objectives need to be formulated by persons who have key roles within the program who have an idea of what constitute reasonable expectations. Fourth, the evaluation design involves decisions about the data collection process: what information will be gathered, what forms will be required, who will be responsible for its collection, and what will be required for pooling and entering data on a district-wide basis? Finally, responsibilities for the analysis, interpretation, and reporting of evaluation results need to be defined.

Chapter 23 | # Supplements

Supplement 23.1, "Implementation Checklist VI," summarizes the major activities that are associated with the program evaluation task.

Supplement 23.2, "Sample Goals and Objectives," presents examples of impact, process, and outcome goals and objectives for students, staff, parents, and community populations.

Supplement 23.1

IMPLEMENTATION CHECKLIST VI:
Program Evaluation

TASK: *To design, develop, and implement a process for evaluating the program's impact, outcomes, and process.*

IMPLEMENTATION ACTIVITY	RESPONSIBILITY OF:	RESOURCES NEEDED:	COMPLETION DATE:
A. Define an Evaluation Process 1. Designate responsibilities for coordinating evaluation at each building level and district-wide; 2. Determine scope of evaluation activity 3. Develop goals and objectives for the implementation process 4. Develop impact, outcome, and process goals for students, staff, parents, and the community 5. Develop impact, outcome, and process objectives for students, staff, parents, and the community 6. Develop consistent, standardized evaluation materials B. Implement Evaluation Process 1. Collect data at regular intervals 2. Meet regularly to discuss and interpret data 3. Develop written analysis of evaluation results C. Report on program progress and evaluation results to staff, parents, the community, and the Board of Education D. Meet regularly to discuss needs for change indicated by evaluation results			

Supplement 23.2

SAMPLE GOALS AND OBJECTIVES

Several examples of goals and their associated objectives for a hypothetical school's student assistance program are given below. Sample impact, outcome, and process goals and objectives are listed for students, staff, parents, and community populations. The samples are intended to demonstrate the difference between goals and objectives and between the impact, outcome, and process areas. Actual goals and objectives may differ considerably from the examples given below.

The list begins with an example of process goals and objectives relating to the implementation process as opposed to the program's operation.

PROCESS GOALS AND OBJECTIVES
FOR PROGRAM IMPLEMENTATION

GOAL 1. To widen the awareness of key school and community groups concerning the need for and nature of a student assistance program.

    Objective 1.1. By June 15, 1987 a Core Committee will have been formed consisting of school and community representatives.

    Objective 1.2. By July 15, 1987, a preliminary needs assessment will have been conducted by Core Committee members.

    Objective 1.3. By August 1, 1987 the Core Committee will have assembled a list of local AODA resources.

GOAL 2. To develop appropriate alcohol and other drug abuse philosophy and policy language.

    Objective 2.1. By July 1, 1987 Core Committee members will have reviewed existing AODA policy and made recommendations for changes.

    Objective 2.2. By August 1, 1987 Core Committee members will draft new policy and philosophy language.

    Objective 2.3. By October 15, 1987 the draft of policy language will have been reviewed by all school staff.

GOAL 3. To design a student assistance program and secure its endorsement by the Board of Education

    Objective 3.1. By October 1, 1987 Core Teams will have been formed in each building.

    Objective 3.2. By November 1, 1987 the need for support groups in each building will have been established.

    Objective 3.3. By December 1, 1987 the Core Committee will have completed a program implementation plan.

    Objective 3.4. By January 15, 1988 the Board of Education will have endorsed philosophy and policy language and funding for the program.

GOAL 4. To form a joint school/community Core Group and conduct Core Group training

Objective 4.1. By October 30, 1987 a district-wide joint school/community Core Group will have been formed.

Objective 4.2. By November 1, 1987 Core Group members will attend a five-day Core Group training workshop.

GOAL 5. To promote awareness of the student assistance program among students, staff, parents, and the community

Objective 5.1. By February 15, 1988 all staff will have attended a one-day inservice on the Student Assistance Program.

Objective 5.2. By March 30, 1988 classroom presentations will have been given to all students.

GOAL 6. To plan and conduct an evaluation of the program's impact, outcomes, and process relating to students, staff, parents, and the community.

Objective 6.1. A program evaluation plan will be completed by April 1, 1988.

Objective 6.2. By July 1, 1988 a progress report will be submitted to the Board of Education.

SAMPLE IMPACT GOALS AND OBJECTIVES

STUDENTS:

GOAL 1. To identify students who are affected by or concerned about others' drug and alcohol use.

Objective 1.1. By June 1, 1988, 400 students (4 per cent) will have indicated an interest in Affected/Concerned Others Groups as a result of classroom presentations by Core Team members.

STAFF:

GOAL 1. To inform staff of the existence of the student assistance program.

Objective 1.1. By February 15, 1988 90 per cent of the staff will be able to identify the Student Assistance Program staff and services in their respective buildings.

PARENTS:

GOAL 1. To inform parents of the Student Assistance Program.

Objective 1.1. By March 30, 1988 all parents will have received a mailing of an informational brochure on the Student Assistance Program.

COMMUNITY:

GOAL 1. To inform community agencies of the existence of the Student Assistance Program.

Objective 1.1. By April 1, 1988 Core Team members will have made personal presentations to 25 community groups and service organizations.

SAMPLE OUTCOME GOALS AND OBJECTIVES

STUDENTS:

GOAL 1. To decrease the alcohol and other drug use patterns of students referred to the Student Assistance Program.

Objective 1.1. By June 1, 1988, 75 per cent of the students referred to the Student Assistance Program will demonstrate reductions in the kinds, amounts, and frequencies of drugs used

GOAL 2. To decrease absenteeism among students referred to the Student Assistance Program.

Objective 2.1. By June 1, 1988 75 per cent of the students referred to the Student Assistance Program will demonstrate decreases in absenteeism.

STAFF:

GOAL 1. To increase referrals of students to the Student Assistance Program by staff.

Objective 1.1. By June 1, 1988, 80 students will have been formally referred to the Student Assistance Program staff using the Staff Referral Form.

PARENTS:

GOAL 1. To increase parent referrals to the Student Assistance Program.

Objective 1.1. By June 1, 1988 10 per cent of referrals will come through parent contacts with Student Assistance Program staff.

GOAL 2. To increase parent awareness of the services of the Student Assistance Program.

Objective 2.1. By June 1, 1988 75 per cent of a parent sample will indicate an awareness of the Student Assistance Program as demonstrated on a questionnaire.

COMMUNITY:

GOAL 1. To increase community awareness of the Student Assistance Program.

Objective 1.1. By October 15, 1987 50 per cent of a sample of non-parent community representatives will demonstrate an awareness of the Student Assistance Program as demonstrated by questionnaire.

SAMPLE PROCESS GOALS AND OBJECTIVES

STUDENTS:

GOAL 1. To identify and assist students with AODA-related problems.

Objective 1.1. By June 1, 1988 5 per cent of the student body will have been identified and provided SAP services by the Core Teams.

Objective 1.2. By January 15, 1988 the attendance and academic progress records of all students will be monitored by the building administrator.

GOAL 2. To provide support services for students with AODA-related problems

Objective 2.1. By June 1, 1988 Affected Others Groups will be available in all buildings.

Objective 2.2. By June 1, 1988 Use-focussed and Recovery Support Groups will be available in all secondary buildings.

STAFF:

GOAL 1. To provide training to Core Team members and others with formal roles in the SAP

Objective 1.1. By September 1, 1987, 25 Core Team members will have participated in a five-day Core Group training workshop.

Objective 1.2. By November 1, 1987 18 Core Team members will have completed training in support group facilitation skills.

PARENTS:

GOAL 1. To provide community education workshops for parents on alcohol and other drug abuse

Objective 1.1. By June 1, 1988 three drug and alcohol awareness nights, conducted by Core Group members, will have been attended by 80 parents.

GOAL 2. To provide support services to parents concerned about alcohol and other drug abuse.

Objective 2.1. By June 1, 1988, a Parents Al-Anon support groups will have been started and attended by 10 parents.

COMMUNITY

GOAL 1. To assess the level of adolescent AODA services in the community

Objective 1.1. By June 1, 1988 a Youth AODA Service Committee will have been formed of the school/community Group and AODA service representatives.

Objective 1.2. By September 15, 1988 the Youth AODA Service Committee will present written recommendations to the Core Group and the Board of Education.

Part Five

Program Maintenance

While much school and community energy is invested in the initial implementation of the Student Assistance Program model, considerable energy is also required to maintain the program. Much of the initial activity has been devoted to widening the sphere of involvement and participation, and in increasing the awareness of participants concerning alcohol and other drug abuse. Most often, resistance to the program in the beginning is due to inadequate information concerning the nature and scope of AODA problems, not just as to how they affect students, but also as to how they affect everyone in the school and the community. To the extent that involvement in the program is experienced at a personal as well as professional level, the initial resistance is replaced by enthusiasm and energy.

Following the initial implementation activity, the operational phase of the program begins. While the boundary between "implementation" and "operation" is admittedly artificial, the operational phase coincides with the implementation of services to students: identification, assessment, support, and so on. The operation of the program is often experienced personally. The energy and enthusiasm generated as implementers experience success in the implementation steps is increased as they begin to experience the outcomes: the staff begins referring; student self-referrals increase; kids start going to treatment and getting well; people in the school feel mutually supported; they begin to feel the "empowering" aspects of the program through the success of individual and cooperative efforts; there is less tolerance for drug and alcohol abuse in and by the community.

Experience shows, however, that the program cannot run by itself. The members of the district-wide Core Group as well as members of the individual Core Teams in each school building will need to engage themselves in maintaining and expanding the level of energy, commitment, and involvement in the program. The process of implementing the program can be thought of as being parallel to the process of treatment. The process of maintaining the program parallels the ongoing process of recovery.

Chapter 24 discusses some of the most important aspects of maintaining the school's student assistance program. Program maintenance involves anticipating a number of program pitfalls, or recognizing them, when they appear, and taking steps to overcome them. As Figure 18.1 in Chapter 18 illustrates, the implementation process is cyclical, not linear. Program maintenance tasks tend to be the same as those involved in program implementation. The maintenance process thus involves examining, revising, and expanding the program in terms of same task areas involved in its initial implementation. In many programs, one of the broader maintenance goals is to broaden the program to include services for student problems other than those created by drug and alcohol abuse and dependency: child abuse, suicide, unwanted pregnancy, etc.

Programs inevitably "run down." Personal, professional, and financial energies become expended. Other issues, initiatives, and crises arise which compete for the attention of staff, the administration, and the community. Consequently, programs which have been in operation for several years experience a need for "revitalization:" activities designed to replenish individual and system resources and to recapture the enthusiasm which accompanied the program's initial implementation and operation.

Supplement 24.1, "Self Maintenance," deals with staff issues. Many programs experience a loss of energy, resources, direction, and commitment due to the phenomenon of staff "burnout." Personal experiences with AODA-related problems is often what sparks the initial involvement of school staff in the student assistance program. The same experiences which create dedication and commitment can also place the staff at risk for burnout. Burnout can manifest itself within individuals and also at the level of the system as a whole. Maintaining the student assistance program entails taking preventive as well as curative measures at both levels.

Chapter 24 | Program Maintenance Issues

In terms of concrete planning and implementation issues, we have encouraged those implementing the Student Assistance Program model to think in terms of at least a three-year process. Thinking about the program and presenting it to the Board of Education and the community in this way emphasizes the long-term commitments that will be required to effectively help students with drug and alcohol problems as well as others.

To follow through with the recovery analogy, the implementation, operation, and maintenance issues can be likened to the phases of recovery for individuals and families. Primary treatment is the brief but intense and often painful period of recognizing the nature of the problem and adopting a new and unfamiliar manner of living and the knowledge and skills necessary to support it. While encountering and surmounting the pitfalls, early recovery entails practicing and gaining familiarity with a healthier lifestyle. These form a foundation for the long-term recovery. Secure in a new, drug-free lifestyle, individuals and families acquire the strengths to take the risks for further growth.

The implementation process is similarly complex; just getting the program off the ground can become the major focus of the energies of those involved, requiring, as it does, examining past behavior and organizational patterns, confronting resistance and denial, and changing entrenched, comfortable responses. While the major implementation tasks can often be accomplished within one year, those implementing the program should be prepared to devote time to addressing the various pitfalls which might become apparent during the first year or so. As the school and its staff become comfortable with the program and begin to experience its successes, revitalizing the program and broadening its focus and impact emerge as the most frequent maintenance needs over the long term.

Pitfalls

All programs will encounter problems and pitfalls during their first years of operation. It is impossible, in the implementation phase, to anticipate or resolve all of the problems which might arise; it is understandable that some areas may be overlooked, or the solution to some problems postponed. The following are a few of the more common pitfalls for which the SAP staff should be alert early during the early stages of the program's operation.

1. Insufficient administrative support. At either the building or district-level, insufficient administrative support can cause the program to be implemented narrowly or incompletely, or to be discontinued altogether. Individual building administrators may regard dealing with student drug and alcohol problems as the province of pupil services staff, may fail to become involved in Core Teams, or avoid participating in Core Group training. Where individual administrators have not been involved in the implementation and training process, they may not fully support the SAP/AODA policy, may circumvent or undermine disciplinary and referral procedures, fail to provide leadership and advocacy for the program with other staff in the building, and fail to support the SAP staff in dealing with parents. Support groups, for example, require smooth working relationships and contacts between students, group leaders, classroom teachers, and parents. The building administrator's firm and vocal support for support group policies and procedures is necessary for them to operate effectively.

At the district level, failure to secure the support and involvement of other administrators and the board of education may also compromise the program, allow it to fade away, or jeopardize its existence. Funding issues, for example, will arise annually, and the student assistance program will be competing with other efforts for limited and scarce resources. To the extent that board members have not been involved in or kept informed of the program, they may make funding decisions in the absence of vital information about the program's successes, impact on students, and support from the community. In some communities, the program has been jeopardized or discontinued because staff and/or community resistance has resulted in a crisis which the board of education was insufficiently prepared to deal with constructively. It is unfortunate but understandable that a given district may vote to discontinue its student assistance program in response to a small but vocal group of parents, supported by a misguided local press, alleging that the program invades the privacy of children and families.

2. Parent consent issues. Support groups inevitably require policies regarding the need for parental information and/or permission which are consistent throughout the district. Failing to develop such guidelines leaves the district with no way to respond rationally, confidently, or consistently to expressions of parent and staff concern over a student's group involvement.

To the extent that the school and the staff have not dealt with negative and judgemental attitudes regarding drug and alcohol abuse, it will be difficult to communicate about such issues to parents and the community with clarity, accuracy, and confidence. Fears concerning parent involvement often preoccupy those implementing the program and can interfere with its operation. Such fears may often consist of the staff's projections of their own fears of confronting those with alcohol and other drug-related problems. Avoiding dealing with parent consent, or adopting a "tell all" policy which conflicts with confidentiality may often be the result.

Clear policies on whether or not to seek parental consent for student participation in various program activities, and a clear understanding of the rationale behind them, can prevent a number of problems from arising or assist the school district and the staff in responding to them appropriately. The failure to develop them can open the district and its student assistance program to legitimate challenges.

3. Secrecy. Understanding that drug and alcohol-related problems are often stigmatized will lead SAP staff to adopt a well-intentioned concern for protecting students' privacy. Similarly, issues involving the confidentiality of student records and privileged communications also adds to the need for limiting communication about students in the program. Respect for privacy and the need to follow legal guidelines protecting confidences can often be exaggerated. As a result, the program can unwittingly contribute to the air of shame and secrecy which traditionally surrounds drug and alcohol-related problems. For example, guarding the identity of students in support groups contributes to the climate of secrecy in a program, and only reinforces the strength of the very "no talk rules" the program seeks to eradicate. While the information disclosed in support groups is confidential, the fact that a student is in a group is not, so long as the name of the group does not label the student as having a specific problem. Similarly, a statement that a student "is in the Student Assistance Program" by itself violates neither his privacy or confidentiality. Similarly, rebuffing teachers' requests for information about a student in the program with claims of "confidentiality" only undermines working relationships and contributes to the view that the student assistance program is the province of an isolated "clique."

4. Isolation. Program staff can often become trapped within their concerns for confidentiality, by the feeling that they alone are qualified to deal effectively with student AODA concerns, and by the cohesiveness they feel as members of the Core Team. In addition, some other staff members feel that since they were not a part of the initial Core Team, there is no way for them to participate or become involved in the student assistance program. There are instances where this message has been explicitly communicated by the program staff. Expressions of interest in getting involved are sometimes met with statements that "everything has been done." Support groups, too, can sometimes become identified as the only component of the student assistance program. Those leading support groups can sometimes lose sight of the contributions and role of teachers, coaches, principals, guidance counselors, and others who work with students on a daily basis.

As a result, it is important to establish close working relationships between the program staff and others in the school and to encourage them to become involved in the program (see Supplement 17.1).

5. "Burnout." Many programs experience a high rate of turnover among SAP Counselor/Coordinators, support group leaders, and other Core Team members. While it usually appears after several years of a program, staff "burnout" is something that can be anticipated and prevented. Burnout occurs where program staff spend a great deal of time being constantly available to provide help, support, and nurturance to students and have not made provisions for adequate self-care. It is important that those involved in the program find formal ways of supporting themselves and each other. One of the values of the Core Team approach is that team members constitute an informal support network for sharing tasks, problems, successes, and failures. Support groups for group facilitators are strongly recommended, as are regular meetings, on a district-wide basis, of other members of the Core Teams and the Core Group.

"Unless the person assigned the nurturing role receives the same care and attention he/she so generously extends to those in need, sooner or later that healer will falter and burnout."
(Carroll 1979, p. 319)"

Burnout also occurs where staff involvement in the program remains entirely uncompensated, or taken for granted, unrecognized or uncelebrated. The day-to-day involvement in serious and sometimes life-threatening problems can lead SAP staff members to lose sight of the progress that has been made or of individual successes. On a district-wide level, something as simple as an annual banquet to celebrate the program, its staff, and its student participants can help to revitalize the program and shift attention from problems to accomplishments.

6. Preoccupation with resistance. Focussing primarily on the resistance of staff, students, or the community is one of the best ways to divert attention from the fact that the majority of persons in the school and in the community support the program. Focussing on resistance usually stops action. Because the subject of drug and alcohol abuse is one of the more emotionally charged areas the school can deal with, and because learning to confront these problems successfully entails risk, there is a tendency to exaggerate the significance or misinterpret the scope of resistance. Allowing the resistance of a few staff members, for example, to play a significant role in planning staff inservices is to give a disproportionate degree of power to a minority. Empowering the denial system is a form of enabling. Similarly, fearing the real or imagined resistance to the program by certain groups (e.g., coaches, clergy) may lead to a decision to exclude them from planning and participation in the program. Such exclusions can create resistance where there was none, strengthen it, or miss a significant opportunity to reduce it. On the other hand, schools discover that it becomes much more possible to implement a program, a policy, a strategy, or an activity when they focus on the degree of support there is.

7. Failure to accept limitations. Discouragement can debilitate a program and its staff members if they and the district have not defined realistic personal, professional, and programmatic limitations. The fact is that all students cannot be helped; not every student or family will respond to the school's best efforts; there will always be resistant families, staff, and students; and resources of time and money will always be scarce compared to the degree of student need, etc. Failing to define and redefine limitations on a personal, professional, and program level leads to the development of unrealistic expectations for all involved, and increasingly frequent feelings of inadequacy when these expectations cannot be met. Those involved in the program should be engaged in regularly redefining the limits of the program.

8. Confusing school/community boundaries. Although a student assistance program should be a "joint school/community effort," there are boundary issues between the two. The student assistance program is located in the school, but requires the advice and support of the community. Likewise, community efforts are located in the community, but benefit from the advice and support of the school staff. Some programs have suffered when these boundaries are not recognized. Core Group members, for example, who are also school staff, may find that they are overextended when the Group begins identifying community action tasks. These tasks may more legitimately be the province of community representatives. Similarly, community members of the Core Group may wish to implement changes in the school's program, forgetting that the school system is an interdependent but separate component of the community.

9. Failure to address staff needs. Specifically, this refers to the need for an Employee Assistance Program which recognizes that staff and their families also have problems which require an enlightened approach to assistance. More generally, however, it means taking into account that a great many staff members are chemically dependent, are spouses or parents of chemically dependent family members, or are adult children of alcoholics. Many times resistance, fears about confidentiality and legal liability, and fears about becoming involved in the program have their basis more in these personal issues than in objective concerns about "the school's role." As much effort has to go into educating staff and making them feel safe with such issues as goes into working with students.

10. Shrinking involvement. One of the best ways to get people to drop out of Core Teams, school/community task forces, or Chemical groups is to give them nothing to do. People will only listen to speakers or watch films for so long. Many people join such organizations with great initial enthusiasm but lose interest because the group has no concrete agenda. Thus, it is important for in-school committees and community groups alike to blend information and awareness functions with an orientation toward the accomplishment of specific tasks (put out a newsletter, purchase a film, belong to a 'speakers bureau,' visit a treatment program, distribute literature, lobby for changes in local ordinances, etc. See Supplement 17.1).

Program Maintenance Tasks

During initial implementation it is important to avoid allowing the student assistance program to be seen as part of the "program of the year" syndrome. That is, implementers must develop within the school the perception that the program will be part of the school's day-to-day functioning for a long time to come. The chief maintenance goal during the second and third years of a program will be maintaining the energy, commitment, enthusiasm, and level of activity of the first year. To accomplish this, attention will often need to be focussed on keeping the program visible and

on expanding the program by encouraging others to become involved and providing additional services. Some maintenance activities may be designed to address the pitfalls described above. Depending on the scope of initial program activity, maintenance tasks might involve expanding the program to all grade levels and school buildings, providing additional types of support groups or increasing their numbers, and so on.

The district can be guided in its program maintenance efforts by the Student Assistance Program Implementation Checklists (Supplement 18.1 through 23.1). In addition to guiding initial efforts, the checklists can be used to identify areas that were originally overlooked, postponed, or are in need of additional attention during the maintenance phase. In a sense, maintenance begins as a result of the information discovered through evaluating the program during its first year. Major maintenance tasks for the second and following years could be categorized in terms of the tasks addressed during implementation.

1. Planning and Organizing. The primary task here during initial implementation involved widening the numbers of people involved and enhancing their awareness of AODA-related issues. During maintenance it is important to keep the program visible by regularly and frequently reporting on its progress. The evaluation of the program's first year should provide a great deal of data concerning the program's impact (how many students were served), outcome or effectiveness (how have students benefited because of their participation), and process (what services were offered and how well policies and procedures are working). This information should be shared with the Board of Education as well as with staff members in each building and with the community as a whole. Since one of the major areas of concentration during program maintenance involves promoting the visibility of the program, efforts should be made to appear regularly before each of these groups.

2. Policy Development. The first year's experience will typically reveal areas where the school's AODA policy is deficient, or where it requires expansion. A co-curricular code, for example, may involve too much deliberation during the initial implementation phase, and might have been postponed until the second year. Athletic codes, or training rules, will also typically need to be changed to be consistent with the SAP/AODA policy and procedures. Weak or tentative language concerning parental permission and involvement may also be strengthened in the light of the first year's experience.

3. Program Design. A major effort should be made to expand the membership of the Core Teams in individual buildings as well as of the district-wide Core

Group. The level of activity during the first year of operation often justifies reevaluating the roles and responsibilities of the SAP Coordinator and SAP Program Director, and increasing the amount of time they devote to program-specific duties. In addition, most schools discover that they need to make major revisions in day-to-day procedures in working with referred students even during the program's first year. They will need to evaluate the functioning of the Core Teams and the level of support from key staff members in each building as well as on a district-wide basis. Working relationships with chemical dependency screening, assessment, and treatment agencies can also be examined and strengthened. Setting goals for the following year is a program maintenance task that involves examining the design of the program. Finally, the Student Assistance Program should by now be a formal part of the annual school district budget. Appearing before the school board with a report on the first year's experience, revisions of the program, and a request for continuation funding is a program design task.

Support groups are an important part of the student assistance program which need continuous evaluation and revision as part of program design. Decisions need to be made concerning revising group goals, assessment and screening procedures, meeting schedules, materials, criteria for selecting group facilitators, as well as many other concrete issues. Experience may dictate the need for more groups and group leaders. Use-focussed or Recovery Support Groups, whose implementation might have been delayed, may now need to begin. Experience with Use-focussed Groups often teaches the need to screen students more carefully and to involve parents earlier in the assessment/ intervention process. Some school discover that local AODA-agencies may be willing to assume greater responsibility for providing Personal Change Groups, leaving the school free to concentrate more fully on Drug Information Groups and Drug Free Support Groups. Similarly, the school may now be in a better position to develop or support the formation of Alateen and/or Alatot meetings in the community, family treatment programs for alcohol and other drug abuse, and other services. To the extent that evaluating the AODA continuum of care is a program design task, the school may be able to devote energies in the second and subsequent years to advocacy for improvements in the availability or appropriateness of local AODA treatment services for youth and their families.

Most student assistance programs will begin taking steps to "broaden the brush" by integrating services for other student problems into the program. Experience seems to support the contention that a firm basis in understanding the dynamics of denial, enabling, confrontation, assessment, intervention, etc., formed by focussing on AODA-related issues initially, assists with the effective management of students who have non-AODA-related problems. A major program design task for maintaining the program consists of asking how each of the major program functions will be carried out for other student concerns: child abuse and neglect, unplanned pregnancy, suicide, separation and divorce, coping with grief and loss, and stress management. Each of these problems have also been effectively dealt with through support groups.

4. Core Group Development. If the impetus for developing its student assistance program has come primarily from within the school, the district-wide, joint school/community Core Group which emerged during program implementation may have retained a school focus. Once the school's program is securely in place, effort is frequently directed to expanding the community membership in the Core group and focussing its energies on community-wide issues. The Core Group may assist other service-providing segments of the community (juvenile justice, health and social services, etc.) in developing more effective AODA-related services for youth. Core Groups with this community focus are often responsible for starting an adolescent chemical dependency treatment unit in a local hospital, increasing the funding for local AODA assessment agencies, the provision of police liaison officers in the schools, and so on.

Training is another of the major areas which will require ongoing effort. School staff and community members who are new members of the Core Group will need intensive Core Group training. In addition, those with special roles in the program may need advanced training in adolescent assessment skills, group facilitation skills, intervention techniques, or in methods of working with parents. As a result of its first year experience, a district may also identify training needs associated with special issues and/or populations: working with elementary age children, leading use-focussed groups, special issues relating to athletes, or the needs of ethnic minorities.

5. Program Promotion. It cannot be overstressed that visibility is one of the keys to successfully maintain the student assistance program from year to year. Steps need to be taken to continue the program's visibility within each building, at the district level, and among students, staff, parents, and the community at large. It is impossible to talk too often or too openly about the program as well as about AODA issues. Visibility and openness not only keep energy and interest alive, but also erode the forces of secrecy and denial which persist from initial program implementation. Where people feel free to speak openly about AODA issues they are less likely to confuse confidentiality and respect for privacy with "secrecy." Thus, openness contributes to a positive climate, to program credibility, and to the incidence of parent, peer, and self referrals.

Staff in each building will need continuing inservice education. The school should devote time to inservice training in basic AODA concepts, referral skills, integrating AODA topics with classroom teaching, designing AODA prevention activities, and implementing an AODA curriculum at the building and district-wide levels.

Efforts to keep the program visible before students should also continue. The development of sophisticated student/parent workshops, for example, for students in athletics and other extracurricular activities often often awaits the development of clear co-curricular codes and procedures to implement them. The school should also continue efforts on behalf of parents, such as continuing to hold parent awareness nights, and to distribute SAP brochures.

6. *Program Evaluation*. All of the maintenance tasks rely on the evaluation of the program's progress thus far, and upon formulating plans and goals for future in the light of past experience. Evaluation thus becomes an important maintenance task by itself. Initial experience with the program's operation will undoubtedly clarify the areas in which evaluation needs to be expanded, simplified, and focussed. Often, for example, there emerges a need to develop more consistent district-wide procedures and formats for the collection of data. If it has not done so as yet, the school may decide to begin utilizing its computer resources for gathering and storing program-related information. All of the data significant to the effective operation of the program can easily be managed using software that is readily available for personal computers found in the majority of school districts. In addition, the school may wish to begin gathering information in order to answer questions oriented more toward research than toward program evaluation.

By anticipating major pitfalls which jeopardize the program's continuing effectiveness and attending to maintenance tasks in the major implementation areas, the school system can not only keep the program energetic and active but more importantly can continue to provide help to students who have drug and alcohol and other problem and to strengthen those aspects of individuals and the environment which preclude their development or progression.

Program Revitalization

In addition to the normal activities that are a part of ongoing maintenance, many programs are beginning to identify a need for what they term "revitalization." The perception that a student assist-

ance program is in need of revitalization sometimes comes about as a result of staff turnover. Program Administrators and SAP Coordinaor/Counselors are promoted or leave the district. Principals, coaches, teachers, pupil services staff, and other Core Team members often change buildings, change jobs, or move to other districts. With time, Core Groups can become more engaged in pursuits other than alcohol or other drug abuse, can lose direction, or can lose community members and interest. Revitalization can also become necessary because overall enthusiasm for the program has waned and dropped far below the levels of excitement characteristic of its inception. Occasionally, too, the student assistance program subsystem itself begins to exhibit signs of system "burnout" which mimic those of individual burnout. A number of strategies may be needed to revitalize the program, recreating and mobilizing the energies that originally characterized it.

Training. Additional training for Core Team and Core Group members has been utilized to infuse new energy into a program. As in the usual maintenance task, new members of Core Teams and Core Groups will need to be exposed to the same intensive AODA training as original members. Existing members of the SAP staff may also require advanced training in assessment and intervention skills, in working with children of alcoholics, or in group facilitation skills generally. Recovering students, who have been in a Recovery Support Group for longer than a year, may present a challenge to group facilitators to deal with issues beyond the task of just staying straight. If a school system has been relying exclusively upon one source of training, identifying and utilizing new training resources can contribute fresh perspectives to the student assistance program.

The school may also find it useful to locate or develop an "exchange program" with local adolescent AODA assessment and adolescent chemical dependency treatment programs. The agency may be willing, for example, to implement an intensive, short-term internship program which allows school staff to become directly involved and immersed in the process of treating adolescents. AODA agency staff can also benefit from spending a comparable time in the school setting on a full-time basis, in order to better understand the needs and limitations of working with students in the educational setting.

Celebration. Recovery is a gift and a loud joy. Finding a means of acknowledging and celebrating the individual efforts of students, families, and the SAP staff is not only intrinsically desireable but also helps to recapture the program's original enthusiasm and energy. Some schools have held an end-of-the-year banquet to which all of those who have participated in or benefitted from the program are invited: Board of Education members, Core Team and Core Group members, the SAP staff, support group leaders, students who have been in support groups, contributors, community AODA agency staff, and so on. Recognition awards are given to those who have contributed significantly to the program; students and/or family members are invited to give "testimonials." Programs can feature a well-known speaker in the field of recovery. Such a public, open, joyous and proud demonstration of gratitude not only validates the individual efforts of all concerned, but helps to further remove the stigma and shame that accompanies drug and alcohol-related problems.

"Recovery is a gift and a loud joy."

Staff Issues. Even the best student assistance program can fall victim to the conflicts and dysfunctions which can afflict any organization or system. Unless identified and addressed, the individual and systemic signs of burnout will not only undermine the program's effectiveness but begin to poison individual efforts. While a program can help to resolve some staff conflicts and mistrust issues, it can also foreground or create others. Old issues, attitudes, and personality conflicts may not be resolved by having to work cooperatively in Core Teams, for example. New conflicts may arise over the handling of individual cases, or over more global issues such as policy language, philosophical orientations, or the direction of the program. In some cases, those who work most closely day-to-day with students, such as support group leaders, do not acquire the visibility with the school or the community that may accompany the Program Director or the SAP Coordinator(s).

Program revitalization may literally require that Core Team members seek outside help to facilitate the identification, discussion, and resolution of interpersonal issues which have begun to compromise the program's effectiveness and to undermine personal satisfactions with it. The emergence of this need often accompanies a change from an outcome oriented to a process oriented approach to the program. In other words, much of the activity undertaken to implement, operaqte, and initially maintain the student assistance program may have been devoted to achieving specific outcomes and goals. The belief that observable outcomes are what is really important if one is to be seen as influential often predominates. Later, there may be a need to focus more on the program's process, to become interested in what the system is doing and how it does it, in the nature and quality of relationships, and in the validation of personal effort. An outside consultant is often required to facilitate the interpersonal interactions among Core Team members or others as

they begin to focus their awareness on themselves and on the nature of various resistences to interacting with each other more openly and honestly.

Chapter 24 | # Supplement

Supplement 24.1, "Self Maintenance: Who Helps the Helpers?" explores some of the problems presented by the phenomenon of "burnout" as it affects student assistance programs. It covers the symptoms, causes and treatment of the burnout syndrome in individuals and examines some preventive steps.

Burnout is also examined at the student assistance program's system level. The system itself can begin to exhibit symptoms of burnout, many of which provide the context for, or "enable," burnout in individuals within the program. Symptoms, causes, treatment, and preventive measures are also examined at this level.

Burnout symptoms are presented in a checklist format which can be used by program staff in assessing the presence of these dynamics in themselves and in the programs they function within.

Supplement 24.1

SELF-MAINTENANCE: WHO HELPS THE HELPERS?

There are many facets of "burnout" upon which authorities agree. First, those most susceptible to "burning out" are people who work in human services or in helping roles. Many such individuals must invest intense emotional effort in others who are severely troubled. Moreover, many of those in helping roles have a heavy personal investment in or dedication to their work, so that progress or the lack of it in one's students is easily translated in one's own personal adequacy or failure. Many school staff members become involved in the student assistance program because of direct personal experience with drug and alcohol abuse and chemical dependency. Some are recovering alcoholics or addicts, others are adult children of alcoholics, and still others have been affected by the chemical dependency in their own children, other family members, colleagues, or friends. Their dedication to recovery, empathy, love for kids, and the wisdom which proceeds from having a shared experience with many students can contribute to their effectiveness and their effort. Unfortunately, these can often also become the attributes which lead helpers to place others needs first and self-care second.

It is important that those who become involved in the student assistance program and who also have firsthand experience with such problems examine the degree to which these experiences can place them at risk for burning out. Sharon Wegscheider (1981), for example, has pointed out how the "Family Hero" can carry the self-defeating self-denial of this role into adulthood and into characteristic "helping" roles and professions. Familiarity with the work of Woititz (1983) and Gravitz and Bowden (1985) can also help affected family members to avoid allowing these personal strengths to become self-defeating. For individuals who have personal AODA-related experience, "burnout" is often a synonym for "relapse."

Secondly, recent work has emphasized that the dynamics of burnout are characteristic of systems as well as of individuals within them. In other words, "burning out" has to do with the mutual interaction between the individual and the system within which he works. Causative, preventive, and remedial factors must therefore be addressed in the system as well as in the individual.

Finally, as White points out, "the type of burnout each staff member is most vulnerable to can be predicted based on the individual's prior history of stress management and the degree to which the program will encourage or inhibit this style" (White 1978, p. 3).

An examination of the factors associated with burnout which follows makes clear the potential for burning out within a Student Assistance Program. Those most susceptible to burnout are those with formal roles within the program, those with coordinative responsibilities, and those who work most closely and frequently with student AODA-related problems: counselors, group facilitators, and so on. The symptoms, causal factors, and implications for the prevention and treatment of burnout within individuals are examined first. The same dynamics are described next as they apply to the system context. The symptoms, adapted from White (1978a, b) and Carroll (1979), may be used as a checklist to assess the presence of burnout symptoms within individuals and/or the system.

BURNOUT AND THE INDIVIDUAL HELPER

SAP Coordinator/Counselors, support group leaders, and others who have daily, face-to-face contact with students who have drug and alcohol-related problems (and their families) often show high rates of turnover, sometimes as soon as the first year of a program's operation. The signs of burning out can include physical, psychological, and social symptoms.

Physical Symptoms

[   ] 1. Feelings of exhaustion and fatigue;

[   ] 2. Being unable to shake a cold;

[   ] 3. Feeling physically run-down;

[   ] 4. Frequent headaches and gastrointestinal disturbances;

[   ] 5. Sudden weight loss or gain;

[   ] 6. Insomnia or frequent difficulty in sleeping;

[   ] 7. Increase in blood pressure;

[   ] 3. Shortness of breath;

[   ] 9. Increased susceptibility to various illnesses, including flu and the common cold;

Psychological Symptoms

[   ] 1. Increased feelings of depression, exhaustion, hopelessness, disillusionment, or boredom;

[   ] 2. Feelings of being trapped in one's job; helplessness;

[   ] 3. Self-doubt about one's effectiveness or the value of one's work; feelings of inadequacy;

[   ] 4. Feelings of isolation;

[   ] 5. Feeling unappreciated for one's hard work and dedication;

[   ] 6. Feeling taken for granted or simply ignored;

[   ] 7. Increased rigidity, stubbornness, judgemental thinking;

[   ] 8. Hyper-irritability; quickness to anger;

[   ] 9. Loss of one's initial enthusiasm for the job;

[   ] 10. Increased suspiciousness and mistrust of others;

[   ] 11. Loss of charisma; loss of control over the expression of feelings;

[   ] 12. Change from optimism to pessimism and cynicism;

[   ] 13. Change from basic acceptance and respect to rejection and disrespect for friends and colleagues;

[   ] 14. Change from flexible, creative thinking to mechanical thinking;

[   ] 15. Increased alcohol or other drug use, gambling, and/or overeating;

[   ] 16. Diminished control over one's basic drives, such as hunger and sex;

[   ] 17. Significant decrease in judgement and reasoning, including the inability to consider the likely consequences of certain acts.

Social Symptoms

[   ] 1. Significant decrement in the ability to relate to students as individuals, especially in a caring and constructive manner;

[   ] 2. Tendency to respond to students in terms of labels or stereotypes (e.g., "He's one of the little sociopaths in my drug group this afternoon");

[   ] 3. Withdrawing and isolating oneself from others;

[   ] 4. Overbonding with other staff, seeking to satisfy basic needs (recognition, friendship, love, and sex) almost exclusively through contacts with other program staff;

[   ] 5. Severing long-term relationships (e.g., through divorce);

[   ] 6. Increased sexual promiscuity;

[   ] 7. Increased interpersonal conflicts, both at school and at home;

[   ] 8. Centering one's life around the job or the program, by working an inordinate number of hours and then justifying this behavior as a form of "dedication" to the program and as a reflection of just how important one is to the school or the program;

[   ] 9. Taking repeated risks that endanger one's physical and psychological well-being.

CAUSATIVE FACTORS

1. Existing physical illnesses that lower strength, energy, and resistance to stress;

2. Existing maladaptive, self-destructive, or compulsive behavior patterns;

3. Inadequate education and training to perform one's role in the program;

4. Unresolved personal issues around alcohol and other drug abuse or dependency, resulting in (a) compulsive overachievement to cover basic feelings of inadequacy, (b) compulsive need to make restitution for past mistakes, (c) over-identification with students; and/or, (d) contempt for students in the program;

5. Inability or refusal to seek or accept assistance from others;

6. Failure to define or inability to admit personal and professional limitations.

7. Inability or unwillingness to communicate to others in the program about signs or symptoms of burning out.

"TREATMENT" FOR INDIVIDUALS

1. Provide relief from stress through time-outs or time off without implying weakness or

failure (e.g., not permitting group leaders to lead two consecutive groups: one semester on and one semester off);

2. Provide additional education and training; permit program staff to attend conferences or visit programs in other school districts;

3. Examine sources of stress and make use of sources of support to develop better stress management techniques (e.g., attendance at Al-Anon and/or implementation of a support group for group facilitators);

4. Pay attention to physical symptoms; have a thorough physical examination.

PREVENTION FOR INDIVIDUALS

1. Engage in regular physical exercise to maintain health and to reduce stress;

2. Utilize relaxation techniques to prevent the buildup or tension, anxiety, and stress;

3. Acquire training in how to structure time, organize work, set realistic goals and expectations, define personal, professional, and program limits;

4. Acquire training in how to maintain some distance between oneself and students without jeopardizing the helping relationship; learn how to "let go."

5. Learn how to identify and replenish personal resources, strengths, and potentials;

6. Identify or create and utilize support systems both within the school system and the program and outside in the community (e.g., establish a support group within the school for SAP staff, and attend Al-Anon);

7. Promote and cultivate a circle of associates within which one can discuss the appearance of burnout symptoms without fear that one's performance in the program will be judged.

BURNOUT AT THE SYSTEM LEVEL

Just as there are signs of burnout apparent in individuals, some aspects of the student assistance program and/or the larger system of which it is a part can exhibit signs of distress.

Symptoms of System Burnout

[   ] 1. There is a significant decrement in the quality of services to students, even though the statistical reports continue to look good;

[   ] 2. Individuals in various parts of the program interrelate in a distrusting, competitive, and hostile manner;

[   ] 3. Bureaucratic "turf" becomes more sharply defined and jealously guarded, impairing the program's ability to effectively manage students; there is mistrust between principals, counselors, SAP Coordinator/Counselor(s), support group facilitators, etc.

[   ] 4. Authority conflicts emerge more frequently and with greater rancor; perception of "roles" becomes confused with power and control issues;

[   ] 5. Important program decisions are more frequently made by one individual or by an increasingly isolated, elitist group which less and less seeks meaningful input from others;

[   ] 6. Communications within the program or between those in the program are poor; program staff become increasingly isolated from others in the school;

[   ] 7. Staff morale deteriorates; program staff express increased feelings of mutual disrespect and distrust, resulting in each side demanding that their rights and responsibilities be codified in writing;

[   ] 8. Program staff miss or show up late for important meetings;

[   ] 9. Absenteeism increases; there is an abnormal use of sick leave;

[   ] 10. Staff turnover increases, with a briefer length of stay in performing various program roles; staff members "drop out;"

[   ] 11. Additional work is assigned without adequate compensation in pay or through job restructuring; increases in work loads are justified by appeals to the staff's dedication, commitment, or talent;

[   ] 12. Relationships between the student assistance program and other service systems grow worse (funding sources, advisory or governing boards, community groups, AODA assessment and treatment programs, etc.);

CAUSATIVE FACTORS OF SYSTEM BURNOUT

1. Frequent, repeated experiences with "treatment failure," due to unrealistic expectations of students or of the program;

2. Internal and external pressures to constantly examine one's motives and actions to assure that one is behaving in a correct and proper manner; attributing student failure to staff members' competence;

3. Maintaining a constant demand to provide students with a high degree of caring and emotional availability; (e.g., implementing more support groups rather than placing some students on a waiting list);

4. Failure of the system to provide qualified program coordinators and/or program administration;

5. Failure to provide program staff with appropriate training to enable them to adequately perform the tasks expected of them;

6. Creating an atmosphere of competition, distrust, and non-support;

7. Failure to compensate or adequately recognize staff effort;

8. Focussing attention consistently on the scope of problems rather than periodically focussing on successes, progress, and changes brought about by the program.

9. Failure to support program staff when they take risky positions that are yet consistent with policy; (e.g., "Are you sure you smelled alcohol on her breath?");

SYSTEM-LEVEL "TREATMENT"

1. Change the program's structure, policies, expectations, goals, and/or operating procedures to minimize sources of stress;

2. Make formal provision for staff nurturance activities such as "guilt-free" time-outs, changes in one's program role, formal recognition of individual efforts, etc.;

3. Obtain training and consultation from competent individual's from outside the system who can facilitate the free, open, and confidential discussion among SAP staff members concerning personal and system-related problems;

4. Prevent the same individuals from consistently overworking;

5. Interrupt program services or components for a short period of time (e.g., suspend support groups for a semester);

6. Insure that staff are adequately compensated for their efforts, either through increased payment, decreased work loads in other areas, or public recognition;

SYSTEM-LEVEL PREVENTION

1. Place strict limits on the amount of time individuals can devote to the program and strictly enforce them;

2. Rotate staff among various roles within the program (e.g., encourage group facilitators to lead different groups; rotate program coordination among three or four Core Team members);

3. Establish more "part-time" roles within the program; share duties among those on the Core Team within each building;

4. Implement staff support systems, or change existing staff meetings to permit SAP staff to socialize informally, to clarify program goals, confer about problems, etc.;

5. Provide retreats for program staff, preferably away from the school system or community, where they can replenish energy and discuss feelings about the program, their roles, and their students;

6. Provide training to staff on how to identify and recover from burnout symptoms;

7. Obtain outside consultation to guard against the stifling effects of a rigid internal program ideology;

8. Cultivate the participation of volunteers.

Chapter 25 | Conclusion

A recent Gallup Poll reported that 74% of the public agreed with the statement that alcoholism is an illness. Those directly involved in the field of alcohol and other drug abuse as well as the public at large can today often take for granted that those who are affected by alcohol and other drug abuse and chemical dependency can find help. Most people know someone who has been in treatment. Hundreds of agencies and multi-million dollar buildings have been erected for the treatment of chemical dependency in individuals, and of codependency in children and other family members. Celebrities, Presidents and First Ladies publicly speak of alcoholism as a disease or of treatment experiences. We have national institutes on alcohol and drug abuse.

It was not always so. The roots of student assistance programs lie not in these but elsewhere. It is easy to forget where the roots of student assistance programs really are. Many of us trace our involvement in developing and implementing student assistance programs to their obvious namesakes — Employee Assistance Programs — which grew up in the early 1970's. The Employee Assistance Program model, however, has its roots in Occupational Alcoholism Programs which developed in the 1940's. OAP's, however, owe their existence to the birth and early success of Alcoholics Anonymous in the 1930's. It was discovering that a person could recover from alcoholism, and not just be subject to brief periods of abstinence followed by an even more calamitous relapse, that led employers to adopt concerted efforts to identify and refer those with drinking problems. Thus, it is possible to trace the lineage of student assistance programs directly back to the emergence of Alcoholics Anonymous and to the *fact* that recovery was now possible, predictable, and within the grasp of anyone.

The Student Assistance Program model has its roots, historically as well as spiritually, in Alcoholics Anonymous and in the fact of recovery. Recovery has to remain the theme of student assistance programs as well as the motivation behind them. Debates over whether student assistance programs are or should be primarily prevention or intervention largely miss the point. Recovery, whether in historical or practical terms, is always *prior* to prevention and intervention. Before we can become personally or professionally adequate to prevent or to intervene we must examine and change the ways in which we have been affected by alcohol and other drug abuse and chemical dependency, for they have surely affected the attitudes, beliefs, feelings, and behavior of all of us, whether through intimate personal experience or through merely growing up in a culture which stigmatizes such problems and those who have them.

Much of the success in learning to deal with AODA problems proceeds from the depth to which one has accepted that alcoholism and other chemical dependencies are illnesses which are not the result of personal fault or blame. Much of the failure to help or be helpful can be attributed to the fear and outright denial of such an acceptance, requiring, as it does, giving up the safety of judgements. Alcoholism, it seems, is about the only illness about which most people — professional and layperson alike — often think They already know enough. The crucial role which attitudes play in accounting for our differential response to chemical as opposed to other problems is instructive. Adolescent suicide, for example, is a tragic and dismaying problem for all of us. In the average school system where there is a suicide, all of the resources of the school are frequently mobilized to educate staff in postvention to ease the pain of survivors, and in the intervention and prevention strategies which testify to the value placed on even one adolescent life. Another student, busted in school for using drugs to postpone the effects of withdrawal or to medicate the despair in his life, would more often than not result in the passage of a school policy to expel him.

Individuals can recover from chemical dependency, and we know how to do that. Families can recover from chemical dependency, and we know how to do that. Systems can also recover from the effects of drug abuse and dependency and we are beginning to learn how to do that.

APPENDIX A

RESOURCES

Al-Anon/Alateen Family Group Headquarters
P. O. Box 182
Madison Square Station
New York, NY 10010
(212) 683-1771

Alcoholics Anonymous World Services, Inc.
468 Park Avenue South
P. O. Box 459
Grand Central Station
New York, NY 10017
(212) 686-1100

National Association of Leadership
for Student Assistance Programs (NALSAP)
1704 Mayflower Street
New Holstein, WI 53061

National Clearinghouse for Alcohol
Information (NCALI)
Box 2345
Rockville, MD 20852
(301) 468-2600

National Council on Alcoholism (NCA)
733 Third Avenue
New York, NY 10017

National Institute on Alcohol Abuse
and Alcoholism (NIAAA)
5600 Fishers Lane
Parklawn Building
Rockville, MD 20852

National Clearinghouse for Drug Abuse
Information (NCDAI)
Room 10A-56
5600 Fishers Lane
Rockville, MD 20857

National Institute on Drug Abuse (NIDA)
5600 Fishers Lane
Rockville, MD 20857

Tough Love
P.O. Box 70
Sellersville, PA 18960

National Association of Children of Alcoholics
31706 Coast Highway
Suite 201
South Laguna, CA 92677
(714) 499-3889

APPENDIX B

NATIONAL ASSOCIATION OF LEADERSHIP FOR STUDENT ASSISTANCE PROGRAMS

The National Association of Leadership for Student Assistance Programs (NALSAP) was established in 1987 as a non-profit, professional membership organization. It was incorporated to formally acknowledge the growth of Student Assistance Programs on a national scale and to recognize the SAP model as a highly effective response to students who are affected by drug and alcohol abuse and related problems.

The Association provides an opportunity to meet, collaborate, and relate to other student assistance programs and professionals, offers opportunities to present papers and workshops at regional and national conferences, to assist in the promotion of effective SAP models, and to share resources.

Among the initial purposes of the Association are the following:

- To promote the establishment of a multidisciplinary approach to the development of student assistance programming

- To promote comprehensive, joint school/community programs for prevention, early identification, intervention, and rehabilitation of students with alcohol/drug-related problems from the preschool through college levels;

- To promote and provide national, regional, state, and local leadership and training;

- To provide a national forum for resource sharing, centralized communications for program issues, and a vehicle for generating and disseminating pertinent knowledge and materials;

- To identify national trends and coordinate with other regional and national organizations dealing with issues relevant to student assistance programming.

For further information, or to apply for membership, contact the NALSAP (see Appendix A).

Bibliography

A Growing Concern: How to Provide Services for Children from Alcoholic Families. Rockville, MD.: National Institute on Alcohol Abuse and Alcoholism, 1983.

Ackerman, Robert J. 1978. *Children of Alcoholics: A Guidebook for Educators, Therapists, and Parents.* Holmes Beach, FL: Learning Publications, Inc.

Alcoholics Anonymous. New York: Alcoholics Anonymous World Services, Inc., 1939.

Alibrandi, Tom. *Young Alcoholics.* Minneapolis, MN: Comp Care Publications, 1978.

Alschuler, Alfred, Kathleen Phillips, and Gerald Weinstein. "Self-Knowledge Education as an Approach to Drug Abuse Education." In *Humanizing Preservice Teacher Education: Strategies for Alcohol and Drug Abuse Prevention.* Washington D. C.: Erie Clearinghouse on Teacher Education, December, 1977.

Altman, Kerry Paul. "The Role-Taking Interview: An Assessment Technique for Adolescents." *Adolescence.* 20:80 (1985): 845-851.

Anderson, Gary L., Sara Krebsbach, and Susan Fredlund. *The Student Assistance Program: The Wisconsin Experience.* Madison, WI: Department of Health and Social Services, 1986. (Available from the De Paul Training Institute, 4143 So. 13th Street, Milwaukee, WI 53220, at a cost of $4.00 to cover printing and mailing).

Barnes, Grace M. and John W. Welte. "Patterns and Predictors of Alcohol Use among 7-12th Grade Students in New York State. *Journal of Studies on Alcohol.* 47:1 (1986): 53-62.

Baumrind, Diana and Kenneth A. Moselle. "A Developmental Perspective on Adolescent Drug Abuse." *Alcohol and Substance Abuse in Adolescence.* 4:3,4 (1985): 41-67.

Benson, Pete L., et al. *Report on 1983 Survey on Drug Use and Drug-Related Attitudes.* Minneapolis, MN: Search Institute, 1983.

Beschner, George M. "The Problem of Adolescent Drug Abuse: An Introduction to Intervention Strategies." In Friedman and Beschner, eds. (1985), pp. 1-12.

Beschner, George M. and Alfred S. Friedman, eds. *Youth Drug Abuse.* Lexington, Mass.: D.C. Heath and Company, 1979.

Biddle, Bruce J., et al. "Social Determinants of Adolescent Drinking." *Journal of Studies on Alcohol.* 41:3 (1980): 215-241.

Biek, Joan, R.N. "Screening Test for Identifying Adolescents Adversely Affected by a Parental Drinking Problem." *Journal of Adolescent Health Care.* 2: (1981): 107-113.

Black, Claudia. *My Dad Loves Me, My Dad Has a Disease.* Newport Beach, CA.: ACT, 1979.

_____. *It Will Never Happen to Me.* Denver: M. A. C., Printing, 1981.

Bosma, W. G. "Alcoholism and Teenagers." *Maryland State Medical Journal.* 24:6 (1975): 62-68.

Botvin, Gilbert J. et al. "Prevention of Alcohol Misuse Through the Development of Personal and Social Competence: A Pilot Study."*Journal of Studies on Alcohol.* 45 (1985): 550-552.

Brook, David W. et al. "Editorial: Adolescent Alcohol and Substance Use and Abuse: A Cause for Concern or Complacency." *Alcohol and Substance Abuse in Adolescence.* 4:3,4 (1985): 1-7.

Budenz, Daniel T. *Relapse to Alcohol/Drug Addiction.* Middleton, Wisconsin: Progressive Literature, 1979.

Burnside, Mary A., et al. "Alcohol Use by Adolescents in Disrupted Families." *Alcoholism: Clinical and Experimental Research.* 10:3 (1986): 274-278.

Carroll, Jerome F. "Staff Burnout as a Form of Ecological Dysfunction." *Contemporary Drug Problems.* 8 (Summer, 1979): 207-225.

Clayton, Richard R., and Christian Ritter. "The Epidemiology of Alcohol and Drug Abuse Among Adolescents." *Alcohol and Substance Abuse in Adolescence.* 4:3,4 (1985): 69-97.

Cohen, Allan Y. "Drug Treatment in School and Alternative School Settings." In Friedman and Beschner, eds. (1985), pp. 178-194.

Cohen, Allan Y. and Yoav Santos. "Youth Drug Abuse and Education: Empirical and Theoretical Considerations." In Beschner and Friedman, eds., pp. 229-254.

Confidentiality of Alcohol and Drug Abuse Patient Records. Federal Law Title 42 Public Health. *Federal Register.* Volume 40 C.F.R. 27802, July 1, 1975.

Cook, Paddy S. and Robert C. Petersen. "Individualizing Adolescent Drug Abuse Treatment." In Friedman and Beschner, eds. (1985), pp. 80-93.

Cotton, N. "The Familial Incidence of Alcoholism: A Review." *Journal of Studies on Alcohol.* 40 (1979): 89-116.

Crewe, Charles. *A Look at Relapse.* Center City, Minnesota: Hazelden Foundation, Inc., 1974.

Daley, Dennis. *Relapse Prevention Workbook.* Holmes Beach, Florida: Learning Publications, Inc., 1986.

Deutsch, Charles. *Broken Bottles Broken Dreams.* New York: Teachers College Press, 1982.

DiCicco, Lena et al. 1984a. "Group Experiences for Children of Alcoholics." *Alcohol Health and Research World.* (Summer, 1984): pp. 20-24.

—————, et al. 1984b. "Identifying the Children of Alcoholic Parents from Survey Responses." *Journal of Alcohol and Drug Education.* 30:1 (1984): 1-17.

Donovan, John E., and Richard Jessor. "Adolescent Problem Drinking: Psychosocial Correlates in a National Sample Study." *Journal of Studies on Alcohol* 39:9 (1978): 1506-1524.

Engs, Ruth C., and David J. Hanson. "The Drinking Patterns and Problems of College Students: 1983." *Journal of Alcohol and Drug Education.* 31:1 (1985): 65-81.

Essex, Nathan and Harold Bishop. "Use These Ten Principles to Refine School Board Policies." *American School Board Journal.* 173:11 (1986): 29-30.

Etherington, Terri. "Teens More Aware of Alcohol, Cocaine Risks." *The Journal.* 14:3 (March, 1985): 2.

Farley, Edward C., Yoav Santos, and David W. Speck. "Multiple Drug-Abuse Patterns of Youths in Treatment." In Beschner and Friedman, eds., pp. 149-168.

Forster, Brenda. "Upper Middle Class Adolescent Drug Use: Patterns and Factors." *Advances in Alcohol and Substance Abuse.* 4:2 (1984): 27-36.

French, John F. and Nancy J. Kaufman, eds. *Handbook for Prevention Evaluation.* Rockville, Maryland: National Institute on Drug Abuse, 1983.

French, John F., Court C. Fisher and Samuel J. Costa, Jr., eds. *Working With Evaluators: A Guide for Drug Abuse Prevention Program Managers.* Rockville, Maryland: National Institute on Drug Abuse, 1983.

Friedman, Alfred S. 1985a. "Referral and Diagnosis of Adolescent Substance Abusers." In Friedman and Beschner, eds. (1985), pp. 66-79.

Friedman, Alfred S. and George M. Beschner, eds. 1985b. *Treatment Services for Adolescent Substance Abusers.* Rockville, Maryland: National Institute on Drug Abuse, 1985.

Friedman, Alfred S. et al. 1985c. "Predicting From Earlier Substance Abuse and Earlier Grade Point Average to Failure to Graduate from High School." *Journal of Alcohol and Drug Education.* 31:1 (1985): 25-31.

Friel, John C. "Co-Dependency Assessment Inventory." *Focus on Family.* 8:3 (May/June, 1985): 20-21.

Galanter, Marc, ed. *Recent Developments in Alcoholism.* Vol. I. New York:Plenum Press, 1983.

Gold, Mark S., M.E. *800-COCAINE.* New York: Bantam Books, 1984.

_____, et al. 1985. "Adolescent Cocaine Abusers: Confronting the Epidemic." *Seminars in Adolescent Medicine.* (December, 1985).

_____, et al. 1986. "Cocaine Update: From Bench to Bedside." *Controversies in Alcoholism and Substance Abuse.* (1986): 35-60.

Goodstadt, Michael S. et al. "Factors Associated with Cannabis Nonuse and Cessation of Use." *Addictive Behaviors.* 11 (1986): 275-286.

Gorski, Terrence T. 1976a. "Denial Patterns: A System for Understanding the Alcoholic's Behavior." Harvey, IL: Ingalls Memorial Hospital, [mimeograph]

_____. 1976b. "The Denial Process and Human Disease." Harvey, IL: Ingalls Memorial Hospital, 1976. [mimeograph]

_____. 1980. "Dynamics of Relapse." *EAP Digest.* (1980): 16-49.

Gorski, Terrence T. and Merlene Miller. *Counseling for Relapse Prevention.* Independence, Missouri: Independence Press, 1982.

Gravitz, Herbert L. and Julie D. Bowden. 1985a. *Guide to Recovery: A Book for Adult Children of Alcoholics.* Holmes Beach, FL.: Leaning Publications, Inc., 1985.

_____. 1985b. "Recovery Continuum for Adult Children of Alcoholics." *Focus on Family.* (May/June, 1985): 6-7.

Green, Bert I. and Marvin Pasch. "Observing the Birth of the Hatch Amendment Regulations: Lessons for the Education Profession." *Educational Leadership.* (January, 1986): 42-48.

Green, Judith. "Overview of Adolescent Drug Use." In Beschner and Friedman, eds., pp. 17-44.

Hampden-Turner, Charles. *Maps of the Mind*. New York: Collier Books, 1981.

Hendin, Herbert, M.D., and Ann Pollinger Haas. "The Adaptive Significance of Chronic Marijuana Use for Adolescents and Adults." *Alcohol and Substance Abuse in Adolescence*. 4:3,4 (1985): 99-115.

Hubbard, R. L., E. R. Cavanaugh, S. G. Craddock, and J. V. Rachal. "Characteristics, Behaviors, and Outcomes for Youth in the TOPS." In Friedman and Beschner, eds. (1985): 49-65.

Huberty, David J. and Jeffrey D. Malmquist. "Adolescent Chemical Dependency." *Perspectives in Psychiatric Care*. 16 (1978): 1978.

Hutchinson, Roger L. and Tom J. Little. "A Study of Alcohol and Drug Usage by Nine-Through Thirteen-Year-Old Children in Central Indiana." *Journal of Alcohol and Drug Education*. 40 (1985): 83-87.

Jackson, Joan K. "The Adjustments of the Family to the Crisis of Alcoholism." *Quarterly Journal of Studies on Alcohol*. 15 (1954): 562-586.

Jellinek, E. M. "Heredity of the Alcoholic." In Jellinek, E. M., Ed. *Alcohol, Science and Society*. Westport, CN: Greenwood Press, 1945. 105-114.

Johnson, Vernon. *I'll Quit Tomorrow*. New York: Harper and Row, 1980.

————. *Intervention: How to Help Someone Who Doesn't Want Help*. Minneapolis: The Johnson Institute, 1986.

Johnston, Lloyd D., et al. 1980. *Highlights from Student Drug Use in America 1975-1980*. Rockville, MD: National Institute on Drug Abuse, 1980.

Johnston, Lloyd D., et al. 1985. *Use of Licit and Illicit Drugs by America's High School Students: 1975-1984*. Rockville, MD.: National Institute on Drug Abuse.

Julien, Robert M. *A Primer of Drug Action*. New York: W. H. Freeman and Company, 1985.

Kandel, Denise B. "On Processes of Peer Influences in Adolescent Drug Use: A Developmental Perspective." *Alcohol and Substance Abuse in Adolescence*. 4:3,4 (1985): 139-163.

Kanfer, Frederick H. "Self-Management Methods." In Kanfer, Frederick H. and Arnold P. Goldstein, eds. *Helping People Change*. New York: Pergamon Press, Inc., 1975, pp. 309-356.

Kirk, Raymond S. "Drug Use Among Rural Youth." In Beschner and Friedman, eds., pp. 379-408.

Knop, Joachim, MD., et al. "A Prospective Study of Young Men at Risk for Alcoholism: School Behavior and Achievement." *Journal of Studies on Alcohol*. 46:4 (1985): 273-277.

Kopp, Sheldon. *If You Meet the Buddha on the Road, Kill Him!* New York: Bantam Books, 1972.

Kornblith, Alice B. "Multiple Drug Abuse Involving Nonopiate, Nonalcoholic Substances. I. Prevalence." *The International Journal of the Addictions*. 16:2 (1981): 197-232.

Krupski, Ann Marie. *Inside the Adolescent Alcoholic*. Center City, MN: Hazelden, 1982.

Kurtz, Ernest. *Not-God: A History of Alcoholics Anonymous*. Center City, MN: Hazelden, 1979.

Laundergan, J. Clark. *The Outcome of Treatment*. Center City, MN.: Hazelden Foundation, 1982.

Lenhart, Susan D. and John S. Wodarski. "Comprehensive Program for Student Alcohol Abuse: A Group Approach." *Journal of Alcohol and Drug Education*. 31:2 (1985): 36-44.

466

Lettieri, Dan J. "Drug Abuse: A Review of Explanations and Models of Explanation." *Alcohol and Substance Abuse in Adolescence.* 4:3,4 (1985): 9-40.

Lettieri, Dan J. and Jacqueline P. Ludford, eds. *Drug Abuse and the American Adolescent.* Rockville, MD: National Institute on Drug Abuse, 1981. [NIDA Research Monograph 38]

Licarione, Margaret. "Conducting Group Therapy with Chemically Dependent Adolescents." In Friedman and Beschner, eds. (1985), pp. 150-163.

Lowman, Cherry. "Facts for Planning No. 2. Alcohol Use as an Indicator of Psychoactive Drug Use Among the Nation's Senior High School Students." *Alcohol Health and Research World.* 6:2 (Winter, 1981/82): 41-46.

Luft, Joseph. *Group Process: An Introduction to Group Dynamics.* Palo Alto, CA.: National Press Books, 1966.

Marks, S. J., Leslie H. Daroff, and Samuel Granick. "Basic Individual Counseling for Drug Abusers." In Friedman and Beschner, eds. (1985), pp. 94-111.

Marshall, Shelly. Young, Sober, and Free. Center City, MN: Hazelden, 1978.

Mayer, J.E. and W. J. Filstead. "The Adolescent Alcohol Involvement Scale." *Journal of Studies on Alcohol.* 40 (1979): 291-300.

Maykut, Madelaine O. *Health Consequences of Abuse and Chronic Marijuana Use.* New York: Pergamon Press, 1984.

McAuliffe, Robert M. and Mary Boesen McAuliffe. 1975a. *The Essentials of Chemical Dependency.* Volume I. Minneapolis, MN: The American Chemical Dependency Society, 1975.

_____. 1975b. *Essentials for the Diagnosis of Chemical Dependency.* Volume II. Minneapolis, MN: The American Chemical Dependency Society, 1975.

McCabe, John M. "Child's Consent to Treatment." Report Prepared for the National Institute on Alcohol Abuse and Alcoholism. Rockville, MD.: NIAAA, 1977. [mimeograph, National Clearinghouse for Alcohol Information # 028325].

McCabe, Thomas R. *Victims No More.* Center City, MN: Hazelden. 1978.

McHolland, James D. "Strategies for Dealing with Resistant Adolescents." *Adolescence.* 20:78 (Summer, 1985): 349-368.

McLaughlin, Robert J. et al. "Psychosocial Correlates of Alcohol Use at Two Age Levels During Adolescence." *Journal of Studies on Alcohol.* 46:3 (1985): 212-218.

Milam, James R. and Katherine Ketcham. *Under the Influence.* Seattle: Madrona Publishers, 1981.

Miller, J. D., et al. *National Survey on Drug Use: Main Findings.* Rockville, MD: National Institute on Drug Abuse, 1983.

Minard, Sally. "Family Systems Model in Organizational Consultation." *Family Process.* 15 (September, 1976): 313-320.

Moberg, D. Paul. "Identifying Adolescents with Alcohol Problems: A Field Test of the Adolescent Alcohol Involvement Scale." *Journal of Studies on Alcohol.* 44:4 (1983): 701-721.

Moursund, Janet. *The Process of Counseling and Therapy.* Englewood Cliffs, New Jersey: Prentice-Hall, Inc., 1985.

NASADAD Alcohol and Drug Abuse Report: Special Report. January-February. Washington, D. C.: National Association of State Alcohol and Drug Abuse Directors, (January-February), 1986.

NIAAA. 1984. Fifth Special Report to the Congress on Alcohol and Health. Washington, D.C.: U. S. Department of Health and Human Services.

NIAAA. 1985. Alcoholism: An Inherited Disease. Rockville, Maryland: U. S. Department of Health and Human Services, 1985.

NIDA. 1976. "Correlate Research Review." (Prevention Branch, Division of Resource Development): Rockville, MD. 20857, 1976.

—————. 1979. "Prevention Briefing Book." (Prevention Branch, Division of Resource Development): Rockville, MD. 20857, 1979.

Newcomb, Michael D. and P. M. Bentler. "Cocaine Use among Adolescents: Longitudinal Associations with Social Context, Psychopathology, and Use of Other Substances." *Addictive Behaviors.* 11 (1986): 263-273.

Nurco, David N., Norma Wegner, and Philip Stephenson. *Manual for Working with Parents of Adolescent Drug Abusers.* Rockville, MD.: NIDA Treatment Research Report, DHSS Publication No. (ADM) 82-1209, 1982.

O'Malley, Stephanie S., Kate B. Carey, and Stephen A, Maisto. "Validity of Young Adults' Reports of Parental Drinking Practices." *Journal of Studies on Alcohol.* 47:5 (1986): 433-435.

Pandina, Robert J., et al. 1981. "Estimation of Substance Use Involvement: Theoretical Considerations and Empirical Findings." *The International Journal of the Addictions.* 16:1 (1981): 1-24.

—————, et al. 1983. "Psychosocial Correlates of Alcohol and Drug Use of Adolescent Students and Adolescents in Treatment." *Journal of Studies on Alcohol.* 44:6 (1983): 950-973.

Petersen, Dennis R. "Pharmacogenetic Approaches to the Neuropharmacology of Ethanol." In Galanter, ed., pp. 49-69.

Pilat, Joanne M., and John W. Jones. "Identification of Children of Alcoholics: Two Empirical Studies." *Alcohol Health and Research World.* (Winter, 1984/1985): 27-33.

Potter-Effron, Patricia S. and Ronald T. "Treating the Family of the Chemically Dependent Adolescent: The Enabling Inventory and Other Techniques for Responsibility." *Alcoholism Treatment Quarterly.* 3:1 (1986): 59-72.

Prather, Hugh. *There Is a Place Where You Are Not Alone.* New York: Doubleday & Company, 1980.

Rist, Marilee C. "Surveillance and Security Are Putting Student Rights at Risk." *The Executive Educator.* (September, 1986): 18-21, 30.

Santo, Yoav. "The Methodology of the National Youth Polydrug Study (NYPS)." In Beschner and Friedman, eds., pp. 129-146.

Satir, Virginia. *Peoplemaking.* Palo Alto, CA.: Science and Behavior Books, Inc., 1972.

Sendor, Benjamin. "Good News: Courts Uphold 'Reasonable' Searches." *The American School Board Journal.* (March, 1986): 24.

Services for Children of Alcoholics: Research Monograph No. 4. Rockville, MD: National Institute on Alcohol Abuse and Alcoholism, 1981.

Sheppard, Margaret A., Deborah Wright, and Michael S. Goodstadt. "Peer Pressure and Drug UseExploding the Myth." *Adolescence*. 20:80 (Winter, 1980): 949-958.

Sher, Kenneth J. and Carol Descutner. "Reports of Paternal Alcoholism: Reliability across Siblings." *Addictive Behaviors*. 11 (1986): 25-30.

Simon, Sidney B., Leland W. Howe and Howard Kirschenbaum. *Values Clarification*. New York: Hart Publishing Company, Inc., 1972.

Single, E., D. Kandel, and R. Faust. "Patterns of Multiple Drug Use in High School." *Journal of Health and Social Behavior*. 15 (1975): 344-357.

Small, Jacquelyn and Sidney Wolf. "Beyond Absintence." *Alcohol Health and Research World*. (1978): 32-36.

Smart, Reginald. "Young Alcoholics in Treatment: Their Characteristics and Recovery Rates at Follow-up." *Alcoholism Clin. Exp. Res. 3* (1979): 19-23.

Splitt, David A. "School Law." *The Executive Educator*. (April, 1986): 14.

Spotts, James V., and Franklin C. Shontz. "A Theory of Adolescent Substance Abuse." *Alcohol and Substance Abuse in Adolescence*. 4:3,4 (1985): 117-137.

Tarter, Ralph E., Arthur Alterman, and Kathleen Edwards. "Alcoholic Denial: A Biopsychological Interpretation." *Journal of Studies on Alcohol*. 45:3 (1984), 214-218.

_____. "Vulnerability to Alcoholism in Men: A Behavior-Genetic Perspective." *Journal of Studies on Alcohol*. 46:4 (1985), 329-356.

Team Up for Prevention with America's Young Athletes. Washington D. C.: U. S. Department of Justice, Drug Enforcement Administration, 1984.

Tiebout, Harry, M. D. "Surrender Versus Compliance in Therapy." Quarterly *Journal of Studies on Alcohol*. 14 (1953): 58-68.

_____. "The Ego Factors in Surrender in Alcoholism." *Quarterly Journal of Studies on Alcohol*. 15 (1954): 610-621.

Topel, Helga. "Biochemical Basis for Alcoholism." *Alcohol*. 2 (1985): 711-788.

Vannicelli, Marsha. "Group Psychotherapy with Alcoholics: Special Techniques." *Journal of Studies on Alcohol*. 43:1 (1982): 17-37.

Wegscheider, Sharon. 1981. *Another Chance: Hope and Health for the Alcoholic Family*. Palo Alto: Science and Behavior Books.

Wegscheider-Cruse, Sharon. 1985. *Choicemaking*. Pompano Beach, FL: Health Communications, Inc.

Werner, Emmy E. "Resilient Offspring of Alcoholics: A Longitudinal Study from Birth to Age 18." *Journal of Studies on Alcohol*. 47:1 (1986): 34-40.

Wertz, Dan C. and Thomas C. Bigley, Jr. "Mobilizing a Community to Challenge Adolescent Substance Abuse: An Educator's Perspective." *Journal of Alcohol and Drug Education*. 31:1 (1985): 1-7.

West, Peg. *Protective Behaviors*. Madison, WI.: Madison Metropolitan School District, 1982.

White, William A. 1978a. *A Systems Response to Staff Burn-out*. Rockville, Maryland: HCS, Inc.

_____. 1978b. *Incest in the Organizational Family: The Unspoken Issue in Staff and Program Burn-out*. Rockville, MD.: HCS, Inc.

Winkelman, Jack L. and Sheila C. Harbet. "Drug Education: A Student-Centered Approach." *Journal of Alcohol and Drug Education*. 31:1 (Fall, 1985): 17-24.

Woititz, Janet G. *Adult Children of Alcoholics*. Hollywood, FL.: Health Communications, Inc., 1983.

Wright, Loyd. S. "High School Polydrug Users and Abusers." *Adolescence*. 20:80 (Spring, 1985): 853-861.

Yalom, Irvin. *The Theory and Practice of Group Psychotherapy*. New York: Basic Books, Inc., 1975.

York, Phyllis, and David York. *Tough Love: A Self-Help Manual for Parents Troubled by Teenage Behavior*. Sellersville, PA: Community Service Foundation, 1980.

Zucker, Robert A. and Thomas C. Harford. "National Study of the Demography of Adolescent Drinking Practices in 1980." *Journal of Studies on Alcohol*. 4 (1983): 974-985.